Philosophy
of
Woman

Philosophy
of
Woman

AN ANTHOLOGY
OF CLASSIC AND CURRENT CONCEPTS

SECOND EDITION

Edited by
MARY BRIODY MAHOWALD

HACKETT PUBLISHING COMPANY

Second edition 1983

Copyright © 1978, 1983 by Hackett Publishing Company

Printed in the United States of America

Cover design by Jackie Lacy
Interior design by James N. Rogers

For further information, please address
Hackett Publishing Company
P.O. Box 44937
Indianapolis, Indiana 46204

Library of Congress Cataloging in Publication Data

Main entry under title:

Philosophy of woman.

    Bibliography: p.
    1. Women—Addresses, essays, lectures. I. Mahowald,
Mary Briody.
HQ1206.P46   1983   305.4'2   83–8433
ISBN 0–915144–49–2
ISBN 0–915144–48–4 (pbk.)

To my very dear friends
Maureen, Lisa, Michael, and Tony—
for the clarity and courage
to be who we are

Contents

viii CONTENTS

Preface

"The proper study of mankind is man."
Alexander Pope, Essay on Man

Surely when Pope penned the above line, he intended "mankind" and "man" to be interpreted generically. Nonetheless, in most philosophical sources for such study, the concept of man has been construed primarily if not exclusively as male, while the concept of woman has been considered only peripherally, uncritically, or not at all. The main purpose of this book is to reduce the resultant conceptual gap by providing means to a clearer, more complete understanding of humankind. In other words, my purpose is largely remedial.

A second aim is pertinent to the problem of woman's status in today's society. Undoubtedly, each of us has opinions regarding this issue. At the heart of any justification for these opinions is the need for clarification of the concept of woman. Similarly, at the heart of any defensible rejection of others' opinions is the need for clarification of their concepts. The material here presented is meant to evoke such clarifications and an assessment of the related concepts, along with their presuppositions and implications. In this sense, my purpose is propaedeutic to examination and determination of specific issues relevant to women.

The "proper study" for which this collection serves as source is appropriately pursuable by men as well as women. For either sex, analysis of the concept of woman may elucidate the rational basis of behavior toward half the human race, and expose the consistency between various elements of that concept.

In the selections which follow I have attempted to represent major philosophical influences of the past and present. My concern in choosing these has been to provide a wide range of philosophical positions, and to draw from opposing approaches to the topic. I have included classical, biblical, and psychoanalytical sources—because I believe that present concepts of woman may be better understood and evaluated in their light. Of course, any of the thinkers here represented may profitably be studied in conjunction with a more extended concentration on her or his overall set of views. In fact, a comparison among these views is quite appropriate.

There are those who think that current interest in the study of woman is a fad. An optimistic implication of that notion is that someday the "specialness" or "unusualness" of studying women will disappear. While I doubt that such a hope will ever be realized, I see no sound basis for construing the study of woman as less vital or endurable than the study of man. Accordingly, my more realistic hope in making this material accessible is to facilitate a less inadequate understanding of human nature.

Acknowledgments

Family, students, friends and colleagues—all have contributed to this second edition. In particular I wish to acknowledge the ongoing, helpful input and encouragement from members of the Society for Women in Philosophy, and (until I left there last year) from students and colleagues of the Department of Philosophy and Women's Studies Program at Indiana University, Indianapolis. I also wish to thank Frances Hackett, William Hackett and James Rogers for their frank and friendly manner of facilitating a second edition. Since moving to Cleveland, I have another name to add to the list of those to thank: Miriam Rosenthal, M.D., who reviewed the material from psychoanalytic literature.

I offer special gratitude to the following publishers who granted permission to reprint many of the articles and excerpts herein; for without these the book would not exist:

McGraw-Hill Book Company for "The Stereotype" by Germaine Greer, from *The Female Eunuch* by Germaine Greer, © 1970, 1971; Curtis Brown, Ltd. for "Our Revolution Is Unique" by Betty Friedan, ALL RIGHTS RESERVED; *Quick Fox* for "Radical Feminism" by Ti-Grace Atkinson; Farrar, Strauss & Giroux, Inc. for "What Is Woman?" from *The Manipulated Man* by Esther Vilar, © 1972; Coward, McCann & Geohegan, Inc. for "The Liberated Woman" from *The Liberated Woman and Other Americans* by Midge Decter; Princeton University Press for "Diary of the Seducer" by Søren Kierkegaard, from Søren Kierkegaard, *Either/Or* vol. 1, trans. David F. Swenson and Lillian Marvin Swenson, with Revisions and a Foreword by Howard A. Johnson (copyright 1944 © 1959) by Princeton University Press, Princeton Paperbacks, 1971; E. P. Dutton for the excerpts from *Thus Spake Zarathustra* by Friedrich Nietzsche, trans. A. Tille, in Everyman's Library Edition; Alfred A. Knopf, Inc. for the excerpt from *The Second Sex* by Simone de Beauvoir, trans. H. M. Parshley, copyright 1972 by Alfred A. Knopf, Inc.; International Publishers, 381 Park Avenue South, New York, N. Y., for Friedrich Engels's "Origin of the Family" and for V. I. Lenin's "The Emancipation of Women"; Beacon Press for "Nature and Revolution" from *Counterrevolution and Revolt* by Herbert Marcuse, copyright © 1972 by Herbert Marcuse; Liveright Publishing Corporation for *Marriage and Morals* by Bertrand Russell, copyright 1929 by Horace Liveright, Inc., copyright renewed 1957 by Bertrand Russell; Teachers College Press for "Marriage" from *The Emile of Jean-Jacques Rousseau,* trans. and ed. by William Boyd, copyright 1962, by arrangement with William Heinemann, Ltd.; The University of California Press for the two excerpts from Immanuel Kant, copyright 1960 by *The Regents of the University of California;* George Allen & Unwin for "The Ethical World" and "Guilt and Destiny" by G. W. F. Hegel, from *Phenomenology of Mind,* trans. J. B. Baillie; Hackett Publishing Company for the excerpt from Plato's *Republic,* Book V; Catholic University of America Press for the selections by Augustine, from the *Fathers of the Church* Series; The Loeb Classical Library and Harvard University Press for the selections by Aristotle, from *Generations of Animals,* trans. A. L. Peck, 1942; Random House, Inc. for "On the First Man" from *Basic Writings of Saint Thomas Aquinas,* edited by Anton Pegis, copyright 1945 and renewed 1973 by Random House, Inc.; W. W. Norton & Company, Inc. for "Femininity," reprinted from *New Introductory Lectures on Psychoanalysis* by Sigmund Freud, translated by James Strachey, copyright © 1965, 1964 by James Strachey, copyright 1933 by Sigmund Freud, copyright renewed 1961 by W. J. H. Sprott; Princeton University Press for "Marriage as a Psychological Relationship" from *The Collected Works of C. G. Jung,* trans. R. F. C. Hull, Bollingen Series XX, Vol. 17: *The Development of Personality,* copyright 1954 by Princeton University Press, copyright © renewed 1982 by Princeton University Press; W. W. Norton & Company, Inc. for "Feminine Psychology" from *New Ways in Psychoanalysis* by Karen Horney, M.D., copyright 1939 by W. W. Norton & Company, Inc., copyright renewed 1966 by Marianne von Eckhardt, Renate Mintz, and Brigitte Swarzenski; *The Holy Cross Quarterly* for "Woman—a Philosophical Analysis" by Hilde Hein; Science History Publications for "A Contemporary Approach to Sex Identity" by Christine Allen, from *Values & the Quality of Life,* W. Shea and J. King-Farlow, eds., New York, 1976; Basic Books, Inc., Publishers, New York, for Chapter 10, "Natural Law Language and Women" by Christine Pierce, in *Women in Sexist Society: Studies in Power and Powerlessness,* edited by Vivian Gornick and Barbara K. Moran, copyright 1971 by Basic Books, Inc.; The University of Chicago Press for "Sex Roles: the Argument from Nature" by Joyce Trebilcot, reprinted from *Ethics* 85 (1975); Cambridge University Press for "Because You Are a Woman" by Joseph R. Lucas, reprinted from *Philosophy* 48, April 1973; Cambridge University Press for "Woman's Place" by Trudy R. Govier, reprinted from Philosophy 49, 1974; Pathfinder Press for "Women: Caste, Class, or Oppressed Sex?" by Evelyn Reed, in *Problems of Women's Liberation,* copyright 1970 by Pathfinder Press; G. P. Putnam's Sons for "The Woman Question: Phi-

losophy of Liberation and the Liberation of Philosophy" by Carol
C. Gould, in *Women in Philosophy* by Carol Gould and Max Wartofsky, copyright 1976 by Carol Gould and Max Wartofsky.

May 1983   MARY BRIODY MAHOWALD
Case Western Reserve University

Introduction

The Need for Clarity

Imagine each of the following situations:

(1) a professor having an affair with a graduate student;
(2) a housekeeper calling the plumber to repair a leak;
(3) a distraught parent consulting with the school principal;
(4) a corporation executive dictating a letter to a secretary;
(5) an operating room nurse assisting a surgeon.

As you mentally picture the above relationships, you are likely to envision a man in the role of professor, plumber, principal, executive, and surgeon, and a woman in each of the corresponding roles. Considering the words involved more carefully, however, it is obvious that none of the persons designated is identified by sex. Consequently, all the relationships described could conceivably be the reverse of the arrangement first imagined, or could occur between members of either sex exclusively. Why, then, do we tend to assign genders where words fail to specify them? One plausible explanation is that our concept of woman fails to encompass activities or roles that are properly assignable to either sex. In other words, our concept of woman is unwarrantably restrictive.

Like most modern and classical languages, English has a single term, "man," which may be interpreted to include *or* exclude female members of the species *Homo sapiens*. As a result, this term, and its equivalents in other languages, has long been the source of ambiguity in oral as well as written discourse about man, woman, and human nature. Obviously, the mere fact that the term *may* be applied to woman is not sufficient grounds for judging that it *is* applied to woman. In the selections which follow, you may be surprised to note the number of influential authors whose views on "man" have been construed as applicable to both sexes, yet whose remarks—on closer inspection—simply do not or cannot apply to those "men" who are women.

To facilitate correct interpretation of the material in this book, we subsequently distinguish between the concept of man as male and the concept of man as an individual of either sex or of humankind generally. Hereafter, then, the term "man" should be construed as referring only to individual male persons, while the terms "human" or "person" are used for women or men, or both. Hopefully, where the selections do not observe as clear a distinction,

1

the different concepts may be distinguished through textual and contextual analyses.

Concepts of Woman and Conceptual Analysis

Since we approach our topic from a philosophical perspective, we ought to recognize the limits of such an investigation. Unlike empirical scientists, philosophers do not examine the world directly, but scrutinize various ways of thinking about the world. In other words, they are interested in analyzing concepts. When we study the philosophy of woman, then, we direct our attention not to women themselves, but to ways of thinking about them; we wish to understand our understanding of woman.

As a particular way of thinking about something, a concept is related to other ways of thinking about things. Hence, the concept of woman is necessarily connected with other concepts such as those of man and human nature. Yet each way of thinking about things is also distinct or separable from other ways; for example, the concept of woman seems totally unrelated to concepts of nuclear fission or of geometric progression. Of course, which concepts are essentially associated with others, and which are essentially dissociated from them depends upon the specific concepts involved. Certain apparently unrelated concepts may be construed as essential to a particular concept of woman. For example, consider the concept of physical weight or mass: some specific quantitative range or average (of weight or mass) may be viewed as necessary to a concept of woman as a bodily being, particularly where such a concept is contrasted with a corresponding concept of man as a bodily being.

A cursory perusal of this book reveals such recurrent themes as freedom, equality, happiness, love, sex, and marriage. While these concepts are pertinent to the meaning of woman and her role in society, they are also subject to various interpretations. For example, John Stuart Mill's concept of happiness as an expected result of sex equality is quite different from the happiness which Simone de Beauvoir suggests may be forfeited through human (including woman's) liberation. Or, the meaning of love, criticized by Mary Wollstonecraft as an obstacle to women's virtue, clearly contrasts with the meaning which Thomas Aquinas attaches to love as the form of woman's (and anyone's) virtue. In order to clarify and understand each author's concept of woman it is important both to identify the crucially related concepts and to elucidate their meanings as fully as possible.

The challenge of philosophy is to overcome what the Austrian philosopher Ludwig Wittgenstein calls the "bewitchment of our intelligence by means of language." The selections which follow contain many possibilities for such bewitchment. To discern and overcome them you will need (among other things) to recognize that conceptual disagreements are sometimes masked by equivocation —that is, through use of terms which take on different meanings in different contexts; and to recognize that, conversely, conceptual agreements may be obscured by univocal use of terms which have conflicting meanings. The term "woman" is an apt candidate for either usage; for while the term is typically used to designate any adult female person, it is also used as a synonym for "wife" (from which its original meaning derives). Conceptual analysis entails careful scrutiny of such terms so that the underlying meanings may be discerned despite possible ambiguity and inconsistency of language. While concepts entail positions about the things we think about, such positions are logical rather than existential. It remains possible that a particular concept conflicts with experience or behavior—even when consistency between thought and action is considered desirable. Thus my concepts of woman and of human nature may be shown to be consistent with each other, while my actual behavior toward women conflicts with my view of human nature. On the other hand, my concepts of human nature and of woman may be inconsistent, while my behavior toward women accords with my concept of human nature.

In introducing the philosophical selections in this book I have briefly indicated the author's general philosophical approach and concept of human nature. These are crucial considerations in light of two legitimate assumptions: (1) that each author's concept of woman ought to be consistent with her/his concept of human nature or person, and (2) the author's overall philosophical context (for example, Plato's idealism, Hume's empiricism, Schopenhauer's voluntarism, Mill's utilitarianism) provides grounds for determining the validity of the corresponding views about human nature, man or woman. While such assumptions are appropriate, it is also appropriate to acknowledge their status as assumptions. In fact, a generally helpful question to ask as we assess our own and others' views is—what assumption or set of assumptions lies at the root of these concepts or judgments? Although warrantable assumptions may not ultimately be provable, awareness of them may enlighten us as to the values and priorities which infuse the premises of logical argument and rational behavior.

From Now to Now: a Nonchronological Sequence

The order of the selections reflects a progression of thought from surface considerations to deeper levels of understanding. We begin with extant popular concepts in order to evoke realization of the need for clarity not only in our concepts of woman and human nature, but also in related concepts such as freedom and equality. Differences between feminist and antifeminist views as well as between diverse interpretations of both can only be recognized in light of these fundamental concepts. For example, the "freedom" which Betty Friedan wants for women is quite different from the "freedom" which antifeminist Esther Vilar imputes to women as manipulators of men. With regard to equality, radical feminist Ti-Grace Atkinson criticizes traditional feminism as "caught in the dilemma of demanding equal treatment for unequal functions, because it is unwilling to challenge political (functional) classification by sex." Thus "equality" for radical feminists means total elimination of sex roles, while "equality" for moderate feminists entails societal adjustments to the special needs of women.

After grappling with such diverse popular concepts we proceed to a consideration of available philosophical approaches to the meaning of woman in contemporary society. Section II briefly explains utilitarian, existential, Marxist, and analytic perspectives, illustrating each through specific representatives. Although Bertrand Russell is a representative of analytic philosophy, the selection from *Marriage and Morals* is not intended as a sample of his analytic work, since Russell himself regarded such issues as beyond the scope of analytic method. On the other hand, most contemporary philosophers (cf. section VI) do regard their writing as analytic, and their views ought to be assessed in that light.

The next section of the book projects what prominent philosophers of the past have had to say about women. Mary Wollstonecraft is the least known name here, but reasons for her relative obscurity are themselves relevant to this collection. In eighteenth-century England, Wollstonecraft's opportunities for developing her full potential were extremely limited by her sex. Given her lack of formal education and early death through complications due to childbirth, it is amazing that Wollstonecraft was able to produce and publish so much of such worth.

Chronologically we proceed backward to examine the classical and Christian roots of current concepts. Since Plato so influenced the thought of Augustine, and Aristotle that of Aquinas, I present these thinkers in that order. Biblical and psychoanalytic sources are then provided. While these writings are not strictly philosophical, it is clear that their ideas continue to have great impact on popular concepts as well as philosophical reflection on woman. The last section illustrates the present stage of philosophical inquiry about women, and the prologue suggests a context for continuing to act out the drama. If and when we succeed in clarifying our concepts of woman and rendering them consistent with our concepts of human nature, we may be philosophically free to devote ourselves full time to ethical/social issues relevant to women.

I

REPRESENTATIVE
POPULAR CONCEPTS

Great philosophers exert their widest influence through those who popularize their thought. Often the popularizers are unaware that they have assimilated their ideas from philosophical sources. While the popular style is usually more lively and appealing than that of the philosophers, its appeal is sometimes bought at the price of precision, thoroughness, or cogency of argument. Such flaws illustrate the problem which this book is intended to help you probe.

Since popular authors reflect and affect the ideas of their contemporaries, it is appropriate to consider their statements about woman. Analysis of their divergent views will reveal both the need and importance of clarifying the concept of woman.

In this section, the first reading describes the stereotype of woman, i.e., the meaning that society assigns to women, and reinforces through media and mores. The next two selections elaborate moderate and radical feminist proposals for eliminating the stereotype in thought and practice. The last two readings represent a reactionary defense of the stereotype as an instance of women's liberation.

FEMINIST VIEWS

Feminists such as Greer, Atkinson, and Friedan generally present their concepts of person or of human nature by negation rather than by affirmation. In other words, they base their criticisms of the present status of women on a notion of what should be the case for women as human beings. Human nature is thus construed as the possibility of developing the unique potential that belongs to every individual. It is a potential that is not, or ought not to be, defined or confined by one's sex or societal "role."

For Friedan, dehumanization occurs to the extent that the feminine mystique (the pervasive but mistaken notion that women are totally fulfilled through the role of "housewife-mother") prevents the development of woman's potential. For Greer, the "de-womanizing" or "castration" of women is the equivalent of dehumanization. Atkinson stresses that the essential rationality of human nature involves a "constructive imagination" which is repeatedly frustrated by the gap between what we can do and what we can imagine done. While their attitudes towards men differ considerably, the three feminists concur that men are also dehumanized to the extent that they conform to a stereotypic or oppressive role in society. As Greer puts it in the last paragraph of *The Female Eunuch:*

> The first significant discovery we shall make as we racket along our female road to freedom is that men are not free, . . . that slaves enslave their masters, and by securing our own manumission we may show men the way they could follow when they jumped off their own treadmill.

GERMAINE GREER

Germaine Greer (1939–) has been director of the Tulsa Center for the Study of Women's Literature since 1979. Before receiving her Ph.D. degree in Shakespeare at Cambridge, Greer taught high school to underprivileged girls, an experience she found both inspiring and instructive. In reading the selection below, you will learn why Greer labels anyone who conforms to the stereotype a "female eunuch." Her own concept of woman denies those stereotypical qualities. "The Stereotype" is an excerpt from *The Female Eunuch*, pp. 47–55.

GERMAINE GREER   'The Stereotype'

In that mysterious dimension where the body meets the soul the stereotype is born and has her being. She is more body than soul, more soul than mind. To her belongs all that is beautiful, even the very word beauty itself. All that exists, exists to beautify her. The sun shines only to burnish her skin and gild her hair; the wind blows only to whip up the color in her cheeks; the sea strives to bathe her; flowers die gladly so that her skin may luxuriate in their essence. She is the crown of creation, the masterpiece. The depths of the sea are ransacked for pearl and coral to deck her; the bowels of the earth are laid open that she might wear gold, sapphires, diamonds and rubies. Baby seals are battered with staves, unborn lambs ripped from their mothers' wombs, millions of moles, muskrats, squirrels, minks, ermines, foxes, beavers, chinchillas, ocelots, lynxes, and other small and lovely creatures die untimely deaths that she might have furs. Egrets, ostriches and peacocks, butterflies and beetles yield her their plumage. Men risk their lives hunting leopards for her coats, and crocodiles for her handbags and shoes. Millions of silkworms offer her their yellow labors; even the seamstresses roll seams and whip lace by hand, so that she might be clad in the best that money can buy.

The men of our civilization have stripped themselves of the fineries of the earth so that they might work more freely to plunder the universe for treasures to deck my lady in. New raw materials, new processes, new machines are all brought into her service. My lady must therefore be the chief spender as well as the chief symbol of spending ability and monetary success. While her mate toils in his factory, she totters about the smartest streets and plushiest hotels with his fortune upon her back and bosom, fingers and wrists, continuing that essential expenditure in his house which is her frame and her setting, enjoying that silken idleness which is the necessary condition of maintaining her mate's prestige and her qualification to demonstrate it. Once upon a time only the aristocratic lady could lay claim to the title of crown of creation: only her hands were white enough, her feet tiny enough, her waist narrow enough, her hair long and golden enough; but every well-to-do burgher's wife set herself up to ape my lady and to follow fashion, until my lady was forced to set herself out like a gilded doll overlaid with monstrous rubies and pearls like pigeons' eggs. Nowadays the Queen of England still considers it part of her royal female role to sport as much of the family jewelry as she can manage at any one time on all public occasions, although the male monarchs have escaped such showcase duty, which devolves exclusively upon their wives.

At the same time as woman was becoming the showcase for wealth and caste, while men were slipping into relative anonymity and "handsome is as handsome does," she was emerging as the central emblem of western art. For the Greeks the male and female body had beauty of a human, not necessarily a sexual, kind; indeed they may have marginally favored the young male form as the most powerful and perfectly proportioned. Likewise the Romans showed no bias towards the depiction of femininity in their predominantly monumental art. In the Renaissance the female form began to predominate, not only as the mother in the predominant emblem of *madonna col bambino*, but as an aesthetic study in herself. At first naked female forms took their changes in crowd scenes or diptychs of Adam and Eve, but gradually Venus claims ascendancy, Mary Magdalene ceases to be wizened and emaciated, and becomes nubile and ecstatic, portraits of anonymous young women, chosen only for their prettiness, begin to appear, are gradually disrobed, and renamed Flora or Primavera. Painters begin to paint their own wives and mistresses and royal consorts as voluptuous beauties, divesting them of their clothes if desirable, but not of their jewelry. Susanna keeps her bracelets on in the bath, and Hélène Fourment keeps ahold of her fur as well!

What happened to women in painting happened to her in poetry as well. Her beauty was celebrated in terms of the riches which clustered around her: her hair was gold wires, her brow ivory, her lips ruby, her teeth gates of pearl, her breasts alabaster veined with lapis lazuli, her eyes as black as jet. The fragility of her loveliness was emphasized by the inevitable comparisons with the rose, and she was urged to employ her beauty in love-making before it withered on the stem. She was for consumption; other sorts of imagery spoke of her in terms of cherries and cream, lips as sweet as honey and skin white as milk, breasts like cream uncrudded, hard as apples. Some celebrations yearned over her finery as well, her lawn more transparent than morning mist, her lace as delicate as gossamer, the baubles that she toyed with and the favors that she gave. Even now we find the thriller hero describing his classy dames' elegant suits, cheeky hats, well-chosen accessories and footwear; the imagery no longer dwells on jewels and flowers but the consumer emphasis is the same. The mousy secretary blossoms into the feminine stereotype when she reddens her lips, lets down her hair, and puts on something frilly.

Nowadays women are not expected, unless they are Paola di Liegi or Jackie Onassis, and then only on gala occasions, to appear with a king's ransom deployed upon their bodies, but they are required to look expensive, fashionable, well-groomed, and not to be seen in the same dress twice. If the duty of the few may have become less onerous, it has also become the duty of the many. The stereotype marshals an army of servants. She is supplied with cosmetics, underwear, foundation garments, stockings, wigs, postiches and hairdressing as well as her outer garments, her jewels and furs. The effect is to be built up layer by layer, and it is expensive. Splendor has given way to fit, line and cut. The spirit of competition must be kept up, as more and more women struggle towards the top drawer, so that the fashion industry can rely upon an expanding market. Poorer women fake it, ape it, pick up on the fashions a season too late, use crude effects, mistaking the line, the sheen, the gloss of the high-class article for a garish simulacrum. The business is so complex that it must be handled by an expert. The paragons of the stereotype must be dressed, coifed and painted by the experts and the style-setters, although they may be encouraged to give heart to the housewives studying their lives in pulp magazines by claiming a lifelong fidelity to their own hair and soap and water. The boast is more usually discouraging than otherwise, unfortunately.

As long as she is young and personable, every woman may cherish the dream that she may leap up the social ladder and dim the sheen of luxury by sheer natural loveliness; the few examples of such a feat are kept before the eye of the public. Fired with hope, optimism and ambition, young women study the latest forms of the stereotype, set out in *Vogue, Nova, Queen* and other glossies, where the mannequins stare from among the advertisements for fabulous real estate, furs and jewels. Nowadays the uniformity of the year's fashions is severely affected by the emergence of the pert female designers who direct their appeal to the working girl, emphasizing variety, comfort, and simple, striking effects. There is no longer a single face of the year: even Twiggy has had to withdraw into marketing and rationed personal appearances, while the Shrimp works mostly in New York. Nevertheless the stereotype is still supreme. She has simply allowed herself a little more variation.

The stereotype is the Eternal Feminine. She is the Sexual Object sought by all men, and by all women. She is of neither sex, for she has herself no sex at all. Her value is solely attested by the demand she excites in others. All she must contribute is her existence. She need achieve nothing, for she is the reward of achievement. She need never give positive evidence of her moral character because virtue is assumed from her loveliness, and her passivity. If any man who has no right to her be found with her she will not be punished, for she is morally neuter. The matter is solely one of male rivalry. Innocently she may drive men to madness and war. The more trouble she can cause, the more her stocks go up, for possession of her means more the more demand she excites. Nobody wants a girl whose beauty is imperceptible to all but him; and so men welcome the stereotype because it directs their taste into the most commonly recognized areas of value, although they may protest because some aspects of it do not tally with their fetishes. There is scope in the stereotype's variety for most fetishes. The leg man may follow miniskirts, the tit man can encourage see-through blouses and plunging necklines, although the man who likes fat women may feel constrained to enjoy them in secret. There are stringent limits to the variations on the stereotype, for nothing must interfere with her function as sex object. She may wear leather, as long as she cannot actually handle a motorbike: she may wear rubber, but it ought not to indicate that she is an expert diver or waterskier. If she wears athletic clothes the purpose is to underline her unathleticism. She may sit astride a horse, looking soft and curvy, but she must not crouch over its neck with her rump in the air.

Because she is the emblem of spending ability and the chief spender, she is also the most effective seller of this world's goods. Every survey ever held has shown that the image of an attractive woman is the most effective advertising gimmick. She may sit astride the mudguard of a new car, or step into it ablaze with jewels; she may lie at a man's feet stroking his new socks; she may hold the petrol pump in a challenging pose, or dance through woodland glades in slow motion in all the glory of a new shampoo; whatever she does her image sells. The gynolatry of our civilization is written large upon its face, upon hoardings, cinema screens, television, newspapers, magazines, tins, packets, cartons, bottles, all consecrated to the reigning deity, the female fetish. Her dominion must not be thought to entail the rule of women, for she is not a woman. Her glossy lips and mat complexion, her unfocused eyes and flawless fingers, her extraordinary hair all floating and shining, curling and gleaming, reveal the inhuman triumph of cosmetics, lighting, focusing and printing, cropping and composition. She sleeps unruffled, her lips red and juicy and closed, her eyes as crisp and black as if new painted, and her false lashes immaculately curled. Even when she washes her face with a new and creamier toilet soap her expression is as tranquil and vacant and her paint as flawless as ever. If ever she should appear tousled and troubled, her features are miraculously smoothed to their proper veneer by a new washing powder or a bouillon cube. For she is a doll: weeping, pouting or smiling, running or reclining, she is a doll. She is an idol, formed of the concatentation of lines and masses, signifying the lineaments of satisfied impotence. Her essential quality is castratedness. She absolutely must be young, her body hairless, her flesh bouyant, and *she must not have a sexual organ*. No musculature must distort the smoothness of the lines of her body, although she may be painfully slender or warmly cuddly. Her expression must betray no hint or humor, curiosity or intelligence, although it may signify hauteur to an extent that is actually absurd, or smoldering lust, very feebly signified by drooping eyes and a sullen mouth (for the stereotype's lust equals irrational submission), or, most commonly, vivacity and idiot happiness. Seeing that the world despoils itself for this creature's benefit she must be happy; the entire structure would topple if she were not. So the image of woman appears plastered on every surface imaginable, smiling interminably. An apple pie evokes a glance of tender beatitude, a washing machine causes hilarity, a cheap box of chocolates brings forth meltingly joyous gratitude, a Coke is the cause of a rictus of unutterable brilliance, even a new stick-on bandage is saluted by a smirk of satisfaction. A real woman licks her lips and opens her mouth and flashes her teeth when photographers appear; *she* must arrive at the premiere of her husband's film in a paroxysm of delight, or his success might be murmured about. The occupational hazard of being a Playboy Bunny is the aching facial muscles brought on by the obligatory smiles.

So what is the beef? Maybe I couldn't make it. Maybe I don't have a pretty smile, good teeth, nice tits, long legs, a cheeky arse, a sexy voice. Maybe I don't know how to handle men and increase my market value, so that the rewards due to the feminine will accrue to me. Then again, maybe I'm sick of the masquerade. I'm sick of pretending eternal youth. I'm sick of belying my own intelligence, my own will, my own sex. I'm sick of peering at the world through false eyelashes, so everything I see is mixed with a shadow of bought hairs; I'm sick of weighting my head with a dead mane, unable to move my neck freely, terrified of rain, of wind, of dancing too vigorously in case I sweat into my lacquered curls. I'm sick of the Powder Room. I'm sick of pretending that some fatuous male's self-important pronouncements are the objects of my undivided attention, I'm sick of going to films and plays when someone else wants to, and sick of having no opinions of my own about either. I'm sick of being a transvestite. I refuse to be a female impersonator. I am a woman, not a castrate.

April Ashley was born male. All the information supplied by genes, chromosomes, internal and external sexual organs added up to the same thing. April was a man. But he longed to be a woman. He longed for the stereotype, not to embrace, but to be. He wanted soft fabrics, jewels, furs, makeup, the love and protection of men. So he was impotent. He couldn't fancy women at all, although he did not particularly welcome homosexual addresses. He did not think of himself as a pervert, or even as a transvestite, but as a woman cruelly transmogrified into manhood. He tried to die, became a female impersonator, but eventually found a doctor in Casablanca who came up with a more acceptable alternative. He was to be castrated, and his penis used as the lining of a surgically constructed cleft, which would be a vagina. He would be infertile, but that has never affected the attribution of femininity. April returned to England, resplendent. Massive hormone treatment had eradicated his beard, and formed tiny breasts: he had grown his hair and bought feminine clothes during the time he had worked as an impersonator. He became a model, and began to illustrate the feminine stereotype as he was perfectly qualified to do, for he was elegant, voluptuous, beautifully groomed, and in love with his own image. On an ill-fated day he married the heir to a peerage, the Hon. Arthur Corbett, acting out the highest achievement of the feminine dream, and went to live with him in a villa in Marbella. The marriage was never consummated. April's incompetence as a woman is what we must expect from a castrate, but it is not so very different after all from the impotence of feminine women, who submit to sex without desire, with only the infantile pleasure of cuddling and affection, which is their favorite reward. As long as the

feminine stereotype remains the definition of the female sex, April
Ashley is a woman, regardless of the legal decision ensuing from
her divorce. She is as much a casualty of the polarity of the sexes
as we all are. Disgraced, unsexed April Ashley is our sister and our
symbol.

*　　　*　　　*

BETTY FRIEDAN

Betty Friedan (1921–   ) first achieved prominence in 1963 through
her best-selling *The Feminine Mystique.* Her thesis there is that
"the core of the problem for women today is not sexual but a problem of identity—a stunting of growth that is perpetuated by the
feminine mystique." In 1967 Friedan became the founding president of the National Organization of Women (NOW), which is the
largest feminist group in the United States. In describing the reformist principles of NOW in the selection that follows, Friedan
also enunciates her concept of the woman who is a feminist. "Our
Revolution is Unique" is excerpted from *Voices of the New Feminism,* ed. by Mary Lou Thompson, pp. 32–43.

BETTY FRIEDAN　'Our Revolution
Is Unique'

We new feminists have begun to define ourselves—existentially—
through action. We have learned that while we had much to learn
from the black civil rights movement and their revolution against
economic and racial oppression, our own revolution is unique: it
must define its own ideology.

We can cut no corners, we are, in effect, where the black revolution was perhaps fifty years ago; but the speed with which our
revolution is moving now is our unearned historical benefit from
what has happened in that revolution. Yet there can be no illusion
on our part that a separatist ideology copied from black power will
work for us. Our tactics and strategy and, above all, our ideology
must be firmly based in the historical, biological, economic, and
psychological reality of our two-sexed world, which is not the same

as the black reality and different also from the reality of the first feminist wave.

Thanks to the early feminists, we who have mounted this second stage of the feminist revolution have grown up with the right to vote, little as we may have used it for our own purposes. We have grown up with the right to higher education and to employment, and with some, not all, of the legal rights of equality. Insofar as we have moved on the periphery of the mainstream of society, with the skills and the knowledge to command its paychecks, even if insufficient; and to make decisions, even if not consulted beyond housework; we begin to have a self-respecting image of ourselves, as women, not just in sexual relation to men, but as full human beings in society. We are able, at least some of us, to see men, in general or in particular, without blind rancor or hostility, and to face oppression as it reveals itself in our concrete experience with politicians, bosses, priests, or husbands. We do not need to suppress our just grievances. We now have enough courage to express them. And yet we are able to conceive the possibility of full affirmation for man. Man is not the enemy, but the fellow victim of the present half-equality. As we speak, act, demonstrate, testify, and appear on television on matters such as sex discrimination in employment, public accommodations, education, divorce-marriage reform, or abortion repeal, we hear from men who feel they can be freed to greater self-fulfillment to the degree that women are released from the binds that now constrain them.

This sense of freeing men as the other half of freeing women has always been there, even in the early writings of Mary Wollstone-craft, Elizabeth Stanton, and the rest; our action-created new awareness has confirmed this.

Another point we are conscious of in the new feminism is that we are a revolution for all, not for an exceptional few. This, above all, distinguishes us from those token spokeswomen of the period since women won the vote, the Aunt Toms who managed to get a place for themselves in society, and who were, I think, inevitably seduced into an accommodating stance, helping to keep the others quiet. We are beginning to know that no woman can achieve a real break-through alone, as long as sex discrimination exists in employment, under the law, in education, in mores, and in denigration of the image of women.

Even those of us who have managed to achieve a precarious success in a given field still walk as freaks in "man's world" since every profession—politics, the church, teaching—is still structured as man's world. Walking as a freak makes one continually self-conscious, apologetic, if not defiant, about being a woman. One is made to feel there are three sexes—men, other women, and myself. The successful woman may think, "I am the exception, the 'brilliant' one with the rare ability to be an anthropologist, author, actress, broker, account executive, or television commentator; but you drones out there, you watch the television set. And what better use can you make of your life than doing the dishes for your loved ones?"

We cannot say that all American women want equality, because we know that women, like all oppressed people, have accepted the traditional denigration by society. Some women have been too much hurt by denigration from others, by self-denigration, by lack of the experiences, education, and training needed to move in society as equal human beings, to have the confidence that they can so move in a competitive society. They say they don't want equality —they have to be happy, adjust to things as they are. Such women find us threatening. They find equality so frightening that they must wish the new feminists did not exist. And yet we see so clearly from younger women and students that to the degree that we push ahead and create opportunities for movement in society, in the process creating the "new women" who are *people first*, to that degree the threat will disappear.

We do not speak for every woman in America, but we speak for the *right* of every woman in America to become all she is capable of becoming—on her own and/or in partnership with a man. And we already know that we speak not for a few, not for hundreds, not for thousands, but for millions—especially for millions in the younger generation who have tasted more equality than their elders. We know this simply from the resonance, if you will, that our actions have aroused in society. . . .

As an example of the new feminism in action, consider the matter of abortion law repeal. . . . What right has any man to say to any woman, "You must bear this child?" What right has any state to say it? The child-bearing decision is a woman's right and not a technical question needing the sanction of the state, nor should the state control access to birth control devices.

This question can only really be confronted in terms of the basic personhood and dignity of woman, which is violated forever if she does not have the right to control her own reproductive process. And the heart of this idea goes far beyond abortion and birth control.

Women, almost too visible as sex objects in this country today, are at the same time invisible people. As the Negro was the invisible man, so women are the invisible people in America today. To be taken seriously as people, women have to share in the decisions of government, of politics, of the church—not just to cook the church supper, but to preach the sermon; not just to look up the zip codes and address the envelopes, but to make the political decisions; not just to do the housework of industry, but to make some of the executive decisions. Women, above all, want to say what their own lives are going to be, what their own personalities are going to be, not permitting male experts to define what is "feminine" or isn't or should be.

The essence of the denigration of women is their definition as sex objects. And to confront our inequality, we must confront our own self-denigration and our denigration by society in these terms.

Am I saying therefore, that women must be liberated from sex? No. I am saying that sex will only be liberated, will only cease to be a sniggering dirty joke and an obsession in this society, when women are liberated, self-determining people, liberated to a creativity beyond motherhood, to a full human creativity.

Nor am I saying that women must be liberated from motherhood. I am saying that motherhood will only be liberated to be a joyous and responsible human act, when women are free to make, with full conscious choice and full human responsibility, the decision to be mothers. Then and only then, will they be able to embrace motherhood without conflict. When they are able to define themselves as people, not just as somebody's mother, not just as servants of children, not just as breeding receptacles, but as people for whom motherhood is a freely chosen part of life, and for whom creativity has many dimensions, as it has for men. . . .

I maintain that motherhood is a bane and a curse, or at least partly that, as long as women are forced to be mothers—and only mothers—against their will. Women today are forced to live too much through their children and husband—too dependent on them, and, therefore, forced to take too much varied resentment, vindictiveness, inexpressible resentment, and rage out on their husbands and their children.

Perhaps the least understood fact of American political life is the enormous buried violence of women in this country today. Like all oppressed people, women have been taking their violence out on their own bodies, in all the maladies with which they plague the doctors' offices and the psychonanalysts. They have been taking out their violence inadvertently and in subtle and in insidious ways on their children and on their husbands. And sometimes, they are not so subtle, for the battered child syndrome that we are hearing more and more about in our hospitals is almost always to be found in the instance of unwanted children, and women are doing the battering, as much or more than men.

Man, we have said, is not the enemy. Men will only be truly liberated, to love women and to be fully themselves, when women are liberated to be full people. Until that happens, men are going to bear the burden and the guilt of the destiny they have forced upon women, the suppressed resentment of that passive stage—the steril-

ity of love, when love is not between two fully active, fully partici-
pant, fully joyous people, but has in it the element of exploitation.
And men will also not be fully free to be all they can be as long as
they must live up to an image of masculinity that denies to a man
all the tenderness and sensitivity that might be considered feminine. Men have in them enormous capacities that they have to repress and fear in themselves, in living up to this obsolete and brutal
man-eating, lion-killing, Ernest Hemingway image of masculinity
—the image of all-powerful masculine superiority. All the burdens
and responsibilities that men are supposed to shoulder alone, make
them, I think, resent women's pedestal, while the burden to women
is enforced passivity.

So the real sexual revolution is not the cheap headlines in the
papers—at what age boys and girls go to bed with each other and
whether they do it with or without the benefit of marriage. That's
the least of it. The real sexual revolution is the emergence of
women from passivity, from thingness, to full self-determination,
to full dignity. And insofar as they can do this, men are also emerging from the stage of identification with brutality and masters to
full and sensitive complete humanity.

A revolutionary theory that's adequate to the current demand of
the sexual revolution must also address itself to the concrete realities of our society. We can only transcend the reality of the institutions that oppress us by confronting them in our actions now; confronting reality, we change it; we begin to create alternatives, not
in abstract discussion, but here and now.

Some women who call themselves revolutionaries get into abstractions. They say, "What's really wrong is marriage altogether.
What's really wrong is having babies altogether; let's have them in
test tubes. Man is the oppressor, and women are enslaved. We don't
want jobs because who wants to be equal to men who aren't free.
All jobs today are just a rat race anyway."

Now we are rationalizing in radical terms of the extremists of the
women's liberation ideology. This is a rationalization for inaction,
because in the end we're going to weep and go home and yell at
our husbands and make life miserable for a while, but we'll eventually conclude that it's hopeless, that nothing can be done.

If we are going to address ourselves to the need for changing the
social institutions that will permit women to be free and equal individuals, participating actively in their society and changing that
society—with men—then we must talk in terms of what is possible,
and not accept what is as what must be. In other words, don't talk
to me about test tubes because I am interested in leading a revolution for the foreseeable future of my society. And I have a certain
sense of optimism that things can be changed.

Twenty-five years from now test-tube babies may be a reality. But it is my educated guess as an observer of the scene—both from what I know of psychology and what I've observed of actual women and men, old and young, conservative and radical, in this country and other countries—that for the foreseeable future people are going to want to enjoy sexual relationships and control the procreative act and make more responsible, human decisions whether and when to have babies.

We need not accept marriage as it's currently structured with the implicit idea of man, the breadwinner, and woman, the housewife. There are many different ways we could posit marriage. But there seems to be a reasonable guess that men and women are going to want relationships of long-term intimacy tied in with sexual relationship, although we can certainly posit a larger variety of sex relationships than now seem conventional. And it's not possible, much less conducive to health, happiness, or self-fulfillment, for women or men to completely suppress their sexual needs.

We can change institutions, but it is a fantasy deviation from a really revolutionary approach to say that we want a world in which there will be no sex, no marriage, that in order for women to be free they must have a manless revolution. We have to deal with the world of reality if we are going to have a real revolution.

I don't happen to think that women and men are so completely different that it is impossible for us to see each other as human beings. I think that it is as possible for men to put themselves finally in woman's place by an act of empathy or by guilt or by awareness of human rights as it has been possible for some whites to do for blacks. But it's perhaps not much more possible than that, though there are more bonds between men and women, and really men's stake in this revolution is greater, because a woman can make a man's life hell if it isn't solved. But I think it would be as much of a mistake to expect men to hand this to women as to consider all men as the enemy, all men as oppressors. This revolution can have the support of men, but women must take the lead in fighting it as any other oppressed group has had to.

I think that it is possible in education to create and disseminate the radical ideology that is needed to influence the great change in expectations and institutions for the revolution of women. In the education of women, I think it is nonsense to keep talking about optional life styles and the freedom of choice that American women have. They do not have them, and we should face this right away. You cannot tell a woman aged eighteen to twenty that she can make a choice to just stay home all her life with her children, her friends, and her husband. This girl is going to live close to a hundred years. There won't be children home to occupy her all her life. If she has intelligence and the opportunity for education it is telling her simply, "Put yourself in a garbage can, except for the years when you have a few little children at home."

The so-called second choice and option—go to school, then have children, stay out for twenty years and then get a job or go back to school—is not satisfactory either. I am not denying the need for occupational therapy for women of my generation who've had to do it this way, but any woman who has run the continuing education gamut knows the limitations of occupational therapy. Women have to do what they can, but they have enormous problems trying to get back after ten or fifteen years. They are mainly just a pool of semi-employable labor and have to be grateful for whatever they can get. Actually only a token few have been involved in these programs.

Some have the idea that there is another choice—and it is immediately implicit that this is a very freakish and exceptional choice—which is to be single-minded about a career like a man. The idea is, don't marry, don't have children, if you really want a demanding profession. Of course, if you do it this way, forget equality for women. I don't want to forget equality for women. I don't accept for most women the necessity of making a choice that no man has to make. This is not to say that women are not to have a free choice to have children or not to have children, to marry or not to marry; but the idea that this choice has to be influenced by professional or political pursuits, that you are going to be sexually frustrated by choosing to be a scientist, is nonsense.

It is a perversion of the new feminism for some to exhort those who would join this revolution to cleanse themselves of sex and the need for love or to refuse to have children. This not only means a revolution with very few followers—but is a cop-out from the problem of moving in society for the *majority* of women, who do want love and children. To enable *all* women, not just the exceptional few, to participate in society we must confront the fact of life—as a temporary fact of most women's lives today—that women do give birth to children. But we must challenge the idea that a woman is primarily responsible for raising children. Man and society have to be educated to accept their responsibility for that role as well. And this is first of all a challenge to education. . . .

Tokenism is worse than nothing. Tokenism is pretending that something is happening, to divert effort from the things that could really make something happen. It is terribly interesting to watch the experiments in continuing education at colleges like Radcliffe and Sarah Lawrence, but they have involved only a limited number of women. *This revolution has got to be for everybody.* Most women who want to get into graduate school simply can't get in at all because many universities won't accept women for part-time study when they've got enough men applying for full-time study.

Let's talk about what could be done that isn't just tinkering or tokenism. Every university should have a child-care center. A child development department in any university that doesn't address itself to this need is not confronting its own professional challenge. Another thing we could do, which NOW is trying to do, is to tackle sex discrimination in the universities in the broadest sense. If we get sex into Title VI as well as Title VII of the Civil Rights Act, so that sex discrimination in education is outlawed as well as race discrimination, we could then demand the removal of government contracts from any university that discriminated against women in assigning fellowships. We could then establish, by going to the Supreme Court, that it was discrimination against women not to give them maternity leave rather than requiring them to drop out of medical school. It is as much discrimination against women not to give them a maternity leave as it would be unconscionable to make a boy who has to go into military service lose his chance to get back into graduate school. And it is discrimination against a woman for the graduate school not to have a child-care center, much less not to give her a scholarship or fellowship. If more than a very few women are to enjoy equality, we have an absolute responsibility to get serious political priority for child-care centers, to make it possible for women not to have to bow out of society for ten or fifteen years when they have children. Or else we are only going to be talking of equal opportunities for a few. . . .

We must overcome our diversity of varied political beliefs. Our common commitment is to equality for women. And we are not single-issue people; we want a voice for all women, to raise our voices in decision making on all matters from war and peace to the kinds of cities we're going to inhabit. Many large issues concern all of us; on these things we may differ. We will surmount this. Political power is necessary to change the situation of the oppressed 51 per cent, to realize the power potential in the fact that women *are* 51 per cent.

We will do it by getting into city hall ourselves, or by getting into Congress ourselves, regardless of whether our political party is Republican or Democratic or Peace and Freedom. We're only going to do it by getting there ourselves; that's the nitty-gritty of self-determination for us. . . .

We must begin to use the power of our actions: to make women finally *visible* as people in America, as conscious political and social power; to change our society *now*, so all women can move freely, as people, in it.

✿   ✿   ✿

TI-GRACE ATKINSON

In 1968 Ti-Grace Atkinson (1938–   ) resigned the presidency of the New York chapter of NOW because of "irreconcilable ideological conflicts" within the organization. The manifesto of "The Feminists," which she subsequently helped to found, names men as "the enemies and the Oppressors of women." Because the institution of marriage is "inherently inequitable" and a "primary formalization of the persecution of women," it is to be rejected "both in theory *and in practice*" by any radical feminist. The "institutions" of love and heterosexual sex are also to be destroyed, since they constitute obstacles to the development of women as human beings. "Radical Feminism" is excerpted from *Amazon Odyssey*, pp. 47–63.

TI-GRACE ATKINSON   'Radical Feminism'

Almanina Barbour, a black militant woman in Philadelphia, once pointed out to me: "The Women's Movement is the first in history with a war on and no enemy." I winced. It was an obvious criticism. I fumbled about in my mind for an answer. Surely the enemy must have been defined at some time. Otherwise, what had we been shooting at for the last couple of years? into the air?

Only two responses came to me, although in looking for those two I realized that it was a question carefully avoided. The first and by far the most frequent answer was "society." The second, infrequently and always furtively, was "men."

If "society" is the enemy, what could that mean? If women are being oppressed, there's only one group left over to be doing the oppressing: men. Then why call them "society?" Could "society" mean the "institutions" that oppress women? But institutions must be maintained, and the same question arises: by whom? The answer to "who is the enemy?" is so obvious that the interesting issue quickly becomes "why has it been avoided?"

The master might tolerate many reforms in slavery but none that would threaten his essential role as master. Women have known this, and since "men" and "society" are in effect synonymous, they have feared confronting him. Without this confrontation and a detailed understanding of what *his* battle strategy has been that has kept us so successfully pinned down, the "Women's Movement" is worse than useless. It invites backlash from men, and no progress for women.

There has never been a feminist analysis. While discontent among women and the attempt to resolve this discontent have often implied that women form a class, no political or *causal* class analysis have followed. To rephrase my last point, the persecution of women has never been taken as the starting point for a political analysis of society.

Considering that the last massing of discontent among women continued some 70 years (1850–1920) and spread the world and that the recent accumulation of grievances began some three years ago here in America, the lack of a structural understanding of the problem is at first sight incomprehensible. It is the understanding of the *reasons* for this devastating omission and for the *implications* of the problem that forces one to "radical feminism."

Women who have tried to solve their problems as a class have proposed not solutions but dilemmas. The traditional feminists want equal rights for women with men. But on what grounds? If women serve a different *function* from men in society, wouldn't this necessarily affect women's "rights?" For example, do *all* women have the "right" not to bear children? Traditional feminism is caught in the dilemma of demanding equal treatment for unequal functions, because it is unwilling to challenge political (functional) classification by sex.

Radical women, on the other hand, grasp that women as a group somehow fit into a political analysis of society, but err in refusing to explore the significance of the fact that women form a class, the uniqueness of this class, and the implications of this description to the system of political classes. Both traditional feminists and radical women have evaded questioning any part of their *raison d'etre:* women are a class, and the terms that make up this initial assumption must be examined.

The feminist dilemma is that it is as women—or "females"—that women are persecuted, just as it was as slaves—or "blacks"—that slaves were persecuted in America. In order to improve their condition, those individuals who are today defined as women must eradicate their own definition. Women must, in a sense, commit suicide, and the journey from womanhood to a society of individuals is hazardous. The feminist dilemma is that we have the most to do, and the least to do it with. We must create, as no other group in history has been forced to do, from the very beginning.

The "battle of the sexes" is a commonplace, both over time and distance. But it is an inaccurate description of what has been happening. A "battle" implies some balance of powers, whereas when one side suffers all the losses, such as in some kinds of raids (often referred to as the "rape" of an area), that is called a *massacre.* Women have been massacred as human beings over history, and this desiny is entailed by their definition. As women begin massing together, they take the first step from *being* massacred to *engaging in* battle (resistance). Hopefully, this will eventually lead to negotiations—in the very far future—and peace.

When any person or group of persons is being mistreated or, to continue our metaphor, is being attacked, there is a succession of responses or investigations.

    (1) depending on the severity of the attack (short of an attack on life), the victim determines how much damage was done and what it was done with
    (2) where is the attack coming from? —from whom? —located where?
    (3) how can you win the immediate battle? —defensive measures? —holding actions?
    (4) why did he attack you?
    (5) how can you win (end) the war? —offensive measures. —moving within his boundaries.

These first five questions are necessary but should be considered diplomatic maneuvers. They have never been answered by the so-called "Women's Movement," and for this reason I think one cannot properly call that Movement "political." It could not have had any direction relevant to women as a class.

If diplomacy fails, that is, if your enemy refuses to stop attacking you, you must force him to stop. This requires a strategy, and this strategy requires a map of the relevant landscape, including such basic information as

    (1) who is the enemy?
    (2) where is he located?
    (3) is he getting outside support? —material? —manpower? —from whom?
    (4) where are his forces massed?
    (5) what's the best ammunition to knock them out?
    (6) what weapons is he using?
    (7) how can you counteract them?
    (8) what is your plan of attack on him to force diplomatic negotiations? —program of action (including priorities). —techniques.

I am using some military terminology, and this may seem incongruous. But why should it? We accept the phrase "battle of the sexes." It is the proposal that *women* fight *back* that seems incongruous. It has been necessary to program women's psychic structure to nonresistance on their own behalf—for obvious reasons—they make up over half the population of the world.

Without a programmatic analysis, the "Women's Movement" has been as if running blindly in the general direction of where they *guess* the last missile that just hit them was based. For the first two years of the last organizing, I was very active in this running-blind approach. It's true that we were attacking evils, but why *those* particular evils? Were they the central issues in the persecution of women? There was no map so I couldn't be sure, but I could see no reason to believe that we knew what the key issues were, much less that we were hitting them.

It became increasingly clear to me that we were incorporating many of our external problems (e.g., power hierarchies) into our own movement, and in understanding this and beginning to ask myself some of the obvious questions I've listed above, I came to the conclusion that at this time the most radical *action* that any woman or group of women could take was a feminist analysis. The implications of such an analysis is a greater threat to the opposition to human rights for women than all the actions and threatened actions put together up until this time by women.

With this introduction to the significance of a feminist analysis, I will outline what we have so far.

As I mentioned before, the *raison d'etre* of all groups formed around the problem of women is that women are a class. What is meant by that? What is meant by "women" and what is meant by "class"?

Does "women" include all women? Some groups have been driven back from the position of *all* women to some proposed "special" class such as "poor" women and eventually concentrated more on economic class than sexual class. But if we're interested in women and how women *qua* women are oppressed, this class must include *all* women.

What separates out a particular individual from other individuals as a "woman?" We recognize it's a sexual separation and that this separation has two aspects, "sociological" and "biological." The term for the sociological function is "woman" (wifman); the term for the biological function is "female" (to suckle). Both terms are descriptive of functions in the interests of someone other than the possessor.

And what is meant by "class?" We've already briefly covered the meaning as the characteristic by which certain individuals are grouped together. In the "Women's Movement" or "feminism," individuals group together to *act* on behalf of women as a class in opposition to the *class* enemies of women. It is the interaction between classes that defines political action. For this reason I call the feminist analysis a *causal class analysis.*

We have established that women are a political class characterized by a sexual function. It is clear that women, at the present time at any rate, have the *capacity* to bear children. But the question arises: "how did this biological classification become a political classification?" How or why did this elaborate superstructure of coercion develop on top of a capacity (which normally implies choice)?

It is generally agreed that women were the first political class. (Children do not properly constitute a political class since the relevant characteristic of its members [namely, age] is unstable for any given member by definition.) "Political" classes are usually defined as classes treated by other classes in some special manner distinct from the way other classes are treated. What is frequently omitted is that "political" classes are *artificial;* they define persons *with* certain capacities by those capacities, changing the contingent to the necessary, thereby appropriating the *capacities* of an individual as a *function* of society. (Definition of "political class" = individuals grouped together by other individuals as a function of the grouping individuals, depriving the grouped individuals of their human status.) A "function" of society cannot be a free individual: exercising the minimal human rights of physical integrity and freedom of movement.

If women were the first political class, and political classes must be defined by individuals outside that class, who defined them, and why, and how? It is reasonable to assume that at some period in history the population was politically undifferentiated; let's call that mass "Mankind" (generic).

The first dichotomous division of this mass is said to have been on the grounds of sex: male and female. But the genitals *per se* would be no more grounds for the human race to be divided in two than skin color or height or hair color. The genitals, in connection with a particular activity, have the *capacity* for the initiation of the reproductive process. But, I submit, it was because one half the human race bears the *burden* of the reproductive *process* and because man, the "rational" animal, had the wit to take advantage of that that the childbearers, or the "beasts of burden," were corralled into a political class. The biologically contingent burden of childbearing was equivocated into a political (or necessary) penalty, thereby modifying those individuals' definition thereby defined from the human to the functional—or animal.

There is no justification for using any individual as a function of others. Didn't *all* members of society have the right to decide if they even wanted to reproduce? Because one half of humanity was and still is forced to bear the burden of reproduction at the will of the other half, the first political class is defined not by its sex—sexuality was only relevant originally as a means to reproduction—but by the function of being the *container* of the reproductive process.

Because women have been taught to believe that men have protective feelings toward women (men have protective feelings toward their functions [property], *not* other human beings!), we women are shocked by these discoveries and ask ourselves *why* men took and continue to take advantage of us.

Some people say that men are naturally, or biologically, aggressive. But this leaves us at an impasse. If the values of society are power-oriented, there is no chance that men would agree to be medicated into an humane state.

The other alternative that has been suggested is to eliminate men as biologically incapable of humane relationships and therefore a menace to society. I can sympathize with the frustration and rage that leads to this suggestion.

But the proposal to eliminate men, as I understand it, assumes that men constitute a kind of social disease, and that by "men" is meant those individuals with certain typical genital characteristics. These genital characteristics are held to determine the organism in every biochemical respect thus determining the psychic structure as well. It may be that as in other mental derangements, and I do believe that men behave in a mentally deranged manner toward women, there is a biochemical correspondence, but this would be ultimately behaviorally determined, not genetically.

I believe that the sex roles—both male and female—must be destroyed, not the individuals who happen to possess either a penis or a vagina, or both, or neither. But many men I have spoken with see little to choose from between the two positions and feel that without the role they'd just as soon die.

Certainly it is the master who resists the abolition of slavery, especially when he is offered no recompense in power. I think that the *need* men have for the role of Oppressor is the source and foundation of all human oppression. Men suffer from a disease peculiar to Mankind which I call "metaphysical cannibalism." Men must, at the very least, cooperate in curing themselves.

Perhaps the pathology of oppression begins with just that characteristic which distinguishes Mankind from the other species: rationality. It has been proposed before that the basic condition of Man is *Angst:* the knowledge and constant awareness that He will die. Man, so the theory goes, is thus trapped by existence in an inescapable dilemma. My proposal is more fundamental.

Man is not aware of the possibility of death until He is able to put together certain abstractions, e.g., descriptions of events, with the relevant descriptive connectives. It requires a fairly sophisticated intellect to be able to extrapolate from the description of an event to one's own condition, that is, from another person's *experience* to one's own essential definition. If, instead of asking ourselves what particular conclusion rationality might arrive at, we ask what the nature of this distinguishing human characteristic is, we come to a more fundamental question.

The distinction between the nature of the animal and human brain seems to be that while an animal can imagine, that is, can mentally image some object before its eyes in some familiar situation, an animal cannot *construct* with its imagination. An animal cannot imagine a new situation made up of ingredients combined together for the first time with each ingredient initiating consequences for the other ingredients to produce the new situation.

Man's rationality is distinguished by its "constructive imagination," and this constructive imagination has been a mixed blessing. The first experience of Man in His existence is usually called "awareness" or "consciousness"; we are *sensible;* our senses are operating unrestricted by external coercions. (So far our description is also true of animals.)

What probably is first *known* to us as a distinct thing is our own body, since it is the object most consistently within our perception. As we see other objects with parts similar to our first object of perception, I think we can observe our first operation of rationality. We "imagine" that the second observation has *consequences* for the first observation. We see another human being as physically complete and autonomous (powerful) and ourselves as abbreviated thus incomplete (powerless). We can never see ourselves as fleshly integral units. We feel and sense and analogize that we are each independent units, but we can never completely perceive *ourselves* as such. Each of us begins with this initial insecurity.

Rational action (intention) requires some sense of individual autonomy. We have choice only to the degree that we are physically free, and every Man by His nature feels ambiguity on this point. In addition, Man realizes early in His maturity that there is an enormous gap between what He can do and what He can *imagine* done. The powers of His body and the powers of His mind are in conflict within one organism; they are mockeries of each other. This second factor adds frustration to the first factor of insecurity.

We now posit Man as insecure and frustrated. He has two needs:

(1) substance, as autonomous body—necessarily outside Himself, and

(2) the alleviation of His frustration (the suppression of feeling) through anger—oppression.

When we understand these two consequences peculiar to Man's nature, we can begin to understand the nature of "politics."

Man feels the need of something, like Himself, as an "extension." This presents a problem since *all* Men suffer this same need. All Men are looking for potency—the substantive power to close the gap between their bodily and mental powers. It seems clear that, once the resolution takes this external direction, some Men—ideally half (thus, one for each)—would have to catch *other* Men in some temporary depression of consciousness (when matured, rationality or constructive imagination) and at some physical disadvantage. This temporary depletion of Self provides the opportunity to simultaneously devour the mind of a member of the selected class and to appropriate their substance to oneself.

It is this process that I call "metaphysical cannibalism." It is to eat one's own kind, especially that aspect considered most potent to the victim while alive—its constructive imagination. This process absorbs the free will of the victim and destroys the evidence that the aggressor and the victim are the Same. The principle of metaphysical cannibalism seemed to meet both needs of Man: to gain potency (power) and to vent frustration (hostility).

Some psychic relief was achieved by one half the human race at the expense of the other half. Men neatly decimated Mankind by one half when they took advantage of the *social* disability of those Men who bore the burden of the reproductive process. Men invaded the being of those individuals now defined as functions, or "females," appropriated their human characteristic, and occupied their bodies. The original "rape" was political, the robbing of one half of Mankind of its humanity. The sexual connotations to the term no doubt grew out of the characterizations made later of the Men in the original action.

This original rape in its essential features has been reenacted and rationalized and justified ever since. First, those Men called women have been anchored to their position as victim by men devising numerous direct variations on women's capture, consolidating women's imprisonment. Second, men have devised indirect variations on the original crime via the principle of oppression against other Men. But all of these variations—what we call class systems and their supportive institutions—are motivated by Man's nature, and all political change will result in nothing but other variations on metaphysical cannibalism—rape—until we find a human and equitable alternative to Man's dilemma.

The male-female distinction was the beginning of the role system, wherein some persons function for others. This primary distinction should properly be referred to as the Oppressor (male)—Oppressed (female) distinction, the first political distinction. Women were the first political class and the beginning of the class system.

Certainly in the pathology of oppression, it is the agent of oppression who must be analyzed and dealt with. He is responsible for the cultivation and spread of the disease.

Still a question arises: how is it that, once the temporary susceptibility to disease (aggression) has passed, the patient does not spontaneously recover? It must be that the external attack aggravates in the victim a latent disorganization which grows and flourishes in response to and finally in tandem with the pathology imposed from outside. This disease, drawn out and cultivated from within, can finally maintain the original victim in a pathological state with few external pressures.

I proposed that the latent disorganization in "females" is the same disorganization—dilemma—from which "males" opted for metaphysical cannibalism. The role of the Oppressor (the male role) is to attempt to resolve his dilemma at the expense of others by destroying their humanity (appropriating the rationality of the Oppressed). The role of the Oppressed (the female-woman role) is to resolve her dilemma by self-destruction (bodily destruction or insanity).

Given an Oppressor—the will for power—the natural response for its counterpart, the Oppressed (given any shade of remaining Self-consciousness), is Self-annihilation. Since the purpose and nature of metaphysical cannibalism is the appropriation *of* and extension *to* substance, bodily self-destruction is uncommon in comparison with mental escapes.

While men can "cannibalize" the consciousness of women as far as human Self-construction for the woman is concerned, men get no direct use from this except insofar as they *believe* it gives them magic powers. But rationality imprisoned must destroy itself.

Metaphysical cannibalism does not solve the dilemma posed by human rationality for either the Oppressor or the Oppressed. The Oppressor can only whet his appetite for power by external measures (like drugs to dull the symptom of pain) and thus increases his disease and symptoms. The Oppressed floats into a limbo of un-Consciousness—driven there by the immobilization of her vital organ, rejecting life but not quite dead, sensible enough to still feel the pain.

The most common female escape is the psychopathological condition of love. It is a euphoric state of fantasy in which the victim transforms her oppressor into her redeemer. She turns her natural hostility toward the aggressor against the remnants of herself—her Consciousness—and sees her counterpart in contrast to herself as all-powerful (as he is by now at her expense).

The combination of his power, her self-hatred, and the hope for a life that is self-justifying—the goal of all living creatures—results in a yearning for her stolen life—her Self—that is the delusion and poignancy of love. "Love" is the natural response of the victim to the rapist.

What is extremely difficult and "unnatural," but necessary, is for the Oppressed to cure themselves (destroy the female role), to throw off the Oppressor, and to help the Oppressor to cure himself (to destroy the male role). It is superhuman, but the only alternative—the elimination of males as a biological group—is subhuman.

Politics and political theory revolve around this paradigm case of the Oppressor and the Oppressed. The theory and the practices can be divided into two parts: those institutions that directly reinforce the paradigm case of oppression, and those systems and institutions that reinforce the principle later extrapolated from this model.

       ❁   ❁   ❁

ANTIFEMINIST VIEWS

Proponents and opponents of "women's liberation" tend to use a similar vocabularly, but attach different meanings to key terms. For example, Ti-Grace Atkinson and Kate Millet define women as the oppressed class, while Norman Mailer labels man the prisoner of sex; Germaine Greer describes the unliberated woman as a female eunuch, while Midge Decter insists that feminists subtly seek a new form of chastity.

Like Norman Mailer, Esther Vilar sees men as oppressed and unfree. Man, she asserts, is "a human being who works," and who by working "supports himself, his wife, and his wife's children." In keeping with his exclusively functional position in society, his dress and appearance are simple and serviceable. "Like a child condemned to play the same game for the rest of his life," man is manipulated by woman to work in her behalf. By acquiescing to this degrading situation, he obtains security and pleasure. Aware that "life-long freedom is a fate worse than slavery, . . . man is always searching for someone or something to enslave him, . . . and, as a rule, his choice falls upon a woman." Which men are exploited by which women generally depends upon their earning power. "The more desirable women in their own class are always being snatched out from under their noses by men who happen to earn more."

Decter is less specific than Vilar in defining man, but it is possible to describe Decter's concept by way of contrast with her view of woman, whether "liberated" or "unliberated." For example, in the following selection it seems clear that Decter considers man less free than woman. Her inclination is to see both sexes conforming to the traditional stereotypes such as Greer describes. Despite the defects of women which Decter focuses upon and criticizes, she would probably prefer a concept of human nature broad enough to include both sexes.

ESTHER VILAR

Born in Buenos Aires, Esther Vilar (1935–   ) was trained as a physician, and spent a year as staff doctor at a Bavarian hospital. At various times she has worked as a translator, salesperson, assembly line operator, shoe model, and secretary. Of the divorce which ended her two-year marriage, Vilar remarked that she broke not with the man but with marriage as an institution. Reporters attested that the former spouses remained close friends. "What Is Woman?" is excerpted from *The Manipulated Man,* pp. 13–21.

ESTHER VILAR   'What Is Woman?'

A woman, as we have already said, is, in contrast to a man, a human being who does not work. One might leave it at that, for there isn't much more to say about her, were the basic concept of "human being" not so general and inexact in embracing both "man" and "woman."

Life offers the human being two choices: animal existence—a lower order of life—and spiritual existence. In general, a woman will choose the former and opt for physical well-being, a place to breed, and an opportunity to indulge unhindered in her breeding habits.

At birth, men and women have the same intellectual potential; there is no primary difference in intelligence between the sexes. It is also a fact that potential left to stagnate will atrophy. Women do not use their mental capacity: they deliberately let it disintegrate. After a few years of sporadic training, they revert to a state of irreversible mental torpor.

Why do women not make use of their intellectual potential? For the simple reason that they do not need to. It is not essential for their survival. Theoretically it is possible for a beautiful woman to have less intelligence than a chimpanzee and still be considered an acceptable member of society.

By the age of twelve at the latest, most women have decided to become prostitutes. Or, to put it another way, they have planned a future for themselves which consists of choosing a man and letting him do all the work. In return for his support, they are prepared to let him make use of their vagina at certain given moments. The minute a woman has made this decision she ceases to develop her mind. She may, of course, go on to obtain various degrees and diplomas. These increase her market value in the eyes of men, for men believe that a woman who can recite things by heart must also *know and understand* them. But any real possibility of communication between the sexes ceases at this point. Their paths are divided forever.

One of man's worst mistakes, and one he makes over and over again, is to assume that woman is his equal, that is, a human being of equal mental and emotional capacity. A man may observe his wife, listen to her, judge her feelings by her reactions, but in all this he is judging her only by outward symptoms, for he is using his *own* scale of values.

He knows what *he* would say, think, and do if he were in her shoes. When he looks at her depressing ways of doing things, he assumes there must be something that prevents her from doing what he himself would have done in her position. This is natural, as he considers himself the measure of all things—and rightly so— if humans define themselves as beings capable of abstract thought.

When a man sees a woman spending hours cooking, washing dishes, and cleaning, it never occurs to him that such jobs probably make her quite happy since they are exactly at her mental level. Instead he assumes that this drudgery prevents her from doing all those things which he himself considers worthwhile and desirable. Therefore, he invents automatic dishwashers, vacuum cleaners, and precooked foods to make her life easier and to allow her to lead the dream life he himself longs for.

But he will be disappointed: rarely using the time she has gained to take an active interest in history, politics, or astrophysics, woman bakes cakes, irons underclothes, and makes ruffles and frills for blouses or, if she is especially enterprising, covers her bathroom with flower decals. It is natural, therefore, that man assumes such things to be the essential ingredients of *gracious living*. This idea must have been instilled by woman, as he himself really doesn't mind if his cakes are store-bought, his underpants unironed, or his bathroom devoid of flowery patterns. He invents cake mixes to liberate her from drudgery, automatic irons and toilet-paper holders already covered with flower patterns to make gracious living easier to attain—and still women take no interest in serious literature, politics, or the conquest of the universe. For her, this newfound leisure comes at just the right moment. At last she can take an interest in *herself:* since a longing after intellectual achievements is alien to her, she concentrates on her external appearance.

Yet even this occupation is acceptable to man. He really loves his wife and wants her happiness more than anything in the world. Therefore, he produces non-smear lipstick, waterproof mascara, home permanents, no-iron frilly blouses, and throwaway underwear—always with the same aim in view. In the end, he hopes, this being whose needs seem to him so much more sensitive, so much more refined, will gain freedom—freedom to achieve in *her* life the ideal state which is *his* dream: to live the life of a *free* man.

Then he sits back and waits. Finally, as woman does not come to him of her own free will, he tries to tempt her into his world. He offers her coeducation, so that she is accustomed to his way of life from childhood. With all sorts of excuses, he gets her to attend his universities and initiates her into the mysteries of his own discoveries, hoping to awaken her interest in the wonders of life. He gives her access to the very last male strongholds, thereby relinquishing traditions sacred to him by encouraging her to make use of her right to vote in the hope that she will change the systems of government he has managed to think up so laboriously, according to her own ideas. Possibly he even hopes that she will be able to create peace in the world—for, in his opinion, women are a pacifist influence.

In all this he is so determined and pigheaded that he fails to see what a fool he is making of himself—ridiculous by his own standards, not those of women, who have absolutely no sense of humor.

No, women do not laugh at men. At most they get irritated. The old institutions of house and home are not yet so obviously outdated and derelict that they can't justify relinquishing all their intellectual pursuits and renouncing all their claims to better jobs. One does wonder, however, what will happen when housework is still further mechanized, when there are *enough* good nursery schools nearby, or when—as must occur before long—men discover that children themselves are not essential.

If only man would stop for one moment in his heedless rush toward progress and think about this state of affairs, he would inevitably realize that his efforts to give woman a sense of mental stimulation have been totally in vain. It is true that woman gets progressively more elegant, more well-groomed, more "cultured," but her demands on life will always be material, never intellectual.

Has she ever made use of the mental processes he teaches at his universities to develop her own theories? Does she do independent research in the institutes he has thrown open to her? Someday it will dawn on man that woman does not read the wonderful books with which he has filled his libraries. And though she may well admire his marvelous works of art in museums, she herself will rarely create, only copy. Even the plays and films, visual exhortations to woman on her own level to liberate herself, are judged only by their entertainment value. They will never be a first step to revolution.

When a man, believing woman his equal, realizes the futility of her way of life, he naturally tends to think that it must be *his* fault, that *he* must be suppressing *her*. But in our time women are no longer subject to the will of men. Quite the contrary. They have been given every opportunity to win their independence and if, after all this time, they have not liberated themselves and thrown off their shackles, we can only arrive at one conclusion: there are no shackles to throw off.

It is true that men love women, but they also despise them. Anyone who gets up in the morning fresh and ready to conquer new worlds (with infrequent success, admittedly, because he has to earn a living) is bound to despise someone who simply isn't interested in such pursuits. Contempt may even be one of the main reasons for his efforts to further the mental development of a woman. He feels ashamed of her and assumes that she, too, must be ashamed of herself. So, being a gentleman, he tries to help.

Men seem incapable of realizing that women entirely lack ambition, desire for knowledge, and need to prove themselves, all things which, to him, are a matter of course. They allow men to live in a world apart because they do not want to join them. Why should they? The sort of independence men have means nothing to women, because women don't feel dependent. They are not even embarrassed by the intellectual superiority of men because they have no ambition in that direction.

There is one great advantage which women have over men: *they have a choice*—a choice between the life of a man and the life of a dim-witted, parasitic luxury item. There are too few women who would not select the latter. Men do not have this choice.

If women really felt oppressed by men, they would have developed hate and fear for them, as the oppressed always do, but women do not fear men, much less hate them. If they really felt humiliated by men's mental superiority, they would have used every means in their power to change the situation. If women really felt unfree, surely, at such a favorable time in their history, they would have broken free of their oppressors.

In Switzerland, one of the most highly developed countries of the world, where until recently women were not allowed to vote, in a certain canton, it is reported, the majority of women were against introducing the vote for women. The Swiss men were shattered, for they saw in this unworthy attitude yet another proof of centuries of male oppression.

How very wrong they were! Women feel anything but oppressed by men. On the contrary, one of the many depressing truths about the relationship between the sexes is simply that man hardly exists in a woman's world: Man is not even powerful enough to revolt against. Woman's dependence on him is only material, of a "physical" nature, something like a tourist's dependence on an airline, a café proprietor's on his espresso machine, a car's on gasoline, a television set's on electric current. Such dependencies hardly involve agonizing.

Ibsen, who suffered from the same misapprehensions as other men, meant his *Doll's House* to be a kind of manifesto for the freedom of women. The premiére in 1880 certainly shocked *men,* and they determined to fight harder to improve women's position.

For women themselves, however, the struggle for emancipation as usual took shape in a change of style: for a while they delighted in their often-laughed-at-masquerade as suffragettes.

Later on, the philosophy of Sartre made a similarly profound impression on women. As proof that they understood it completely, they let their hair grow down to their waists and wore black pullovers and trousers.

Even the teachings of the Chinese Communist leader Mao Tsetung were a success—the Mao look lasted for a whole season.

*   *   *

MIDGE DECTER

Midge Decter (1927–   ) has characterized herself (in her *Liberal Parents, Radical Children*) as "a member of what must be called America's professional, or enlightened, liberal middle class." Born in the midwest and educated under a strong religious influence, Decter has fulfilled "roles" of wife and mother while maintaining editorial positions for such journals as *Commentary* and *Harper's.* Besides the book from which the following is excerpted (*The Liberated Woman and Other Americans,* pp. 86–95), Decter has also collected her articles about women into a volume entitled *The New Chastity and Other Arguments against Women's Liberation.*

MIDGE DECTER   'The Liberated Woman'

BEING A WOMAN

.   .   .   .

What had brought this girl to such a pass? She was the pride, if the puzzle, of all who had a hand in her growing up. She was the envy of childhood friends. Even the society against whose "values" she had inveighed was eager to pronounce her, through all its media and honored spokesmen, a superior being to any it had heretofore produced. Nothing either—not even the once operative but now vanished notion of the beginner's apprenticeship to his elders—had stood externally between her and her personal ambition. Moreover, out in the real world, as in school and at home nothing produced by this ambition would go without at least its due measure of attention. The question of marriage, the question of having children, were now entirely in her own keeping. Yet she saw herself, felt herself, believed herself to be, oppressed. Oppressed by the parents who had always stood in awe of the possibility of her unhappiness; oppressed by the schools which had tracked themselves according to the contours of her particular capacities; oppressed by the working world which had issued her its most solemn invitation; and oppressed above all by the men who had wished to enter with her into some more or less negotiable pact of mutual advantage.

Partly, of course, she felt oppressed because she was invited to do so by the expression all around her of the same feeling in others. Movements like Women's Lib always have some degree of that circularity about them. Which is to say, in addition to being expressions of a deep dissatisfaction, they do themselves constitute a culture of dissatisfaction, which gives it style and sanction among the semblables and *soeurs* of their leaders. And who would not, enjoying something less than divine happiness, be both soothed and excited by the idea that he was indeed a victim?

Still, there must have been, had to have been, a very fertile ground in her own anxieties for all those public discontents to have taken hold there so quickly. A good deal of that anxiety had to do with her need to make a mark in the world. She had for the first time in her life suffered its very real pangs during her freshman year in college, when, bereft of a public identity, she had found herself quite unexpectedly with the need among strangers to, as it were, introduce herself. Such a demand must have existed for college freshmen everywhere and at all times, but no one had been less prepared for it by life than she. Convinced by the attitude of those around her that there would be no let or hindrance to her achievement, she was given to feel, on the other side, no corresponding pinch of necessity. Her condition in fact approached not the least workable definition of freedom: a state in which all the options are open. She could succeed or get by; she could prepare herself to be fully self-supporting, to play some luxuriously "creative" if dependent role, or to enhance herself culturally and spiritually for a life of marriage and homemaking. She could stay in school or she could leave, to the disappointment of family and friends perhaps, but with none of the opprobrium attaching to what for a young man would have constituted the very definition of failure, future as well as present. Therefore she had to choose and in choosing, state something voluntarily on a definition of herself. This crisis as it was first enacted in school was, as we have seen, short-lived. Not only because she took the option to succeed but because, given her charm and school's commitment to the idea of what would be the best for her, the institution itself became implicated in her making the "right" choice. There was, then, no genuine settlement, only a deferral of the problem.

Her one brief job counted for very little in this particular connection. For one thing she had not got herself this job, it was given to her. For another, in her almost immediate decision not to throw in her lot with the magazine's lay the possibility to disregard altogether the question of her performance there. So what she actually knew of jobs she knew from hearsay. First, there was a crucial childhood memory: women sitting in the kitchen mornings over coffee, complaining of the dullness of the days with nothing but children for company while "he" was off in the city, mysteriously but no doubt profitably—and certainly no doubt pleasurably— spending his time "among people." The men who returned home each night had looked in the ordinary way of things tired from a day's work and often worried. Their conversation bespoke anything but a life of far-off adventure—they spoke of money a good deal, of problems, of enemies and allies. But the impression had been fixed: jobs were some kind of preserve of the privileged, they were meant to be interesting.

Then there were the jobs of her friends. Those among them who had been best—*i.e.*, most liberally—educated seemed to have the least satisfying of these. Either, the complaint ran, the job was too routine and boring, or it involved too many worries about things its holder preferred not to have to worry about—too much attention to precise detail, say, or being answerable to too many angry people when something went wrong. Funnily enough, though it was one of the cardinal planks in the feminist platform, very few of the complaints aired in her hearing had to do with money, except as an aspect of the appreciation or lack of appreciation being shown by management for the true qualifications and talents of the complainant. Nor did she ever hear a tale of someone's demanding more money at the risk of her resignation and being turned down.

What she heard most about, though she did not articulate it to herself in so simple a fashion, were problems of status. The girls she knew who were secretaries resented being called secretaries, they would without hesitation trade ten dollars a week for some title that to a hearer would gloss over their exact position in a hierarchy, and they seemed to resent most bitterly of all those (to their mind) housewifely services they were expected to provide, such as procuring coffee, buying gifts, making reservations. And most of them refused absolutely to work for other women. For it was difficult enough to "serve" a man, but someone differentiated from them only by position and title was nearly intolerable. Those, on the other hand, who had jobs carrying independent responsibility tended to be even more restive, for either the work was found to contain too large a component of drudgery or the pay to be insufficiently honorific or—and this is a very common complaint, she'd so briefly made it herself—the purposes of the enterprise for which they were asked to assume some measure of responsibility were uncongenial to them.

She never heard men issuing such complaints as these, except for that special breed of men she had always in her mind's privacy dubbed "losers"—who, no matter what they did, archly or self-righteously pronounced themselves superior to it and thereby were justified and ennobled in their failure. And putting all these things together—the "interestingness" of work to men, its obvious drudgery and lack of dignity for women—the conclusion was inevitable: the status of women was that of inferiors, they were not being handed a fair portion of that which had been preempted by and was being desperately held as the nearly exclusive preserve of men.

She had, to be sure, known men whose every day on the job involved them in a swallowing of pride, or at least the resignation to a good deal of unpleasantness, and who claimed to have no choice on the grounds of their need to support themselves and others. At college she had even met young men whose choice of studies and future career had hinged on some consideration of what was likely to yield the best return in terms of both money and conditions of work—though there were clearly many fewer of these than there had once been—and for them she and her friends had tended to feel a certain contempt. If there was, then, something of a logical flaw involved in training oneself for a life of monied leisure, in the study, say, of the English novel, only to find oneself bitter about being thought unqualified in spirit as well as training for valuable work, such a flaw was not taken by her friends to be their own. The world had been misrepresented to them, they said; or, more commonly now, the world, precisely in its unwillingness to make proper use of their superior endowments, was an evil place and must be forced to mend its ways.

For herself, a free-lance writer, the problem posed itself somewhat differently. She could not, in the actual conditions of work, claim to be discriminated against. She must inevitably sit down all by herself and face her typewriter. The product of this confrontation had to be judged immediately and found adequate or inadequate. Both the level and quantity of her production were up to her. But her difficulties were immense. She found she could not always do what she intended, and there were times when she would not meet her assignments at all. She often had to undergo that extremely painful experience for writers of having her work emended, altered, questioned, under what she came to feel was an altogether arbitrary editorial eye. In high school, then college, she had heard nothing but praise for whatever she was able to do. Now she was often

criticized: editors rejected her, or people took exception to, um-
brage at, something she'd published. She started to tighten up more
and more at her typewriter. Once, for a period of four or five
months, she was unable to write a sentence.

She began to tell herself that the real difficulty lay in the world's
expectations of her. The people around her, thinking of her inevitably as a wife and mother, did not care if she wrote or not. Her
lover, pretending sympathy, demanded that he have clean shirts
and a made bed—her contribution to the upkeep of the common
household thus being made equal to her attention to her own concerns. Editors, pretending interest in her, seemed to keep raising
the ante on her performance, asking her to take on more and more
ambitious projects and to be responsible to more and a wider range
of subjects that intimidated her. To this last, she responded with
an ever greater concentration on those subjects where her expertise
might not be challenged. Finally, with a large assist from Women's
Liberation itself, she found it most satisfying to write only about
herself.

Primary among the things she wrote about herself was a continuing discussion, carried on through symposia in virtually all the
major national magazines, of her attitude to men and sex. She might
have suspected there was something slightly redolent of the exploitation of women in the sudden spate of requests to discourse
in public on the facts and circumstances of her own sexual temperament, but she did not. In the light of the overwhelming importance
the matter had come to assume in her own eyes, she took its importance for others as a matter of course. Whatever reservation she
might have had about exposing not only herself but all the men
she'd slept with or refused to sleep with vanished under the impact
of the knowledge that her experience, far from being private, was
exemplary. She told of her unhappiness as a sexual object, of the
lack of satisfaction with her so-called freedom; she described the
humiliations of her abortion. Her declarations began to feed on
themselves, and she truly warmed to her subject.

No one, not even her lovers, was as likely to be taken aback by
her revelations as her own parents, particularly her mother. The
sexual freedom she had been granted since early girlhood was
something that not only had cost them the guilt of discovering in
themselves a certain old-fashioned emotional resistance to it that
had to be suppressed in the name of principle and fairness of mind,
but had brought them considerable pain of simple envy. The freedom so largely denied to and so valiantly striven for by her mother
—which striving formed the basis of a vow that her own daughter's
sexuality would not be distorted by adult hypocrisy and purpose-
less social punishment—had been her generation's very definition
of sexual equality: the right to live within a single standard of

sexual conduct and the corresponding right to demand, as well as to give, sexual pleasure. Now here was her daughter, untortured by the longings that had once imposed upon herself the need for deceit and deviousness, assisted and supported in the realization of her true nature, claiming that it was precisely the possibility to have a wide sexual experience that constituted the major block to women's equality. For, said her daughter in effect, for a girl to be sexually active entangled her all the more with male egos and desires. And to seek pleasure in sex was to involve oneself in judgments of success and failure that were essentially male, and not female, in character. A woman permitted honestly to seek her own needs, as men had since time immemorial been permitted to seek theirs, would be demanding love and respect for and consideration of her person, rather than the direct satisfaction of a lust she was in any case not sure she had ever felt.

Her lover's response to this was not so much to be taken aback as to feel a curious relief mingled with rage and guilt. His boyhood, too—and until this moment he had not realized to how great an extent—had been held in thrall to the myth of the new sexual freedom of women. His success with girls, for instance, had been measured not by the number of them he could bring to submission but by the degree of sexual satisfaction he could bring each or any of them to. Each sexual encounter had been a test of his prowess not as a hunter but as a provider. So to have stalked and overcome his prey was not the end but only the beginning of his labors. To this end, he, too, had been successively monogamous, disciplining the lust which now need shame him only by its most flagrant weaknesses— its impatience and its reluctance to differentiate individuals. With the result, as he said to himself bitterly, that the woman to whom he had given most of himself—to the point, if she had asked it, of marriage—was now telling the world what she had never in deepest intimacy told him: that it had all been for naught. As his rage was that of having been betrayed, so his relief was that of knowing what it was, finally, that stood at the center of those delicate negotiations on which he had lavished so much anxiety, so much deluded consciousness. His guilt grew out of the suspicion that, withal, her problem was his responsibility, that had he but succeeded with her . . . mental habits, especially with respect to sex, after all, die hard; he thought, however, that if she called him selfish oppressor long enough and often enough, he might yet rid himself of that guilt.

As for her, the satisfactions of her new burst of self-expression blinded her to the fact that in the act of announcing women to be the equals of men, what she was really saying was that women were very different from men and that they wanted fundamentally different things. Nor was she aware that in her denunciation of men

for keeping her from her true freedom what she was really denouncing them for was their having submitted to an earlier set of
female demands, demands which had failed to bring her true happiness, demands she felt enslaved to rather than liberated by, and
which she would abjure but knew not now in the name of what.

It is virtually an axiom of human nature that we will not know
that which we are not forced to know. Thus given her upbringing
and education, our heroine has attained to womanhood knowing
very little about men and women. She need not know, for an elementary start, that the sexual revolution which oppresses her is a
revolution made in her behalf by other women, wrested from men
and assented to by them—as is always the politics of such cases—in
the face of the power of the revolutionaries, and not from some
notion of particular advantage to themselves. Nor need she, child
of a marriage whose manners bespoke equality of husband and
wife, know that marriage and children are not things imposed on
women by men but quite the other way around. She would in fact
be outraged by the proposition, taught in no school either of learning or life ever attended by her, that marriage is not a psychic relationship but a transaction: in which a man foregoes the operations
of his blind boyhood lust, and agrees to undertake the support and
protection of a family and receives in exchange the ease and comforts of home.

Above all, being a creature of the sixties rather than the fifties,
she need not know that freedom is an end in itself, a value whose
strongest connections are thus not with happiness but with responsibility. The freedom granted her by society is, in so short a time
as it has been demanded, remarkably equal to that enjoyed by
men. It is the freedom to make certain choices and take the consequences. If she wishes to devote herself to marriage, she may do so.
If she wishes instead to pursue a career, she may do so. If there
are difficulties put in the way of the latter—of which her sex may
or may not be one but is certainly not the only one and is often indeed not the one she complains of—she is free to attempt to overcome them. If she opts to have both marriage and a career, she
will put herself in the way of certain inevitable practical difficulties,
the managing of which will on the other hand also widen her
options for gratification.

Perhaps most important, if she wishes not to be a sexual object,
she may refrain from being one. What, after all, is to stop her from
setting her own social and emotional price on her sexual complicity
and then simply waiting for the man, if any, who is willing to pay
it? If the price should be deemed too high, that also would be a
freely chosen consequence. Or she might accept the implication of
most of the pronouncements of Women's Liberation and simply
remain chaste, thereby restoring to herself that uniquely feminine

power over men which many women so cavalierly made light of in their struggle for equality. Freedom, runs a social theory thought by her educators too stodgy to trouble her pretty head with, can only be granted by others in theory; its realization can lie only in one's enactment of it.

To judge from what she says and does, however—finding only others at fault for her predicaments, speaking always of herself as a means of stating the general case, shedding tears as a means of negotiation—the freedom she truly seeks is of a rather different kind. It is a freedom demanded by children and enjoyed by no one: the freedom from all difficulty. If in the end her society is at fault for anything, it is for allowing her to grow up with the impression that this is something possible to ask. Even the good fairies who attended her birth would never have dared so far.

RELATED READINGS

Since pertinent material is constantly increasing, the following list should be regarded as merely representative of current views. Some sources constitute classical renditions of their differing perspectives (e.g., Betty Friedan's and Norman Mailer's); others offer philosophical analyses of feminist and antifeminist views. An annotated bibliography of this material is available in *Women and Feminism in American History: A Guide to Information Sources* by Elizabeth Tingley and Donald Tingley. Detroit: Gale Publishers, 1981.

Andelin, Helen. *Fascinating Womanhood.* New York: Bantam Books, 1965.

Bullough, Vern L., and Bullough, Bonnie. *The Subordinate Sex.* Urbana: University of Illinois Press, 1973.

Cade, Toni, ed. *The Black Woman.* New York: Mentor Books, 1970.

Chafe, William H. *Women and Equality.* New York: Oxford University Press, 1977.

Daly, Mary. *Gyn-Ecology: The Metaethics of Radical Feminism.* Boston: Beacon Press, 1979.

Decter, Midge. *The New Chastity and Other Arguments against Women's Liberation.* New York: Coward, McCann and Geoghegan, Inc., 1972.

Firestone, Shulamith. *The Dialectic of Sex.* New York: Bantam Books, 1970.

Freeman, Jo, ed. *Women: a Feminist Perspective.* Palo Alto: Mayfield Publishing Company, 1975.

Friedan, Betty. *The Feminine Mystique.* New York: Dell Publishing Company, 1963.

————. *It Changed My Life.* New York: Random House, 1976.

————. *The Second Stage.* New York: Summit Press, 1981.

Frye, Marilyn. "Male Chauvinism: A Conceptual Analysis," In *Philosophy and Sex,* edited by Robert Baker and Frederick Elliston, pp. 65–79. Buffalo: Prometheus Books, 1976.

Goldberg, Steven. *The Inevitability of Patriarchy.* New York: William Morrow and Company, Inc., 1973.

Gilder, George. *Sexual Suicide.* New York: Quadrangle Books, 1973.

Gornick, Vivian, and Moran, Barbara K., eds. *Woman in Sexist Society.* New York: Basic Books, 1971.

Harding, Sandra. "Feminism: Reform or Revolution?" In *Women and Philosophy,* edited by Carol Gould and Marx Wartofsky, pp. 271–284. New York: G.P. Putnam and Sons, 1976.

Hein, Hilde. "On Reaction and the Women's Movement." In *Women and Philosophy,* edited by Carol Gould and Marx Wartofsky, pp. 248–270. New York: G.P. Putnam and Sons, 1976.

Jaggar, Alison, and Struhl, Paula, eds. *Feminist Frameworks.* New York: McGraw-Hill Book Company, 1978.

Koedt, Anne, and Firestone, Shulamith, eds. *Notes from the Third Year: Women's Liberation.* New York, 1972.

Lakhoff, Robin. *Language and Women's Place.* New York: Harper and Row Publishers, Inc., 1975.

Lerna, Gerda. *The Female Experience.* Indianapolis: Bobbs-Merrill and Company, Inc., 1977.

Lifton, Robert J., ed. *The Woman in America.* Boston: Beacon Press, 1967.

Lynn, Mary D., ed. *Women's Liberation in the Twentieth Century.* New York: John Wiley, 1975.

Mahowald, Mary B. "Feminism: Individualistic or Communalistic?" In *Freedom* (*Proceedings of the American Catholic Philosophical Association*), vol. 50, pp. 219–228, 1976.

Mailer, Norman. *The Prisoner of Sex.* Boston: Little, Brown and Company, 1971.

Marine, Gene. *A Male Guide to Women's Liberation.* New York: Holt, Rinehart and Winston, Inc., 1972.

McBride, Angela B. *Living with Contradictions: A Married Feminist.* New York: Harper and Row Publishers, Inc., 1975.

Mitchell, Juliet. *Psychoanalysis and Feminism.* New York: Pantheon Books, 1974.

Miller, Casey, and Swift, Kate. *Words and Women.* New York: Doubleday and Company, 1976.

Millett, Kate. *Sexual Politics.* New York: Doubleday and Company, 1970.

Morgan, Marabel. *The Total Woman*. Old Tappan, New Jersey: Fleming H. Revell Company, 1973.

Morgan, Robin, ed. *Sisterhood Is Powerful*. New York: Vintage Books, 1970.

Mount, Eric. *The Feminine Factor*. Richmond, Virginia: John Knox Press, 1973.

Reeves, Nancy. *Womenkind: Beyond the Stereotypes*. Chicago: Aldine Publishing Company, 1971.

Roberts, Joan I., ed. *Beyond Intellectual Sexism*. New York: David McKay Company, Inc., 1976.

Roszak, Betty, and Roszak, Theodore. *Masculine/Feminine*. New York: Harper Colophon Books, 1969.

Schafly, Phyllis. *The Power of the Positive Woman*. New York: Arlington House, 1977.

Steinem, Gloria, and Chester G. *Wonder Woman*. New York: Holt, Rinehart and Winston, Inc., 1974.

Thompson, Mary Lou, ed. *Voices of the New Feminism*. Boston: Beacon Press, 1970.

II

RECENT PHILOSOPHICAL APPROACHES

Authors included in this section represent several strains of philosophical emphases: utilitarian, existential, marxist, and analytic. From their differing perspectives the selections all reflect concern about the rights and liberty of individuals. Except for Nietzsche and Kierkegaard, this concern extends to members of both sexes. Thus the overall thrust, in contrast to that of most earlier philosophers, is supportive of today's feminist principles.

THE UTILITARIAN CONTEXT

In general, a utilitarian philosophy attempts to uphold the value of both the individual and society, while insisting that empirical consequences are (or ought to be) the criteria according to which we establish priorities for moral and political decisions. Like Jeremy Bentham, his philosophical mentor, JOHN STUART MILL (1806–1873) affirmed that the greatest good for society is constituted by the greatest happiness or pleasure for the greatest number of individuals. Unlike Bentham, however, Mill maintained that the pleasures which may justify ethical action differ qualitatively as well as quantitatively. For example, merely sensual delights are in fact inferior to intellectual or aesthetic modes of pleasure. Moreover, it is futile to pursue happiness directly, or for oneself alone. "[P]aradoxical as the assertion may be," Mill claimed, "the conscious ability to do without happiness gives the best prospect of realizing such happiness as is attainable." To secure happiness for ourselves, then, we must seek primarily to promote the well-being of others.

Mill's personal life provides an intriguing example of consistency with his utilitarian ethics. Mill was a bachelor, and Harriett Taylor was a wife and mother of two when they met in their early twenties. Despite the deep rapport of intellect and sentiment which soon developed between them, it was not until twenty-one years later (two years after John Taylor's death) that they married. Harriet characterized her relationship both to her husband and to Mill during those years as that of a *Seelenfreundin* (a spiritual friend).

45

Their decision not to break up the Taylor family through divorce seems to have been motivated by concern to promote the greatest happiness for the greatest number.

Mill's Concept of Human Nature

In his famous essay *On Liberty*, which Mill describes as a joint production with Harriet Taylor, the liberty defended is a liberty of conscience (of thought and feeling), of tastes and pursuits, and of association. The only grounds which justify limitation of any individual's liberty in these regards are self-protection and the prevention of harm to others. Since human nature is essentially free and fundamentally good, every individual has the right to seek happiness according to her or his own capacity, while respecting and supporting the right of others to do the same. Freedom, according to Mill, is a prerequisite for human happiness and progress. Contentment or satisfaction is possible for those who become inured to living in shackles, but such individuals cannot experience genuine happiness until they are actually free.

Before marrying Harriet Taylor, Mill formally renounced whatever legal advantages might accrue to him by reason of the marriage contract. "There is no natural inequality between the sexes, except perhaps in bodily strength; even that admits of doubt, and if bodily strength is to be the measure of superiority, mankind are no better than savages." Equality, however, should not be confused with sameness. The proper relationship between the sexes, as among all individuals, with their inevitable diversity, is one of complementarity, or "reciprocal superiority." Each of us has something unique and superior to contribute to one another.

The following is excerpted from an essay first published in 1869. Although Harriet had died eleven years earlier, Mill thus described her contribution to the work: "[A]ll that is most striking and profound belongs to my wife; coming from the fund of thought which had been made common to us both, by our innumerable conversations and discussions on a topic which filled so large a place in our minds."

JOHN STUART MILL   The Subjection of Women

The object of this Essay is to explain as clearly as I am able, the grounds of an opinion which I have held from the very earliest period when I had formed any opinions at all on social or political matters, and which, instead of being weakened or modified, has been constantly growing stronger by the progress of reflection and the experience of life: That the principle which regulates the existing social relations between the two sexes—the legal subordination of one sex to the other—is wrong in itself, and now one of the chief hindrances to human improvement; and that it ought to be replaced by a principle of perfect equality, admitting no power or privilege on the one side, nor disability on the other. . . .

The generality of a practice is in some cases a strong presumption that it is, or at all events once was, conducive to laudable ends. This is the case, when the practice was first adopted, or afterwards kept up, as a means to such ends, and was grounded on experience of the mode in which they could be most effectually attained. If the authority of men over women, when first established, had been the result of a conscientious comparison between different modes of constituting the government of society; if, after trying various other modes of social organization—the government of women over men, equality between the two, and such mixed and divided modes of government as might be invented—it had been decided, on the testimony of experience, that the mode in which women are wholly under the rule of men, having no share at all in public concerns, and each in private being under the legal obligation of obedience to the man with whom she has associated her destiny, was the arrangement most conducive to the happiness and well being of both; its general adoption might then be fairly thought to be some evidence that, at the time when it was adopted, it was the best: though even then the considerations which recommended it may, like so many other primeval social facts of the greatest importance, have subsequently, in the course of ages, ceased to exist. But the state of the case is in every respect the reverse of this. In the first place, the opinion in favour of the present system, which entirely subordinates the weaker sex to the stronger, rests upon theory only; for there never has been trial made of any other: so that experience, in the sense in which it is vulgarly opposed to theory, cannot be pretended to have pronounced any verdict. And in the second place, the adoption of this system of inequality never was the result of deliberation, or forethought, or any social ideas, or any notion whatever of what conduced to the benefit of humanity or the good order of society. It arose simply from the fact that from the very earliest twilight of human society, every woman (owing to the value attached to her by men, combined with her inferiority in muscular strength) was found in a state of bondage to some man. Laws and systems of polity always begin by recognising the relations they find already existing between individuals. . . .

So true is it that unnatural generally means only uncustomary, and that everything which is usual appears natural. The subjection of women to men being a universal custom, any departure from it quite naturally appears unnatural. But how entirely, even in this case, the feeling is dependent on custom, appears by ample experience. Nothing so much astonishes the people of distant parts of the world, when they first learn anything about England, as to be told that it is under a queen: the thing seems to them so unnatural as to be almost incredible. To Englishmen this does not seem in the least degree unnatural, because they are used to it; but they do feel it unnatural that women should be soldiers or members of parliament. In the feudal ages, on the contrary, war and politics were not thought unnatural to women, because not unusual. . . .

But, it will be said, the rule of men over women differs from all these others in not being a rule of force: it is accepted voluntarily; women make no complaint, and are consenting parties to it.

In the first place, a great number of women do not accept it. Ever since there have been women able to make their sentiments known by their writings (the only mode of publicity which society permits to them), an increasing number of them have recorded protests against their present social condition. . . .

How many more women there are who silently cherish similar aspirations, no one can possibly know; but there are abundant tokens how many *would* cherish them, were they not so strenuously taught to repress them as contrary to the proprieties of their sex. It must be remembered, also, that no enslaved class ever asked for complete liberty at once. . . . It is a political law of nature that those who are under any power of ancient origin, never begin by complaining of the power itself, but only of its oppressive exercise. There is never any want of women who complain of ill usage by their husbands. There would be infinitely more, if complaint were not the greatest of all provocatives to a repetition and increase of the ill usage. . . .

Men do not want solely the obedience of women, they want their sentiments. All men, except the most brutish, desire to have, in the woman most nearly connected with them, not a forced slave but a willing one, not a slave merely, but a favourite. They have therefore put everything in practice to enslave their minds. . . .

All women are brought up from the earliest years in the belief that their ideal of character is the very opposite to that of men; not self-will, and government by self-control, but submission, and yielding to the control of others. All the moralities tell them that it is the duty of women, and all the current sentimentalities that it is their nature, to live for others; to make complete abnegation of themselves, and to have no life but in their affections. And by their affections are meant the only ones they are allowed to have—those to the men with whom they are connected, or to the children who constitute an additional and indefeasible tie between them and a man. When we put together three things—first, the natural attraction between opposite sexes; secondly, the wife's entire dependence on the husband, every privilege or pleasure she has being either his gift, or depending entirely on his will; and lastly, that the principal object of human pursuit, consideration, and all objects of social ambition, can in general be sought or obtained by her only through him, it would be a miracle if the object of being attractive to men had not become the polar star of feminine education and formation of character. And, this great means of influence over the minds of women have been acquired, an instinct of selfishness made men avail themselves of it to the utmost as a means of holding women in subjection, by representing to them meekness, submissiveness, and resignation of all individual will into the hands of a man, as an essential part of sexual attractiveness. . . .

The preceding considerations are amply sufficient to show that custom, however universal it may be, affords in this case no presumption, and ought not to create any prejudice, in favour of the arrangements which place women in social and political subjection to men. But I may go farther, and maintain that the course of history, and the tendencies of progressive human society, afford not only no presumption in favour of this system of inequality of rights, but a strong one against it; and that, so far as the whole course of human improvement up to this time, the whole stream of modern tendencies, warrants any inference on the subject, it is, that this relic of the past is discordant with the future, and must necessarily disappear. . . .

Neither does it avail anything to say that the *nature* of the two sexes adapts them to their present functions and position, and renders these appropriate to them. Standing on the ground of common sense and the constitution of the human mind, I deny that any one knows, or can know, the nature of the two sexes, as long as they have only been seen in their present relation to one another. If men had ever been found in society without women, or women without men, or if there had been a society of men and women in which the women were not under the control of the men, something might have been positively known about the mental and moral differences which may be inherent in the nature of each. What is now called the nature of women is an eminently artificial thing—the result of forced repression in some directions, unnatural stimulation in others. It may be asserted without scruple, that no other class of dependents have had their character so entirely distorted from its natural proportions by their relation with their masters. . . .

Even the preliminary knowledge, what the differences between the sexes now are, apart from all questions as to how they are made what they are, is still in the crudest and most incomplete state. . . .

It is a subject on which nothing final can be known, as long as those who alone can really know it, women themselves, have given but little testimony, and that little, mostly suborned. . . .

It is only a man here and there who has any tolerable knowledge of the character even of the women of his own family. I do not mean, of their capabilities; these nobody knows, not even themselves, because most of them have never been called out. I mean their actually existing thoughts and feelings. Many a man thinks he perfectly understands women, because he has had amatory relations with several, perhaps with many of them. If he is a good observer, and his experience extends to quality as well as quantity, he may have learnt something of one narrow department of their nature—an important department, no doubt. But of all the rest of it, few persons are generally more ignorant, because there are few from whom it is so carefully hidden. The most favourable case which a man can generally have for studying the character of a woman, is that of his own wife: for the opportunities are greater, and the cases of complete sympathy not so unspeakably rare. And in fact, this is the source from which any knowledge worth having on the subject has, I believe, generally come. But most men have not had the opportunity of studying in this way more than a single case: accordingly one can, to an almost laughable degree, infer what a man's wife is like, from his opinions about women in general. . . .

[E]ven if he could study many women of one rank, or of one country, he would not thereby understand women of other ranks or countries; and even if he did, they are still only the women of a single period of history; we may safely assert that the knowledge which men can acquire of women, even as they have been and are, without reference to what they might be, is wretchedly imperfect and superficial, and always will be so, until women themselves have told all they have to tell. . . . One thing we may be certain of—that what is contrary to women's nature to do, they never will be made to do by simply giving their nature free play. . . . What women by nature cannot do, it is quite superfluous to forbid them from doing. What they can do, but not so well as the men who are their competitors, competition suffices to exclude them from. . . . If women have a greater natural inclination for some things than for others, there is no need of laws or social inculcation to make the majority of them do the former in preference to the latter. . . .

The general opinion of men is supposed to be, that the natural vocation of a woman is that of a wife and mother. I say, is supposed to be, because, judging from acts—from the whole of the present constitution of society—one might infer that their opinion was the direct contrary. They might be supposed to think that the alleged natural vocation of women was of all things the most repugnant to their nature; insomuch that if they are free to do anything else—if any other means of living, or occupation of their time and faculties, is open, which has any chance of appearing desirable to them— there will not be enough of them who will be willing to accept the condition said to be natural to them. If this is the real opinion of men in general, it would be well that it should be spoken out. I should like to hear somebody openly enunciating the doctrine (it is already implied in much that is written on the subject)—"It is necessary to society that women should marry and produce children. They will not do so unless they are compelled. Therefore it is necessary to compel them." . . .

I am far from pretending that wives are in general no better treated than slaves; but no slave is a slave to the same lengths, and in so full a sense of the word, as a wife is. Hardly any slave, except one immediately attached to the master's person, is a slave at all hours and all minutes; in general he has, like a soldier, his fixed task, and when it is done, or when he is off duty, he disposes within certain limits, of his own time, and has a family life into which the master rarely intrudes. . . .

Surely, if a woman is denied any lot in life but that of being the personal bodyservant of a despot, and is dependent for everything upon the chance of finding one who may be disposed to make a favourite of her instead of merely a drudge, it is a very cruel aggravation of her fate that she should be allowed to try this chance only once. The natural sequel and corollary from this state of things would be, that since her all in life depends upon obtaining a good master, she should be allowed to change again and again until she finds one. I am not saying that she ought to be allowed this privilege. That is a totally different consideration. The question of divorce, in the sense involving liberty of remarriage, is one into which it is foreign to my purpose to enter. All I now say, is that to those to whom nothing but servitude is allowed, the free choice of servitude is the only, though a most insufficient, alleviation. . . . If married life were all that it might be expected to be, looking to the laws alone, society would be a hell upon earth. Happily there are both feelings and interests which in many men exclude, and in most, greatly temper, the impulses and propensities which lead to tyranny. . . . [B]ecause men in general do not inflict, nor women suffer, all the misery which could be inflicted and suffered if the full power of tyranny with which the man is legally invested were acted on; the defenders of the existing form of the institution think that all its iniquity is justified, and that any complaint is merely quarrelling with the evil which is the price paid for every great good.

Meanwhile, laws and institutions require to be adapted, not to good men, but to bad. Marriage is not an institution designed for a select few. Men are not required, as a preliminary to the marriage ceremony, to prove by testimonials that they are fit to be trusted with the exercise of absolute power. . . . [T]here are all grades of goodness and wickedness in men, down to those whom no ties will bind, and on whom society has no action but through its *ultima ratio*, the penalties of the law. In every grade of this descending scale are men to whom are committed all the legal powers of a husband. The vilest malefactor has some wretched woman tied to him, against whom he can commit any atrocity except killing her, and, if tolerably cautious, can do that without much danger of the legal penalty. . . .

What is it then, which really tempers the corrupting effects of the power, and makes it compatible with such amount of good as we actually see? Mere feminine blandishments, though of great effect in individual instances, have very little effect in modifying the general tendencies of the situation; for their power only lasts while the woman is young and attractive, often only while her charm is new, and not dimmed by familiarity; and on many men they have not much influence at any time. The real mitigating causes are, the personal affection which is the growth of time, in so far as the man's nature is susceptible of it, and the woman's character sufficiently congenial with his to excite it; their common interests as regards the children, and their general community of interest as concerns third persons (to which however there are very great limitations); the real importance of the wife to his daily comforts and enjoyments, and the value he consequently attaches to her on his personal account, which, in a man capable of feeling for others, lays the foundation of caring for her on her own; and lastly, the influence naturally acquired over almost all human beings by those near to their persons. . . . Through these various means, the wife frequently exercises even too much power over the man; she is able to affect his conduct in things in which she may not be qualified to influence it for good—in which her influence may be not only unenlightened, but employed on the morally wrong side. . . . But neither in the affairs of families nor in those of states is power a compensation for the loss of freedom. Her power often gives her what she has no right to, but does not enable her to assert her own rights. . . . There are, no doubt, women, as there are men, whom equality of consideration will not satisfy; with whom there is no peace while any will or wish is regarded but their own. Such persons are a proper subject for the law of divorce. They are only fit to live alone, and no human beings ought to be compelled to associate their lives with them.

[T]he true virtue of human beings is fitness to live together as equals; claiming nothing for themselves but what they as freely concede to every one else; regarding command of any kind as an exceptional necessity, and in all cases a temporary one; and pre-

ferring, whenever possible, the society of those with whom leading
and following can be alternate and reciprocal. . . . The family,
justly constituted, would be the real school of the virtues of freedom. . . . It will always be a school of obedience for the children,
of command for the parents. What is needed is, that it should be
a school of sympathy in equality, of living together in love, without
power on one side or obedience on the other. This it ought to be
between the parents. . . .

[W]hatever would be the husband's or wife's if they were not
married, should be under their exclusive control during marriage;
which need not interfere with the power to tie up property by settlement, in order to preserve it for children. Some people are senti-
mentally shocked at the idea of a separate interest in money matters, as inconsistent with the ideal fusion of two lives into one. For
my own part, I am one of the strongest supporters of community
of goods, when resulting from an entire unity of feeling in the owners, which makes all things common between them. But I have no
relish for a community of goods resting on the doctrine, that what
is mine is yours but what is yours is not mine; and I should prefer
to decline entering into such a compact with any one, though I
were myself the person to profit by it. . . .

When the support of the family depends, not on property, but
on earnings, the common arrangement, by which the man earns
the income and the wife superintends the domestic expenditure,
seems to be in general the most suitable division of labour between
the two persons. If, in addition to the physical suffering of bearing
children, and the whole responsibility of their care and education
in early years, the wife undertakes the careful and economical
application of the husband's earnings to the general comfort of the
family; she takes not only her fair share, but usually the larger
share, of the bodily and mental exertion required by their joint
existence. If she undertakes any additional portion, it seldom re-
lieves her from this, but only prevents her from performing it properly. The care which she is herself disabled from taking of the children and the household, nobody else takes . . . .

In an otherwise just state of things, it is not, therefore, I think,
a desirable custom, that the wife should contribute by her labour
to the income of the family. In an unjust state of things, her doing
so may be useful to her, by making her of more value in the eyes
of the man who is legally her master; but, on the other hand, it
enables him still farther to abuse his power, by forcing her to work,
and leaving the support of the family to her exertions, while he
spends most of his time in drinking and idleness. The *power* of
earning is essential to the dignity of a woman, if she has not independent property. But if marriage were an equal contract . . . it
would not be necessary for her protection, that during marriage she

should make this particular use of her faculties. Like a man when he chooses a profession, so, when a woman marries, it may in general be understood that she makes choice of the management of a household, and the bringing up of a family, as the first call upon her exertions, during as many years of her life as may be required for the purpose; and that she renounces, not all other objects and occupations, but all which are not consistent with the requirements of this. . . . But the utmost latitude ought to exist for the adaptation of general rules to individual suitabilities; and there ought to be nothing to prevent faculties exceptionally adapted to any other pursuit, from obeying their vocation notwithstanding marriage: due provision being made for supplying otherwise any falling-short which might become inevitable, in her full performance of the ordinary functions of mistress of a family. These things, if once opinion were rightly directed on the subject, might with perfect safety be left to be regulated by opinion, without any interference of law.

.   .   .   .

[T]he generality of the male sex cannot yet tolerate the idea of living with an equal. Were it not for that, I think that almost every one, in the existing state of opinion in politics and political economy, would admit the injustice of excluding half the human race from the greater number of lucrative occupations, and from almost all high social functions. . . . when anything is forbidden to women, it is thought necessary to say, and desirable to believe, that they are incapable of doing it, and that they depart from their real path of success and happiness when they aspire to it. But to make this reason plausible (I do not say valid), . . . [i]t is not sufficient to maintain that women on the average are less gifted than men on the average, with certain of the higher mental faculties, or that a smaller number of women than of men are fit for occupations and functions of the highest intellectual character. It is necessary to maintain that no women at all are fit for them, and that the most eminent women are inferior in mental faculties to the most mediocre of the men on whom those functions at present devolve. For if the performance of the function is decided either by competition, or by any mode of choice which secures regard to the public interest, there needs to be no apprehension that any important employments will fall into the hands of women inferior to average men, or to the average of their male competitors. The only result would be that there would be fewer women than men in such employments; a result certain to happen in any case, if only from the preference always likely to be felt by the majority of women for the one vocation in which there is nobody to compete with them. . . . [N]ot a few merely, but many women have proved themselves capable of everything, perhaps without a single exception, which is done by men, and of doing it successfully and creditably. The utmost that can be said is, that there are many things which none of them have succeeded in doing as well as they have been done by some men—many in which they they have not reached the very highest rank. But there are extremely few, dependent only on mental faculties, in which they have not attained the rank next to the highest. . . .

Are we so certain of ways finding a man made to our hands for any duty or function of social importance which falls vacant, that we lose nothing by putting a ban upon one-half of mankind, and refusing before hand to make their faculties available, however distinguished they may be? And even if we could do without them, would it be consistent with justice to refuse to them their fair share of honour and distinction, or to deny to them the equal moral right of all human beings to choose their occupation (short of injury to others) according to their own preferences, at their own risk? Nor is the injustice confined to them: it is shared by those who are in a position to benefit by their services. To ordain that any kind of persons shall not be physicians, or shall not be advocates, or shall not be members of parliament, is to injure not them only, but all who employ physicians or advocates, or elect members of parliament, and who are deprived of the stimulating effect of greater competition on the exertions of the competitors, as well as restricted to narrower range of individual choice.

[A]ny woman, who succeeds in an open profession, proves by that very fact that she is qualified for it. And in the case of public offices, if the political system of the country is such as to exclude unfit men, it will equally exclude unfit women: while if it is not, there is no additional evil in the fact that the unfit persons whom it admits may be either women or men. As long therefore as it is acknowledged that even a few women may be fit for these duties, the laws which shut the door on those exceptions cannot be justified by any opinion which can be held respecting the capacities of women in general. . . .

Let us consider the special nature of the mental capacities most characteristic of a woman of talent. They are all of a kind which fits them for practice, and makes them tend towards it. What is meant by a woman's capacity of intuitive perception? It means, a rapid and correct insight into present fact. . . . With equality of experience and of general faculties, a woman usually sees much more than a man of what is immediately before her. Now this sensibility to the present, is the main quality on which the capacity for practice, as distinguished from theory, depends. . . . I admit that there can be no good practice without principles, and that the predominant place which quickness of observation holds among a woman's faculties, makes her particularly apt to build over-hasty generalizations upon her own observation; though at the same time no less ready in rectifying those generalizations, as her observation takes a wider range. But the corrective to this defect, is access to the experience of the human race; general knowledge—exactly the thing which education can best supply. A woman's mistakes are specifically those of a clever self-educated man, who often sees what men trained in routine do not see, but falls into errors for want of knowing things which have long been known. . . .

[T]his gravitation of women's minds to the present, to the real, to actual fact, while in its exclusiveness it is a source of errors, is also a most useful counteractive of the contrary error. . . . A woman seldom runs wild after an abstraction. The habitual direction of her mind to dealing with things as individuals rather than in groups, and (what is closely connected with it) her more lively interest in the present feelings of persons, which makes her consider first of all, in anything which claims to be applied to practice, in what manner persons will be affected by it—these two things make her extremely unlikely to put faith in any speculation which loses sight of individuals, and deals with things as if they existed for the benefit of some imaginary entity, some mere creation of the mind, not resolvable into the feelings of living beings. Women's thoughts are thus as useful in giving reality to those of thinking men, as men's thoughts in giving width and largeness to those of women. In depth, as distinguished from breadth, I greatly doubt if even now, women, compared with men, are at any disadvantage.

Let us now consider another of the admitted superiorities of clever women, greater quickness of apprehension. . . . He who has not his faculties under immediate command, in the contingencies of action, might as well not have them at all. He may be fit to criticize, but he is not fit to act. Now it is in this that women, and the men who are most like women, confessedly excel. It will be said, perhaps, that the greater nervous susceptibility of women is a disqualification for practice, in anything but domestic life, by rendering them mobile, changeable, too vehemently under the influence of the moment, incapable of dogged perseverance, unequal and uncertain in the power of using their faculties. . . . Much of all this is the mere overflow of nervous energy run to waste, and would cease when the energy was directed to a definite end. Much is also the result of conscious or unconscious cultivation; as we see by the almost total disappearance of "hysterics" and fainting fits, since they have gone out of fashion.

Women who in their early years have shared in the healthful physical education and bodily freedom of their brothers, and who obtain a sufficiency of pure air and exercise in after-life, very rarely have any excessive susceptibility of nerves which can disqualify them for active pursuits. There is indeed a certain proportion of persons, in both sexes, in whom an unusual degree of nervous sensibility is constitutional, and of so marked a character as to be the feature of their organization which exercises the greatest influence over the whole character of the vital phenomena. . . . We will assume this as a fact: and let me then ask, are men of nervous temperament found to be unfit for the duties and pursuits usually followed by men? If not, why should women of the same temperament be unfit for them? The peculiarities of the temperament are, no doubt, within certain limits, an obstacle to success in some employments, though an aid to it in others. But when the occupation is suitable to the temperament, and sometimes even when it is unsuitable, the most brilliant examples of success are continually given by the men of high nervous sensibility. . . . [P]eople of this temperament are particularly apt for what may be called the executive department of the leadership of mankind. They are the material of great orators, great preachers, impressive diffusers of moral influences. . . .

To so ridiculous an extent are the notions formed of the nature of women, mere empirical generalizations, framed, without philosophy or analysis, upon the first instances which present themselves, that the popular idea of it is different in different countries, according as the opinions and social circumstances of the country have given to the women living in it any specialty of development or non-development. An Oriental thinks that women are by nature peculiarly voluptuous; see the violent abuse of them on this ground in Hindoo writings. An Englishman usually thinks that they are by nature cold. The sayings about women's fickleness are mostly of French origin; from the famous distich of Francis the First, upward and downward. In England it is a common remark, how much more constant women are than men. Inconstancy has been longer reckoned discreditable to a woman, in England than in France; and Englishwomen are besides, in their inmost nature, much more subdued to opinion. . . .

I have said that it cannot now be known how much of the existing mental differences between men and women is natural, and how much artificial; whether there are any natural differences at all; or, supposing all artificial causes of difference to be withdrawn, what natural character would be revealed. I am not about to attempt what I have pronounced impossible: but doubt does not forbid conjecture, and where certainty is unattainable, there may yet be the means of arriving at some degree of probability. . . .

Let us take, then, the only marked case which observation affords, of apparent inferiority of women to men, if we except the merely physical one of bodily strength. No production in philosophy, science, or art, entitled to the first rank, has been the work of a woman. Is there any mode of accounting for this, without supposing that women are naturally incapable of producing them?

In the first place, we may fairly question whether experience has afforded sufficient grounds for an induction. It is scarcely three generations since women, saving very rare exceptions, have begun to try their capacity in philosophy, science, or art. It is only in the present generation that their attempts have been at all numerous; and they are even now extremely few, everywhere but in England and France. It is a relevant question, whether a mind possessing the requisites of first-rate eminence in speculation or creative art could have been expected, on the mere calculation of chances, to turn up during that lapse of time, among the women whose tastes and personal position admitted of their devoting themselves to these pursuits. In all things which there has yet been time for—in all but the very highest grades in the scale of excellence, especially in the department in which they have been longest engaged, literature (both prose and poetry)—women have done quite as much, have obtained fully as high prizes as many of them, as could be expected from the length of time and the number of competitors. . . .

If we consider the works of women in modern times, and contrast them with those of men, either in the literary or the artistic department, such inferiority as may be observed resolves itself essentially into one thing: but that is a most material one; deficiency of originality. . . . Thoughts original, in the sense of being unborrowed—of being derived from the thinker's own observations or intellectual processes—are abundant in the writings of women. But they have not yet produced any of those great and luminous new ideas which form an era in thought, nor those fundamentally new conceptions in art, which open a vista of possible effects not before thought of, and found a new school. . . . This is the sort of inferiority which their works manifest: for in point of execution, in the detailed application of thought, and the perfection of style, there is no inferiority. . . .

It no doubt often happens that a person, who has not widely and accurately studied the thoughts of others on a subject, has by natural sagacity a happy intuition, which he can suggest, but cannot prove, which yet when matured may be an important addition to knowledge: but even then, no justice can be done to it until some other person, who does possess the previous acquirements, takes it in hand, tests it, gives it a scientific or practical form, and fits it into its place among the existing truths of philosophy or science. Is it supposed that such felicitous thoughts do not occur to women? They occur by hundreds to every woman of intellect. But they are mostly lost, for want of a husband or friend who has the other knowledge which can enable him to estimate them properly and bring them before the world: and even when they are brought before it, they generally appear as his ideas, not their real author's. Who can tell how many of the most original thoughts put forth by male writers, belong to a woman by suggestion, to themselves only by verifying and working out? If I may judge by my own case, a very large proportion indeed.

If we turn from pure speculation to literature in the narrow sense of the term, and the fine arts, there is a very obvious reason why women's literature is, in its general conception and in its main features, an imitation of men's. Why is the Roman literature, as critics proclaim to satiety, not original but an imitation of the Greek? Simply because the Greeks came first. If women lived in a different country from men, and had never read any of their writings, they would have had a literature of their own. As it is, they have not created one, because they found a highly advanced literature already created. . . . All women who write are pupils of the great male writers. . . . What years are to a gifted individual, generations are to a mass. If women's literature is destined to have a different collective character from that of men, depending on any difference of natural tendencies, much longer time is necessary than has yet elapsed, before it can emancipate itself from the influence of accepted models, and guide itself by its own impulses. But if, as I believe, there will not prove to be any natural tendencies common to women, and distinguishing their genius from that of men, yet every individual writer among them has her individual tendencies, which at present are still subdued by the influence of precedent and example: and it will require generations more, before their individuality is sufficiently developed to make head against the influence. . . .

There are other reasons, besides those which we have now given, that help to explain why women remain behind men, even in the pursuits which are open to both. For one thing, very few women have time for them. This may seem a paradox; it is an undoubted social fact. The time and thoughts of every woman have to satisfy great previous demands on them for things practical. There is, first, the superintendence of the family and the domestic expenditure, which. . . . presents questions for consideration and solution, foreseen and unforeseen, at every hour of the day. . . . If a woman is of a rank and circumstances which relieve her in a measure from these cares, she has still devolving on her the management for the whole family of its intercourse with others—of what is called society, and the less the call made on her by the former duty, the greater is always the development of the latter. . . .

There is another consideration to be added to all these . . . an ardent desire of celebrity. Nothing less is commonly a sufficient stimulus to undergo the long and patient drudgery, which, in the case even of the greatest natural gifts, is absolutely required for great eminence. . . . Now, whether the cause be natural or artificial, women seldom have this eagerness for fame. . . . The influence they seek is over those who immediately surround them. . . . I do not at all believe that it is inherent in women. It is only the natural result of their circumstances. The love of fame in men is encouraged by education and opinion, . . . and is stimulated by the access which fame gives to all objects of ambition, including even the favour of women; while to women themselves all these objects are closed, and the desire of fame itself considered daring and unfeminine. . . .

As for moral differences, considered as distinguished from intellectual, the distinction commonly drawn is to the advantage of women. They are declared to be better than men; an empty compliment, which must provoke a bitter smile from every woman of spirit, since there is no other situation in life in which it is the established order, and considered quite natural and suitable, that the better should obey the worse.

.   .   .   .

What good are we to expect from the changes proposed in our customs and institutions? Would mankind be at all better off if women were free? If not, why disturb their minds, and attempt to make a social revolution in the name of an abstract right? . . . To which let me first answer, the advantage of having the most universal and pervading of all human relations regulated by justice instead of injustice. The vast amount of this gain to human nature, it is hardly possible, by any explanation or illustration, to place in a stronger light than it is placed by the bare statement, to any one who attaches a moral meaning to words. All the selfish propensities, the self-worship, the unjust self-preference, which exist among mankind, have their source and root in, and derive their principal nourishment from, the present constitution of the relation between men and women. Think what it is to a boy, to grow up to manhood in the belief that without any merit or any exertion of his own, . . . by the mere fact of being born a male he is by right the superior of all and every one of an entire half of the human race: including probably some whose real superiority to himself he has daily or hourly occasion to feel. . . . What must be the effect on his character, of this lesson? It is an exact parallel to the feeling of a hereditary king that he is excellent above others by being born a king, or a noble by being born a noble. . . . Above all, when the feeling of being raised above the whole of the other sex is combined with personal authority over one individual among them; the situation, if a school of conscientious and affectionate forbearance to those whose strongest points of character are conscience and affection, is to men of another quality a regularly constituted Academy or Gymnasium for training them in arrogance and overbearingness. . . .

The second benefit to be expected from giving to women the free use of their faculties, by leaving them the free choice of their employments, and opening to them the same field of occupation and the same prizes and encouragements as to other human beings, would be that of doubling the mass of mental faculties available for the higher service of humanity. Where there is now one person qualified to benefit mankind and promote the general improvement, as a public teacher, or an administrator of some branch of public or social affairs, there would then be a chance of two. . . .

This great accession to the intellectual power of the species, and to the amount of intellect available for the good management of its affairs, would be obtained, partly, through the better and more complete intellectual education of women, which would then improve *pari passu* with that of men. Women in general would be brought up equally capable of understanding business, public affairs, and the higher matters of speculation, with men in the same class of society; and the select few of the one as well as of the other sex, who were qualified not only to comprehend what is done or thought by others, but to think or do something considerable themselves, would meet with the same facilities for improving and training their capacities in the one sex as in the other. In this way the widening of the sphere of action for women would operate for good, by raising their education to the level of that of men, and making the one participate in all improvements made in the other. . . .

Besides the addition to the amount of individual talent available for the conduct of human affairs, which certainly are not at present so abundantly provided in that respect that they can afford to dispense with one-half of what nature proffers; the opinion of women would then possess a more beneficial, rather than a greater, influence upon the general mass of human belief and sentiment. I say a more beneficial, rather than a greater influence; for the influence of women over the general tone of opinion has always, or at least from the earliest known period, been very considerable. The influence of mothers on the early character of their sons, and the desire of young men to recommend themselves to young women, have in all recorded times been important agencies in the formation of character, and have determined some of the chief steps in the progress of civilization. . . . The other mode in which the effect of women's opinion has been conspicuous, is by giving a powerful stimulus to those qualities in men, which, not being themselves trained in, it was necessary for them that they should find in their protectors. Courage, and the military virtues generally, have at all times been greatly indebted to the desire which men felt of being admired by women: and the stimulus reaches far beyond this one class of eminent qualities, since, by a very natural effect of their position, the best passport to the admiration and favour of women has always been to be thought highly of by men. . . .

It is often said that in the classes most exposed to temptation, a man's wife and children tend to keep him honest and respectable, both by the wife's direct influence, and by the concern he feels for their future welfare. This may be so, and no doubt often is so, with those who are more weak than wicked; and this beneficial influence would be preserved and strengthened under equal laws. . . . But when we ascend higher in the scale, we come among a totally different set of moving forces. The wife's influence tends, as far as it goes, to prevent the husband from falling below the common standard of approbation of the country. It tends quite as strongly to hinder him from rising above it. The wife is the auxiliary of the common public opinion. . . . If he differs in his opinion from the mass—if he sees truths which have not yet dawned upon them, or if, feeling in his heart truths which they nominally recognize, he would like to act up to those truths more conscientiously than the generality of mankind—to all such thoughts and desires, marriage is the heaviest of drawbacks, unless he be so fortunate as to have a wife as much above the common level as he himself is. . . .

There is another very injurious aspect in which the effect, not of women's disabilities directly, but of the broad line of difference which those disabilities create between the education and character of a woman and that of a man, requires to be considered. Nothing can be more unfavourable to that union of thought and inclinations which is the ideal of married life. . . . While women are so unlike men, it is not wonderful that selfish men should feel the need of arbitrary power in their own hands, to arrest *in limine* the life-long conflict of inclinations, by deciding every question on the side of their own preference.

[T]hough it may stimulate the amatory propensities of men, it does not conduce to married happiness, to exaggerate by differences of education whatever may be the native differences of the sexes. . . .

What a difference there must be in the society which the two persons will wish to frequent, or be frequented by! Each will desire associates who share their own tastes: the persons agreeable to one, will be indifferent or positively disagreeable to the other. . . . They cannot help having different wishes as to the bringing up of the children: each will wish to see reproduced in them their own tastes and sentiments: and there is either a compromise, and only a half-satisfaction to either, or the wife has to yield—often with bitter suffering; and, with or without intention, her occult influence continues to counterwork the husband's purposes.

It would of course be extreme folly to suppose that these differences of feeling and inclination only exist because women are brought up differently from men, and that there would not be differences of taste under any imaginable circumstances. But there is nothing beyond the mark in saying that the distinction in bringing-up immensely aggravates those differences, and renders them wholly inevitable. . . .

[W]hen each of two persons, instead of being a nothing, is a something; when they are attached to one another, and are not too much unlike to begin with; the constant partaking in the same things, assisted by their sympathy, draws out the latent capacities of each for being interested in the things which were at first interesting only to the other; and works a gradual assimilation of the tastes and characters to one another, partly by the insensible modification of each, but more by a real enriching of the two natures, each acquiring the tastes and capacities of the other in addition to its own. . . .

What marriage may be in the case of two persons of cultivated faculties, identical in opinions and purposes, between whom there exists that best kind of equality, similarity of powers and capacities with reciprocal superiority in them—so that each can enjoy the luxury of looking up to the other, and can have alternately the pleasure of leading and of being led in the path of development—I will not attempt to describe. To those who can conceive it, there is no need; to those who cannot, it would appear the dream of an enthusiast. But I maintain, with the profoundest conviction, that this, and this only, is the ideal of marriage; and that all opinions, customs and institutions which favour any other notion of it, or turn the conceptions and aspirations connected with it into any other direction, by whatever pretences they may be coloured, are relics of primitive barbarism. The moral regeneration of mankind will only really commence, when the most fundamental of the social relations is placed under the rule of equal justice, and when human beings learn to cultivate their strongest sympathy with an equal in rights and in cultivation.

Thus far, the benefits which it has appeared that the world would gain by ceasing to make sex a disqualification for privileges and a badge of subjection, are social rather than individual; consisting in an increase of the general fund of thinking and acting power, and an improvement in the general conditions of the association of men with women. But it would be a grievous understatement of the case to omit the most direct benefit of all, the unspeakable gain in private happiness to the liberated half of the species; the difference to them between a life of subjection to the will of others, and a life of rational freedom. After the primary necessities of food and raiment, freedom is the first and strongest want of human nature.

❋   ❋   ❋

THE EXISTENTIALIST CONTEXT

"Existentialism" is a term that can better be described than defined. Basically, the "existence" about which the existentialist is concerned is human existence, and the focus of that concern is human subjectivity or freedom. Historically, existentialism involves a reaction against an overemphasis on reason and the capability of reason for solving all human problems. Certain aspects of life, the existentialist insists, are entirely inexplicable by reason; certain values for the individual cannot and need not be rationally deduced or justified. Freedom is the assertion of power over reason and nature; it is the condition of life's responsibility and risk. Such an emphasis on freedom suggests an advocacy of liberation for women. But this is not the case for Kierkegaard and Nietzsche, as will be clear from the selections below. De Beauvoir's views on the issue seem to be more consistent with the existentialist position.

SØREN KIERKEGAARD's (1813–1855) writings about woman may or may not have been influenced by a rigidly religious background and an extremely melancholy disposition. For a time his melancholy was lightened through love for and engagement to Regina Olsen. But Kierkegaard broke the engagement, even while claiming he still loved Regina. In subsequent writings he attempted to explain his decision to remain unmarried. For Kierkegaard, commitment to God required his renunciation of marriage.

FRIEDRICH NIETZSCHE (1844–1900) was also brought up in a strongly religious household. After the death of his father, a Lutheran pastor, this household was composed entirely of women. In contrast to Kierkegaard, Nietzsche developed an antireligious attitude. To him (in *Joyful Wisdom*) we owe the popular antitheistic declaration: "God is dead."

SIMONE DE BEAUVOIR (1908–   ) draws upon her own experience in elaborating her concept of woman. Despite efforts of home and boarding school to mold her to the traditional feminine role (see her *Memoirs of a Dutiful Daughter*), she decided early in adult life to acquire and maintain a professional stature and independence through her teaching and writing, without the concomitant roles of wife and mother. It is now abundantly clear that she succeeded in that resolve. Among de Beauvoir's numerous works are the award-winning novel *The Mandarins* (1954), and more recently a well-acclaimed critical analysis of society's maltreatment of the elderly, *The Coming of Age* (1972). In all her works, the social dimension of de Beauvoir's existentialist interpretation is apparent. As an author, she claims to have derived the greatest personal satisfaction from the book specifically addressed to the subject of woman, *The Second Sex*.

Kierkegaard's Concept of Human Nature

For Kierkegaard, "existence" is a category relating to the free individual, actualized through the self-commitment of a radical choice between alternatives. To be human is to define oneself through such choices. The levels of alternatives constitute a progression from a subhuman level of existence (before choice) to a transcendence of reason, through faith. The first stage is that of the aesthetic, who has decided to live his life in pursuit of sensual enjoyment (Don Juan, for example). Inevitably, he cannot sustain the pleasure he seeks, and this leads him either to despair or to move to an ethical level of existence. If he chooses to live ethically his life is thereafter governed by reason. His acceptance of universal moral standards and obligations provides him with a sense of permanence, wholeness, and consistency. A typical instance of this decision is marriage, which necessarily involves renunciation and ordering of the sexual impulse. Eventually, however, the ethical person confronts the inadequacy of reason in grappling with life's problems. At that point, he is aware of a religious vocation: an invitation to live entirely by faith in the midst of objective uncertainty. If he chooses to take the "leap of faith," he fulfills his highest human capacity through his religious commitment. Unfortunately, claims Kierkegaard, woman is incapable of such commitment. "[T]o be able to be related to the Christian task," he writes, "it is necessary to be a man, [because] a man's hardness and strength are required to be able to bear just the stress of the task."

In the selection which follows an aesthete name Johannes reflects on the meaning of woman. His "diary" recounts his successful seduction of Cordelia, whom he subsequently deserts. "When a girl has given away everything," he writes, "then she is weak, then she has lost everything. For a man guilt is a negative moment; for a woman it is the value of her being. Now all resistance is impossible, and only as long as that is present is it beautiful to love. . . ."

"Diary of the Seducer" is excerpted from Kierkegaard's *Either/ Or*, vol. 1.

SØREN KIERKEGAARD   'Diary of the Seducer'

.   .   .   .

Woman will always offer an inexhaustible fund of material for reflection, an eternal abundance for observation. The man who feels no impulse toward the study of woman may, as far as I am concerned, be what he will; one thing he certainly is not, he is no aesthetician. This is the glory and divinity of aesthetics, that it enters into relation only with the beautiful: it has to do essentially only with fiction and the fair sex. It makes me glad and causes my heart to rejoice when I represent to myself how the sun of feminine loveliness diffuses its rays into an infinite manifold, refracting itself in a confusion of tongues, where each individual woman has her little part of the whole wealth of femininity, yet so that her other characteristics harmoniously center about this point. In this sense feminine beauty is infinitely divisible. But the particular share of beauty which each one has must be present in a harmonious blending, for otherwise the effect will be disturbing, and it will seem as if Nature had intended something by this woman, but nothing ever came of it.

My eyes can never weary of surveying this peripheral manifold, these scattered emanations of feminine beauty. Each particular has its little share, and yet is complete in itself, happy, glad, beautiful. Every woman has her share: the merry smile, the roguish glance, the wistful eye, the pensive head, the exhuberant spirits, the quiet sadness, the deep foreboding, the brooding melancholy, the earthy homesickness, the unbaptized movements, the beckoning brows, the questioning lips, the mysterious forehead, the ensnaring curls, the concealing lashes, the heavenly pride, the earthly modesty, the angelic purity, the secret blush, the light step, the airy grace, the languishing posture, the dreamy yearning, the inexplicable sighs, the willowy form, the soft outlines, the luxuriant bosom, the swelling hips, the tiny foot, the dainty hand. —Each woman has her own traits, and the one does not merely repeat the other. And when I have gazed and gazed again, considered and again considered this multitudinous variety, when I have smiled, sighed, flattered, threatened, desired, tempted, laughed, wept, hoped, feared, won, lost—then I shut up my fan, and gather the fragments into a unity, the parts into a whole. Then my soul is glad, my heart beats, my passion is aflame. This one woman, the only woman in all the world, she must belong to me, she must be mine. Let God keep his heaven, if only I can keep her. I know full well what I choose; it is something so great that heaven itself must be the loser by such a division, for what would be left to heaven if I keep her? The faithful Mohammedans will be disappointed in their hopes when in their Paradise they embrace pale, weak shadows; for warm hearts they cannot find, since all the warmth of the heart is concentrated in her breast; they will yield themselves to be a comfortless despair when they find pale lips, lustreless eyes, a lifeless bosom, a limp pressure of the hand; for all the redness of the lips and the fire of the eye and the heaving of the bosom and the promise of the hand and the foreboding of the sigh and the seal of the kiss and the trembling of the touch and the passion of the embrace—all, all are concentrated in her, who lavishes on men a wealth sufficient for a whole world, both for time and eternity.

Thus I have often reflected upon this matter; but every time I conceive woman thus, I become warm, because I think of her as warm. And though in general, warmth is accounted a good sign, it does not follow that my mode of thinking will be granted the respectable predicate that it is solid. Hence I shall now for variety's sake attempt, myself being cold, to think coldly of woman. I shall attempt to think of woman in terms of her category. Under what category must she be conceived? Under the category of being for another. But this must not be understood in the bad sense, as if the woman who is for me is also for another. Here as always in abstract thinking, it is essential to refrain from every reference to experience; for otherwise as in the present case, I should find, in the most curious manner, that experience is both for and against me. Woman is therefore being for another. Here as always, experience is a most curious thing, because its nature is always to be both for and against. Here again, but from another side, it will be necessary not to let oneself be disturbed by experience, which teaches that it is a rare thing to find a woman who is in truth a being for another, since a great many are in general absolutely nothing, either for themselves or for others. Woman shares this category with Nature, and, in general, with everything feminine. Nature as a whole exists only for another; not in the teleological sense, so that one part of Nature exists for another part, but so that the whole of Nature is for an Other—for the Spirit. In the same way with the particulars. The life of the plant, for example, unfolds in all naiveté its hidden charms and exists only for another. In the same way a mystery, a charade, a secret, a vowel, and so on, has being only for another. And from this it can be explained why, when God created Eve, he caused a deep sleep to fall upon Adam; for woman is the dream of man. In still another way the story teaches that woman is a being for another. It tells, namely, that Jehovah created Eve from a rib taken from the side of man. Had she been taken from man's brain, for example, woman would indeed still have been a being for an-

other; but it was not the intention to make her a figment of the
brain, but something quite different. She became flesh and blood,
but this causes her to be included under the category of Nature,
which is essentially being for another. She awakens first at the
touch of love; before that time she is a dream, yet in her dream life
we can distinguish two stages: in the first, love dreams about her;
in the second, she dreams about love.

As being for another, woman is characterized by pure virginity.
Virginity is, namely, a form of being, which, in so far as it is a
being for itself, is really an abstraction, and only reveals itself to
another. The same characterization also lies in the concept of
female innocence. It is therefore possible to say that woman in this
condition is invisible. As is well known, there existed no image of
Vesta, the goddess who most nearly represented feminine virginity.
This form of existence is, namely, jealous for itself aesthetically,
just as Jehovah is ethically, and does not desire that there should
be any image or even any notion of one. This is the contradiction,
that the being which is for another *is* not, and only becomes visible,
as it were, by the interposition of another. Logically, this contradiction will be found to be quite in order, and he who knows how
to think logically will not be disturbed by it, but will be glad in it.
But whoever thinks illogically will imagine that whatever is a being
for another *is,* in the finite sense in which one can say about a
particular thing: that is something for me.

This being of woman (for the word *existence* is too rich in meaning, since woman does not persist in and through herself) is rightly
described as charm, an expression which suggests plant life; she is
a flower, as the poets like to say, and even the spiritual in her is
present in a vegetative manner. She is wholly subject to Nature,
and hence only aesthetically free. In a deeper sense she first becomes free by her relation to man, and when man courts her properly, there can be no question of a choice. Woman chooses, it is
true, but if this choice is thought of as the result of a long deliberation, then this choice is unfeminine. Hence it is, that it is a humilia-
tion to receive a refusal, because the individual in question has
rated himself too high, has desired to make another free without
having the power.—In this situation there is deep irony. That which
merely exists for another has the appearance of being predominant:
man sues, woman chooses. The very concept of woman requires
that she be the vanquished; the concept of man, that he be the victor; and yet the victor bows before the vanquished. And yet this is
quite natural, and it is only boorishness, stupidity, and lack of
erotic sensibility to take no notice of that which immediately yields
in this fashion. It has also a deeper ground. Woman is, namely,
substance, man is reflection. She does not therefore choose indepen-

dently; man sues, she chooses. But man's courtship is a question, and her choice only an answer to a question. In a certain sense man is more than woman, in another sense he is infinitely less.

This being for another is the true virginity. If it makes an attempt to be a being for itself, in relation to another being which is being for it, then the opposition reveals itself in an absolute coyness; but this opposition shows at the same time that woman's essential being is being for another. The diametrical opposite to absolute devotion is absolute coyness, which in a converse sense is invisible as the abstraction against which everything breaks, without the abstraction itself coming to life. Femininity now takes on the character of an abstract cruelty, the caricature in its extreme form of the intrinsic feminine brittleness. A man can never be so cruel as a woman. Consult mythologies, fables, folk-tales, and you will find this view confirmed. If there is a description of a natural force whose mercilessness knows no limits, it will always be a feminine nature. Or one is horrified at reading about a young woman who callously allows all her suitors to lose their lives, as so often happens in the folk-tales of all nations. A Bluebeard slays all the women he has loved on their bridal night, but he does not find his happiness in slaying them; on the contrary, his happiness has preceded, and in this lies the concreteness; it is not cruelty for the sake of cruelty. A Don Juan seduces them and runs away, but he finds no happiness at all in running away from them, but rather in seducing them; consequently, it is by no means this abstract cruelty.

Thus, the more I reflect on this matter, I see that my practice is in perfect harmony with my theory. My practice has always been impregnated with the theory that woman is essentially a being for another. Hence it is that the moment has here such infinite significance; for a being for another is always the matter of a moment. It may take a longer, it may take a short time before the moment comes, but as soon as it has come, then that which was originally a being for another assumes the character of relative being, and then all is over. I know very well that husbands say that the woman is also in another sense a being for another, that she is everything to her husband through life. One must make allowance for husbands. I really believe that it is something which they mutually delude one another into thinking. Every class in society generally has certain conventional customs, and especially certain conventional lies. Among these must be reckoned this sailor's yarn. To be a good judge of the moment is not so easy a matter, and he who misjudges it is in for boredom for the rest of his life. The moment is everything, and in the moment, woman is everything; the consequences I do not understand. Among these consequences is the begetting of children. Now I fancy that I am a fairly consistent thinker, but if I were to think until I became crazy, I am not a man who could think this consequence; I simply do not understand it; to understand it requires a husband.

*   *   *

Nietzsche's Concept of Human Nature

For Nietzsche, man (male?) "is something which must be surpassed; man is a bridge and not a goal." He is "a rope stretched between animal and Superman—a rope over an abyss." The abyss is the irrationality of the world, which can only be transcended through the "Will to Power." This will is an intrinsic quality of the individual through which he affirms life—his life, rather than the life of humanity, or another's life. Man's goal is to be "Superman," to acquire a personal individualistic excellence through fulfillment of his will to power. Since God is dead, this goal is now possible. The assertion of the will to power, which is the life of man, occurs only because certain individuals are thus controllable; they are controllable because they are naturally inferior.

"Of Womenkind, Old and Young" and "Of Child and Marriage" are excerpted from *Thus Spake Zarathustra;* "Our Virtues" is excerpted from *Beyond Good and Evil.*

FRIEDRICH NIETZSCHE 'Of Womenkind, Old and Young'

Wherefore stealest thou so timidly through the twilight, Zarathustra? And what hidest thou so carefully beneath thy mantle?

Is it some treasure that hath been given thee? Or a child born unto thee? Or walkest thou now thyself in the ways of thieves, thou friend of the wicked?—

Verily, my brother! said Zarathustra, it is a treasure that hath been given me: a little truth it is that I carry.

But it is unruly as a young child, and if I hold not its mouth it crieth over-loud.

As this day I went my way alone at the hour of sunset I met a little old woman who spake thus to my soul:

Much hath Zarathustra spoken even unto us women, but never spake he unto us of woman.

And I answered her: Of woman must one speak only to men.

Speak also to me of woman, she said, I am old enough to forget it forthwith.

And I, assenting, spake thus to the little old woman:

All in woman is a riddle, and all in woman hath one answer—that is child-bearing.

Man is for woman a means: the end is ever the child. But what is woman for man?

Two things true man desireth: danger and play. Therefore desireth he woman as the most dangerous of playthings.

Man shall be trained for war, and woman for the recreation of the warrior: all else is folly.

Over-sweet fruits—the warrior loveth them not. Therefore he loveth woman; bitter is even the sweetest woman.

Woman understandeth children better than man, but man is more childlike than woman.

In true man a child lieth hidden: it longeth to play. Up, ye women, discover me the child in man!

Let woman be a plaything pure and delicate as a jewel, illumined with the virtues of a world that is yet to come.

Let the beam of a star shine in your love! Let your hope be, Would I might give birth to the Superman!

Let there be valour in your love! Assail with your love him that maketh you afraid.

In your love let your honour be! Little else knoweth woman of honour. But let it be your honour ever to love more than ye be loved, and never to be second.

Let man fear woman when she loveth: then will she sacrifice all, and naught else hath value for her.

Let man fear woman when she hateth: for in the depth of his soul man is but evil, but woman is base.

Whom hateth woman most?—Thus spake the iron to the loadstone: I hate thee most because thou drawest but are not strong enough to draw me to thee.

Man's happiness is, I will. Woman's happiness is, He will.

Behold, this moment hath the world been perfected;—thus deemeth every woman when she obeyeth with all her love.

Woman must obey and find depth to her surface. Surface is woman's nature, foam tossed to and fro on shallow water.

But deep is man's nature, his current floweth in subterranean caverns: woman divineth his power, but understandeth it not.

Then the little old woman answered me: Many fine things saith Zarathustra, and especially for them that are young enough.

A strange thing is this—Zarathustra knoweth little of women, and yet is he right regarding them! Is this because with women nothing is impossible?

And now take as thanks a little truth. I am old enough to speak it!

Wrap it well and keep its mouth shut: else will it cry over-loud, this little truth.

Give me, woman, thy little truth, I said. And thus spake the little old woman:

Thou goest to women? Remember thy whip!—

Thus spake Zarathustra.

     ✿ ✿ ✿

FRIEDRICH NIETZSCHE   'Of Child and Marriage'

I have a question for thee alone, my brother: I cast it as a plummet into thy soul that I may know how deep it be.

Thou art young and desirest child and marriage. But I ask thee, Art thou a man that *may* desire a child?

Art thou victor, self-subduer, master of thy senses, lord of thy virtues? Thus do I ask thee.

Or speak the beast and blind need in thy desire? Or loneliness? Or self-discord?

I would that thy victory and thy freedom desired a child. So thou shouldest build living monuments to thy victory and thy liberation.

Thou shalt build beyond thyself. But first I would have thee be built thyself—perfect in body and soul.

Thou shalt propagate thyself not only *onwards* but *upwards!* Thereto may the garden of marriage assist thee!

Thou shalt create a higher body, a primal motion, a self-rolling wheel—thou shalt create a creator.

Marriage: this call I the will of two to create that one which is more than they that created him. Marriage call I reverence of the one for the other as for them that possess such a will.

Let this be the meaning and truth of thy marriage. But that which the much-too-many call marriage, the superfluous ones—alas, what call I that?

Alas! this double poverty of soul! Alas! this double uncleanness of souls! Alas! this double despicable ease!

Marriage they call it; and they say their marriage is made in heaven.

As for me, I love it not, this heaven of the superfluous! Nay, I love them not, these beasts entrapped in heavenly snares!

Far from me also be the God that cometh halting to bless that He joined not together!

Laugh not at such marriages! What child hath not cause to weep over its parents?

Worthy meseemed such an one, and ripe for the meaning of earth, but when I beheld his wife earth seemed to me a madhouse.

Yea, I would the earth would quake whenever a saint mateth with a goose.

Such an one went forth in quest of truth like a hero, and his prize at length was a little dressed-up lie. He calleth it his marriage.

Such another was reserved in society and chose fastidiously. But suddenly he forever lowered his company: he calleth this his marriage.

A third sought a serving-wench with an angel's virtues. But suddenly he became the serving-wench of a woman, and now needeth himself to become an angel!

All buyers have I found cautious and cunning of eye. Yet even the most cunning buyeth his wife in a sack.

Many brief follies—that ye call love. And your marriage maketh an end of many brief follies with one long stupidity.

Your love for woman, and woman's love for man: alas, would they were sympathy for suffering and hidden deities! But commonly two beasts find one another out.

Even your best love is but a rapturous likeness, an anguished ardour. It is a torch to light you to higher paths.

Some day ye shall love beyond yourselves! *Learn,* then, how to love! To that end were ye compelled to drink the bitter cup of your love.

Bitterness is in the cup even of the best love: thus causeth it desire for the Superman: thus it maketh thee to thirst, the creator!

Creative thirst, an arrow of desire for the Superman: say, my brother, is this thy will to marriage?

Holy call I such a will and such a marriage.

Thus spake Zarathustra.

*   *   *

FRIEDRICH NIETZSCHE   'Our Virtues'

231

Learning changes us; it does what all nourishment does which also does not merely "preserve"—as physiologists know. But at the bottom of us, really "deep down," there is, of course, something unteachable, some granite of spiritual *fatum,* of predetermined decision and answer to predetermined selected questions. Whenever a cardinal problem is at stake, there speaks an unchangeable "this is I"; about man and woman, for example, a thinker cannot relearn but only finish learning—only discover ultimately how this is "settled in him." At times we find certain solutions of problems that inspire strong faith in *us;* some call them henceforth *their* "convictions." Later—we see them only as steps to self-knowledge, sign-posts to the problem we *are*—rather, to the great stupidity we are, to our spiritual *fatum,* to what is *unteachable* very "deep down."

After this abundant civility that I have just evidenced in relation to myself I shall perhaps be permitted more readily to state a few truths about "woman as such"—assuming that it is now known from the outset how very much these are after all only—*my* truths.

232

Woman wants to become self-reliant—and for that reason she is beginning to enlighten men about "woman as such": *this* is one of the worst developments of the general *uglification* of Europe. For what must these clumsy attempts of women at scientific self-exposure bring to light! Woman has much reason for shame; so much pendantry, superficiality, schoolmarmishness, petty presumption, petty licentiousness and immodesty lies concealed in woman—one only needs to study her behavior with children!—and so far all this was at bottom best repressed and kept under control by *fear* of man. Woe when "the eternally boring in woman"—she is rich in that!—is permitted to venture forth! When she begins to unlearn thoroughly and on principle her prudence and art—of grace, of play, of chasing away worries, of lightening burdens and taking things lightly—and her subtle aptitude for agreeable desires!

Even now female voices are heard which—holy Aristophanes!—are frightening: they threaten with medical explicitness what woman *wants* from man, first and last. Is it not in the worst taste when woman sets about becoming scientific that way? So far enlightenment of this sort was fortunately man's affair, man's lot—we remained "among ourselves" in this; and whatever women write about "woman," we may in the end reserve a healthy suspicion whether woman really *wants* enlightenment about herself—whether she *can* will it—

Unless a woman seeks a new adornment for herself that way—I do think adorning herself is part of the Eternal-Feminine?—she surely wants to inspire fear of herself—perhaps she seeks mastery. But she does not *want* truth: what is truth to woman? From the beginning, nothing has been more alien, repugnant, and hostile to

woman than truth—her great art is the lie, her highest concern is
mere appearance and beauty. Let us men confess it: we honor and
love precisely *this* art and *this* instinct in woman—we who have
a hard time and for our relief like to associate with beings under
whose hands, eyes, and tender follies our seriousness, our gravity
and profundity almost appear to us like folly.

Finally I pose the question: has ever a woman conceded profundity to a woman's head, or justice to a woman's heart? And is it
not true that on the whole "woman" has so far been despised most
by woman herself—and by no means by us?

We men wish that woman should not go on compromising herself
through enlightenment—just as it was man's thoughtfulness and
consideration for woman that found expression in the church de-
cree: *mulier taceat in ecclesia!*[1] It was for woman's good when
Napoleon gave the all too eloquent Madame de Stael to understand: *mulier taceat in politicis!*[2] And I think it is a real friend of
women that counsels them today: *mulier taceat de muliere!*[3]

233

It betrays a corruption of the instincts—quite apart from the fact
that it betrays bad taste—when a woman adduces Madame Roland
or Madame de Stael or Monsieur George Sand, of all people, as if
they proved anything in *favor* of "woman as such." Among men
these three are the three *comical* women as such—nothing more!—
and precisely the best involuntary *counterarguments* against emancipation and feminine vainglory.

234

Stupidity in the kitchen; woman as cook: the gruesome thought-
lessness to which the feeding of the family and of the master of the
house is abandoned! Woman does not understand what food *means*
—and wants to be cook. If woman were a *thinking* creature, she, as
cook for millennia, would surely have had to discover the greatest
physiological facts, and she would have had to gain possession of
the art of healing. Bad cooks—and the utter lack of reason in the
kitchen—have delayed human development longest and impaired
it most: nor have things improved much even today. A lecture for
finishing-school girls.

1. Woman should be silent in church.

2. Woman should be silent when it comes to politics.

3. Woman should be silent about woman.

235

There are expressions and bull's-eyes of the spirit, there are epigrams, a little handful of words, in which a whole culture, a whole society is suddenly crystallized. Among these belongs the occasional remark of Madame de Lambert to her son: *"mon ami, ne vous permettez jamais que de folies, qui vous feront grand plaisir"*[4] —incidentally the most motherly and prudent word ever directed to a son.

236

What Dante and Goethe believed about woman—the former when he sang, *"ella guardava suso, ed io in lei,"*[5] and the latter when he translated this, "the Eternal-Feminine attracts us *higher*" —I do not doubt that every nobler woman will resist this faith, for she believes the same thing about the Eternal-Masculine—

237

SEVEN EPIGRAMS ON WOMAN

How the longest boredom flees, when a man comes on his knees!

Science and old age at length give weak virtue, too, some strength.

Black dress and a silent part make every woman appear—smart.

Whom I thank for my success? God;—and my dear tailoress.

Young: flower-covered den. Old: a dragon denizen.

Noble name, the legs are fine, man as well: that he were mine!

Ample meaning, speech concise—she-ass, watch for slippery ice!

237a

Men have so far treated women like birds who had strayed to them from some height: as something more refined and vulnerable, wilder, stranger, sweeter, and more soulful—but as something one has to lock up lest it fly away.

4. "My friend, permit yourself nothing but follies—that will give you great pleasure."

5. "She looked up, and I at her."

238

To go wrong on the fundamental problem of "man and woman," to deny the most abysmal antagonism between them and the necessity of an eternally hostile tension, to dream perhaps of equal rights, equal education, equal claims and obligations—that is a *typical* sign of shallowness, and a thinker who has proved shallow in this dangerous place—shallow in his instinct—may be considered altogether suspicious, even more—betrayed, exposed: probably he will be too "short" for all fundamental problems of life, of the life yet to come, too, and incapable of attaining *any* depth. A man, on the other hand, who has depth, in his spirit as well as in his desires, including that depth of benevolence which is capable of severity and hardness and easily mistaken for them, must always think about woman as *Orientals* do: he must conceive of woman as a possession, as property that can be locked, as something predestined for service and achieving her perfection in that. Here he must base himself on the tremendous reason of Asia, on Asia's superiority in the instincts, as the Greeks did formerly, who were Asia's best heirs and students: as is well known, from Homer's time to the age of Pericles, as their culture *increased* along with the range of their powers, they also gradually became *more severe,* in brief, more Oriental, against woman. *How* necessary, *how* logical, *how* humanely desirable even, this was—is worth pondering.

239

In no age has the weaker sex been treated with as much respect by men as in ours: that belongs to the democratic inclination and basic taste, just like disrespectfulness for old age. No wonder that this respect is immediately abused. One wants more, one learns to demand, finally one almost finds this tribute of respect insulting, one would prefer competition for rights, indeed even a genuine fight: enough, woman loses her modesty. Let us immediately add that she also loses taste. She unlearns her *fear* of man: but the woman who "unlearns fear" surrenders her most womanly instincts.

That woman ventures forth when the aspect of man that inspires fear—let us say more precisely, when the *man* in man is no longer desired and cultivated—that is fair enough, also comprehensible enough. What is harder to comprehend is that, by the same token—woman degenerates. This is what is happening today: let us not deceive ourselves about that.

Wherever the industrial spirit has triumphed over the military and aristocratic spirit, woman now aspires to the economic and legal self-reliance of a clerk: "woman as clerk" is inscribed on the gate to the modern society that is taking shape now. As she thus takes possession of new rights, aspires to become "master" and writes the "progress" of woman upon her standards and banners, the opposite development is taking place with terrible clarity: *woman is retrogressing.*

Since the French Revolution, woman's influence in Europe has *decreased* proportionately as her rights and claims have increased; and the "emancipation of woman," insofar as that is demanded and promoted by women themselves (and not merely by shallow males) is thus seen to be an odd symptom of the increasing weakening and dulling of the most feminine instincts. There is *stupidity* in this movement, an almost masculine stupidity of which a woman who had turned out well—and such women are always prudent— would have to be thoroughly ashamed.

To lose the sense for the ground on which one is most certain of victory; to neglect practice with one's proper weapons; to let oneself go before men, perhaps even "to the point of writing a book," when formerly one disciplined oneself to subtle and cunning humility; to work with virtuous audacity against men's faith in a basically different ideal that he takes to be *concealed* in woman, something Eternally-and-Necessarily-Feminine—to talk men emphatically and loquaciously out of their notion that woman must be maintained, taken care of, protected, and indulged like a more delicate, strangely wild, and often pleasant domestic animal; the awkward and indignant search for everything slavelike and serflike that has characterized woman's position in the order of society so far, and still does (as if slavery were a counterargument and not instead a condition of every higher culture, every enhancement of culture)—what is the meaning of all this if not a crumbling of feminine instincts, a defeminization?

To be sure, there are enough imbecilic friends and corrupters of woman among the scholarly asses of the male sex who advise woman to defeminize herself in this way and to imitate all the stupidities with which "man" in Europe, European "manliness," is sick: they would like to reduce woman to the level of "general education," probably even of reading the newspapers and talking about politics. Here and there they even want to turn women into freethinkers and scribblers—as if a woman without piety would not seem utterly obnoxious and ridiculous to a profound and godless man.

Almost everywhere one ruins her nerves with the most pathological and dangerous kind of music (our most recent German music) and makes her more hysterical by the day and more incapable of her first and last profession—to give birth to strong children. Altogether one wants to make her more "cultivated" and, as is said, make the weaker sex *strong* through culture—as if history did not teach us as impressively as possible that making men "cultivated" and making them weak—weakening, splintering, and sicklying over the *force of the will*—have always kept pace, and that the most powerful and influential women of the world (most recently Napolean's mother) owed their power and ascendancy over men to the force of their will—and not to schoolmasters!

What inspires respect for woman, and often enough even fear, is her *nature,* which is more "natural" than man's, the genuine, cunning suppleness of a beast of prey, the tiger's claw under the glove, the naiveté of her egoism, her uneducability and inner wildness, the incomprehensibility, scope, and movement of her desires and virtues—

What, in spite of all fear, elicits pity for this dangerous and beautiful cat "woman" is that she appears to suffer more, to be more vulnerable, more in need of love, and more condemned to disappointment than any other animal. Fear and pity: with these feelings man has so far confronted woman, always with one foot in tragedy which tears to pieces as it enchants.

What? And this should be the end? And the breaking of woman's magic spell is at work? The "borification" of woman is slowly dawning? O Europe! Europe! We know the horned animal you always found most attractive; it still threatens you! Your old fable could yet become "history"—once more an immense stupidity might become master over you and carry you off. And this time no god would hide in it; no, only an "idea," a "modern idea"!—

*   *   *

De Beauvoir's Concept of Human Nature

In *The Second Sex,* de Beauvoir defines her philosophical perspective as that of "existentialist ethics." From that perspective, human beings are necessarily viewed as unique individuals and subjects; as such, they live ethically to the degree that they realize their freedom. In an important earlier work, *The Ethics of Ambiguity,* de Beauvoir delineates the ways in which persons fall short of fulfilling their own humanity through apathy, childish submission, introversion, and extroversion. The ethical person recognizes that the human situation is irremediably ambiguous or absurd, but refuses to acquiesce or surrender to the ambiguity. Instead, the moral man or woman transcends the ambiguity through the activity of freedom. According to de Beauvoir, "freedom must project itself

toward its own reality through a content whose value it establishes." Through the choices we make, we create our own values.
To abstain from or avoid these choices by merely conforming to the
values of others is to be immoral.

A rather common argument against the existentialist emphasis on
individual freedom is that it implies an anarchic society, a chaos
of clashes among egoistic pursuers of values. In the thought of de
Beauvoir, this argument cannot be sustained, for freedom requires
that (a) we assume full responsibility for our choices, and (b) we
treat other persons as free also. In fact, "no existence can be validly
fulfilled," de Beauvoir writes, "if it is limited to itself." Hence, "to
will oneself free is also to will others free." In the following passage
de Beauvoir explains her concept rather succinctly:

> to be free is not to have the power to do anything you like; it
> is to be able to surpass the given towards an open future; the
> existence of others as a freedom defines my situation and is
> even the condition of my own freedom. I am oppressed if I
> am thrown into prison, but not if I am kept from throwing my
> neighbor into prison.

The following material is excerpted from the Introduction and
Conclusion of *The Second Sex*.

SIMONE de BEAUVOIR   The Second Sex

. . . [W]hat is a woman?

To state the question is, to me, to suggest, at once, a preliminary
answer. The fact that I ask it is in itself significant. A man would
never get the notion of writing a book on the peculiar situation of
the human male[1]. But if I wish to define myself, I must first of all
say: "I am a woman"; on this truth must be based all further discussion. A man never begins by presenting himself as an individual
of a certain sex; it goes without saying that he is a man. The terms
masculine and *feminine* are used symmetrically only as a matter
of form, as on legal papers. In actuality the relation of the two sexes
is not quite like that of two electrical poles, for man represents both
the positive and the neutral, as is indicated by the common use of
man to designate human beings in general; whereas woman represents only the negative, defined by limiting criteria, without recip-

1. The Kinsey Report [Alfred C. Kinsey and others: *Sexual Behavior in the
Human Male* (W. B. Saunders Co., 1948)] is no exception, for it is limited to
describing the sexual characteristics of American men, which is quite a different matter.

rocity. In the midst of an abstract discussion it is vexing to hear a man say: "You think thus and so because you are a woman"; but I know that my only defense is to reply: "I think thus and so because it is true," thereby removing my subjective self from the argument. It would be out of the question to reply: "And you think the contrary because you are a man," for it is understood that the fact of being a man is no peculiarity. A man is in the right in being a man; it is the woman who is in the wrong. It amounts to this: just as for the ancients there was an absolute vertical with reference to which the oblique was defined, so there is an absolute human type, the masculine. Woman has ovaries, a uterus; these peculiarities imprison her in her subjectivity, circumscribe her within the limits of her own nature. It is often said that she thinks with her glands. Man superbly ignores the fact that his anatomy also includes glands, such as the testicles, and that they secrete hormones. He thinks of his body as a direct and normal connection with the world, which he believes he apprehends objectively, whereas he regards the body of woman as a hindrance, a prison, weighed down by everything peculiar to it. "The female is a female by virtue of a certain *lack* of qualities," said Aristotle; "we should regard the female nature as afflicted with a natural defectiveness." And St. Thomas for his part pronounced woman to be an "imperfect man," an "incidental" being. This is symbolized in Genesis where Eve is depicted as made from what Bossuet called "a supernumerary bone" of Adam.

Thus humanity is male and man defines woman not in herself but as relative to him; she is not regarded as an autonomous being. Michelet writes: "Woman, the relative being. . . ." And Benda is most positive in his *Rapport d'Uriel:* "The body of man makes sense in itself quite apart from that of woman, whereas the latter seems wanting in significance by itself. . . . Man can think of himself without woman. She cannot think of herself without man." And she is simply what man decrees; thus she is called "the sex," by which is meant that she appears essentially to the male as a sexual being. For him she is sex—absolute sex, no less. She is defined and differentiated with reference to man and not he with reference to her; she is the incidental, the inessential as opposed to the essential. He is the Subject, he is the Absolute—she is the Other.[2]

2. E. Lévinas expresses this idea most explicitly in his essay *Temps et l' Autre.* "Is there not a case in which otherness, alterity [altérité], unquestionably marks the nature of a being, as its essence, an instance, of otherness not consisting purely and simply in the opposition of two species of the same genus? I think that the feminine represents the contrary in its absolute sense, this contrariness being in no wise affected by any relation between it and its correlative and thus remaining absolutely other. Sex is not a certain specific difference . . . no more is the sexual difference a mere contradiction. . . . Nor

The category of the *Other* is as primordial as consciousness itself. In the most primitive societies, in the most ancient mythologies, one finds the expression of a duality—that of the Self and the Other. This duality was not originally attached to the division of the sexes; it was not dependent upon any empirical facts. . . .

. . . Otherness is a fundamental category of human thought.

Thus it is that no group ever sets itself up as the One without at once setting up the Other over against itself. If three travelers chance to occupy the same compartment, that is enough to make vaguely hostile "others" out of all the rest of the passengers on the train. In small-town eyes all persons not belonging to the village are "strangers" and suspect; to the native of a country all who inhabit other countries are "foreigners"; Jews are "different" for the anti-Semite, Negroes are "inferior" for American racists, aborigines are "natives" for colonists, proletarians are the "lower class" for the privileged. . . . No subject will readily volunteer to become the object, the inessential; it is not the Other who, in defining himself as the Other, establishes the One. The Other is posed as such by the One in defining himself as the One. But if the Other is not to regain the status of being the One, he must be submissive enough to accept this alien point of view.

. . . . If woman seems to be the inessential which never becomes the essential, it is because she herself fails to bring about this change. Proletarians say "We"; Negroes also. Regarding themselves as subjects, they transform the bourgeois, the whites, into "others." But women do not say "We," except at some congress of feminists or similar formal demonstration; men say "women," and women use the same word in referring to themselves. They do not authentically assume a subjective attitude. The proletarians have accomplished the revolution in Russia, the Negroes in Haiti, the Indo-Chinese are battling for it in Indo-China; but the women's effort has never been anything more than a symbolic agitation. They have gained only what men have been willing to grant; they have taken nothing, they have only received.

The reason for this is that women lack concrete means for organizing themselves into a unit which can stand face to face with the

---

does this difference lie in the duality of two complementary terms, for two complementary terms imply a preexisting whole. . . . Otherness reaches its full flowering in the feminine, a term of the same rank as consciousness but of opposite meaning."

I suppose that Lévinas does not forget that woman, too, is aware of her own consciousness, or ego. But it is striking that he deliberately takes a man's point of view, disregarding the reciprocity of subject and object. When he writes that woman is mystery, he implies that she is mystery for man. Thus his description, which is intended to be objective, is in fact an assertion of masculine privilege.

correlative unit. They have no past, no history, no religion of their own; and they have no such solidarity of work and interest as that of the proletariat. They are not even promiscuously herded together in the way that creates community feeling among the American Negroes, the ghetto Jews, the workers of Saint-Denis, or the factory hands of Renault. They live dispersed among the males, attached through residence, housework, economic condition, and social standing to certain men—fathers or husbands—more firmly than they are to other women. If they belong to the bourgeoisie, they feel solidarity with men of that class, not with proletarian women; if they are white, their allegiance is to white men, not to Negro women. The proletariat can propose to massacre the ruling class, and a sufficiently fanatical Jew or Negro might dream of getting sole possession of the atomic bomb and making humanity wholly Jewish or black; but woman cannot even dream of exterminating the males. The bond that unites her to her oppressors is not comparable to any other. The division of the sexes is a biological fact, not an event in human history. Male and female stand opposed within a primordial *Mitsein,* and woman has not broken it. The couple is a fundamental unity with its two halves riveted together, and the cleavage of society along the line of sex is impossible. Here is to be found the basic trait of woman: she is the Other in a totality of which the two components are necessary to one another.

... To decline to be the Other, to refuse to be a party to the deal —this would be for women to renounce all the advantages conferred upon them by their alliance with the superior caste. Man-the-sovereign will provide woman-the-liege with material protection and will undertake the moral justification of her existence; thus she can evade at once both economic risk and the metaphysical risk of a liberty in which ends and aims must be contrived without assistance. Indeed, along with the ethical urge of each individual to affirm his subjective existence, there is also the temptation to forgo liberty and become a thing. This is an inauspicious road, for he who takes it—passive, lost, ruined—becomes henceforth the creature of another's will, frustrated in his transcendence and deprived of every value. But it is an easy road; on it one avoids the strain involved in undertaking an authentic existence. When man makes of woman the *Other,* he may, then, expect her to manifest deep-seated tendencies toward complicity. Thus, woman may fail to lay claim to the status of subject because she lacks definite resources, because she feels the necessary bond that ties her to man regardless of reciprocity, and because she is often very well pleased with her role as the *Other.* . . . People have tirelessly sought to prove that woman is superior, inferior, or equal to man. Some say that, having been created after Adam, she is evidently a secondary being; others say on the contrary that Adam was only a rough draft and that God succeeded in producing the human being in perfection when He created Eve. Woman's brain is smaller; yes, but it is relatively larger. Christ was made a man; yes, but perhaps for his greater humility. Each argument at once suggests its opposite, and both are often fallacious. If we are to gain understanding, we must get out of these ruts; we must discard the vague notions of superiority, inferiority, equality which have hitherto corrupted every discussion of the subject and start afresh. . . .

But it is doubtless impossible to approach any human problem with a mind free from bias. The way in which questions are put, the points of view assumed, presuppose a relativity of interest; all characteristics imply values, and every objective description, so called, implies an ethical background. Rather than attempt to conceal principles more or less definitely implied, it is better to state them openly at the beginning. This will make it unnecessary to specify on every page in just what sense one uses such words as *superior, inferior, better, worse, progress, reaction,* and the like. If we survey some of the works on woman, we note that one of the points of view most frequently adopted is that of the public good, the general interest; and one always means by this the benefit of society as one wishes it to be maintained or established. For our part, we hold that the only public good is that which assures the private good of the citizens; we shall pass judgment on institutions according to their effectiveness in giving concrete opportunities to individuals. But we do not confuse the idea of private interest with that of happiness, although that is another common point of view. Are not women of the harem more happy than women voters? Is not the housekeeper happier than the working-woman? It is not too clear just what the word *happy* really means and still less what true values it may mask. There is no possibility of measuring the happiness of others, and it is always easy to describe as happy the situation in which one wishes to place them.

In particular those who are condemned to stagnation are often pronounced happy on the pretext that happiness consists in being at rest. This notion we reject, for our perspective is that of existentialist ethics. Every subject plays his part as such specifically through exploits or projects that serve as a mode of transcendence; he achieves liberty only through a continual reaching out toward other liberties. There is no justification for present existence other than its expansion into an indefinitely open future. Every time transcendence falls back into immanence, stagnation, there is a degradation of existence into the *"en-soi"*—the brutish life of subjection to given conditions—and of liberty into constraint and contingence. This downfall represents a moral fault if the subject consents to it; if it is inflicted upon him, it spells frustration and oppression. In both cases it is an absolute evil. Every individual concerned to justify his existence feels that his existence involves an undefined need to transcend himself, to engage in freely chosen projects.

Now, what peculiarly signalizes the situation of woman is that she—a free and autonomous being like all human creatures—nevertheless finds herself living in a world where men compel her to assume the status of the Other. They propose to stabilize her as object and to doom her to immanence since her transcendence is to be overshadowed and forever transcended by another ego (*conscience*) which is essential and sovereign. The drama of woman lies in this conflict between the fundamental aspirations of every subject (*ego*)—who always regards the self as the essential—and the compulsions of a situation in which she is the inessential. How can a human being in woman's situation attain fulfillment? What roads are open to her? Which are blocked? How can independence be recovered in a state of dependency? What circumstances limit woman's liberty and how can they be overcome? These are the fundamental questions on which I would fain throw some light. This means that I am interested in the fortunes of the individual as defined not in terms of happiness but in terms of liberty.

Quite evidently this problem would be without significance if we were to believe that woman's destiny is inevitably determined by physiological, psychological, or economic forces. Hence I shall discuss first of all the light in which woman is viewed by biology, psychoanalysis, and historical materialism. Next I shall try to show exactly how the concept of the "truly feminine" has been fashioned —why woman has been defined as the Other—and what have been the consequences from man's point of view. Then from woman's point of view I shall describe the world in which women must live; and thus we shall be able to envisage the difficulties in their way as, endeavoring to make their escape from the sphere hitherto assigned them, they aspire to full membership in the human race.

.   .   .   .

We have seen that in spite of legends no physiological destiny imposes an eternal hostility upon Male and Female as such; even the famous praying mantis devours her male only for want of other food and for the good of the species: it is to this, the species, that all individuals are subordinated, from the top to the bottom of the scale of animal life. Moreover, humanity is something more than a mere species: it is a historical development; it is to be defined by the manner in which it deals with its natural, fixed characteristics, its *facticité*. Indeed, even with the most extreme bad faith in the world, it is impossible to demonstrate the existence of a rivalry between the human male and female of a truly physiological nature. Further, their hostility may be allocated rather to that intermediate terrain between biology and psychology: psychoanalysis. Woman, we are told, envies man his penis and wishes to castrate him; but the childish desire for the penis is important in the life of the adult woman only if she feels her femininity as a mutilation; and then it is as a symbol of all the privileges of manhood that she wishes to appropriate the male organ. We may readily agree that her dream of castration has this symbolic significance: she wishes, it is thought, to deprive the male of his transcendence.

But her desire, as we have seen, is much more ambiguous: she wishes, in a contradictory fashion, *to have* this transcendence, which is to suppose that she at once respects it and denies it, that she intends at once to throw herself into it and keep it within herself. This is to say that the drama does not unfold on a sexual level; further, sexuality has never seemed to us to define a destiny, to furnish in itself the key to human behavior, but to express the totality of a situation that it only helps to define. The battle of the *sexes* is not immediately implied in the anatomy of man and woman. The truth is that when one evokes it, one takes for granted that in the timeless realm of Ideas a battle is being waged between those vague essences the Eternal Feminine and the Eternal Masculine; and one neglects the fact that this titanic combat assumes on earth two totally different forms, corresponding with two different moments of history.

The woman who is shut up in immanence endeavors to hold man in that prison also; thus the prison will be confused with the world, and woman will no longer suffer from being confined there: mother, wife, sweetheart are the jailers. Society, being codified by man, decrees that woman is inferior: she can do away with this inferiority only by destroying the male's superiority. She sets about mutilating, dominating man, she contradicts him, she denies his truth and his values. But in doing this she is only defending herself; it was neither a changeless essence nor a mistaken choice that doomed her to immanence, to inferiority. They were imposed upon her. All oppression creates a state of war. And this is no exception. The existent who is regarded as inessential cannot fail to demand the re-establishment of her sovereignty.

Today the combat takes a different shape; instead of wishing to put man in a prison, woman endeavors to escape from one; she no longer seeks to drag him into the realms of immanence but to emerge, herself, into the light of transcendence. Now the attitude of the males creates a new conflict; it is with a bad grace that the man lets her go. He is very well pleased to remain the sovereign subject, the absolute superior, the essential being; he refuses to accept his companion as an equal in any concrete way. She replies to his lack of confidence in her by assuming an aggressive attitude.

It is no longer a question of a war between individuals each shut up in his or her sphere: a caste claiming its rights goes over the top and it is resisted by the privileged caste. Here two transcendences are face to face; instead of displaying mutual recognition, each free being wishes to dominate the other.

This difference of attitude is manifest on the sexual plane as on the spiritual plane. The "feminine" woman in making herself prey tries to reduce man, also, to her carnal passivity; she occupies herself in catching him in her trap, in enchanting him by means of the desire she arouses in him in submissively making herself a thing. The emancipated woman, on the contrary, wants to be active, a taker, and refuses the passivity man means to impose on her. Thus Elise and her emulators deny the values of the activities of virile type; they put the flesh above the spirit, contingence above liberty, their routine wisdom above creative audacity. But the "modern" woman accepts masculine values: she prides herself on thinking, taking action, working, creating, on the same terms as men; instead of seeking to disparage them, she declares herself their equal. In so far as she expresses herself in definite action, this claim is legitimate, and male insolence must then bear the blame. But in men's defense it must be said that women are wont to confuse the issue. A Mabel Dodge Luhan intended to subjugate D. H. Lawrence by her feminine charms so as to dominate him spiritually thereafter; many women, in order to show by their successes their equivalence to men, try to secure male support by sexual means; they play on both sides, demanding old-fashioned respect and modern esteem, banking on their old magic and their new rights. It is understandable that a man becomes irritated and puts himself on the defensive; but he is also double-dealing when he requires woman to play the game fairly while he denies them the indispensable trump cards through distrust and hostility. Indeed, the struggle cannot be clearly drawn between them, since woman is opaque in her very being; she stands before man not as a subject but as an object paradoxically endued with subjectivity; she takes herself simultaneously as *self* and as *other*, a contradiction that entails baffling consequences. When she makes weapons at once of her weakness and of her strength, it is not a matter of designing calculation: she seeks salvation spontaneously in the way that has been imposed on her, that of passivity, at the same time when she is actively demanding her sovereignty; and no doubt this procedure is unfair tactics, but it is dictated to her by the ambiguous situation assigned her. Man, however, becomes indignant when he treats her as a free and independent being and then realizes that she is still a trap for him; if he gratifies and satisfies her in her posture as prey, he finds her claims to autonomy irritating; whatever he does, he feels tricked and she feels wronged.

The quarrel will go on as long as men and women fail to recognize each other as peers; that is to say, as long as femininity is perpetuated as such. Which sex is the more eager to maintain it? Woman, who is being emancipated from it, wishes none the less to retain its privileges; and man, in that case, wants her to assume its limitations. "It is easier to accuse one sex than to excuse the other," says Montaigne. It is vain to apportion praise and blame. The truth is that if the vicious circle is so hard to break, it is because the two sexes are each the victim at once of the other and of itself. Between two adversaries confronting each other in their pure liberty, an agreement could be easily reached: the more so as the war profits neither. But the complexity of the whole affair derives from the fact that each camp is giving aid and comfort to the enemy; woman is pursuing a dream of submission, man a dream of identification. Want of authenticity does not pay: each blames the other for the unhappiness he or she has incurred in yielding to the temptations of the easy way; what man and woman loathe in each other is the shattering frustration of each one's own bad faith and baseness.

We have seen why men enslaved women in the first place; the devaluation of femininity has been a necessary step in human evolution, but it might have led to collaboration between the two sexes; oppression is to be explained by the tendency of the existent to flee from himself by means of identification with the other, whom he oppresses to that end. In each individual man that tendency exists today; and the vast majority yield to it. The husband wants to find himself in his wife, the lover in his mistress, in the form of a stone image; he is seeking in her the myth of his virility, of his sovereignty, of his immediate reality. "My husband never goes to the movies," says his wife, and the dubious masculine opinion is graved in the marble of eternity. But he is himself the slave of his double: what an effort to build up an image in which he is always in danger! In spite of everything his success in this depends upon the capricious freedom of women: he must constantly try to keep this propitious to him. Man is concerned with the effort to appear male, important, superior; he pretends so as to get pretense in return; he, too, is aggressive, uneasy; he feels hostility for women because he is afraid of them, he is afraid of them because he is afraid of the personage, the image, with which he identifies himself. What time and strength he squanders in liquidating, sublimating, transferring complexes, in talking about women, in seducing them, in fearing them! He would be liberated himself in their liberation. But this is precisely what he dreads. And so he obstinately persists in the mystifications intended to keep woman in her chains.

That she is being tricked, many men have realized. "What a misfortune to be a woman! And yet the misfortune, when one is a woman, is at bottom not to comprehend that it is one." says Kierkegaard.[3] For a long time there have been efforts to disguise this misfortune. For example, guardianship has been done away with: women have been given "protectors," and if they are invested with the rights of the old-time guardians, it is in woman's own interest. To forbid her working, to keep her at home, is to defend her against herself and to assure her happiness. We have seen what poetic veils are thrown over her monotonous burdens of housekeeping and maternity: in exchange for her liberty she has received the false treasures of her "femininity." Balzac illustrates this maneuver very well in counseling man to treat her as a slave while persuading her that she is a queen. Less cynical, many men try to convince themselves that she is really privileged. There are American sociologists who seriously teach today the theory of "low-class gain." In France, also, it has often been proclaimed—although in a less scientific manner—that the workers are very fortunate in not being obliged to "keep up appearances" and still more so the bums who can dress in rags and sleep on the sidewalks, pleasures forbidden to the Count de Beaumont and the Wendels. Like the carefree wretches gaily scratching at their vermin, like the merry Negroes laughing under the lash and those joyous Tunisian Arabs burying their starved children with a smile, woman enjoys that incomparable privilege: irresponsibility. Free from troublesome burdens and cares, she obviously has "the better part." But it is disturbing that with an obstinate perversity—connected no doubt with original sin—down through the centuries and in all countries, the people who have the better part are always crying to their benefactors: "It is too much! I will be satisfied with yours!" But the munificent capitalists, the generous colonists, the superb males, stick to their guns: "Keep the better part, hold on to it!"

It must be admitted that the males find in woman more complicity than the oppressor usually finds in the oppressed. And in bad faith they take authorization from this to declare that she has *desired* the destiny they have imposed on her. We have seen that all the main features of her training combine to bar her from the roads of revolt and adventure. Society in general—beginning with her respected parents—lies to her by praising the lofty values of love, devotion, the gift of herself, and then concealing from her the fact that neither lover nor husband nor yet her children will be in-

3. *In Vino Veritas.* He says further: "Politeness is pleasing—essentially—to woman, and the fact that she accepts it without hesitation is explained by nature's care for the weaker, for the unfavored being, and for one to whom an illusion means more than a material compensation. But this illusion, precisely, is fatal to her. . . . To feel oneself freed from distress thanks to something imaginary, to be the dupe of something imaginary, is that not a still deeper mockery? . . . Woman is very far from being *verwahrlost* (neglected), but in another sense she is, since she can never free herself from the illusion that nature has used to console her."

clined to accept the burdensome charge of all that. She cheerfully
believes these lies because they invite her to follow the easy slope:
in this others commit their worst crime against her; throughout her
life from childhood on, they damage and corrupt her by designating as her true vocation this submission, which is the temptation of
every existent in the anxiety of liberty. If a child is taught idleness
by being amused all day long and never being led to study, or
shown its usefulness, it will hardly be said, when he grows up, that
he chose to be incapable and ignorant; yet this is how woman is
brought up, without ever being impressed with the necessity of
taking charge of her own existence. So she readily lets herself come
to count on the protection, love, assistance, and supervision of others, she lets herself be fascinated with the hope of self-realization
without *doing* anything. She does wrong in yielding to the temptation; but man is in no position to blame her, since he has led her
into the temptation. When conflict arises between them, each will
hold the other responsible for the situation; she will reproach him
with having made her what she is: "No one taught me to reason or
to earn my own living"; he will reproach her with having accepted
the consequences: "You don't know anything, you are an incompe-
tent," and so on. Each sex thinks it can justify itself by taking the
offensive; but the wrongs done by one do not make the other innocent.

The innumerable conflicts that set men and women against one
another come from the fact that neither is prepared to assume all
the consequenses of this situation which the one has offered and the
other accepted. The doubtful concept of "equality in inequality,"
which the one uses to mask his despotism and the other to mask her
cowardice, does not stand the test of experience: in their exchanges,
woman appeals to the theoretical equality she has been guaranteed,
and man the concrete inequality that exists. The result is that in
every association an endless debate goes on concerning the ambiguous meaning of the words *give* and *take:* she complains of giving
her all, he protests that she takes his all. Woman has to learn that
exchanges—it is a fundamental law of political economy—are based
on the value the merchandise offered has for the buyer, and not for
the seller: she has been deceived in being persuaded that her worth
is priceless. The truth is that for man she is an amusement, a pleasure, company, an inessential boon; he is for her the meaning, the
justification of her existence. The exchange, therefore, is not of two
items of equal value.

This inequality will be especially brought out in the fact that the
time they spend together—which fallaciously seems to be the same
time—does not have the same value for both partners. During the
evening the lover spends with his mistress he could be doing
something of advantage to his career, seeing friends, cultivating

business relationships, seeking recreation; for a man normally integrated in society, time is a positive value: money, reputation, pleasure. For the idle, bored woman, on the contrary, it is a burden she wishes to get rid of; when she succeeds in killing time, it is a benefit to her: the man's presence is pure profit. In a liaison what most clearly interests the man, in many cases, is the sexual benefit he gets from it: if need be, he can be content to spend no more time with his mistress than is required for the sexual act; but—with exceptions—what she, on her part, wants is to kill all the excess time she has on her hands; and—like the storekeeper who will not sell potatoes unless the customer will take turnips also—she will not yield her body unless her lover will take hours of conversation and "going out" into the bargain. A balance is reached if, on the whole, the cost does not seem too high to the man, and this depends, of course, on the strength of his desire and the importance he gives to what is to be sacrificed. But if the woman demands—offers—too much time, she becomes wholly intrusive, like the river overflowing its banks, and the man will prefer to have nothing rather than too much. Then she reduces her demands; but very often the balance is reached at the cost of a double tension: she feels that the man has "had" her at a bargain, and he thinks her price is too high. This analysis, of course, is put in somewhat humorous terms; but— except for those affairs of jealous and exclusive passions in which the man wants total possession of the woman—this conflict constantly appears in cases of affection, desire, and even love. He always has "other things to do" with his time; whereas she has time to burn; and he considers much of the time she gives him not as a gift but as a burden.

As a rule he consents to assume the burden because he knows very well that he is on the privileged side, he has a bad conscience; and if he is of reasonable good will he tries to compensate for the inequality by being generous. He prides himself on his compassion, however, and at the first clash he treats the woman as ungrateful and thinks, with some irritation: "I'm too good for her." She feels she is behaving like a beggar when she is convinced of the high value of her gifts, and that humiliates her.

Here we find the explanation of the cruelty that woman often shows she is capable of practicing; she has a good conscience because she is on the unprivileged side; she feels she is under no obligation to deal gently with the favored caste, and her only thought is to defend herself. She will even be very happy if she has occasion to show her resentment to a lover who has not been able to satisfy all her demands: since he does not give her enough, she takes savage delight in taking back everything from him. At this point the wounded lover suddenly discovers the value *in toto* of a liaison each moment of which he held more or less in contempt: he is ready to promise her everything, even though he will feel exploited again when he has to make good. He accuses his mistress of blackmailing him: she calls him stingy; both feel wronged.

Once again it is useless to apportion blame and excuses: justice can never be done in the midst of injustice. A colonial administrator has no possibility of acting rightly toward the natives, nor a general toward his soldiers; the only solution is to be neither colonist nor military chief; but a man could not prevent himself from being a man. So there he is, culpable in spite of himself and laboring under the effects of a fault he did not himself commit; and here she is, victim and shrew in spite of herself. Sometimes he rebels and becomes cruel, but then he makes himself an accomplice of the injustice, and the fault becomes really his. Sometimes he lets himself be annihilated, devoured, by his demanding victim; but in that case he feels duped. Often he stops at a compromise that at once belittles him and leaves him ill at ease. A well-disposed man will be more tortured by the situation than the woman herself: in a sense it is always better to be on the side of the vanquished; but if she is well-disposed also, incapable of self-sufficiency, reluctant to crush the man with the weight of her destiny, she struggles in hopeless confusion.

In daily life we meet with an abundance of these cases which are incapable of satisfactory solution because they are determined by unsatisfactory conditions. A man who is compelled to go on materially and morally supporting a woman whom he no longer loves feels he is victimized; but if he abandons without resources the woman who has pledged her whole life to him, she will be quite as unjustly victimized. The evil originates not in the perversity of individuals—and bad faith first appears when each blames the other—it originates rather in a situation against which all individual action is powerless. Women are "clinging," they are a dead weight, and they suffer for it; the point is that their situation is like that of a parasite sucking out the living strength of another organism. Let them be provided with living strength of their own, let them have the means to attack the world and wrest from it their own subsistence, and their dependence will be abolished—that of man also. There is no doubt that both men and women will profit greatly from the new situation.

A world where men and women would be equal is easy to visualize, for that precisely is what the Soviet Revolution *promised*: women raised and trained exactly like men were to work under the same conditions[4] and for the same wages. Erotic liberty was to be

___

4. That certain too laborious occupations were to be closed to women is not in contradiction to this project. Even among men there is an increasing effort

recognized by custom, but the sexual act was not to be considered a "service" to be paid for; woman was to be *obliged* to provide herself with other ways of earning a living; marriage was to be based on a free agreement that the spouses could break at will; maternity was to be voluntary, which meant that contraception and abortion were to be authorized and that, on the other hand, all mothers and their children were to have exactly the same rights, in or out of marriage; pregnancy leaves were to be paid for by the State, which would assume charge of the children, signifying not that they would be *taken away* from their parents, but that they would not be *abandoned* to them.

But is it enough to change laws, institutions, customs, public opinion, and the whole social context, for men and women to become truly equal? "Women will always be women," say the skeptics. Other seers prophesy that in casting off their femininity they will not succeed in changing themselves into men and they will become monsters. This would be to admit that the woman of today is a creation of nature; it must be repeated once more that in human society nothing is natural and that woman, like much else, is a product elaborated by civilization. The intervention of others in her destiny is fundamental: if this action took a different direction, it would produce a quite different result. Woman is determined not by her hormones or by mysterious instincts, but by the manner in which her body and her relation to the world are modified through the action of others than herself. The abyss that separates the adolescent boy and girl has been deliberately opened out between them since earliest childhood; later on, woman could not be other than what she *was made*, and that past was bound to shadow her for life. If we appreciate its influence, we see clearly that her destiny is not predetermined for all eternity.

We must not believe, certainly, that a change in woman's economic condition alone is enough to transform her, though this factor has been and remains the basic factor in her evolution; but until it has brought about the moral, social, cultural, and other consequences that it promises and requires, the new woman cannot appear. At this moment they have been realized nowhere, in Russia no more than in France or the United States; and this explains why the woman of today is torn between the past and the future. She appears most often as a "true woman" disguised as a man, and she feels herself as ill at ease in her flesh as in her masculine garb. She must shed her old skin and cut her own new clothes. This she

---

to obtain adaptation to profession; their varying physical and mental capacities limit their possibilities of choice; what is asked is that, in any case, no line of sex or caste be drawn.

could do only through a social evolution. No single educator could fashion a *female human being* today who would be the exact homologue of the *male human being;* if she is raised like a boy, the young girl feels she is an oddity and thereby she is given a new kind of sex specification. Stendhal understood this when he said: "The forest must be planted all at once." But if we imagine, on the contrary, a society in which the equality of the sexes would be concretely realized, this equality would find new expression in each individual.

If the little girl were brought up from the first with the same demands and rewards, the same severity and the same freedom, as her brothers, taking part in the same studies, the same games, promised the same future, surrounded with women and men who seemed to her undoubted equals, the meanings of the castration complex and of the Oedipus complex would be profoundly modified. Assuming on the same basis as the father the material and moral responsibility of the couple, the mother would enjoy the same lasting prestige; the child would perceive around her an androgynous world and not a masculine world. Were she emotionally more attracted to her father—which is not even sure—her love for him would be tinged with a will to emulation and not a feeling of powerlessness; she would not be oriented toward passivity. Authorized to test her powers in work and sports, competing actively with the boys, she would not find the absence of the penis —compensated by the promise of a child—enough to give rise to an inferiority complex; correlatively, the boy would not have a superiority complex if it were not instilled into him and if he looked up to women with as much respect as to men.[5] The little girl would not seek sterile compensation in narcissism and dreaming, she would not take her fate for granted; she would be interested in what she was *doing,* she would throw herself without reserve into undertakings.

I have already pointed out how much easier the transformation of puberty would be if she looked beyond it, like the boys, toward a free adult future: menstruation horrifies her only because it is an abrupt descent into femininity. She would also take her young eroticism in much more tranquil fashion if she did not feel a frightened disgust for her destiny as a whole; coherent sexual information would do much to help her over this crisis. And thanks to coeducational schooling, the august mystery of Man would have no occa-

5. I knew a little boy of eight who lived with his mother, aunt, and grandmother, all independent and active women, and his weak old half-crippled grandfather. He had a crushing inferiority complex in regard to the feminine sex, although he made efforts to combat it. At school he scorned comrades and teachers because they were miserable males.

sion to enter her mind: it would be eliminated by everyday familiarity and open rivalry.

Objections raised against this system always imply respect for sexual taboos; but the effort to inhibit all sex curiosity and pleasure in the child is quite useless; one succeeds only in creating repressions, obsessions, neuroses. The excessive sentimentality, homosexual fervors, and platonic crushes of adolescent girls, with all their train of silliness and frivolity, are much more injurious than a little childish sex play and a few definite sex experiences. It would be beneficial above all for the young girl not to be influenced against taking charge herself of her own existence, for then she would not seek a demigod in the male—merely a comrade, a friend, a partner. Eroticism and love would take on the nature of free transcendence and not that of resignation; she could experience them as a relation between equals. There is no intention, of course, to remove by a stroke of the pen all the difficulties that the child has to overcome in changing into an adult; the most intelligent, the most tolerant education could not relieve the child of experiencing things for herself; what could be asked is that obstacles should not be piled gratuitously in her path. Progress is already shown by the fact that "vicious" little girls are no longer cauterized with a red-hot iron. Psychoanalysis has given parents some instruction, but the conditions under which, at the present time, the sexual training and initiation of woman are accomplished are so deplorable that none of the objections advanced against the idea of a radical change could be considered valid. It is not a question of abolishing in woman the contingencies and miseries of the human condition, but of giving her the means for transcending them.

Woman is the victim of no mysterious fatality; the peculiarities that identify her as specifically a woman get their importance from the significance placed upon them. They can be surmounted, in the future, when they are regarded in new perspectives. Thus, as we have seen, through her erotic experience woman feels—and often detests—the domination of the male; but this is no reason to conclude that her ovaries condemn her to live forever on her knees. Virile aggressiveness seems like a lordly privilege only within a system that in its entirety conspires to affirm masculine sovereignty; and woman *feels* herself profoundly passive in the sexual act only because she already *thinks* of herself as such. Many modern women who lay claim to their dignity as human beings still envisage their erotic life from the standpoint of a tradition of slavery: since it seems to them humiliating to lie beneath the man, to be penetrated by him, they grow tense in frigidity. But if the reality were different, the meaning expressed symbolically in amorous gestures and postures would be different, too: a woman who pays and dominates her lover can, for example, take pride in her superb idleness and consider that she is enslaving the male who is actively exerting himself. And here and now there are many sexually well-balanced couples whose notions of victory and defeat are giving place to the idea of an exchange.

As a matter of fact, man, like woman, is flesh, therefore passive, the plaything of his hormones and of the species, the restless prey of his desires. And she, like him, in the midst of the carnal fever, is a consenting, a voluntary gift, an activity; they live out in their several fashions the strange ambiguity of existence made body. In those combats where they think they confront one another, it is really against the self that each one struggles, projecting into the partner that part of the self which is repudiated; instead of living out the ambiguities of their situation, each tries to make the other bear the abjection and tries to reserve the honor for the self. If, however, both should assume the ambiguity with a clear-sighted modesty, correlative of an authentic pride, they could see each other as equals and would live out their erotic drama in amity. The fact that we are human beings is infinitely more important than all the peculiarities that distinguish human beings from one another; it is never the given that confers superiorities: "virtue," as the ancients called it, is defined at the level of "that which depends on us." In both sexes is played out the same drama of the flesh and the spirit, of finitude and transcendence; both are gnawed away by time and laid in wait for by death, they have the same essential need for one another; and they can gain from their liberty the same glory. If they were to taste it, they would no longer be tempted to dispute fallacious privileges, and fraternity between them could then come into existence.

I shall be told that all this is utopian fancy, because woman cannot be "made over" unless society has first made her really the equal of man. Conservatives have never failed in such circumstances to refer to that vicious circle; history, however, does not revolve. If a caste is kept in a state of inferiority, no doubt it remains inferior; but liberty can break the circle. Let the Negroes vote and they become worthy of having the vote; let woman be given responsibilities and she is able to assume them. The fact is that oppressors cannot be expected to make a move of gratuitous generosity; but at one time the revolt of the oppressed, at another time even the very evolution of the privileged caste itself, creates new situations; thus men have been led, in their own interest, to give partial emancipation to women: it remains only for women to continue their ascent, and the successes they are obtaining are an encouragement for them to do so. It seems almost certain that sooner or later they will arrive at complete economic and social equality, which will bring about an inner metamorphosis.

However this may be, there will be some to object that if such a world is possible it is not desirable. When woman is "the same" as her male, life will lose its salt and spice. This argument, also, has lost its novelty: those interested in perpetuating present conditions are always in tears about the marvelous past that is about to disappear, without having so much as a smile for the young future. It is quite true that doing away with the slave trade meant death to the great plantations, magnificent with azaleas and camellias, it meant ruin to the whole refined Southern civilization. The attics of time have received its rare odd laces along with the clear pure voices of the Sistine *castrati,* and there is a certain "feminine charm" that is also on the way to the same dusty repository. I agree that he would be a barbarian indeed who failed to appreciate exquisite flowers, rare lace, the crystal-clear voice of the eunuch, and feminine charm.

When the "charming woman" shows herself in all her splendor, she is a much more exalting object than the "idiotic paintings, overdoors, scenery, showman's garish signs, popular chromos," that excited Rimbaud; adorned with the most modern artifices, beautified according to the newest techniques, she comes down from the remoteness of the ages, from Thebes, from Crete, from Chichén-Itzá; and she is also the totem set up deep in the African jungle; she is a helicopter and she is a bird; and there is this, the greatest wonder of all: under her tinted hair the forest murmur becomes a thought, and words issue from her breasts. Men stretch forth avid hands toward the marvel, but when they grasp it it is gone; the wife, the mistress, speak like everybody else through their mouths: their words are worth just what they are worth; their breasts also. Does such a fugitive miracle—and one so rare—justify us in perpetuating a situation that is baneful for both sexes? One can appreciate the beauty of flowers, the charm of women, and appreciate them at their true value; if these treasures cost blood or misery, they must be sacrificed.

But in truth this sacrifice seems to men a peculiarly heavy one; few of them really wish in their hearts for woman to succeed in making it; those among them who hold woman in contempt see in the sacrifice nothing for them to gain, those who cherish her see too much that they would lose. And it is true that the evolution now in progress threatens more than feminine charm alone: in beginning to exist for herself, woman will relinquish the function as double and mediator to which she owes her privileged place in the masculine universe; to man, caught between the silence of nature and the demanding presence of other free beings, a creature who is at once his like and a passive thing seems a great treasure. The guise in which he conceives his companion may be mythical, but the experiences for which she is the source or the pretext are none the less real: there are hardly any more precious, more intimate, more ardent. There is no denying that feminine dependence, inferiority, woe, given women their special character; assuredly woman's autonomy, if it spares men many troubles, will also deny them many conveniences; assuredly there are certain forms of the sexual adventure which will be lost in the world of tomorrow. But this does not mean that love, happiness, poetry, dream, will be banished from it.

Let us not forget that our lack of imagination always depopulates the future; for us it is only an abstraction; each one of us secretly deplores the absence there of the one who was himself. But the humanity of tomorrow will be living in its flesh and in its conscious liberty; that time will be its present and it will in turn prefer it. New relations of flesh and sentiment of which we have no conception will arise between the sexes; already, indeed, there have appeared between men and women friendships, rivalries, complicities, comradeships—chaste or sensual—which past centuries could not have conceived. To mention one point, nothing could seem to me more debatable than the opinion that dooms the new world to uniformity and hence to boredom. I fail to see that this present world is free from boredom or that liberty ever creates uniformity.

To begin with, there will always be certain differences between man and woman; her eroticism, and therefore her sexual world, have a special form of their own and therefore cannot fail to engender a sensuality, a sensitivity, of a special nature. This means that her relations to her own body, to that of the male, to the child, will never be identical with those the male bears to his own body, to that of the female, and to the child; those who make much of "equality in difference" could not with good grace refuse to grant me the possible existence of differences in equality. Then again, it is institutions that create uniformity. Young and pretty, the slaves of the harem are always the same in the sultan's embrace; Christianity gave eroticism its savor of sin and legend when it endowed the human female with a soul; if society restores her sovereign individuality to woman, it will not thereby destroy the power of love's embrace to move the heart.

It is nonsense to assert that revelry, vice, ecstasy, passion, would become impossible if man and woman were equal in concrete matters; the contradictions that put the flesh in opposition to the spirit, the instant to time, the swoon of immanence to the challenge of transcendence, the absolute of pleasure to the nothingness of forgetting, will never be resolved; in sexuality will always be materialized the tension, the anguish, the joy, the frustration, and the triumph of existence. To emancipate woman is to refuse to confine her to the relations she bears to man, not to deny them to her; let her have her independent existence and she will continue none the less to exist for him *also:* mutually recognizing each other as subject, each will yet remain for the other an *other*. The reciprocity of their relations will not do away with the miracles—desire, possession, love, dream, adventure—worked by the division of human beings into two separate categories; and the words that move us—giving, conquering, uniting—will not lose their meaning. On the contrary, when we abolish the slavery of half of humanity, together with the whole system of hypocrisy that it implies, then the "division" of humanity will reveal its genuine significance and the human couple will find its true form. "The direct, natural, necessary relation of human creatures is the *relation of man to woman*," Marx has said.[6] "The nature of this relation determines to what point man himself is to be considered as a *generic being*, as mankind; the relation of man to woman is the most natural relation of human being to human being. By it is shown, therefore, to what point the *natural* behavior of man has become *human* or to what point the *human* being has become his *natural* being, to what point his *human nature* has become his *nature*."

The case could not be better stated. It is for man to establish the reign of liberty in the midst of the world of the given. To gain the supreme victory, it is necessary, for one thing, that by and through their natural differentiation men and women unequivocally affirm their brotherhood.

*   *   *

THE MARXIST CONTEXT

In general, Marxist theory involves a greater emphasis upon society than upon the individual. It would be a mistake, however, to construe that emphasis as denying rights and freedom to the individual, even though some supposedly Marxist instances of modern government seem to support that interpretation. Totalitarian regimes are basically inconsistent with the social teachings of Marx, particularly in his early writings. While some scholars consider the later writings a departure from the earlier ones, the majority insist that Marx was consistent, and that the politically radical views of the later period such as those expressed in *Capital* can only be understood correctly in the light of his earlier humanistic concepts.

Both Karl Marx (1818–83) and Friedrich Engels (1820–95) were products of German bourgeois society. Their life-long friendship began in 1844 in Paris, where Marx had gone to escape political pressures evoked by his radical writings. A key theme in Marx's

6. *Philosophical Works,* Vol. VI (Marx's italics).

manuscripts of this period is his denunciation of previous philosophers for having engaged exclusively in speculation about the world, thereby neglecting their primary responsibility for affecting social change. Through his own study of history, Marx had become convinced that the most effective way to improve society was through economics; he therefore embarked upon a thorough study of that subject as a tool through which to fulfill what he believed to be the proper function of philosophy.

Subsequently both Marx and Engels lived in England, where Marx labored long years in the composition of *Capital*. He supported his family on the pittance received from occasional articles, supplemented by the generosity of Engels, who managed his father's textile business in London. In fundamental agreement with Marx's ideas, Engels thus sought to contribute financially to their actualization. His writings also reflect his accord with Marx's theory.

One of the most influential converts to Maxism was another product of the bourgeoisie—Vladimir Lenin (1870–1924). As a youth in Russia, Lenin had become involved in the "intelligentsia," a politically radical discussion circle, for whom the writings of Marx and Engels were an important source and inspiration. Two early events are revealing with regard to Lenin's later social attitudes: (1) When his older brother Alex was arrested and executed for involvement in a plot to kill the Tsar, Lenin refused to seek personal retribution or revenge; only the universal interests, those of every member of society, could justify retaliation for such an act; (2) In 1887 Lenin was expelled from law school for his part in a minor student demonstration. Without benefit of teachers or classes, he studied on his own and passed the required examinations with the highest possible grades: he thus exhibited a determined will as well as a keen intellect, powers he fully utilized in behalf of the oppressed.

As a result of his efforts to form a Russian Marxist organization, Lenin was arrested and imprisoned first at St. Petersburg, then in Siberia, for over four years. Upon his release he continued his subversive efforts from exile, principally by writings and building up a political party. Not until 1917, when revolution in Russia erupted spontaneously through the downfall of the Tsar, did Lenin return to his native land, where he eventually succeeded in establishing and leading the Communist Party. In all these activities, Lenin saw himself as applying to Russia the ideas and idealism of Marx.

Marx's Concept of Human Nature

Marx's philosophy is sometimes called a dialectical materialism. The dialectic derives from Hegel; basically, it means a view of reality and history as a progressive process of interaction between opposing forces. Society is continually advancing through its varying forms, towards the fullest realization of our human potential. The materialism of Marx involves the claim that all reality is matter or nature, even human reality. This does not imply a denial of human consciousness, but allows that this consciousness be defined as a complex arrangement of matter. In other words, human beings are composed of the same "stuff" (matter) as are plants and animals and minerals, but they differ from those instances of matter in that they exhibit consciousness.

Hence, to be human, for Marx, is to be a very special kind of "dialectical matter"; it is to be a being whose consciousness allows him or her to affect as well as be affected by the world. To be human is to be a producer, and not a mere product, in the midst of nature. Marx's use of the term "production" extends to any work of human beings, including works of art and intellect To be human is also to be related to other persons in a truly human, that is, a free and intelligent, manner. Dehumanization of individuals or society occurs wherever human beings are treated as products or means of production rather than as producers, or whenever they are alienated, or cut off from free interaction with other persons. According to Marx, such dehumanization inevitably occurs within the capitalistic economic system.

In his early writings, Marx had described the man-woman relationship as a gauge for the level of humanization achieved by a society. For example, wherever prostitution is practiced, women are used as objects of pleasure for men; similarly, capitalistic producers use the working class as means of obtaining economic profit for themselves. The following selection, written by Engels after Marx's death, applies Marx's criterion to a critique of the modern family.

Engel's "Origin of the Family" is excerpted from *Origin of the Family, Private Property and the State.*

FRIEDRICH ENGELS 'Origin of the Family'

If we consider the most primitive known forms of family . . . the form of sexual intercourse can only be described as promiscuous—promiscuous in so far as the restrictions later established by custom did not yet exist. . . .

According to Morgan, from this primitive state of promiscuous intercourse there developed, probably very early:

1. THE CONSANGUINE FAMILY,
THE FIRST STAGE OF THE FAMILY

Here the marriage groups are separated according to generations: all the grandfathers and grandmothers within the limits of
the family are all husbands and wives of one another; so are also
their children, the fathers and mothers; the latter's children will
form a third circle of common husbands and wives; and their children, the great-grandchildren of the first group, will form a fourth.
In this form of marriage, therefore, only ancestors and progeny,
and parents and children, are excluded from the rights and duties
(as we should say) of marriage with one another. . . .

2. THE PUNALUAN FAMILY

If the first advance in organization consisted in the exclusion of
parents and children from sexual intercourse with one another, the
second was the exclusion of sister and brother. On account of the
greater nearness in age, this second advance was infinitely more
important, but also more difficult, than the first. It was effected
gradually, beginning probably with the exclusion from sexual intercourse of one's own brothers and sisters (children of the same
mother) first in isolated cases and then by degrees as a general
rule (even in this century exceptions were found in Hawaii), and
ending with the prohibition of marriage even between collateral
brothers and sisters, or, as we should say, between first, second,
and third cousins. It affords, says Morgan, "a good illustration of
the operation of the principle of natural selection." There can be
no question that the tribes among whom inbreeding was restricted
by this advance were bound to develop more quickly and more
fully than those among whom marriage between brothers and
sisters remained the rule and the law. . . .

In all forms of group family, it is uncertain who is the father of
a child; but it is certain who its mother is. Though she calls *all*
the children of the whole family her children and has a mother's
duties toward them, she nevertheless knows her own children from
the others. It is therefore clear that in so far as group marriage prevails, descent can only be proved on the *mother's* side and that
therefore only the *female* line is recognized. And this is in fact the
case among all peoples in the period of savagery or in the lower
stage of barbarism. It is the second great merit of Bachofen that
he was the first to make this discovery. To denote this exclusive
recognition of descent through the mother and the relations of inheritance which in time resulted from it, he uses the term "mother
right," which for the sake of brevity I retain. The term is, however,
ill-chosen, since at this stage of society there cannot yet be any talk
of "right" in the legal sense. . . .

3. THE PAIRING FAMILY

A certain amount of pairing, for a longer or shorter period, already occurred in group marriage or even earlier; the man had a chief wife among his many wives (one can hardly yet speak of a favorite wife), and for her he was the most important among her husbands. . . . [T]hese customary pairings were bound to grow more stable as the gens developed and the classes of "brothers" and "sisters" between whom marriage was impossible became more numerous. The impulse given by the gens to the prevention of marriage between blood relatives extended still further.

. . . The increasing complication of these prohibitions made group marriages more and more impossible; they were displaced by the *pairing family*. In this stage, one man lives with one woman, but the relationship is such that polygamy and occasional infidelity remain the right of the men, even though for economic reasons polygamy is rare, while from the woman the strictest fidelity is generally demanded throughout the time she lives with the man and adultery on her part is cruelly punished. The marriage tie can, however, be easily dissolved by either partner; after separation, the children still belong as before to the mother alone. . . .

Thus the history of the family in primitive times consists in the progressive narrowing of the circle, originally embracing the whole tribe, within which the two sexes have a common conjugal relation. The continuous exclusion, first of nearer, then of more and more remote relatives, and at last even of relatives by marriage, ends by making any kind of group marriage practically impossible. Finally, there remains only the single, still loosely linked pair, the molecule with whose dissolution marriage itself ceases. This in itself shows what a small part individual sex love, in the modern sense of the word, played in the rise of monogamy. . . .

The pairing family, itself too weak and unstable to make an independent household necessary or even desirable, in no wise destroys the communistic household inherited from earlier times. Communistic housekeeping, however, means the supremacy of women in the house; just as the exclusive recognition of the female parent, owing to the impossibility of recognizing the male parent with certainty, means that the women—the mothers—are held in high respect. One of the most absurd notions taken over from 18th century enlightenment is that in the beginning of society woman was the slave of man. Among all savages and all barbarians of the lower and middle stages, and to a certain extent of the upper stage also, the position of women is not only free, but honorable. . . .

The communistic household, in which most or all of the women belong to one and the same gens, while the men come from various gentes, is the material foundation of that supremacy of the women which was general in primitive times. . . . The reports of travelers and missionaries, I may add, to the effect that women among savages and barbarians are overburdened with work in no way contradict what has been said. The division of labor between the two sexes is determined by quite other causes than by the position of woman in society. Among peoples where the women have to work far harder than we think suitable, there is often much more real respect for women than among our Europeans. The lady of civilization, surrounded by false homage and estranged from all real work, has an infinitely lower social position than the hard-working woman of barbarism, who was regarded among her people as a real lady (lady, *frowa*, *Frau*—mistress) and who was also a lady in character.

. . . In the single pair the group was already reduced to its final unit, its two-atom molecule: one man and one woman. Natural selection, with its progressive exclusions from the marriage community, had accomplished its task; there was nothing more for it to do in this direction. Unless new, *social* forces came into play, there was no reason why a new form of family should arise from the single pair. But these new forces did come into play. . . . [T]he domestication of animals and the breeding of herds had developed a hitherto unsuspected source of wealth and created entirely new social relations. . . .

Once it had passed into the private possession of families and there rapidly begun to augment, this wealth dealt a severe blow to the society founded on pairing marriage and the matriarchal gens. Pairing marriage had brought a new element into the family. By the side of the natural mother of the child is placed its natural and attested father with a better warrant of paternity, probably, than that of many a "father" today. According to the division of labor within the family at that time, it was the man's part to obtain food and the instruments of labor necessary for the purpose. He therefore also owned the instruments of labor, and in the event of husband and wife separating, he took them with him, just as she retained her household goods. Therefore, according to the social custom of the time, the man was also the owner of the new source of subsistence, the cattle, and later of the new instruments of labor, the slaves. But according to the custom of the same society, his children could not inherit from him. . . .

Thus on the one hand, in proportion as wealth increased it made the man's position in the family more important than the woman's, and on the other hand created an impulse to exploit this strengthened position in order to overthrow, in favor of his children, the traditional order of inheritance. This, however, was impossible so long as descent was reckoned according to mother right. Mother right, therefore, had to be overthrown, and overthrown it was. . . .

The overthrow of mother right was the *world historical defeat of the female sex*. The man took command in the home also; the woman was degraded and reduced to servitude; she became the slave of his lust and a mere instrument for the production of children. This degraded position of the woman, especially conspicuous among the Greeks of the heroic and still more of the classical age, has gradually been palliated and glossed over, and sometimes clothed in a milder form; in no sense has it been abolished.

The establishment of the exclusive supremacy of the man shows its effects first in the patriarchal family, which now emerges as an intermediate form. Its essential characteristic is not polygyny, of which more later, but "the organization of a number of persons, bond and free, and into a family under paternal power for the purpose of holding lands and for the care of flocks and herds. . . . (In the Semitic form) the chiefs, at least, lived in polygamy. . . . Those held to servitude and those employed as servants lived in the marriage relation" [Morgan, 1963: 474].

Its essential features are the incorporation of unfree persons and paternal power; hence the perfect type of this form of family is the Roman. The original meaning of the word "family" (*familia*) is not that compound of sentimentality and domestic strife which forms the ideal of the present-day philistine; among the Romans it did not at first even refer to the married pair and their children but only to the slaves. *Famulus* means domestic slave, and *familia* is the total number of slaves belonging to one man. As late as the time of Gaius, the *familia, id est patrimonium* (family, that is, the patrimony, the inheritance) was bequeathed by will. The term was invented by the Romans to denote a new social organism whose head ruled over wife and children and a number of slaves, and was invested under Roman paternal power with rights of life and death over them all.

> This term, therefore, is no older than the ironclad family system of the Latin tribes, which came in after field agriculture and after legalized servitude, as well as after the separation of the Greeks and Latins [Morgan, 1963: 478].

Marx adds:

> The modern family contains in germ not only slavery (*servitus*) but also serfdom, since from the beginning it is related to agricultural services. It contains *in miniature* all the contradictions which later extend throughout society and its state.

Such a form of family shows the transition of the pairing family to monogamy. In order to make certain of the wife's fidelity and therefore of the paternity of the children, she is delivered over unconditionally into the power of the husband; if he kills her, he is only exercising his rights.

With the patriarchal family, we enter the field of written history, a field where comparative jurisprudence can give valuable help. And it has in fact brought an important advance in our knowledge. We owe to Maxim Kovalevsky (*Tableau, etc.* 60–100) the proof that the patriarchal household community, as we still find it today among the Serbs and the Bulgars under the name of *zádruga* (which may be roughly translated "bond of friendship") or *bratstvo* (brotherhood), and in a modified form among the Oriental peoples, formed the transitional stage between the matriarchal family deriving from group marriage and the single family of the modern world. . . .

4. THE MONOGAMOUS FAMILY

It develops out of the pairing family, as previously shown, in the transitional period between the upper and middle stages of barbarism; its decisive victory is one of the signs that civilization is beginning. It is based on the supremacy of the man, the express purpose being to produce children of undisputed paternity; such paternity is demanded because these children are later to come into their father's property as his natural heirs. It is distinguished from pairing marriage by the much greater strength of the marriage tie, which can no longer be dissolved at either partner's wish. As a rule, it is now only the man who can dissolve it and put away his wife. The right of conjugal infidelity also remains secured to him, at any rate by custom (the *Code Napoléon* explicitly accords it to the husband as long as he does not bring his concubine into the house), and as social life develops he exercises his right more and more; should the wife recall the old form of sexual life and attempt to revive it, she is punished more severely than ever. . . .

This is the origin of monogamy as far as we can trace it back among the most civilized and highly developed people of antiquity. It was not in any way the fruit of individual sex love, with which it had nothing whatever to do; marriages remained as before marriages of convenience. It was the first form of the family to be based not on natural but on economic conditions—on the victory of private property over primitive, natural communal property. The Greeks themselves put the matter quite frankly: the sole exclusive aims of monogamous marriage were to make the man supreme in the family and to propagate, as the future heirs to his wealth, children indisputably his own. Otherwise, marriage was a burden, a duty which had to be performed whether one liked it or not to gods, state, and one's ancestors. In Athens the law exacted from the man not only marriage but also the performance of a minimum of so-called conjugal duties.

Thus when monogamous marriage first makes its appearance in history, it is not as the reconciliation of man and woman, still less as the highest form of such a reconciliation. Quite the contrary, monogamous marriage comes on the scene as the subjugation of the one sex by the other; it announces a struggle between the sexes unknown throughout the whole previous prehistorical period. In an old unpublished manuscript written by Marx and myself in 1846, I find the words: "The first division of labor is that between man and woman for the propagation of children." And today I can add: The first class opposition that appears in history coincides with the development of the antagonism between man and woman in monogamous marriage, and the first class oppression coincides with that of the female sex by the male. Monogamous marriage was a great historical step forward; nevertheless, together with slavery and private wealth, it opens the period that has lasted until today in which every step forward is also relatively a step backward, in which prosperity and development for some is won through the misery and frustration of others. It is the cellular form of civilized society in which the nature of the oppositions and contradictions fully active in that society can be already studied.

The old comparative freedom of sexual intercourse by no means disappeared with the victory of pairing marriage or even of monogamous marriage:

> The old conjugal system, now reduced to narrower limits by the gradual disappearance of the punaluan groups, still environed the advancing family, which it was to follow to the verge of civilization. . . . It finally disappeared in the new form of hetaerism, which still follows mankind in civilization as a dark shadow upon the family [Morgan, 1963: 511].

By "hetaerism" Morgan understands the practice, *coexistent with monogamous marriage,* of sexual intercourse between men and unmarried women outside marriage, which, as we know, flourishes in the most varied forms throughout the whole period of civilization and develops more and more into open prostitution. . . .

But a second contradiction thus develops within monogamous marriage itself. At the side of the husband who embellishes his existence with hetaerism stands the neglected wife. And one cannot have one side of this contradiction without the other, any more than a man has a whole apple in his hand after eating half. But that seems to have been the husbands' notion, until their wives taught them better. With monogamous marriage, two constant social types, unknown hitherto, make their appearance on the scene

—the wife's attendant lover and the cuckold husband. The husbands had won the victory over the wives, but the vanquished magnanimously provided the crown. Together with monogamous marriage and hetaerism, adultery became an unavoidable social institution—denounced, severely penalized, but impossible to suppress. At best, the certain paternity of the children rested on moral conviction as before, and to solve the insoluble contradiction the *Code Napoléon*, Article 312, decreed: "*L'enfant conçu pendant le mariage a pour pére le mari*," the father of a child conceived during marriage is—the husband. Such is the final result of three thousand years of monogamous marriage.

Thus, wherever the monogamous family remains true to its historical origin and clearly reveals the antagonism between the man and the woman expressed in the man's exclusive supremacy, it exhibits in miniature the same oppositions and contradictions as those in which society has been moving, without power to resolve or overcome them, ever since it split into classes at the beginning of civilization. I am speaking here, of course, only of those cases of monogamous marriage where matrimonial life actually proceeds according to the original character of the whole institution but where the wife rebels against the husband's supremacy. Not all marriages turn out thus, as nobody knows better than the German philistine who can no more assert his rule in the home than he can in the state and whose wife, with every right, wears the trousers he is unworthy of. . . .

[I]f monogamy was the only one of all the known forms of the family through which modern sex love could develop, that does not mean that within monogamy modern sexual love developed exclusively or even chiefly as the love of husband and wife for each other. That was precluded by the very nature of strictly monogamous marriage under the rule of the man. Among all historically active classes—that is, among all ruling classes—matrimony remained what it had been since the pairing marriage, a matter of convenience which was arranged by the parents. The first historical form of sexual love as passion, a passion recognized as natural to all human beings (at least if they belonged to the ruling classes), and as the highest form of the sexual impulse—and that is what constitutes its specific character—this first form of individual sexual love, the chivalrous love of the middle ages, was by no means conjugal. Quite the contrary, in its classic form among the Provençals, it heads straight for adultery, and the poets of love celebrated adultery. . . .

Nowadays there are two ways of concluding a bourgeois marriage. In Catholic countries the parents, as before, procure a suitable wife for their young bourgeois son, and the consequence is, of course, the fullest development of the contradiction inherent in monogamy: the husband abandons himself to hetaerism and the wife to adultery. Probably the only reason why the Catholic Church abolished divorce was because it had convinced itself that there is no more a cure for adultery than there is for death. In Protestant countries, on the other hand, the rule is that the son of a bourgeois family is allowed to choose a wife from his own class with more or less freedom; hence there may be a certain element of love in the marriage as, indeed, in accordance with Protestant hypocrisy is always assumed for decency's sake. Here the husband's hetaerism is a more sleepy kind of business, and adultery by the wife is less the rule. But since in every kind of marriage people remain what they were before and since the bourgeois of Protestant countries are mostly philistines, all that this Protestant monogamy achieves, taking the average of the best cases, is a conjugal partnership of leaden boredom, known as "domestic bliss." . . .

In both cases, however the marriage is conditioned by the class position of the parties and is to that extent always a marriage of convenience. In both cases this marriage of convenience turns often enough into the crassest prostitution—sometimes of both partners, but far more commonly of the woman, who only differs from the ordinary courtesan in that she does not let out her body on piecework as a wage worker but sells it once and for all into slavery.

And of all marriages of convenience Fourier's words hold true: "As in grammar two negatives make an affirmative, so in matrimonial morality two prostitutions pass for a virtue."[1] Sex love in the relationship with a woman becomes and can only become the real rule among the oppressed classes, which means today among the proletariat—whether this relation is officially sanctioned or not. But here all the foundations of typical monogamy are cleared away. Here there is no property, for the preservation and inheritance of which monogamy and male supremacy were established; hence there is no incentive to make this male supremacy effective. What is more, there are no means of making it so. Bourgeois law, which protects this supremacy, exists only for the possessing class and their dealings with the proletarians. The law costs money and, on account of the worker's poverty, it has no validity for his relation to his wife. Here quite other personal and social conditions decide. And now that large-scale industry has taken the wife out of the home onto the labor market and into the factory, and made her often the breadwinner of the family, no basis for any kind of male supremacy is left in the proletarian household, except, perhaps, for something of the brutality toward women that has spread since the introduction of monogamy. The proletarian family is therefore no longer monogamous in the strict sense, even where there is passionate love and firmest loyalty on both sides and maybe all the bless-

1. Charles Fourier, *Théorie de l'Unité Universelle*, Paris, 1841–45, III, 120.

ings of religious and civil authority. Here, therefore, the eternal attendants of monogamy, hetaerism and adultery, play only an almost vanishing part. The wife has in fact regained the right to dissolve the marriage, and if two people cannot get on with one another, they prefer to separate. In short, proletarian marriage is monogamous in the etymological sense of the word, but not at all in its historical sense.

Our jurists, of course, find that progress in legislation is leaving women with no further ground of complaint. Modern civilized systems of law increasingly acknowledge first, that for a marriage to be legal it must be a contract freely entered into by both partners and secondly, that also in the married state both partners must stand on a common footing of equal rights and duties. If both these demands are consistently carried out, say the jurists, women have all they can ask.

This typically legalist method of argument is exactly the same as that which the radical republican bourgeois uses to put the proletarian in his place. The labor contract is to be freely entered into by both partners. But it is considered to have been freely entered into as soon as the law makes both parties equal on *paper*. The power conferred on the one party by the difference of class position, the pressure thereby brought to bear on the other party—the real economic position of both—that is not the law's business. Again, for the duration of the labor contract, both parties are to have equal rights in so far as one or the other does not expressly surrender them. That economic relations compel the worker to surrender even the last semblance of equal rights—here again, that is no concern of the law.

In regard to marriage, the law, even the most advanced, is fully satisfied as soon as the partners have formally recorded that they are entering into the marriage of their own free consent. What goes on in real life behind the juridical scenes, how this free consent comes about—that is not the business of the law and the jurist. . . .

As regards the legal equality of husband and wife in marriage, the position is no better. The legal inequality of the two partners bequeathed to us from earlier social conditions is not the cause but the effect of the economic oppression of the woman. In the old communistic household, which comprised many couples and their children, the task entrusted to the women of managing the household was as much a public, a socially necessary industry as the procuring of food by the men. With the patriarchal family and still more with the single monogamous family, a change came. Household management lost its public character. It no longer concerned society. It became a *private service;* the wife became the head servant, excluded from all participation in social production. Not until the coming of modern large-scale industry was the road to social production opened to her again—and then only to the proletarian wife. But it was opened in such a manner that, if she carries out her duties in the private service of her family, she remains excluded from public production and unable to earn; and if she wants to take part in public production and earn independently, she cannot carry out family duties. And the wife's position in the factory is the position of women in all branches of business, right up to medicine and the law. The modern individual family is founded on the open or concealed domestic slavery of the wife, and modern society is a mass composed of these individual families as its molecules.

In the great majority of cases today, at least in the possessing classes, the husband is obliged to earn a living and support his family, and that in itself gives him a position of supremacy without any need for special legal titles and privileges. Within the family he is the bourgeois, and the wife represents the proletariat. In the industrial world, the specific character of the economic oppression burdening the proletariat is visible in all its sharpness only when all special legal privileges of the capitalist class have been abolished and complete legal equality of both classes established. The democratic republic does not do away with the opposition of the two classes; on the contrary, it provides the clear field on which the fight can be fought out. And in the same way, the peculiar character of the supremacy of the husband over the wife in the modern family, the necessity of creating real social equality between them and the way to do it, will only be seen in the clear light of day when both possess legally complete equality of rights. Then it will be plain that the first condition for the liberation of the wife is to bring the whole female sex back into public industry, and that this in turn demands that the characteristic of the monogamous family as the economic unit of society be abolished.

We thus have three principal forms of marriage which correspond broadly to the three principal stages of human development: for the period of savagery, group marriage; for barbarism, pairing marriage; for civilization, monogamy supplemented by adultery and prostitution. Between pairing marriage and monogamy intervenes a period in the upper stage of barbarism when men have female slaves at their command and polygamy is practiced.

As our whole presentation has shown, the progress which manifests itself in these successive forms is connected with the peculiarity that women, but not men, are increasingly deprived of the sexual freedom of group marriage. In fact, for men group marriage actually still exists even to this day. What for the woman is a crime entailing grave legal and social consequences is considered honorable in a man or, at the worst, a slight moral blemish which he cheerfully bears. But the more the hetaerism of the past is changed in our time by capitalist commodity production and brought into conformity with it, the more, that is to say, it is transformed into undisguised prostitution, the more demoralizing are its effects. And it demoralizes men far more than women. Among women, prostitution degrades only the unfortunate ones who become its victims, and even these by no means to the extent commonly believed. But it degrades the character of the whole male world. A long engagement particularly is in nine cases out of ten a regular preparatory school for conjugal infidelity.

We are now approaching a social revolution in which the economic foundations of monogamy as they have existed hitherto will disappear just as surely as those of its complement—prostitution. Monogamy arose from the concentration of considerable wealth in the hands of a single individual—a man—and from the need to bequeath this wealth to the children of that man and of no other. For this purpose, the monogamy of the woman was required, not that of the man, so this monogamy of the woman did not in any way interfere with open or concealed polygamy on the part of the man. But by transforming by far the greater portion, at any rate, of permanent, heritable wealth—the means of production—into social property, the coming social revolution will reduce to a minimum all this anxiety about bequeathing and inheriting. Having arisen from economic causes, will monogamy then disappear when these causes disappear?

One might answer, not without reason: far from disappearing, it will on the contrary begin to be realized completely. For with the transformation of the means of production into social property there will disappear also wage labor, the proletariat, and therefore the necessity for a certain—statistically calculable—number of women to surrender themselves for money. Prostitution disappears; monogamy, instead of collapsing, at last becomes a reality—also for men.

In any case, therefore, the position of men will be very much altered. But the position of women, of *all* women, also undergoes significant change. With the transfer of the means of production into common ownership, the single family ceases to be the economic unit of society. Private housekeeping is transformed into a social industry. The care and education of the children becomes a public affair; society looks after all children alike, whether they are legitimate or not. This removes all the anxiety about the "consequences," which today is the most essential social—more as well as economic—factor that prevents a girl from giving herself completely to the man she loves. Will not that suffice to bring about the gradual growth of unconstrained sexual intercourse and with it a more tolerant public opinion in regard to a maiden's honor and a woman's shame? And finally, have we not seen that in the modern world monogamy and prostitution are indeed contradictions, but inseparable contradictions, poles of the same state of society? Can prostitution disappear without dragging monogamy with it into the abyss?

Here a new element comes into play, an element which at the time when monogamy was developing existed at most in embryo—individual sex love. . . .

Our sex love differs essentially from the simple sexual desire, the Eros, of the ancients. In the first place, it assumes that the person loved returns the love; to this extent the woman is on an equal footing with the man, whereas in the Eros of antiquity she was often not even asked. Secondly, our sex love has a degree of intensity and duration which makes both lovers feel that non-possession and separation are a great, if not the greatest, calamity; to possess one another, they risk high stakes, even life itself. In the ancient world this happened only, if at all, in adultery. And finally, there arises a new moral standard in the judgment of a sexual relationship. We do not only ask, was it within or outside marriage, but also, did it spring from love and reciprocated love or not? Of course, this new standard has fared no better in feudal or bourgeois practice than all the other standards of morality—it is ignored. But neither does it fare any worse. It is recognized, like all the rest, in theory, on paper. And for the present more than this cannot be expected. . . .

In the vast majority of cases . . . marriage remained up to the close of the middle ages what it had been from the start—a matter which was not decided by the partners. In the beginning, people were already born married—married to an entire group of the opposite sex. In the later forms of group marriage similar relations probably existed, but with the group continually contracting. In the pairing marriage it was customary for the mothers to settle the marriages of their children; here, too, the decisive considerations are the new ties of kinship which are to give the young pair a stronger position in the gens and tribe. And when, with the preponderance of private over communal property and the interest in its bequeathal father right and monogamy gained supremacy, the dependence of marriages on economic considerations became complete. The *form* of marriage by purchase disappears; the actual practice is steadily extended until not only the woman but also the man acquires a price—not according to his personal qualities but according to his property. That the mutual affection of the people concerned should be the one paramount reason for marriage, outweighing everything else, was and always had been absolutely unheard of in the practice of the ruling classes; that sort of thing only happened in romance—or among the oppressed classes, who did not count.

Such was the state of things encountered by capitalist production when it began to prepare itself, after the epoch of geographical discoveries, to win world power by world trade and manufacture. One would suppose that this manner of marriage exactly suited it, and so it did. And yet—there are no limits to the irony of history—capitalist production itself was to make the decisive breach in it. By changing all things into commodities, it dissolved all inherited and traditional relationships, and in place of time-honored custom and historic right, it set up purchase and sale, "free" contract. And the English jurist H. S. Maine thought he had made a tremendous discovery when he said that our whole progress in comparison with former epochs consisted in the fact that we had passed "from status to contract," from inherited to freely contracted conditions—which, in so far as it is correct was already in *The Communist Manifesto* [Chapter II].

But a contract requires people who can dispose freely of their persons, actions, and possessions and meet each other on the footing of equal rights. To create these "free" and "equal" people was one of the main tasks of capitalist production. Even though at the start it was carried out only half-consciously, and under a religious disguise at that, from the time of the Lutheran and Calvinist Reformation the principle was established that man is only fully responsible for his actions when he acts with complete freedom of will, and that it is a moral duty to resist all coercion to an immoral act. But how did this fit in with the hitherto existing practice in the arrangement of marriages? Marriage according to the bourgeois conception was a contract, a legal transaction, and the most important one of all because it disposed of two human beings, body and mind, for life. Formally, it is true, the contract at that time was entered into voluntarily; without the assent of the persons concerned, nothing could be done. But everyone knew only too well how this assent was obtained and who were the real contracting parties in the marriage. But if real freedom of decision was required for all other contracts, then why not for this? Had not the two young people to be coupled also the right to dispose freely of themselves, of their bodies and organs? Had not chivalry brought sex love into fashion, and was not its proper bourgeois form, in contrast to chivalry's adulterous love, the love of husband and wife? And if it was the duty of married people to love each other, was it not equally the duty of lovers to marry each other and nobody else? Did not this right of the lovers stand higher than the right of parents, relations, and other traditional marriage brokers and match-makers? . . .

So it came about that the rising bourgeoisie, especially in Protestant countries where existing conditions had been most severely shaken, increasingly recognized freedom of contract also in marriage, and carried it into effect in the manner described. Marriage remained class marriage, but within the class the partners were conceded a certain degree of freedom of choice. And on paper, in ethical theory and in poetic description, nothing was more immutably established than that every marriage is immoral which does not rest on mutual sexual love and really free agreement of husband and wife. In short, the love marriage was proclaimed as a human right, and indeed not only as a *droit de l'homme,* one of the rights of man, but also, for once in a way, as *droit de la femme,* one of the rights of woman.

This human right, however, differed in one respect from all other so-called human rights. While the latter in practice remain restricted to the ruling class (the bourgeoisie) and are directly or indirectly curtailed for the oppressed class (the proletariat), in the case of the former the irony of history plays another of its tricks. The ruling class remains dominated by the familiar economic influences and therefore only in exceptional cases does it provide instances of really freely contracted marriages, while among the oppressed class, as we have seen, these marriages are the rule.

Full freedom of marriage can therefore only be generally established when the abolition of capitalist production and of the property relations created by it has removed all the accompanying economic considerations which still exert such a powerful influence on the choice of a marriage partner. For then there is no other motive left except mutual inclination.

And as sexual love is by its nature exclusive—although at present this exclusiveness is fully realized only in the woman—the marriage based on sexual love is by its nature individual marriage. We have seen how right Bachofen was in regarding the advance from group marriage to individual marriage as primarily due to the women. Only the step from pairing marriage to monogamy can be put down to the credit of the men, and historically the essence of this was to make the position of the women worse and the infidelities of the men easier. If now the economic considerations also disappear which made women put up with the habitual infidelity of their husbands—concern for their own means of existence and still more for their children's future—then, according to all previous experience, the equality of woman thereby achieved will tend infinitely more to make men really monogamous than to make women polyandrous.

But what will quite certainly disappear from monogamy are all the features stamped upon it through its origin in property relations; these are, in the first place, supremacy of the man and secondly, the indissolubility of marriage. The supremacy of the man in marriage is the simple consequence of his economic supremacy, and with the abolition of the latter will disappear of itself. The indissolubility of marriage is partly a consequence of the economic situation in which monogamy arose, partly tradition from the period when the connection between this economic situation and monogamy was not fully understood and was carried to extremes under a religious form. Today it is already broken through at a thousand points. If only the marriage based on love is moral, then also only the marriage is moral in which love continues. But the intense emotion of individual sex love varies very much in duration from one individual to another, especially among men, and if affection definitely comes to an end or is supplanted by a new passionate love, separation is a benefit for both partners as well as for society—only people will then be spared having to wade through the useless mire of a divorce case.

What we can now conjecture about the way in which sexual relations will be ordered after the impending overthrow of capitalist production is mainly of a negative character, limited for the most part to what will disappear. But what will there be new? That will be answered when a new generation has grown up: a generation of men who never in their lives have known what it is to buy a woman's surrender with money or any other social instrument of power; a generation of women who have never known what it is to give themselves to a man from any other considerations than real love or to refuse to give themselves to their lover from fear of the economic consequences. When these people are in the world, they will care precious little what anybody today thinks they ought to do; they will make their own practice and their corresponding public opinion about the practice of each individual—and that will be the end of it.

*　　*　　*

Lenin's Concept of Human Nature

Like Marx and Engels, Lenin viewed human nature from a materialistic perspective. Although human being are comprised of mind and matter, the former is dependent upon the latter. Each person is essentially a social being, having a primary moral responsibility to promote the egalitarian interests of every member of society. In pursuing that end, the responsibility of the individual is proportionate to an awareness of obstacles to the universal interests, and to the varying competence of each individual for overcoming those obstacles. For example, Lenin himself, because of the advantages of his bourgeois background, natural talent, and education, considered himself more responsible for correcting the inequities of society than the typically uneducated proletarian peasant, who had become inured to oppression.

For Lenin, the ideal of an egalitarian society is so good in itself that it justifies revolution as means to its accomplishment. Nonetheless, violence and bloodshed are permitted only where indispensable for implementing the ideal, and never for the sake of merely procuring or maintaining dictatorial power. History discloses Lenin's effort, during the last few months of his life, to prevent Josef Stalin's assumption of the party's leadership. It appears that Lenin anticipated and disapproved the excessive exercise of power that followed in the Stalinist purges. Lenin wrote and spoke often about the necessity and means for emancipating women in society. His comments, spread over a range of years and documents, are collected in a book entitled *The Emancipation of Women*. The following selection is drawn from that collection; its main part is an interview with Lenin on the "*Woman Question*," conducted by the German communist, Clara Zetkin.

❋　　❋　　❋

V. I. LENIN　The Emancipation of Women

Capitalism and Female Labour

Modern capitalist society is the hiding place of numerous cases of poverty and oppression that are not immediately visible. The scattered families of middle class people, artisans, factory workers, clerks and the lower civil servants, are indescribably poor and barely make ends meet in the *best* of times. Millions and millions of women in such families live (or rather drag out an existence) as household slaves, striving with a desperate daily effort to feed and clothe their families on a few coppers, economising in everything except their own labour.

It is from among these women that the capitalists are most eager to engage workers who work at home and who are prepared for a monstrously low wage to "earn" an extra crust of bread for themselves and their families. It is from among them that the capitalists of all countries (like the slave owners of antiquity and the feudal lords of the Middle Ages) choose any number of concubines at the most "favourable" price. No "moral indignation" (hypocritical in ninety-nine cases out of a hundred) about prostitution can do anything to prevent this commerce in women's bodies; as long as wage slavery exists, prostitution must inevitably continue. Throughout the history of society all the oppressed and exploited classes have always been compelled (their exploitation consists in this) to hand over to the oppressors, first, their unpaid labour and, secondly, their women to be the concubines of the "masters".

Slavery, feudalism and capitalism are alike in this respect. Only the *form* of the exploitation changes, the exploitation remains.

. . . .

The conditions that make it impossible for the oppressed classes to "exercise" their democratic rights are not the exception under capitalism; they are typical of the system. In most cases the right of divorce will remain unrealisable under capitalism, for the oppressed sex is subjugated economically. No matter how much democracy there is under capitalism, the woman remains a "domestic slave", a slave locked up in the bedroom, nursery, kitchen. . . . The fuller the freedom of divorce, the clearer will women see that the source of their "domestic slavery" is capitalism, not lack of rights.

. . . .

Soviet Power and the Status of Women

The status of women makes clear in the most striking fashion the difference between bourgeois and socialist democracy. . . .

In a bourgeois republic (i.e., where there is private ownership of land, factories, shares, etc.), be it the most democratic republic, women have never had equal rights, *anywhere in the world, in any one of the more advanced countries.* And this despite the fact that more than 125 years passed since the French (bourgeois-democratic) Revolution.

In words bourgeois democracy promises equality and freedom, but in practice *not a single* bourgeois republic, even the more advanced, has granted women (half the human race) and men complete equality in the eyes of the law, or delivered women from dependence on and the oppression of the male.

Bourgeois democracy is the democracy of pompous phrases, solemn words, lavish promises and high-sounding slogans about *freedom and equality,* but in practice all this cloaks the lack of freedom and the inequality of women, the lack of freedom and the inequality for the working and exploited people.

. . . .

[N]ot a single democratic party in the world, not even in the most advanced bourgeois republic, has done in decades so much as a hundredth part of what we did in our very first year in power. We actually razed to the ground the infamous laws placing women in a position of inequality, restricting divorce and surrounding it with disgusting formalities, denying recognition to children born out of wedlock, enforcing a search for their fathers, etc., laws numerous survivals of which, to the shame of the bourgeoisie and of capitalism, are to be found in all civilised countries. We have a thousand times the right to be proud of what we have done in this field. But the more *thoroughly* we clear the ground of the lumber of the old, bourgeois laws and institutions, the more we realise that we have only cleared the ground to build on, but are not yet building.

Notwithstanding all the laws emancipating woman, she continues to be a *domestic slave,* because *petty housework* crushes, strangles, stultifies and degrades her, chains her to the kitchen and the nursery, and she wastes her labour on barbarously unproductive, petty, nerve-racking, stultifying and crushing drudgery. The real *emancipation of women,* real communism, will begin only where and when an all-out struggle begins (led by the proletariat wielding the state power) against this petty housekeeping, or rather when its *wholesale transformation* into a large-scale socialist economy begins.

Do we in practice pay sufficient attention to this question, which in theory every Communist considers indisputable? Of course not. Do we take proper care of the *shoots* of communism which already exist in this sphere? Again the answer is *no.* Public catering establishments, nurseries, kindergartens—here we have examples of these shoots, here we have the simple, everyday means, involving nothing pompous, grandiloquent or ceremonial, which can *really emancipate women,* really lessen and abolish their inequality with men as regards their role in social production and public life. These means are not new, they (like all the material prerequisites for socialism) were created by large-scale capitalism. But under capitalism they remained, first, a rarity, and secondly—which is particularly important—either *profit-making* enterprises, with all the worst features of speculation, profiteering, cheating and fraud, or "acrobatics of bourgeois charity", which the best workers rightly hated and despised.

.   .   .   .

An Interview on the Woman Question

"The first proletarian dictatorship is truly paving the way for the complete social equality of women. . . . I understand that in Hamburg a gifted Communist woman is bringing out a newspaper for prostitutes, and is trying to organise them for the revolutionary struggle. Now Rosa, a true Communist, felt and acted like a human being when she wrote an article in defence of prostitutes who have landed in jail for violating a police regulation concerning their sad trade. They are unfortunate double victims of bourgeois society.

Victims, first, of its accursed system of property and, secondly, of its accursed moral hypocrisy. There's no doubt about this. Only a coarse-grained and short-sighted person could forget this. To understand this is one thing, but it is quite another thing—how shall I put it?—to organise the prostitutes as a special revolutionary guild contingent and publish a trade union paper for them. Are there really no industrial working women left in Germany who need organising, who need a newspaper, who should be enlisted in your struggle? This is a morbid deviation. It strongly reminds me of the literary vogue which made a sweet madonna out of every prostitute. Its origin was sound too: social sympathy, and indignation against the moral hypocrisy of the honourable bourgeoisie. But the healthy principle underwent bourgeois corrosion and degenerated. The question of prostitution will confront us even in our country with many a difficult problem. Return the prostitute to productive work, find her a place in the social economy—that is the thing to do. . . . I have been told that at the evenings arranged for reading and discussion with working women, sex and marriage problems come first. . . . Freud's theory has now become a fad. I mistrust sex theories expounded in articles, treatises, pamphlets, etc.— in short, the theories dealt with in that specific literature which sprouts so luxuriantly on the dung heap of bourgeois society. I mistrust those who are always absorbed in the sex problems, the way an Indian saint is absorbed in the contemplation of his navel. It seems to me that this superabundance of sex theories, which for the most part are mere hypotheses, and often quite arbitrary ones, stems from a personal need. It springs from the desire to justify one's own abnormal or excessive sex life before bourgeois morality and to plead for tolerance towards oneself. This veiled respect for bourgeois morality is as repugnant to me as rooting about in all that bears on sex. No matter how rebellious and revolutionary it may be made to appear, it is in the final analysis thoroughly bourgeois. Intellectual and others like them are particularly keen on this. There is no room for it in the Party, among the class-conscious, fighting proletariat."

". . . Why is the approach to this problem inadequate and un-Marxist? Because sex and marriage problems are not treated as only part of the main social problem. Conversely, the main social problem is presented as a part, an appendage to the sex problem. The important point recedes into the background. Thus not only is this question obscured, but also thought, and the class-consciousness of working women in general, is dulled.

"Besides, and this isn't the least important point, Solomon the Wise said there is a time for everything. I ask you, is this the time to keep working women busy for months at a stretch with such questions as as how to love or be loved, how to woo or be wooed?

This, of course, with regard to the 'past, present and future', and among the various races. And it is proudly styled historical material. Nowadays all the thoughts of Communist women, of working women, should be centred on the proletarian revolution, which will lay the foundation, among other things, for the necessary revision of material and sexual relations. . . .

"I was also told that sex problems are a favourite subject in your youth organisations too, and that there are hardly enough lecturers on this subject. This nonsense is especially dangerous and damaging to the youth movement. It can easily lead to sexual excesses, to overstimulation of sex life and to wasted health and strength of young people. You must fight that too. There is no lack of contact between the youth movement and the women's movement. Our Communist women everywhere should cooperate methodically with young people. This will be a continuation of motherhood, will elevate it and extend it from the individual to the social sphere. Women's incipient social life and activities must be promoted, so that they can outgrow the narrowness of their philistine, individualistic psychology centred on home and family. But this is incidental.

"In our country, too, considerable numbers of young people are busy 'revising bourgeois conceptions and morals' in the sex question. And let me add that this involves a considerable section of our best boys and girls, of our truly promising youth. It is as you have just said. In the atmosphere created by the aftermath of war and by the revolution which has begun, old ideological values, finding themselves in a society whose economic foundations are undergoing a radical change, perish, and lose their restraining force. New values crystallise slowly, in the struggle. With regard to relations between people, and between man and woman, feelings and thoughts are also becoming revolutionised. New boundaries are being drawn between the rights of the individual and those of the community, and hence also the duties of the individual. Things are still in complete, chaotic ferment. The direction and potentiality of the various contradictory tendencies can still not be seen clearly enough. It is a slow and often very painful process of passing away and coming into being. All this applies also to the field of sexual relations, marriage, and the family. The decay, putrescence, and filth of bourgeois marriage with its difficult dissolution, its licence for the husband and bondage for the wife, and its disgustingly false sex morality and relations fill the best and most spiritually active of people with the utmost loathing.

"The coercion of bourgeois marriage and bourgeois legislation on the family enhance the evil and aggravate the conflicts. It is the coercion of 'sacrosanct' property. It sanctifies venality, baseness, and dirt. The conventional hypocrisy of 'respectable' bourgeois society takes care of the rest. People revolt against the prevailing abominations and perversions. And at a time when mighty nations are being destroyed, when the former power relations are being disrupted, when a whole social world is beginning to decline, the sensations of the individual undergo a rapid change. A stimulating thirst for different forms of enjoyment easily acquires an irresistible force. Sexual and marriage reforms in the bourgeois sense will not do. In the sphere of sexual relations and marriage, a revolution is approaching—in keeping with the proletarian revolution. Of course, women and young people are taking a deep interest in the complex tangle of problems which have arisen as a result of this. Both the former and the latter suffer greatly from the present messy state of sex relations. Young people rebel against them with the vehemence of their years. This is only natural. Nothing could be falser than to preach monastic self-denial and the sanctity of the filthy bourgeois morals to young people. However, it is hardly a good thing that sex, already strongly felt in the physical sense, should at such a time assume so much prominence in the psychology of young people. The consequences are nothing short of fatal. . . .

"Youth's altered attitude to questions of sex is of course 'fundamental', and based on theory. Many people call it 'revolutionary' and 'communist'. They sincerely believe that this is so. I am an old man, and I do not like it. I may be a morose ascetic, but quite often this so-called 'new sex life' of young people—and frequently of the adults too—seems to me purely bourgeois and simply an extension of the good old bourgeois brothel. All this has nothing in common with free love as we Communists understand it. No doubt you have heard about the famous theory that in communist society satisfying sexual desire and the craving for love is as simple and trivial as 'drinking a glass of water'. A section of our youth has gone mad, absolutely mad, over this 'glass-of-water theory'. It has been fatal to many a young boy and girl. Its devotees assert that it is a Marxist theory. I want no part of the kind of Marxism which infers all phenomena and all changes in the ideological superstructure of society directly and blandly from its economic basis, for things are not as simple as all that. A certain Frederick Engels has established this a long time ago with regard to historical materialism.

"I consider the famous 'glass-of-water' theory as completely un-Marxist and, moreover, as anti-social. It is not only what nature has given but also what has become culture, whether of a high or low level, that comes into play in sexual life. Engels pointed out in his *Origin of the Family* how significant it was that the common sexual relations had developed into individual sex love and thus became purer. The relations between the sexes are not simply the expression of a mutual influence between economics and a physical want deliberately singled out for physiological examination. It would be rationalism and not Marxism to attempt to refer the change in these relations directly to the economic basis of society in isolation from its connection with the ideology as a whole. To be sure, thirst has to be quenched. But would a normal person normally lie down in the gutter and drink from a puddle? Or even from a glass whose edge has been greased by many lips? But the social aspect is more important than anything else. The drinking of water is really an individual matter. But it takes two people to make love, and a third person, a new life, is likely to come into being. This deed has a social complexion and constitutes a duty to the community.

"As a Communist I have no liking at all for the 'glass-of-water' theory, despite its attractive label: 'emancipation of love.' Besides, emancipation of love is neither a novel nor a communistic idea. You will recall that it was advanced in fine literature around the middle of the past century as 'emancipation of the heart'. In bourgeois practice it materialised into emancipation of the flesh. It was preached with greater talent than now, though I cannot judge how it was practised. Not that I want my criticism to breed asceticism. That is farthest from my thoughts. Communism should not bring asceticism, but joy and strength, stemming, among other things, from a consummate love life. Whereas today, in my opinion, the obtaining plethora of sex life yields neither joy nor strength. On the contrary, it impairs them. This is bad, very bad, indeed, in the epoch of revolution.

"Young people are particularly in need of joy and strength. Healthy sports, such as gymnastics, swimming, hiking, physical exercises of every description and a wide range of intellectual interests is what they need, as well as learning, study and research, and as far as possible collectively. This will be far more useful to young people than endless lectures and discussions on sex problems and the so-called living by one's nature. *Mens sana in corpore sano.* Be neither monk nor Don Juan, but not anything in between either, like a German philistine. . . . I will not vouch for the reliability or the endurance of women whose love affair is intertwined with politics, or for the men who run after every petticoat and let themselves in with every young female. No, no, that does not go well with revolution. . . .

"The revolution calls for concentration and rallying of every nerve by the masses and by the individual. It does not tolerate orgiastic conditions so common among d'Annunzio's decadent heros and heroines. Promiscuity in sexual matters is bourgeois. It is a sign of degeneration. The proletariat is a rising class. It does not need an intoxicant to stupefy or stimulate it, neither the intoxicant of sexual laxity or of alcohol. It should and will not forget the vileness, the filth and the barbarity of capitalism. It derives its strongest inspiration to fight from its class position, from the communist ideal.

What it needs is clarity, clarity, and more clarity. Therefore, I repeat, there must be no weakening, no waste and no dissipation of energy. Self-control and self-discipline are not slavery; not in matters of love either. . . . We want to separate organisations of communist women! She who is a Communist belongs as a member to the Party, just as he who is a Communist. They have the same rights and duties. There can be no difference of opinion on that score. However, we must not shut our eyes to the facts. The Party must have organs—working groups, commissions, committees, sections or whatever else they may be called—with the specific purpose of rousing the broad masses of women, bringing them into contact with the Party and keeping them under its influence. This naturally requires that we carry on systematic work among the women. We must teach the awakened women, win them over for the proletarian class struggle under the leadership of the Communist Party, and equip them for it. When I say this I have in mind not only proletarian women, whether they work in mills or cook the family meal. I also have in mind the peasant women and the women of the various sections of the lower middle class. They, too, are victims of capitalism, and more than ever since the war. The lack of interest in politics and the otherwise anti-social and backward psychology of these masses of women, the narrow scope of their activities and the whole pattern of their lives are undeniable facts. It would be silly to ignore them, absolutely silly. We must have our own groups to work among them, special methods of agitation, and special forms of organisation. This is not bourgeois 'feminism'; it is a practical revolutionary expediency. . . .

We cannot exercise the dictatorship of the proletariat without having millions of women on our side. Nor can we engage in communist construction without them. We must find a way to reach them. We must study and search in order to find this way.

"It is therefore perfectly right for us to put forward demands for the benefit of women. This is not a minimum programme, nor a programme of reform in the Social-Democratic sense, in the sense of the Second International. It does not go to show that we believe the bourgeoisie and its state will last forever, or even for a long time. Nor is it an attempt to pacify the masses of women with reforms and to divert them from the path of revolutionary struggle. It is nothing of the sort, and not any sort of reformist humbug either. Our demands are no more than practical conclusions, drawn by us from the crying needs and disgraceful humiliations that weak and underprivileged woman must bear under the bourgeois system. We demonstrate thereby that we are aware of these needs and of the oppression of women, that we are conscious of the privileged position of the men, and that we hate—yes, hate—and want to remove whatever oppresses and harasses the working woman, the wife of the worker, the peasant woman, the wife of the little man, and even in many respects the woman of the propertied classes. The rights and social measures we demand of bourgeois society for women are proof that we understand the position and interests of women and that we will take note of them under the proletarian dictatorship. Naturally, not as soporific and patronising reformists. No, by no means. But as revolutionaries who call upon the women to take a hand as equals in the reconstruction of the economy and of the ideological superstructure."

[I]n our propaganda we must not make a fetish out of our demands for women. No, we must fight now for these and now for other demands, depending on the existing conditions, and naturally always in association with the general interests of the proletariat.

"Every tussle of this kind sets us at loggerheads with the respectable bourgeois clique and its no less respectable reformist lackeys. This compels the latter either to fight under our leadership—which they do not want—or to drop their disguise. Thus, the struggle fences us off from them and shows our communist face. It wins us the confidence of the mass of women, who feel themselves exploited, enslaved and crushed by the domination of the man, by the power of their employers and by bourgeois society as a whole. Betrayed and abandoned by all, working women come to realise that they must fight together with us. Must I avow, or make you avow, that the struggle for women's rights must also be linked with our principal aim—the conquest of power and the establishment of the dictatorship of the proletariat? At present, this is, and will continue to be, our alpha and omega. That is clear, absolutely clear. But the broad masses of working women will not feel irresistibly drawn to the struggle for state power if we harp on just this one demand, even though we may blare it forth on the trumpets of Jericho. No, a thousand times no! We must combine our appeal politically in the minds of the female masses with the sufferings, the needs and the wishes of the working women. They should all know what the proletarian dictatorship will mean to them—complete equality of rights with men, both legal and in practice, in the family, the state and in society, and that it also spells the annihilation of the power of the bourgeoisie. . . .

"Soviet Russia casts a new light on our demands for women. Under the dictatorship of the proletariat they are no longer an object of struggle between the proletariat and the bourgeoisie. Once they are carried out, they serve as bricks for the building of communist society. This shows the women on the other side of the border the decisive importance of the conquest of power by the proletariat. The difference between their status here and there must be demonstrated in bold relief in order to win the support of the masses of women in the revolutionary class struggles of the proletariat. Mobilisation of the female masses, carried out with a clear understanding of principles and a firm organisational basis, is a vital question for the Communist Parties and their victories. But let us not deceive ourselves. Our national sections still lack the proper understanding of this question. They adopt a passive, wait-and-see attitude when it comes to creating a mass movement of working women under communist leadership. They do not realize that developing and leading such a mass movement is an important part of all Party activity, as much as half of all the Party work. Their occasional recognition of the need and value of a purposeful, strong and numerous communist women's movement is but platonic lip-service rather than a steady concern and task of the Party.

"They regard agitation and propaganda among women and the task of rousing and revolutionising them as of secondary importance, as the job of just the women Communists. None but the latter are rebuked because the matter does not move ahead more quickly and strongly. This is wrong, fundamentally wrong! It is outright separatism. It is equality of women *á rebours,* as the French say, i.e., equality reversed. What is at the bottom of the incorrect attitude of our national sections? (I am not speaking of Soviet Russia.) In the final analysis, it is an underestimation of women and of their accomplishments. That's just what it is! Unfortunately, we may still say of many of our comrades, 'Scratch the Communist and a philistine appears.' To be sure, you have to scratch the sensitive spots,—such as their mentality regarding women. Could there be any more palpable proof than the common sight of a man calmly watching a woman wear herself out with trivial, monotonous, strength- and time-consuming work, such as her housework, and watching her spirit shrinking, her mind growing dull, her heartbeat growing faint, and her will growing slack? It goes without saying that I am not referring to the bourgeois ladies who dump all housework and the care for their children on the hired help. What I say applies to the vast majority of women, including the wives of workers, even if these spend the day at the factory and earn money.

"Very few husbands, not even the proletarians, think of how much they could lighten the burdens and worries of their wives, or relieve them entirely, if they lent a hand in this 'women's work'. But no, that would go against the 'privilege and dignity of the husband'. He demands that he have rest and comfort. The domestic life of the woman is a daily sacrifice of self to a thousand insignificant trifles. The ancient rights of her husband, her lord and master, survive unnoticed. Objectively, his slave takes her revenge. Also in concealed form. Her backwardness and her lack of understanding for her husband's revolutionary ideals act as a drag on his fighting spirit, on his determination to fight. They are like tiny worms, gnawing and undermining imperceptibly, slowly but surely. I know

the life of the workers, and not only from books. Our communist work among the masses of women, and our political work in
general, involves considerable educational work among the men.
We must root out the old slave-owner's point of view, both in the
Party and among the masses. That is one of our political tasks, a
task just as urgently necessary as the formation of a staff composed
of comrades, men and women, with thorough theoretical and practical training for Party work among working women. . . .

"The government of the proletarian dictatorship—jointly with the
Communist party and the trade unions of course—makes every
effort to overcome the backward views of men and women and thus
uproot the old, non-communist psychology. It goes without saying
that men and women are absolutely equal before the law. A sincere
desire to give effect to this equality is evident in all spheres. We
are enlisting women to work in the economy, the administration,
legislation and government. All courses and educational institutions
are open to them, so that they can improve their professional and
social training. We are organising community kitchens and public
dining-rooms, laundries and repair shops, crèches, kindergartens,
children's homes and educational institutions of every kind. In
brief, we are quite in earnest about carrying out the requirements
of our programme to shift the functions of housekeeping and education from the individual household to society. Woman is thus being
relieved from her old domestic slavery and all dependence on her
husband. She is enabled to give her capabilities and inclinations
full play in society. Children are offered better opportunities for
their development than at home. We have the most progressive
female labour legislation in the world, and it is enforced by author-
ised representatives of organised labour. We are establishing maternity homes, mother-and-child homes, mothers' health centres,
courses for infant and child care, exhibitions of mother and child
care, and the like. We are making every effort to provide for needy
and unemployed women.

"We know perfectly well that all this is still too little, considering the needs of the working women, and that it is still far from
sufficient for their real emancipation. Yet it is an immense stride
forward from what there was in tsarist and capitalist Russia. Moreover, it is a lot as compared with the state of affairs where capitalism still holds undivided sway. It is a good start in the right direction, and we shall continue to develop it consistently, and with all
available energy, too. . . . Because with each day that passes it
becomes clearer that we cannot make progress without the millions
of women. Think what this means in a country where the peasants
comprise a solid 80% of the population. Small peasant farming implies individual housekeeping and the bondage of women. You
will be far better off than we are in this respect, provided your

proletarians at last grasp that the time is historically ripe for seizure of power, for revolution. In the meantime, we are not giving way to despair, despite the great difficulties. Our forces grow as the latter increase. Practical necessity will also impel us to find new ways of emancipating the masses of women. In combination with the Soviet state, comradely solidarity will accomplish wonders. To be sure, I mean comradely solidarity in the communist, not in the bourgeois, sense, in which it is preached by the reformists, whose revolutionary enthusiasm has evaporated like the smell of cheap vinegar. Personal initiative, which grows into, and fuses with collective activity, should accompany comradely solidarity. Under the proletarian dictatorship the emancipation of women through the realisation of communism will proceed also in the countryside. In this respect I expect much from the electrification of our industry and agriculture. That is a grand scheme! The difficulties in its way are great, monstrously great. Powerful forces latent in the masses will have to be released and trained to overcome them. Millions of women must take part in this."

*   *   *

HERBERT MARCUSE

The three leading influences on the thought of Herbert Marcuse (1898–1979) are Hegel, Marx, and Freud. Although he rejected Hegel's vision of the Absolute Spirit, together with its "spiritualistic" view of human nature and society. Marcuse embraced the Hegelian dialectic and concept of history as a march towards freedom. On the whole Marcuse endorsed Marx's criticisms of philosophy and society, but extended his own critique to various expressions of marxism as well as capitalism. For Marcuse the working class ". . . no longer appears to be the living contradiction of the established society." Rather, the source of exploitation is the very concept of, and instinct towards, domination—a domination which dehumanizes not only the oppressed but also the oppressor. From Freud, Marcuse draws his notion that the overcoming of repression through the "rationality of gratification" is the ideal of individuals and for society.

Marcuse's Concept of Human Nature

In *One-Dimensional Man*, Marcuse describes the caricature of human nature which oppressive and repressive forces within society have created. Basically, one-dimensionality means the reduction of human nature to the dimension of objectivity; in other words, it is the denial of subjectivity or freedom to individuals. Marcuse maintains that human nature is in reality dialectical, i.e., it consists of the interaction between the free subject and the objective world, including other subjects. Such a view tends to identify the real and the ideal, invoking the latter as criterion for critique of dehumanizing conditions in society.

Dehumanization occurs not only through deprivation of freedom but also through denial of human capacities for rationality and happiness. Both are crucial factors for Marcuse. Accordingly, he construes the *eros* which impels us towards pleasure as entirely compatible with the *logos* of human reason. Indeed, he speculates about the possibility of a

> knowledge [which] will no longer disturb pleasure. Perhaps it can even become pleasure, which the ancient idea of *nous* had dared to see. . . .

Such a goal is one which Marcuse himself views as achievable, but only insofar as we succeed in overcoming one-dimensionality through freedom.

The following selection is excerpted from *Counterrevolution and Revolt*. Boston: Beacon Press, 1972, pp. 59–78.

HERBERT MARCUSE   'Nature and Revolution'

The novel historical pattern of the coming revolution is perhaps best reflected in the role played by a new sensibility in radically changing the "style" of the opposition. I have sketched out this new dimension in *An Essay on Liberation;* here I shall attempt to indicate what is at stake, namely, a new relation between man and nature—his own, and external nature. The radical transformation of nature becomes an integral part of the radical transformation of society. Far from being a mere "psychological" phenomenon in groups or individuals, the new sensibility is the medium in which social change becomes an individual need, the mediation between the political practice of "changing the world" and the drive for personal liberation.

What is happening is the discovery (or rather, rediscovery) of nature as an ally in the struggle against the exploitative societies in which the violation of nature aggravates the violation of man.

The discovery of the liberating forces of nature and their vital role in the construction of a free society becomes a new force in social change.

What is involved in the liberation of nature as a vehicle of the liberation of man?

This notion refers to (1) *human* nature: man's primary impulses and senses as foundation of his rationality and experience and (2) *external* nature: man's existential environment, the "struggle with nature" in which he forms his society. It must be stressed from the beginning that, in both of these manifestations, nature is a historical entity: man encounters nature as transformed by society, subjected to a specific rationality which became, to an ever-increasing extent, technological, instrumentalist rationality, bent to the requirements of capitalism. And this rationality was also brought to bear on man's own nature, on his primary drives. To recall only two characteristic contemporary forms of the adaptation of primary drives to the needs of the established system: the social steering of *aggressiveness* through transferring the aggressive act to technical instruments, thus reducing the sense of guilt; and the social steering of *sexuality* through controlled desublimation, the plastic beauty industry, which leads to a reduction of the sense of guilt and thus promotes "legitimate" satisfaction.

Nature is a part of history, an object of history; therefore, "liberation of nature" cannot mean returning to a pretechnological stage, but advancing to the use of the achievements of technological civilization for freeing man and nature from the destructive abuse of science and technology in the service of exploitation. Then, certain lost qualities of artisan work may well reappear on the new technological base.

In the established society, nature itself, ever more effectively controlled, has in turn become another dimension for the control of man: the extended arm of society and its power. Commercialized nature, polluted nature, militarized nature cut down the life environment of man, not only in an ecological but also in a very existential sense. It blocks the erotic cathexis (and transformation) of his environment: it deprives man from finding himself in nature, beyond and this side of alienation; it also prevents him from recognizing nature as a *subject* in its own right—a subject with which to live in a common human universe. This deprivation is not undone by the opening of nature to massive fun and togetherness, spontaneous as well as organized—a release of frustration which only adds to the violation of nature.

Liberation of nature is the recovery of the life-enhancing forces in nature, the sensuous aesthetic qualities which are foreign to a life wasted in unending competitive performances: they suggest the new qualities of *freedom*. No wonder then that the "spirit of capitalism" rejects or ridicules the idea of liberated nature, that it relegates this idea to the poetic imagination. Nature, if not left alone and protected as "reservation," is treated in an aggressively scientific way: it is there for the sake of domination; it is value-free matter, material. This notion of nature is a *historical* a priori, pertaining to a specific form of society. A free society may well have a very different a priori and a very different object; the development of the scientific concepts may be grounded in an experience of nature as a totality of life to be protected and "cultivated," and technology would apply this science to the reconstruction of the environment of life.

Domination of man through the domination of nature: the concrete link between the liberation of man and that of nature has become manifest today in the role which the ecology drive plays in the radical movement. The pollution of air and water, the noise, the encroachment of industry and commerce on open natural space have the physical weight of enslavement, imprisonment. The struggle against them is a political struggle; it is obvious to what extent the violation of nature is inseparable from the economy of capitalism. At the same time, however, the political function of ecology is easily "neutralized" and serves the beautification of the Establishment. Still, the physical pollution practiced by the system must be combated here and now—just as its mental pollution. To drive ecology to the point where it is no longer containable within the capitalist framework means first extending the drive *within* the capitalist framework.[1]

The relation between nature and freedom is rarely made explicit in social theory. In Marxism too, nature is predominantly an object, the adversary in man's "struggle with nature," the field for the ever more rational development of the productive forces.[2] But in this form, nature appears as that which capitalism has *made* of nature: matter, raw material for the expanding and exploiting administration of men and things. Does this image of nature conform to that of a free society? Is nature only a productive force—or does it also exist *"for its own sake"* and, in *this* mode of existence, for *man?*

In the treatment of *human* nature, Marxism shows a similar tendency to minimize the role of the natural basis in social change—a tendency which contrasts sharply with the earlier writings of Marx. To be sure, "human nature" would be different under socialism to the degree to which men and women would, for the first time

1. See Murray Bookchin, "Ecology and Revolutionary Thought" and "Towards a Liberatory Technology," in *Post-Scarcity Anarchism* (Berkeley: Ramparts Press, 1971).

2. See Alfred Schmidt, *Der Begriff der Natur in der Lehre von Marx* (Frankfurt: Europäische Verlagsanstalt, 1962).

in history, develop and fulfill their own needs and faculties in association with each other. But this change is to come about almost as a by-product of the new socialist institutions. Marxist emphasis on the development of political consciousness shows little concern with the roots of liberation in individuals, i.e., with the roots of social relationships there where individuals most directly and profoundly experience their world and themselves: in their *sensibility*, in their instinctual needs.

In *An Essay on Liberation,* I suggested that without a change in this dimension, the old Adam would be reproduced in the new society, and that the construction of a free society *presupposes* a break with the familiar experience of the world: with the mutilated sensibility. Conditioned and "contained" by the rationality of the established system, sense experience tends to "immunize" man against the very unfamiliar experience of the possibilities of human freedom. The development of a radical, nonconformist sensibility assumes vital political importance in view of the unprecedented extent of social control perfected by advanced capitalism: a control which reaches down into the instinctual and physiological level of existence. Conversely, resistance and rebellion, too, tend to activate and operate on this level.

"Radical sensibility": the concept stresses the active, constitutive role of the senses in shaping reason, that is to say, in shaping the categories under which the world is ordered, experienced, changed. The senses are not merely passive, receptive: they have their own "syntheses" to which they subject the primary data of experience. And these syntheses are not only the pure "forms of intuition" (space and time) which Kant recognized as an inexorable a priori *ordering* of sense data. There are perhaps also other syntheses, far more concrete, far more "material," which may constitute an empirical (i.e., historical) a priori of experience. Our world emerges not only in the pure forms of time and space, but also, and *simultaneously*, as a totality of sensuous qualities—object not only of the eye (synopsis) but of *all* human senses (hearing, smelling, touching, tasting). It is this qualitative, elementary, unconscious, or rather preconscious, constitution of the world of experience, it is this primary experience itself which must change radically if social change is to be radical, qualitative change.

II

The subversive potential of the sensibility, and nature as a field of liberation are central themes in Marx's *Economic and Philosophic Manuscripts.* They have been reread and reinterpreted again and again, but these themes have been largely neglected. Recently, the Manuscripts served to justify the concept of "humanistic socialism" in opposition to the bureaucratic-authoritarian Soviet model; they provided a powerful impetus in the struggle against Stalinism and post-Stalinism. I believe that in spite of their "pre-scientific" character, and in spite of the prevalence of Feuerbach's philosophic naturalism, these writings espouse the most radical and integral idea of socialism, and that precisely here, "nature" finds its place in the theory of revolution.

I recall briefly the principal conception of the Manuscripts. Marx speaks of the "complete emancipation of all human senses and qualities"[3] as the feature of socialism: only this emancipation is the "transcendence of private property." This means the emergence of a new type of man, different from the human subject of class society in his very nature, in his physiology: "the *senses* of the social man are *other* than those of the non-social man."[4]

"Emancipation of the senses" implies that the senses become "practical" in the reconstruction of society, that they generate new (socialist) relationships between man and man, man and things, man and nature. But the senses become also "sources" of a new (socialist) *rationality:* freed from that of exploitation. The emancipated senses would repel the instrumentalist rationality of capitalism while preserving and developing its achievements. They would attain this goal in two ways: *negatively*—inasmuch as the Ego, the other, and the object world would no longer be experienced in the context of aggressive acquisition, competition, and defensive possession; *positively*—through the "human appropriation of nature," i.e., through the transformation of nature into an environment (medium) for the human being as "species being"; free to develop the specifically human faculties: the creative, aesthetic faculties.

"Only through the objectively unfolded richness of man's essential being is the richness of subjective human sensibility (a musical ear, an eye for beauty of form—in short, *senses* capable of human gratification, senses affirming themselves as essential powers of man) either cultivated or brought into being."[5] The emancipated senses, in conjunction with a natural science proceeding on their basis, would guide the "human appropriation" of nature. Then, nature would have "lost its mere utility,"[6] it would appear not merely as stuff—organic or inorganic matter—but as life force in its

3. Karl Marx, *The Economic and Philosophic Manuscripts of 1844,* Dirk J. Struik, ed. (New York: International Publishers, 1964), p. 139.

4. *Ibid.,* p. 141.

5. *Ibid.,* p. 141.

6. *Ibid.,* p. 139.

own right, as subject-object;[7] the striving for life is the substance common to man and nature. Man would then form a living object. The senses would "relate themselves to the thing for the sake of the thing. . . ."[8] And they can do so only inasmuch as the thing itself is objectified human *Verhalten:* objectification of human relationships and is thus itself humanly related to man.[9]

This outrageously unscientific, metaphysical notion foreshadows the mature materialistic theory: it grasps the world of things as objectified human labor, shaped by human labor. Now if this forming human activity produces the technical and natural environment of an acquisitive and repressive society, it will also produce a dehumanized nature; and radical social change will involve a radical transformation of nature.

Also of the *science* of nature? Nature as manifestation of subjectivity: the idea seems inseparable from teleology—long since taboo in Western science. Nature as object per se fitted all too well into the universe of the capitalist treatment of matter to allow discarding the taboo. It seemed entirely justified by the increasingly effective and profitable mastery of nature which was achieved under this taboo.

Is is true that the recognition of nature as a subject is metaphysical teleology incompatible with scientific objectivity? Let us take Jacques Monod's statement of the meaning of objectivity in science:

> What I have tried to show . . . is that the scientific attitude implies what I call the postulate of objectivity—that is to say, the fundamental postulate that there is no plan, that there is no intention in the universe.[10]

The idea of the liberation of nature stipulates no such plan or intention in the universe: liberation is the possible plan and intention

7. "The sun is the object of the plant . . . just as the plant is an object for the sun. . . ." *Ibid.,* p. 181.

8. *Ibid.,* p. 139.

9. For the sake of the thing"—an illustration:
In Yugoslavia, they sell wooden cuttings boards which, on one side, are painted with very colorful, pretty flower patterns; the other side is unpainted. The boards bear the imprint: "don't hurt my pretty face, use other side." Childish anthropomorphism? Certainly. But can we perhaps imagine that the people who had this idea, and those users who pay attention to it, have a quite natural, instinctual aversion against violence and destruction, that they have indeed a "human relation" to matter, that matter to them is part of the *life* environment and thus assumes traits of a living object?

10. Interview with the *New York Times,* March 15, 1971.

of human beings, brought to bear upon nature. However, it does stipulate that nature is susceptible to such an undertaking, and that there are forces in nature which have been distorted and suppressed—forces which could support and enhance the liberation of man. This capacity of nature may be called "chance," or "blind freedom," and it may give good meaning to the human effort to redeem this blindness—in Adorno's words: to help nature "to open its eyes," to help it "on the poor earth to become what perhaps it would like to be."[11]

Nature as subject without teleology, without "plan" and "intention": this notion goes well with Kant's "purposiveness without purpose." The most advanced concepts of the Third Critique have not yet been explored in their truly revolutionary significance. The aesthetic form in art has the aesthetic form in nature (*das Naturschöne*) as its correlate, or rather desideratum. If the idea of beauty pertains to nature as well as to art, this is not merely an analogy, or a human idea imposed on nature—it is the insight that the aesthetic form, as a token of freedom, is a mode (or moment?) of existence of the human as well as the natural universe, an objective quality. Thus Kant attributes the beautiful in nature to nature's "capacity to form itself, in its freedom, also in an aesthetically purposive way, according to chemical laws. . . ."[12]

The Marxian conception understands nature as a universe which becomes the congenial medium for human gratification to the degree to which nature's *own* gratifying forces and qualities are recovered and released. In sharp contrast to the capitalist exploitation of nature, its "human appropriation" would be nonviolent, nondestructive: oriented on the life-enhancing, sensuous, aesthetic qualities inherent in nature. Thus transformed, "humanized," nature would respond to man's striving for fulfillment, nay, the latter would not be possible without the former. Things have their "inherent measure" (*inhärentes Mass*):[13] this measure is *in* them, is the potential enclosed in them; only man can free it and, in doing so, free his own human potential. Man is the only being who can "form things in accordance with the laws of beauty."[14]

Aesthetics of liberation, beauty as a "form" of freedom: it looks as if Marx has shied away from this anthropomorphist, idealistic conception. Or is this apparently idealistic notion rather the *enlargement of the materialistic base?* For "man is directly a *natural*

11. Theodor W. Adorno, *Aesthetische Theorie* (Frankfurt/Main: Suhrkamp, 1970), pp. 100, 107.

12. *Critique of Judgment,* S 58.

13. Marx, *loc. cit.,* p. 114.

14. *Ibid.*

being; he is a corporeal, living, real, sensuous, objective being" who has "real, sensuous objects" as the objects of his life.[15] And his senses ("like those organs which are directly social in their form")[16] are active, practical in the "appropriation" of the object world; they express the social existence of man, his "objectification." This is no longer Feuerbach's "naturalism" but, on the contrary, the extension of Historical Materialism to a dimension which is to play a vital role in the liberation of man.

There is, however, a definite internal limit to the idea of the liberation of nature through "human appropriation." True, the aesthetic dimension is a vital dimension of freedom; true, it repels violence, cruelty, brutality, and by this token will become an essential quality of a free society, not as a separate realm of "higher culture," but as a driving force and *motive* in the *construction* of such a society. And yet, certain brute facts, unconquered and perhaps unconquerable facts, call for skepticism. Can the human appropriation of nature ever achieve the elimination of violence, cruelty, and brutality in the daily sacrifice of animal life for the physical reproduction of the human race? To treat nature "for its own sake" sounds good, but it is certainly not for the sake of the animal to be eaten, nor probably for the sake of the plant. The end of this war, the perfect peace in the animal world—this idea belongs to the Orphic myth, not to any conceivable historical reality. In the face of the suffering inflicted by man on man, it seems terribly "premature" to campaign for universal vegetarianism or synthetic foodstuffs; as the world is, priority must be on *human* solidarity among human beings. And yet, no free society is imaginable which does not, under its "regulative idea of reason," make the concerted effort to reduce consistently the suffering which man imposes on the animal world.

Marx's notion of a human appropriation of nature retains something of the *hubris* of domination. "Appropriation," no matter how human, remains appropriation of a (living) object by a subject. It offends that which is essentially other than the appropriating subject, and which exists precisely as object in its own right—that is, as subject! The latter may well be hostile to man, in which case the relation would be one of struggle; but the struggle may also subside and make room for peace, tranquillity, fulfillment. In this case, not appropriation but rather its negation would be the non-exploitative relation: surrender, "letting-be," acceptance . . . But such surrender meets with the impenetrable resistance of matter; nature is not a manifestation of "spirit," but rather its essential *limit*.

15. *Ibid.,* p. 181.
16. *Ibid.,* p. 139.

III

Although the historical concept of nature as a dimension of social change does not imply teleology and does not attribute a "plan" to nature, it does conceive of nature as subject-object: as a *cosmos* with its own potentialities, necessities, and chances. And these potentialities can be, not only in the sense of their value-free function in theory and practice, but also as bearers of *objective values.* These are envisaged in such phrases as "violation of nature," "suppression of nature." Violation and suppression then mean that human action against nature, man's interrelation with nature, offends against certain objective *qualities* of nature—qualities which are essential to the enhancement and fulfillment of life. And it is on such objective grounds that the liberation for man to his own humane faculties is linked to the liberation of nature—that "truth" is attributable to nature not only in a mathematical but also in an existential sense. The emancipation of man involves the recognition of such truth in things, in nature. The Marxian vision recaptures the ancient theory of knowledge as *recollection:* "science" as the rediscovery of the true *Forms* of things, distorted and denied in the established reality, the perpetual *materialistic core of idealism.* The "idea," as the term for these Forms, is not a "mere" idea, but an image illuminating what is false, distorted in the way in which things are "given," what is missing in their familiar perception, in the mutilated experience which is the work of society.

Recollection thus is not remembrance of a Golden Past (which never existed), of childhood innocence, primitive man, et cetera. Recollection as epistemological faculty rather is synthesis, reassembling the bits and fragments which can be found in the distorted humanity and distorted nature. This recollected material has become the domain of the imagination, it has been sanctioned by the repressive societies in art, and as "poetic truth"—poetic truth only, and therefore not much good in the actual transformation of society. These images may well be called "innate ideas" inasmuch as they cannot possibly be given in the immediate experience which prevails in the repressive societies. They are given rather as the *horizon* of experience under which the immediately given forms of things appears as "negative," as denial of their inherent possibilities, their truth. But in this sense, they are "innate" in man as *historical* being; they are themselves historical because the possibilities of liberation are always and everywhere historical possibilities. Imagination, *as knowledge,* retains the insoluble tension between idea and reality, the potential and the actual. This is the *idealistic core* of dialectical materialism: the transcendence of freedom beyond the given forms. In this sense too, Marxian theory is the historical heir of German Idealism.

Freedom thus becomes a "regulative concept of reason" guiding the practice of changing reality in accordance with its "idea," i.e., its own potentialities—to make reality free for its truth. Dialectical materialism understands freedom as historical, empirical transcendence, as a force of social change, transcending its immediate form also in a socialist society—not toward ever more production, not toward Heaven or Paradise, but toward an ever more peaceful, joyful struggle with the inexorable resistance of society and nature. This is the philosophical core of the theory of the permanent revolution.

As such force, freedom is rooted in the primary drives of men and women, it is the vital need to enhance their life instincts. Prerequisite is the capacity of the senses to experience not only the "given" but also the "hidden" qualities of things which would make for the betterment of life. The radical redefinition of sensibility as "practical" desublimates the idea of freedom without abandoning its transcendent content: the senses are not only the basis for the *epistemological* constitution of reality, but also for its *transformation*, its *subversion* in the interest of liberation.

Human freedom is thus rooted in the human *sensibility*: the senses do not only "receive" what is given to them, in the form in which it appears, they do not "delegate" the transformation of the given to another faculty (the understanding); rather, they discover or *can* discover by themselves, in their "practice," new (more gratifying) possibilities and capabilities, forms and qualities of things, and can urge and guide their realization. The emancipation of the senses would make freedom what it is not yet: a sensuous need, an objective of the Life Instincts (*Eros*).

In a society based on alienated labor, human sensibility is *blunted*: men perceive things only in the forms and functions in which they are given, made, used by the existing society; and they perceive only the possibilities of transformation as defined by, and confined to, the existing society.[17] Thus, the existing society is *reproduced* not only in the mind, the consciousness of men, but *also in their senses*; and no persuasion, no theory, no reasoning can break this prison, unless the fixed, petrified *sensibility* of the individuals is *"dissolved," opened to a new dimension of history,* until the oppressive familiarity with the given object world is broken—broken in a *second alienation*: that from the alienated society.

Today, in the revolt against the "consumer society," sensibility strives to become "practical," the vehicle for radical reconstruction, for new ways of life. It has become a force in the *political*

17. For the following see my *An Essay on Liberation* (Boston: Beacon Press, 1969), pp. 36 ff

struggle for liberation.[18] And that means: the individual emancipation of the senses is supposed to be the beginning, even the foundation, of *universal* liberation, the free society is to take roots in new instinctual needs. How is this possible? How can "humanity," human solidarity as *"concrete universal"* (and not as abstract value), as real force, as "praxis," originate in the individual sensibility; how can objective freedom originate in the most subjective faculties of man?

We are faced with the *dialectic* of the universal and the particular: how can the human sensibility, which is *principium individuationis,* also generate a *universalizing* principle?

I refer again to the philosophical treatment of this problem in German idealism: here is the intellectual origin of the Marxian concept. For *Kant:* a universal sensorium (the pure forms of intuition) constitutes the one unified framework of sense experience, thus validating the universal categories of the understanding. For *Hegel:* reflection on the content and mode of *my* immediate sense certainty reveals the "We" in the "I" of intuition and perception. When the still unreflected consciousness has reached the point where it becomes conscious of itself and its relation to its objects, where it has experienced a "trans-sensible" world "behind" the sensuous appearance of things, it discovers that *we* ourselves are behind the curtain of appearance. And this "we" unfolds as social reality in the struggle between Master and Servant for "mutual recognition."

This is the turning point on the road that leads from Kant's effort to reconcile man and nature, freedom and necessity, universal and particular, to Marx's materialistic solution: Hegel's *Phenomenology* breaks with Kant's transcendental conception: history and society enter into the theory of knowledge (and into the very structure of knowledge) and do away with the "purity" of the a priori; the materialization of the idea of freedom begins. But a closer look shows that the same tendency was already present in Kant's philosophy: in the development from the First to the Third Critique.

1) In the *First Critique,* the freedom of the subject is present only in the epistemological syntheses of the sense data; freedom is relegated to the transcendental Ego's pure syntheses: it is the power of the a priori by virtue of which the transcendental subject constitutes the objective world of experience; theoretical knowledge.

2) In the *Second Critique,* the realm of *praxis* is reached with the stipulation of the autonomy of the moral person: his power to

18. The fight for the Peoples Park in Berkeley, which was met with brute force by the armed guardians of law and order, shows the explosion of sensibility in political action.

originate causation without breaking the universal causation which governs nature: necessity. The price: subjection of the sensibility to the categorical imperative of reason. The relation between human freedom and natural necessity remains obscure.

3) In the *Third Critique,* man and nature are joined in the aesthetic dimension, the rigid "otherness" of nature is reduced, and Beauty appears as "symbol of morality." The union of the realm of freedom and that of necessity is here conceived not as the mastery of nature, not as bending nature to the purposes of man, but as attributing to nature an ideal purposiveness "of its own: a purposiveness without purpose."

But it is only the *Marxian* conception which, while preserving the critical, transcendent element of idealism, uncovers the material, historical ground for the reconciliation of human freedom and natural necessity; subjective and objective freedom. This union presupposes liberation: the revolutionary *praxis* which is to abolish the institutions of capitalism and to replace them by socialist institutions and relationships. But in this transition, the emancipation of the senses must accompany the emancipation of consciousness, thus involving the *totality* of human existence. The individuals themselves must change in their very instincts and sensibilities if they are to build, in association, a *qualitatively* different society. But why the emphasis on *aesthetic* needs in this reconstruction?

IV

It is not just in passing and out of exuberance that Marx speaks of the formation of the object world "in accordance with the laws of beauty" as a feature of free human practice. Aesthetic qualities are essentially nonviolent, nondomineering (I shall come back to it in Chapter III)—qualities which, in the domain of the arts, and in the repressive use of the term "aesthetic" as pertaining to the sublimated "higher culture" only, are divorced from the social reality and from "practice" as such. The revolution would undo this repression and recapture aesthetic needs as a subversive force, capable of counteracting the dominating aggressiveness which has shaped the social and natural universe. The faculty of being "receptive," "passive," is a precondition of freedom: it is the ability to see things in their own right, to experience the joy enclosed in them, the erotic energy of nature—an energy which is there to be liberated; nature, too, awaits the revolution! This receptivity is itself the soil of creation: it is opposed, not to productivity, but to *destructive* productivity.

The latter has been the ever more conspicuous feature of male domination: inasmuch as the "male principle" has been the ruling mental and physical force, a free society would be the "definite negation" of this principle—it would be a *female* society. In this sense, it has nothing to do with matriarchy of any sort; the image of the woman as mother is itself repressive; it transforms a biological fact into an ethical and cultural value and thus it supports and justifies her social repression. At stake is rather the ascent of Eros over aggression, in men *and* women; and this means, in a male-dominated civilization, the "femalization" of the male. It would express the decisive change in the instinctual structure: the weakening of primary aggressiveness which, by a combination of biological and social factors, has governed the patriarchal culture.

In this transformation, the Women's Liberation Movement becomes a radical force to the degree to which it transcends the entire sphere of aggressive needs and performances, the entire social organization and division of functions. In other words, the movement becomes radical to the degree to which it aims, not only at equality *within* the job and value structure of the *established* society (which would be the equality of dehumanization) but rather at a change in the structure itself (the basic demands of equal opportunity, equal pay, and release from full-time household and child care are a prerequisite). Within the established structure, neither men nor women are free—and the dehumanization of men may well be greater than that of women since the former suffer not only the conveyor belt and assembly line but also the standards and "ethics" of the "business community."

And yet, the liberation of women would be more sweeping than that of men because the repression of women has been constantly fortified by the social use of their biological constitution. The bearing of children, being a mother, is supposed to be not only their natural function but also the fulfillment of their "nature"—and so is being a wife, since the reproduction of the species occurs within the framework of the monogamous patriarchal family. Outside this framework, the woman is still predominantly a plaything or a temporary outlet for sexual energy not consummated in marriage.

Marxian theory considers sexual exploitation as the primary, original exploitation, and the Women's Liberation Movement fights the degradation of the woman to a "sexual object." But it is difficult to overcome the feeling that here, repressive qualities characteristic of the bourgeois-capitalist organization of society enter into the fight against this organization. Historically, the image of the woman as sexual object, and her exchange value on the market, devalue the earlier repressive images of the woman as mother and wife. These earlier images were essential to the bourgeois ideology during a period of capitalist development now left behind: the period where some "inner-worldly asceticism" was still operative in the dynamic of the economy. In comparison, the present image of the woman as sexual object is a *desublimation* of bourgeois morality—

characteristic of a "higher stage" of capitalist development. Here, too, the commodity form is universalized: it now invades formerly sanctified and protected realms. The (female) body, as seen and plastically idealized by *Playboy*, becomes desirable merchandise with a high exchange value. Disintegration of bourgeois morality, perhaps—but *cui bono?* To be sure, this new body image promotes sales, and the plastic beauty may not be the real thing, but they stimulate aesthetic-sensuous needs which, in their development, must become incompatible with the body as instrument of alienated labor. The male body, too, is made the object of sexual image creation—also plasticized and deodorized . . . clean exchange value. After the secularization of religion, after the transformation of ethics into Orwellian hypocrisy—is the "socialization" of the body as sexual object perhaps one of the last decisive steps toward the completion of the exchange society: the completion which is the beginning of the end?

Still, the publicity with the body (at present, the female body) as object is dehumanizing, the more so since it plays up to the dominant male as the aggressive subject for whom the female is there, to be taken, to be laid. It is in the nature of sexual relationships that both, male and female, are object *and* subject at the same time; erotic and aggressive energy are fused in both. The surplus-aggression of the male is socially conditioned—as is the surplus-passivity of the female. But beneath the social factors which determine male aggressiveness and female receptivity, a *natural* contrast exists: it is the woman who "embodies," in a literal sense, the promise of peace, of joy, of the end of violence. Tenderness, receptivity, sensuousness have become features (or mutilated features) of her body—features of her (repressed) humanity. These female qualities may well be socially determined by the development of capitalism. The process is truly dialectical.[19] Although the reduction of the concrete individual faculties to abstract labor power established an abstract equality between men and women (equality before the machine), this abstraction was less complete in the case of women. They were employed in the material process of production to a lesser extent than men. Women were fully employed in the household, the family, which was supposed to be the sphere of realization for the bourgeois individual. However, this sphere was isolated from the productive process and thus contributed to the women's mutilation. And yet, this isolation (separation) from the alienated work world of capitalism enabled the woman to remain less brutalized by the Performance Principle, to remain closer to her sensibility: more human than men. That this image (and reality) of the

19. This dialectic is the center of Angela Davis's paper *Marxism and Women's Liberation* (not yet published). Written in jail, this paper is the work of a great woman, militant, intellectual.

woman has been determined by an aggressive, male-dominated society does not mean that this determination must be rejected, that the liberation of women must overcome the female "nature." The equalization of male and female would be regressive: it would be a new form of female acceptance of a male principle. Here too the historical process is dialectical: the patriarchal society has created a female image, a female counter-force, which may still become one of the gravediggers of patriarchal society. In this sense too, the woman holds the promise of liberation. It is the woman who, in Delacroix' painting, holding the flag of the revolution, leads the people on the barricades. She wears no uniform; her breasts are bare, and her beautiful face shows no trace of violence. But she has a rifle in her hand—for the end of violence is still to be fought for. . . .

✿   ✿   ✿

THE ANALYTIC CONTEXT

In contrast to existentialism, which has been strongly influenced by Descartes and the German idealists, modern analytic philosophy derives largely from the empirical tradition of Hume. Its method, which has given rise to diverse interpretations and applications, describes the predominant philosophical approach in the United States and other English-speaking countries.

The method of analysis starts with data obtained through experience, and commonly accepted as knowledge. In order to explicate this complex bulk of data, the analytic philosopher formulates propositions (expressed judgments). Within any set of related propositions, a recognition of logical interdependence and redundancies enables the philosopher to reduce the propositions to their simplest formulation. The propositions are then arranged according to the inferential relationship that one bears to the other, so that their appropriate deductive sequence is manifest. ("Deductive" describes a process of reasoning from a general proposition to a less general proposition.) Formal syllogisms illustrate the deductive sequence. Each deductive chain of inference depends logically upon some initial premise or premises, which may or may not be provable. "The discovery of these premises," writes Bertrand Russell, "belongs to philosophy." In other words, the philosophical method of logical analysis entails reasoning from complex and relatively concrete propositions to those that are simpler and more abstract.

Like his godfather, John Stuart Mill, Bertrand Russell (1872–1970) was a financially independent aristocrat whose early focus on mathematics influenced a life-long devotion to logic. In his *Principia Mathematica* of 1910, Russell attempted (with his co-author Alfred North Whitehead) to show that pure mathematics is reducible to logic, because its primary principles are logical premises, and its concepts definable in logical terms or symbols. As Russell extended his study of logic to the philosophical arena, he insisted on recognition of philosophy's limits, especially by distinguishing between judgments that are empirically or logically demonstrable, and those that are ultimately reliant upon opinion or taste. The latter group includes metaphysical judgments, much of ethics, and social and political theory. Although Russell did not refrain from making statements in these areas, he considered them quite outside the scope of philosophy.

Another point of similarity with Mill is Russell's persistent dedication to the cause of individual rights and freedom. Not only did Russell write extensively on particular social issues; he also actively campaigned in support of his convictions. For example, in 1907 he ran for Parliament on behalf of women's suffrage; in 1918 he was imprisoned for six months because of his public opposition to the war. The latter issue also illustrates Russell's willingness to alter his views where further thought or evidence suggested he should do so. Despite his earlier pacifism, he concurred with efforts to resist Hitler's dominating influence in Europe. Once hostilities had ceased, his predominant interest was the promotion of world government and nuclear disarmament.

Russell's Concept of Human Nature

Russell categorized his own views of human nature and society in *What I Believe,* a book in which he summarized those views. The categorization is appropriate. Belief, for Russell, describes the status of judgments that are not obtained through certainly reliable methods. What Russell purports to believe is that

> Man is a part of Nature. . . . His body, like other matter, is composed of electrons and protons, which, so far as we know, obey the same laws as those not forming part of animals or plants. . . . Electrons and protons, like the soul, are logical fictions; each is really a history, a series of events, not a single persistent entity.

Such belief is in keeping with Russell's later (1945) definition: "A person is a certain series of experiences." Among these experiences are "thoughts." "What we call our 'thoughts,'" Russell observes, seem to depend upon the organization of tracks in the brain in the same sort of way in which journeys depend upon roads and railways. . . . All the evidence goes to show that what we regard as our mental life is bound up with brain structure and organized bodily energy.

Although human beings are part of Nature they are nonetheless capable of transcending Nature through the determination of values. In this respect, persons are greater than Nature. "Nature in itself," Russell claims, "is neutral, neither good nor bad. . . ." Only human beings can create or confer value so as to make their lives "good." For Russell himself, "[t]he good life is one inspired by love and guided by knowledge." It is a life conditioned by freedom and productive of happiness for individuals as well as for society. The function of the state is to facilitate "the good life" for all persons. An essential criterion in fulfilling this function is justice; that is, "the recognition of the equal claims of all human beings."

Most of the following excerpt is drawn from Chapter 7 of *Marriage and Morals*.

BERTRAND RUSSELL   Marriage and Morals

THE LIBERATION OF WOMEN

The emancipation of women is part of the democratic movement; it begins with the French Revolution, which, as we have already seen, altered the laws of inheritance in a sense favourable to daughters. Mary Wollstonecraft's "Vindication of the Rights of Women" (1792) is a product of the ideas that caused and were caused by the French Revolution. From her time down to the present day the claim of women to equality with men has been asserted with continually increasing emphasis and success. John Stuart Mill's "Subjection of Women" is a very persuasive and well-reasoned book, which had a great influence upon the more thoughtful members of the generation immediately following his own. My father and mother were disciples of his, and my mother used to make speeches in favour of votes for women in the sixties.

. . . [T]he rapidity with which women in most civilized countries have acquired their political rights is without parallel in the past, considering the immense magnitude of the change in outlook that has been involved. The abolition of slavery is more or less analogous, but after all slavery did not exist in European countries in modern times, and did not concern anything so intimate as the relations of men and women.

The causes of this sudden change are, I think, twofold: on the one hand there was the direct influence of democratic theory, which made it impossible to find any logical answer to the demands of women; on the other hand there was the fact that a continually increasing number of women were engaged in making their own living outside the home, and did not depend for the comfort of their daily lives upon the favour of fathers and husbands. This situation, of course, reached its height during the war, when a very large part of the work usually performed by men had to be undertaken by women. Before the war one of the objections commonly urged against votes for women was that women would tend to be pacifists. During the war they gave a large-scale refutation of this charge, and the vote was given to them for their share in the bloody work. To the idealistic pioneers, who had imagined that women were going to raise the moral tone of politics, this issue may have been disappointing, but it seems to be the fate of idealists to obtain what they have struggled for in a form which destroys their ideals. The rights of women did not, of course, in fact depend upon any belief that women were morally or in any other way superior to men; they depended solely upon their rights as human beings, or rather upon the general argument in favour of democracy. But as always happens when an oppressed class or nation is claiming its rights, advocates sought to strengthen the general argument by the contention that women had peculiar merits, and these merits were generally represented as belonging to the moral order.

The political emancipation of women, however, concerns our theme only indirectly; it is their social emancipation that is important in connection with marriage and morals. In early days, and in the East down to our own time, the virtue of women was secured by segregating them. No attempt was made to give them inward self-control, but everything was done to take away all opportunity for sin. In the West this method was never adopted wholeheartedly, but respectable women were educated from their earliest years so as to have a horror of sexual intercourse outside marriage. As the methods of this education became more and more perfected, the outward barriers were more and more removed. Those who did most to remove the outward barriers were convinced that the inward barriers would be sufficient. It was thought, for example, that the chaperon was unnecessary, since a nice girl who had been well brought up would never yield to the advances of young men whatever opportunities of yielding might be allowed her. It was generally held by respectable women when I was young that sexual intercourse was displeasing to the great majority of women, and was only endured within marriage from a sense of duty; holding this view, they were not unwilling to risk a greater degree of freedom for their daughters than had seemed wise in more realistic ages.

The results have perhaps been somewhat different from what was anticipated, and the difference has existed equally as regards wives and as regards unmarried women. The women of the Victorian age were, and a great many women still are, in a mental prison. This prison was not obvious to consciousness, since it consisted of subconscious inhibitions. The decay of inhibitions, which has taken place among the young of our own time, has led to the reappearance in consciousness of instinctive desires which has been buried beneath mountains of prudery. This is having a very revolutionary effect upon sexual morality, not only in one country or in one class, but in all civilized countries and in all classes.

The demand for equality between men and women concerned itself from the first not only with political matters but also with sexual morality. The attitude of Mary Wollstonecraft was thoroughly modern, but she was not imitated in this respect by the subsequent pioneers of women's rights. They, on the contrary, were for the most part very rigid moralists, whose hope was to impose upon men the moral fetters which hitherto had only been endured by women. Ever since 1914, however, young women, without much theorizing, have taken a different line. The emotional excitement of the war was no doubt the precipitating cause of this new departure, but it would have come before very long in any case. The motives of female virtue in the past were chiefly the fear of hellfire and fear of pregnancy; the one was removed by the decay of theological orthodoxy, the other by contraceptives. For some time traditional morality managed to hold out through the force of custom and mental inertia, but the shock of the war caused these barriers to fall. Modern feminists are no longer so anxious as the feminists of thirty years ago to curtail the "vices" of men; they ask rather that what is permitted to men shall be permitted also to them. Their predecessors sought equality in moral slavery, whereas they seek equality in moral freedom.

This whole movement is as yet in a very early phase, and it is impossible to say how it will develop. Its adherents and practitioners as yet are mostly quite young. They have very few champions among persons of weight and importance. The police, the law, the Church and their parents are against them whenever the facts come to the knowledge of these repositories of power, but in general the young have the kindness to conceal the facts from those to whom they would cause pain. Writers who . . . proclaim the facts are thought by the old to be libelling the young, though the young remain unconscious of being libelled.

A situation of this sort is, of course, very unstable. It is a question which of two things will happen first: either the old will become aware of the facts and will set to work to deprive the young of their new-won freedom, or the young, growing up, will themselves acquire positions of dignity and importance, which will make it possible to give the sanction of authority to the new morality. . . .

Let us, however, pause a moment to consider the logical implications of the demand that women should be the equals of men. Men have from time immemorial been allowed in practice, if not in theory, to indulge in illicit sexual relations. It has not been expected of a man that he should be a virgin on entering marriage, and even after marriage, infidelities are not viewed very gravely if they never come to the knowledge of a man's wife and neighbours. The possibility of this system has depended upon prostitution. This institution, however, is one which it is difficult for a modern to defend, and few will suggest that women should acquire the same rights as men through the establishment of a class of male prostitutes for the satisfaction of women who wish, like their husbands, to seem virtuous without being so. Yet it is quite certain that in these days of late marriage only a small percentage of men will remain continent until they can afford to set up house with a woman of their own class. And if unmarried men are not going to be continent, unmarried women, on the ground of equal rights will claim that they also need not be continent. To the moralists this situation is no doubt regrettable. Every conventional moralist who takes the trouble to think it out will see that he is committed in practice to what is called the double standard, that is to say, the view that sexual virtue is more essential in a woman than in a man. It is all very well to argue that his theoretical ethic demands continence of men also. To this there is the obvious retort that the demand cannot be enforced on the men since it is easy for them to sin secretly. The conventional moralist is thus committed against his will not only to an inequality as between men and women, but also to the view that it is better for a young man to have intercourse with prostitutes than with girls of his own class, in spite of the fact that with the latter, though not with the former, his relations are not mercenary and may be affectionate and altogether delightful. Moralists, of course, do not think out the consequences of advocating a morality which they know will not be obeyed; they think that so long as they do not advocate prostitution they are not responsible for the fact that prostitution is the inevitable outcome of their teaching. This, however, is only another illustration of the well-known fact that the professional moralist in our day is a man of less than average intelligence.

In view of the above circumstances, it is evident that so long as many men for economic reasons find early marriage impossible, while many women cannot marry at all, equality as between men and women demands a relaxation in the traditional standards of feminine virtue. If men are allowed prenuptial intercourse (as in fact they are), women must be allowed it also. And in all countries where there is an excess of women it is an obvious injustice that those women who by arithmetical necessity must remain unmarried should be wholly debarred from sexual experience. Doubtless the pioneers of the women's movement had no such consequences in view, but their modern followers perceive them clearly, and whoever opposes these deductions must face the fact that he or she is not in favour of justice to the female sex.

A very clear-cut issue is raised by this question of the new morality versus the old. If the chastity of girls and the faithfulness of wives is no longer to be demanded, it becomes necessary either to have new methods of safeguarding the family or else to acquiesce in the breakup of the family. It may be suggested that the procreation of children should only occur within marriage, and that all extra-marital sexual intercourse should be rendered sterile by the use of contraceptives. In that case husbands might learn to be as tolerant of lovers as Orientals are of eunuchs. The difficulty of such a scheme as yet is that it requires us to place more reliance on the efficacy of contraceptives and the truthfulness of wives than seems rational; this difficulty may, however, be diminished before long. The other alternative compatible with the new morality is the decay of fatherhood as an important social institution, and the taking over of the duties of the father by the State. In particular cases where a man felt sure of his paternity and fond of the child, he might, of course, voluntarily undertake to do what fathers now normally do in the way of financial support for the mother and child; but he would not be obliged to do so by law. Indeed all children would be in the position in which illegitimate children of unknown paternity are now, except that the State, regarding this as the normal case, would take more trouble with their nurture than it does at present.

If, on the other hand, the old morality is to be reestablished, certain things are essential; some of them are already done, but experience shows that these alone are not effective. The first essential is that the education of girls should be such as to make them stupid and superstitious and ignorant; this requisite is already fulfilled in schools over which the churches have any control. The next requisite is a very severe censorship upon all books giving information on sex subjects; this condition also is coming to be fulfilled in England and in America, since the censorship, without change in the law, is being tightened up by the increasing zeal of the police. These conditions, however, since they exist already, are clearly insufficient. The only thing that will suffice is to remove from younger women all opportunity of being alone with men: girls must be forbidden to earn their living by work outside the home; they must never be allowed an outing unless accompanied by their mother or an aunt; the regrettable practice of going to dances without a chaperon must be sternly stamped out. It must be illegal for an unmarried woman under fifty to possess a motor-car, and perhaps it would be wise to subject all unmarried women once a month to medical examination by police doctors, and to send to a penitentiary all such as were found to be not virgins. The use of contraceptives must, of course, be eradicated, and it must be illegal in conversation with unmarried women to throw doubt upon the dogma of eternal damnation. These measures, if carried out vigorously for a hundred years or more, may perhaps do something to stem the rising tide of immorality. I think, however, that in order to avoid the risk of certain abuses, it would be necessary that all policemen and all medical men should be castrated. Perhaps it would be wise to carry this policy a step further, in view of the inherent depravity of the male character. I am inclined to think that moralists would be well advised to advocate that all men should be castrated, with the exception of ministers of religion.

It will be seen that there are difficulties and objections whichever course we adopt. If we are to allow the new morality to take its course, it is bound to go further than it has done, and to raise difficulties hardly as yet appreciated. If, on the other hand, we attempt in the modern world to enforce restrictions which were possible in a former age, we are led into an impossible stringency of regulation, against which human nature would soon rebel. This is so clear that, whatever the dangers or difficulties, we must be content to let the world go forward rather than back. For this purpose we shall need a genuinely new morality. I mean by this that obligations and duties will still have to be recognized, though they may be very different from the obligations and duties recognized in the past.

.   .   .   .

In a rational ethic, marriage would not count as such in the absence of children. A sterile marriage should be easily dissoluble, for it is through children alone that sexual relations become of importance to society, and worthy to be taken cognizance of by a legal institution. This, of course, is not the view of the Church, which, under the influence of St. Paul, still views marriage rather as the alternative to fornication than as the means to the procreation of children.

.   .   .   .

It is . . . possible for a civilized man and woman to be happy in marriage, although if this is to be the case a number of conditions must be fulfilled. There must be a feeling of complete equality on both sides; there must be no interference with mutual freedom; there must be the most complete physical and mental intimacy; and there must be a certain similarity in regard to standards of values. (It is fatal, for example, if one values only money while the other values only good work.) Given all these conditions, I believe marriage to be the best and most important relation that can exist between two human beings. If it has not often been realized hitherto, that is chiefly because husband and wife have regarded themselves as each other's policeman. If marriage is to achieve its possibilities, husbands and wives must learn to understand that whatever the law may say, in their private lives they must be free.

.   .   .   .

The importance of the family, as it exists at present, in the psychology of mothers is very difficult to estimate. I think that during pregnancy and lactation a woman has, as a rule, a certain instinctive tendency to desire a man's protection—a feeling, no doubt, inherited from the anthropoid apes. Probably a woman who, in our present rather harsh world, has to dispense with this protection tends to become somewhat unduly combative and self-assertive. These feelings, however, are only in part instinctive. They would be greatly weakened, and in some cases wholly abolished, if the State gave adequate care to expectant and nursing mothers and to young children. I think perhaps the chief harm that would be done to women by abolition of the father's place in the home would be the diminution in the intimacy and seriousness of their relations with the male sex. Human beings are so constructed that each sex has much to learn from the other, but mere sex relations, even when they are passionate, do not suffice for these lessons. Cooperation in the serious business of rearing children, and companionship through the long years involved, bring about a relation more important and more enriching to both parties than any that would exist if men had no responsibility for their children. And I do not think that mothers who live in a purely feminine atmosphere, or whose contacts with men are trivial, will, except in a minority of cases, be quite so good for their children from the point of view of emotional education as those who are happily married and cooperating at each stage with their husbands. One must, however, in a great many cases set other considerations over against these. If a woman is actively unhappy in her marriage—and this, after all, is by no means an uncommon occurrence—her unhappiness makes it very difficult for her to have the right kind of emotional poise in dealing with her children. In such cases she could undoubtedly be

a better mother if she were quit of the father. We are thus led to
the entirely trivial conclusion that happy marriages are good, while
unhappy ones are bad.

. . . There is a theory that the desire for children is commoner
among women than among men, but my own impression, for what
it is worth, is exactly the contrary. In a very large number of modern marriages, the children are a concession on the part of the
woman to the man's desires. A woman, after all, has to face labour
and pain and possible loss of beauty in order to bring a child into
the world, whereas a man has no such grounds for anxiety. A man's
reasons for wishing to limit his family are generally economic; these
reasons operate equally with the woman, but she has her own
special reasons as well. The strength of the desire men feel for children is evident when one considers the loss of material comfort that
professional men deliberately incur when they undertake to educate a family in the expensive manner that their class considers
necessary.

. . . My belief, is, . . . though I put it forward with some hesitation, that the elimination of paternity as a recognized social relation would tend to make men's emotional life trivial and thin,
causing in the end a slowly growing boredom and despair. . . .

.   .   .   .

[T]he development of feminism among married women is likely,
in the not distant future, even within the framework of capitalist
society, to lead to the elimination of one if not both parents from
the care of the young in the wage-earning class.

The revolt of women against the domination of men is a movement which, in its purely political sense, is practically completed,
but in its wider aspects is still in its infancy. Gradually its remoter
effects will work themselves out. The emotions which women are
supposed to feel are still, as yet, a reflection of the interests and
sentiments of men. You will read in the works of male novelists
that women find physical pleasure in suckling their young; you
can learn by asking any mother of your acquaintance that this is
not the case, but until women had votes no man ever thought of
doing so. Maternal emotions altogether have been so long slob-
bered over by men who saw in them subconsciously the means to
their own domination that a considerable effort is required to arrive
at what women sincerely feel in this respect. Until very recently,
all decent women were supposed to desire children, but to hate sex.
Even now, many men are shocked by women who frankly state that
they do not desire children. Indeed, it is not uncommon for men to
take it upon themselves to deliver homilies to such women. So long
as women were in subjection, they did not dare to be honest about

their own emotions, but professed those which were pleasing to the male. We cannot, therefore, argue from what has been hitherto supposed to be women's normal attitude towards children, for we may find that as women become fully emancipated their emotions turn out to be, in general, quite different from what has hitherto been thought. I think that civilization, at any rate as it has hitherto existed, tends greatly to diminish women's material feelings. It is probable that a high civilization will not in future be possible to maintain unless women are paid such sums for the production of children as to make them feel it is worth while as a money-making career. If that were done, it would, of course, be unnecessary that all women, or even a majority, should adopt this profession. It would be one profession among others, and would have to be undertaken with professional thoroughness. These, however, are speculations. The only point in them that seems fairly certain is that feminism in its later developments is likely to have a profound influence in breaking up the patriarchal family, which represents man's triumph over woman in prehistoric times.

❀   ❀   ❀

RELATED READINGS

de Beauvoir, Simone. *The Ethics of Ambiguity*. New York: Citadel Press, 1948.

————. *Memoirs of a Dutiful Daughter*. Trans. by James Kirkup. Baltimore: Penguin Books, 1974.

Bebel, August. *Women and Socialism*. Trans. by H. B. Adams Walther. New York: AMS Press, 1976.

Collins, Margery L. and Pierce, Christine. "Holes and Slime: Sexism in Sartre's Psychoanalysis." In *Women and Philosophy*, edited by C. Gould and M. Wartofsky. New York: G. P. Putnam and Sons, 1976, pp. 112–127.

Durant, W. J. "Bertrand Russell on Marriage and Morals." In *Adventures in Genius*. New York: Simon and Schuster, 1931.

Eisenstein, Zillah R. (ed.) *Capitalist Patriarchy and the Case for Socialist Feminism*. New York: Monthly Review Press, 1978.

Frisbe, Sandra. "Women and the Will to Power," *Gnosis*, vol. 1, no. 2 (Spring 1975), pp. 1–10.

de Goncourt, Edmond and de Goncourt, Jules. *The Woman of the Eighteenth Century*, trans. by J. LeClercq and R. Roeder. New York: Minton, Balch and Company, 1927.

Guettel, Charnie. *Marxism and Feminism.* Toronto: Women's Press, 1974.

Hayek, Friedrich A. *John Stuart Mill and Harriet Taylor: Their Friendship and Subsequent Marriage.* Chicago: University of Chicago Press, 1951.

Held, Virginia. "Marx, Sex, and the Transformation of Society." In *Women and Philosophy,* edited by C. Gould and M. Wartofsky. New York: G. P. Putnam and Sons, 1976, pp. 168–184.

Honeycutt, Karen. "Clara Zetkin: A Socialist Approach to the Problem of Women's Oppression." *Feminist Studies* 3 (Spring-Summer 1976), pp. 131–144.

Jenness, Linda (ed.). *Feminism and Socialism.* New York: Pathfinder Press, 1972.

Kainz, Howard P. "The Relationship of Dread to Spirit in Man and Woman, according to Kierkegaard." *The Modern Schoolman* XLVII, 1 (Nov. 1969), pp. 1–13.

Kollontai, Alexandra. *Sexual Relations and the Class Struggle.* Trans. by Alix Holt. Bristol, England: The Falling Wall Press, 1972.

Leighton, Jean. *Simone de Beauvoir on Woman.* Rutherford, New Jersey: Fairleigh Dickinson University Press, 1975.

Mahowald, Mary B. "Freedom vs. Happiness, and 'Women's Lib.'" *Journal of Social Philosophy* VI, 2 (April 1975), pp. 10–13.

Marcuse, Herbert. "Marxism and Feminism." *Women's Studies* 2 (1974), pp. 279-288.

Marx, Karl et al. *The Woman Question.* Selections from the Writings of Marx, Lenin and Stalin. New York: International Publishers, 1951.

Mill, John Stuart. *Autobiography of John Stuart Mill.* New York: Columbia University Press, 1960.

Mill, John Stuart and Mill, Harriet Taylor. *Essays on Sex Equality.* Edited by Alice S. Rossi. Chicago: University of Chicago Press, 1970.

Mitchell, Juliet. "Marxism and Women's Liberation." *Social Praxis* 1 (1973), pp. 11–22.

Pappe, H. O. *John Stuart Mill and the Harriet Taylor Myth.* Parkville: Melbourne University Press, 1961.

Parsons, Katherine. "Nietzsche and Moral Change." *Feminist Studies* 2 (1974), pp. 57–76.

Reed, Evelyn. *Is Biology Woman's Destiny?* New York: Pathfinder Press, 1972.

──────. *Problems of Women's Liberation.* New York: Pathfinder Press, 1969.

Rowbotham, Sheila. *Women, Resistance and Revolution.* London: Allen Lane The Penguin Press, 1972.

Russell, Bertrand. "The Status of Women." *The Bertrand Russell Archives,* 1974, pp. 3–12.

Scott, Hilda. *Does Socialism Liberate Women?* Boston: Beacon Press, 1974.

Stern, Bernhard J. "Engels on the Family." In *A Centenary of Marxism.* Edited by Samuel Bernstein. New York: Science and Society, 1948, pp. 42–64.

Stern, Karl. "Kierkegaard." In *The Flight from Woman.* New York: Farrar, Straus and Giroux, 1965, pp. 199–226.

Trotsky, Leon. *Women and the Family.* New York: Pathfinder Press, 1970.

Vicinus, Martha (ed.). *Suffer and Be Still / Women in the Victorian Age.* Bloomington: Indiana University Press, 1972.

Williford, Miriam. "Bentham on the Rights of Women." *Journal of the History of Ideas* 36 (1975), pp. 167–176.

III
EARLIER PHILOSOPHERS' VIEWS

In general, the authors in this section exemplify the spirit of the Enlightenment through their concern with the human subject and with the moral and social life of that subject. However, their common concern is reflected through differing philosophies: empiricism, rationalism, and idealism, and consequently through differing views of human nature. Except in the case of Mary Wollstonecraft, specific remarks about women occur only peripherally or secondarily to the writer's main philosophical contributions, which include elaborations on the meaning of man. It is useful to compare or contrast concepts of person and of woman in the same writer, for such concepts have continued quite beyond the lifespan of their author.

Jean-Jacques Rousseau provides a link between the thinkers here presented. John Locke seems to have anticipated Rousseau's social contract theory in its view of primitive human nature. David Hume attempted, rather unsuccessfully, to befriend Rousseau by offering him sanctuary in England when his works had evoked hostile reaction in France and Switzerland. Immanuel Kant admits to having been greatly impressed by the works of Rousseau, whose *Emile* he had read before writing the *Observations* from which our selection is excerpted. Mary Wollstonecraft devotes much space in *The Vindication of the Rights of Women* to a critique of Rousseau's thoughts in *Emile*. G. W. F. Hegel read Rousseau's writings during his student days, and Arthur Schopenhauer cites Rousseau as an author whose views on women support his own.

JOHN LOCKE

Like other philosophers of his day, John Locke (1632–1704) was especially concerned with the problem of human knowledge. While he agreed with Cartesian criticism of the scholastic tradition as obscure and unproductive, he rejected the theory of innate ideas, insisting that the mind is a *tabula rasa* (blank slate) prior to experience. In his famous *Treatise concerning Human Understanding* Locke distinguishes between primary qualities, as powers inherent in real things, and secondary qualities, as the ways through which primary qualities are perceived by a subject. Sensation and reflection are the twin sources of experience, providing us with ideas that may be simple or complex. An idea is defined as "the *object* of the understanding when a man thinks," and knowledge consists in our perception of agreement or disagreement among ideas. Three kinds of knowledge are accessible to human beings: intuitive knowledge of oneself, demonstrative knowledge of God, and sensitive knowledge of the external world.

Locke's Concept of Human Nature

Locke defines a person as "a thinking, intelligent being, that has reason and reflection and can consider itself as itself, the same thinking thing in different times and places." The basis for one's sense of self is thus bodily continuity, as perceived by consciousness. In anticipation of Rousseau, Locke views the state of nature as a situation in which human beings are free and equal, with no common authority over them. They are also naturally prone to communicate with others; hence, language is "the great instrument and common tie of society."

According to Locke, the specific purpose for which people join together is "the material preservation of their lives, liberties and estates, which I call by the general name property." In other words our natural independence and desire for (as well as right to) property are bound to cause social conflicts which require the mediation of government for their resolution. Governments are thus designed to promote the common good. Since they represent the will of the majority of the people, the people retain the right to alter their mode of representation, even in extreme cases, through rebellion.

That Locke saw no need to avoid religious sources in philosophical writing is evident in the selection that follows. Among his peers this was intellectually acceptable, since the Bible was generally regarded as a source of truth not only about God but also about the world and human nature.

The following are excerpted from *Two Treatises of Government*, Book II: Of Civil Government, in *The Works of John Locke, Esq.*, Vol. II, ch. VI and VII. London: Printed for S. Birt, D. Browne, T. Longman, J. Shuckburgh, C. Hitch and L. Hawes, J. Hodges, J. Oswald, A. Millar, J. and J. Rivington, J. Ward, and M. Cooper, M.DCC.LI, pp. 181-2, 184-5, 188-91.

JOHN LOCKE   'Of Paternal Power'

It may perhaps be censured as an impertinent criticism, in a discourse of this nature, to find fault with words and names, that have obtained in the world: and yet possibly it may not be amiss to offer new ones, when the old are apt to lead men into mistakes, as this of *paternal power* probably has done, which seems so to place the power of parents over their children wholly in the *father*, as if the *mother* had no share in it; whereas, if we consult reason or revelation, we shall find, she has an equal title. This may give one reason to ask, whether this might not be more properly called *parental power?* for whatever obligation nature and the right of generation lays on children, it must certainly bind them equal to both the concurrent causes of it. And accordingly we see the positive law of God everywhere joins them together, without distinction, when it commands the obedience of children, *Honour thy father and thy mother*, Exod. xx. 12. *Whosoever curseth his father or his mother*, Lev. xx. 9. *Ye shall fear every man his mother and his father*, Lev. xix. 3. *Children, obey your parents*, &c. Eph. vi. 1. is the style of the Old and New Testament.

Had but this one thing been well considered, without looking any deeper into the matter, it might perhaps have kept men from running into those gross mistakes, they have made, about this power of parents; which, however it might, without any great harshness, bear the name of absolute dominion, and regal authority, when under the title of *paternal power* it seemed appropriated to the father, would yet have sounded but oddly, and in the very name shown the absurdity, if this supposed absolute power over children had been called *parental;* and thereby have discovered, that it belonged to the *mother* too: for it will but very ill serve the turn of those men, who contend so much for the absolute power and authority of the *fatherhood*, as they call it, that the mother should have any share in it; and it would have but ill supported the *monarchy* they contend for, when by the very name it appeared, that that fundamental authority, from whence they would derive their government of a single person only, was not placed in one, but two persons jointly. But to let this of names pass.

Though I have said above, *Chap. II. That all men by nature are equal,* I cannot be supposed to understand all sorts of *equality:* age or *virtue* may give men a just precedency: *excellency of parts* and *merit* may place others above the common level: *birth* may subject some, and *alliance* or *benefits* others, to pay an observance to those to whom nature, gratitude, or other respects, may have made it due: and yet all this consists with the *equality*, which all men are in, in respect of jurisdiction or dominion one over another; which was the *equality* I there spoke of, as proper to the business in hand, being that *equal right,* that every man hath, *to his natural freedom*, without being subjected to the will or authority of any other man. . . .

The *freedom* then of man, and liberty of acting according to his own will, is *grounded on* his having *reason*, which is able to instruct him in that law he is to govern himself by, and make him know how far he is left to the freedom of his own will. To turn him loose to an unrestrained liberty, before he has reason to guide him, is not the allowing him the privilege of his nature to be free; but to thrust him out amongst brutes, and abandon him to a state as wretched, and as much beneath that of a man, as theirs. This is that which puts the *authority* into the *parents'* hands to govern the *minority* of their children. God hath made it their business to employ this care on their offspring, and hath placed in them suitable inclinations of tenderness and concern to temper this power, to apply it, as his wisdom designed it, to the children's good, as long as they should need to be under it.

But what reason can hence advance this care of the *parents* due to their off-spring into an *absolute arbitrary dominion* of the father, whose power reaches no farther, than by such a discipline, as he finds most effectual, to give such strength and health to their bodies, such vigour and rectitude to their minds, as may best fit his children to be most useful to themselves and others; and, if it be necessary to his condition, to make them work, when they are able, for their own subsistence. But in this power the *mother* too has her share with the *father*.

Nay, this *power* so little belongs to the *father* by any peculiar right of nature, but only as he is guardian of his children, that when he quits his care of them, he loses his power over them, which goes along with their nourishment and education, to which it is inseparably annexed; and it belongs as much to the *foster-father* of an exposed child, as to the natural father of another. So little power does the bare *act of begetting* give a man over his issue; if all his care ends there, and this be all the title he hath to the name and authority of a father. And what will become of this *paternal power* in that part of the world, where one woman hath more than one husband at a time? or in those parts of *America*, where, when the husband and wife part, which happens frequently, the children are all left to the mother, follow her, and are wholly under her care and provision? If the father die whilst the children are young, do they not naturally everywhere owe the same obedience to their *mother*, during their minority, as to their father were he alive? and will any one say, that the mother hath a legislative power over her children? that she can make standing rules, which shall be of perpetual obligation, by which they ought to regulate all the concerns of their property, and bound their liberty all the course of their lives? or can she inforce the observation of them with capital punishments? for this is the proper *power of the magistrate*, of which the father hath not so much as the shadow. His command over his children is but temporary, and reaches not their life or property. . . .

❋   ❋   ❋

JOHN LOCKE   Of Political and Civil Society

God having made man such a creature, that in his own judgment, it was not good for him to be alone, put him under strong obligations of necessity, convenience, and inclination to drive him into *society*, as well as fitted him with understanding and language to continue and enjoy it. The *first society* was between man and wife, which gave beginning to that between parents and children; to which, in time, that between master and servant came to be added: and though all these might, and commonly did meet together, and make up but one family, wherein the master or mistress of it had some sort of rule proper to a family; each of these, or all together, came short of *political society*, as we shall see, if we consider the different ends, ties, and bounds of each of these.

Conjugal society is made by a voluntary compact between man and woman; and tho' it consist chiefly in such a communion and right in one another's bodies as is necessary to its chief end, procreation; yet it draws with it mutual support and assistance, and a communion of interests too, as necessary not only to unite their care and affection, but also necessary to their common off-spring, who have a right to be nourished, and maintained by them, till they are able to provide for themselves.

For the end of *conjunction, between male and female,* being not barely procreation, but the continuation of the species; this conjunction betwixt male and female ought to last, even after procreation, so long as is necessary to the nourishment and support of the young ones, who are to be sustained by those that got them, till they are able to shift and provide for themselves. This rule, which the infinite wise maker hath set to the works of his hands, we find the inferior creatures steadily obey. In those viviparous animals which feed on grass, the *conjunction between male and female* lasts no longer than the very act of copulation; because the teat of the dam being sufficient to nourish the young, till it be able to feed on grass, the male only begets, but concerns not himself for the female or young, to whose sustenance he can contribute nothing. But in beasts of prey the *conjunction* lasts longer: because the dam not being able well to subsist herself, and nourish her numerous offspring by her own prey alone, a more laborious, as well as more dangerous way of living, than by feeding on grass, the assistance of the male is necessary to the maintenance of their common family, which cannot subsist till they are able to prey for themselves, but by the joint care of male and female. The same is to be observed in all birds, (except some domestic ones, where plenty of food excuses the cock from feeding, and taking care of the young brood) whose young needing food in the nest, the cock and hen continue mates, till the young are able to use their wing, and provide for themselves.

And herein I think lies the chief, if not the only reason, *why the male and female in mankind are tied to a longer conjunction* than other creatures, *viz.* because the female is capable of conceiving, and *de facto* is commonly with child again, and brings forth too a new birth, long before the former is out of a dependency for support on his parents' help, and able to shift for himself, and has all the assistance that is due to him from his parents: whereby the father, who is bound to take care for those he hath begot, is under an obligation to continue in conjugal society with the same woman longer than other creatures, whose young being able to subsist of themselves, before the time of procreation returns again, the conjugal bond dissolves of itself, and they are at liberty, till *Hymen* at his usual anniversary season summons them again to choose new mates. Wherein one cannot but admire the wisdom of the great Creator, who having given to man foresight, and an ability to lay up for the future, as well as to supply the present necessity, hath made it necessary, that *society of man and wife should be more lasting*, than of male and female amongst other creatures; that so their industry might be encouraged, and their interest better united, to make provision and lay up goods for their common issue, which uncertain mixture, or easy and frequent solutions of conjugal society would mightily disturb.

But tho' these are ties upon *mankind*, which make the *conjugal bonds* more firm and lasting in man, than the other species of animals; yet it would give one reason to enquire, why this *compact*, where procreation and education are secured, and inheritance taken care for, may not be made determinable, either by consent, or at a certain time, or upon certain conditions, as well as any other voluntary compacts, there being no necessity in the nature of the thing, nor to the ends of it, that it should always be for life; I mean, to such as are under no restraint of any positive law, which ordains all such contracts to be perpetual.

But the husband and wife, though they have but one common concern, yet having different understandings, will unavoidably sometimes have different wills too; it therefore being necessary that the last determination, *i. e.* the rule, should be placed somewhere; it naturally falls to the man's share, as the abler and the stronger. But this reaching but to the things of their common interest and property, leaves the wife in the full and free possession of what by contract is her peculiar right, and gives the husband no more power over her life than she has over his; the *power of the husband* being so far from that of an absolute monarch, that the *wife* has in many cases a liberty to separate from him, where natural right, or their contract allows it; whether that contract be made by themselves in the state of nature, or by the customs or laws of the country they live in; and the children upon such separation fall to the father or mother's lot, as such contract does determine.

For all the ends of *marriage* being to be obtained under politic government, as well as in the state of nature, the civil magistrate doth not abridge the right or power of either naturally necessary to those ends, *viz.* procreation and mutual support and assistance whilst they are together; but only decides any controversy that may arise between man and wife about them. If it were otherwise, and that absolute *sovereignty* and power of life and death naturally belonged to the husband, and were *necessary to the society between man and wife*, there could be no matrimony in any of those countries where the husband is allowed no such absolute authority. But the ends of matrimony requiring no such power in the husband, the condition of *conjugal society* put it not in him, it being not at all necessary to that state. *Conjugal society* could subsist and attain its ends without it; nay, community of goods, and the power over them, mutual assistance and maintenance, and other things belonging to *conjugal society*, might be varied and regulated by that contract which unites man and wife in that society, as far as may consist with procreation and the bringing up of children till they could shift for themselves; nothing being necessary to any society, that is not necessary to the ends for which it is made. . . .

Let us therefore consider a *master of a family* with all these subordinate relations of *wife, children, servants,* and *slaves,* united under the domestic rule of a family; which, what resemblance soever it may have in its order, offices, and number too, with a little common-wealth, yet is very far from it, both in its constitution, power and end: or if it must be thought a monarchy, and the *paterfamilias* the absolute monarch in it, absolute monarchy will have but a very shattered and short power, when it is plain, by what has been said before, that the *master of the family* has a very distinct and differently limited *power,* both as to time and extent, over those several persons that are in it; for excepting the slave (and the family is as much a family, and his power as *paterfamilias* as great, whether there be any slaves in his family or no) he has no legislative power of life and death over any of them, and none too but what a *mistress of a family* may have as well as he. And he certainly can have no absolute power over the whole *family,* who has but a very limited one over every individual in it. But how a *family,* or any other society of men, differ from that which is properly *political society,* we shall best see, by considering wherein *political society* itself consists.

❊   ❊   ❊

DAVID HUME

The philosophy of David Hume (1711–1776), like that of Locke, is generally labeled as "empiricism" because of its emphasis on experience as the sole source of knowledge. Unlike other empiricists, however, Hume pursued the logic of their position to its radical implications: a critique of the principle of causality, and a denial of the possibility of certain or "scientific" knowledge about the world. Through association of ideas, Hume claimed, human beings tend to assign metaphysical causes to the data they experience. But such imputative judgments can never be entirely accounted for by reason, since the cause-effect relationship upon which they are based cannot be strictly demonstrated. Accordingly, even the most reliable scientific conclusions are mere statements of probability. Instead of interpreting such judgments as unfailing certitudes, Hume maintains that we ought to preserve a healthy skepticism regarding all assertions about reality.

Hume's Concept of Human Nature

For Hume, the study of human nature constitutes the central concern of philosophy. The experimental method appropriate to this task is one based entirely on empirical data, including that of introspection, with conclusions that are open-ended. In light of this approach, Hume insisted that convictions about existence are not a matter of knowledge but of natural belief. Imagination, he maintained, is the source of belief in independent bodies, including our own, and memory plays a key role in establishing each one's sense of personal identity. As memory represents separate past perceptions in a chain of resemblance, imagination tends to (falsely) interpret their relation as a continuity which signifies identity of the self. According to Hume, "self or person is not any one impression, but that to which our several impressions and ideas *are supposed* to have a reference." (Italics added.) The supposition is natural but unwarranted, since there is no provable underlying identity in the succession of perceptions that constitutes the mind.

With regard to "liberty," Hume observes another instance of the tendency to attribute existential status to an unprovable cause of experienced effects. "By liberty," he asserts, "we can only mean *a power of acting or not acting according to the determinations of the will*." The will is described as "the internal impression we feel and are conscious of, when we knowingly give rise to any new motion of our body, or new perception of our mind." Hume regards his definition of liberty as one "in which all men agree," and considers such liberty "also essential to morality."

As Hume uses it, the term "passion" refers to the entire sweep of human emotions and affections. Since reason alone is incapable of producing action or volition, he asserts that "[r]eason is, and ought only to be the slave of the passions" in questions of conduct. Hume seems to have thought that basic sentiments of morality were common to all individuals, and should be trusted. His moral ideal can readily be elaborated through epithets such as "*sociable, good-natured, humane, merciful, grateful, friendly, generous, beneficent,* or their equivalents." Such descriptives, Hume claims, "are known in all languages, and universally express the highest merit which human nature is capable of attaining."

"Of Love and Marriage" and "Of Polygamy and Divorce" are excerpted from *Essays, Moral, Political and Literary,* edited by T. H. Green and T. H. Gross, pp. 383–88 of vol. II, and pp. 231–39 of vol. I.

"Of Chastity and Modesty" is from Hume's *Treatise of Human Nature,* edited by L. A. Selby-Bigge. Oxford at the Clarendon Press, 1888, pp. 570–573.

DAVID HUME   'Of Love and Marriage'

I know not whence it proceeds, that women are so apt to take amiss every thing which is said in disparagement of the married state; and always consider a satyr upon matrimony as a satyr upon themselves. Do they mean, that they are the parties principally concerned, and that if a backwardness to enter into that state should prevail in the world, they would be the greatest sufferers? Or, are they sensible, that misfortunes and miscarriages of the married state are owing more to their sex than to ours? I hope they do not intend to confess either of these two particulars, or to give such an advantage to their adversaries, the men, as even to allow them to suspect it.

I have often had thoughts of complying with this humour of the fair sex, and of writing a panegyric upon marriage: But, in looking around for materials, they seemed to be of so mixed a nature, that at the conclusion of my reflections, I found that I was as much disposed to write a satyr, which might be placed on the opposite pages of the panegyric: And I am afraid, that as satyr is, on most occasions, thought to contain more truth than panegyric, I should have done their cause more harm than good by this expedient. To misrepresent facts is what, I know, they will not require of me. I must be more a friend to truth, than even to them, where their interests are opposite.

I shall tell the women what it is our sex complains of most in the married state; and if they be disposed to satisfy us in this particular, all the other differences will easily be accommodated. If I be not mistaken, 'tis their love of dominion, which is the ground of the quarrel; tho' 'tis very likely, that they will think it an unreasonable love of it in us, which makes us insist so much upon that point. However this may be, no passion seems to have more influence on female minds, than this for power; and there is a remarkable instance in history of its prevailing above another passion, which is the only one that can be supposed a proper counterpoise for it. We are told, that all the women in Scythia once conspired against the men, and kept the secret so well, that they executed their design before they were suspected. They surprised the men in drink, or asleep; bound them all fast in chains; and having called a solemn council of the whole sex, it was debated what expedient should be used to improve the present advantage, and prevent their falling again into slavery. To kill all the men did not seem to be the relish of any part of the assembly, notwithstanding the injuries formerly received; and they were afterwards pleased to make a great merit of this lenity of theirs. It was, therefore, agreed to put out the eyes of the whole male sex, and thereby resign in all future time the vanity which they could draw from their beauty, in order to secure their authority. We must no longer pretend to dress and show, said they; but then we shall be free from slavery. We shall hear no more tender sighs; but in return we shall hear no more imperious commands. Love must forever leave us; but he will carry subjection along with him.

'Tis regarded by some as an unlucky circumstance, since the women were resolved to maim the men, and deprive them of some of their senses, in order to render them humble and dependent, that the sense of hearing could not serve their purpose, since 'tis probable the females would rather have attacked that than the sight: And I think it is agreed among the learned, that, in a married state, 'tis not near so great an inconvenience to lose the former sense as the latter. However this may be, we are told by modern anecdotes, that some of the Scythian women did secretly spare their husbands' eyes; presuming, I suppose, that they could govern them as well by means of that sense as without it. But so incorrigible and untractable were these men, that their wives were all obliged, in a few years, as their youth and beauty decayed, to imitate the example of their sisters; which it was no difficult matter to do in a state where the female sex had once got the superiority.

I know not if our Scottish ladies derive any thing of this humour from their Scythian ancestors; but, I must confess that I have often been surprised to see a woman very well pleased to take a fool for her mate, that she might govern with the less control; and could not but think her sentiments, in this respect, still more barbarous than those of the Scythian women above-mentioned; as much as the eyes of the understanding are more valuable than those of the body.

But to be just, and to lay the blame more equally, I am afraid it is the fault of our sex, if the women be so fond of rule, and that if we did not abuse our authority, they would never think it worth while to dispute it. Tyrants, we know, produce rebels; and all history informs us, that rebels, when they prevail, are apt to become tyrants in their turn. For this reason, I could wish there were no pretensions to authority on either side; but that every thing was carried on with perfect equality, as between two equal members of the same body. And to induce both parties to embrace those amicable sentiments, I shall deliver to them Plato's account of the origin of love and marriage.

Mankind, according to that fanciful philosopher, were not, in their original, divided into male and female, as at present; but each individual person was a compound of both sexes, and was in himself both husband and wife, melted down into one living creature. This union, no doubt, was very entire, and the parts very well adjusted together, since there resulted a perfect harmony betwixt the male and female, altho' they were obliged to be inseparable companions. And so great were the harmony and happiness flowing from it, that the Androgynes (for so Plato calls them) or Men-Women, became insolent upon their prosperity, and rebelled against the Gods. To punish them for this temerity, Jupiter could contrive no better expedient, than to divorce the male-part from the female, and make two imperfect beings of the compound, which was before so perfect. Hence the origin of men and women, as distinct creatures. But notwithstanding this division, so lively is our remembrance of the happiness which we enjoyed in our primaeval state, that we are never at rest in this situation; but each of these halves is continually searching thro' the whole species to find the other half, which was broken from it: And when they meet, they join again with the greatest fondness and sympathy. But it often happens, that they are mistaken in this particular; that they take for their half what no way corresponds to them; and that the parts do not meet nor join in with each other, as is usual in fractures. In this case the union was soon dissolved, and each part is set loose again to hunt for its lost half, joining itself to every one whom it meets, by way of trial, and enjoying no rest till its perfect sympathy with its partners shows that it has at last been successful in its endeavours.

Were I disposed to carry on this fiction of Plato, which accounts for the mutual love betwixt the sexes in so agreeable a manner, I would do it by the following allegory.

When Jupiter had separated the male from the female, and had quelled their pride and ambition by so severe an operation, he could not but repent him of the cruelty of his vengeance, and take compassion on poor mortals, who were now become incapable of any repose or tranquility. Such cravings, such anxieties, such necessities arose, as made them curse their creation, and think existence itself a punishment. In vain had they recourse to every other occupation and amusement. In vain did they seek after every pleasure of sense, and every refinement of reason. Nothing could fill that void, which they felt in their hearts, or supply the loss of their partner, who was so fatally separated from them. To remedy this disorder, and to bestow some comfort, at least, on the human race in their forlorn situation, Jupiter sent down Love and Hymen, to collect the broken halves of human kind, and piece them together in the best manner possible. These two deities found such a prompt disposition in mankind to unite again in their primaeval state, that they proceeded on their work with wonderful success for some time; till at last, from many unlucky accidents, dissension arose betwixt them. The chief counsellor and favourite of Hymen was Care, who was continually filling his patron's head with prospects of futurity; a settlement, family, children, servants; so that little else was regarded in all the matches *they* made. On the other hand, *Love* had chosen Pleasure for his favourite, who was as pernicious a counsellor as the other, and would never allow *Love* to look beyond the present momentary gratification, or the satisfying of the prevailing inclination. These two favourites became, in a little time, irreconcileable enemies, and made it their chief business to undermine each other in all their undertakings. No sooner had *Love* fixed upon two halves, which he was cementing together, and forming to a close union, but *Care* insinuates himself; and bringing Hymen along with him, dissolves the union produced by love, and joins each half to some other half, which he had provided for it. To be revenged of this, *Pleasure* creeps in upon a pair already joined by Hymen; and calling *Love* to his assistance, they under hand contrive to join each half by secret links, to halves, which Hymen was wholly unacquainted with. It was not long before this quarrel was felt in its pernicious consequences; and such complaints arose before the throne of Jupiter, that he was obliged to summon the offending parties to appear before him, in order to give an account of their proceedings. After hearing the pleadings on both sides, he ordered an immediate reconcilement betwixt Love and Hymen, as the only expedient for giving happiness to mankind: And that he might be sure this reconcilement should be durable, he laid his strict injunctions on them never to join any halves without consulting their favourites *Care* and *Pleasure,* and obtaining the consent of both to the conjunction. Where this order is strictly observed, the *Androgyne* is perfectly restored, and the human race enjoy the same happiness as in their primaeval state. The seam is scarce perceived that joins the two beings; but both of them combine to form one perfect and happy creature.

*   *   *

DAVID HUME   'Of Polygamy and Divorce'

As marriage is an engagement entered into by mutual consent, and has for its end the propagation of the species, it is evident, that it must be susceptible of all the variety of conditions, which consent establishes, provided they be not contrary to this end.

A man, in conjoining himself to a woman, is bound to her according to the terms of his engagement: In begetting children, he is bound, by all the ties of nature and humanity, to provide for their subsistence and education. When he has performed these two parts of duty, no one can reproach him with injustice or injury. And as the terms of his engagement, as well as the methods of subsisting his offspring, may be various, it is mere superstition to imagine, that marriage can be entirely uniform, and will admit only of one mode or form. Did not human laws restrain the natural liberty of men, every particular marriage would be as different as contracts or bargains of any other kind or species.

As circumstances vary, and the laws purpose different advantages, we find, that, in different times and places, they impose different conditions on this important contract. In Tonquin, it is usual for the sailors, when the ships come into harbour, to marry for the season; and notwithstanding this precarious engagement, they are assured, it is said, of the strictest fidelity to their bed, as well as the whole management of their affairs, from those temporary spouses.

I cannot, at present, recollect my authorities; but I have somewhere read, that the republic of Athens, having lost many of its citizens by war and pestilence, allowed every man to marry two wives, in order the sooner to repair the waste which had been made by these calamities. The poet Euripides happened to be coupled to two noisy Vixens who so plagued him with their jealousies and quarrels, that he became ever after a professed *woman-hater;* and is the only theatrical writer, perhaps the only poet, that ever entertained an aversion to the sex.

In that agreeable romance, called *the History of the* Sevarambians, where a great many men and a few women are supposed to be shipwrecked on a desert coast; the captain of the troop, in order to obviate those endless quarrels which arose, regulates their marriages after the following manner: He takes a handsome female to himself alone; assigns one to every couple of inferior officers; and to five of the lowest rank he gives one wife in common.

The ancient Britons had a singular kind of marriage, to be met with among no other people. Any number of them, as ten or a dozen, joined in a society together, which was perhaps requisite for mutual defence in those barbarous times. In order to link this society the closer, they took an equal number of wives in common; and whatever children were born, were reputed to belong to all of them, and were accordingly provided for by the whole community.

Among the inferior creatures, nature herself, being the supreme legislator, prescribes all the laws which regulate their marriages, and varies those laws according to the different circumstances of the creature. Where she furnishes, with ease, food and defence to the newborn animal, the present embrace terminates the marriage; and the care of the offspring is committed entirely to the female. Where the food is of more difficult purchase, the marriage continues for one season, till the common progeny can provide for itself; and the union immediately dissolves, and leaves each of the parties free to enter into a new engagement at the ensuing season. But nature, having endowed man with reason, has not so exactly regulated every article of his marriage contract, but has left him to adjust them, by his own prudence, according to his particular circumstances and situation. Municipal laws are a supply to the wisdom of each individuual; and, at the same time, by restraining the natural liberty of men, make private interest submit to the interest of the public. All regulations, therefore, on this head are equally lawful, and equally conformable to the principles of nature; though they are not all equally convenient, or equally useful to society. The laws may allow of polygamy, as among the *Eastern* nations; or of voluntary divorces, as among the Greeks and Romans; or they may confine one man to one woman, during the whole course of their lives, as among the modern Europeans. It may not be disagreeable to consider the advantages and disadvantages, which result from each of these institutions.

The advocates for polygamy may recommend it as the only effectual remedy for the disorders of love, and the only expedient for freeing men from that slavery to the females, which the natural violence of our passions has imposed upon us. By this means alone can we regain our right of sovereignty; and, sating our appetite, re-establish the authority of reason in our minds, and, of consequence, our own authority in our families. Man, like a weak sovereign, being unable to support himself against the wiles and intrigues of his subjects, must play one faction against another, and become absolute by the mutual jealousy of the females. *To divide and to govern* is an universal maxim; and by neglecting it, the Europeans undergo a more grievous and a more ignominious slavery than the Turks or Persians, who are subjected indeed to a sovereign, that lies at a distance from them, but in their domestic affairs rule with an uncontrollable sway.

On the other hand, it may be urged with better reason, that this sovereignty of the male is a real usurpation, and destroys that nearness of rank, not to say equality, which nature has established between the sexes. We are, by nature, their lovers, their friends, their patrons: Would we willingly exchange such endearing appellations, for the barbarous title of master and tyrant?

In what capacity shall we gain by this inhuman proceeding? As lovers, or as husbands? The *lover*, is totally annihilated; and courtship, the most agreeable scene in life, can no longer have place, where women have not the free disposal of themselves, but are bought and sold, like the meanest animal. The *husband* is as little a gainer, having found the admirable secret of extinguishing every part of love, except its jealously. No rose without its thorn; but he must be a foolish wretch indeed, that throws away the rose and preserves only the thorn.

But the Asiatic manners are as destructive to friendship as to love. Jealously excludes men from all intimacies and familiarities with each other. No one dares bring his friend to his house or table, lest he bring a lover to his numerous wives. Hence all over the east, each family is as much separate from another, as if they were so many distinct kingdoms. No wonder then, that Solomon, living like an eastern prince, with his seven hundred wives, and three hundred concubines, without one friend, could write so pathetically concerning the vanity of the world. Had he tried the secret of one wife or mistress, a few friends, and a great many companions, he might have found life somewhat more agreeable. Destroy love and friendship; what remains in the world worth accepting?

The bad education of children, especially children of condition, is another unavoidable consequence of these eastern institutions. Those who pass the early part of life among slaves, are only qualified to be, themselves, slaves and tyrants; and in every future intercourse, either with their inferiors or superiors, are apt to forget the natural equality of mankind. What attention, too, can it be supposed a parent, whose seraglio affords him fifty sons, will give to instilling principles of morality or science into a progeny, with

whom he himself is scarcely acquainted, and whom he loves with
so divided an affection? Barbarism, therefore, appears, from reason
as well as experience, to be the inseparable attendant of polygamy.

To render polygamy more odious, I need not recount the frightful
effects of jealously, and the constraint in which it holds the fair-sex
all over the east. In those countries men are not allowed to have
any commerce with the females, not even physicians, when sickness
may be supposed to have extinguished all wanton passions in the
bosoms of the fair, and, at the same time, has rendered them unfit
objects of desire. . . .

. . . But it will, perhaps, appear strange, that, in a European
country, jealously can yet be carried to such a height, that it is indecent so much as to suppose that a woman of rank can have feet
or legs. Witness the following story, which we have from very good
authority. When the mother of the late king of Spain was on her
road towards Madrid, she passed through a little town in Spain,
famous for its manufactory of gloves and stockings. The magistrates
of the place thought they could not better express their joy for the
reception of their new queen, than by presenting her with a sample
of those commodities, for which alone their town was remarkable.
The *major domo,* who conducted the princess, received the gloves
very graciously: But when the stockings were presented, he flung
them away with great indignation, and severely reprimanded the
magistrates for this egregious piece of indecency. *Know,* says he,
that a queen of Spain has no legs. The young queen, who, at that
time, understood the language but imperfectly, and had often been
frightened with stories of Spanish jealousy, imagined that they
were to cut off her legs. Upon which she fell a crying, and begged
them to conduct her back to Germany; for that she never could
endure the operation: And it was with some difficulty they could
appease her. Philip IV. is said never in his life to have laughed
heartily, but at the recital of this story.

Having rejected polygamy, and matched one man with one
woman, let us now consider what duration we shall assign to their
union, and whether we shall admit of those voluntary divorces,
which were customary among the Greeks and Romans. Those who
would defend this practice may employ the following reasons.

How often does disgust and aversion arise after marriage, from
the most trivial accidents, or from an incompatibility of humour;
where time, instead of curing the wounds, proceeding from mutual
injuries, festers them every day the more, by new quarrels and
reproaches? Let us separate hearts, which were not made to associate together. Each of them may, perhaps, find another for which it
is better fitted. At least, nothing can be more cruel than to preserve,
by violence, an union, which, at first, was made by mutual love,
and is now, in effect, dissolved by mutual hatred.

But the liberty of divorces is not only a curet to hatred and domestic quarrels: It is also an admirable preservative against them,
and the only secret for keeping alive that love, which first united
the married couple. The heart of man delights in liberty: The very
image of constraint is grievous to it: When you would confine it
by violence, to what would otherwise have been its choice, the inclination immediately changes, and desire is turned into aversion.
If the public interest will not allow us to enjoy in polygamy that
variety, which is so agreeable in love: at least, deprive us not of
that liberty, which is so essentially requisite. In vain you tell me,
that I had my choice of the person, with whom I would conjoin
myself. I had my choice, it is true, of my prison; but this is but a
small comfort, since it must still be a prison.

Such are the arguments which may be urged in favour of divorces: But there seem to be these three unanswerable objections
against them. *First,* What must become of the children, upon the
separation of the parents? Must they be committed to the care of
a step-mother; and instead of the fond attention and concern of a
parent, feel all the indifference or hatred of a stranger or an enemy?
These inconveniences are sufficiently felt, where nature has made
the divorce by the doom inevitable to all mortals: And shall we seek
to multiply those inconveniences, by multiplying divorces, and
putting it in the power of parents, upon every caprice, to render
their posterity miserable?

Secondly, If it be true, on the one hand, that the heart of man
naturally delights in liberty, and hates every thing to which it is
confined; it is also true, on the other, that the heart of man naturally
submits to necessity, and soon loses an inclination, when there appears an absolute impossibility of gratifying it. These principles of
human nature, you'll say, are contradictory: But what is man but
a heap of contradictions! Though it is remarkable, that, where
principles are, after this manner, contrary in their operation, they
do not always destroy each other; but the one or the other may
predominate on any particular occasion, according as circumstances are more or less favourable to it. For instance, love is a
restless and impatient passion, full of caprices and variations: arising in a moment from a feature, from an air, from nothing, and suddenly extinguishing after the same manner. Such a passion requires
liberty above all things; and therefore Eloisa had reason, when, in
order to preserve this passion, she refused to marry her beloved
Abelard.

> How oft, when prest to marriage, have I said,
> Curse on all laws but those which love has made;
> Love, free as air, at sight of human ties,
> Spreads his light wings, and in a moment flies.

But *friendship* is a calm and sedate affection, conducted by reason and cemented by habit; springing from long acquaintance and mutual obligations; without jealousies or fears, and without those feverish fits of heat and cold, which cause such an agreeable torment in the amorous passion. So sober an affection, therefore, as friendship, rather thrives under constraint, and never rises to such a height, as when any strong interest or necessity binds two persons together, and gives them some common object of pursuit. We need not, therefore, be afraid of drawing the marriage-knot, which chiefly subsists by friendship, the closest possible. The amity between the persons, where it is solid and sincere, will rather gain by it: And where it is wavering and uncertain, this is the best expedient for fixing it. How many frivolous quarrels and disgusts are there, which people of common prudence endeavour to forget, when they lie under a necessity of passing their lives together; but which would soon be inflamed into the most deadly hatred were they pursued to the utmost, under the prospect of an easy separation?

In the *third* place, we must consider, that nothing is more danerous than to unite two persons so closely in all their interests and concerns, as man and wife, without rendering the union entire and total.

The least possibility of a separate interest must be the source of endless quarrels and suspicions. The wife, not secure of her establishment, will still be driving some separate end or project; and the husband's selfishness, being accompanied with more power, may be still more dangerous.

Should these reasons against voluntary divorces be deemed insufficient, I hope no body will pretend to refuse the testimony of experience. At the time when divorces were most frequent among the Romans, marriages were most rare; and Augustus was obliged, by penal laws, to force men of fashion into the married state: A circumstance which is scarcely to be found in any other age or nation. The more ancient laws of Rome, which prohibited divorces, are extremely praised by Dionysius Halycarnassaeus. Wonderful was the harmony, says the historian, which this inseparable union of interests produced between married persons; while each of them considered the inevitable necessity by which they were linked together, and abandoned all prospect of any other choice or establishment.

The exclusion of polygamy and divorces sufficiently recommends our present European practice with regard to marriage.

❖   ❖   ❖

DAVID HUME   'Of Chastity and Modesty'

If any difficulty attend this system concerning the laws of nature and nations, 'twill be with regard to the universal approbation or blame, which follows their observance or transgression, and which some may not think sufficiently explain'd from the general interests of society. To remove, as far as possible, all scruples of this kind, I shall here consider another set of duties, *viz.* the *modesty* and *chastity* which belong to the fair sex: And I doubt not but these virtues will be found to be still more conspicuous instances of the operation of those principles, which I have insisted on.

There are some philosophers, who attack the female virtues with great vehemence, and fancy they have gone very far in detecting popular errors, when they can show, that there is no foundation in nature for all that exterior modesty, which we require in the expressions, and dress, and behaviour of the fair sex. I believe I may spare myself the trouble of insisting on so obvious a subject, and may proceed, without farther preparation, to examine after what manner such notions arise from education, from the voluntary conventions of men, and from the interest of society.

Whoever considers the length and feebleness of human infancy, with the concern which both sexes naturally have for their offspring, will easily perceive, that there must be an union of male and female for the education of the young, and that this union must be of considerable duration. But in order to induce the men to impose on themselves this restraint, and undergo cheerfully all the fatigues and expences, to which it subjects them, they must believe, that the children are their own, and that their natural instinct is not directed to a wrong object, when they give a loose to love and tenderness. Now if we examine the structure of the human body, we shall find, that this security is very difficult to be attain'd on our part; and that since, in the copulation of the sexes, the principle of generation goes from the man to the woman, an error may easily take place on the side of the former, tho' it be utterly impossible with regard to the latter. From this trivial and anatomical observation is deriv'd that vast difference betwixt the education and duties of the two sexes.

Were a philosopher to examine the matter *a priori*, he would reason after the following manner. Men are induc'd to labour for the maintenance and education of their children, by the persuasion that they are really their own; and therefore 'tis reasonable, and even necessary, to give them some security in this particular. This security cannot consist entirely in the imposing of severe punishments on any transgressions of conjugal fidelity on the part of the wife; since these public punishments cannot be inflicted without legal proof, which 'tis difficult to meet with in this subject. What restraint, therefore, shall we impose on women, in order to counterbalance so strong a temptation as they have to infidelity? There seems to be no restraint possible, but in the punishment of bad fame or reputation; a punishment, which has a mighty influence on the human mind, and at the same time is inflicted by the world upon surmises, and conjectures, and proofs, that would never be receiv'd in any court of judicature. In order, therefore, to impose a due restraint on the female sex, we must attach a peculiar degree of shame to their infidelity, above what arises merely from its injustice, and must bestow proportionable praises on their chastity.

But tho' this be a very strong motive to fidelity, our philosopher would quickly discover, that it would not alone be sufficient to that purpose. All human creatures, especially of the female sex, are apt to over-look remote motives in favour of any present temptation: The temptation is here the strongest imaginable: Its approaches are insensible and seducing: And a woman easily finds, or flatters herself she shall find, certain means of securing her reputation, and preventing all the pernicious consequences of her pleasures. 'Tis necessary, therefore, that, beside the infamy attending such licences, there should be some preceding backwardness or dread, which may prevent their first approaches, and may give the female sex a repugnance to all expressions, and postures, and liberties, that have an immediate relation to that enjoyment.

Such would be the reasonings of our speculative philosopher: But I am persuaded, that if he had not a perfect knowledge of human nature, he would be apt to regard them as mere chimerical speculations, and would consider the infamy attending infidelity, and backwardness to all its approaches, as principles that were rather to be wish'd than hop'd for in the world. For what means, would he say, of persuading mankind, that the transgressions of conjugal duty are more infamous than any other kind of injustice, when 'tis evident they are more excusable, upon account of the greatness of the temptation? And what possibility of giving a backwardness to the approaches of a pleasure, to which nature has inspir'd so strong a propensity; and a propensity that 'tis absolutely necessary in the end to comply with, for the support of the species?

But speculative reasonings, which cost so much pains to philosophers, are often form'd by the world naturally, and without reflection: As difficulties, which seem unsurmountable in theory, are easily got over in practice. Those, who have an interest in the fidelity of women, naturally disapprove of their infidelity, and all the approaches to it. Those, who have no interest, are carried along with the stream. Education takes possession of the ductile minds of the fair sex in their infancy. And when a general rule of this kind is once establish'd, men are apt to extend it beyond those principles, from which it first arose. Thus bachelors, however debauch'd, cannot choose but be shock'd with any instance of lewdness or impudence in women. And tho' all these maxims have a plain reference to generation, yet women past child-bearing have no more privilege in this respect, than those who are in the flower of their youth and beauty. Men have undoubtedly an implicit notion, that all those ideas of modesty and decency have a regard to generation; since they impose not the same laws, *with the same force,* on the male sex, where that reason takes not place. The exception is there obvious and extensive, and founded on a remarkable difference, which produces a clear separation and disjunction of ideas. But as the case is not the same with regard to the different ages of women, for this reason, tho' men know, that these notions are founded on the public interest, yet the general rule carries us beyond the original principle, and makes us extend the notions of modesty over the whole sex, from their earliest infancy to their extremest old-age and infirmity.

Courage, which is the point of honour among men, derives its merit, in a great measure, from artifice, as well as the chastity of women; tho' it has also some foundation in nature, as we shall see afterwards.

As to the obligations which the male sex lie under, with regard to chastity, we may observe, that according to the general notions of the world, they bear nearly the same proportion to the obligations of women, as the obligations of the law of nations do to those of the law of nature. 'Tis contrary to the interest of civil society, that men should have an *entire* liberty of indulging their appetites in venereal enjoyment: But as this interest is weaker than in the case of the female sex, the moral obligation, arising from it, must be proportionably weaker. And to prove this we need only appeal to the practice and sentiments of all nations and ages.

❖   ❖   ❖

JEAN-JACQUES ROUSSEAU

The philosophy of Jean-Jacques Rousseau (1712-1778) emphasizes society as the means through which human beings are civilized. Ironically, Rousseau's own disposition, as reported by biographers, was extremely erratic and irascible. However, to dismiss his ideas simply on the basis of his personal flaws is to commit what logicians call the genetic fallacy. We ought instead to follow the example of Mary Wollstonecraft, who distinguished between the man and his ideas, evaluating the latter so as to discern what truth might be contained therein. Rousseau's principal philosophical contribution involves his focus on the individual and liberty, rather than on universal principles or changeless values.

Rousseau's Concept of Human Nature

In his *Discourse on the Origin of Inequality among Men,* Rousseau describes "primitive" man, or man "in the state of nature" as essentially free and good. Freedom, for Rousseau, is *the* fundamental difference between man and brute, more fundamental even than reason or understanding. But freedom is limited the minute an individual becomes socialized. Hence, primitive man is asocial, i.e., indifferent to others. Rousseau pictures such a person

> wandering up and down the forests, without industry, without speech and without hunger, an equal stranger to war and to all ties, neither standing in need of his fellow-creatures nor having any desire to hurt them.

Self-love is another trait of human nature in its primitive state. This is a passion which becomes good or evil according to the circumstances in which it develops. Compassion naturally arises through the extension of self-love to others; it is a virtue contributing to the preservation on the whole species. Conscience, which for Rousseau means a love of order, is an innate principle of justice and virtue, and which also derives from self-love. Egoism should not be identified with self-love, for "in the true state of nature, egoism does not exist."

Gradually, as free individuals claimed private property and required others to respect their ownership, the original natural equality of men disappeared. Rousseau describes the resulting social order as a "sacred right which serves as the basis of all other rights." Within that order *natural* freedom and equality are inevitably lost, but man gains *civil* liberty and equality by freely entering into a social contract. The "general will" defines the limit of civil liberty. Civil equality occurs to the extent that all citizens share the same duties and right. Within society, then, freedom and equality are *relative*, whereas for primitive man they were absolute. Summarily, Rousseau's contrasting concept can be put as follows:

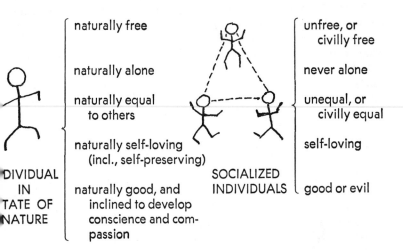

naturally free

naturally alone

naturally equal
   to others

naturally self-loving
   (incl., self-preserving)

naturally good, and
   inclined to develop
   conscience and com-
   passion

INDIVIDUAL
IN
STATE OF
NATURE

unfree, or
   civilly free

never alone

unequal, or
   civilly equal

self-loving

good or evil

SOCIALIZED
INDIVIDUALS

The following selection illustrates Rousseau's philosophy of education. Given the author's essentially positive view of primitive
human nature, the responsibility of the educator is never to impede
but always to facilitate the natural development of the individual.
The task "to form the man of nature" is so comprehensive that a
full-time private tutor is required. Rousseau sees the ideal tutor introducing his student to the best of life's experiences, fostering but
never coercing the growth of virtue and reason. The education of
Sophie is treated only with reference to preparing the ideal mate
for Emile. Sophie represents any woman.

"Marriage" is excerpted from *The Emile of Jean-Jacques Rousseau*, translated by William Boyd.

JEAN-JACQUES ROUSSEAU   'Marriage'

Sophie should be as typically woman as Emile is man. She must
possess all the characteristics of humanity and of womanhood
which she needs for playing her part in the physical and the moral
order. Let us begin by considering in what respects her sex and
ours agree and differ.

In everything that does not relate to sex the woman is as the
man: they are alike in organs, needs and capacities. In whatever
way we look at them the difference is only one of less or more. In
everything that relates to sex there are correspondences and differ-

ences. The difficulty is to determine what in their constitution is due to sex and what is not. All we know with certainty is that the common features are due to the species and the differences to sex. From this twofold point of view we find so many likenesses and so many contrasts that we cannot but marvel that nature has been able to create two beings so much alike with constitutions so different.

The sameness and the difference cannot but have an effect on mentality. This is borne out by experience and shows the futility of discussions about sex superiorities and inequalities. A perfect man and a perfect woman should no more resemble each other in mind than in countenance: and perfection does not admit of degrees.

In the mating of the sexes each contributes in equal measure to the common end but not in the same way. From this diversity comes the *first* difference which has to be noted in their personal relations. It is the part of the one to be active and strong, and of the other to be passive and weak. Accept this principle and it follows in the *second* place that woman is intended to please man. If the man requires to please the woman in turn the necessity is less direct. Masterfulness is his special attribute. He pleases by the very fact that he is strong. This is not the law of love, I admit. But it is the law of nature, which is more ancient than love.

If woman is made to please and to be dominated, she ought to make herself agreeable to man and avoid provocation. Her strength is in her charms and through them she should constrain him to discover his powers and make use of them. The surest way of bringing these powers into active operation is to make it necessary by her resistance.

In this way self-esteem is added to desire and the man triumphs in the victory which the woman has compelled him to achieve. Out of this relation comes attack and defence, boldness on the one side and timidity on the other, and in the end the modesty and sense of shame with which nature has armed the weak for the subjugation of the strong.

Hence as a *third* consequence of the different constitution of the sexes, the stronger may appear to be master, and yet actually be dependent on the weaker: not because of a superficial practice of gallantry or the prideful generosity of the protective sex, but by reason of an enduring law of nature. By giving woman the capacity to stimulate desires greater than can be satisfied, nature has made man dependent on woman's good will and constrained him to seek to please her as a condition of her submission. Always there remains for man in his conquest the pleasing doubt whether strength has mastered weakness, or there has been a willing subjection; and the woman has usually the guile to leave the doubt unresolved.

Men and women are unequally affected by sex. The male is only a male at times; the female is a female all her life and can never forget her sex.

Plato in his *Republic* gives women the same physical training as men. That is what might be expected. Having made an end of private families in his state and not knowing what to do with the women, he found himself compelled to make men of them. That wonderful genius provided for everything in his plans, and went out of his way to meet an objection that nobody was likely to make, while missing the real objection. I am not speaking about the so-called community of wives, so often charged against him by people who have not read him. What I refer to is the social promiscuity which ignored the differences of sex by giving men and women the same occupations, and sacrificed the sweetest sentiments of nature to the artificial sentiment of loyalty which could not exist without them. He did not realise that the bonds of convention always develop from some natural attachment: that the love one has for his neighbours is the basis of his devotion to the state; that the heart is linked with the great fatherland through the little fatherland of the home; that it is the good son, the good husband, the good father, that makes the good citizen.

Once it has been shown that men and women are essentially different in character and temperament, it follows that they ought not to have the same education. In accordance with the direction of nature they ought to co-operate in action, but not to do the same things. To complete the attempt we have been making to form the man of nature, we must now go on to consider how the fitting mate for him is to be formed.

If you want right guidance, always follow the leadings of nature. Everything that characterises sex should be respected as established by nature. Men's pride leads them astray when, comparing women with themselves, they say, as they are continually doing, that women have this or that defect, which is absent in men. What would be defects in men are good qualities in women, which are necessary to make things go on well. Women on their side never stop complaining that we men make coquettes of them and keep amusing them with trifles in order to maintain our ascendency. What a foolish idea! When have men ever had to do with the education of girls? Who prevents the mother bringing up their daughters as they please? Are we men to blame if girls please us by their beauty and attract us by the art they have learned from their mothers? Well, try to educate them like men. They will be quite willing. But the more they resemble men the less will be their power over men, and the greater their own subjection.

The faculties common to the sexes are not equally shared between them; but take them all in all, they are well balanced. The more womanly a woman is, the better. Whenever she exercises her own proper powers she gains by it: when she tries to usurp ours she becomes our inferior. Believe me, wise mother, it is a mistake to bring up your daughter to be like a good man. Make her a good woman, and you can be sure that she will be worth more for herself and for us. This does not mean that she should be brought up in utter ignorance and confined to domestic tasks. A man does not want to make his companion a servant and deprive himself of the peculiar charms of her company. That is quite against the teaching of nature, which has endowed women with quick pleasing minds. Nature means them to think, to judge, to love, to know and to cultivate the mind as well as the countenance. This is the equipment nature has given them to compensate for their lack of strength and enable them to direct the strength of men.

As I see it, the special functions of women, their inclinations and their duties, combine to suggest the kind of education they require. Men and women are made for each other but they differ in the measure of their dependence on each other. We could get on better without women than women could get on without us. To play their part in life they must earn our esteem. By the very law of nature women are at the mercy of men's judgments both for themselves and for their children. It is not enough that they should be estimable: they must be esteemed. It is not enough that they should be beautiful: they must be pleasing. It is not enough that they should be wise: their wisdom must be recognised. Their honour does not rest on their conduct but on their reputation. Hence the kind of education they get should be the very opposite of men's in this respect. Public opinion is the tomb of a man's virtue by the throne of a woman's.

On the good constitution of the mothers depends that of the children and the early education of men is in their hands. On women too depend the morals, the passions, the tastes, the pleasures, aye and the happiness of men. For this reason their education must be wholly directed to their relations with men. To give them pleasure, to be useful to them, to win their love and esteem, to train them in their childhood, to care for them when they grow up, to give them counsel and consolation, to make life sweet and agreeable for them: these are the tasks of women in all times for which they should be trained from childhood.

TRAINING FOR WOMANHOOD
(1) TO THE AGE OF TEN

From the beginning little girls are fond of dress. Not content with being pretty they want notice taken of them. It is evident from their little airs that they have already got this concern. Almost as

soon as they can understand what is said to them they can be controlled by telling them what people think of them. It would be
foolish to speak that way to little boys and it would not have the
same effect. Provided they are left free to enjoy their games boys
care very little about what anybody thinks of them. It takes much
time and effort to bring them under the same control.

However girls get this first lesson, it is a very good one. The
body, one might say is born before the mind and for that reason
must be trained first. That applies to both sexes but with a difference. In the boys the object of the training is the development of
strength, in the girls the development of graces. Not that these
qualities should be confined to one sex or the other but that they
should differ in the importance attached to them. Women should
have enough strength to do all they have to do gracefully: men
enough skill to do what they have to do with ease.

Excessive softness in women makes men soft. They should not be
sturdy like men but for them, so that they may be the mothers of
sturdy males. From this point of view convents and boarding
schools where the children get homely food and can run about and
play freely in the open air and garden are preferable to the home
where a delicately nurtured girl, always seated in a stuffy room
under her mother's eye, dare not get up to walk or talk or breathe
and is never free for a moment to jump or run or shout or give way
to the natural petulance of her age. This is against all reason. It
can only result in the ruin of both heart and body.

Everything that checks and constrains nature is in bad taste. This
applies to the finery that bedecks the body as much as to the ornaments of the mind. Life, health, sanity, comfort ought to come first.
There can be no grace without freedom and no charm in languor
and illness. Suffering excites pity but it is the bloom of health that
gives pleasure and delight.

Children of the two sexes have many amusements in common,
and that is right since it will be the same when they grow up. But
they have also distinctive tastes. Boys like movement and noise:
their toys are drums, tops and go-carts. Girls would rather have
things that look well and serve for adornment: mirrors, jewels,
dress materials and most of all dolls. The doll is the special plaything of the sex. Here the girls' liking is plainly directed towards
her lifework. For her the art of pleasing finds its physical expression
in dress. That is all a child can acquire of this art.

Look at the little girl, busy with her doll all day long, changing
its trappings, dressing and undressing it hundreds of times, always
on the outlook for new ways of decoration whether good or bad.
Her fingers are clumsy and her taste unformed, but already her
bent is evident. 'But,' you may say, 'she is dressing her doll, not
herself.' No doubt! The fact is that she sees her doll and not herself.

For the time being she herself does not matter. She is absorbed in the doll and her coquetry is expressed through it. But the time will come when she will be her own doll.

Here then right at the beginning is a well-marked taste. You have only to follow it up and give it direction. What the little one wishes most of all is to decorate her doll, to make bows, tippets, sashes, lacework for it. In all this she has to depend on the good will of others for help and it would be more convenient in every way if she could do it herself. Here is a motive for the first lessons given to her. They are not tasks prescribed for her but favours conferred. As a matter of fact nearly all little girls greatly dislike learning to read and write but they are always willing to learn to use the needle. They imagine themselves grown up and think happily of the time when they will be using their talents in adorning themselves.

The first open road is easy to follow. Tapestry which is the amusement of women is not much to the liking of girls, and furnishings, having nothing to do with the person, are remote from their interests. But needlework, embroidery and lacemaking come readily to them. The same willing progress leads on easily to drawing, for this art is not unrelated to that of dressing one's self with good taste. I would not have girls taught to draw landscape or to do figure painting. It will be enough if they draw leaves, flowers, fruit, draperies, anything that can add to the elegance of dress and enable them to make their own embroidery patterns. If it is important for men to confine their studies in the main to everyday knowledge, it is even more important for women whose way of life, though less laborious, does not permit them to devote themselves to the talent of their choice at the expense of their duties.

Whatever the humorists may say, good sense is common to the two sexes. Girls are generally more docile than boys and in any case have more need to be brought under authority. But this does not mean that they should be required to do things without seeing the use of them. The maternal art is to make evident the purpose of everything that is prescribed to them; and this is all the easier to do since the girl's intelligence is more precocious than the boy's. This principle excludes for both boys and girls not only studies which serve no obvious purpose but even those which only become useful at a later stage. If it is wrong to urge a boy to learn to read it is even worse to compel little girls to do so before making them realise the value of reading. After all what need have girls to read and write at an early age? They are not going to have a household to manage for a long time to come. All of them have curiosity enough to make sure that they will learn without compulsion when leisure and the occasion come. Possibly they should learn to count first of all.

Counting has an obvious utility at all stages and much practice is required to avoid errors in calculation. I guarantee that if a little girl does not get cherries at tea-time till she has performed some arithmetical exercise she will very soon learn to count.

Always justify the tasks you impose on young girls but impose them all the same. Idleness and indocility are their most dangerous faults and are most difficult to cure once they are contracted. Not only should girls be careful and industrious but they should be kept under control from an early age. This hardship, if it be a hardship, is inseparable from their sex. All their lives they will be under the hard, unceasing constraints of the proprieties. They must be disciplined to endure them till they come to take them as a matter of course and learn to overcome caprice and bow to authority. If they are inclined to be always busy they should sometimes be compelled to do nothing whatever. To save them from dissipation, caprice and fickleness they must learn above all to master themselves.

Do not let girls get bored with their occupations and turn too keen on their amusements, as happens in the ordinary education where, as Fénelon says, all the bordeom is on the one side and all the pleasure on the other. A girl will only be bored with her tasks if she gets on badly with the people around her. A little one who loves her mother or some darling friend will work in their company day in and day out and never become tired. The constraint put on the child, so far from weakening the affection she has for her mother, will make it stronger; for dependence is a state natural to women, and girls realise that they are made for obedience.

And just because they have, or ought to have, little freedom, they carry the freedom they have to excess. Extreme in all things, they devote themselves to their play with greater zeal than boys. This is the second defect. This zeal must be kept within bounds. It is the cause of several vices peculiar to women, among others the capricious changing of their tastes from day to day. Do not deprive them of mirth, laughter, noise and romping games, but prevent them tiring of one game and turning to another. They must get used to being stopped in the middle of their play and put to other tasks without protest on their part. This daily constraint will produce the docility that women need all their lives. The first and most important quality of a woman is sweetness. Being destined to obey a being so imperfect as man (often with many vices and always with many shortcomings), she must learn to submit uncomplainingly to unjust treatment and marital wrongs. Not for his sake but for her own she must preserve her sweetness.

Girls should always be submissive, but mothers should not always be inexorable. To make a young person docile there is no call to make her unhappy. Indeed I should not be sorry if sometimes she were allowed to exercise a little cunning, not to elude punishment but to escape having to obey. Guile is a natural gift of her sex; and being convinced that all natural dispositions are good and right in themselves I think that this one should be cultivated like the rest. The characteristic cunning with which women are endowed is an equitable compensation for their lesser strength. Without it women would not be the comrade of man but his slave. This talent gives her the superiority that keeps her his equal and enables her to rule him even while she obeys.

TRAINING FOR WOMANHOOD
(2) AFTER THE AGE OF TEN

Fine dress may make a woman outstanding, but it is only the person herself that pleases. The attire that is least noticeable often makes its wearer most noticed. The education of young girls in this respect is utterly wrong. They are promised ornaments for rewards, and taught to love gorgeous apparel. 'How beautiful she is,' people say when a girl is all dressed up. This is quite wrong. Girls should learn that so much finery is only put on to hide defects, and that the triumph of beauty is to shine by itself. If I saw a young girl strutting like a peacock in gay garments I should show myself disturbed by this disguising of her figure. I should remark: 'What a pity she is so over-dressed. Do you not think she could do with something simpler? Is she pretty enough to dispense with this or that?' Perhaps she would then be the first to want the ornamentation removed so that she might be judged on her merits.

The first thing that young persons notice as they grow up is that external adornment is not enough, if they lack accomplishments of their own. They cannot make themselves beautiful, and it is too soon for them to play the coquette; but they are old enough to have graceful gestures, an attractive accent, a self-possessed bearing, a light step, and gracious manners. At this stage the voice improves in range, strength and tone, the arms develop, the movements become more confident; and with all this comes the discovery that there is an art by which they can win attention in any situation. From this point sewing and industry no longer suffice of themselves. New talents make their appearance and their usefulness is recognised.

I know that austere teachers are against teaching girls singing or dancing or any of the arts of pleasing. Secular songs, they say, are wicked. Dancing is an invention of the devil. A young girl should find entertainment enough in work and prayer. Strange entertainments these for a child of ten! For my part I greatly fear that the little saints who have been compelled to spend their childhood in prayer will occupy their youth in quite different ways and make up for what they missed in girlhood when they marry. We should consider what befits age as well as befits sex. A young girl should not live like her grandmother. She should be lively and merry. She should dance and sing as much as she likes and enjoy all the innocent pleasures of her age. . . .

The question is sometimes raised whether girls should be taught by masters or mistresses. Personally I would rather they had no need for either but should learn of themselves what they are strongly inclined to learn. In the arts which have pleasure as their object anyone can teach a young girl—father or mother, sister or brother, girl friends, governesses, her mirror, above all her own taste. Taste is formed by industry and the natural gifts. By its means the mind is gradually opened to the idea of beauty in all its forms, and ultimately to those moral notions allied to beauty. This is perhaps one reason why the sentiments of decency and propriety are acquired by girls sooner than by boys. They certainly do not come from their governesses.

The art of speech takes first place among the pleasing arts. It is the mind with its succession of feelings and ideas that imparts life and variety to the countenance and inspires the talk that keeps the attention fixed on one object. That, I believe, is why young girls so quickly learn to chatter agreeably and put expression into their talk, even before they feel it. And that is why men find it amusing to listen to them so soon: they are waiting for the first gleam of intelligence to break through feeling.

The chatter of girls should not be curbed by the hard question that one puts to boys: 'What's the good of that?' but rather by the other question that is no more easy to answer: 'What will be the effect of that?' In the early years before they can distinguish good and evil, or pass judgment on other people, girls should make it a rule for themselves to say only agreeable things to those with whom they are talking. What makes this rule difficult in practice is that it must always be kept subordinate to our first rule: 'Never tell a lie.'

It is obvious that if male children cannot form any true idea of religion it is still more beyond the comprehension of girls. For that very reason I would speak to them about it at an earlier age, for if it were necessary to wait till they were able to discuss these profound questions the chances are that they would never be mentioned at all. Just as a woman's conduct is subject to public opinion, so is her faith subject to authority. Every girl should have her mother's religion, and every woman her husband's. Not being able to judge for themselves in such matters, they should accept the conviction of fathers and husbands as they accept that of the church. . . .

It is of less consequence that girls should learn their religion young than that they should learn it well and still more that they love it. If you make it onerous and are always depicting God as angry with them, if in His name you impose on them a great many disagreeable duties which they never see you fulfil yourself, what can they think but that learning the catechism and praying to God are duties for little girls and will wish to be grown up like you to escape this obligation? Example is all important. Without it you will never make any impression on children.

When you explain the articles of faith let it be in the form of direct instruction and not by question and answer. Girls should only answer what they think themselves and not what has been prescribed for them. . . .

[M]etaphysical questions are not for a little girl to answer. . . . Don't make your girls theologians and dialecticians. Accustom them to feel themselves always under the eyes of God, and to live as they will be glad to have lived when they appear before Him. That is the true religion, the only one incapable of abuse, impiety or fanaticism. . . .

It is well to keep in mind that up to the age when reason becomes active and the growth of sentiment makes conscience speak, good or bad for young women is only what those around them so regard. What they are told to do is good: what they are forbidden is bad. That is all they have to know. From this it is evident how important is the choice of those who are to be with them and exercise authority over them, even more than in the case of boys. But in due course the moment will come when they begin to form their own judgment and then the plan of their education must be changed. We cannot leave them with social prejudices as the only law of their lives. For all human beings there is a rule of conduct which comes before public opinion. All other rules are subject to the inflexible direction of this rule. Even prejudices must be judged by it, and it is only in so far as the values of men are in accord with it that they are entitled to have authority over us. This rule is conscience, the inner conviction (*sentiment*). Unless the two rules are in concord in women's education, it is bound to be defective. Personal conviction without regard for public opinion will fail to give them that fineness of soul which puts the hallmark of worldly honour on good conduct; and public opinion lacking personal conviction will only make false, dishonest women with a sham virtue. For the co-ordination of the two guides to right living, women need to cultivate a faculty to arbitrate between them, to prevent conscience going astray on the one hand and correct the errors of prejudice on the other. This faculty is reason. But at the mention of reason all sorts of questions arise. Are women capable of sound reasoning? It is necessary for them to cultivate it? If they do cultivate it, will it be of any use to them in the functions imposed on them? Is it compatible with a becoming simplicity?

The reason that brings a man to a knowledge of his duties is not very complex. The reason that brings a woman to hers is simpler still. The obedience and loyalty she owes to her husband and the tender care she owes her children are such obvious and natural consequences of her position that she cannot without bad faith refuse to listen to the inner sentiment which is her guide, nor fail to recognise her duty in her natural inclination. Since she depends on her own conscience and on the opinion of other people she must learn to compare and harmonise the two rules. This can best be done by cultivating her understanding and her reason.

SOPHIE
The Outcome of the Right Education

Let us now look at the picture of Sophie which has been put before Emile, the image he has of the woman who can make him happy.

Sophie is well born and has a good natural disposition. She has a feeling heart which sometimes makes her imagination difficult to control. Her mind is acute rather than precise: her temper easy but variable; her person ordinary but pleasing. Her countenance gives indication of a soul—with truth. Some girls have good qualities she lacks and others have the qualities she possesses in fuller measure; but none has these qualities better combined in a happy character. Without being very striking, she interests and charms, and it is difficult to say why.

Sophie is fond of dress and has taste enough to dress well. She dislikes rich clothes and her own always combine simplicity with elegance. She does not know which are the fashionable colours, but she knows to perfection those that suit herself. No girl gives less sign of careful dressing and yet no piece of hers has been selected casually. Her dress is modest in appearance but coquettish in effect. She does not display her charms, but hides them in such a way as to appeal to the imagination.

Sophie has natural talents. She is aware of them and has not neglected them. But not having been in a position to give much thought to their cultivation, she has been content to exercise her sweet voice in singing with truth and taste, and her little feet in walking with an easy grace. She has had no singing teacher but her father, and no dancing mistress but her mother. A neighbouring organist has given her a few lessons in playing accompaniments on the harpsichord, which she has practised alone. But music for her is a taste rather than a talent, and she cannot play a tune by note.

What Sophie knows best and has been most carefully taught are the tasks of her own sex, even those like dressmaking, not usually thought necessary. There is no kind of needlework she cannot do, but she has a special preference for lace-making because it calls for a pleasing pose, as well as grace and lightness in the fingers. She has also applied herself to all the details of the household. She understands cookery and kitchen work. She knows the prices of provisions and can judge their qualities. She can keep accounts and is her mother's housekeeper. At the same time, she does not take equal pleasure in all her duties. For example, though she likes nice food she is not fond of cooking, and is rather disgusted with some of its details. For the same reason she has always been unwilling to inspect the garden. The soil seems to her dirty, and when she sees the dunghill she imagines she feels a smell. This defect she owes to her mother, according to whom cleanliness is one of the first obligations imposed on a woman by nature. The result is that cleaning takes up an undue amount of Sophie's time.

Sophie's mind is pleasing but not brilliant, solid but not deep. She has always something attractive to say to those who talk with her, but lacks the conversational adornments we associate with cultured women. Her mind has been formed, not only by reading but by conversation with her father and mother and by her own reflections on the little bit of the world she has seen. She is too sensitive to preserve a perfect evenness of temper, but too sweet to allow this to be troublesome to other people. It is only herself that is hurt.

She is religious, but her religion is reasonable and simple, with few dogmas and still fewer observances. The essential observance for her is morality, and she devotes her life to the service of God by doing good. In all the instructions they have given her on this subject her parents have accustomed her to a respectful submission. 'My daughter,' they say to her, 'this knowledge is not for one of your age. When the time comes your husband will instruct you.' Apart from that, they are content to dispense with long pious talks, and only preach to her by their example.

The love of virtue is her ruling passion. She loves virtue, because it is the glory of a woman and the only road to true happiness; because, also, it is dear to her respected father and her tender mother. These sentiments inspire her with an enthusiasm that uplifts the soul and keeps all her young inclinations in subjection to the noble passion for virtue. She will be chaste and good till her last breath. . . .

A pupil of nature like Emile, she is better suited for him than any other woman. She is indeed his woman, his equal in birth and merit, his inferior in fortune. Her special charm only reveals itself gradually, as one comes to know her, and her husband will appreciate it more than anyone. Her education is in no way exceptional. She has taste without study, talents without art, judgment without knowledge. Her mind is still vacant but has been trained to learn: it is well-tilled land only waiting for the grain. What a pleasing ignorance! Happy is the man destined to instruct her. She will be her husband's disciple, not his teacher. Far from wanting to impose her tastes on him, she will share his. . . .

'My children,' I say to them as I take them both by the hand, . . . 'I have often thought that if it were possible to prolong the happiness of love in marriage we would have a heaven on earth. Would you like me to tell you what in my belief is the only way to secure that?' . . . 'It is to go on being lovers after you are married.' . . . 'Knots which are too tightly drawn break. That is what happens to the marriage tie when too great a strain is put on it. The faithfulness required of a married couple is the most sacred of all obligations but the power it gives one partner over the other is too great. Constraint and love go ill together, and the pleasures of marriage are not to be had on demand. It is impossible to make a duty of tender affection and to treat the sweetest pledges of love as a right. What right there is comes from mutual desire: nature knows no other. Neither belongs to the other except by his or her own good will. Both must remain master of their persons and their caresses.

'When Emile became your husband, Sophie, he became your head and by the will of nature you owe him obedience. But when the wife is like you it is good for the husband to be guided by her: that is also the law of nature and it gives you as much authority over his heart as his sex gives him over your person. Make yourself dear to him by your favours and respected by your refusals. On these terms you will get his confidence; he will listen to your advice and settle nothing without consulting you. After love has lasted a considerable time a sweet habit takes its place, and the attraction of confidence succeeds the transports of passion. When you cease to be Emile's mistress you will be his wife and sweetheart and the mother of his children, and you will enjoy the closest intimacy. Remember that if your husband lives happily with you, you will be a happy woman.'

'Dear Emile,' I say to the young husband, 'all through life a man has need of a counsellor and guide. . . . From this time on, Sophie is your tutor.'

*   *   *

IMMANUEL KANT

Although the life style of Immanuel Kant (1724–1804) was conservative and uneventful, his *Weltanschauung* (world view) was a radical and thoroughly systematic innovation in philosophy. In developing his transcendental idealism, he assimilated the fundamental emphases of both the rationalist and empiricist schools that preceded him. Basically, Kant distinguished between noumena or things-in-themselves, and phenomena or things-as-they-appear. Since experience is the only source of our knowledge, the phenomena or appearances are all that we know, while the noumena or the reality beyond appearance remain unknowable. We may make valid claims about reality, but these are postulates rather than certain judgments. The three fundamental ideas of reality which reason continually attempts to fathom are God, freedom, and immortality. Of these, freedom is the only idea whose corresponding reality can be known through experience (the experience of obligation provokes an awareness of freedom as the condition for our obligation); and even then, Kant maintains we can know *that* freedom is without knowing *what* it is.

The philosophy of Kant is elaborated most completely and clearly in his critical writings (mainly, his *Critique of Pure Reason, Critique of Practical Reason,* and *Critique of Judgment*), which were written later than the selection that follows. However, while the *Critiques* represent a difference in style, method and content, they never contradict Kant's basic claims in the *Observations on the Feeling of the Beautiful and Sublime.*

Kant's Concept of Human Nature

For Kant, the only unconditioned good is the good will residing within a person. It is conditionless because its decisions are universalizable, which means that the goods chosen are intended to hold for all individuals. This leads to Kant's famous "categorical imperative": to act in whatever way you would will anyone in your situation to act. Persons ought always to be treated as ends in themselves, and never merely as means.

As its title implies, the *Observations* was never intended as an exhaustive systematic study of human nature. Nonetheless, its second section treats "Of the Attributes of the Beautiful and Sublime in Man in General." The two attributes refer to the chief kinds of finer human feelings. The "sublime" is that which arouses esteem and admiration; it is always great and simple. In contrast, the "beautiful" arouses love and joy; it may be small or ornamented. The sublime may be terrifying, noble, or splendid; the beautiful may be merely pretty (outwardly only), or properly beautiful (internally and externally). The sight of a snow-covered mountain peak is sublime; the sight of a flower-strewn meadow is beautiful.

Individuals are both beautiful and sublime. A melancholy person generally is more sublime in his make-up, while a sanguine person is more beautiful; a choleric person has the appearance rather than the substance of sublimity, while a phlegmatic person has neither attribute to a discernible degree. "Friendship," claims Kant, "has mainly the character of the sublime, but love between the sexes, that of the beautiful." The interplay between the two attributes affects the moral component of individual and social life.

"Of the Distinction of the Beautiful and Sublime in the Interrelations of the Two Sexes" is Section Three of *Observations on the Feeling of the Beautiful and Sublime*," translated by John T. Goldthwait.

IMMANUEL KANT 'Of the Distinction of the Beautiful and Sublime in the Interrelations of the Two Sexes'

He who first conceived of woman under the name of the *fair sex* probably wanted to say something flattering, but he has hit upon it better than even he himself might have believed. For without taking into consideration that her figure in general is finer, her features more delicate and gentler, and her mien more engaging and more expressive of friendliness, pleasantry, and kindness than in the male sex, and not forgetting what one must reckon as a secret magic with which she makes our passion inclined to judgments favorable to her—even so, certain specific traits lie especially in the personality of this sex which distinguish it clearly from ours and chiefly result in making her known by the mark of the beautiful. On the other side, we could make a claim on the title of the *noble sex*, if it were not required of a noble disposition to decline honorific titles and rather to bestow than to receive them. It is not to be understood by this that woman lacks noble qualities, or that the male sex must do without beauty completely. On the contrary, one expects that a person of either sex brings both together, in such a way that all the other merits of a woman should unite solely to enhance the character of the beautiful, which is the proper reference point; and on the other hand, among the masculine qualities the sublime clearly stands out as the criterion of his kind. All judgments of the two sexes must refer to these criteria, those that praise as well as those that blame; all education and instruction must have these before its eyes, and all efforts to advance the moral perfection of the one or the other—unless one wants to disguise the charming distinction that nature has chosen to make between the two sorts of human being. For here it is not enough to keep in mind that we are dealing with human beings; we must also remember that they are not all alike.

Women have a strong inborn feeling for all that is beautiful, elegant, and decorated. Even in childhood they like to be dressed up, and take pleasure when they are adorned. They are cleanly and very delicate in respect to all that provokes disgust. They love pleasantry and can be entertained by trivialities if only these are merry and laughing. Very early they have a modest manner about themselves, know how to give themselves a fine demeanor and be self-possessed—and this at an age when our well-bred male youth is still unruly, clumsy, and confused. They have many sympathetic sensations, good-heartedness, and compassion, prefer the beautiful to the useful, and gladly turn abundance of circumstance into parsimony, in order to support expenditure on adornment and glitter. They have very delicate feelings in regard to the least offense, and are exceedingly precise to notice the most trifling lack of attention and respect toward them. In short, they contain the chief cause in human nature for the contrast of the beautiful qualities with the noble, and they refine even the masculine sex.

I hope the reader will spare me the reckoning of the manly qualities, so far as they are parallel to the feminine, and be content only to consider both in comparison with each other. The fair sex has just as much understanding as the male, but it is a *beautiful understanding*, whereas ours should be a *deep understanding*, an expression that signifies identity with the sublime.

To the beauty of all actions belongs above all the mark that they display facility, and appear to be accomplished without painful toil. On the other hand, strivings and surmounted difficulties arouse admiration and belong to the sublime. Deep meditation and a long-sustained reflection are noble but difficult, and do not well befit a person in whom unconstrained charms should show nothing else than a beautiful nature. Laborious learning or painful pondering, even if a woman should greatly succeed in it, destroy the merits that are proper to her sex, and because of their rarity they can make of her an object of cold admiration; but at the same time they will weaken the charms with which she exercises her great power over the other sex. A woman who has a head full of Greek . . . or carries on fundamental controversies about mechanics . . . might as well even have a beard; for perhaps that would express more obviously the mien of profundity for which she strives. The beautiful understanding selects for its objects everything closely related to the finer feeling, and relinquishes to the diligent, fundamental, and deep understanding abstract speculations or branches of knowledge useful but dry. A woman therefore will learn no geometry; of the principle of sufficient reason or the monads she will know only so much as is needed to perceive the salt in a satire which the insipid grubs of our sex have censured. The fair can leave Descartes his vortices to whirl forever without troubling themselves about them. . . . In history they will not fill their heads with battles, nor in geography with fortresses, for it becomes them just as little to reek of gunpowder as it does the males to reek of musk.

It appears to be a malicious stratagem of men that they have wanted to influence the fair sex to this perverted taste. For, well aware of their weakness before her natural charms and of the fact that a single sly glance sets them more in confusion than the most difficult problem of science, so soon as woman enters upon this taste they see themselves in a decided superiority and are at an advantage that otherwise they hardly would have, being able to succor their vanity in its weakness by a generous indulgence toward her. The content of woman's great science, rather, is humankind, and among humanity, men. Her philosophy is not to reason, but to sense. In the opportunity that one wants to give to women to cultivate their beautiful nature, one must always keep this relation before his eyes. One will seek to broaden their total moral feeling and not their memory, and that of course not by universal rules but by some judgment upon the conduct that they see about them. The examples one borrows from other times in order to examine the influence the fair sex has had in culture, the various relations to the masculine in which it has stood in other ages or in foreign lands, the character of both so far as it can be illustrated by these, and the changing taste in amusements—these comprise her whole history and geography. For the ladies, it is well to make it a pleasant diversion to see a map setting forth the entire globe or the principal parts of the world. This is brought about by showing it only with the intention of portraying the different characters of peoples that dwell there, and the differences of their taste and moral feeling, especially in respect to the effect these have upon the relations of the sexes—together with a few easy illustrations taken from the differences of their climates, or their freedom or slavery. It is of little consequence whether or not the women know the particular subdivisions of these lands, their industry, power, and sovereigns. Similarly, they will need to know nothing more of the cosmos than is necessary to make the appearance of the heavens on a beautiful evening a stimulating sight to them, if they can conceive to some extent that yet more worlds, and in them yet more beautiful creatures, are to be found. Feeling for expressive painting and for music, not so far as it manifests artistry but sensitivity—all this refines or elevates the taste of this sex, and always has some connection with moral impulses. Never a cold and speculative instruction but always feelings and those indeed which remain as close as possible to the situation of her sex. Such instruction is very rare because it demands talents, experience, and a heart full of feeling;

and a woman can do very well without any other, as in fact without this she usually develops very well by her own efforts.

The virtue of a woman is a *beautiful virtue.* That of the male sex should be a *noble virtue.* Women will avoid the wicked not because it is unright, but because it is ugly; and virtuous actions mean to them such as are morally beautiful. Nothing of duty, nothing of compulsion, nothing of obligation! Woman is intolerant of all commands and all morose constraint. They do something only because it pleases them, and the art consists in making only that please them which is good. I hardly believe that the fair sex is capable of principles, and I hope by that not to offend, for these are also extremely rare in the male. But in place of it Providence has put in their breast kind and benevolent sensations, a fine feeling for propriety, and a complaisant soul. One should not at all demand sacrifices and generous self-restraint. A man must never tell his wife if he risks a part of his fortune on behalf of a friend. Why should he fetter her merry talkativeness by burdening her mind with a weighty secret whose keeping lies solely upon him? Even many of her weaknesses are, so to speak, *beautiful faults.* Offense or misfortune moves her tender soul to sadness. A man must never weep other than magnanimous tears. Those he sheds in pain or over circumstances of fortune make him contemptible. *Vanity,* for which one reproaches the fair sex so frequently, so far as it is a fault in that sex, yet is only a beautiful fault. For—not to mention that the men who so gladly flatter a woman would be left in a strait if she were not inclined to take it well—by that they actually enliven their charms. This inclination is an impulsion to exhibit pleasantness and good demeanor, to let her merry wit play, to radiate through the changing devices of dress, and to heighten her beauty. Now in this there is not at all any offensiveness toward others, but rather so much courtesy, if it is done with good taste, that to scold against it with peevish rebukes is very ill-bred. A woman who is too inconstant and deceitful is called a coquette; which expression yet has not so harsh a meaning as what, with a changed syllable, is applied to man, so that if we understand each other, it can sometimes indicate a familiar flattery. If vanity is a fault that in a woman much merits excuse, a *haughty bearing* is not only as reproachable in her as in people in general, but completely disfigures the character of her sex. For this quality is exceedingly stupid and ugly, and is set completely in opposition to her captivating, modest charms. Then such a person is in a slippery position. She will suffer herself to be judged sharply and without any pity; for whoever presumes an esteem invites all around him to rebuke. Each disclosure of even the least fault gives everyone a true joy, and the word *coquette* here loses its mitigated meaning. One must always distinguish between vanity and conceit. The first seeks approbation and to some extent honors those on whose account it gives itself the trouble. The second believes itself already in full possession of approbation, and because it never strives to gain any, it wins none.

If a few ingredients of vanity do not deform a woman in the eyes of the male sex, still, the more apparent they are, the more they serve to divide the fair sex among themselves. Then they judge one another very severely, because the one seems to obscure the charms of the other, and in fact, those who make strong presumptions of conquest actually are seldom friends of one another in a true sense.

Nothing is so much set against the beautiful as disgust, just as nothing sinks deeper beneath the sublime than the ridiculous. On this account no insult can be more painful to a man than being called a *fool,* and to a woman, than being called *disgusting.* The English *Spectator* maintains that no more insulting reproach could be made to a man than if he is considered a liar, and to a woman none more bitter than if she is held unchaste. I will leave this for what it is worth so far as it is judged according to strictness in morals. But here the question is not what of itself deserves the greatest rebuke, but what is actually felt as the harshest of all. And to that point I ask every reader whether, when he sets himself to thinking upon this matter, he must not assent to my opinion. . . .

[N]*eatness,* which of course well becomes any person, in the fair sex belongs among the virtues of first rank and can hardly be pushed too high among them, although in a man it sometimes rises to excess and then becomes trifling.

Sensitivity to *shame* is a secrecy of nature addressed to setting bounds to a very intractable inclination, and since it has the voice of nature on its side, seems always to agree with good moral qualities even if it yields to excess. Hence it is most needed, as a supplement to principles, for there is no instance in which inclination is so ready to turn Sophist, subtly to devise complaisant principles, as in this. But at the same time it serves to draw a curtain of mystery before even the most appropriate and necessary purposes of nature, so that a too familiar acquaintance with them might not occasion disgust, or indifference at least, in respect to the final purpose of an impulse onto which the finest and liveliest inclinations of human nature are grafted. This quality is especially peculiar to the fair sex and very becoming to it. There is also a coarse and contemptible rudeness in putting delicate modesty to embarrassment or annoyance by the sort of vulgar jests called obscenities. However, although one may go as far around the secret as one ever will, the sexual inclination still ultimately underlies all her remaining charms, and a woman, ever as a woman, is the pleasant object of a well-mannered conversation; and this might perhaps explain why otherwise polite men occasionally take the liberty to let certain fine allusions show through, by a little mischief in their jests, which make us call them *loose* or *waggish*. Because they neither affront by searching glances nor intend to injure anyone's esteem, they believe it justified to call the person who receives it with an indignant or brittle mien *a prude*. I mention this practice only because it is generally considered as a somewhat bold trait in polite conversation, and also because in point of fact much wit has been squandered upon it; however, judgment according to moral strictness does not belong here, because what I have to observe and explain in the sensing of the beautiful is only the appearances.

The noble qualities of this sex, which still, as we have already noted, must never disguise the feeling of the beautiful, proclaim themselves by nothing more clearly and surely than by *modesty*, a sort of noble simplicity and innocence in great excellences. Out of it shines a quiet benevolence and respect toward others, linked at the same time with a certain *noble trust* in oneself, and a reasonable self-esteem that is always to be found in a sublime disposition. Since this fine mixture at once captivates by charms and moves by respect, it puts all the remaining shining qualities in security against the mischief of censure and mockery. Persons of this temperament also have a heart for friendship, which is a woman can never be valued highly enough, because it is so rare and moreover must be so exceedingly charming.

As it is our purpose to judge concerning feelings, it cannot be unpleasant to bring under concepts, if possible, the difference of the impression that the form and features of the fair sex make on the masculine. This complete fascination is really overlaid upon the sex instinct. Nature pursues its great purpose, and all refinements that join together, though they may appear to stand as far from that as they will, are only trimmings and borrow their charm ultimately from that very source. A healthy and *coarse taste*, which always stays very close to this impulse, is little tempted by the charms of demeanor, of facial features, of eyes, and so on, in a woman, and because it really pertains only to sex, it oftentimes sees the delicacy of others as empty flirting.

If this taste is not fine, nevertheless it is not on that account to be disdained. For the largest part of mankind complies by means of it with the great order of nature, in a very simple and sure way. Through it the greatest number of marriages are brought about, and indeed by the most diligent part of the human race; and because the man does not have his head full of fascinating expressions, languishing eyes, noble demeanor, and so forth, and understands nothing of all this, he becomes that much the more attentive to householders' virtues, thrift and such, and to the dowry. As for what relates to the somewhat finer taste, one whose account it might be necessary to make a distinction among the exterior charms of women, this is fixed either upon what in the form and the expression of the face is moral, or upon what is non-moral. In respect to the last-named sort of pleasantness, a lady is called *pretty*. A well-proportioned figure, regular features, colors of eyes and face which contrast prettily, beauties pure and simple which are also pleasing in a bouquet and gain a cool approbation. The face itself says nothing, although it is pretty, and speaks not to the heart. What is moral in the expression of the features, the eyes, and mien pertains to the feeling either of the sublime or of the beautiful. A woman in whom the agreeableness beseeming her sex particularly makes manifest the moral expression of the sublime is called *beautiful* in the proper sense; so far as the moral composition makes itself discernible in the mien or facial features, she whose features show qualities of beauty is *agreeable,* and if she is that to a high degree, *charming.* The first, under a mien of composure and a noble demeanor, lets the glimmer of a beautiful understanding play forth through discreet glances, and as in her face she portrays a tender feeling and a benevolent heart, she seizes possession of the affection as well as the esteem of a masculine heart. The second exhibits merriment and wit in laughing eyes, something of fine mischief, the playfulness of jest and sly coyness. She charms, while the first moves; and the feeling of love of which she is capable and which she stimulates in others is fickle but beautiful, whereas the feeling of the first is tender, combined with respect, and constant. I do not want to engage in too detailed an analysis of this sort, for in doing so the author always appears to depict his own inclination. I shall still mention, however, that the liking many women have for a healthy but pale color can be explained here. For this generally accompanies a disposition of more inward feeling and delicate sensation, which belongs to the quality of the sublime; whereas the rosy and blooming complexion proclaims less of the first, but more of the joyful and merry disposition—but it is more suitable to vanity to move and to arrest, than to charm and to attract. On the other hand there can be very pretty persons completely without moral feeling and without any expression that indicates feeling; but they will neither move nor charm, unless it might be the coarse taste of which we have made mention, which sometimes grows somewhat more refined and then also selects after its fashion. It is too bad that this sort of beautiful creatures easily fall into the fault of *conceit,* through the consciousness of the beautiful figure their mirror shows them, and from a lack of finer sensations, for then they make all indifferent to them except the flatterer, who has ulterior motives and contrives intrigues.

Perhaps by following these concepts one can understand something of the different effect the figure of the same woman has upon the tastes of men. I do not concern myself with what in this impression relates too closely to the sex impulse and may be of a piece with the particular sensual illusion with which the feeling of everyone clothes itself, because it lies outside the compass of finer taste. Perhaps . . . the figure that make the first impression, at the time when this impulse is still new and is beginning to develop, remains the pattern all feminine figures in the future must more or less follow so as to be able to stir the fanciful ardor, whereby a rather coarse inclination is compelled to choose among the different objects of a sex. Regarding the somewhat finer taste, I affirm that the sort of beauty we have called the *pretty figure* is judged by all men very much alike, and that opinions about it are not so different as one generally maintains. . . . [I]t appears that, as greatly as the caprice of taste in . . . different quarters of the world may diverge, still, whatever is once known in any of these as especially pretty will also be considered the same in all the others. But whenever what is moral in the features mingles in the judgment upon the fine figure, the taste of different men is always very different, both because their moral feeling itself is dissimilar, and also on account of the different meaning that the expression of the face may have in every fancy. One finds that those formations that at first glance do not have any particular effect, because they are not pretty in any decided way, generally appear far more to captivate and to grow constantly more beautiful as soon as they begin to please upon nearer acquaintance. On the other hand, the pretty appearance that proclaims itself at once is later received with greater indifference. This probably is because moral charms, when they are evident, are all the more arresting because they are set in operation only on the occasion of moral sensations, and let themselves be discovered in this way, each disclosure of a new charm causing one to suspect still more of these; whereas all the agreeable features that do not at all conceal themselves, after exercising their entire effect at the beginning, can subsequently do nothing more than to cool off the enamored curiosity and bring it gradually to indifference. . . .

Finally age, the great destroyer of beauty, threatens all these charms; and if it proceeds according to the natural order of things, gradually the sublime and noble qualities must take the place of the beautiful, in order to make a person always worthy of a greater respect as she ceases to be attractive. In my opinion, the whole perfection of the fair sex in the bloom of years should consist in the beautiful simplicity that has been brought to its height by a refined simplicity that has been brought to its height by a refined feeling toward all that is charming and noble. Gradually, as the claims upon charms diminish, the reading of books and the broadening of insight could refill unnoticed the vacant place of the Graces with the Muses, and the husband should be the first instructor. Nevertheless, when the epoch of growing old, so terrible to every woman, actually approaches, she still belongs to the fair sex, and that sex disfigures itself if in a kind of despair of holding this character longer, it gives way to a surly and irritable mood.

An aged person who attends a gathering with a modest and friendly manner, is sociable in a merry and sensible way, favors with a pleasant demeanor the pleasures of youth in which she herself no longer participates, and, as she looks after everything, manifests contentment and benevolence toward the joys that are going on around her, is yet a finer person than a man of like age and perhaps ever more attractive than a girl, although in another sense. Indeed the platonic love might well be somewhat too mystical, which an ancient philosopher asserted when he said of the object of his inclination, "The Graces reside in her wrinkles, and my soul seems to hover upon my lips when I kiss her withered mouth"; but such claims must be relinquished. An old man who acts infatuated is a fool, and the like presumptions of the other sex at that age are disgusting. It never is due to nature when we do not appear with a good demeanor, but rather to the fact that we turn her upside down.

In order to keep close to my text, I want to undertake a few reflections on the influence one sex can have upon the other, to beautify or ennoble its feeling. Woman has a superior feeling for the beautiful, so far as it pertains to herself; but for the noble, so far as it is encountered in the male sex. Man on the other hand has a decided feeling for the noble, which belongs to his qualities, but for the beautiful, so far as it is to be found in woman. From this it must follow that the purposes of nature are directed still more to ennoble man, by the sexual inclination, and likewise still more to beautify woman. A woman is embarrassed little that she does not possess certain high insights, that she is timid, and not fit for serious employments, and so forth; she is beautiful and captivates, and that is enough. On the other hand, she demands all these qualities in a man, and the sublimity of her soul shows itself only in that she knows to treasure these noble qualities so far as they are found in him. How else indeed would it be possible that so many grotesque male faces, whatever merits they may possess, could gain such well-bred and fine wives! Man on the other hand is much more delicate in respect to the beautiful charms of woman. By their fine figure, merry naiveté, and charming friendliness he is sufficiently repaid for the lack of book learning and for other deficiencies that he must supply by his own talents. Vanity and fashion can give these natural drives a false direction and make out of many a male a *sweet gentleman,* but out of a woman either a prude or an Amazon; but still nature always seeks to reassert her own order. One can thereby judge what powerful influences the sexual inclination could have especially upon the male sex, to ennoble it, if instead of many dry instructions the moral feeling of woman were seasonably developed to sense properly what belongs to the dignity and the sublime qualities of the other sex, and were thus prepared to look upon the trifling fops with disdain and to yield to no other qualities than the merits. It is also certain that the power of her charms on the whole would gain through that; for it is apparent that their fascination for the most part works only upon nobler souls; the others are not fine enough to sense them. Just as the poet Simonides said, when someone advised him to let the Thessalians hear his beautiful songs: "These fellows are too stupid to be beguiled by such a man as I am." It has been regarded moreover as an effect of association with the fair sex that men's customs have become gentler, their conduct more polite and refined, and their bearing more elegant; but the advantage of this is only incidental.[1] The principal object is that the man should become more perfect as a man, and the woman as a wife; that is, that the motives of the sexual inclination work according to the hint of nature, still more to ennoble the one and to beautify the qualities of the other. If all comes to the extreme, the man, confident in his merits, will be able to say: "Even if you do not love me, I will constrain you to esteem me," and the woman, secure in the might of her charms, will answer: "Even if you do not inwardly admire me, I will still constrain you to love me." In default of such principles one sees men take on femininity in order to please, and woman occasionally (although much more seldom) affect a masculine demeanor in order to stimulate esteem; but whatever one does contrary to nature's will, one always does very poorly.

In matrimonial life the united pair should, as it were, constitute a single moral person, which is animated and governed by the understanding of the man and the taste of the wife. For not only can one credit more insight founded on experience to the former, and more freedom and accuracy in sensation to the latter; but also, the more sublime a disposition is, the more inclined it is to place the greatest purpose of its exertions in the contentment of a beloved object, and likewise the more beautiful it is, the more it seeks to requite these exertions by complaisance. In such a relation, then, a dispute over precedence is trifling and, where it occurs, is the surest sign of a coarse or dissimilarly matched taste. If it comes to such a state that the question is of the right of the superior to command, then the case is already utterly corrupted; for where the whole union is in reality erected solely upon inclination, it is already half destroyed as soon as the "duty" begins to make itself

1. This advantage itself is really much reduced by the observation that one will have made, that men who are too early and too frequently introduced into company where women sets the tone generally become somewhat trifling, and in male society they are boring or even contemptible because they have lost the taste for conversation, which must be merry, to be sure, but still of actual content—witty, to be sure, but also useful through its earnest discourse.

heard. The presumption of the woman in this harsh tone is extremely ugly, and of the man is base and contemptible in the highest degree. However, the wise order of things so brings it about that all these niceties and delicacies of feeling have their whole strength only in the beginning, but subsequently gradually become duller through association and domestic concerns, and then degenerate into familiar love. Finally, the great skill consists in still preserving sufficient remainders of those feelings so that indifference and satiety do not put an end to the whole value of the employment on whose account it has solely and alone been worth the trouble to enter such a union.

*   *   *

MARY WOLLSTONECRAFT

The name of Mary Wollstonecraft (1759–1797) is not generally included among the ranks of philosophers. Consequently, it may come as a surprise to someone reading her works for the first time to see how rich an intellectual source they provide. Unlike most philosophers, Wollstonecraft could draw on personal experience in describing the nature and role of woman, but her sex also exerted a limiting influence on her philosophical development. The little informal instruction she received was directed entirely toward fulfilment as a wife and mother. Moreover, she died at an age (38 years, of complications due to childbirth) when many major thinkers have yet to produce their greatest works (Kant's brilliant Critiques, for example, did not appear until he had passed fifty). The marvel is that, despite many obstacles and disadvantages, Wollstonecraft produced twelve books and numerous articles. Apparently, not only her words, but her life contained the ideas she wanted to express.

Wollstonecraft's Concept of Human Nature

Probably the work best calculated to prepare for a reading of the following selection is the earlier *A Vindication of the Rights of Men,* which was written in 1790 as a response to Edmund Burke's *Reflections on the Revolution in France.* Arguing against Burke's concept of rights and their underlying assumptions, Wollstonecraft maintained that

The birthright of man [of humankind, or every individual regardless of sex] . . . is such a degree of liberty, civil and religious, as is compatible with the liberty of every other individual with whom he is united in a social compact. . . . It is necessary emphatically to repeat that there are rights which men inherit at their birth, as rational creatures, who were raised above the brute creation by their improvable faculties; and that, in receiving these, not from their forefathers but, from God, prescription can never undermine natural rights.

In his *Reflections* Burke had claimed that "a woman *is* but an animal, and an animal not of the highest order." Wollstonecraft's reply reveals her critical attitude toward the prevailing ("fashionable") feminine behavior:

> If beautiful weakness be interwoven in a woman's frame, if the chief business of her life be (as you insinuate) to inspire love, and Nature has made an eternal distinction between the qualities that dignify a rational being and this animal perfection, her duty and happiness in this life must clash with any preparation for a more exalted state.

A Vindication of the Rights of Men insists that a different concept of woman is both available and necessary to the liberty of humankind:

> But should experience prove that there is a beauty in virtue, a charm in order, which necessarily implies exertion, a depraved sensual taste may give way to a more manly one—and *melting* feelings to rational satisfactions. Both may be equally natural to man; the test is their moral difference, and that point reason alone can decide.
>
> Such a glorious change can only be produced by liberty. Inequality of rank must ever impede the growth of virtue, by vitiating the mind that submits or domineers; that is ever employed to procure nourishment for the body, or amusement for the mind.

Wollstonecraft's concept of human nature anticipates the utilitarian view of the essential freedom and intelligence of every individual. A situation of unequal rights demeans humanity in general, both those whose share of rights is greater as well as those whose rights are less or none.

The following article is excerpted from *A Vindication of the Rights of Woman*.

MARY
WOLLSTONECRAFT A Vindication of the Rights of Woman

... I shall first consider women in the grand light of human creatures, who, in common with men, are placed on this earth to unfold their faculties; and afterwards I shall more particularly point out their peculiar designation. . . .

My own sex, I hope, will excuse me, if I treat them like rational creatures, instead of flattering their *fascinating* graces, and viewing them as if they were in a state of perpetual childhood, unable to stand alone. I earnestly wish to point out in what true dignity and human happiness consists—I wish to persuade women to endeavour to acquire strength, both of mind and body, and to convince them that the soft phrases, susceptibility of heart, delicacy of sentiment, and refinement of taste, are almost synonymous with epithets of weakness, and that those beings who are only the objects of pity and that kind of love, which has been termed its sister, will soon become objects of contempt.

Dismissing, then, those pretty feminine phrases, which the men condescendingly use to soften our slavish dependence, and despising that weak elegancy of mind, exquisite sensibility, and sweet docility of manners, supposed to be the sexual characteristics of the weaker vessel, I wish to shew that elegance is inferior to virtue, that the first object of laudable ambition is to obtain a character as a human being, regardless of the distinction of sex; and that secondary views should be brought to this simple touchstone.

.   .   .   .

In the present state of society it appears necessary to go back to first principles in search of the most simple truths, and to dispute with some prevailing prejudice every inch of ground. To clear my way, I must be allowed to ask some plain questions, and the answers will probably appear as unequivocal as the axioms on which reasoning is built; though, when entangled with various motives of action, they are formally contradicted, either by the words or conduct of men.

In what does man's pre-eminence over the brute creation consist? The answer is as clear as that a half is less than the whole; in Reason.

What acquirement exalts one being above another? Virtue, we spontaneously reply.

For what purpose were the passions implanted? That man by struggling with them might attain a degree of knowledge denied to the brutes; whispers Experience.

Consequently the perfection of our nature and capability of happiness, must be estimated by the degree of reason, virtue, and knowledge, that distinguish the individual, and direct the laws which bind society: and that from the exercise of reason, knowledge and virtue naturally flow, is equally undeniable, if mankind be viewed collectively.

.   .   .   .

[T]he most perfect education, in my opinion, is such an exercise of the understanding as is best calculated to strengthen the body and form the heart. Or, in other words, to enable the individual to attain such habits of virtue as will render it independent. In fact, it is a farce to call any being virtuous whose virtues do not result from the exercise of its own reason. This was Rousseau's opinion respecting men: I extend it to women, and confidently assert that they have been drawn out of their sphere by false refinement, and not by an endeavour to acquire masculine qualities. Still the regal homage which they receive is so intoxicating, that till the manners of the times are changed, and formed on more reasonable principles, it may be impossible to convince them that the illegitimate power, which they obtain, by degrading themselves, is a curse, and that they must return to nature and equality, if they wish to secure the placid satisfaction that unsophisticated affections impart. But for this epoch we must wait—wait, perhaps, till kings and nobles, enlightened by reason, and, preferring the real dignity of man to childish state, throw off their gaudy hereditary trappings: and if then women do not resign the arbitrary power of beauty—they will prove that they have *less* mind than man.

I may be accused of arrogance; still I must declare what I firmly believe, that all the writers who have written on the subject of female education and manners, from Rousseau to Dr. Gregory, have contributed to render women more artificial, weak characters, than they would otherwise have been; and consequently, more useless members of society. I might have expressed this conviction in a lower key; but I am afraid it would have been the whine of affectation, and not the faithful expression of my feelings, of the clear result which experience and reflection have led me to draw. When I come to that division of the subject, I shall advert to the passages that I more particularly disapprove of, in the works of the authors I have just alluded to; but it is first necessary to observe, that my objection extends to the whole purport of those books, which tend, in my opinion, to degrade one half of the human species, and render women pleasing at the expense of every solid virtue.

Though, to reason on Rousseau's ground, if man did attain a degree of perfection of mind when his body arrived at maturity, it might be proper, in order to make a man and his wife *one,* that she should rely entirely on his understanding; and the graceful ivy, clasping the oak that supported it, would form a whole in which strength and beauty would be equally conspicuous. But, alas! husbands, as well as their helpmates, are often only overgrown children; nay, thanks to early debauchery, scarcely men in their outward form—and if the blind lead the blind, one need not come from heaven to tell us the consequence.

Many are the causes that, in the present corrupt state of society, contribute to enslave women by cramping their understandings and sharpening their senses. One, perhaps, that silently does more mischief than all the rest, is their disregard of order.

To do everything in an orderly manner, is a most important precept, which women, who, generally speaking, receive only a disorderly kind of education, seldom attend to with that degree of exactness that men, who from their infancy are broken into method, observe. This negligent kind of guess-work, for what other epithet can be used to point out the random exertions of a sort of instinctive common sense, never brought to the test of reason? prevents their generalizing matters of fact—so that they do to-day, what they did yesterday, merely because they did it yesterday.

This contempt of the understanding in early life has more baneful consequences than is commonly supposed; for the little knowledge which women of strong minds attain, is, from various circumstances, of a more desultory kind than the knowledge of men, and it is acquired more by sheer observations on real life, than from comparing what has been individually observed with the results of experience generalized by speculation. Led by their dependent situation and domestic employments more into society, what they learn is rather by snatches; and as learning is with them, in general, only a secondary thing, they do not pursue any one branch with that persevering ardour necessary to give vigour to the faculties, and clearness to the judgment. In the present state of society, a little learning is required to support the character of a gentleman; and boys are obliged to submit to a few years of discipline. But in the education of women, the cultivation of the understanding is always subordinate to the acquirement of some corporeal accomplishment; even while enervated by confinement and false notions of modesty, the body is prevented from attaining that grace and beauty which relaxed half-formed limbs never exhibit. Besides, in youth their faculties are not brought forward by emulation; and having no serious scientific study, if they have natural sagacity it is turned too soon on life and manners. They dwell on effects, and modifications, without tracing them back to causes; and complicated rules to adjust behaviour are a weak substitute for simple principles.

As a proof that education gives this appearance of weakness to females, we may instance the example of military men, who are, like them, sent into the world before their minds have been stored with knowledge or fortified by principles. The consequences are similar; soldiers acquire a little superficial knowledge, snatched from the muddy current of conversation, and, from continually mixing with society, they gain, what is termed a knowledge of the world; and this acquaintance with manners and customs has frequently been confounded with a knowledge of the human heart. But can the crude fruit of casual observation, never brought to the test of judgment, formed by comparing speculation and experience, deserve such a distinction? Soldiers, as well as women, practice the minor virtues with punctilious politeness. Where is then the sexual difference, when the education has been the same? All the difference that I can discern, arises from the superior advantage of liberty, which enables the former to see more of life.

It is wandering from my present subject, perhaps, to make a political remark; but, as it was produced naturally by the train of my reflections, I shall not pass it silently over.

Standing armies can never consist of resolute robust men; they may be well disciplined machines, but they will seldom contain men under the influence of strong passions, or with very rigorous faculties. And as for any depth of understanding, I will venture to affirm, that it is as rarely to be found in the army as amongst women; and the cause, I maintain, is the same. It may be further observed, that officers are also particularly attentive to their persons, fond of dancing, crowded rooms, adventures, and ridicule. Like the *fair* sex, the business of their lives is gallantry. They were taught to please, and they only live to please. Yet they do not lose their rank in the distinction of sexes, for they are still reckoned superior to women, though in what their superiority consists, beyond what I have just mentioned, it is difficult to discover.

The great misfortune is this, that they both acquire manners before morals, and a knowledge of life before they have, from reflection, any acquaintance with the grand ideal outline of human nature. The consequence is natural; satisfied with common nature, they become a prey to prejudices, and taking all their opinions on credit, they blindly submit to authority. So that, if they have any sense, it is a kind of instinctive glance, that catches proportions, and decides with respect to manners; but fails when arguments are to be pursued below the surface, or opinions analyzed.

May not the same remarks be applied to women? Nay, the argument may be carried still further, for they are both thrown out of a useful station by the unnatural distinctions established in civilized life. Riches and hereditary honours have made cyphers of women to give consequence to the numerical figure; and idleness has produced a mixture of gallantry and despotism into society, which leads the very men who are the slaves of their mistresses to tyrannize over their sisters, wives, and daughters. This is only keeping them in rank and file, it is true. Strengthen the female mind by enlarging it, and there will be an end to blind obedience; but, as blind obedience is ever fought for by power, tyrants and sensualists are in the right when they endeavour to keep women in the dark, because the former only want slaves, and the latter a plaything. The sensualist, indeed, has been the most dangerous of tyrants, and women have been duped by their lovers, as princes by their ministers, whilst dreaming that they reigned over them.

I now principally allude to Rousseau, for his character of Sophia is, undoubtedly, a captivating one, though it appears to me grossly unnatural; however it is not the superstructure, but the foundation of her character, the principles on which her education was built, that I mean to attack; nay, warmly as I admire the genius of that able writer, whose opinions I shall often have occasion to cite, indignation always takes place of admiration, and the rigid frown of insulted virtue effaces the smile of complacency, which his eloquent periods are wont to raise, when I read his voluptuous reveries. Is this the man, who, in his ardour for virtue, would banish all the soft arts of peace, and almost carry us back to Spartan discipline? Is this the man who delights to paint the useful struggles of passion, the triumphs of good dispositions, and the heroic flights which carry the glowing soul out of itself?—How are these mighty sentiments lowered when he describes the pretty foot and enticing airs of his little favourite! But, for the present, I waive the subject, and, instead of severely reprehending the transient effusions of overweening sensibility, I shall only observe, that whoever has cast a benevolent eye on society, must often have been gratified by the sight of humble mutual love, not dignified by sentiment, or strengthened by a union in intellectual pursuits. The domestic trifles of the day have afforded matters for cheerful converse, and innocent caresses have softened toils which did not require great exercise of mind or stretch of thought: yet, has not the sight of this moderate felicity excited more tenderness than respect? An emotion similar to what we feel when children are playing, or animals sporting, whilst the contemplation of the noble struggles of suffering merit has raised admiration, and carried our thoughts to that world where sensation will give place to reason.

Women are, therefore, to be considered either as moral beings, or so weak that they must be entirely subjected to the superior faculties of men.

Let us examine this question. Rousseau declares that a woman should never, for a moment, feel herself independent, that she should be governed by fear to exercise her *natural* cunning, and made a coquettish slave in order to render her a more alluring object of desire, a *sweeter* companion to man, whenever he chooses to relax himself. He carries the arguments, which he pretends to draw from the indications of nature, still further, and insinuates that truth and fortitude, the corner stones of all human virtue should be cultivated with certain restrictions, because, with respect to the female character, obedience is the grand lesson which ought to be impressed with unrelenting rigour.

What nonsense! when will a great man arise with sufficient strength of mind to puff away the fumes which pride and sensuality have thus spread over the subject! If women are by nature inferior to men, their virtues must be the same in quality, if not in degree, or virtue is a relative idea; consequently, their conduct should be founded on the same principles, and have the same aim.

Connected with man as daughters, wives, and mothers, their moral character may be estimated by their manner of fulfilling those simple duties; but the end, the grand end of their exertions should be to unfold their own faculties and acquire the dignity of conscious virtue. They may try to render their road pleasant; but ought never to forget, in common with man, that life yields not the felicity which can satisfy an immortal soul. I do not mean to insinuate that either sex should be so lost in abstract reflections or distant views, as to forget the affections and duties that lie before them, and are, in truth, the means appointed to produce the fruit of life: on the contrary, I would warmly recommend them, even while I assert, that they afford most satisfaction when they are considered in their true, sober light.

Probably the prevailing opinion, that woman was created for man, may have taken its rise from Moses's poetical story; yet, as very few, it is presumed, who have bestowed any serious thought on the subject, ever supposed that Eve was, literally speaking, one of Adam's ribs, the deduction must be allowed to fall to the ground; or, only be so far admitted as it proves that man, from the remotest antiquity, found it convenient to exert his strength to subjugate his companion, and his invention to show that she ought to have her neck bent under the yoke, because the whole creation was only created for his convenience or pleasure.

Let it not be concluded that I wish to invert the order of things; I have already granted, that, from the constitution of their bodies, men seem to be designed by Providence to attain a greater degree of virtue. I speak collectively of the whole sex; but I see not the shadow of a reason to conclude that their virtues should differ in respect to their nature. In fact, how can they, if virtue has only one eternal standard? I must therefore, if I reason consequentially, as strenuously maintain that they have the same simple direction, as that there is a God.

It follows then that cunning should not be opposed to wisdom, little cares to great exertions, or insipid softness, varnished over with the name of gentleness, to that fortitude which grand views alone can inspire.

I shall be told that woman would then lose many of her peculiar graces, and the opinion of a well-known poet might be quoted to refute my unqualified assertion. For Pope has said, in the name of the whole male sex,

"Yet ne'er so sure our passion to create,
As when she touch'd the brink of all we hate."

In what light this sally places men and women, I shall leave to the judicious to determine; meanwhile I shall content myself with observing, that I cannot discover why, unless they are mortal, females should always be degraded by being made subservient to love or lust.

To speak disrespectfully of love is, I know, high treason against sentiment and fine feelings; but I wish to speak the simple language of truth, and rather to address the head than the heart. To endeavour to reason love out of the world, would be to out Quixote Cervantes, and equally offend against common sense; but an endeavour to restrain this tumultuous passion, and to prove that it should not be allowed to dethrone superior powers, or to usurp the sceptre which the understanding should ever coolly wield, appears less wild.

Youth is the season for love in both sexes; but in those days of thoughtless enjoyment provision should be made for the more important years of life, when reflection takes place of sensation. But Rousseau, and most of the male writers who have followed his steps, have warmly inculcated that the whole tendency of female education ought to be directed to one point:—to render them pleasing.

Let me reason with the supporters of this opinion who have any knowledge of human nature, do they imagine that marriage can eradicate the habitude of life? The woman who has only been taught to please will soon find that her charms are oblique sunbeams, and that they cannot have much effect on her husband's heart when they are seen every day, when the summer is passed and gone. Will she then have sufficient native energy to look into herself for comfort, and cultivate her dormant faculties? or, is it not more rational to expect that she will try to please other men; and, in the emotions raised by the expectation of new conquests, endeavour to forget the mortification her love or pride has received? When the husband ceases to be a lover—and the time will inevitably come, her desire of pleasing will then grow languid, or become a spring of bitterness; and love, perhaps, the most evanescent of all passions, gives place to jealousy or vanity.

I now speak of women who are restrained by principle or prejudice; such women, though they would shrink from an intrigue with real abhorrence, yet, nevertheless, wish to be convinced by the homage of gallantry that they are cruelly neglected by their husbands; or, days and weeks are spent in dreaming of the happiness enjoyed by congenial souls till their health is undermined and their spirits broken by discontent. How then can the great art of pleasing be such a necessary study? it is only useful to a mistress; the chaste wife, and serious mother, should only consider her power to please as the polish of her virtues, and the affection of her husband as one of the comforts that render her talk less difficult and her life happier. But, whether she be loved or neglected, her first wish should be to make herself respectable, and not to rely for all her happiness on a being subject to like infirmities with herself.

The worthy Dr. Gregory fell into a similar error. . . . He advises them to cultivate a fondness for dress, because a fondness for dress, he asserts, is natural to them. I am unable to comprehend what either he or Rousseau mean, when they frequently use this indefinite term. If they told us that in a pre-existent state the soul was fond of dress, and brought this inclination with it into a new body, I should listen to them with a half smile, as I often do when I hear a rant about innate elegance. But if he only meant to say that the exercise of the faculties will produce this fondness—I deny it. It is not natural; but arises, like false ambition in men, from a love of power.

Dr. Gregory goes much further; he actually recommends dissimulation, and advises an innocent girl to give the lie to her feelings, and not dance with spirit, when gaiety of heart would make her feet eloquent without making her gestures immodest. In the name of truth and common sense, why should not one woman acknowledge that she can take more exercise than another? or, in other words, that she has a sound constitution; and why, to damp innocent vivacity, is she darkly to be told that men will draw conclusions which she little thinks of?—Let the libertine draw what inference he pleases; but, I hope, that no sensible mother will restrain the natural frankness of youth by instilling such indecent cautions. Out of the abundance of the heart the mother speaketh;

and a wiser than Solomon hath said, that the heart should be made clean, and not trivial ceremonies observed, which it is not very difficult to fulfil with scrupulous exactness when vice reigns in the heart.

Women ought to endeavour to purify their heart; but can they do so when their uncultivated understandings make them entirely dependent on their senses for employment and amusement, when no noble pursuit sets them above the little vanities of the day, or enables them to curb the wild emotions that agitate a reed over which every passing breeze has power? To gain the affections of a virtuous man, is affectation necessary? Nature has given woman a weaker frame than man; but, to ensure her husband's affections, must a wife, who by the exercise of her mind and body whilst she was discharging the duties of a daughter, wife, and mother, has allowed her constitution to retain its natural strength, and her nerves a healthy tone, is she, I say, to condescend to use art and feign a sickly delicacy in order to secure her husband's affection? Weakness may excite tenderness, and gratify the arrogant pride of man; but the lordly caresses of a protector will not gratify a noble mind that pants for, and deserves to be respected. Fondness is a poor substitute for friendship!

In a seraglio, I grant, that all these arts are necessary; the epicure must have his palate tickled, or he will sink into apathy; but have women so little ambition as to be satisfied with such a condition? Can they supinely dream life away in the lap of pleasure, or the languor of weariness, rather than assert their claim to pursue reasonable pleasures and render themselves conspicuous by practising the virtues which dignify mankind? Surely she has not an immortal soul who can loiter life away merely employed to adorn her person, that she may amuse the languid hours, and soften the cares of a fellow-creature who is willing to be enlivened by her smiles and tricks, when the serious business of life is over.

Besides, the woman who strengthens her body and exercises her mind will, by managing her family and practising various virtues, become the friend, and not the humble dependent of her husband; and if she, by possessing such substantial qualities, merit his regard, she will not find it necessary to conceal her affection, not to pretend to an unnatural coldness of constitution to excite her husband's passions. In fact, if we revert to history, we shall find that the women who have distinguished themselves have neither been the most beautiful nor the most gentle of their sex.

Nature, or, to speak with strict propriety, God, has made all things right; but man has sought him out many inventions to mar the work. I now allude to that part of Dr. Gregory's treatise, where he advises a wife never to let her husband know the extent of her sensibility or affection. Voluptuous precaution, and as ineffectual as absurd. Love, from its very nature, must be transitory. To seek for a secret that would render it constant, would be as wild a search as for the philosopher's stone, or the grand panacea: and the discovery would be equally useless, or rather pernicious, to mankind. The most holy band of society is friendship. It has been well said, by a shrewd satirist, "that rare as true love is, true friendship is still rarer."

This is an obvious truth, and the cause not lying deep, will not elude a slight glance of inquiry.

Love, the common passion, in which chance and sensation take place of choice and reason, is, in some degree, felt by the mass of mankind; for it is not necessary to speak, at present, of the emotions that rise above or sink below love. This passion, naturally increased by suspense and difficulties, draws the mind out of its accustomed state, and exalts the affections; but the security of marriage, allowing the fever of love to subside, a healthy temperature is thought insipid, only by those who have not sufficient intellect to substitute the calm tenderness of friendship, the confidence of respect, instead of blind admiration, and the sensual emotions of fondness.

This is, must be, the course of nature,—friendship or indifference inevitably succeeds love. And this constitution seems perfectly to harmonize with the system of government which prevails in the moral world. Passions are spurs to action, and open the mind; but they sink into mere appetites, become a personal and momentary gratification, when the object is gained, and the satisfied mind rests in enjoyment. . . .

If all the faculties of woman's mind are only to be cultivated as they respect her dependence on man; if, when a husband be obtained, she have arrived at her goal, and meanly proud rests satisfied with such a paltry crown, let her grovel contentedly, scarcely raised by her employments above the animal kingdom; but, if, struggling for the prize of her high calling, she look beyond the present scene, let her cultivate her understanding without stopping to consider what character the husband may have whom she is destined to marry. Let her only determine, without being too anxious about present happiness, to acquire the qualities that ennoble a rational being, and a rough inelegant husband may shock her taste without destroying her peace of mind. She will not model her soul to suit the frailties of her companion, but to bear with them: his character may be a trial, but not an impediment to virtue. . . .

I own it frequently happens that women who have fostered a romantic unnatural delicacy of feeling, waste their lives in *imagining* how happy they should have been with a husband who could love them with a fervid increasing affection every day, and all day. But they might as well pine married as single—and would not be a jot more unhappy with a bad husband than longing for a good one. That a proper education; or, to speak with more precision, a well stored mind, would enable a woman to support a single life with dignity, I grant; but that she should avoid cultivating her taste, lest her husband should occasionally shock it, is quitting a substance for a shadow. To say the truth, I do not know of what use is an improved taste, if the individual be not rendered more independent of the casualties of life; if new sources of enjoyment, only dependent on the solitary operations of the mind, are not opened. People of taste, married or single, without distinction, will ever be disgusted by various things that touch not less observing minds. . . .

How women are to exist in that state where there is to be neither marrying or giving in marriage, we are not told. For though moralists have agreed that the tenor of life seems to prove that *man* is prepared by various circumstances for a future state, they constantly concur in advising *woman* only to provide for the present. Gentleness, docility, and a spaniel-like affection are, on this ground, consistently recommended as the cardinal virtues of the sex; and, disregarding the arbitrary economy of nature, one writer has declared that it is masculine for a woman to be melancholy. She was created to be the toy of man, his rattle, and it must jingle in his ears whenever, dismissing reason, he chooses to be amused.

To recommend gentleness, indeed, on a broad basis is strictly philosophical. A frail being should labour to be gentle. But when forbearance confounds right and wrong, it ceases to be a virtue; and, however convenient it may be found in a companion—that companion will ever be considered as an inferior, and only inspire a vapid tenderness, which easily degenerates into contempt. Still, if advice could really make a being gentle, whose natural disposition admitted not of such a fine polish, something towards the advancement of order would be attained; but if, as might quickly be demonstrated, only affectation be produced by this indiscriminate counsel, which throws a stumbling-block in the way of gradual improvement, and true melioration of temper, the sex is not much benefited by sacrificing solid virtues to the attainment of superficial graces, though for a few years they may procure the individual's regal sway.

As a philosopher, I read with indignation the plausible epithets which men use to soften their insults; and, as a moralist, I ask what is meant by such heterogeneous associations, as fair defects, amiable weaknesses, &c? If there be but one criterion of morals, but one archetype for man, women appear to be suspended by destiny. . . , they have neither the unerring instinct of brutes, nor are allowed to fix the eye of reason on a perfect model. They were made to be loved, and must not aim at respect, lest they should be hunted out of society as masculine. . . .

[A]fter surveying the history of woman, I cannot help, agreeing with the severest satirist, considering the sex as the weakest as well as the most oppressed half of the species. What does history disclose but marks of inferiority, and how few women have emancipated themselves from the galling yoke of sovereign man?—So few, that the exceptions remind me of an ingenious conjecture respecting Newton: that he was probably a being of superior order, accidentally caged in a human body. Following the same train of thinking, I have been led to imagine that the few extraordinary women who have rushed in eccentrical directions out of the orbit prescribed to their sex, were *male* spirits, confined by mistake in female frames. But if it be not philosophical to think of sex when the soul is mentioned, the inferiority must depend on the organs; or the heavenly fire, which is to ferment the clay, is not given in equal portions.

But avoiding, as I have hitherto done, any direct comparison of the two sexes collectively, or frankly acknowledging the inferiority of woman, according to the present appearance of things, I shall only insist that men have increased that inferiority till women are almost sunk below the standard of rational creatures. Let their faculties have room to unfold, and their virtues to gain strength, and then determine where the whole sex must stand in the intellectual scale. Yet let it be remembered, that for a small number of distinguished women I do not ask a place. . . .

[I]f they be really capable of acting like rational creatures, let them not be treated like slaves; or, like the brutes who are dependent on the reason of man, when they associate with him; but cultivate their minds, give them the salutary, sublime curb of principle, and let them attain conscious dignity by feeling themselves only dependent on God. Teach them, in common with man, to submit to necessity, instead of giving, to render them more pleasing, a sex to morals.

Further, should experience prove that they cannot attain the same degree of strength of mind, perseverance, and fortitude, let their virtues be the same in kind, though they may vainly struggle for the same degree; and the superiority of man will be equally clear, if not clearer; and truth, as it is a simple principle, which admits of no modification, would be common to both. Nay, the order of society as it is at present regulated, would not be inverted, for woman would then only have the rank that reason assigned her, and arts could not be practised to bring the balance even, much less to turn it.

These may be termed Utopian dreams. Thanks to that Being who impressed them on my soul, and gave me sufficient strength of mind to dare to exert my own reason, till, becoming dependent only on him for the support of my virtue, I view, with indignation, the mistaken notions that enslave my sex.

I love man as my fellow; but his sceptre, real or usurped, extends not to me, unless the reason of an individual demands my homage; and even then the submission is to reason, and not to man. In fact, the conduct of an unaccountable being must be regulated by the operations of its own reason; or on what foundation rests the throne of God?

It appears to me necessary to dwell on these obvious truths, because females have been insulated, as it were; and, while they have been stripped of the virtues that should clothe humanity, they have been decked with artificial graces that enable them to exercise a short-lived tyranny. Love, in their bosoms, taking place of every nobler passion, their sole ambition is to be fair, to raise emotion instead of inspiring respect; and this ignoble desire, like the servility in absolute monarchies, destroys all strength of character. Liberty is the mother of virtue, and if women be, by their very constitution, slaves, and not allowed to breathe the sharp invigorating air of freedom, they must ever languish like exotics, and be reckoned beautiful flaws in nature.

As to the argument respecting the subjection in which the sex has ever been held, it retorts on man. The many have always been enthralled by the few; and monsters, who scarcely have shewn any discernment of human excellence, have tyrannized over thousands of their fellow-creatures. Why have men of superior endowments submitted to such degradation? For, is it not universally acknowledged that kings, viewed collectively, have ever been inferior, in abilities and virtue, to the same number of men taken from the common mass of mankind—yet, have they not, and are they not still treated with a degree of reverence that is an insult to reason? China is not the only country where a living man has been made a God. *Men* have submitted to superior strength to enjoy with impunity the pleasure of the moment—*women* have only done the same, and therefore till it is proved that the courtier, who servilely resigns the birthright of a man, is not a moral agent, it cannot be demonstrated that woman is essentially inferior to man because she has always been subjugated. . . .

Bodily strength from being the distinction of heroes is now sunk into such unmerited contempt that men, as well as women, seem to think it unnecessary: the latter, as it takes from their feminine graces, and from that lovely weakness the source of their undue power; and the former, because it appears inimical to the character of a gentleman.

. . . Yet the contrary, I believe, will appear to be the fact; for, on diligent inquiry, I find that strength of mind has, in most cases, been accompanied by superior strength of body,—natural soundness of constitution,—not that robust tone of nerves and vigour of muscles, which arise from bodily labour, when the mind is quiescent, or only directs the hands. . . .

I will allow that bodily strength seems to give man a natural superiority over woman; and this is the only solid basis on which the superiority of the sex can be built. But I still insist, that not only the virtue, but the *knowledge* of the two sexes should be the same in nature, if not in degree, and that women, considered not only as moral, but rational creatures, ought to endeavour to acquire human virtues (or perfections) by the *same* means as men, instead of being educated like a fanciful kind of *half* being—one of Rousseau's wild chimeras.

But, if strength of body be, with some show of reason, the boast of men, why are women so infatuated as to be proud of a defect? Rousseau has furnished them with a plausible excuse, which could only have occurred to a man, whose imagination had been allowed to run wild, and refine on the impressions made by exquisite senses;—that they might, forsooth, have a pretext for yielding to a natural appetite without violating a romantic species of modesty, which gratifies the price and libertinism of man.

.   .   .   .

I have, probably, had an opportunity of observing more girls in their infancy than J. J. Rousseau—I can recollect my own feelings, and I have looked steadily around me; yet, so far from coinciding with him in opinion respecting the first dawn of the female character, I will venture to affirm, that a girl, whose spirits have not been damped by inactivity, or innocence tainted by false shame, will always be a romp, and the doll will never excite attention unless confinement allows her no alternative. Girls and boys, in short, would play harmlessly together, if the distinction of sex was not inculcated long before nature makes any difference. I will go further, and affirm, as an indisputable fact, that most of the women, in the circle of my observation, who have acted like rational creatures, or shown any vigour of intellect, have accidentally been allowed to run wild—as some of the elegant formers of the fair sex would insinuate. . . .

.   .   .   .

I lament that women are systematically degraded by receiving the trivial attentions, which men think it manly to pay to the sex, when, in fact, they are insultingly supporting their own superiority. It is not condescension to bow to an inferior. So ludicrous, in fact, do these ceremonies appear to me, that I scarcely am able to govern my muscles, when I see a man start with eager and serious solicitude to lift a handkerchief, or shut a door, when the *lady* could have done it herself, had she only moved a pace or two. . . .

Women, commonly called Ladies, are not to be contradicted in company, are not allowed to exert any manual strength; and from them the negative virtues only are expected, when any virtues are expected, patience, docility, good-humour, and flexibility; virtues incompatible with any vigorous exertion of intellect.

. . . .

I wish to sum up what I have said in a few words, for I here throw down my gauntlet, and deny the existence of sexual virtues, not excepting modesty. For man and woman, truth, if I understand the meaning of the word, must be the same; yet the fanciful female character, so prettily drawn by poets and novelists, demanding the sacrifice of truth and sincerity, virtue becomes a relative idea, having no other foundation than utility, and of that utility men pretend arbitrarily to judge, shaping it to their own convenience.

Women, I allow, may have different duties to fulfil; but they are *human* duties, and the principles that should regulate the discharge of them, I sturdily maintain, must be the same.

To become respectable, the exercise of their understanding is necessary, there is no other foundation for independence of character; I mean explicitly to say that they must only bow to the authority of reason, instead of being the *modest* slaves of opinion.

In the superior ranks of life how seldom do we meet with a man of superior abilities, or even common acquirements? The reason appears to me clear, the state they are born in was an unnatural one. The human character has ever been formed by the employments the individual, or class, pursues; and if the faculties are not sharpened by necessity, they must remain obtuse. The argument may fairly be extended to women; for, seldom occupied by serious business, the pursuit of pleasure gives that insignificancy to their character which renders the society of the *great* so insipid. The same want of firmness, produced by a similar cause, forces them both to fly from themselves to noisy pleasures, and artificial passions, till vanity takes place of every social affection, and the characteristics of humanity can scarcely be discerned. Such are the blessings of civil governments, as they are at present organized, that wealth and female softness equally tend to debase mankind, and are produced by the same cause; but allowing women to be rational creatures, they should be incited to acquire virtues which they may call their own, for how can a rational being be ennobled by anything that is not obtained by its *own* exertions?

❖   ❖   ❖

RELATED READINGS

Burns, Steven. "The Humean Female." *Dialogue* 15 (Sept. 1976), pp. 415–424.

Clark, Lorenne. "Women and John Locke; Or, Who Owns the Apples in the Garden of Eden?" *Canadian Journal of Philosophy* 7 (Dec. 1977), pp. 699–724.

Edman, Irwin (ed.). "The Metaphysics of the Love of the Sexes." In *The Philosophy of Schopenhauer*. New York: The Modern Library, Inc., 1928, pp. 337–376.

Flexner, Eleanor. *Mary Wollstonecraft; a Biography.* New York: Coward, McCann and Geoghegan, 1972.

Hill, Thomas E., Fr. "Servility and Self-Respect." *The Monist* 57 (Jan. 1973), pp. 87–104.

Kelso, Ruth. *Doctrine for the Lady of the Renaissance.* Urbana: University of Illinois Press, 1956.

Korsmeyer, Carolyn W. "Reason and Morals in the Early Feminist Movement: Mary Wollstonecraft." In *Women and Philosophy,* ed. by C. Gould and M. Wartofsky. New York: G. P. Putnam and Sons, 1976, pp. 97–111.

Rapaport, Elizabeth. "On the Future of Love: Rousseau and the Radical Feminists." In *Women and Philosophy,* ed. by C. Gould and M. Wartofsky. New York: G. P. Putnam and Sons, 1976, pp. 185–205.

Sachs, Hannelore. *The Renaissance Woman,* trans. by Marianne Herzfeld. New York: McGraw-Hill Book Company, Inc., 1971.

Sahakian, Mabel and Sahakian, William. *Rousseau as Educator.* New York: Twayne Publishing Company, 1974.

Squadrito, Kathy. "Locke on the Equality of the Sexes." *Journal of Social Philosophy* X, 1 (Jan. 1979), pp. 6–11.

Stern, Karl. "Schopenhauer." In *The Flight from Woman.* New York: Farrar, Straus and Giroux, 1965, pp. 107–122.

Wolff, Robert Paul. "There's Nobody Here but Us Persons." In *Women and Philosophy,* ed. by C. Gould and M. Wartofsky. New York: G. P. Putnam and Sons, 1976, pp. 128–144.

Wollstonecraft, Mary. *A Vindication of the Rights of Men.* London: J. Johnson, 1790.

G. W. F. HEGEL

The problem bequeathed by Kant to his philosophical posterity was how to bridge the gap between *noumena* and *phenomena.* To Kant himself, as we have seen, the gap was unbridgeable, but to other idealists (e.g., Fichte, Schelling, and Schopenhauer as well as Hegel), a response to that problem was the foundation for each of their philosophies.

Georg Hegel's (1770–1831) basic response to the Kantian problem was a denial that the problem existed. As an absolute objective idealist, Hegel maintained that reality is ultimately rational, and thus accessible to reason. Reality is also dialectical, exhibiting its process character through ongoing syntheses of opposing (differing) elements. Through logic, philosophy of nature and philosophy of spirit we study the dialectical unfolding of the Idea in thought, matter and time. To Hegel, the more universal the idea, the more fully it presents reality. Since the Absolute Idea manifests itself gradually through us and in us, history discloses an inexorable and continuing progress towards the Absolute, which Hegel identifies with Spirit or Mind (*Geist*).

Hegel's Concept of Human Nature

Human consciousness represents a link between nature and spirit. Unlike other natural organisms, human beings are capable of determining their own destinies through rational freedom. Such determination involves both cognitive and practical factors; among the former are intuition, imagination and memory; among the latter are feeling, instincts and will. According to Hegel, the free individual synthesizes these differing factors through reason, fulfilling his/her own subjective spirit through such free deliberations. In order to actualize the ideal of rational freedom, however, spirit must pass over into the objective order of ethics and history.

The "march towards freedom" which Hegel defines as history consists in settling the conflict between particular wills and the universal will of the Absolute. To the extent that particular agents identify their own interests with those of other individuals, they act both ethically and freely. The individual is related to the state through the family and through civil society. While Hegel did not view any particular state as complete embodiment of the Idea, he construed the State as the sovereign manifestation of Spirit at any given point in time.

The following excerpt is drawn from G. W. F. Hegel, *The Phenomenology of Mind,* trans. by J. B. Baillie. Great Britain: Unwin

Brothers Ltd., Woking 1910 (Revised 1931 by The Macmillan Company), pp. 474–479, 481–482, 496–497.

G. W. F. HEGEL   'The Ethical World'

The divine law which holds sway in the family has also on its side distinctions within itself, the relations among which make up the living process of its realization. Amongst the three relationships, however, of husband and wife, parents and children, brothers and sisters, the relationship of husband and wife is to begin with the primary and immediate form in which one consciousness recognizes itself in another, and in which each knows that reciprocal recognition. Being natural self-knowledge, knowledge of self on the basis of nature and not on that of ethical life, it merely represents and typifies in a figure the life of spirit, and is not spirit itself actually realized. Figurative representation, however, has its reality in an other than it is. This relationship, therefore, finds itself realized not in itself as such, but in the child—an other, in whose coming into being that relationship consists, and with which it passes away. And this change from one generation onwards to another is permanent in and as the life of a nation.

The reverent devotion (*Pietät*) of husband and wife towards one another is thus mixed up with a natural relation and with feeling, and their relationship is not inherently self-complete; similarly, too, the second relationship, the reverent devotion of parents and children to one another. The devotion of parents towards their children is affected with emotion just by their being consciously realized in what is external to themselves (viz. the children), and by their seeing them become something on their own account without this returning to the parents; independent existence on the part of the children remains a foreign reality, a reality all their own. The devotion of children, again, towards their parents is conversely affected by their coming into being from, or having their essential nature in, what is external to themselves (viz. the parents) and passes away; and by their attaining independent existence and a self-consciousness of their own solely through separation from the source whence they came—a separation in which the spring gets exhausted.

Both these relationships are constituted by and hold within the transience and the dissimilarity of the two sides, which are assigned to them.

An unmixed intransitive form of relationship, however, holds between brother and sister. They are the same blood, which, however, in them has entered into a condition of stable equilibrium. They therefore stand in no such natural relation as husband and wife, they do not desire one another; nor have they given to one another, nor received from one another, this independence of individual being; they are free individualities with respect to each other. The feminine element, therefore, in the form of the sister, premonizes and foreshadows most completely the nature of ethical life (*sittliches Wesen*). She does not become conscious of it, and does not actualize it, because the law of the family is her inherent implicit inward nature, which does not lie open to the daylight of consciousness, but remains inner feeling and the divine element exempt from actuality. The feminine life is attached to these household divinities (*Penates*), and sees in them both her universal substance, and her particular individuality, yet so views them that this relation of her individuality to them is at the same time not the natural one of pleasure.

As a daughter, the woman must now see her parents pass away with natural emotion and yet with ethical resignation, for it is only at the cost of this condition that she can come to that individual existence of which she is capable. She thus cannot see her independent existence positively attained in her relation to her parents. The relationships of mother and wife, however, are individualized partly in the form of something natural, which brings pleasure; partly in the form of something negative, which finds simply its own evanescence in those relationships; partly again the individualization is just on that account something contingent which can be replaced by an other particular individuality. In a household of the ethical kind, a woman's relationships are not based on a reference to this particular husband, this particular child, but to *a* husband, to children *in general*,—not to feeling, but to the universal. The distinction between her ethical life (*Sittlichkeit*) (while it determines her particular existence and brings her pleasure) and that of her husband consists just in this, that it has always a directly universal significance for her, and is quite alien to the impulsive condition of mere particular desire. On the other hand, in the husband these two aspects get separated; and since he possesses, as a citizen, the self-conscious power belonging to the universal life, the life of the social whole, he acquires thereby the rights of desire, and keeps himself at the same time in detachment from it. So far, then, as particularity is implicated in this relationship in the case of the wife, her ethical life is not purely ethical; so far, however, as it is ethical, the particularity is a matter of indifference, and the wife is without the moment of knowing herself as *this* particular self in and through an other.

The brother, however, is in the eyes of the sister a being whose nature is unperturbed by desire and is ethically like her own; her recognition in him is pure and unmixed with any sexual relation. The indifference characteristic of particular existence and the ethical contingency thence arising are, therefore, not present in this relationship; instead, the moment of individual selfhood, recognizing and being recognized, can here assert its right, because it is bound up with the balance and equilibrium resulting from their being of the same blood, and from their being related in a way that involves no mutual desire. The loss of a brother is thus irreparable to the sister, and her duty towards him is the highest.[1]

This relationship at the same time is the limit, at which the circumscribed life of the family is broken up, and passes beyond itself. The brother is the member of the family in which its spirit becomes individualized, and enabled thereby to turn towards another sphere, towards what is other than and external to itself, and pass over into consciousness of universality. The brother leaves this immediate, rudimentary, and, therefore, strictly speaking, negative ethical life of the family, in order to acquire and produce the concrete ethical order which is conscious of itself.

He passes from the divine law, within whose realm he lived, over to the human law. The sister, however, becomes, or the wife remains, director of the home and the preserver of the divine law. In this way both the sexes overcome their merely natural being, and become ethically significant, as diverse forms dividing between them the different aspects which the ethical substance assumes. Both these universal factors of the ethical world have their specific individuality in naturally distinct self-consciousnesses, for the reason that the spirit at work in the ethical order is the immediate unity of the substance [of ethical life] with self-consciousness—an immediacy which thus appears as the existence of a natural difference, at once as regards its aspect of reality and of difference. It is that aspect which, in the notion of spiritual reality, came to light as "original determinate nature", when we were dealing with the stage of "Individuality which is real to itself". This moment loses the indeterminateness which it still has there, and the contingent diversity of "constitution" and "capacities". It is now the specific opposition of the two sexes, whose natural character acquires at the same time the significance of their respective ethical determinations.

The distinction of the sexes and of their ethical content remains all the same within the unity of the ethical substance, and its process is just the constant development of that substance. The husband is sent forth by the spirit of the family into the life of the community, and finds there his self-conscious reality. Just as the family thereby finds in the community its universal substance and subsistence, conversely the community finds in the family the formal element of its own realization, and in the divine law its power

1. Cp. *Antigone*, 1. 910.

and confirmation. Neither of the two is alone self-complete. Human law as a living and active principle proceeds from the divine, the law holding on earth from that of the nether world, the conscious from the unconscious, mediation from immediacy; and returns too whence it came. The power of the nether world, on the other hand, finds its realization upon earth; it comes through consciousness to have existence and efficacy.

The universal elements of the ethical life are thus the (ethical) substance *qua* universal, and that substance *qua* particular consciousness. Their universal actuality is the nation and the family; while they get their natural self, and their operative individuality, in man and woman. . . .

The ethical realm remains in this way permanently a world without blot or stain, a world untainted by any internal dissension. So, too, its process is an untroubled transition from one of its powers to the other, in such a way that each preserves and produces the other. We see it no doubt divided into two ultimate elements and their realization: but their opposition is rather the confirming and substantiation of one through the other; and where they directly come in contact with each other as actual factors, their mediating common element is the immediate permeation of the one with the other. The one extreme, universal spirit conscious of itself, becomes, through the individuality of man, linked together with its other extreme, its force and its element, with *unconscious* spirit. On the other hand, divine law is individualized, the unconscious spirit of the particular individual finds its existence, in woman, through the mediation of whom the unconscious spirit comes out of its unrealizedness into actuality, and rises out of the state of unknowing and unknown, into the conscious realm of universal spirit. The union of man with woman constitutes the operative mediating agency for the whole, and constitutes the element which, while separated into the extremes of divine and human law, is, at the same time, their immediate union. This union, again, turns both those first mediate connexions (*Schlusse*) into one and the same synthesis, and unites into one process the twofold movement in opposite directions—one from reality to unreality, the downward movement of human law, organized into independent members, to the danger and trial of death,—the other, from unreality to reality, the upward movement of the law of the nether world to the daylight of conscious existence. Of these movements the former falls to man, the latter to woman. . . .

❃   ❃   ❃

G. W. F. HEGEL 'Guilt and Destiny'

Human law, then, in its universal mode of existence is the community, in its efficient operation in general is the manhood of the community, in its actual efficient operation is the government. It has its being, its process, and its subsistence by consuming and absorbing into itself the separatist action of the household gods (*Penates*), the individualization into insular independent families which are under the management of womankind, and by keeping them dissolved in the fluent continuum of its own nature. The family at the same time, however, is in general its element, the individual consciousness its universal operative basis. Since the community gets itself subsistence only by breaking in upon family happiness, and dissolving [individual] self-consciousness into the universal, it creates its enemy for itself within its own gates, creates it in what it suppresses, and what is at the same time essential to it —womankind in general. Womankind—the everlasting irony in the life of the community—changes by intrigue the universal purpose of government into a private end, transforms its universal activity into a work of this or that specific individual, and perverts the universal property of the state into a possession and ornament for the family. Woman in this way turns to ridicule the grave wisdom of maturity, which, being dead to all particular aims, to private pleasure, personal satisfaction, and actual activity as well, thinks of, and is concerned for, merely what is universal; she makes this wisdom the laughing-stock of raw and wanton youth, an object of derision and scorn, unworthy of their enthusiasm. She asserts that it is everywhere the force of youth that really counts; she upholds this as of primary significance; extols a son as one who is the lord and master of the mother who has borne him; a brother as one in whom the sister finds man on a level with herself; a youth as one through whom the daughter, freed from her dependence (on the family unity), acquires the satisfaction and the dignity of wifehood.

❀   ❀   ❀

ARTHUR SCHOPENHAUER

Arthur Schopenhauer (1788–1860) is generally regarded as a philosopher of pessimism. This is an interesting designation because idealists such as he are more often construed as optimistic.

Actually, there are reasons for both tendencies in Schopenhauer's background: the happy circumstances of his material wealth and gifts of mind, and the tragic circumstances of his father's suicide and the sustained hostility between his mother and himself.

Kant and Hegel exerted a significant influence upon the development of Schopenhauer's philosophy. From Kant he learned and applied the distinction between phenomena and noumena; from Hegel he learned and rejected an exclusively rationalistic interpretation of reality. For Schopenhauer, our "idea" of the world (the world as presented to us empirically or phenomenally) is diverse or many; but metaphysically or noumenally, the world is *one*. Its oneness is ascertained and maintained not through reason but through will. This will—a blind impulse, an incessant striving—is the driving force of the world. The title of Schopenhauer's main work, *The World as Will and Idea*, expresses his fundamental thesis in this regard.

Schopenhauer's Concept of Human Nature

According to Schopenhauer, all organisms possess a will to live. In human nature, the exercise of this will entails reason as a principal means of satisfying biological needs and wants. Knowledge is thus a servant of the human will to live.

The thought of Schopenhauer is called a voluntarism because of its emphasis on will, which is described as totally determinative of individuals and society. In our consciousness of acts already willed, we think ourselves free, but in fact our actions follow inexorably from our noumenal (real) character. Our sense of freedom is the effect of ignorance of the determining causes of our actions. Even apparently drastic changes in personality are traceable to character determination. Suppose, for example, an individual whose acts are generally motivated by desire for financial gain is persuaded that great treasure in heaven is obtainable through the fulfillment of certain "religious" observances. This new conviction may cause the person to behave in a manner radically different from past practice, yet entirely consistent with his or her character.

Schopenhauer's pessimism is evident in his discussion of the will to live as a striving to assert existence at the expense of others. Accordingly, he asserts that "[t]he chief source of the most serious evils which afflict man is man himself." In effect, the world is "a hell which surpasses that of Dante through the fact that one man must be the devil of another." Human desire is itself a form of pain, relieved only momentarily by snatches of happiness. Happiness is both transient and negative, for whatever quenches our desires soon turns into boredom, inclining us to seek one another's company for further relief. The greater our intellectual powers, the more we tend to experience isolation from others, and the greater our capacity for suffering.

Morality, for Schopenhauer, consists in overcoming our natural subservience to the will to live. The just man penetrates the illusion of individuality to the extent that he sets others on the same level with himself. Sympathy, or love, involves recognition that all individuals are really one, as differentiated phenomena of the same undivided will. "All true and pure love," Schopenhauer claims, "is sympathy, and all love which is not sympathy is selfishness."

The following selection is excerpted from Schopenhauer's *Studies in Pessimism*, translated by Thomas Bailey Sanders (1860–1928).

ARTHUR SCHOPENHAUER   'On Women'

Schiller's poem in honour of women, *Wurde der Frauen*, is the result of much careful thought, and it appeals to the reader by its antithetic style and its use of contrast; but as an expression of the true praise which should be accorded to them, it is, I think, inferior to these few words of Jouy's: *Without women the beginning of our life would be helpless; the middle, devoid of pleasure; and the end, of consolation.* The same thing is more feelingly expressed by Byron in *Sardanapalus:*—

> The very first
> Of human life must spring from woman's breast,
> Your first small words are taught you from her lips,
> Your first tears quench'd by her, and your last sighs
> Too often breathed out in a woman's hearing,
> When men have shrunk from the ignoble care
> Of watching the last hour of him who led them.
> (*Act* I. *Scene* 2.)

These two passages indicate the right standpoint for the appreciation of women.

You need only look at the way in which she is formed to see that woman is not meant to undergo great labour, whether of the mind or of the body. She pays the debt of life not by what she does but by what she suffers; by the pains of childbearing and care for the child, and by submission to her husband, to whom she should be a patient and cheering companion.

The keenest sorrows and joys are not for her, nor is she called upon to display a great deal of strength. The current of her life should be more gentle, peaceful and trivial than man's, without being essentially happier or unhappier.

Women are directly fitted for acting as the nurses and teachers of our early childhood by the fact that they are themselves childish, frivolous and short-sighted; in a word, they are big children all their life long—a kind of intermediate stage between the child and the full-grown man, who is man in the strict sense of the word. See how a girl will fondle a child for days together, dance with it and sing to it; and then think what a man, with the best will in the world, could do if he were put in her place.

With young girls Nature seems to have had in view what, in the language of the drama, is called *a coup de théâtre*. For a few years she dowers them with a wealth of beauty and is lavish in her gift of charm, at the expense of the rest of their life, in order that during those years they may capture the fantasy of some man to such a degree that he is hurried into undertaking the honourable care of them, in some form or other, as long as they live—a step for which there would not appear to be any sufficient warranty if reason only directed his thoughts. Accordingly Nature has equipped woman, as she does all her creatures, with the weapons and implements requisite for the safeguarding of her existence, and for just as long as it is necessary for her to have them. Here, as elsewhere, Nature proceeds with her usual economy; for just as the female ant, after fecundation, loses her wings, which are then superfluous, nay, actually a danger to the business of breeding; so, after giving birth to one or two children, a woman generally loses her beauty; probably, indeed, for similar reasons.

And so we find that young girls, in their hearts, look upon domestic affairs or work of any kind as of secondary importance, if not actually as a mere jest. The only business that really claims their earnest attention is love, making conquests, and everything connected with this—dress, dancing, and so on.

The nobler and more perfect a thing is, the later and slower it is in arriving at maturity. A man reaches the maturity of his reasoning powers and mental faculties hardly before the age of twenty-eight; a woman, at eighteen. And then, too, in the case of woman, it is only reason of a sort—very niggard in its dimensions. That is why women remain children their whole life long; never seeing anything but what is quite close to them, cleaving to the present moment, taking appearance for reality, and preferring trifles to matters of the first importance. For it is by virtue of his reasoning faculty that man does not live in the present only, like the brute, but looks about him and considers the past and the future; and this is the origin of prudence, as well as of that care and anxiety which so many people exhibit. Both the advantages and the disadvantages which this involves, are shared in by the

woman to a smaller extent because of her weaker power of reasoning. She may, in fact, be described as intellectually short-
sighted, because, while she has an intuitive understanding of what
lies quite close to her, her field of vision is narrow and does not
reach to what is remote: so that things which are absent or past or
to come have much less effect upon women than upon men. This is
the reason why women are more often inclined to be extravagant,
and sometimes carry their inclination to a length that borders upon
madness. It their hearts women think that it is men's business to
earn money and theirs to spend it—if possible during their husband's life, but, at any rate, after his death. The very fact that their
husband hands them over his earnings for purposes of housekeeping strengthens them in this belief.

However many disadvantages all this may involve, there is at
least this to be said in its favour: that the woman lives more in the
present than the man, and that, if the present is at all tolerable,
she enjoys it more eagerly. This is the source of that cheerfulness
which is peculiar to woman, fitting her to amuse man in his hours of
recreation, and, in case of need, to console him when he is borne
down by the weight of his cares.

It is by no means a bad plan to consult women in matters of
difficulty, as the Germans used to do in ancient times; for their
way of looking at things is quite different from ours, chiefly in the
fact that they like to take the shortest way to their goal, and, in
general, manage to fix their eyes upon what lies before them;
while we, as a rule, see far beyond it, just because it is in front
of our noses. In cases like this, we need to be brought back to the
right standpoint, so as to recover the near and simple view.

Then, again, women are decidedly more sober in their judgment
than we are, so that they do not see more in things than is really
there; whilst, if our passions are aroused, we are apt to see things
in an exaggerated way, or imagine what does not exist.

The weakness of their reasoning faculty also explains why it is
that women show more sympathy for the unfortunate than men
do, and so treat them with more kindness and interest; and why it
is that, on the contrary, they are inferior to men in point of justice,
and less honourable and conscientious. For it is just because their
reasoning power is weak that present circumstances have such a
hold over them, and those concrete things which lie directly before their eyes exercise a power which is seldom counteracted to
any extent by abstract principles of thought, by fixed rules of
conduct, firm resolutions, or, in general, by consideration for the
past and the future, or regard of what is absent and remote. Accordingly, they possess the first and main elements that go to
make a virtuous character, but they are deficient in those secondary

qualities which are often a necessary instrument in the formation of it.

Hence it will be found that the fundamental fault of the female
character is that it has *no sense of justice*. This is mainly due to
the fact, already mentioned, that women are defective in the powers of reasoning and deliberation; but it is also traceable to the position which Nature has assigned to them as the weaker sex. They are
dependent, not upon strength, but upon craft; and hence their instinctive capacity for cunning, and their ineradicable tendency to
say what is not true. For as lions are provided with claws and
teeth, and elephants and boars with tusks, bulls with horns, and the
cuttle fish with its cloud of inky fluid, so Nature has equipped
woman, for her defence and protection, with the arts of dissimulation; and all the power which Nature has conferred upon man in
the shape of physical strength and reason has been bestowed upon
women in this form. Hence dissimulation is innate in woman, and
almost as much a quality of the stupid as of the clever. It is as
natural for them to make use of it on every occasion as it is for
those animals to employ their means of defence when they are attacked; they have a feeling that in doing so they are only within
their rights. Therefore a woman who is perfectly truthful and not
given to dissimulation is perhaps an impossibility, and for this very
reason they are so quick at seeing through dissimulation in others
that it is not a wise thing to attempt it with them. But this fundamental defect which I have stated, with all that it entails, gives
rise to falsity, faithlessness, treachery, ingratitude, and so on. Per-
jury in a court of justice is more often committed by women than
by men. It may, indeed, be generally questioned whether women
ought to be sworn at all. From time to time one finds repeated cases
everywhere of ladies, who want for nothing, taking things from
shop-counters when no one is looking and making off with them.

Nature has appointed that the propagation of the species shall
be the business of men who are young, strong and handsome; so
that the race may not degenerate. This is the firm will and purpose
of Nature in regard to the species, and it finds its expression in the
passions of women. There is no law that is older or more powerful
than this. Woe, then, to the man who sets up claims and interests
that will conflict with it; whatever he may say and do, they will
be unmercifully crushed at the first serious encounter. For the innate rule that governs women's conduct, though it is secret and
unformulated, nay, unconscious in its working, is this: *We are
justified in deceiving those who think they have acquired rights
over the species by paying little attention to the individual, that is,
to us. The constitution and, therefore, the welfare of the species
have been placed in our hands and committed to our care, through*

the control we obtain over the next generation, which proceeds from us; let us discharge our duties conscientiously. But women have no abstract knowledge of this leading principle; they are conscious of it only as a concrete fact; and they have no other method of giving expression to it than the way in which they act when the opportunity arrives. And then their conscience does not trouble them so much as we fancy; for in the darkest recesses of their heart they are aware that, in committing a breach of their duty towards the individual, they have all the better fulfilled their duty towards the species, which is infinitely greater.[1]

And since women exist in the main solely for the propagation of the species, and are not destined for anything else, they live as a rule, more for the species than for the individual, and in their hearts take the affairs of the species more seriously than those of the individual. This gives their whole life and being a certain levity; the general bent of their character is in a direction fundamentally different from that of man; and it is this which produces that discord in married life which is so frequent, and almost the normal state.

The natural feeling between men is mere indifference, but between women it is actual enmity. The reason of this is that trade-jealousy—*odium figulinum*—which, in the case of men, does not go beyond the confines of their own particular pursuit but with women embraces the whole sex; since they have only one kind of business. Even when they meet in the street women look at one another like Guelphs and Ghibellines. And it is a patent fact that when two women make first acquaintance with each other they behave with more constraint and dissimulation than two men who would show in a like case; and hence it is that an exchange of compliments between two women is a much more ridiculous proceeding than between two men. Further, whilst a man will, as a general rule, always preserve a certain amount of consideration and humanity in speaking to others, even to those who are in a very inferior position, it is intolerable to see how proudly and disdainfully a fine lady will generally behave towards one who is in a lower social rank (I do not mean a woman who is in her service), whenever she speaks to her. The reason of this may be that, with women, differences of rank are much more precarious than with us; because, while a hundred considerations carry weight in our case, in theirs there is only one, namely, with which man they have found favour; as also that they stand in much nearer relations with one another than men do, in consequence of the one-sided nature of their calling. This makes them endeavour to lay stress upon differences of rank.

1. A more detailed discussion of the matter in question may be found in my chief work, *Die Welt als Wille und Vorstellung*, vol. ii., ch. 44.

It is only the man whose intellect is clouded by his sexual impulses that could give the name of *the fair sex* to that undersized, narrow-shouldered, broad-hipped, and short-legged race: for the whole beauty of the sex is bound up with this impulse. Instead of calling them beautiful, there would be more warrant for describing women as the unaesthetic sex. Neither for music, nor for poetry, nor for fine art, have they really and truly any sense or susceptibility; it is a mere mockery if they make a pretence of it in order to assist their endeavour to please. Hence, as a result of this, they are incapable of taking a *purely objective interest* in anything; and the reason of it seems to me to be as follows. A man tries to acquire *direct* mastery over things, either by understanding them or by forcing them to do his will. But a woman is always and everywhere reduced to obtaining this mastery *indirectly*, namely through a man; and whatever direct mastery she may have is entirely confined to him. And so it lies in woman's nature to look upon everything only as a means for conquering man; and if she takes an interest in anything else it is simulated—a mere roundabout way of gaining her ends by coquetry and feigning what she does not feel. Hence even Rousseau declared: *Women have, in general, no love of any art; they have no proper knowledge of any; and they have no genius.*[2]

No one who sees at all below the surface can have failed to remark the same thing. You need only observe the kind of attention women bestow upon a concert, an opera, or a play—the childish simplicity, for example, with which they keep on chattering during the finest passages in the greatest masterpieces. If it is true that the Greeks excluded women from their theatres, they were quite right in what they did; at any rate you would have been able to hear what was said upon the stage. In our day, besides, or in lieu of saying, *Let a woman keep silence in the church,* it would be much to the point to say, *Let a woman keep silence in the theatre.* This might, perhaps, be put up in big letters on the curtain.

And you cannot expect anything else of women if you consider that the most distinguished intellects among the whole sex have never managed to produce a single achievement in the fine arts that is really great, genuine, and original; or given to the world any work of permanent value in any sphere. This is most strikingly shown in regard to painting, where mastery of techniques is at least as much within their power as within ours—and hence they are diligent in cultivating it; but still, they have not a single great painting to boast of, just because they are deficient in that objectivity of mind which is so directly indispensable in painting. They never get beyond a subjective point of view. It is quite in

2. Lettre á d'Alembert.

keeping with this that ordinary women have no real susceptibility for art at all; for Nature proceeds in strict sequence—*non facit saltum*. And Huarte in his *Examen de ingenios para las scienzias*— a book which has been famous for three hundred years—denies women the possession of all the higher faculties. The case is not altered by particular and partial exceptions; taken as a whole, women are, and remain, thorough-going philistines, and quite incurable. Hence, with that absurd arrangement which allows them to share the rank and title of their husbands, they are a constant stimulus to his ignoble ambitions. And, further, it is just because they are philistines that modern society, where they take the lead and set the tone, is in such a bad way. Napoleon's saying—that *women have no rank*—should be adopted as the right standpoint in determining their position in society; and as regards their other qualities Chamfort makes the very true remark: *They are made to trade with our own weaknesses and our follies, but not with our reason. The sympathies that exist between them and men are skin-deep only, and do not touch the mind or the feelings or the character.* They form the *sexus sequior*—the second sex, inferior in every respect to the first; their infirmities should be treated with consideration; but to show them great reverence is extremely ridiculous, and lowers us in their eyes. When Nature made two divisions of the human race, she did not draw the line exactly through the middle. These divisions are polar and opposed to each other, it is true; but the difference between them is not qualitative merely, it is also quantitative.

This is just the view which the ancients took of woman, and the view which people in the East take now; and their judgment as to her proper position is much more correct than ours, with our old French notions of gallantry and our preposterous system of reverence—that highest product of Teutonico-Christian stupidity. These notions have served only to make women more arrogant and overbearing; so that one is occasionally reminded of the holy apes in Benares, who in the consciousness of their sanctity and inviolable position think they can do exactly as they please.

But in the West the woman, and especially the *lady*, finds herself in a false position; for woman, rightly called by the ancients *sexus sequior*, is by no means fit to be the object of our honour and veneration, or to hold her head higher than man and be on equal terms with him. The consequences of this false position are sufficiently obvious. Accordingly it would be a very desirable thing if this Number Two of the human race were in Europe also relegated to her natural place, and an end put to that lady-nuisance, which not only moves all Asia to laughter, but would have been ridiculed by Greece and Rome as well. It is impossible to calculate the good effects which such a change would bring about in our social, civil and political arrangements. There would be no necessity for the

Salic law: it would be a superfluous truism. In Europe the *lady*, strictly so-called, is a being who should not exist at all; she should be either a housewife or a girl who hopes to become one; and she should be brought up, not to be arrogant, but to be thrifty and submissive. It is just because there are such people as *ladies* in Europe that the women of the lower classes, that is to say, the great majority of the sex, are much more unhappy than they are in the East. And even Lord Byron says: *Thought of the state of women under the ancient Greeks—convenient enough. Present state, a remnant of the barbarism of the chivalric and the feudal ages—artificial and unnatural. They ought to mind home—and be well fed and clothed—but not mixed in society. Well educated, too, in religion—but to read neither poetry nor politics—nothing but books of piety and cookery. Music—drawing—dancing—also a little gardening and ploughing now and then. I have seen them mending the roads in Epirus with good success. Why not, as well as hay-making and milking?*

The laws of marriage prevailing in Europe consider the woman as the equivalent of the man—start, that is to say, from a wrong position. In our part of the world where monogamy is the rule, to marry means to have one's rights and double one's duties. Now when the laws gave women equal rights with man, they ought to have also endowed her with a masculine intellect. But the fact is that, just in proportion as the honours and privileges which the laws accord to women exceed the amount which Nature gives, there is a diminution in the number of women who really participate in these privileges; and all the remainder are deprived of their natural rights by just so much as is given to the others over and above their share. For the institution of monogamy, and the laws of marriage which it entails, bestow upon the woman an unnatural position of privilege, by considering her throughout as the full equivalent of the man, which is by no means the case; and seeing thus men who are shrewd and prudent very often scruple to make so great a sacrifice and to acquiesce in so unfair an arrangement.

Consequently, whilst among polygamous nations every woman is provided for, where monogamy prevails the number of married women is limited; and there remains over a large number of women without stay or support, who, in the upper classes, vegetate as useless old maids, and in the lower succumb to hard work for which they are not suited; or else become *filles de joie*, whose life is as destitute of joy as it is of honour. But under the circumstances they become a necessity; and their position is openly recognised as serving the special end of warding off temptation from those women favoured by fate, who have found, or may hope to find, husbands. In London alone there are 80,000 prostitutes. What are they but the women, who, under the institution of monogamy, have come off worst? Theirs is a dreadful fate: they are human sacrifices offered up on the altar of monogamy. The women whose wretched position is here described are the inevitable set-off to the European lady with her arrogance and pretension. Polygamy is therefore a real benefit to the female sex if it is taken as a whole. And, from another point of view, there is no true reason why a man whose wife suffers from chronic illness, or remains barren, or has gradually become too old for him, should not take a second. The motives which induce so many people to become converts to Mormonism appear to be just those which militate against the unnatural institution of monogamy.

Moreover, the bestowal of unnatural rights upon women has imposed upon them unnatural duties, and nevertheless a breach of these duties makes them unhappy. Let me explain. A man may often think that his social or financial position will suffer if he marries, unless he makes some brilliant alliance. His desire will then be to win a woman of his own choice under conditions other than those of marriage, such as will secure her position and that of the children. However fair, reasonable, fit and proper these conditions may be, if the woman consents by foregoing that undue amount of privilege which marriage alone can bestow, she to some extent loses her honour, because marriage is the basis of civic society; and she will lead an unhappy life, since human nature is so constituted that we pay an attention to the opinion of other people which is out of all proportion to its value. On the other hand, if she does not consent, she runs the risk either of having to be given in marriage to a man whom she does not like, or of being landed high and dry as an old maid; for the period during which she has a chance of being settled for life is very short. And in view of this aspect of the institution of monogamy, Thomasius' profoundly learned treatise *de Concubinatu* is well worth reading; for it shows that, amongst all nations and in all ages, down to the Lutheran Reformation, concubinage was permitted; nay, that it was an institution which was to a certain extent actually recognised by law, and attended with no dishonour. It was only the Lutheran Reformation that degraded it from this position. It was seen to be a further justification for the marriage of the clergy; and then, after that, the Catholic Church did not dare to remain behindhand in the matter.

There is no use arguing about polygamy; it must be taken as *de facto* existing everywhere, and the only question is as to how it shall be regulated. Where are there, then, any real monogamists? We all live, at any rate, for a time, and most of us, always, in polygamy. And so, since every man needs many women, there is nothing fairer than to allow him, nay, to make it incumbent upon him, to provide for many women. This will reduce woman to her true and natural position as a subordinate being; and the *lady—*

that monster of European civilisation and Teutonico-Christian stupidity—will disappear from the world, leaving only *women,* but no more *unhappy women,* of whom Europe is now full.

In India no woman is ever independent, but in accordance with the law of Manu, she stands under the control of her father, her husband, her brother or her son. It is, to be sure, a revolting thing that a widow should immolate herself upon her husband's funeral pyre; but it is also revolting that she should spend her husband's money with her paramours—the money for which he toiled his whole life long, in the consoling belief that he was providing for his children. Happy are those who have kept the middle course— *medium tenuere beati.*

The first love of a mother for her child is, with the lower animals as with men, of a purely *instinctive* character, and so it ceases when the child is no longer in a physically helpless condition. After that, the first love should give way to one that is based on habit and reason; but this often fails to make its appearance, especially where the mother did not love the father. The love of a father for his child is of a different order, and more likely to last; because it has its foundation in the fact that in the child he recognises his own inner self; that is to say, his love for it is metaphysical in its origin.

In almost all nations, whether of the ancient or the modern world, even amongst the Hottentots, property is inherited by the male descendants alone; it is only in Europe that a departure has taken place; but not amongst the nobility, however. That the property which has cost men long years of toil and effort, and been won with so much difficulty, should afterwards come into the hands of women, who then, in their lack of reason, squander it in a short time, or otherwise fool it away, is a grievance and a wrong, as serious as it is common, which should be prevented by limiting the right of women to inherit. In my opinion the best arrangement would be that by which women, whether widows or daughters, should never receive anything beyond the interest for life on property secured by mortgage, and in no case the property itself, or the capital, except where all male descendants fail. The people who make money are men, not women; and it follows from this that women are neither justified in having unconditional possession of it, nor fit persons to be entrusted with its administration. When wealth, in any true sense of the word, that is to say, funds, houses or land, is to go to them as an inheritance, they should never be allowed the free disposition of it. In their case a guardian should always be appointed; and hence they should never be given the free control of their own children, wherever it can be avoided. The vanity of women, even though it should not prove to be greater than that of men, has this much danger in it that it takes an entirely material direction. They are vain, I mean, of their personal beauty, and then of finery, show and magnificence. That is just why they are so much in their element in society. It is this, too, which makes them so inclined to be extravagant, all the more as their reasoning power is low. Accordingly we find an ancient writer describing woman as in general of an extravagant nature— Γυνὴ τὸ σύνολον ἔστι δαπανηρὸν φύσει.[3] But with men vanity often takes the direction of non-material advantages, such as intellect, learning, courage.

In the *Politics*[4] Aristotle explains the great disadvantage which accrued to the Spartans from the fact that they conceded too much to their women, by giving them the right of inheritance and dower, and a great amount of independence; and he shows how much this contributed to Sparta's fall. May it not be the case in France that the influence of women, which went on increasing steadily from the time of Louis XIII., was to blame for that gradual corruption of the Court and the Government, which brought about the Revolution of 1789, of which all subsequent disturbances have been the fruit? However that may be, the false position which women occupy, demonstrated as it is, in the most glaring way, the institution of the *lady,* is a fundamental defect in our social scheme, and this defect, proceeding from the very heart of it, must spread its baneful influence in all directions.

That woman is by nature meant to obey may be seen by the fact that every woman who is placed in the unnatural position of complete independence, immediately attaches herself to some man, by whom she allows herself to be guided and ruled. It is because she needs a lord and master. If she is young, it will be a lover; if she is old, a priest.

3. Brunck's *Gnomici poetae graeci* v. 115.

4. Bk. I., ch. 9.

IV
ANCIENT AND MEDIEVAL INFLUENCES

In this section we reach into the historical roots of our concepts of human nature and of woman. That these roots are still quite alive is apparent to anyone familiar with the Judaic-Christian tradition which links contemporary thought to its classical sources. While we may personally reject or challenge these sources, the ideas they express have undoubtedly influenced us through the world about us.

Among the Greeks of the fifth century B.C., Plato and Aristotle were principal contributors to an intellectual heritage utilized by medieval theologians in order to teach their religious beliefs. Foremost among the Christian theologians were Augustine and Thomas Aquinas. The former drew heavily upon Plato, the latter upon Aristotle; but both regarded the Bible as an utterly reliable source of truth about God, the world, and human nature.

PLATO

The principal writings of Plato (427–437 B.C.) are dialogues in which Socrates, his teacher, generally articulates the positions of the author. In the *Republic,* from which the following selection is excerpted (Book V, 451c–466d), Plato describes two worlds: a world of forms or ideas, and a world of physical objects or appearances. Since these two worlds are viewed as radically distinct, Plato is often called a dualist. His basic claim, made plausible through the Myth of the Cave (Book VI), is that the world of forms (of immaterial objects) is the real world, while the world of appearances (the world we perceive), is not.

Graphically, this *Weltanschauung* of Plato may be represented as follows:

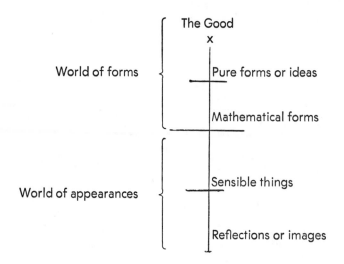

In Book VII of the *Republic*, Plato describes the division of each world: the world of appearances includes material objects (such as your body) and reflections (such as your mirror image); and the world of forms includes mathematical forms or quantitative abstractions (such as square or hypotenuse) and pure forms of qualitative abstractions (such as justice or gentleness). But Plato's dualism denies both reality and intelligibility to anything that is merely physical or material. We can only know that which is real, and reality is immaterial, universal, and unchanging. Our awareness of changing, particular appearances is not knowledge but opinion. As one advances towards the highest form (the Good), one increases in knowledge and reality; thus my body, while not belonging to the world of forms, is closer to that reality than my shadow, and justice is a higher level of being or reality than a circle.

Plato's Concept of Human Nature

Since the real world for Plato is essentially immaterial, human reality is essentially immaterial, or soul. This soul comprises three parts: an appetitive part (desire for sensual fulfillment); a courageous and spirited part (pursuit of honor and fame); and a rational part (the reason, capable of controlling and ordering the other parts). Of these, the last is the immortal part of human nature. Plato regards the body as a kind of prison from which the soul may one day be released through death to live a purely rational life. If you were to find a place for yourself within Plato's world of forms and world of appearances, you might see yourself sitting on a line separating the two worlds, your head in one, and your feet

dangling in the other; through your body you are merely appearance—unreal and unintelligible; through your soul you are truly
human—real and rational.

Plato's Republic is an ideally just state, with a citizenry composed of workers, warriors, and philosopher-rulers or guardians.
Each inhabitant is educated to fulfill the function for which he
or she is best suited by nature. The term "nature" in the *Republic* is
used in several ways: Plato speaks of the nature of an individual
person (male or female), the nature of woman (in general), and
the nature of humankind. For the good of the state, Plato insists
on respecting the natural differences among individuals. The more
universal good for Plato has priority over less universal goods;
thus, the good of one sex or class has a lower priority than the good
of all humankind. The greater good is always the more rational,
immaterial, and unchanging, when contrasted with other goods of
nature. Radical practices such as those recommended for the Republic (for example, community of wives and children, and control
of reproduction) should be assessed in light of this priority. Although Plato's later views concerning women were more conservative (e.g., in *The Laws*), his emphasis on the universal good remained consistent.

PLATO   Republic
(from Book V)

We must now, said I, go back to what should have been said
earlier in sequence. However, this may well be the right way: c
after we have completed the parts that men must play, we
turn to those of women, especially as you call on me to do so.

For men of such a nature and education as we have described there is, in my opinion, no other right way to deal
with wives and children than following the road upon which
we started them. We attempted, in our argument, to establish
the men as guardians of the flock. — Yes.

Let us then give them for the birth and upbringing of chil-   d
dren a system appropriate to that function and see whether it
suits us or not. — How?

Like this: do we think that the wives of our guardian
watchdogs should join in whatever guardian duties the men
fulfill, join them in the hunt, and do everything else in common, or should we keep the women at home as unable to do
so because they must bear and rear their young, and leave to
the men the labour and the whole care of the flock?

e   All things, he said, should be done in common, except that
the women are physically weaker and the men stronger.

And is it possible, I asked, to make use of living creatures
for the same purposes unless you give them the same upbringing and education? — It is not possible.

So if we use the women for the same tasks as the men, they
452   must be taught the same things. — Yes.

Now we gave the men artistic and physical culture. — Yes.

So we must give both also to the women, as well as training
in war, and use them for the same tasks. — That seems to
follow from what you say.

Perhaps, I said, many of the things we are saying, being
contrary to custom, would stir up ridicule, if carried out in
practice in the way we are telling them. — They certainly
would, he said.

What, I asked, is the most ridiculous feature you see in
b   this? Or is it obvious that women should exercise naked in
the palaestra along with the men, not only the young women
but the older women too, as the old men do in the gymnasia
when their bodies are wrinkled and not pleasant to look at
and yet they are fond of physical exercise? — Yes, by Zeus,
he said, it would appear ridiculous as things stand now.

Surely, I said, now that we have started on this argument,
c   we must not be afraid of all the jokes of the kind that the wits
will make about such a change in physical and artistic culture, and not least about the women carrying arms and riding
horses. — You are right, he said.

As we have begun this discussion we must go on to the
tougher part of the law and beg these people not to practise
their own trade of comedy at our expense but to be serious
and to remember that it is not very long since the Greeks
thought it ugly and ridiculous, as the majority of barbarians
still do, for men to be seen naked. When first the cretans and
d   then the Lacedaemonians started their physical training, the
wits of those days could have ridiculed it all, or do you not
think so? — I do.

But I think that after it was found in practice to be better
to strip than to cover up all those parts, then the spectacle
ceased to be looked on as ridiculous because reasonable argument had shown that it was best. This showed that it is foolish
to think anything ridiculous except what is bad, or to try to
e   raise a laugh at any other spectacle than that of ignorance
and evil as being ridiculous, as it is foolish to be in earnest
about any other standard of beauty than that of the good. —
Most certainly.

Must we not first agree whether our proposals are possible

or not? And we must grant an opportunity for discussion to anyone who, in jest or seriously, wishes to argue the point 453 whether female human nature can share all the tasks of the male sex, or none at all, or some but not others, and to which of the two waging war belongs. Would this not be the best beginning and likely to lead to the best conclusion? — Certainly.

Do you then want us to dispute among ourselves on behalf of those others, lest the other side of the argument fall by default? — There is nothing to stop us. b

Let us then speak on their behalf: "Socrates and Glaucon, there is no need for others to argue with you. You yourselves, when you began to found your city, agreed that each person must pursue the one task for which he is fitted by nature." I think we did agree to this, of course. — "Can you deny that a woman is by nature very different from a man?" — Of course not. "And is it not proper to assign a different task to each according to their nature?" — Certainly. "How then are you c not wrong and contradicting yourselves when you say that men and women must do the same things, when they have quite separate natures?" Do you have any defence against that argument, my good friend?

That is not very easy offhand, he said, but I ask and beg you to explain the argument on our side, whatever it is.

It is these and many other difficulties that I foresaw, Glaucon, I said, when I was afraid and hesitated to tackle the law d concerning the acquiring of wives and the upbringing of children. — By Zeus, he said, it does not seem at all easy.

It is not, said I, but the fact is that whether a man falls into a small swimming pool or in the middle of the ocean, he must swim all the same. — Certainly.

So when we must swim too and try to save ourselves from the sea of our argument, hoping that a dolphin will pick us up or we may find some other miraculous deliverance. — It e seems so.

Come now, said I, let us see if we can find a way out. We have agreed that a different nature must follow a different occupation and that the nature of man and woman is different, and we now say that different natures must follow the same pursuits. This is the accusation brought against us. — Surely.

How grand is the power of disputation, Glaucon. — Why? 454

Because, I said, many people fall into it unwittingly and think they are not disputing but conversing because they cannot analyze their subject into its parts, but they pursue mere verbal contradictions of what has been said, thus engaging in a dispute rather than in a conversation.

Many people, he said, have that experience, but does this also apply to us at the present moment?

b   It most certainly does, I said. I am afraid we have indeed unwittingly fallen into disputation. — How?

We are bravely, but in a disputatious and verbal fashion, pursuing the principle that a nature which is not the same must not engage in the same pursuits, but when we assigned different tasks to a different nature and the same to the same nature, we did not examine at all what kind of difference and sameness of nature we had in mind and in what regard we were distinguishing them. — No, we did not look into that.

c   We might therefore just as well, it seems, ask ourselves whether the nature of bald men and long-haired men is the same and not opposite, and then, agreeing that they are opposite, if we allow bald men to be cobblers, not allow long-haired men to be, or again if long-haired men are cobblers, not allow the others to be. — That would indeed be ridiculous.

Is it ridiculous for any other reason than because we did not fully consider their same or different natures in every d respect but we were only watching the kind of difference and sameness which applied to those particular pursuits? For example, a male and a female physician, we said, have the same nature of soul, or do you not think so? — I do.

But a physician and a carpenter have a different nature? — Surely.

Therefore, I said, if the male and the female are seen to be different as regards a particular craft or other pursuit we shall say this must be assigned to one or the other. But if they seem to differ in this particular only, that the female bears children while the male begets them, we shall say that there e has been no kind of proof that a woman is different from a man as regards the duties we are talking about, and we shall still believe that our guardians and their wives should follow the same pursuits. — And rightly so.

Next we shall bid anyone who holds the contrary view to 455 instruct us in this: with regard to what craft or pursuit concerned with the establishment of the city is the nature of man and woman not the same but different? — That is right.

Someone else might very well say what you said a short time ago, that it is not easy to give an immediate reply, but that it would not be at all difficult after considering the question. — He might say that.

Do you then want us to beg the one who raises these ob- b jections to follow us to see whether we can show him that no pursuit connected with the management of the city belongs in particular to a woman? — Certainly.

Come now, we shall say to him, give us an answer: did you mean that one person had a natural ability for a certain pursuit, while another had not, when the first learned it easily, the latter with difficulty? The one, after a brief period of instructions, was able to find things out for himself from what he had learned, while the other, after much instruction, could not even remember what he had learned; the former's body adequately served his mind, while the other's physical reactions opposed his. Are there any other ways in which you distinguished the naturally gifted in each case from those who were not? — No one will say anything else. c

Do you know of any occupation practised by mankind in which the male sex is not superior to the female in all these respects? Or shall we pursue the argument at length by mentioning weaving, baking cakes, cooking vegetables, tasks in which the female sex certainly seems to distinguish itself, and in which it is most laughable of all for women to be inferior to men? d

What you say is true, he said, namely that one sex is much superior to the other in almost everything, yet many women are better than many men in many things, but on the whole it is as you say.

There is therefore no pursuit connected with city management which belongs to woman because she is a woman, or to a man because he is a man, but various natures are scattered in the same way among both kinds of persons. Woman by nature shares all pursuits, and so does man, but in all of them woman is a physically weaker creature than man. — Certainly. e

Shall we then assign them all to men, and none to a woman? — How can we?

One woman, we shall say, is a physician, another is not, one is by nature artistic, another is not. — Quite so.

One may be athletic or warlike, while another is not warlike and has no love of athletics. — I think so. 456

Further, may not one woman love wisdom, another hate it, or one may be high-spirited, another be without spirit? — That too.

So one woman may have a guardian nature, the other not. Was it not a nature with these qualities which we selected among men for our male guardians too? — We did.

Therefore the nature of man and woman is the same as regards guarding the city, except in so far as she is physically weaker, and the man's nature stronger. — So it seems.

Such women must then be chosen along with such men to b

live with them and share their guardianship, since they are
qualified and akin to them by nature. — Certainly.

Must we not assign the same pursuits to the same natures? — The same.

We have come round then to what we said before, and we
agree that it is not against nature to give to the wives of the
guardians an education in the arts and physical culture. —
Definitely not.

c We are not legislating against nature or indulging in mere
wishful thinking since the law we established is in accord
with nature. It is rather the contrary present practice which
is against nature as it seems. — It appears so.

Now we were to examine whether our proposals were possible and the best. — We were.

That they are possible is now agreed? — Yes.

After this we must seek agreement whether they are the
best. — Clearly.

With a view to having women guardians, we should not
have one kind of education to fashion the men, and another
d for the women, especially as they have the same nature to
begin with. — No, not another.

What is your opinion of this kind of thing? — Of what?

About thinking to yourself that one man is better and another worse, or do you think that they are all alike? — Certainly not.

In the city we were establishing, do you think the guardians are made better men by the education they have received,
or the cobblers who were educated for their craft? — Your
question is ridiculous.

e I know, said I. Well, are these guardians not the best of
all the citizens? — By far.

Will then these women guardians not be the best of
women? — That too by far.

Is there anything better for a city than to have the best
possible men and women? — Nothing.

457 And it is the arts and physical culture, as we have described them, which will achieve this? — Of course.

So the institution we have established is not only possible
but also the best. — That is so.

The women then must strip for their physical training,
since they will be clothed in excellence. They must share
in war and the other duties of the guardians about the city,
and have no other occupation; the lighter duties will be assigned to them because of the weakness of their sex. The man
b who laughs at the sight of naked women exercising for the

best of reasons is "plucking the unripe fruit of laughter",
he understands nothing of what he is laughing at, it seems,
nor what he is doing. For it is and always will be a fine saying
that what is beneficial is beautiful, what is harmful is ugly. —
Very definitely.

Let us say then that we have escaped from one wave of
criticism in our discussion of the law about women, and we
have not been altogether swamped when we laid it down
that male and female guardians must share all their duties in   c
common, and our argument is consistent when it states that
this is both possible and beneficial. — It is, he said, certainly
no small wave from which you are escaping.

You will not say this was a big one when you see the one
that follows, I said. — Speak up, then, he said, and let me
see it.

I think, I said, that the law follows from the last and those
that have gone before. — What law?

All these women shall be wives in common to all the men,   d
and not one of them shall live privately with any man; the
children too should be held in common so that no parent
shall know which is his own offspring, and no child shall know
his parent.

This proposal raises far more doubts than the last, both
as to its possibility and its usefulness, he said.

I do not think its usefulness will be disputed, I said, namely
that it is not a great blessing to hold wives in common, and
children too, provided it is possible. I think that most controversy will arise on the question of its possibility. — Both   e
points, he said, will certainly be disputed.

You mean that I will have to fight a combination of arguments. I thought I could escape by running away from one
of them, if you thought the proposal beneficial, and that it
would only remain for me to argue its possibility. — I saw
you running away, he said, but you must explain both.

Well, I said, I must take my punishment. Allow me, however, to indulge myself as if on holiday, as lazy-minded   458
people feast on their own thoughts whenever they take a walk
alone. Instead of finding out how something they desire may
become a reality, such people pass over that question to
avoid wearying themselves by deliberating on what is possible and what is not; they assume that what they desire is
available; they arrange the details and enjoy themselves
thinking about all they will do when it has come to pass, thus
making a lazy mind ever lazier. I am myself at this moment   b
getting soft, and I want to delay consideration of the feasi-

bility of our proposal until later. I will assume that it is feasible and examine, if you will allow me, how the rulers will arrange these things when they happen and I will argue that this will be most beneficial to the city and to the guardians. This I will try to examine along with you, and deal with the other question later, if you permit. — I permit it, he said, carry on with your examination.

c   I think that surely our rulers, if indeed they are worthy of the name, and their auxiliaries as well, will be willing, the latter to do what they are told, the former to give the orders, in part by obeying the laws themselves, and in part, in such matters as we have entrusted to them, by imitating these laws. — That is likely.

You then, as their lawgiver, just as you chose the men, will in the same manner choose the women and provide as far as possible those of the same nature. Since they have their dwellings and meals together and none of them possess any-
d   thing of the kind as private property, they will be together and mix together both in the gymnasia and in the rest of their education and they will, I think, be driven by inborn necessity to have intercourse with one another. Or do you not think that what I say will of necessity happen?

The necessity is not of a mathematical but of an erotic kind, he said, and this is probably stronger in persuading and compelling the mass of the people.

Yes indeed, I said. The next point is, Glaucon, that promiscuity is impious in a city of fortunate people, nor will the
e   rules allow it. — It is not right.

After this we must obviously make marriage as sacred as possible, and sacred marriages will be those which are the most beneficial. — Most certainly.

459   How then will they be most beneficial? Tell me, Glaucon: I see that at home you have hunting dogs and quite a number of pedigree birds. Did you then, by Zeus, pay any attention to their unions and breeding? — In what way? he asked.

In the first place, though they are all of good stock, are there not some who are and prove themselves to be best? — There are.

Do you breed equally from them all, or are you anxious to breed most from the best? — From the best.

b   Further, do you breed from the youngest, or from the oldest, or from those in their prime? — From those in their prime.

And do you think that if they were not bred in this way, your stock of birds and dogs would deteriorate considerably? — I do.

Do you think things are any different in the case of horses and the other animals? — That would indeed be absurd.

Good gracious, my friend, I said, how great is our need for extremely able rulers if the same is true for the human race. — c It is, but what about it?

Because they will need to use a good many drugs. For people who do not need drugs but are willing to follow a diet even an inferior physician will be sufficient, but when drugs are needed, we know that a bolder physician is required. — True, but what do you have in mind?

This, I said: our rulers will probably have to make considerable use of lies and deceit for the good of their subjects. d We said that all such things are useful as a kind of drug. — And rightly so.

This "rightly" will occur frequently in matters of marriage and the bearing of children. — How so?

It follows from our previous agreement that the best men must have intercourse with the best women as frequently as possible, and the opposite is true of the very inferior men and women; the offspring of the former must be reared, but not e the offspring of the latter, if our herd is to be of the highest possible quality. Only the rulers should know of these arrangements, if our herd of guardians is to avoid all dissension as far as possible. — Quite right.

Therefore certain festivals will be established by law at which we shall bring the brides and grooms together; there 460 will also be sacrifices, and our poets must compose hymns to celebrate the marriages. The number of marriages we shall leave to the rulers to decide, in such a way as to keep the number of males as stable as possible, taking into account war, disease, and similar factors so that our city shall, as far as possible, become neither too big nor too small. — Right.

There will have to be some clever lots introduced, so that at each marriage celebration the inferior man we mentioned will blame chance but not the rulers. — Quite so.

The young men who have distinguished themselves in war b or in other ways must be given awards consisting of other prizes and also more abundant permission to sleep with women, so that we may have a good excuse to have as many children as possible begotten by them. — Right.

As the children are born, officials appointed for the purpose — be they men or women or both, since our offices are open to both women and men — will take them. — Yes.

The children of good parents they will take to a rearing c pen in the care of nurses living apart in a certain section of the city; the children of inferior parents, or any child of the others born defective, they will hide, as is fitting, in a secret and unknown place. — Yes, he said, if the breed of the guardians is to remain pure.

d   The nurses will also see to it that the mothers are brought to the rearing pen when their breasts have milk, but take every precaution that no mother shall know her own child; they will provide wet nurses if the number of mothers is insufficient; they will take care that the mothers suckle the children for only a reasonable time; the care of sleepless children and all other troublesome duties will belong to the wet nurses and other attendants.

You are making it very easy, he said, for the wives of the guardians to have children.

And that is fitting, I said. Let us take up the next point of our proposal: We said that the children's parents should be in their prime. — True.

e   Do you agree that a reasonable interpretation of this is twenty years for a woman and thirty years for a man? — Which years?

A woman, I said, is to bear children for the state from the age of twenty to the age of forty, a man after he has passed
461   "his peak as a racer" begets children for the state till he reaches fifty. — This, he said, is the physical and mental peak for both.

If a man either younger or older than this meddles with procreation for the state, we shall declare his offence to be neither pious nor right as he begets for the city a child which, if he remains secret, will be born without benefit of the sacrifices and prayers which priests and priestesses and the whole city utter at every marriage festival, that the children of good and useful parents may always prove themselves better and
b   more useful; but this child is born in darkness, the result of dangerous incontinence. — Right.

The same law will apply, I said, if a man still of begetting years unites with a woman of child-bearing age without the sanction of the rulers; we shall say that he brings to the city an unauthorized and unhallowed bastard. — Quite right.

However, I think that when women and men have passed
c   the age of having children, we shall leave them free to have intercourse with anyone they wish, with these exceptions: for a man, his daughter or mother, or the daughter's daughters, or his mother's female progenitors; for a woman, a son or father, their male issue or progenitors. Having received these instructions they should be very careful not to bring a single child into the light, but if one should be conceived, and forces

its way to the light, they must deal with it knowing that no nurture is available for it.

This too, he said, is sensibly spoken, but how shall they know their fathers and daughters and those other relation- d ships you mentioned?

They have no means of knowing, I said, but all the children who are born in the tenth and seventh month after a man became a bridegroom he will call sons if they are male, daughters if they are female, and they will call him father, and so too he will call their offspring his grandchildren who in turn will call the first group their grandfathers and grand-mothers. Those born during the time when their fathers and mothers were having children they will call their brothers and sisters, so that, as I said, these groups will have no sexual relations with each other. But the law will allow brothers and e sisters to live together if the lot so falls and the Pythian ap-proves. — Quite right.

This then is the holding in common of wives and children for the guardians of your city. We must now confirm in our argument that it conforms with the rest of our constitution 462 and is by far the best. Or how are we to proceed? — In that way, by Zeus.

Is not the first step towards agreement to ask ourselves what we say is the greatest good in the management of the city? At this the lawgiver must aim in making his laws. Also what is the greatest evil. Then we should examine whether the system we have just described follows the tracks of the good and not those of evil. — By all means.

Is there any greater evil we can mention for a city than whatever tears it apart into many communities instead of b one? — There is not.

Do not common feelings of pleasure and pain bind the city together, when as nearly as possible all the citizens equally rejoice or feel pain at the same successes and fail-ures? — Most certainly.

For such feelings to be isolated and private dissolves the city's unity, when some suffer greatly while others greatly c rejoice at the same public or private events. — Of course.

And that sort of thing happens whenever such words as "mine" and "not mine" — and so with "another's" — are not used in unison. — Most certainly.

And the city which most closely resembles the individual? When one of us hurts his finger, the whole organism which binds body and soul together into the unitary system man-aged by the ruling part of it shares the pain at once through-d   out when one part suffers. This is why we say that the man has a pain in his finger, and the same can be said of any part of the man, both about the pain which any part suffers, and its pleasure when it finds relief.

Certainly, he said. As for your question, the best managed city certainly closely resembles such an organism.

And whenever anything good or bad happens to a single
e   one of its citizens, such a city will certainly say that this citizen is a part of itself, and the whole city will rejoice or suffer with him. — That must be so, if it has good laws.

It is time now, I said, for us to return to our own city and to look there for the features we have agreed on, whether it, or any other city, possesses them to the greatest degree. — We must do so.

463   Well then. There are rulers and people in the other cities as well as in this one? — There are.

And they call each other fellow-citizens. — Of course.

Besides the word fellow-citizens, what do the people call the rulers in the other cities?

In many they call them masters, but in democracies they call them by this very name, rulers.

What do the people call them in our city? Besides fellow
b   citizens, what do they call the rulers? — Saviors and helpers.

And what do the rulers call the people? — Providers of food and wages.

What do the rulers call the people in other cities? — Slaves.

And what do the rulers call each other? — Fellow rulers.

And ours? — Fellow guardians.

Can you tell me whether a ruler in the other cities might address one of his fellow rulers as his kinsman and another as an outsider? — Certainly, many could.

He then considers his kinsman, and addresses him, as his
c   own, but not the outsider? — That is so.

What about your guardians? Can any of them consider any other of his fellow guardians an outsider and address him as such?

Not in any way, he said, for when he meets any one of them he will think he is meeting a brother or a sister, a father or a mother, a son or a daughter, their offspring or progenitors.

You put that very well, I said, but, further, tell me this:
d   will you legislate these family relationships as names only, or must they act accordingly in all they do? Must a man show to his fathers the respect, solicitude, and obedience to his parents required by law? Otherwise, if he acts differently, he will fare worse at the hands of gods and men as one whose actions are neither pious nor just. Will these be the sayings

that ring in his ears on the part of all citizens from childhood
both about their fathers, those pointed out to them as such,
and about their other kindred — or will there be other voices?

It will be those, he said; it would be absurd if their lips   e
spoke these names of kindred without appropriate action
following.

So in our city more than any other, when any individual
fares well or badly, they would all speak in unison the words
we mentioned just now, namely that "mine" is doing well,
or "mine" is doing badly. — That also is very true.

And we said that such a belief and its expression are fol-   464
lowed by common feelings of pleasure and pain. — And we
were right.

So our citizens will to the greatest extent share the same
thing which they call "mine," with the result that they in
highest degree share common feelings of pleasure and pain. —
Surely.

And besides other arrangements, the reason for this is the
holding of wives and children in common among the guardians. — More than anything else.

This we agreed was the greatest blessing for a city, and we   b
compared a well run city to the body's reaction to pain or
pleasure in any part of it. — And we were right to agree
on that.

So then the cause of the greatest good for our city has
been shown to be the common ownership of wives and children among the auxiliaries. — Certainly.

And in this we are consistent with what went before, for
we said somewhere that they must have no private houses
or land or any private possessions, that they receive their
upkeep from the other citizens as a wage for their guardian-   c
ship, and that they must all spend it in common, if they are
to be real guardians. — Right.

Does now what we said before and what we are saying
now make them even more real guardians, and prevent them
from tearing the city apart by not calling the same thing
"mine," one man applying the word to one thing and another
to another? One man would then drag into his own house   d
whatever he could get hold of away from the others; another
drag things into his different house to another wife and other
children. This would make for private pleasures and pains at
private events. Our people, on the other hand, will think of
the same thing as their own, aim at the same goal, and, as far
as possible, feel pleasure and pain in unison. — Most certainly.

What follows? Will not lawsuits and mutual accusations
disappear from among them, one might say, since they own

e   nothing but their body, everything else being held in common? Hence they will be spared all the dissension which is due to the possession of wealth, children, and families? — They will inevitably be spared them.

Nor could cases of violence or assault rightly occur among them, for we shall declare that it is a fine and just thing to defend oneself against those of the same age, thus compelling them to keep in good physical condition. — Right.

465   The law is right in this also, that if an angry man satisfied his anger in a personal encounter of this kind, he is less likely to turn to more important quarrels. — Certainly.

An older man will have authority over all the young, and be allowed to chastise them. — Obviously.

It is surely also obvious that a younger man, except by order of the rulers, shall not apply violence of any kind to, nor strike, an older man, nor fail to respect him in other ways. There are two adequate guardians to prevent this, namely shame and fear; shame will prevent him laying hands on his

b   parents, fear because the others will come to the rescue of the victim, some as his sons, some as his brothers, and some as his fathers. — That follows, he said.

So the laws will induce people to live at peace with each other. — Very much so.

And if there is no discord among the guardians there is no danger that the rest of the city will start factions against them or among themselves. — No danger.

c   I hesitate to mention the petty evils they will escape: the poor man's flattery of the rich, the perplexities and sufferings involved in bringing up children and in making the necessary money to feed the household, sometimes borrowing, sometimes denying the debt, in one way or another providing enough money to hand over to their wives and household slaves to dispense; all the various troubles which men endure

d   in these matters are quite obvious and sordid and not worth discussing. — They are clear even to the blind.

They will be free of all these, and they will live a life more blessed than that of Olympian victors. — How?

Olympian victors are considered happy on account of only a small part of the blessings available to our guardians, whose victory is even finer and their upkeep from public funds more complete. The victory they gain is the safety of the whole city and the victor's crown they and their children receive is their nurture and all the necessities of life; they

e   receive rewards from their own city while they live, and at their death they are given a worthy funeral. — Certainly fine rewards.

Remember, said I, that earlier in our discussion someone —
I forget who — shocked us by saying that we did not make
our guardians happy, that while it was in their power to own
all the possessions of our citizens, yet they possessed nothing.
We said at the time that we would investigate later whether   466
this would happen, but that our concern at the time was to
make our guardians true guardians and the city as happy as
we could, and that we would not concentrate our attention
upon one group and make them happy in our city. — I remember.

Well now, if the life of the auxiliaries is indeed much finer
and better than that of Olympian victors, it is not to be compared to that of the cobblers or other craftsmen, or with that   b
of the farmers? — I do not think so.

It is surely right to repeat here what I said then, that, if a
guardian seeks happiness in such a way as not even to be a
guardian nor to be satisfied with a life so stable and moderate
and, as we maintain, so much the best; if a silly and youthful
idea of happiness should come into his mind and set him off
to use his power to appropriate everything in the city as his
own, he will realize the true wisdom of Hesiod's saying that   c
somehow "the half is more than the whole."

If he takes my advice, he said, he will stay with this kind
of life.

You agree then, I said, that the women should be associated
with the men in the way we have described in matters of
education and child bearing, and in the guarding of the other
citizens. Both when they remain in the city and when they   d
go to war they must share the guardians' duties, hunt with
them like hounds, share as far as possible in everything in
every way. In doing so they will be acting for the best, and in
no way contrary to woman's nature as compared with man's,
as they were born to associate with one another. — I agree.

It now remains, I said, for us to determine whether this association can be brought about among human beings as it
can among animals, and how it can be brought about. — You
took the words out of my mouth.

As far as war is concerned, I said, the way they will wage   e
it is clear, I think. — How so?

Men and women will campaign together; moreover they
will take the sturdy among their children with them, in order
that, like the children of other craftsmen, they may observe
the actions which they will perform when they grow up.   467
Moreover, in addition to observing these, they can assist and
help in all the duties of war and attend upon their fathers and
mothers. Have you not noticed in the other crafts how the

children of potters for example assist and observe for a long time before they engage in making pots? — Yes indeed.

Should those craftsmen take more care than the guardians in training their children by suitable experience and observation? — That would be quite ridiculous.

b   Besides, every living creature will fight better in the presence of its young. — That is true, but, Socrates, there is a considerable danger that, if they are defeated, as happens frequently in war, they will lose their children's lives as well as their own, thus making it impossible for the rest of the city to recover.

*   *   *

AUGUSTINE

In the contribution of Greek philosophy to medieval thought, Plato was the most widespread and consistent influence, especially as interpreted through Plotinus by Augustine (354–430). Although Augustine considered faith superior to reason as a source of truth, his views also reflect Plato's rather disparaging attitudes toward the body, as well as Plato's insistence that truth is immutable and immaterial. Augustine's own experience may have been an impetus to the development of negative attitudes toward sex. In 386, after having parted from the woman with whom he had lived for over ten years and who bore him a son, Augustine was converted to Christianity. His conversion constituted a deliberate redirection of a natural inclination toward sensual and sexual gratification. While his taste for intellectual pursuits continued, his energies were thereafter channeled toward the fulfillment of religious and ascetic ideals.

Augustine's Concept of Human Nature

Philosophically, Augustine's concept of human nature is platonic: to be human is to be a soul imprisoned by a body. Theologically, however, Augustine amended this view to accommodate the Scriptural data regarding creation. In his work *The Trinity* Augustine explains his concept of the *imago Dei* ("image of God") in light of the statement in Genesis 1:27 that

God created man in the image of himself, in the image of God he created him, male and female he created them.

As God is immaterial, the *imago Dei* is also immaterial, or soul. As God is Trinity (Father, Son, and Spirit), his human image is also trinitarian through its threefold spiritual powers of memory, understanding, and will. Human beings increase in their likeness to God and in fulfillment of their own human reality to the extent that these powers are directed toward God.

The famous Augustinian dictum "Love, and do what you will" can only be properly understood in the light of the preceding concept of human nature. So understood, it is relevant also to Augustine's description of peace: the "tranquillity of order," which is the goal of all societal relationships (including war). The order to be observed involves a notion of authority as service. In the family, for example,

> they who care for the rest rule—the husband the wife, the parents the children, the masters the servants; and they who are cared for obey—the women their husbands, the children their parents, the servants their masters. But in the family of the just man who lives by faith and is as yet a pilgrim journeying on to the celestial city, even those who rule serve those whom they seem to command. . . .

Only where familial roles and authority are so construed can "domestic peace" prevail.

The excerpt from *The Trinity* is taken from Book XII; "The Good of Marriage" and "Adulterous Marriages" are taken from *Treatises on Marriage and Other Subjects*. The excerpt from *Confessions* is from Book XIII; the excerpt from *The City of God* is from Book XXII.

AUGUSTINE   The Trinity

(from Book XII)

 .   .   .   .   .   .

Why . . . does Scripture make no mention except of male and female in the nature of man that has been made to the image of God? For to complete the image of the Trinity the son should also be added, even though he was still placed in the loins of his father, as the woman was in his side. Or perhaps the woman, too, was already made, and Scripture has combined in a summary statement that of which it will explain more carefully later on, how it was done, and for this reason could not mention the son because he was not yet born? As if the Holy Spirit, who was later to describe the birth of the son in its proper place, could not have also included it in this brief account, just as He afterwards spoke about the woman in the proper place, who was taken from the side of the man, and yet has not failed to make mention of her here.

We ought . . . not to understand man as made to the image of the exalted Trinity, that is, to the image of God, in such a way that the same image is understood to be in three human beings; especially since the Apostle says that the man is the image of God, and consequently should remove the covering from his head, which he warns the woman to use, when he speaks as follows: 'A man indeed ought not to cover his head, because he is the image and glory of God. But the woman is the glory of the man.'

What, then, is to be said about this? If the woman according to her own person completes the image of the Trinity, why is the man still called that image when she has been taken from his side? Or if even one human person out of three can be called the image of God, as each person in the exalted Trinity itself is also God, why is not the woman also the image of God? For this is also the reason why she is commanded to cover her head, which he is forbidden to do because he is the image of God.

But we must see how the words spoken by the Apostle, that not the woman but the man is the image of God, are not contrary to that which is written in Genesis: 'God made man, to the image of God he made him; male and female he made them and blessed them.' For he says that human nature itself, which is complete in both sexes, has been made to the image of God, and he does not exclude the woman from being understood as the image of God. For after he had said that God made man to the image of God, he went on to say: 'He made him male and female,' or at any rate (if we punctuate this passage differently) 'male and female he made them.' In what sense, therefore, are we to understand the Apostle, that the man is the image of God, and consequently is forbidden to cover his head, but the woman is not, and on this account is commanded to do so? The solution lies, I think, in what I already said when discussing the nature of the human mind, namely, that the woman together with her husband is the image of God, so that that whole substance is one image. But when she is assigned as a help-mate, a function that pertains to her alone, then she is not the image of God; but as far as the man is concerned, he is by himself alone the image of God, just as fully and completely as when he and the woman are joined together into one.

As we said of the nature of the human mind, that if as a whole it contemplates the truth, it is the image of God; and when its functions are divided and something of it is diverted to the handling of temporal things, nevertheless that part which consults the truth is the image of God, but that other part, which is directed to the handling of inferior things, is not the image of God. And since the more it has extended itself towards that which is eternal, so much the more is it formed thereby to the image of God, and on that account it is not to be restrained so as to hold itself back and refrain from thence; therefore, the man ought not to cover his head.

But because an all too great advance towards the inferior things is dangerous to that rational knowledge which is concerned with corporeal and temporal things, it ought to have a power over its head; this is indicated by the veil which signifies that it ought to be kept in check. For a sacred and pious meaning is pleasing to the holy angels. For God does not see things according to the measure of time, nor is anything new wrought in His vision and knowledge when anything temporal and transitory takes place, as the senses are affected by such things, whether the carnal senses of animals and men, or even the heavenly senses of the angels.

That the Apostle Paul intended by this distinction between the male and female sex to signify the mystery of a more hidden truth can be understood from this, that he says in another place that she is indeed a widow, who is desolate, without sons and nephews, and yet that she ought to trust in the Lord and continue in prayers night and day; he here indicates that the woman having been seduced and brought into transgression will be saved through childbearing, and then he has added: 'If they shall continue in faith and love and holiness with sobriety' [1 *Tim.* 2.15]. As if it could possibly harm a good widow if she did not have any children, or if those whom she had did not wish to continue in good works!

But because those which are called good works are, as it were, the sons of our life, according to the sense in which it is asked, what is a man's life? that is, how does he conduct himself in temporal things? and because these good works are wont to be practiced chiefly in the offices of mercy, but the works of mercy profit nothing either to the pagans or to the Jews, who do not believe in Christ, or to any heretics or schismatics, in whom faith, charity, and sober holiness are not found, what the Apostle meant to signify is evident, and it is expressed figuratively and mystically, because he was speaking about the veiling of the woman's head, which will remain an empty precept, unless it is referred to some hidden mystery.

For as not only the most true reason, but also the authority of the Apostle himself declares, man was made to the image of God, not according to the form of the body, but according to the rational mind. For it is a vain and degrading thought which represents God as circumscribed and limited by the outlines of corporeal members. Moreover, does not this same blessed Apostle say: 'Be renewed in the spirit of your mind, and put on the new man, him who is created according to God' [*Eph.* 4.23–24], and even more plainly in another place: 'Stripping yourselves of the old man with his deeds, put on the new, who is renewed unto the knowledge of God according to the image of him that created him' [*Cf. Col.* 3.9–10]? If, therefore, we are renewed in the spirit of our mind, and it is precisely the new man who is renewed unto the knowledge of God, according to the image of Him who created him, then no one can doubt that man has been made to the image of Him who created him, not according to the body, nor according to any part of the mind, but according to the rational mind where the knowledge of God can reside.

But according to this renewal we are also made the sons of God through the Baptism of Christ, and when we put on the new man, we certainly put on Christ through faith. Who is it, then, that would exclude women from this fellowship, since they are with us co-heirs of grace, and since the same Apostle says in another place: 'For you are all children of God through faith in Christ Jesus. For whoever have been baptized in Christ, has put on Christ. There is neither Jew nor Greek, there is neither slave nor freeman, there is neither male nor female. For you are all one in Christ Jesus' [*Cf. Gal.* 3.26–28]. Have the believing women, therefore, lost their bodily sex?

But because they are renewed there to the image of God, where there is no sex, man is made there to the image of God, where there is no sex, namely, in the spirit of his mind. Why, then, is the man on that account not bound to cover his head because he is the image and glory of God, but the woman must cover it because she is the glory of the man, just as if the woman were not renewed in the spirit of her mind, who is renewed unto the knowledge of God according to the image of Him who created him? But because she differs from the man by her bodily sex, that part of the reason which is turned aside to regulate temporal things, could be properly symbolized by her corporeal veil; so that the image of God does not remain except in that part of the mind of man in which it clings to the contemplation and consideration of the external reasons, which, as is evident, not only men but also women possess.

❋   ❋   ❋

AUGUSTINE 'Treatises on Marriage and Other Subjects'

THE GOOD OF MARRIAGE

. . . This is what we now say, that according to the present condition of birth and death, which we know and in which we were created, the marriage of male and female is something good. This union divine Scripture so commands that it is not permitted a woman who has been dismissed by her husband to marry again, as long as her husband lives, nor is it permitted a man who has been dismissed by his wife to marry again, unless she who left has died. Therefore, regarding the good of marriage, which even the Lord confirmed in the Gospel, not only because He forbade the dismissal of a wife except for fornication, but also because He came to the marriage when invited, there is merit in inquiring why it is a good.

This does not seem to me to be a good solely because of the procreation of children, but also because of the natural companionship between the two sexes. Otherwise, we could not speak of marriage in the case of old people, especially if they had either lost their children or had begotten none at all. But, in a good marriage, although one of many years, even if the ardor of youths has cooled between man and woman, the order of charity still flourishes between husband and wife. They are better in proportion as they begin the earlier to refrain by mutual consent from sexual intercourse, not that it would afterwards happen of necessity that they would not be able to do what they wished, but that it would be a matter of praise that they had refused beforehand what they were able to do. If, then, there is observed that promise of respect and of services due to each other by either sex, even though both members weaken in health and become almost corpse-like, the chastity of souls rightly joined together continues the purer, the more it has been proved, and the more secure, the more it has been calmed.

Marriage has also this good, that carnal or youthful incontinence, even if it is bad, is turned to the honorable task of begetting children, so that marital intercourse makes something good out of the evil of lust. Finally, the concupiscence of the flesh, which parental affection tempers, is repressed and becomes inflamed more modestly. For a kind of dignity prevails when, as the husband and wife they unite in the marriage act, they think of themselves as mother and father. . . .

. . . If we compare the things themselves, in no way can it be doubted that the chastity of continence is better than the chastity of marriage. Although both, indeed, are a good, when we compare the men, the one who has the greater good than the other is the better. . . .

We must take this into account, too, that it is not right to compare men with men in some one good. For, it can happen that one does not have something that the other has, but he has something that is to be valued more highly. Greater, indeed, is the good of obedience than the good of continence. Marriage is nowhere condemned by the authority of our Scriptures; disobedience, however, is nowhere condoned. . . .

The right question is plainly not whether a virgin thoroughly disobedient should be compared with an obedient married woman, but a less obedient to a more obedient, for there is also nuptial chastity and it is indeed a good, but a lesser one than virginal chastity. Therefore, if the woman who is inferior in the good of obedience in proportion as she is greater in the good of chastity is compared with the other, then he who sees, when he compares chastity itself and obedience, that obedience in a certain way is the mother of all virtues, judges which woman is to be placed first. On this account, then, there can be obedience without virginity, because virginity is of counsel, not of precept. I am speaking of that obedience whereby precepts are obeyed. There can be obedience to precepts without virginity, but there cannot be this obedience without chastity. For it is of the essence of chastity not to commit fornication, not to commit adultery, not to be stained with any illicit intercourse. Whoever do not observe these precepts act against the commands of God and on this account are banished from the virtue of obedience. Virginity can exist by itself without obedience, since a woman can, although accepting the counsel of virginity and guarding her virginity, neglect the precepts; just as we know many sacred virgins who are garrulous, inquisitive, addicted to drink, contentious, greedy, proud. All these vices are against the precepts and destroy them through their sin of disobedience, like Eve herself. Therefore, not only is the obedient person to be preferred to the disobedient one, but the more obedient wife is to be preferred to the less obedient virgin.

ADULTEROUS MARRIAGES

. . . Since the husband and wife are equal as regards the marriage bond, just as 'The wife, while her husband is alive, will be called an adulteress, if she be with another man [Rom. 7.3],' so will the husband also be called an adulterer if, while his wife is living, he is with another woman. . . .

. . . I am making these observations about both sexes, but particularly on account of men who think themselves superior to women, lest they deem themselves their equals in the matter of chastity. They should have taken the lead in chastity, so that their wives would follow them as their heads. But, since the law forbids adultery, if weakness of the flesh should be admitted as an excuse of incontinence, an occasion for losing their souls is offered to many under the guise of a false impunity. Women also have flesh, to whom their husbands are unwilling to make some such allowance, as though it were granted them because they are men. Never believe that something is owed the stronger sex as an honor which is detrimental to chastity, since meet honor is owed to virtue and not to vice. On the contrary, when they demand such great chastity on the part of their wives, who assuredly have flesh, so that, when they go on long journeys away from their wives, they wish them to pass their glowing youth, untarnished by any adulterous relations—in fact, a great many women pass their days most virtuously, particularly the women of Syria, whose husbands, absorbed in business affairs, leave them as young men and hardly return to their old wives in their advanced age—by the very fact that they pretend that they are unable to practice continence they prove more clearly that it is not impossible. For, if the weakness of men could not accomplish this, much less could the weaker feminine sex.

*   *   *

AUGUSTINE   Confessions
(from Book XIII)

. . . Even as in his soul there is one power which is master by virtue of counsel and another made its subject so as to obey, so also for man in the corporeal order there was made woman. Because of her reasonable and intelligent mind she would have equality of nature, but as to bodily sex she would be subject to the male sex, just as the active appetite is made subject, so as to conceive right and prudent conduct from the rational mind.

*   *   *

AUGUSTINE   The City of God
(from Book XXII)

Chapter 17

There are some who think that in the resurrection all will be men, and that women will lose their sex. This view springs from an interpretation of the texts: 'Until we all attain to . . . perfect manhood, to the mature measure of the fullness of Christ' [Eph. 4.13] and 'conformed to the image of the Son of God' [Rom. 8.29]. The interpretation is based on the fact that the man alone was made by God out of the 'slime of the earth,' whereas the woman was made from the man. For myself, I think that those others are more sensible who have no doubt that both sexes will remain in the resurrection. After all, there will then be none of that lust which is the cause of shame in connection with sex, and so, all will be as before the first sin, when the man and the woman were naked and felt no shame. In the resurrection, the blemishes of the body will be gone, but the nature of the body will remain. And, certainly a woman's sex is her nature and no blemish; only, in the resurrection, there will be no conception or child-bearing associated with her nature. Her members will remain as before, with the former purpose sublimated to a newer beauty. There will be no concupiscence to arouse and none will be aroused, but her womanhood will be a hymn to the wisdom of God, who first made her a woman, and to the clemency of God, who freed her from the corruption into which she fell.

Even in the beginning, when woman was made from a rib in the side of the sleeping man, that had no less a purpose than to symbolize prophetically the union of Christ and His Church. . . . Therefore, woman is as much the creation of God as man is. If she was made from the man, this was to show her oneness with him; and if she was made in the way she was, this was to prefigure the oneness of Christ and the Church.

God, then, who made us man and woman will raise us up as man and woman. . . .

What our Lord said was that, in the resurrection, there would be no marriage. He did not say that there would be no women. In the context it would have been an easier answer to the question asked to have said that there would be no women—if that was to be the case in the resurrection. Actually, He affirmed that there would be women when He used the double expression: 'neither marry' (as men do) nor 'be given in marriage' (as in the case of women). In the resurrection, then, there will be those who on earth 'marry' and those who 'are given in marriage.' Only, in heaven there will be no marriage.

*   *   *

ARISTOTLE

Although his philosophy rests on the principles of logic which he developed and elaborated, Aristotle (384–322 B.C.), in contrast to his teacher Plato, is decidedly empiricist in his approach to knowledge. All things in nature, Aristotle asserts, act toward an end. Changes or motion in the physical world are explained through the principles of act and potency, and in individual existents these principles emerge as matter and form. Neither can exist separately; matter is a principle of individuation, and form a principle of intelligibility.

In living things, the form is soul, which Aristotle defines as "principle of life." Plants possess a vegetative soul which enables them to grow and reproduce; animals possess a sentient soul which enables them to propel themselves and respond to sense stimuli. In the Aristotelian hierarchy of souls, the higher organism subsumes capabilities of the lower organism, so that animals also grow and reproduce, and human beings fulfill vegetative and animal (as well as human) functions.

Aristotle's Concept of Human Nature

What makes a human being human, according to Aristotle, is his or her rational soul, the basis for faculties of intellect and will. As rational animals, human beings fulfill their nature, or act according to their proper end, to the extent that they exercise their reason and volition. Knowledge is acquired through a process of conceptualization, or abstraction of a universal essence from a multiplicity of sense experiences. Thus, knowledge depends upon, but is not identical with, experience. Concepts are universal and immaterial; the objects of knowledge are individual and material. Since we only know forms, there is an inevitable gap between our knowledge of existent things and the things themselves.

The will, or rational appetite, inclines us to embrace an apprehended good. Where good is obtained, the result is happiness. On ethical as well as political levels, human beings act in pursuit of happiness. The universal good, which has priority over any merely individual good, produces some degree of happiness or satisfaction for everyone, since it applies to all individuals.

Human beings are also political animals. Their natural social interactions, according to Aristotle, arise from love of the useful, the pleasant, and the good. "Perfect friendship," Aristotle maintains, "is the friendship of men who are good, and alike in virtue; for these wish well alike to each other *qua* good, and they are good in themselves." While such friendships evoke pleasure without seeking it, they occur but rarely because "such men are rare," and there must be equality between the friends.

The following selections—"On the Generation of Animals" and "Politics"—are excerpted, respectively, from *Generation of Animals*, trans. by A. Peck, and *Aristotle's Politics*, trans. by W. Bolland.

ARISTOTLE   'On the Generation of Animals'

We may safely set down as the chief principles of generation the male [factor] and the female [factor]; the male as possessing the principle of movement and of generation, the female as possessing that of matter. One is most likely to be convinced of this by considering how the semen is formed and whence it comes; for although the things that are formed in the course of Nature no doubt take their rise out of semen, we must not fail to notice how the semen itself is formed from the male and the female, since it is because this part is secreted from the male and the female, and because its secretion takes place in them and out of them, that the male and the female are the principles of generation. By a "male" animal we mean one which generates in another, by "female" one which generates in itself. This is why in cosmology too they speak of the nature of the Earth as something female and call it "mother," while they give to the heaven and the sun and anything else of that kind the title of "generator," and "father."

Now male and female differ in respect of their *logos*, in that the power or faculty possessed by the one differs from that possessed by the other; but they differ also in bodily sense, in respect of certain physical parts. They differ in their *logos*, because the male is that which has the power to generate in another (as was stated above), while the female is that which can generate in itself, *i.e.*, it is that out of which the generated offspring, which is present in the generator, comes into being. Very well, then: they are distinguished in respect of their faculty, and this entails a certain function. Now for the exercise of every function instruments are needed, and the instruments for physical faculties are the parts of the body. Hence it is necessary that, for the purpose of copulation and procreation, certain parts should exist, parts that are different from each other, in respect of which the male will differ from the female; for although male and female are indeed used as epithets of the whole of the animal, it is not male or female in respect of the whole of itself, but only in respect of a particular faculty and a particular part—just as it is "seeing" and "walking" in respect of certain parts—and this part is one which is evident to the senses. . . .

. . . A woman is as it were an infertile male; the female, in fact, is female on account of inability of a sort, viz., it lacks the power to concoct semen out of the final state of the nourishment (this is either blood, or its counterpart in bloodless animals) because of the coldness of its nature. . . .

. . . The female, though it does not contribute any semen to generation, yet contributes something, viz., the substance constituting the menstrual fluid. But the same is apparent if we consider the matter generally, from the theoretical standpoint. Thus: there must be that which generates, and that out of which it generates; and even if these two be united in one, at any rate they must differ in kind, and in that the *logos* of each of them is distinct. In those animals in which these two faculties are separate, the body—that is to say the physical nature—of the active partner and of the passive must be different. Thus, if the male is the active partner, the one which originates the movement, and the female *qua* female is the passive one, surely what the female contributes to the semen of the male will be not semen but material. And this is in fact what we find happening; for the natural substance of the menstrual fluid is to be classed as "prime matter." . . .

. . . As for the reason why one comes to be formed, and is, male, and another female (*a*) in so far as this results from *necessity*, *i.e.*, from the proximate motive cause and from what sort of matter, our argument as it proceeds must endeavour to explain; (*b*) in so far as this occurs on account of what is *better*, *i.e.*, on account of the final cause (the Cause "for the sake of which"), the principle is derived from the upper cosmos. What I mean is this. Of the things which are, some are eternal and divine, others admit alike of being and not-being, and the beautiful and the divine acts always, in virtue of its own nature, as a cause which produces that which is *better* in the things which admit of it; while that which is not eternal admits of being [and not-being], and of acquiring a share both in the better and in the worse; also, Soul is better than body, and a thing which has Soul in it is better than one which has not, in virtue of that Soul; and being is better than not-being, and living than not living. These are the causes on account of which generation of animals takes place, because since the nature of a class of this sort is unable to be eternal, that which comes into being is eternal in the manner that is open to it. Now it is impossible for it to be so *numerically,* since the "being" of things is to be found in the particular, and if it really were so, then it would be eternal; it is, however, open to it to be so *specifically.* That is why there is always a *class* of men, of animals, of plants; and since the principle of these is "the male" and "the female," it will surely be for the sake of generation that "the male" and "the female" are present in the individuals which are male and female. And as the proximate motive cause, to which belong the *logos* and the Form, is *better* and more divine in its nature than the Matter, it is *better* also that the superior one should be separate from the inferior one. That is why wherever possible and so far as possible the male is separate from the female, since it is something *better* and more divine in that it is the principle of movement for generated things, while the female serves as their matter. The male, however, comes together with the female and mingles with it for the business of generation, because this is something that concerns both of them. . . .

. . . Just as it sometimes happens that deformed offspring are produced by deformed parents, and sometimes not, so the offspring produced by a female are sometimes female, sometimes not, but male. The reason is that the female is as it were a deformed male; and the menstrual discharge is semen, though in an impure condition; *i.e.,* it lacks one constituent, and one only, the principle of Soul. . . . This principle has to be supplied by the semen of the male, and it is when the female's residue secures this principle that a fetation is formed. . . .

. . . Why does this generative residue, then, not occur in all males, although it occurs in all females? The answer is that an animal is a living body, a body with Soul in it. The female always provides the material, the male provides that which fashions the material into shape; this, in our view, is the specific characteristic of each of the sexes: that is what it means to be male or to be female. Hence, necessity requires that the female should provide the physical part, *i.e.,* a quantity of material, but not that the male should do so, since necessity does not require that the tools should reside in the product that is being made, nor that the agent which uses them should do so. Thus the physical part, the body, comes from the female, and the Soul from the male, since the Soul is the essence of a particular body. . . .

. . . The male and the female are distinguished by a certain ability and inability. Male is that which is able to concoct, to cause to take shape, and to discharge, semen possessing the "principle" of the "form"; and by "principle" I do not mean that sort of principle out of which, as out of matter, an offspring is formed belonging to the same kind as its parent, but I mean the *first motive principle,* whether it is able to act thus in itself or in something else. Female is that which receives the semen, but is unable to cause semen to take shape or to discharge it. And all concoction works by means of heat. Assuming the truth of these two statements, it follows of necessity that male animals are hotter than female ones, since it is on account of coldness and inability that the female is more abundant in blood in certain regions of the body....

Now as the one sex is able and the other is unable to secrete the residue in a pure condition; and as there is an instrument for every ability or faculty, for the one which yields its product in a more finished condition and for the one which yields the same product in a less finished condition; and as male and female stand opposed in this way ("able" and "unable" being used in more senses than one); therefore of necessity there must be an instrument both for the male and for the female; hence the male has the *perineos* and the female has the uterus. Nature gives each one its instrument simultaneously with its ability, since it is *better* done thus. Hence each of these regions of the body gets formed simultaneously with the corresponding secretions and abilities, just as the ability to see does not get perfected without eyes, nor the eye without the ability to see, and just as the gut and the bladder are perfected simultaneously with the ability to form the residues. Now as the stuff out of which the parts are formed is the same as that from which they derive their growth, namely the nourishment, we should expect each of the parts to be formed out of that sort of material and that sort of residue which it is fitted to receive. Secondly, and on the contrary, it is, as we hold, formed in a way out of its opposite. Thirdly, in addition, it must be laid down that, assuming the extinction of a thing means its passing into its opposite condition, then also that which does not get mastered by the agent which is fashioning it must of necessity change over into its opposite condition. With these as our premises it may perhaps be clearer why and by what cause one offspring becomes male and another female. It is this. When the "principle" is failing to gain the mastery and is unable to effect concoction owing to deficiency of heat, and does not succeed in reducing the material into its own proper form, but instead is worsted in the attempt, then of necessity the material must change over into its opposite condition. Now the opposite of the male is the female, and it is opposite in respect of that whereby one is male and the other female. And since it differs in the ability it possesses, so also it differs in the instrument which it possesses. Hence this is the condition into which the material changes over. And when one vital part changes, the whole make-up of the animal differs greatly in appearance and form. This may be observed in the case of eunuchs; the mutilation of just one

part of them results in such a great alteration of their old semblance, and in close approximation to the appearance of the female.
The reason for this is that some of the body's parts are "principles"
and once a principle has been "moved" (*i.e.*, changed), many of
the parts which cohere with it must of necessity change as well.

Let us assume then (1) that "the male" is a principle and is
causal in its nature; (2) that a male is male in virtue of a particular
ability, and a female in virtue of a particular inability; (3) that the
line of determination between the ability and the inability is
whether a thing effects or does not effect concoction of the ultimate
nourishment; (4) that the reason for this lies in the "principle,"
i.e., in the part of the body which possesses the principle of the
natural heat. From this it follows of necessity that, in the blooded
animals, a heart must take shape and that the creature formed is
to be either male or female, and, in the other kinds which have
male and female sexes, the counterpart of the heart. As far, then,
as the principle and the cause of male and female is concerned,
this is what it is and where it is situated; a creature, however, really
is male or female only from the time when it has got the parts by
which female differs from male, because it is not in virtue of some
casual part that it is male or female, any more than it is in virtue
of some casual part that it can see or hear.

To resume then: We repeat that semen has been posited to be
the ultimate residue of the nourishment. (By "ultimate" I mean
that which gets carried to each part of the body—and that too is
why the offspring begotten takes after the parent which has begotten it, since it comes to exactly the same thing whether we
speak of being drawn from every one of the parts or passing into
every one of the parts, though the latter is more correct.) The
semen of the male, however, exhibits a difference, inasmuch as the
male possesses in itself a principle of such a kind as to set up
movement [in the animal as well] and thoroughly to concoct the
ultimate nourishment, whereas the female's semen contains material only. If [the male semen] gains the mastery, it brings [the
material] over to itself; but if it gets mastered, it changes over
either into its opposite or else into extinction. And the opposite of
the male is the female, which is female in virtue of its inability to
effect concoction, and of the coldness of its bloodlike nourishment.
And Nature assigns to each of the residues the part which is fitted
to receive it. Now the semen is a residue, and in the hotter of the
blooded animals, *i.e.*, the males, this is manageable in size and
amount, and therefore in males the parts which receive this residual product are passages; in females, however, on account of
their failure to effect concoction, this residue is a considerable
volume of bloodlike substance, because it has not been matured;
hence there must of necessity be here too some part fitted to receive

it, different from that in the male, and of a fair size. That is why the uterus has these characteristics; and that is the part wherein the female differs from the male. . . .

In human beings, more males are born deformed than females; in other animals, there is no preponderance either way. The reason is that in human beings the male is much hotter in its nature than the female. On that account male embryos tend to move about more than female ones, and owing to their moving about they get broken more, since a young creature can easily be destroyed owing to its weakness. And it is due to this self-same cause that the perfecting of female embryos is inferior to that of male ones, [since their uterus is inferior in condition. In other animals, however, the perfecting of female embryos is not inferior to that of male ones: they are not any later in developing than the males, as they *are* in women], for while still within the mother, the female takes longer to develop than the male does; though once birth has taken place everything reaches its perfection sooner in females than in males—*e.g.*, puberty, maturity, old age—because females are weaker and colder in their nature; and we should look upon the female state as being as it were a deformity, though one which occurs in the ordinary course of nature. While it is within the mother, then, it develops slowly on account of its coldness, since development is a sort of concoction, concoction is effected by heat, and if a thing is hotter its concoction is easy; when, however, it is free from the mother, on account of its weakness it quickly approaches its maturity and old age, since inferior things all reach their end more quickly, and this applies to those which take their shape under the hand of Nature just as much as to the products of the arts and crafts. The reason which I have just stated accounts also for the fact that (a) in human beings twins survive less well if one is male and the other female, but (b) in other animals they survive just as well: in human beings it is contrary to nature for the two sexes to keep pace with each other, male and female requiring unequal periods for their development to take place; the male is bound to be late or the female early; whereas in the other animals equal speed is not contrary to nature. There is also a difference between human beings and the other animals with regard to gestation. Other animals are most of the time in better physical condition, whereas the majority of women suffer discomfort in connexion with gestation. Now the cause of this is to some extent attributable to their manner of life, which is sedentary, and this means that they are full of residue; they have more of it than the other animals. This is borne out by the case of those tribes where the women live a life of hard work. With such women gestation is not so obvious, and they find delivery an easy business. And so do women everywhere who are used to hard work. The reason is that the effort of working uses up the residues, whereas sedentary women have a great deal of such matter in their bodies owing to the absence of effort, as well as to the cessation of the menstrual discharges during gestation, and they find the pains of delivery severe. Hard work, on the other hand, gives the breath (*pneuma*) exercise, so that they can hold it; and it is this which determines whether delivery is easy or difficult. . . .

*   *   *

ARISTOTLE 'Politics'

It is by examining things in their growth from the very beginning that we shall in this, as in other matters, obtain the clearest view. Now, it is necessary, in the first place, to group in couples those elements that cannot exist without each other, such as the female and male united for the sake of reproduction of species (and this union does not come from the deliberate action of the will, but in them, as in the other animals and plants, the desire to leave behind such another as themselves is implanted by nature), and also that which naturally rules, and that which naturally is ruled, connected for the sake of security. For that which has the capacity, in virtue of its intelligence, of looking forward is by nature the ruling and master element, while that which has the capacity, in virtue of its body, of carrying out this will of the superior is the subject and slave by nature. And for this reason the interests of the master and the slave are identical. Now it is by *nature* that the woman and the slave have been marked as separate, for nature produces nothing in a niggard fashion . . . but she makes each individual thing for one end; for it is only thus that each instrument will receive its most perfect development, namely, by subserving not many functions, but one. But among the barbarians the female and slave have the same position as the man; and the reason is that these nations do not possess the naturally ruling element, but, instead, their association becomes that of slave-woman and slave-man: and on this account the poets say, 'It is proper that Greeks should rule over barbarians,' implying that the ideas of barbarian and slave are by nature the same. So from these two forms of association comes the *Family* in its original form. . . .

. . . Every state is composed of Households, and the parts of the Household are those elements of which the household in its turn consists. Now the Household, when complete, consists of slaves and free persons. . . .

There have been seen to be three elements of household government, the first being the rule of the master over slaves, of which we have spoken before, the second that of the father over children, and the third that of the husband over the wife; for to rule both his wife and his children as beings equally free, but not with the same character of rule. His rule over the wife is like that of a magistrate in a free state, over his children it is like that of a king. For both the male is naturally more qualified to lead than the female, unless where some unnatural case occurs, and also the older and more perfect than the younger and imperfect. Now in the government of free states in most cases the positions of ruler and ruled alternate, for there is a tendency that all should be naturally equal and differ in no respect; but, nevertheless, whenever one party rules and the other is ruled, there is a wish that there should be some difference made in garb, titles, honours. . . . But the relation of the male to the female is always of this character and unchanged. But the rule over the children is the rule of a king, for the father is ruler both through affection and seniority, and this is the character of a king's rule; and for this reason Homer was right in addressing Zeus as 'Father of Gods and Men'—Zeus the king of all these. For a king should differ in nature from his subjects, but be still the same in kind; and this is the relation of the elder to the younger, the father to the child.

It is clear, therefore, that the earnest attention of household management is more concerned with living men than with the acquisition of inanimate objects—with the excellence of the former rather than with that of property, to which we give the name of wealth—with the excellence of freemen rather than with that of slaves. Now, in the first place, some one may raise a difficulty with regard to slaves: whether a slave has any excellence beyond that of an instrument and an agent; any other more valuable than these, such as Temperance, Courage, Justice, and any of the other dispositions of that sort; or whether he has none at all beyond bodily services. There is a difficulty either way. For if slaves have such excellence, in what will they differ from freemen? and yet to say that they are not, if they are men with a share of reason, is absurd. The question is very nearly the same in the case of women and children, as to whether they too have excellences, and if a woman ought to be temperate and courageous and just, and if a child is utterly intemperate or wisely temperate or not. And to speak generally, we have now this consideration before us with regard to the natural subject and the natural ruler, have they the same excellence or a distinct kind? For if both ought to share in nobleness of character, why, once and for ever, should one be ruler and the other be subject? for it cannot be that they differ in the matter of greatness or less (i.e. of degree), for to be ruled and to rule differ in kind, but the greater and the less do not. On the other hand, if one ought to possess this nobleness, while the other ought not, it it is a strange state of things. For if, on the one hand, the ruler is not to be temperate and just, how is he to be a good ruler? if, on the other, the subject (is to lack these qualities), how is he to be a good subject? For being, according to our supposition, utterly intemperate and cowardly, he will do none of those things that he should do. It is obvious, then, that while it is necessary for both parties to have their share of excellence, there must still be different kinds of excellence, just as there are also different kinds of those who are naturally subject to rule. And this has led us directly to the consideration of the Soul: for in the soul there is by nature an element that rules and also an element that is ruled; and in these we recognise distinction of excellence—the excellence, to wit, of that which possesses reason, and the excellence of that which lacks it. It is clear, then, that the same rule holds good in the other cases also, so that most things in the world are rulers or ruled by Nature's direction. For in different method does the free element rule the slave, the male the female, the man the child; and while in all of these are there present their separate shares of soul, these are present in each in a different manner. For the slave, speaking generally, has not the deliberative faculty, but the woman has it, though without power to be effective; the child has it, but in an imperfect degree. Similarly, then, must it necessarily be with regard to the moral virtues also. We must suppose that all ought to have some share in them, though not in the same way, but only so far as each requires for the fulfillment of his own function. Therefore the ruler should have moral excellence in its perfect form (for his function is strictly that of the master builder, and *reason* is the master builder), and each of the rest (the subordinates) should have just as much as falls to him. And so it is clear that moral excellence belongs to all the classes we have mentioned: and yet the same kind of temperance does not belong to woman and man, nor the same courage and justice (as Socrates thought), but the one is the courage of the ruler, the other the courage of the subject. And similarly with the other virtues. . . .

Since every household is part of a state, . . . it is necessary that we should have our eye on the constitution in educating our children and wives; if so be that it is of importance towards the State being good that both the children should be good and the women good; and important it must necessarily be. For women are half the free population; and it is from children that grow the members of the constitution.

❀   ❀   ❀

THOMAS AQUINAS

In contrast with most medieval theologians, Thomas Aquinas (1225–1274) used Aristotle rather than Plato as his main philosophical source. As a result, some of his views were considered sufficiently radical to warrant their official condemnation by church authorities. The influence of Aristotle is evident in Aquinas' emphases on experience as the basis of knowledge and on the essential unity of form and matter in individuals.

A crucial contribution of Aquinas himself to philosophy is his notion of the act of existence (sometimes called *esse*, which literally means "to be") as the principle of individual unity in all things, even God. For creatures, this concept involves a distinction between "what a thing is" (its general essence or nature or species; e.g., a human being's "humanness") and "that it is" (its particular existence as a unique individual). In the Creator, however, essence and existence are the same. Hence, God alone is utterly simple.

Since Aquinas construed his role as that of Christian theologian and teacher, his primary concern in his writings was to elicit an understanding of Christian beliefs. For example, his main work, from which the following selection is taken, is neither pure philosophy nor an apology (a rational defense of faith); it is rather, as its title implies (Summa Theologica means "highest theology"), a work written by a believer for believers. Accordingly, the starting point is faith data, or revelation (the Bible), and philosophy is used as a rational tool for understanding and explaining what is already believed.

Aquinas' Concept of Human Nature

Since Aquinas subscribed to the Aristotelian concept of human nature as an essential union of body and soul, he considered death the proof of human mortality, and held that the separated soul which continues to exist after death does not truly constitute a person. But Aquinas also believed in the Christian doctrine of resurrection of the body through reunion with the soul sometime after death. This belief supported his argument for personal immortality in a life subsequent to that resurrection.

For Aquinas, each human being is a union of his or her human essence (which includes soul and body) and existence (which is not to be identified with soul or body). "What you are" is not to be equated with "that you are" because your essence was conceived within the divine mind before it was given existence through creation. From the perspective of his Christian faith Aquinas also considered human nature as oriented toward a supernatural end, that is, an end which can neither be conceived nor achieved through mere human capability. To Aquinas, then, to be a person is to be a rational animal whose origin and end is God.

THOMAS AQUINAS   'On the First Man'

Question XCII

THE PRODUCTION OF WOMAN

(In Four Articles)

We must next consider the production of the woman. Under this head there are four points of inquiry: (1) Whether woman should have been made in that first production of things? (2) Whether woman should have been made from man? (3) Whether of man's rib? (4) Whether woman was made immediately by God?

First Article

WHETHER WOMAN SHOULD HAVE BEEN MADE IN THE FIRST PRODUCTION OF THINGS?

We proceed thus to the First Article:—

Objection 1. It would seem that woman should not have been made in the first production of things. For the Philosopher says that the *female is a misbegotten male.*[1] But nothing misbegotten or defective should have been in the first production of things. Therefore woman should not have been made at that first production.

Obj. 2. Further, subjection and limitation were a result of sin, for to the woman was it said after sin (*Gen. iii.* 16): *Thou shalt be under the man's power;* and Gregory says that, *Where there is no sin, there is no inequality.*[2] But woman is naturally of less strength and dignity than man, *for the agent is always more honorable than the patient,* as Augustine says.[3] Therefore woman should not have been made in the first production of things before sin.

1. *De Gener. Anim.*, II, 3 (737a 27).

2. *Moral.* XXI, 15 (PL 76, 203).

3. *De Genesi ad Litt.*, XII, 16 (PL 34, 467).

Obj. 3. Further, occasions of sin should be cut off. But God foresaw that woman would be an occasion of sin to man. Therefore He should not have made woman.

On the contrary, It is written (*Gen. ii.* 18): *It is not good for man to be alone; let us make him a helper like to himself.*

I answer that, It was necessary for woman to be made, as the Scripture says, as *a helper* to man; not, indeed, as a helpmate in other works, as some say, since man can be more efficiently helped by another man in other works; but as a helper in the work of generation. This can be made clear if we observe the mode of generation carried out in various living things. Some living things do not possess in themselves the power of generation, but are generated by an agent of another species; and such are those plants and animals which are generated, without seed, from suitable matter through the active power of the heavenly bodies. Others possess the active and passive generative power together, as we see in plants which are generated from seed. For the noblest vital function in plants is generation, and so we observe that in these the active power of generation invariably accompanies the passive power. Among perfect animals, the active power of generation belongs to the male sex, and the passive power to the female. And as among animals there is a vital operation nobler than generation, to which their life is principally directed, so it happens that the male sex is not found in continual union with the female in perfect animals, but only at the time of coition; so that we may consider that by coition the male and female are one, as in plants they are always united, even though in some cases one of them preponderates, and in some the other. But man is further ordered to a still nobler work of life, and that is intellectual operation. Therefore there was greater reason for the distinction of these two powers in man; so that the female should be produced separately from the male, and yet that they should be carnally united for generation. Therefore directly after the formation of woman, it was said: *And they shall be two in one flesh* (*Gen. ii.* 24).

Reply Obj. 1. As regards the individual nature, woman is defective and misbegotten, for the active power in the male seed tends to the production of a perfect likeness according to the masculine sex; while the production of woman comes from defect in the active power, or from some material indisposition, or even from some external influence, such as that of a south wind, which is moist, as the Philosopher observes.[4] On the other hand, as regards universal human nature, woman is not misbegotten, but is included in nature's intention as directed to the work of generation. Now the universal intention of nature depends on God, Who is the universal

4. Aristotle, *De Gener. Anim.*, IV, 2 (766b 33).

Author of nature. Therefore, in producing nature, God formed not only the male but also the female.

Reply Obj. 2. Subjection is twofold. One is servile, by virtue of which a superior makes use of a subject for his own benefit; and this kind of subjection began after sin. There is another kind of subjection, which is called economic or civil, whereby the superior makes use of his subjects for their own benefit and good; and this kind of subjection existed even before sin. For the good of order would have been wanting in the human family if some were not governed by others wiser than themselves. So by such a kind of subjection woman is naturally subject to man, because in man the discernment of reason predominates. Nor is inequality among men excluded by the state of innocence, as we shall prove.

Reply Obj. 3. If God had deprived the world of all those things which proved an occasion of sin, the universe would have been imperfect. Nor was it fitting for the common good to be destroyed in order that individual evil might be avoided; especially as God is so powerful that He can direct any evil to a good end.

Second Article

WHETHER WOMAN SHOULD HAVE BEEN MADE FROM MAN?

We proceed thus to the Second Article:—

Objection 1. It would seem that woman should not have been made from man. For sex belongs both to man and animals. But in the other animals the female was not made from the male. Therefore neither should it have been so with man.

Obj. 2. Further, things of the same species are of the same matter. But male and female are of the same species. Therefore, as man was made of the slime of the earth, so woman should have been made of the same, and not from man.

Obj. 3. Further, woman was made to be a helpmate to man in the work of generation. But close relationship makes a person unfit for that office; and hence near relations are debarred from intermarriage, as is written (*Lev. xviii.* 6). Therefore woman should not have been made from man.

On the contrary, It is written (*Ecclus. xvii.* 5): *He created of him,* that is, out of man, *a helpmate like to himself,* that is, woman.

I answer that, When all things were first made, it was more suitable for woman to be formed from man than for this to happen in other animals. First, in order thus to give the first man a certain dignity consisting in this, that as God is the principle of the whole universe, so the first man, in likeness to God, was the principle of the whole human race. Hence Paul says that *God made the whole human race from one* (*Acts xvii.* 26). Secondly, that man might love woman all the more, and cleave to her more closely, knowing her to be fashioned from himself. Hence it is written (*Gen. ii.* 23, 24): *She was taken out of man, wherefore a man shall leave father and mother, and shall cleave to his wife.* This was most necessary in the human species, in which the male and female live together for life; which is not the case with other animals. Thirdly, because, as the Philosopher says, the human male and female are united, not only for generation, as with other animals, but also for the purpose of domestic life, in which each has his or her particular duty, and in which the man is the head of the woman.[5] Therefore it was suitable for the woman to be made out of man, as out of her principle. Fourthly, there is a sacramental reason for this. For by this is signified that the Church takes her origin from Christ. Therefore the Apostle says (*Ephes. v.* 32): *This is a great sacrament; but I speak in Christ and in the Church.*

Reply Obj. 1. is clear from the foregoing.

Reply Obj. 2. Matter is that from which something is made. Now created nature has a determinate principle, and since it is determined to one thing, it has also a determinate mode of proceeding. Therefore from determinate matter it produces something in a determinate species. On the other hand, the divine power, being infinite, can produce things of the same species out of any matter, such as a man from the slime of the earth, and a woman from a man.

Reply Obj. 3. A certain affinity arises from natural generation, and this is an impediment to matrimony. Woman, however, was not produced from man by natural generation, but by the divine power alone. Hence Eve is not called the daughter of Adam. And so this argument does not prove.

Third Article

WHETHER THE WOMAN WAS FITTINGLY MADE FROM THE RIB OF MAN?

We proceed thus to the Third Article:—

Objection 1. It would seem that woman should not have been formed from the rib of man. For the rib was much smaller than the woman's body. Now from a smaller thing a larger thing can be made only—either by addition (and then the woman ought to have been described as made out of that which was added, rather than out of the rib itself);—or by rarefaction, because, as Augustine says: *A body cannot increase in bulk except by rarefaction.*[6] But woman's

5. *Eth.,* VIII, 12 (1162a 19).

6. *De Genesi ad Litt.,* X, 26 (PL 34, 428).

body is not more rarefied than man's—at least, not in the proportion of a rib to Eve's body. Therefore Eve was not formed from a rib of Adam.

Obj. 2. Further, in those things which were first created there was nothing superfluous. Therefore a rib of Adam belonged to the integrity of his body. So, if a rib was removed, his body remained imperfect; which is unreasonable to suppose.

Obj. 3. Further, a rib cannot be removed from man without pain. But there was no pain before sin. Therefore it was not right for a rib to be taken from the man, that Eve might be made from it.

On the contrary, It is written (*Gen. ii.* 22): *God built the rib, which He took from Adam, into a woman.*

I answer that, It was right for a woman to be made from a rib of man. First, to signify the social union of man and woman, for the woman should neither use authority over man, and so she was not made from his head; nor was it right for her to be subject to man's contempt as his slave, and so she was not made from his feet. Secondly, for the sacramental signification; for from the side of Christ sleeping on the Cross the Sacraments flowed—namely, blood and water—on which the Church was established.

Reply Obj. 1. Some say that woman's body was formed by a material increase, without anything being added, in the same way as our Lord multiplied the five loaves. But this is quite impossible. For such an increase of matter would either be by a change of the very substance of the matter itself, or by a change of its dimensions. It was not by a change of the substance of the matter, both because matter, considered in itself, is quite unchangeable, since it has a potential existence, and has nothing but the nature of a subject; and because multiplication and size are extraneous to the essence of matter itself. And so, the multiplication of matter is quite unintelligible, as long as the matter itself remains the same without anything added to it, unless it receives greater dimensions. This implies rarefaction, which is for the same matter to receive greater dimensions, as the Philosopher says.[7] To say, therefore, that the same matter is enlarged, without being rarefied, is to combine contradictories—viz., the definition without the absence of the thing defined.

Therefore, as no rarefaction is apparent in such multiplications of matter, we must admit an addition of matter, either by creation or, what is more probable, by conversion. Hence Augustine says that *Christ filled five thousand men with five loaves in the same way as from a few seeds He produces the harvest of corn*[8]—that is,

7. *Phys.*, IV, 9 (217a 25).

8. *Tract.* XXIV, super *Ioann.*, VI, 2 (PL 35, 1593).

by transformation of the nourishment. Nevertheless, we say that the crowds were fed with five loaves, or that woman was made from the rib, because an addition was made to the already existing matter of the loaves and of the rib.

Reply Obj. 2. The rib belonged to the integral perfection of Adam, not as an individual, but as the principle of the human race; just as the semen belongs to the perfection of the begetter, and is released by a natural and pleasurable operation. Much more, therefore, was it possible that by the divine power the body of woman should be produced from the man's rib.

From this it is clear how to answer the third objection.

Fourth Article

WHETHER WOMAN WAS FORMED IMMEDIATELY BY GOD?

We proceed thus to the Fourth Article:—

Objection 1. It would seem that woman was not formed immediately by God. For no individual is produced immediately by God from another individual alike in species. But woman was made from man, who is of the same species. Therefore she was not made immediately by God.

Obj. 2. Further, Augustine says that corporeal things are governed by God through the angels. But woman's body was formed from corporeal matter. Therefore it was made through the ministry of the angels, and not immediately by God.

Obj. 3. Further, those things which pre-exist in creatures in their causal principles are produced by the power of some creature, and not immediately by God. But woman's body was produced in its causal principles among the first created works, as Augustine says. Therefore it was not produced immediately by God.

On the contrary, Augustine says, in the same work: *God alone, to Whom all nature owes its existence, could form or fashion woman from man's rib.*[9]

I answer that, As was said above, the natural generation of every species is from some determinate matter. Now the matter whence man is naturally begotten is the human semen of man or woman. Therefore an individual of the human species cannot be generated naturally from any other matter. Now God alone, the author of nature, can bring an effect into being outside the ordinary course of nature. Therefore God alone could produce either man from the slime of the earth, or woman from the rib of man.

Reply Obj. 1. This argument is good when an individual is be-

9. *De Genesi ad Litt.,* IX, 15 (PL 34, 403).

gotten, by natural generation, from that which is like it in species.

Reply Obj. 2. As Augustine says, we do not know whether the angels were employed by God in the formation of woman; but it is certain that, as the body of man was not formed by the angels from the slime of the earth, so neither was the body of woman formed by them from the man's rib.

Reply Obj. 3. As Augustine says: *The first creation of things did not demand that woman should be made thus; it made it possible for her to be thus made.*[10] Therefore the body of woman pre-existed according to these causal principles in the first works of God, not according to an active potentiality, but according to a passive potentiality ordered to the active power of God.

. . . .

Question 93   *Fourth Article*

WHETHER THE IMAGE OF GOD IS FOUND IN EVERY MAN?

. . . .

Objection 1. It would seem that the image of God is not found in every man. For the Apostle says that *man is the image of God, but woman is the image of man* (I *Cor. xi.* 7). Therefore, as woman is an individual of the human species, it is clear that every individual is not an image of God. . . .

Reply Obj. 1. The image of God, in its principal signification, namely the intellectual nature, is found both in man and in woman. Hence after the words, *To the image of God He created him,* it is added, *Male and female He created them* (*Gen. i.* 27). Moreover it is said *them* in the plural, as Augustine remarks, lest it should be thought that both sexes were united in one individual. But in a secondary sense the image of God is found in man, and not in woman, for man is the beginning and end of woman, just as God is the beginning and end of every creature. So when the Apostle had said that *man is the image and glory of God, but woman is the glory of man,* he adds his reason for saying this: *For man is not of woman, but woman of man; and man was not created for woman, but woman for man.*

. . . .

10. *Op. cit.,* IX, 18 (PL 34, 407).

Sixth Article

WHETHER THE IMAGE OF GOD IS IN MAN AS REGARDS THE MIND ONLY?

. . . *Obj.* 2. Further, it is written (*Gen. i.* 27): *God created man to His own image; to the image of God He created him; male and female He created them.* But the distinction of male and female is in the body. Therefore the image of God is also in the body, and not only in the mind.

. . . *Reply Obj.* 2. As Augustine says, some have thought that the image of God was not in man individually, but severally. They held that *the man represents the Person of the Father; that those born of man denote the person of the Son; and that woman is a third person in likeness to the Holy Ghost, since she so proceeded from man as not to be his son or daughter.* All of this is manifestly absurd. First, because it would follow that the Holy Ghost is the principle of the Son, just as woman is the principle of man's offspring; secondly, because one man would be to the image of only one Person; thirdly, because in that case Scripture should not have mentioned the image of God in man until after the birth of offspring. Therefore we must observe that when Scripture had said, *to the image of God He created him,* it added, *male and female He created them,* not to imply that the image of God came through the distinction of sex, but that the image of God belongs to both sexes, since it is in the mind, wherein there is no distinction of sexes. Therefore the Apostle (*Col. iii.* 10), after saying, *According to the image of Him that created him,* added, *Where there is neither male nor female.* . . .

Question 94   *Fourth Article*

WHETHER MAN IN HIS FIRST STATE COULD HAVE BEEN DECEIVED?

.   .   .   .

Objection 1. It would seem that man in his first state could have been deceived. For the Apostle says (1 *Tim. ii.* 14) that *the woman being seduced was in the transgression.*

Obj. 2. Further, the Master of the *Sentences* says that *woman was not frightened at the serpent speaking, because she thought that he had received the faculty of speech from God.*[11] But this was untrue. Therefore before sin woman was deceived. . . .

11. Peter Lombard, *Sent.,* II, xxi, 4 (I, 405).

Reply Obj. 1. Though woman was deceived before she sinned in deed, still it was not till she had already sinned by interior pride. For Augustine says that *woman would not have believed the words of the serpent, had she not already acquiesced in the love of her own power, and in a presumption of self-conceit.*[12]

Reply Obj. 2. Woman thought that the serpent had received this faculty, not as acting in accordance with nature, but by virtue of some supernatural operation. We need not, however, follow the Master of the *Sentences* in this point.

Question 96   *Third Article*

WHETHER IN THE STATE OF INNOCENCE MEN WOULD HAVE BEEN EQUAL?

.   .   .   .

On the contrary, It is written (*Rom. xiii.* I): *The things which are of God, are well ordered.* But order consists chiefly in inequality, for Augustine says: *Order disposes things equal and unequal in their proper place.*[13] Therefore in the first state, which would have been most proper and orderly, inequality would exist.

I answer that, We must needs admit that in the first state there would have been some inequality, at least as regards sex, because generation depends upon diversity of sex; and likewise as regards age, for some would have been born of others, nor would sexual union have been sterile.

Moreover, as regards the soul, there would have been inequality as to justice and knowledge. For man worked, not of necessity, but of his own free choice, by virtue of which man can apply himself, more or less, to action, desire or knowledge. Hence some would have made a greater advance in justice and knowledge than others.

There could also have been bodily disparity. For the human body was not entirely exempt from the laws of nature, so as not to receive from exterior sources more or less advantage and help, since it was likewise dependent on food wherewith to sustain life.

So we may say that, according to the climate, or the movement of the stars, some would have been born more robust in body than others, and also greater, and more beautiful, and in all ways better disposed; so that, however, in those who were thus surpassed, there would have been no defect or fault either in soul or body.

12. *De Genesi ad Litt.*, XI, 30 (PL 34, 445).

13. *De Civit. Dei*, XIX, 13 (PL 41, 640).

RELATED READINGS

Alexander, William M. "Sex and Philosophy in Augustine." *Augustinian Studies* 5 (1974), pp. 197–208.

Annas, Julia. "Plato's Republic and Feminism." *Philosophy* 51 (July 1976), pp. 307–321.

Beard, Mary R. *Woman as Force in History.* New York: Collier Books, 1962.

Calvert, Brian. "Plato and the Equality of Women." *Phoenix* 29 (1975), pp. 231–243.

Clark, Stephen R. "Appendix B: The Sexes." In *Aristotle's Man.* Oxford: Clarendon Press, 1975, pp. 206–211.

Cumming, Alan. "Pauline Christianity and Greek Philosophy: A Study of the Status of Women." *Journal of the History of Ideas* 34 (1973), pp. 517–528.

Dickason, Anne. "Anatomy and Destiny: The Role of Biology in Plato's Views of Women. In *Women and Philosophy,* ed. by C. Gould and M. Wartofsky. New York: G. P. Putnam's Sons, 1976, pp. 45–53.

Donaldson, James. *Woman: Her Position and Influence in Ancient Greece and Rome, and among the Early Christians.* New York: Longmans, Green and Company, 1907.

Fortenbaugh, W. W. "On Plato's Feminism in Republic V." *Apeiron* 9 (Nov. 1975), pp. 1–4.

Gage, Matilda J. *Woman, Church, and State: A Historical Account of the Status of Woman through the Christian Ages, with Reminiscences of the Matriarchate.* New York: Arno Press, 1972.

Garside, Christine. "Can a Woman Be Good in the Same Way as a Man?" *Dialogue* 10 (Sept. 1971), pp. 534–544.

————. "Plato on Women." *Feminist Studies* 2 (1975), pp. 131–138.

Hageman, Alice L. (ed). *Sexist Religion and Women in the Church.* New York: Association Press, 1974.

Koltun, Elizabeth (ed.). *The Jewish Woman.* New York: Schocken Books, 1976.

Morris, Joan. *The Lady Was a Bishop.* New York: The Macmillan Company, 1973.

Meyer, Hans. "The Human Person," *The Philosophy of St. Thomas Aquinas,* trans. by F. Eckhoff. St. Louis: B. Herder Book Company, 1946, pp. 204–210.

Okin, Susan, "Philosopher Queens and Private Wives: Plato on Women and the Family." *Philosophy and Public Affairs* 6 (Summer 1977), pp. 345–369.

Osborne, Martha Lee. "Plato's Unchanging View of Woman: A

Denial that Anatomy Spells Destiny." *Philosophical Forum* 6 (Summer 1975), pp. 447–452.

Ostheimer, Anthony. *The Family: a Thomistic Study in Social Philosophy*. Washington: Catholic University of America Press, 1939.

Pierce, Christine. "Equality: Republic V." *The Monist* 57 (Jan. 1973), pp. 1–11.

Pomeroy, Sarah. "Feminism in Book V of Plato's *Republic.*" *Apeiron* 8 (1974), pp. 32–34.

————. *Goddesses, Whores, Wives, and Slaves: Women in Classical Antiquity*. New York: Schocken Books, 1975.

Power, Eileen Edna. *Medieval Women*. New York: Cambridge University Press, 1975.

Ruether, Rosemary (ed.). *Religion and Sexism Images of Woman in the Jewish and Christian Traditions*. New York: Simon and Schuster, 1974.

Saxonhouse, Arlene W. "The Philosopher and the Female in the Political Thought of Plato." *Political Theory* 4 (May 1976), pp. 195–212.

Tavard, George H. *Women in Christian Tradition*. South Bend: University of Notre Dame Press, 1974.

Vlastos, Gregory. "The Status of Persons in Platonic Justice: Women." *Carus Lectures*. La Salle, Illinois: Open Court Press, 1976.

Whitbeck, Caroline. "Theories of Sex Difference." *Women and Philosophy*, ed. by C. Gould and M. Wartofsky. New York: G. P. Putnam and Sons, 1976, pp. 54–80.

V
BIBLICAL AND
PSYCHOANALYTIC SOURCES

Although the selections that follow are not drawn from the writings of philosophers as such, the ideas presented have undoubtedly exerted a great influence on current thought. Consequently, whether or not we subscribe to these ideas, we cannot adequately understand or evaluate prevalent concepts of woman without adverting to them. Furthermore, as we have seen in the preceding selections, many important philosophers of past and present utilize biblical and psychoanalytic sources in elaborating their own views. To some the Bible provides a source of truth to confirm their arguments; to others it is a compilation of errors to be refuted. Similarly, despite the crucial role of Freud in the psychoanalytic tradition, his ideas have evoked both approval and disapproval on the part of peers and followers. Excerpts from dissident psychoanalysts are included in order to exemplify diverse assessments of his work.

THE BIBLE

Most Scripture scholars concur that there are several authors for the Book of Genesis, and the selection below supports that judgment; for example, Chapters 1 and 2 present two different accounts of creation, and Chapters 4 and 5 provide differing genealogies. The Song of Songs is a series of love poems generally attributed to King Solomon.

The letters of Paul are primarily his response to particular situations in particular communities that he had converted to Christianity. One problem among the Corinthian Christians with which Paul was concerned was sexual immorality; Chapter 7 of his first letter to them forms a part of his response to that problem. Another issue was that of authority, both at home and at worship; Chapter 11 (below) gives Paul's advice on the question of authority in the husband/wife relationship. Although scholars do not all agree that

the Letter to the Ephesians was authored by Paul, its content as
here excerpted is basically in accord with Paul's sentiments in
1 Cor. 11.

The Bible's Concept(s) of Human Nature

To appreciate biblical conceptions of woman, man and human
nature, we need to be aware of the religious presuppositions that
underlie these concepts. One such presupposition is the doctrine
of creation, which maintains that all things owe their origin and
continued existence to God. While this belief is also logically ten-
able for one who believes in biological evolution, it involves a con-
fession that existence is ultimately contingent, that is, dependent
upon a supreme being. In contrast with the Platonic tradition, the
notion of creation implies a positive regard for the physical world,
as the work of a Creator who "saw that it was good" (Gen. 1: 25).

A second presupposition or belief is humankind's need for and
hope of being saved. Leaving aside the question of what constitutes
salvation, the "need" and "hope" are paradoxical aspects—the first
involving an admission of human limitation, the second an expectation that the limitation is overcome through divine redemption. In
this context human freedom is restricted from within through natural limitations and from without through ultimate dependence on
God.

The selections from the Old Testament represent contrasting
views of human sexuality. In Genesis, God's punishment to Eve,
the prototypical woman, is her sexual desire for man, her domination by him, and the pain of childbirth. The Song of Solomon, on
the other hand, extols the joy and beauty of sexual love, depicting
both bride and bridegroom as aggressive, passionate lovers. The
husband/wife relationship, as here described, is usually seen as an
allegory for the relationship between God and Israel, or (for Christians) between Christ and the Church. Paul's letter to the Ephesians also employs this allegory, advising husbands to love their
wives as Christ loved the Church.

That the human body is to be regarded with particular reverence
among the works of creation is clear from both Testaments. In
Genesis, for example, we read that God created "man" in his own
image and give "him" (or "them") dominion over other creatures
(Gen. 1: 26). Since it is the whole person that is God's creature,
one does not *have* a body, but *is* the union of soul and body. In the
New Testament, the idea of respect for the body is reinforced
through the doctrine of the incarnation, of God assuming flesh in
Christ, who was conceived by and born of a woman. Various passages indicate that every human body is deserving of reverence;
for example, Paul's reminder to the Corinthians: "Your body, you

know, is the temple of the Holy Spirit" (1 Cor. 6:19). Belief in "resurrection of the body" (i.e., its reunion with the soul sometime after death) also illustrates the essential connection between body and soul.

The excerpts following are drawn from *The Holy Bible*, Revised Standard Version, Genesis 1–5, Song of Solomon, 1 Corinthians 7, 11 and Ephesians 5.

THE HOLY BIBLE   Genesis 1–5

1 In the beginning God created the heavens and the earth. The earth was without form and void, and darkness was upon the the face of the deep; and the Spirit of God was moving over the face of the waters.

3 And God said, "Let there be light"; and there was light. And God saw that the light was good; and God separated the light from the darkness. God called the light Day, and the darkness he called Night. And there was evening and there was morning, one day.

6 And God said, "Let there be a firmament in the midst of the waters, and let it separate the waters from the waters." And God made the firmament and separated the waters which were under the firmament from the waters which were above the firmament. And it was so. And God called the firmament Heaven. And there was evening and there was morning, a second day.

9 And God said, "Let the waters under the heavens be gathered together into one place, and let the dry land appear." And it was so. God called the dry land Earth, and the waters that were gathered together he called Seas. And God saw that it was good. And God said, "Let the earth put forth vegetation, plants yielding seed, and fruit trees bearing fruit in which is their seed, each according to its kind, upon the earth." And it was so. The earth brought forth vegetation, plants yielding seed according to their own kinds, and trees bearing fruit in which is their seed, each according to its kind. And God saw that it was good. And there was evening and there was morning, a third day.

14 And God said, "Let there be lights in the firmament of the heavens to separate the day from the night; and let them be for signs and for seasons and for days and years, and let them be lights in the firmament of the heavens to give light upon the earth." And it was so. And God made the two great lights, the greater light to rule the day, and the lesser light to rule the night; he made the stars also. And God set them in the firmament of the heavens to give light upon the earth, to rule over the day and

over the night, and to separate the light from the darkness. And God saw that it was good. And there was evening and there was morning, a fourth day.

20 And God said, "Let the waters bring forth swarms of living creatures, and let birds fly above the earth across the firmament of the heavens." So God created the great sea monsters and every living creature that moves, with which the waters swarm, according to their kinds, and every winged bird according to its kind. And God saw that it was good. And God blessed them, saying, "Be fruitful and multiply and fill the waters in the seas, and let birds multiply on the earth." And there was evening and there was morning, a fifth day.

24 And God said "Let the earth bring forth living creatures according to their kinds: cattle and creeping things and beasts of the earth according to their kinds." And it was so. And God made the beasts of the earth according to their kinds and the cattle according to their kinds, and everything that creeps upon the ground according to its kind. And God saw that it was good.

26 Then God said, "Let us make man in our image, after our likeness; and let them have dominion over the fish of the sea, and over the birds of the air, and over the cattle, and over all the earth, and over every creeping thing that creeps upon the earth." So God created man in his own image, in the image

of God he created him; male and female he created them. And God blessed them, and God said to them, "Be fruitful and multiply, and fill the earth and subdue it; and have dominion over the fish of the sea and over the birds of the air and over every living thing that moves upon the earth." And God said, "Behold, I have given you every plant yielding seed which is upon the face of all the earth and every tree with seed in its fruit; you shall have them for food. And to every beast of the earth, and to every bird of the air, and to everything that creeps on the earth, everything that has the breath of life, I have given every green plant for food." And it was so. And God saw everything that he had made, and behold, it was very good. And there was evening and there was morning, a sixth day.

2 Thus the heavens and the earth were finished, and all the host of them. And on the seventh day God finished his work which he had done, and he rested on the seventh day from all his work which he had done. So God blessed the seventh day and hallowed it, because on it God rested from all his work which he had done in creation.

4 These are the generations of the heavens and the earth when they were created.

In the day that the LORD God made the earth and the heavens, when no plant of the field was yet in the earth and no herb of the field had yet sprung up—for the LORD God had not caused it to rain upon the earth, and there was no man to till the ground; but a mist went up from the earth and watered the whole face of the ground—then the LORD God formed man and dust from the ground, and breathed into his nostrils the breath of life; and man became a living being. And the LORD God planted a garden in Eden, in the east, and there he put the man whom he had formed. And out of the ground the LORD God made to grow every tree that is pleasant to the sight and good for food, the tree of life also in the midst of the garden, and the tree of the knowledge of good and evil. . . .

15 The LORD God took the man and put him in the garden of Eden to till it and keep it. And the LORD God commanded the man, saying, "You may freely eat of every tree of the garden; but of the tree of the knowledge of good and evil you shall not eat, for in the day that you eat of it you shall die."

18 Then the LORD God said, "It is not good that the man should be alone; I will make him a helper fit for him." So out of the ground the LORD God formed every beast of the field and every bird of the air, and brought them to the man to see what he would call them; and whatever the man called every living creature, that was its name. The man gave names to all cattle, and to the birds of the air, and to every beast of the field; but for the man there was not found a helper fit for him. So the LORD God caused a deep sleep to fall upon the man, and while he slept took one of his ribs and closed up its place with flesh; and the rib which the LORD God had taken from the man he made into a woman and brought her to the man. Then the man said,

"This at last is bone of my bones
    and flesh of my flesh;
she shall be called Woman,
    because she was taken out of
    Man."

Therefore a man leaves his father and his mother and cleaves to his wife, and they become one flesh. And the man and his wife were both naked, and were not ashamed.

3 Now the serpent was more subtle than any other wild creature that the LORD God had made. He said to the woman, "Did God say, 'You shall not eat of any tree of the garden'?" And the woman said to the serpent, "We may eat of the fruit of the trees of the garden; but God said, "You shall not eat of the fruit of the tree which is in the midst of the garden, neither shall you touch it, lest you die." But the serpent said to the woman, "You will not die. For God knows that when you eat of it your eyes will be opened, and you will be like God, knowing good and evil." So when the woman saw that the tree was good for food, and that it was a delight to the eyes, and that the tree was to be desired to make one wise, she took of its fruit and ate; and she also gave

some to her husband, and he ate. Then the eyes of both were opened, and they knew that they were naked; and they sewed fig leaves together and made themselves aprons.

8 And they heard the sound of the LORD God walking in the garden in the cool of the day, and the man and his wife hid themselves from the presence of the LORD God among the trees of the garden. But the LORD God called to the man, and said to him, "Where are you?" And he said "I heard the sound of thee in the garden, and I was afraid, because I was naked; and I hid myself." He said, "Who told you that you were naked? Have you eaten of the tree of which I commanded you not to eat?" The man said, "The woman whom thou gavest to be with me, she gave me fruit of the tree, and I ate." Then the LORD God said to the woman, "What is this that you have done?" The woman said, "The serpent beguiled me, and I ate." The LORD God said to the serpent,

"Because you have done this,
    cursed are you above all
        cattle,
    and above all wild animals;
upon your belly you shall go,
    and dust you shall eat
    all the days of your life.
I will put enmity between you
        and the woman,
    and between your seed and
        her seed;
he shall bruise your head,
    and you shall bruise his
        heel."

To the woman he said,
"I will greatly multiply your
        pain in childbearing;
    in pain you shall bring forth
        children,
yet your desire shall be for
        your husband,
    and he shall rule over you."
And to Adam he said,
"Because you have listened to
        the voice of your wife,
    and have eaten of the tree
of which I commanded you,
    'You shall not eat of it,'
cursed is the ground because
        of you;
    in toil you shall eat of it all
        the days of your life;
thorns and thistles it shall
        bring forth to you;
    and you shall eat the plants
        of the field.
In the sweat of your face
    you shall eat bread
till you return to the ground,
    for out of it you were taken;
you are dust,
    and to dust you shall
        return."

20 The man called his wife's name Eve, because she was the mother of all living. And the LORD God made for Adam and for his wife garments of skins, and clothed them.

22 Then the LORD God said, "Behold, the man has become like one of us, knowing good and evil; and now, lest he put forth his hand and take also of the tree of life, and eat, and live for ever"— therefore the LORD God sent him forth from the garden of Eden, to till the ground from which he was taken. He drove out the man; and at the east of

the garden of Eden he placed the cherubim, and a flaming sword which turned every way, to guard the way to the tree of life.

4 Now Adam knew Eve his wife, and she conceived and bore Cain, saying, "I have gotten a man with the help of the LORD." . . .

5 This is the book of the generations of Adam. When God created man, he made him in the likeness of God. Male and female he created them, and he blessed them and named them Man when they were created. When Adam had lived a hundred and thirty years, he became the father of a son in his own likeness, after his image, and named him Seth. The days of Adam after he became the father of Seth were eight hundred years; and he had other sons and daughters. Thus all the days that Adam lived were nine hundred and thirty years; and he died.

✿   ✿   ✿

THE HOLY BIBLE   The Song of Solomon

2 I am a rose of Sharon,
  a lily of the valleys.

As a lily among brambles,
  so is my love among
  maidens.

As an apple tree among the
  trees of the wood,
  so is my beloved among
  young men.
With great delight I sat in his
  shadow,
  and his fruit was sweet to
  my taste.
He brought me to the
  banqueting house,
  and his banner over me was
  love.
Sustain me with raisins,
  refresh me with apples;
  for I am sick with love.

O that his left hand were
  under my head,
  and that his right hand
  embraced me!
I adjure you, O daughters of
  Jerusalem,
  by the gazelles or the hinds
  of the field,
that you stir not up nor
  awaken love
until it please.

The voice of my beloved!
  Behold, he comes,
leaping upon the mountains,
  bounding over the hills.
My beloved is like a gazelle,
  or a young stag.
Behold, there he stands
  behind our wall,
gazing in at the windows,
  looking through the lattice.

My beloved speaks and says
to me:
"Arise, my love, my fair one,
and come away;
for lo, the winter is past,
the rain is over and gone.
The flower appear on the
earth,
the time of singing has
come,
and the voice of the
turtledove
is heard in our land.
The fig tree puts forth its figs,
and the vines are in
blossom;
they give forth fragrance.
Arise, my love, my fair one,
and come away.

3 Upon my bed by night
I sought him whom my soul
loves;
I sought him, but found him
not;
I called him, but he gave
no answer.
"I will rise now and go about
the city,
in the streets and in the
squares;
I will seek him whom my soul
loves."
I sought him, but found
him not.
The watchmen found me,
as they went about in the
city.
"Have you seen him whom
my soul loves?"
Scarcely had I passed them,
when I found him whom
my soul loves.
I held him, and would not let
him go
until I had brought him
into my mother's house,

and into the chamber of her
that conceived me.
I adjure you, O daughters of
Jerusalem,
by the gazelles or the hinds
of the field,
that you stir not up nor
awaken love
until it please.

What is that coming up from
the wilderness,
like a column of smoke,
perfumed with myrrh and
frankincense,
with all the fragrant
powders of the merchant?
Behold, it is the litter of
Solomon!
About it are sixty mighty men
of the mighty men of Israel.
all girt with swords
and expert in war,
each with his sword at his
thigh,
against alarms by night.
King Solomon made himself a
palanquin
from the wood of Lebanon.
He made its posts of silver,
its back of gold, its seat of
purple;
it was lovingly wrought
within
by the daughters of
Jerusalem.
Go forth, O daughters of Zion,
and behold King Solomon,
with the crown with which
his mother crowned him
on the day of his wedding,
on the day of the gladness
of his heart.

5 I come to my garden, my
sister, my bride,

I gather my myrrh with my
    spice,
I eat my honeycomb with
    my honey,
I drink my wine with my
    milk.

Eat, O friends, and drink:
    drink deeply, O lovers!

I slept, but my heart was
    awake.
Hark! my beloved is knocking.
"Open to me, my sister, my
    love,
    my dove, my perfect one;
for my head is wet with dew,
    my locks with the drops of
    the night."
I had put off my garment,
    how could I put it on?
I had bathed my feet,
    how could I soil them?
My beloved put his hand to
    the latch,
    and my heart was thrilled
    within me.
I arose to open to my beloved,
    and my hands dripped with
    myrrh,
my fingers with liquid myrrh,
    upon the handles of the
    bolt.
I opened to my beloved,
    but my beloved had turned
    and gone.
My soul failed me when he
    spoke.
I sought him, but found him
    not;
    I called him, but he gave no
    answer.
The watchmen found me,
    as they went about in the
    city;
they beat me, they wounded

me,
    they took away my mantle,
    those watchmen of the
    walls.
I adjure you, O daughters of
    Jerusalem,
    if you find my beloved,
that you tell him
    I am sick with love.

What is your beloved more
    than another beloved,
    O fairest among women?
What is your beloved more
    than another beloved,
    that you thus adjure us?

My beloved is all radiant and
    ruddy,
    distinguished among ten
    thousand.
His head is the finest gold;
    his locks are wavy,
    black as a raven.
His eyes are like doves
    beside springs of water,
bathed in milk,
    fitly set.
His cheeks are like beds of
    spices,
    yielding fragrance.
His lips are lilies,
    distilling liquid myrrh.
His arms are rounded gold,
    set with jewels.
His body is ivory work,
    encrusted with sapphires,
His legs are alabaster
    columns,
    set upon bases of gold.
His appearance is like
    Lebanon,
    choice as the cedars.
His speech is most sweet,
    and he is altogether
    desirable.

This is my beloved and this is
my friend,
O daughters of Jerusalem.

7 How graceful are your
feet in sandals,
O queenly maiden!
Your rounded thighs are like
jewels,
the work of a master hand.
Your navel is a rounded bowl
that never lacks mixed
wine.
Your belly is a heap of wheat,
encircled with lilies.
Your two breasts are like two
fawns,
twins of a gazelle.
Your neck is like an ivory
tower.
Your eyes are pools in
Heshbon,
by the gate of Bath-rab'bim.
Your nose is like a tower of
Lebanon,
overlooking Damascus.
Your head crowns you like
Carmel,
and your flowing locks are
like purple;
a king is held captive in
the tresses.
How fair and pleasant you
are,
O loved one, delectable
maiden!
You are stately as a palm tree,
and your breasts are like its
clusters.
I say I will climb the palm
tree
and lay hold of its branches.
Oh, may your breasts be like
clusters of the vine,
and the scent of your
breath like apples,

and your kisses like the best
wine
that goes down smoothly,
gliding over lips and teeth.

I am my beloved's,
and his desire is for me.
Come, my beloved,
let us go forth into the
fields,
and lodge in the villages;
let us go out early to the
vineyards,
and see whether the vines
have budded,
whether the grape blossoms
have opened
and the pomegranates are
in bloom.
There I will give you my love.
The mandrakes give forth
fragrance,
and over our doors are all
choice fruits,
new as well as old,
which I have laid up for
you, O my beloved.

8 O that you were like a
brother to me,
that nursed at my mother's
breast!
If I met you outside, I would
kiss you,
and none would despise
me.
I would lead you and bring
you
into the house of my
mother,
and into the chamber of her
that conceived me.
I would give you spiced wine
to drink,
the juice of my
pomegranates.

O that his left hand were
  under my head,
and that his right hand
  embraced me!
I adjure you, O daughters of
  Jerusalem,
that you stir not up nor
  awaken love
until it please.

Who is that coming up from
  the wilderness,
leaning upon her beloved?
Under the apple tree I
  awakened you.
There your mother was in
  travail with you,

there she who bore you was
  in travail.

Set me as a seal upon your
  heart,
as a seal upon your arm;
for love is strong as death,
  jealousy is cruel as the
  grave.
Its flashes are flashes of fire,
  a most vehement flame.
Many waters cannot quench
  love,
neither can floods drown it.
If a man offered for love
  all the wealth of his house,
  it would be utterly scorned.

❋   ❋   ❋

THE HOLY BIBLE   Ephesians 5

5 Therefore be imitators of God, as beloved children. And walk in love, as Christ loved us and gave himself up for us, a fragrant offering and sacrifice to God. . . .

21 Be subject to one another out of reverence for Christ. Wives, be subject to your husband, as to the Lord. For the husband is the head of the wife as Christ is the head of the church, his body, and is himself its Savior. As the church is subject to Christ, so let wives also be subject in everything to their husbands. Husbands, love your wives, as Christ loved the church and gave himself up for her, that he might sanctify her, having cleansed her by the washing of water with the word, that he might present the church to himself in splendor, without spot or wrinkle or any such thing, that she might be holy and without blemish. Even so husbands should love their wives as their own bodies. He who loves his wife loves himself. For no man ever hates his own flesh, but nourishes and cherishes it, as Christ does the church, because we are members of his body. "For this reason a man shall leave his father and mother and be joined to his wife, and the two shall become one flesh." This mystery is a profound one, and I am saying that it refers to Christ and the church; however, let each one of

you love his wife as himself, and
let the wife see that she respects

her husband.

❧   ❧   ❧

THE HOLY BIBLE   1 Corinthians 7

7 Now concerning the mat-
ters about which you wrote.
It is well for a man not to touch
a woman. But because of the
temptation to immorality, each
man should have his own wife
and each woman her own husband. The husband should give
to his wife her conjugal rights,
and likewise the wife to her husband. For the wife does not rule
over her own body, but the husband does; likewise the husband
does not rule over his own body,
but the wife does. Do not refuse
one another except perhaps by
agreement for a season, that you
may devote yourselves to prayer;
but then come together again,
lest Satan tempt you through
lack of self-control. I say this by
way of concession, not of command. I wish that all were as I
myself am. But each has his own
special gift from God, one of
one kind and one of another.

8 To the unmarried and the
widows I say that it is well for
them to remain single as I do.
But if they cannot exercise self-
control, they should marry. For
it is better to marry than to be
aflame with passion.

10 To the married I give
charge, not I but the Lord, that
the wife should not separate

from her husband (but if she
does, let her remain single or
else be reconciled to her husband)—and that the husband
should not divorce his wife.

12 To the rest I say, not the
Lord, that if any brother has a
wife who is an unbeliever, and
she consents to live with him,
he should not divorce her. If any
woman has a husband who is an
unbeliever, and he consents to
live with her, she should not divorce him. For the unbelieving
husband is consecrated through
his wife, and the unbelieving
wife is consecrated through her
husband. Otherwise, your children would be unclean, but as
it is they are holy. But if the unbelieving partner desires to separate, let it be so; in such a case
the brother or sister is not bound.
For God has called us to peace.
Wife, how do you know whether
you will save your husband?
Husband, how do you know
whether you will save your wife?

17 Only, let every one lead
the life which the Lord has assigned to him, and in which God
has called him. This is my rule
in all the churches. Was any one
at the time of his call already
circumcised? Let him not seek
to remove the marks of circum-

cision. Was any one at the time of his call uncircumcised? Let him not seek circumcision. For neither circumcision counts for anything nor uncircumcision, but keeping the commandments of God. Every one should remain in the state in which he was called. Were you a slave when called? Never mind. But if you can gain your freedom, avail yourself of the opportunity. For he who was called in the Lord as a slave is a freedman of the Lord. Likewise he who was free when called is a slave of Christ. You were bought with a price; do not become slaves of men. So, brethren, in whatever state each was called, there let him remain with God.

25 Now concerning the unmarried, I have no command of the Lord, but I give my opinion as one who by the Lord's mercy is trustworthy. I think that in view of the present distress it is well for a person to remain as he is. Are you bound to a wife? Do not seek to be free. Are you free from a wife? Do not seek marriage. But if you marry, you do not sin, and if a girl marries she does not sin. Yet those who marry will have worldly troubles, and I would spare you that. I mean, brethren, the appointed time has grown very short; from now on, let those who have wives live as though they had none, and those who mourn as though they were not mourning, and those who rejoice as though they were not rejoicing, and those who buy as though they had no goods, and those who

deal with the world as though they had no dealings with it. For the form of this world is passing away.

32 I want you to be free from anxieties. The unmarried man is anxious about the affairs of the Lord, how to please the Lord; but the married man is anxious about worldly affairs, how to please his wife, and his interests are divided. And the unmarried woman or girl is anxious about the affairs of the Lord, how to be holy in body and spirit; but the married woman is anxious about worldly affairs, how to please her husband. I say this for your own benefit, not to lay any restraint upon you, but to promote good order and to secure your undivided devotion to the Lord.

36 If any one thinks that he is not behaving properly toward his betrothed, if his passions are strong, and it has to be, let him do as he wishes: let them marry —it is no sin. But whoever is firmly established in his heart, being under no necessity but having his desire under control, and has determined this in his heart, to keep her as his betrothed, he will do well. So that he who marries his betrothed does well; and he who refrains from marriage will do better.

39 A wife is bound to her husband as long as he lives. If the husband dies, she is free to be married to whom she wishes, only in the Lord. But in my judgment she is happier if she remains as she is. And I think that I have the Spirit of God.

✿   ✿   ✿

THE HOLY BIBLE   1 Corinthians 11

11 Be imitators of me, as I am of Christ.

2 I commend you because you remember me in everything and maintain the traditions even as I have delivered them to you. But I want you to understand that the head of every man is Christ, the head of a woman is her husband, and the head of Christ is God. Any man who prays or prophesies with his head covered dishonors his head, but any woman who prays or prophesies with her head unveiled dishonors her head—it is the same as if her head were shaven. For if a woman will not veil herself, then she should cut off her hair; but if it is disgraceful for a woman to be shorn or shaven, let her wear a veil. For a man ought not to cover his head, since he is the image and glory of God; but woman is the glory of man. (For man was not made from woman, but woman from man. Neither was man created for woman, but woman for man.) That is why a woman ought to have a veil on her head, because of the angels. (Nevertheless, in the Lord woman is not independent of man nor man of woman; for as woman was made from man, so man is now born of woman. And all things are from God.) Judge for yourselves; is it proper for a woman to pray to God with her head uncovered? Does not nature itself teach you that for a man to wear long hair is degrading to him, but if a woman has long hair, it is her pride? For her hair is given to her for a covering. If any one is disposed to be contentious, we recognize no other practice, nor do the churches of God. . . .

✿   ✿   ✿

RELATED READINGS

Bassett, Marion Preston. *A New Sex Ethics and Marriage Structure; Discussed by Adam and Eve.* New York: Philosophical Library, 1961.

Boldrey, Richard and Boldrey, Joyce. *Chauvinist or Feminist? Paul's View of Women.* Grand Rapids: Baker Book House, 1976.

Carmody, Denise L. *Women and World Religions.* Nashville: Abingdon Press, 1979.

Christ, Carol and Plaskow, Judith. *Womanspirit Rising: A Feminist Reader in Religion.* New York: Harper and Row Publishing Company, 1979.

Daly, Mary. *Beyond God the Father.* Boston: Beacon Press, 1973.

Fischer, James A. *God Said: Let There Be Woman: A Study of Biblical Women.* New York: Alba House, 1979.

Jewett, Paul K. *Man as Male and Female.* Grand Rapids: William B. Eerdmans Publishing Company, 1975.

Koltun, Elizabeth (ed.). *The Jewish Woman.* New York: Schocken Books, 1976.

Kress, Robert. *Whither Womankind?* St. Meinrad, Indiana: Abbey Press, 1975.

Lightfoot, Neil R. The Role of Women: *New Testament Perspectives.* Memphis: Student Association Press, 1978.

Maimonides, Moses. *The Code of Maimonides,* vol. 4, Book IV of the Code, "The Book of Women." New Haven: Yale University Press, 1972.

Mikhail, Mona N. *Images of Islamic Women: Fact and Fiction.* Metuchen, New Jersey: Scarecrow Press, 1978.

Mollenkott, Virginia R. *Women, Men, and the Bible.* Nashville: Abingdon Press, 1977.

Morris, Joan. *The Lady Was a Bishop.* New York: Macmillan Company, Inc., 1973.

Ochs, Carol. *Behind the Sex of God.* Boston: Beacon Press, 1977.

Otwell, John H. *And Sarah Laughed: The Status of Woman in the Old Testament.* Philadelphia: Westminster Press, 1977.

Pape, Dorothy. *In Search of God's Ideal Woman.* Downers Grove, Illinois: Inter-Varsity Press, 1976.

Plaskow, Judith and Romero, Joan Arnold (eds.). *Women and Religion.* Missoula, Montana: Scholar's Press, 1974.

Raccagni, Michelle. *The Modern Arab Woman.* Metuchen, New Jersey: Scarecrow Press, Inc., 1978.

Ruether, Rosemary. *The Image of Women in the Judeo-Christian Tradition.* New York: Simon and Schuster, Inc., 1972.

――――. *New Woman New Earth, Sexist Ideologies and Human Liberation.* New York: The Seabury Press, Inc., 1975.

―――― (ed.). *Religion and Sexism.* Images of Woman in the Jewish and Christian Traditions. New York: Simon and Schuster, Inc., 1974.

Russell, Letty M. *Human Liberation in a Feminist Perspective—a Theology.* Philadelphia: Westminster Press, 1974.

――――. *The Liberating Word: A Guide to Non-Sexist Interpretation of the Bible.* Philadelphia: Westminster Press, 1976.

Scanzoni, Letha and Hardesty, Nancy. *All We're Meant to Be: a Biblical Approach to Women's Liberation.* Waco, Texas: Word Books, 1975.

Stanton, Elizabeth Cady. *The Woman's Bible*. Seattle: Coalition on Women and Religion, 1974.

Swidler, Arlene. *Woman in a Man's Church*. New Jersey: Paulist Press, 1972.

PSYCHOANALYTIC THEORY

While there are diverse interpretations of psychoanalytic theory, these share certain claims about human nature and about a method for explaining mental functioning and human behavior. Basic to this theory is the role of the unconscious in psychic determinism. The human psyche is generally viewed as consisting of three structures: the id, the ego, and the superego, which interact and overlap in processes such as repression, projection, and transference. For each individual there are psychosexual stages of development: oral, anal, and genital, each describing an area of the body which is particularly responsive to pleasureable stimulation for a certain period; these correspond with stages of personality development in both sexes. Psychoanalytic therapy is designed to assist the individual to recall episodes of the past that lie buried in the unconscious. Supposedly, where such events have triggered undesirable behavior, recognition of their occurrence facilitates the overcoming of their debilitating influence.

SIGMUND FREUD

As founder of psychoanalysis, Sigmund Freud (1856–1939) not only elaborated its key concepts but precipitated much controversy because of the novelty and boldness of his ideas. In Freud's view the task of the ego is to reconcile the individual demands of the id with the social/moral demands of the superego; the healthy individual is one for whom as many demands as possible are fulfilled in light of the reality principle. Two basic human impulses, sexuality and aggression, account for personality differences from infancy through adulthood. An Oedipus complex explains how the initial bonding between infant and mother leads to repression of rivalry felt towards the parent of the same sex. The concept of penis envy is Freud's way of characterizing a little girl's reaction to her realization that she lacks the sexual organ of her male counterpart. Obviously this concept is suggestive of a broader level of application regarding female/male relations.

The following excerpts are taken from *New Introductory Lec-*

tures in Psychoanalysis, translated and edited by James Strachey. New York: W. W. Norton and Company, Inc., 1965, Lecture XXXIII, pp. 112–135.

SIGMUND FREUD 'Femininity'

To-day's lecture . . . brings forward nothing but observed facts, almost without any speculative additions, and it deals with a subject which has a claim on your interest second almost to no other. Throughout history people have knocked their heads against the riddle of the nature of femininity—

> Häupter in Hieroglyphenmützen,
> Häupter in Turban und schwarzem Barett,
> Perückenhäupter und tausend andre
> Arme, schwitzende Menschenhäupter. . . .[1]

Nor will *you* have escaped worrying over this problem—those of you who are men; to those of you who are women this will not apply—you are yourselves the problem. When you meet a human being, the first distinction you make is 'male or female?' and you are accustomed to make the distinction with unhesitating certainty. Anatomical science shares your certainty at one point and not much further. The male sexual product, the spermatozoon, and its vehicle are male; the ovum and the organism that harbours it are female. In both sexes organs have been formed which serve exclusively for the sexual functions; they were probably developed from the same [innate] disposition into two different forms. Besides this, in both sexes the other organs, the bodily shapes and tissues, show the influence of the individual's sex, but this is inconstant and its amount variable; these are what are known as secondary sexual characters. Science next tells you something that runs counter to your expectations and is probably calculated to confuse your feelings. It draws your attention to the fact that portions of the male sexual apparatus also appear in women's bodies, though in an atrophied state, and vice versa in the alternative case. It regards their occurrence as indications of *bisexuality,* as though

---

1. Heads in hieroglyphic bonnets,
   Heads in turbans and black birettas,
   Heads in wigs and thousand other
   Wretched, sweating heads of humans. . . .
       (Heine, *Nordsee* [Second Cycle, VII, 'Fragen'].)

an individual is not a man or a woman but always both—merely a certain amount more the one than the other. You will then be asked to make yourselves familiar with the idea that the proportion in which masculine and feminine are mixed in an individual is subject to quite considerable fluctuations. Since, however, apart from the very rarest cases, only one kind of sexual product—ova or semen—is nevertheless present in one person, you are bound to have doubts as to the decisive significance of those elements and must conclude that what constitutes masculinity or femininity is an unknown characteristic which anatomy cannot lay hold of.

Can psychology do so perhaps? We are accustomed to employ 'masculine' and 'feminine' as mental qualities as well, and have in the same way transferred the notion of bisexuality to mental life. Thus we speak of a person, whether male or female, as behaving in a masculine way in one connection and in a feminine way in another. But you will soon perceive that this is only giving way to anatomy or to convention. You cannot give the concepts of 'masculine' and 'feminine' *any* new connotation. The distinction is not a psychological one; when you say 'masculine', you usually mean 'active', and when you say 'feminine', you usually mean 'passive'. Now it is true that a relation of the kind exists. The male sex-cell is actively mobile and searches out the female one, and the latter, the ovum, is immobile and waits passively. This behaviour of the elementary sexual organisms is indeed a model for the conduct of sexual individuals during intercourse. The male pursues the female for the purpose of sexual union, seizes hold of her and penetrates into her. But by this you have precisely reduced the characteristic of masculinity to the factor of aggressiveness so far as psychology is concerned. You may well doubt whether you have gained any real advantage from this when you reflect that in some classes of animals the females are the stronger and more aggressive and the male is active only in the single act of sexual union. This is so, for instance, with the spiders. Even the functions of rearing and caring for the young, which strike us as feminine *par excellence,* are not invariably attached to the female sex in animals. In quite high species we find that the sexes share the task of caring for the young between them or even that the male alone devotes himself to it. Even in the sphere of human sexual life you soon see how inadequate it is to make masculine behaviour coincide with activity and feminine with passivity. A mother is active in every sense towards her child; the act of lactation itself may equally be described as the mother suckling the baby or as her being sucked by it. The further you go from the narrow sexual sphere the more obvious will the 'error of superimposition'[2] become. Women can display

2. [I.e. mistaking two different things for a single one.]

great activity in various directions, men are not able to live in company with their own kind unless they develop a large amount of passive adaptability. If you now tell me that these facts go to prove precisely that both men and women are bisexual in the psychological sense, I shall conclude that you have decided in your own minds to make 'active' coincide with 'masculine' and 'passive' with 'feminine'. But I advise you against it. It seems to me to serve no useful purpose and adds nothing to our knowledge.

One might consider characterizing femininity psychologically as giving preference to passive aims. This is not, of course, the same thing as passivity; to achieve a passive aim may call for a large amount of activity. It is perhaps the case that in a woman, on the basis of her share in the sexual function, a preference for passive behaviour and passive aims is carried over into her life to a greater or lesser extent, in proportion to the limits, restricted or far-reach ing, within which her sexual life thus serves as a model. But we must beware in this of underestimating the influence of social customs, which similarly force women into passive situations. All this is still far from being cleared up. There is one particularly constant relation between femininity and instinctual life which we do not want to overlook. The suppression of women's aggressiveness which is prescribed for them constitutionally and imposed on them socially favours the development of powerful masochistic impulses, which succeed, as we know, in binding erotically the destructive trends which have been diverted inwards. Thus masochism, as people say, is truly feminine. But if, as happens so often, you meet with masochism in men, what is left to you but to say that these men exhibit very plain feminine traits?

And now you are already prepared to hear that psychology too is unable to solve the riddle of femininity. The explanation must no doubt come from elsewhere, and cannot come till we have learnt how in general the differentiation of living organisms into two sexes came about. We know nothing about it, yet the existence of two sexes is a most striking characteristic of organic life which distinguishes it sharply from inanimate nature. However, we find enough to study in those human individuals who, through the possession of female genitals, are characterized as manifestly or predominantly feminine. In conformity with its peculiar nature, psychoanalysis does not try to describe what a woman is—that would be a task it could scarcely perform—but sets about enquiring how she comes into being, how a woman develops out of a child with a bisexual disposition. In recent times we have begun to learn a little about this, thanks to the circumstance that several of our excellent women colleagues in analysis have begun to work at the question. The discussion of this has gained special attractiveness from the distinction between the sexes. For the ladies, whenever some comparison seemed to turn out unfavourable to their sex, were able to utter a suspicion that we, the male analysts, had been unable to overcome certain deeply-rooted prejudices against what was feminine, and that this was being paid for in the partiality of our researches. We, on the other hand, standing on the ground of bisexuality, had no difficulty in avoiding impoliteness. We had only to say: 'This doesn't apply to *you*. You're the exception; on this point you're more masculine than feminine.'

We approach the investigation of the sexual development of women with two expectations. The first is that here once more the constitution will not adapt itself to its function without a struggle. The second is that the decisive turning-points will already have been prepared for or completed before puberty. Both expectations are promptly confirmed. Furthermore, a comparison with what happens with boys tells us that the development of a little girl into a normal woman is more difficult and more complicated, since it includes two extra tasks, to which there is nothing corresponding in the development of a man. Let us follow the parallel lines from their beginning. Undoubtedly the material is different to start with in boys and girls: it did not need psycho-analysis to establish that. The difference in the structure of the genitals is accompanied by other bodily differences which are too well known to call for mention. Differences emerge too in the instinctual disposition which give a glimpse of the later nature of women. A little girl is as a rule less aggressive, defiant and self-sufficient; she seems to have a greater need for being shown affection and on that account to be more dependent and pliant. It is probably only as a result of this pliancy that she can be taught more easily and quicker to control her excretions: urine and faeces are the first gifts that children make to those who look after them, and controlling them is the first concession to which the instinctual life of children can be induced. One gets an impression, too, that little girls are more intelligent and livelier than boys of the same age; they go out more to meet the external world and at the same time form stronger object-cathexes. I cannot say whether this lead in development has been confirmed by exact observations, but in any case there is no question that girls cannot be described as intellectually backward. These sexual differences are not, however, of great consequence: they can be outweighed by individual variations. For our immediate purposes they can be disregarded.

Both sexes seem to pass through the early phases of libidinal development in the same manner. It might have been expected that in girls there would already have been some lag in aggressiveness in the sadistic-anal phase, but such is not the case. Analysis of children's play has shown our women analysts that the aggressive impulses of little girls leave nothing to be desired in the way of abundance and violence. With their entry into the phallic phase the differences between the sexes are completely eclipsed by their agreements. We are now obliged to recognize that the little girl is a little man. In boys, as we know, this phase is marked by the fact that they have learnt how to derive pleasurable sensations from their small penis and connect its excited state with their ideas of sexual intercourse. Little girls do the same thing with their still smaller clitoris. It seems that with them all their masturbatory acts are carried out on this penis-equivalent, and that the truly feminine vagina is still undiscovered by both sexes. It is true that there are a few isolated reports of early vaginal sensations as well, but it could not be easy to distinguish these from sensations in the anus or vestibulum; in any case they cannot play a great part. We are entitled to keep to our view that in the phallic phase of girls the clitoris is the leading erotogenic zone. But it is not, of course, going to remain so. With the change to femininity the clitoris should wholly or in part hand over its sensitivity, and at the same time its importance, to the vagina. This would be one of the two tasks which a woman has to perform in the course of her development, whereas the more fortunate man has only to continue at the time of his sexual maturity the activity that he has previously carried out at the period of the early efflorescence of his sexuality.

We shall return to the part played by the clitoris; let us now turn to the second task with which a girl's development is burdened. A boy's mother is the first object of his love, and she remains so too during the formation of his Oedipus complex and, in essence, all through his life. For a girl too her first object must be her mother (and the figures of wet-nurses and foster-mothers that merge into her). The first object-cathexes occur in attachment to the satisfaction of the major and simple vital needs, and the circumstances of the care of children are the same for both sexes. But in the Oedipus situation the girl's father has become her love-object, and we expect that in the normal course of development she will find her way from this paternal object to her final choice of an object. In the course of time, therefore, a girl has to change her erotogenic zone and her object—both of which a boy retains. The question then arises of how this happens: in particular, how does a girl pass from her mother to an attachment to her father? or, in other words, how does she pass from her masculine phase to the feminine one to which she is biologically destined?

It would be a solution of ideal simplicity if we could suppose that from a particular age onwards the elementary influence of the mutual attraction between the sexes makes itself felt and impels the small woman towards men, while the same law allows the boy to continue with his mother. We might suppose in addition that in this the children are following the pointer given them by the sexual preference of their parents. But we are not going to find things so easy; we scarcely know whether we are to believe seriously in the power of which poets talk so much and with such enthusiasm but which cannot be further dissected analytically. We have found an answer of quite another sort by means of laborious investigations, the material for which at least was easy to arrive at. For you must know that the number of women who remain till a late age tenderly dependent on a paternal object, or indeed on their real father, is very great. We have established some surprising facts about these women with an intense attachment of long duration to their father. We knew, of course, that there had been a preliminary stage of attachment to the mother, but we did not know that it could be so rich in content and so long-lasting, and could leave behind so many opportunities for fixations and dispositions. During this time the girl's father is only a troublesome rival; in some cases the attachment to her mother lasts beyond the fourth year of life. Almost everything that we find later in her relation to her father was already present in this earlier attachment and has been transferred subsequently on to her father. In short, we get an impression that we cannot understand women unless we appreciate this phase of their pre-Oedipus attachment to their mother.

We shall be glad, then, to know the nature of the girl's libidinal relations to her mother. The answer is that they are of very many different kinds. Since they persist through all three phases of infantile sexuality, they also take on the characteristics of the different phases and express themselves by oral, sadistic-anal and phallic wishes. These wishes represent active as well as passive impulses; if we relate them to the differentiation of the sexes which is to appear later—though we should avoid doing so as far as possible— we may call them masculine and feminine. Besides this, they are completely ambivalent, both affectionate and of a hostile and aggressive nature. The latter often only come to light after being changed into anxiety ideas. It is not always easy to point to a formulation of these early sexual wishes; what is most clearly expressed is a wish to get the mother with child and the corresponding wish to bear her a child—both belonging to the phallic period and sufficiently surprising, but established beyond doubt by analytic observation. The attractiveness of these investigations lies in the surprising detailed findings which they bring us. Thus, for instance, we discover the fear of being murdered or poisoned, which may later form the core of a paranoic illness, already present in this pre-Oedipus period, in relation to the mother. Or another case: you will recall an interesting episode in the history of analytic research which caused me many distressing hours. In the period in which the main interest was directed to discovering infantile sexual traumas, almost all my women patients told me that they had been seduced by their father. I was driven to recognize in the end that these reports were untrue and so came to understand that hysterical symptoms are derived from phantasies and not from real occurrences. It was only later that I was able to recognize in this phantasy of being seduced by the father the expression of the typical Oedipus complex in women. And now we find the phantasy of seduction once more in the pre-Oedipus prehistory of girls; but the seducer is regularly the mother. Here, however, the phantasy touches the ground of reality, for it was really the mother who by her activities over the child's bodily hygiene inevitably stimulated, and perhaps even roused for the first time, pleasurable sensations in her genitals.

I have no doubt you are ready to suspect that this portrayal of the abundance and strength of a little girl's sexual relations with her mother is very much overdrawn. After all, one has opportunities of seeing little girls and notices nothing of the sort. But the objection is not to the point. Enough can be seen in the children if one knows how to look. And besides, you should consider how little of its sexual wishes a child can bring to preconscious expression or communicate at all. Accordingly we are only within our rights if we study the residues and consequences of this emotional world in retrospect, in people in whom these processes of development had attained a specially clear and even excessive degree of expansion. Pathology has always done us the service of making discernible by isolation and exaggeration conditions which would remain concealed in a normal state. And since our investigations have been carried out on people who were by no means seriously abnormal, I think we should regard their outcome as deserving belief.

We will now turn our interest on to the single question of what it is that brings this powerful attachment of the girl to her mother to an end. This, as we know, is its usual fate: it is destined to make room for an attachment to her father. Here we come upon a fact which is a pointer to our further advance. This step in development does not involve only a simple change of object. The turning away from the mother is accompanied by hostility; the attachment to the mother ends in hate. A hate of that kind may become very striking and last all through life; it may be carefully overcompensated later on; as a rule one part of it is overcome while another part persists. Events of later years naturally influence this greatly. We will restrict ourselves, however, to studying it at the time at which the girl turns to her father and to enquiring into the motives for it. We are then given a long list of accusations and grievances against the mother which are supposed to justify the child's hostile feelings; they are of varying validity which we shall not fail to examine. A number of them are obvious rationalizations and the true sources of enmity remain to be found. I hope you will be interested if on this occasion I take you through all the details of a psycho-analytic investigation.

The reproach against the mother which goes back furthest is that she gave the child too little milk—which is construed against her as lack of love. Now there is some justification for this reproach in our families. Mothers often have insufficient nourishment to give their children and are content to suckle them for a few months, for half or three-quarters of a year. Among primitive peoples children are fed at their mother's breast for two or three years. The figure of the wet-nurse who suckles the child is as a rule merged into the mother; when this has not happened, the reproach is turned into another one—that the nurse, who fed the child so willingly, was sent away by the mother too early. But whatever the true state of affairs may have been, it is impossible that the child's reproach can be justified as often as it is met with. It seems, rather, that the child's avidity for its earliest nourishment is altogether insatiable, that it never gets over the pain of losing its mother's breast. I should not be surprised if the analysis of a primitive child, who could still suck at its mother's breast when it was already able to run about and talk, were to bring the same reproach to light. The fear of being poisoned is also probably connected with the withdrawal of the breast. Poison is nourishment that makes one ill. Perhaps children trace back their early illnesses too to this frustration. A fair amount of intellectual education is a prerequisite for believing in chance; primitive people and uneducated ones, and no doubt children as well, are able to assign a ground for everything that happens. Perhaps originally it was a reason on animistic lines. Even to-day in some strata of our population no one can die without having been killed by someone else—preferably by the doctor. And the regular reaction of a neurotic to the death of someone closely connected with him is to put the blame on himself for having caused the death.

The next accusation against the child's mother flares up when the next baby appears in the nursery. If possible the connection with oral frustration is preserved: the mother could not or would not give the child any more milk because she needed the nourishment for the new arrival. In cases in which the two children are so close in age that lactation is prejudiced by the second pregnancy, this reproach acquires a real basis, and it is a remarkable fact that a child, even with an age difference of only 11 months, is not too young to take notice of what is happening. But what the child grudges the unwanted intruder and rival is not only the suckling but all the other signs of maternal care. It feels that it has been dethroned, despoiled, prejudiced in its rights; it casts a jealous hatred upon the new baby and develops a grievance against the faithless mother which often finds expression in a disagreeable change in its behaviour. It becomes 'naughty', perhaps, irritable and disobedient and goes back on the advances it has made towards controlling its excretions. All of this has been very long familiar and is accepted as self-evident; but we rarely form a correct idea of the strength of these jealous impulses, of the tenacity with which they persist and of the magnitude of their influence on later development. Especially as this jealousy is constantly receiving fresh nourishment in the later years of childhood and the whole shock is repeated with the birth of each new brother or sister. Nor does it make much difference if the child happens to remain the mother's preferred favourite. A child's demands for love are immoderate, they make exclusive claims and tolerate no sharing.

An abundant source of a child's hostility to its mother is provided by its multifarious sexual wishes, which alter according to the phase of the libido and which cannot for the most part be satisfied. The strongest of these frustrations occur at the phallic period, if the mother forbids pleasurable activity with the genitals—often with severe threats and every sign of displeasure—activity to which, after all, she herself had introduced the child. One would think these were reasons enough to account for a girl's turning away from her mother. One would judge, if so, that the estrangement follows inevitably from the nature of children's sexuality, from the immoderate character of their demand for love and the impossibility of fulfilling their sexual wishes. It might be thought indeed that this first love-relation of the child's is doomed to dissolution for the very reason that it is the first, for these early object-cathexes are regularly ambivalent to a high degree. A powerful tendency to aggressiveness is always present beside a powerful love, and the more passionately a child loves its object the more sensitive does it become to disappointments and frustrations from that object; and in the end the love must succumb to the accumulated hostility. Or the idea that there is an original ambivalence such as this in erotic cathexes may be rejected, and it may be pointed out that it is the special nature of the mother-child relation that leads, with equal inevitability, to the destruction of the child's love; for even the mildest upbringing cannot avoid using compulsion and introducing restrictions, and any such intervention in the child's liberty must provoke as a reaction an inclination to rebelliousness and aggressiveness. A discussion of these possibilities might, I think, be most interesting; but an objection suddenly emerges which forces our interest in another direction. All these factors—the slights, the disappointments in love, the jealousy, the seduction followed by prohibition—are, after all, also in operation in the relation of a *boy* to his mother and are yet unable to alienate him from the maternal object. Unless we can find something that is specific for girls and is not present or not in the same way present in boys, we shall not have explained the termination of the attachment of girls to their mother.

I believe we have found this specific factor, and indeed where we expected to find it, even though in a surprising form. Where we expected to find it, I say, for it lies in the castration complex. After all, the anatomical distinction [between the sexes] must express itself in psychical consequences. It was, however, a surprise to learn from analyses that girls hold their mother responsible for their lack of a penis and do not forgive her for their being thus put at a disadvantage.

As you hear, then, we ascribe a castration complex to women as well. And for good reasons, though its content cannot be the same as with boys. In the latter the castration complex arises after they have learnt from the sight of the female genitals that the organ which they value so highly need not necessarily accompany the body. At this the boy recalls to mind the threats he brought on himself by his doings with that organ, he begins to give credence to them and falls under the influence of fear of castration, which will be the most powerful motive force in his subsequent development. The castration complex of girls is also started by the sight of the genitals of the other sex. They at once notice the difference and, it must be admitted, its significance too. They feel seriously wronged, often declare that they want to 'have something like it too', and fall a victim to 'envy for the penis', which will leave ineradicable traces on their development and the formation of their character and which will not be surmounted in even the most favourable cases without a severe expenditure of psychical energy. The girl's recognition of the fact of her being with a penis does not by any means imply that she submits to the fact easily. On the contrary, she continues to hold on for a long time to the wish to get something like it herself and she believes in that possibility for improbably long years; and analysis can show that, at a period when knowledge of reality has long since rejected the fulfillment of the wish as unattainable, it persists in the unconscious and retains a considerable cathexis of energy. The wish to get the longed-for penis eventually in spite of everything may contribute to the motives that drive a mature woman to analysis, and what she may reasonably expect from analysis—a capacity, for instance, to carry on an intellectual profession—may often be recognized as a sublimated modification of this repressed wish.

One cannot very well doubt the importance of envy for the penis. You may take it as an instance of male injustice if I assert that envy and jealousy play an even greater part in the mental life of women than of men. It is not that I think these characteristics are absent in men or that I think they have no other roots in women than envy for the penis; but I am inclined to attribute their greater amount in women to this latter influence. Some analysts, however, have shown an inclination to depreciate the importance of this first instalment of penis-envy in the phallic phase. They are of opinion that what we find of this attitude in women is in the main a secondary structure which has come about on the occasion of later conflicts by regression to this early infantile impulse. This, however, is a general problem of depth psychology. In many patho-logical—or even unusual—instinctual attitudes (for instance, in all sexual perversions) the question arises of how much of their strength is to be attributed to early infantile fixations and how much to the influence of later experiences and developments. In such cases it is almost always a matter of complemental series such as we put forward in our discussion of the aetiology of the neuroses. Both factors play a part in varying amounts in the causation; a less on the one side is balanced by a more on the other. The infan-tile factor sets the pattern in all cases but does not always deter-mine the issue, though it often does. Precisely in the case of penis-envy I should argue decidedly in favour of the preponderance of the infantile factor.

The discovery that she is castrated is a turning-point in a girl's growth. Three possible lines of development start from it: one leads to sexual inhibition or to neurosis, the second to change of character in the sense of a masculinity complex, the third, finally, to normal femininity. We have learnt a fair amount, though not everything, about all three.

The essential content of the first is as follows: the little girl has hitherto lived in a masculine way, has been able to get pleasure by the excitation of her clitoris and has brought this activity into relation with her sexual wishes directed towards her mother, which are often active ones; now, owing to the influence of her penis-envy, she loses her enjoyment in her phallic sexuality. Her self-love is mortified by the comparison with the boy's far superior equipment and in consequence she renounces her masturbatory satisfaction from her clitoris, repudiates her love for her mother and at the same time not infrequently represses a good part of her sexual trends in general. No doubt her turning away from her mother does not occur all at once, for to begin with the girl regards her castration as an individual misfortune, and only gradually ex-tends it to other females and finally to her mother as well. Her love was directed to her *phallic* mother; with the discovery that her mother is castrated it becomes possible to drop her as an object, so that the motives for hostility, which have long been accumulat-ing, gain the upper hand. This means, therefore, that as a result of the discovery of women's lack of a penis they are debased in value for girls just as they are for boys and later perhaps for men.

You all know the immense aetiological importance attributed by our neurotic patients to their masturbation. They make it responsible for all their troubles and we have the greatest difficulty in persuading them that they are mistaken. In fact, however, we ought to admit to them that they are right, for masturbation is the executive agent of infantile sexuality, from the faulty development of which they are indeed suffering. But what neurotics mostly blame is the masturbation of the period of puberty; they have mostly forgotten that of early infancy, which is what is really in question. I wish I might have an opportunity some time of explaining to you at length how important all the factual details of early masturbation become for the individual's subsequent neurosis or character: whether or not it was discovered, how the parents struggled against it or permitted it, or whether he succeeded in suppressing it himself. All of this leaves permanent traces on his development. But I am on the whole glad that I need not do this. It would be a hard and tedious task and at the end of it you would put me in an embarrassing situation by quite certainly asking me to give you some practical advice as to how a parent or educator should deal with the masturbation of small children. From the development of girls, which is what my present lecture is concerned with, I can give you the example of a child herself trying to get free from masturbating. She does not always succeed in this. If envy for the penis has provoked a powerful impulse against clitoridal masturbation but this nevertheless refuses to give way, a violent struggle for liberation ensues in which the girl, as it were, herself takes over the role of her deposed mother and gives expression to her entire dissatisfaction with her inferior clitoris in her efforts against obtaining satisfaction from it. Many years later, when her masturbatory activity has long since been suppressed, an interest still persists which we must interpret as a defence against a temptation that is still dreaded. It manifests itself in the emergence of sympathy for those to whom similar difficulties are attributed, it plays a part as a motive in contracting a marriage and, indeed, it may determine the choice of a husband or lover. Disposing of early infantile masturbation is truly no easy or indifferent business.

Along with the abandonment of clitoridal masturbation a certain amount of activity is renounced. Passivity now has the upper hand, and the girl's turning to her father is accomplished principally with the help of passive instinctual impulses. You can see that a wave of development like this, which clears the phallic activity out of the way, smooths the ground for femininity. If too much is not lost in the course of it through repression, this femininity may turn out to be normal. The wish with which the girl turns to her father is no doubt originally the wish for the penis which her mother has refused her and which she now expects from her father. The feminine situation is only established, however, if the wish for a penis is replaced by one for a baby, if, that is, a baby takes the place of a penis in accordance with an ancient symbolic equivalence. It has not escaped us that the girl has wished for a baby earlier, in the undisturbed phallic phase: that, of course, was the meaning of her playing with dolls. But that play was not in fact an expression of her femininity; it served as an identification with her mother with the intention of substituting activity for passivity. *She* was playing the part of her mother and the doll was herself: now she could do with the baby everything that her mother used to do with her. Not until the emergence of the wish for a penis does the doll-baby become a baby from the girl's father, and thereafter the aim of the most powerful feminine wish. Her happiness is great if later on this wish for a baby finds fulfilment in reality, and quite especially so if the baby is a little boy who brings the longed-for penis with him. Often enough in her combined picture of 'a baby from her father' the emphasis is laid on the baby and her father left unstressed. In this way the ancient masculine wish for the possession of a penis is still faintly visible through the femininity now achieved. But perhaps we ought rather to recognize this wish for a penis as being *par excellence* a feminine one.

With the transference of the wish for a penis-baby on to her father, the girl has entered the situation of the Oedipus complex. Her hostility to her mother, which did not need to be freshly created, is now greatly intensified, for she becomes the girl's rival, who receives from her father everything that she desires from him. For a long time the girl's Oedipus complex concealed her pre-Oedipus attachment to her mother from our view, though it is nevertheless so important and leaves such lasting fixations behind it. For girls the Oedipus situation is the outcome of a long and difficult development; it is a kind of preliminary solution, a position of rest which is not soon abandoned, especially as the beginning of the latency period is not far distant. And we are now struck by a difference between the two sexes, which is probably momentous, in regard to the relation of the Oedipus complex to the castration complex. In a boy the Oedipus complex, in which he desires his mother and would like to get rid of his father as being a rival, develops naturally from the phase of his phallic sexuality. The threat of castration compels him, however, to give up that attitude. Under the impression of the danger of losing his penis, the Oedipus complex is abandoned, repressed and, in the most normal cases, entirely destroyed, and a severe super-ego is set up as its heir. What happens with a girl is almost the opposite. The castration complex prepares for the Oedipus complex instead of destroying it; the girl is driven out of her attachment to her mother through the influence of her envy for the penis and she enters the Oedipus situation as though into a haven of refuge. In the absence of fear of castration the chief motive is lacking which leads boys to surmount the Oedipus complex. Girls remain in it for an indeterminate length of time; they demolish it late and, even so, incompletely. In these circumstances the formation of the super-ego must suffer; it cannot attain the strength and independence which give it its cultural significance, and feminists are not pleased when we point out to them the effects of this factor upon the average feminine character.

To go back a little. We mentioned as the second possible reaction to the discovery of female castration the development of a powerful masculinity complex. By this we mean that the girl refuses, as it were, to recognize the unwelcome fact and, defiantly rebellious, even exaggerates her previous masculinity, clings to her clitoridal activity and takes refuge in an identification with her phallic mother or her father. What can it be that decides in favour of this outcome? We can only suppose that it is a constitutional factor, a greater amount of activity, such as is ordinarily characteristic of a male. However that may be, the essence of this process is that at this point in development the wave of passivity is avoided which opens the way to the turn towards femininity. The extreme achievement of such a masculinity complex would appear to be the influencing of the choice of an object in the sense of manifest homosexuality. Analytic experience teaches us, to be sure, that female homosexuality is seldom or never a direct continuation of infantile masculinity. Even for a girl of this kind it seems necessary that she should take her father as an object for some time and enter the Oedipus situation. But afterwards, as a result of her inevitable disappointments from her father, she is driven to regress into her early masculinity complex. The significance of these disappointments must not be exaggerated; a girl who is destined to become feminine is not spared them, though they do not have the same effect. The predominance of the constitutional factor seems indisputable; but the two phases in the development of female homosexuality are well mirrored in the practices of homosexuals, who play the parts of mother and baby with each other as often and as clearly as those of husband and wife. . . .

. . . the development of femininity remains exposed to disturbance by the residual phenomena of the early masculine period. Regressions to the fixations of the pre-Oedipus phases very frequently occur; in the course of some women's lives there is a repeated alternation between periods in which masculinity or femininity gains the upper hand. Some portion of what we men call 'the enigma of women' may perhaps be derived from this expression of bisexuality in women's lives. But another question seems to have become ripe

for judgement in the course of these researches. We have called
the motive force of sexual life 'the libido'. Sexual life is dominated
by the polarity of masculine–feminine; thus the notion suggests
itself of considering the relation of the libido to this antithesis. It
would not be surprising if it were to turn out that each sexuality
had its own special libido appropriated to it, so that one sort of
libido would pursue the aims of a masculine sexual life and another sort those of a feminine one. But nothing of the kind is true.
There is only one libido, which serves both the masculine and the
feminine sexual functions. To it itself we cannot assign any sex;
if, following the conventional equation of activity and masculinity,
we are inclined to describe it as masculine, we must not forget
that it also covers trends with a passive aim. Nevertheless the juxta-
position 'feminine libido' is without any justification. Furthermore,
it is our impression that more constraint has been applied to the
libido when it is pressed into the service of the feminine function,
and that—to speak teleologically—Nature takes less careful account
of its [that function's] demands than in the case of masculinity.
And the reason for this may lie—thinking once again teleologically—
in the fact that the accomplishment of the aim of biology has been
entrusted to the aggressiveness of men and has been made to
some extent independent of women's consent.

The sexual frigidity of women, the frequency of which appears
to confirm this disregard, is a phenomenon that is still insufficiently
understood. Sometimes it is psychogenic and in that case accessible
to influence; but in other cases it suggests the hypothesis of its
being constitutionally determined and even of there being a con-
tributory anatomical factor.

I have promised to tell you of a few more psychical peculiarities
of mature femininity, as we come across them in analytic observation. We do not lay claim to more than an average validity for these
assertions; nor is it always easy to distinguish what should be
ascribed to the influence of the sexual function and what to social
breeding. Thus, we attribute a larger amount of narcissism to
femininity, which also affects women's choice of object, so that
to be loved is a stronger need for them than to love. The effect of
penis-envy has a share, further, in the physical vanity of women,
since they are bound to value their charms more highly as a late
compensation for their original sexual inferiority. Shame, which is
considered to be a feminine characteristic *par excellence* but is
far more a matter of convention than might be supposed, has as
its purpose, we believe, concealment of genital deficiency. We are
not forgetting that at a later time shame takes on other functions.
It seems that women have made few contributions to the discoveries and inventions in the history of civilization; there is, however,
one technique which they may have invented—that of plaiting and

weaving. If that is so, we should be tempted to guess the unconscious motive for the achievement. Nature herself would seem to have given the model which this achievement imitates by causing the growth at maturity of the pubic hair that conceals the genitals. The step that remained to be taken lay in making the threads adhere to one another, while on the body they stick into the skin and are only matted together. If you reject this idea as fantastic and regard my belief in the influence of lack of a penis on the configuration of femininity as an *idée fixe*, I am of course defenceless.

The determinants of women's choice of an object are often made unrecognizable by social conditions. Where the choice is able to show itself freely, it is often made in accordance with the narcissistic ideal of the man whom the girl had wished to become. If the girl has remained in her attachment to her father—that is, in the Oedipus complex—her choice is made according to the paternal type. Since, when she turned from her mother to her father, the hostility of her ambivalent relation remained with her mother, a choice of this kind should guarantee a happy marriage. But very often the outcome is of a kind that presents a general threat to such a settlement of the conflict due to ambivalence. The hostility that has been left behind follows in the train of the positive attachment and spreads over on to the new object. The woman's husband, who to begin with inherited from her father, becomes after a time her mother's heir as well. So it may easily happen that the second half of a woman's life may be filled by the struggle against her husband, just as the shorter first half was filled by her rebellion against her mother. When this reaction has been lived through, a second marriage may easily turn out very much more satisfying. Another alteration in a woman's nature, for which lovers are unprepared, may occur in a marriage after the first child is born. Under the influence of a woman's becoming a mother herself, an identification with her own mother may be revived, against which she had striven up till the time of her marriage, and this may attract all the available libido to itself, so that the compulsion to repeat reproduces an unhappy marriage between her parents. The difference in a mother's reaction to the birth of a son or a daughter shows that the old factor of lack of a penis has even now not lost its strength. A mother is only brought unlimited satisfaction by her relation to a son; this is altogether the most perfect, the most free from ambivalence of all human relationships. A mother can transfer to her son the ambition which she has been obliged to suppress in herself, and she can expect from him the satisfaction of all that has been left over in her of her masculinity complex. Even a marriage is not made secure until the wife has succeeded in making her husband her child as well and in acting as a mother to him.

A woman's identification with her mother allows us to distinguish two strata: the pre-Oedipus one which rests on her affectionate attachment to her mother and takes her as a model, and the later one from the Oedipus complex which seeks to get rid of her mother and take her place with her father. We are no doubt justified in saying that much of both of them is left over for the future and that neither of them is adequately surmounted in the course of development. But the phase of the affectionate pre-Oedipus attachment is the decisive one for a woman's future: during it preparations are made for the acquisition of the characteristics with which she will later fulfil her role in the sexual function and perform her invaluable social tasks. It is in this identification too that she acquires her attractiveness to a man, whose Oedipus attachment to his mother it kindles into passion. How often it happens, however, that it is only his son who obtains what he himself aspired to! One gets an impression that a man's love and a woman's are a phase apart psychologically.

The fact that women must be regarded as having little sense of justice is no doubt related to the predominance of envy in their mental life; for the demand for justice is a modification of envy and lays down the condition subject to which one can put envy aside. We also regard women as weaker in their social interests and as having less capacity for sublimating their instincts than men. The former is no doubt derived from the dissocial quality which unquestionably characterizes all sexual relations. Lovers find sufficiency in each other, and families too resist inclusion in more comprehensive associations. The aptitude for sublimation is subject to the greatest individual variations. On the other hand I cannot help mentioning an impression that we are constantly receiving during analytic practice. A man of about thirty strikes us as a youthful, somewhat unformed individual, whom we expect to make powerful use of the possibilities for development opened up to him by analysis. A woman of the same age, however, often frightens us by her psychical rigidity and unchangeability. Her libido has taken up final positions and seems incapable of exchanging them for others. There are no paths open to further development; it is as though the whole process had already run its course and remains thenceforward insusceptible to influence—as though, indeed, the difficult development to femininity had exhausted the possibilities of the person concerned. As therapists we lament this state of things, even if we succeed in putting an end to our patient's ailment by doing away with her neurotic conflict.

That is all I had to say to you about femininity. It is certainly incomplete and fragmentary and does not always sound friendly.

But do not forget that I have only been describing women in so far as their nature is determined by their sexual function. It is true that that influence extends very far; but we do not overlook the fact that an individual woman may be a human being in other respects as well. If you want to know more about femininity, enquire from your own experiences of life, or turn to the poets, or wait until science can give you deeper and more coherent information.

        ❁   ❁   ❁

C. G. JUNG

After several years of friendly collaboration Carl Gustav Jung (1875–1961) broke with Freud to found his own school of analytical psychology. Jung's approach involved distinctions between predominantly extroverted and introverted personalities, and between four functions of personality—sensation, thinking, feeling, and intuition, which are present in differing proportions in different people. Each individual possesses a "persona" (cf. superego), i.e., a socially imposed mask behind which the true ego resides, and a "shadow" (cf. id), i.e., a rejected set of desires, emotions and attitudes imprisoned in the unconscious. A third major force in personality is the "image," which determines how the opposite sex is perceived. In man this image of the feminine is called the *anima;* in woman the image of the masculine is the *animus.* Jung viewed the anima as particularly related to the function of feeling, and the animus to thinking, supposing that feeling is generally more dominant in woman, and thinking in man.

The following selection is from *The Development of Personality,* translated by R. F. C. Hull. Princeton: Princeton University Press, 1954, pp. 198–201.

C. G. JUNG   'Marriage as a Psychological Relationship'

Every man carries within him the eternal image of woman, not the image of this or that particular woman, but a definite feminine image. This image is fundamentally unconscious, an hereditary factor of primordial origin engraved in the living organic system of the man, an imprint or "archetype" of all the ancestral experiences of the female, a deposit, as it were, of all the impressions ever made by woman—in short, an inherited system of psychic adaptation. Even if no women existed, it would still be possible, at any given time, to deduce from this unconscious image exactly how a woman would have to be constituted psychically. The same is true of the woman: she too has her inborn image of man. Actually, we know from experience that it would be more accurate to describe it as an image of *men,* whereas in the case of the man it is rather the image of *woman.* Since this image is unconscious, it is always unconsciously projected upon the person of the beloved, and is one of the chief reasons for passionate attraction or aversion. I have called this image the "anima," and I find the scholastic question *Habet mulier animam?* especially interesting, since in my view it is an intelligent one inasmuch as the doubt seems justified. Woman has no anima, no soul, but she has an *animus.* The anima has an erotic, emotional character, the animus a rationalizing one. Hence most of what men say about feminine eroticism, and particularly about the emotional life of women, is derived from their own anima projections and distorted accordingly. On the other hand, the astonishing assumptions and fantasies that women make about men come from the activity of the animus, who produces an inexhaustible supply of illogical arguments and false explanations.

Anima and animus are both characterized by an extraordinary many-sidedness. In a marriage it is always the contained who projects this image upon the container, while the latter is only partially able to project his unconscious image upon his partner. The more unified and simple this partner is, the less complete the projection. In which case, this highly fascinating image hangs as it were in mid air, as though waiting to be filled out by a living person. There are certain types of women who seem to be made by nature to attract anima projections; indeed one could almost speak of a definite "anima type." The so-called "sphinx-like" character is an indispensable part of their equipment, also an equivocalness, an intriguing elusiveness—not an indefinite blur that offers nothing, but an indefiniteness that seems full of promises, like the speaking silence of a Mona Lisa. A woman of this kind is both old and young, mother and daughter, of more than doubtful chastity, childlike, and yet endowed with a naïve cunning that is extremely disarming to men. Not every man of real intellectual power can be an animus, for the animus must be a master not so much of fine ideas as of fine words—words seemingly full of meaning which purport to leave a great deal unsaid. He must also belong to the "misunderstood" class, or be in some way at odds with his environment, so that the idea of self-sacrifice can insinuate itself. He must be a rather questionable hero, a man with possibilities, which is not to say that an animus projection may not discover a real hero long before he has become perceptible to the sluggish wits of the man of "average intelligence."

For man as well as for woman, in so far as they are "containers," the filling out of this image is an experience fraught with consequences, for it holds the possibility of finding one's own complexities answered by a corresponding diversity. Wide vistas seem to open up in which one feels oneself embraced and contained. I say "seem" advisedly, because the experience may be two-faced. Just as the animus projection of a woman can often pick on a man of real significance who is not recognized by the mass, and can actually help him to achieve his true destiny with her moral support, so a man can create for himself a *femme inspiratrice* by his anima projection. But more often it turns out to be an illusion with destructive consequences, a failure because his faith was not sufficiently strong. To the pessimists I would say that these primordial psychic images have an extraordinarily positive value, but I must warn the optimists against blinding fantasies and the likelihood of the most absurd aberrations.

One should on no account take this projection for an individual and conscious relationship. In its first stages it is far from that, for it creates a compulsive dependence based on unconscious motives other than the biological ones. Rider Haggard's *She* gives some indication of the curious world of ideas that underlies the anima projection. They are in essence spiritual contents, often in erotic disguise, obvious fragments of a primitive mythological mentality that consists of archetypes, and whose totality constitutes the collective unconscious. Accordingly, such a relationship is at bottom collective and not individual. (Benoît, who created in *L'Atlantide* a fantasy figure similar even in details to "She," denies having plagiarized Rider Haggard.)

If such a projection fastens on to one of the marriage partners, a collective spiritual relationship conflicts with the collective biological one and produces in the container the division or disintegration I have described above. If he is able to hold his head above water, he will find himself through this very conflict. In that case the projection, though dangerous in itself, will have helped him to pass from a collective to an individual relationship. This amounts to full conscious realization of the relationship that marriage brings. Since the aim of this paper is a discussion of the psychology of marriage, the psychology of projection cannot concern us here. It is sufficient to mention it as a fact.

One can hardly deal with the psychological marriage relationship without mentioning, even at the risk of misunderstanding, the nature of its critical transitions. As is well known, one understands nothing psychological unless one has experienced it oneself. Not that this ever prevents anyone from feeling convinced that his own judgment is the only true and competent one. This disconcerting fact comes from the necessary over-valuation of the momentary content of consciousness, for without this concentration of attention one could not be conscious at all. Thus it is that every period of life has its own psychological truth, and the same applies to every stage of psychological development. There are even stages which only the few can reach, it being a question of race, family, education, talent, and passion. Nature is aristocratic. The normal man is a fiction, although certain generally valid laws do exist. Psychic life is a development that can easily be arrested on the lowest levels. It is as though every individual had a specific gravity, in accordance with which he either rises, or sinks down, to the level where he reaches his limit. His views and convictions will be determined accordingly. No wonder, then, that by far the greater number of marriages reach their upper psychological limit in fulfilment of the biological aim, without injury to spiritual or moral health. Relatively few people fall into deeper disharmony with themselves. Where there is a great deal of pressure from outside, the conflict is unable to develop much dramatic tension for sheer lack of energy. Psychological insecurity, however, increases in proportion to social security, unconsciously at first, causing neuroses, then consciously, bringing with it separations, discord, divorces, and other marital disorders. On still higher levels, new possibilities of psychological development are discerned, touching on the sphere of religion where critical judgment comes to a halt.

Progress may be permanently arrested on any of these levels, with complete unconsciousness of what might have followed at the next stage of development. As a rule graduation to the next stage is barred by violent prejudices and superstitious fears. This, however, serves a most useful purpose, since a man who is compelled by accident to live at a high level too high for him becomes a fool and a menace.

Nature is not only aristocratic, she is also esoteric. Yet no man of understanding will thereby be induced to make a secret of what he knows, for he realizes only too well that the secret of psychic development can never be betrayed, simply because that development is a question of individual capacity.

❧   ❧   ❧

KAREN HORNEY

After fifteen years of consistently attempting to apply Freud's theories in behalf of her patients, Karen Horney (1885–1952) publicly articulated her points of disagreement with the founder of psychoanalysis. Like Jung, Horney rejects Freud's insistence on the centrality of the sexual drive in determining human personality. "When we relinquish this one-sided emphasis on genesis," she writes,

> we recognize that the connection between later peculiarities and earlier experiences is more complicated than Freud assumes: there is no such thing as an isolated repetition of isolated experiences; but the entirety of infantile experiences combines to form a certain character structure. . . .

To Horney the character structure that determines human personality is not the inevitable outcome of instinctual impulses, modified by the environment; rather it involves the activity of the ego in response to all of life's conditions, both internal and external. Instead of the pleasure principle, Horney speaks of a "striving for safety" as the motivation for human behavior. The "new therapeutic goal" which she endorses is "to restore the individual to himself, to help him regain his spontaneity and find his center of gravity in himself."

The following selection is from *New Ways in Psychoanalysis*. New York: W. W. Norton and Company, Inc., 1939, Ch. VI, pp. 101–119.

KAREN HORNEY   'Feminine Psychology'

Freud believes that psychic peculiarities and difficulties in the two sexes are engendered by bisexual trends in both of them. His contention is, briefly, that many psychic difficulties in man are due to his rejection of "feminine" trends in himself, and that many peculiarities in woman are due to her essential wish to be a man. Freud has elaborated this thought in more detail for the psychology of woman than for that of man, and therefore I shall discuss only his views of feminine psychology.

According to Freud the most upsetting occurrence in the development of the little girl is the discovery that other human beings have a penis, while she has none. "The discovery of her castration is the turning point in the life of the girl."[1] She reacts to this discovery with a definite wish to have a penis too, with the hope that it will still grow, and with an envy of those more fortunate beings who possess one. In the normal development penis-envy does not continue as such; after recognizing her "deficiency" as an unalterable fact, the girl transfers the wish for a penis to a wish for a child. "The hoped-for possession of a child is meant as a compensation for her bodily defect."[2]

Penis-envy is originally a merely narcissistic phenomenon, the girl feeling offended because her body is less completely equipped than the boy's. But it has also a root in object relations. According to Freud the mother is the first sexual object for the girl as well as for the boy. The girl wishes to have a penis not only for the sake of narcissistic pride, but also because of her libidinal desires for the mother, which, in so far as they are genital in nature, have a masculine character. Not recognizing the elemental power of heterosexual attraction, Freud raises the question as to why the girl has any need at all to change her attachment to the father. He gives two reasons for this change in affection: hostility toward the mother, who is held responsible for the lack of a penis, and a wish to obtain this desired organ from the father. "The wish with which girls turn to their father is, no doubt, ultimately the wish for the penis." Thus originally both boys and girls know only one sex: the masculine.

Penis-envy is assumed to leave ineradicable traces in woman's development; even in the most normal development it is overcome only by a great expenditure of energy. Woman's most significant attitudes or wishes derive their energy from her wish for a penis. Some of Freud's principal contentions intended to illustrate this may be briefly enumerated.

Freud considers the wish for a male child to be woman's strongest wish, because the wish for a child is heir to the wish for a penis. The son represents a sort of wish-fulfillment in the sense of penis possession. "The only thing that brings a mother undiluted satisfaction is her relation to a son: the mother can transfer to her son all the ambition which she has had to suppress in herself and she can hope to get from him the satisfaction of all that has remained to her of her masculinity complex."

Happiness during pregnancy, particularly when neurotic disturbances that are otherwise present subside during this time, is

1. Sigmund Freud, *New Introductory Lectures on Psychoanalysis* (1933), chapter on "The Psychology of Women." The following interpretation of Freud's point of view is based primarily on this source.

2. Karl Abraham, "Ausserungsformen des weiblichen Kastrationskomplexes" in *Internationale Zeitschrift für Psychoanalyse* (1921).

referred to as symbolic gratification in the possession of a penis (the penis being the child). When the delivery is delayed for functional reasons, it is suspected that the woman does not want to separate herself from the penis-child. On the other hand, motherhood may be rejected because it is a reminder of femininity. Similarly, depressions and irritations occurring during menstruation are regarded as the result of menstruation being a reminder of femininity. Cramps in menstruation are often interpreted as the result of fantasies in which the father's penis has been swallowed.

Disturbances in the relationship to men are regarded as ultimate results of penis-envy. As women turn to men mainly in the expectation of receiving a gift (penis-child), or in the expectation of having all their ambitions fulfilled, they easily turn against men if they fail to live up to such expectations. Envy of men may show itself also in the tendency to surpass them or in any kind of disparaging or in a striving for independence in so far as it implies disregarding man's help. In the sexual sphere the refutation of the feminine role may appear openly after defloration; the latter may arouse animosity to the partner because it is experienced as a castration.

In fact, there is scarcely any character trait in woman which is not assumed to have an essential root in penis-envy. Feminine inferiority feelings are regarded as an expression of contempt for the woman's own sex because of the lack of a penis. Freud believes that woman is more vain than man and attributes this to her necessity for compensation for the lack of a penis. Woman's physical modesty is born ultimately of a wish to hide the "deficiency" of her genitals. The greater role of envy and jealousy in woman's character is a direct outcome of penis-envy. Her tendency toward envy accounts for woman having "too little sense of justice," as well as for her "preference for mental and occupational interests belonging to the sphere of men."[3] Practically all of woman's ambitious strivings suggest to Freud her wish for a penis as the ultimate driving force. Also ambitions which are usually regarded as specifically feminine, such as the wish to be the most beautiful woman or the wish to marry the most prominent man, are, according to Abraham, expressions of penis-envy.

Although the concept of penis-envy is related to anatomical differences it is nevertheless contradictory to biological thinking. It would require tremendous evidence to make it plausible that woman, physically built for specifically female functions, should be psychically determined by a wish for attributes of the other sex. But actually the data presented for this contention are scant, consisting of three main observations.

3. Karl Abraham, *op. cit.*

First, it is pointed out that little girls often express the wish to have a penis or the hope that it will still grow. There is no reason, however, to think that this wish is any more significant than their equally frequent wish to have a breast; moreover the wish for a penis may be accompanied by a kind of behavior which in our culture is regarded as feminine.

It is also pointed out that some girls before puberty not only may wish to be a boy, but through their tomboyish behavior may indicate that they really mean it. Again, however, the question is whether we are justified in taking these tendencies at their face value; when they are analyzed we may find good reasons for the apparently masculine wishes: opposition, despair at not being attractive as a girl, and the like. As a matter of fact, since girls have been brought up with greater freedom this kind of behavior has become rare.

Finally, it is pointed out that adult women may express a wish to be a man, sometimes explicitly, sometimes by presenting themselves in dreams with a penis or penis symbol; they may express contempt for women and attribute existing inferiority feelings to being a woman; castrative tendencies may be manifest or may be expressed in dreams, in disguised or undisguised form. These latter data, however, though their occurrence is beyond doubt, are not as frequent as is suggested in some analytical writings. Also they are true only of neurotic women. Finally, they permit of a different interpretation and hence are far from proving the contention beyond dispute. Before discussing them critically let us first try to understand how it is that Freud and many other analysts see such overwhelming evidence for the decisive influence of penis-envy on woman's character.

In my estimation two main factors account for this conviction. On the basis of theoretical biases—which coincide to some extent with existing cultural prejudices—the analyst regards the following trends in women patients as off-hand suggestive of underlying penis-envy: tendencies to boss man, to berate him, to envy his success, to be ambitious themselves, to be self-sufficient, to dislike accepting help. I suspect that these trends are sometimes imputed to underlying penis-envy without further evidence. Further evidence may easily be found, however, in simultaneous complaints about feminine functions (such as menstruation) or frigidity, or in complaints about a brother having been preferred, or in a tendency to point out certain advantages of man's social position, or in dream symbols (a woman carrying a stick, slicing a sausage).

In reviewing these trends, it is obvious that they are characteristic of neurotic men as well as of neurotic women. Tendencies toward dictatorial power, toward egocentric ambition, toward envying and berating others are never-failing elements in present-day neuroses though the role they assume in a neurotic structure varies.

Furthermore, observation of neurotic women shows that all the trends in question appear toward other women or toward children as well as toward men. It appears dogmatic to assume that their expression in relation to others is merely a radiation from their relation to men.

Finally, as to dream symbols, any expression of wishes for masculinity is taken at its face value instead of being regarded skeptically for a possible deeper meaning. This procedure is contrary to the customary analytical attitude and can be ascribed only to the determining power of theoretical preconceptions.

Another source feeding the analyst's conviction of the significance of penis-envy lies not in himself but in his women patients. While some women patients are not impressed by interpretations which point to penis-envy as the origin of their troubles, others take them up readily and quickly learn to talk about their difficulties in terms of femininity and masculinity, or even to dream in symbols fitting this kind of thinking. These are not necessarily patients who are particularly gullible. Every experienced analyst will notice whether a patient is docile and suggestible and by analyzing these trends will diminish errors springing from that source. And some patients view their problems in terms of masculinity and femininity without any suggestion from the analyst, for naturally one cannot exclude the influence of literature. But there is a deeper reason why many patients gladly seize upon explanations offered in terms of penis-envy: these explanations present comparatively harmless and simple solutions. It is so much easier for a woman to think that she is nasty to her husband because, unfortunately, she was born without a penis and envies him for having one than to think, for instance, that she has developed an attitude of righteousness and infallibility which makes it impossible to tolerate any questioning or disagreement. It is so much easier for a patient to think that nature has given her an unfair deal than to realize that she actually makes excessive demands on the environment and is furious whenever they are not complied with. It seems thus that the theoretical bias of the analyst may coincide with the patient's tendency to leave her real problems untouched.

If wishes for masculinity may screen repressed drives, what then renders them fit to serve in this way?

Here we come to see cultural factors. The wish to be a man, as Alfred Adler has pointed out, may be the expression of a wish for all those qualities or privileges which in our culture are regarded as masculine, such as strength, courage, independence, success, sexual freedom, right to choose a partner. To avoid misunderstanding let me state explicitly that I do not mean to say that penis-envy is nothing but a symbolic expression of the wish to have the qualities regarded as masculine in our culture. This would not be plausible, because wishes to have these qualities need not be repressed and hence do not require a symbolic expression. A symbolic expression is necessary only for tendencies or feelings shoved out of awareness.

What then are the repressed strivings which are covered up by the wish for masculinity? The answer is not an all-embracing formula but must be discovered from an analysis of each patient and each situation. In order to discover the repressed strivings it is necessary not to take at face value a woman's tendency in one way or another to base her inferiority feelings on the fact that she is a woman; rather it must be pointed out to her that every person belonging to a minority group or to a less privileged group tends to use that status as a cover for inferiority feelings of various sources, and that the important thing is to try to find out these sources. According to my experience, one of the most frequent and effective sources is a failure to live up to certain inflated notions about the self, notions which in turn are necessary because various unrecognized pretenses have to be covered up.

Furthermore, it is necessary to bear in mind the possibility that the wish to be a man may be a screen for repressed ambition. In neurotic persons ambition may be so destructive that it becomes loaded with anxiety and hence has to be repressed. This is true of men as well as of women but as a result of the cultural situation a repressed destructive ambition in a woman may express itself in the comparatively harmless symbol of a wish to be a man. What is required of psychoanalysis is to uncover the egocentric and destructive elements in the ambition and to analyze not only what led up to this kind of ambition but also what consequences it has for the personality in the way of inhibitions to love, inhibitions to work, envy of competitors, self-belittling tendencies, fear of failure and of success.[4] The wish to be a man drops out of the patient's associations as soon as we tackle the underlying problems of her ambition and exalted opinion about what she is or should be. It is then no longer possible for her to hide behind the symbolic screen of masculinity wishes.

In short, interpretations in terms of penis-envy bar the way to an understanding of fundamental difficulties, such as ambition, and of the whole personality structure linked up with them. That such interpretations befog the real issue is my most stringent objection to them, particularly from the therapeutic angle. And I have the same objection to the assumed importance of bisexuality in man's psychology. Freud believes that in man's psychology what corre-

4. *Cf.* Karen Horney, *The Neurotic Personality of Our Time* (1937), chs. 10–12.

sponds to penis-envy is his "struggle against the passive or feminine attitude toward other men."[5] He calls this fear the "repudiation of femininity" and makes it responsible for various difficulties which in my estimation belong to the structure of types who need to appear perfect and superior.

Freud has made two other suggestions, closely interrelated, concerning inherent feminine characteristics. One is that femininity has "some secret relationship with masochism."[6] The other is that the basic fear in woman is that of losing love, and that this fear corresponds to the fear of castration in man.

Helene Deutsch has elaborated Freud's assumption and generalized it in calling masochism the elemental power in feminine mental life. She contends that what woman ultimately wants in intercourse is to be raped and violated; what she wants in mental life is to be humiliated; menstruation is significant to the woman because it feeds masochistic fantasies; childbirth represents the climax of masochistic satisfaction. The pleasures of motherhood, inasmuch as they include certain sacrifices and a concern for the children, constitute a long drawn out masochistic gratification. Because of these masochistic striving women, according to Deutsch, are more or less doomed to be frigid unless in intercourse they are or feel raped, injured or humiliated.[7] Rado holds that woman's preference for masculinity is a defense against feminine masochistic strivings.[8]

Since according to psychoanalytic theory psychic attitudes are molded after sexual attitudes, the contentions concerning a specifically feminine basis of masochism have far-reaching implications. They entail the postulate that women in general, or at least the majority of them, essentially desire to be submissive and dependent. In support of these views is the impression that in our culture masochistic trends are more frequent in women than in men. But it must be remembered that the available data concern only neurotic women.

Many neurotic women have masochistic notions about intercourse, such as that women are prey to man's animal desires, that they have to sacrifice themselves and are debased by the sacrifice.

5. Sigmund Freud, "Analysis Terminable and Interminable," *op. cit.*

6. Sigmund Freud, *New Introductory Lectures.*

7. Helene Deutsch, "The Significance of Masochism in the Mental Life of Women" (Part I, "Feminine Masochism in Its Relation to Frigidity") in *International Journal of Psychoanalysis* (1930).

8. Sandor Rado, "Fear of Castration in Women" in *Psychoanalytic Quarterly* (1933).

There may be fantasies about being physically injured by intercourse. A few neurotic women have fantasies of masochistic satisfaction in childbirth. The great number of mothers who play the role of martyr and continually emphasize how much they are sacrificing themselves for the children may certainly be proof that motherhood can offer a masochistic satisfaction to neurotic women. There are also neurotic girls who shrink from marriage because they visualize themselves as enslaved and abused by the potential husband. Finally, masochistic fantasies about the sexual role of woman may contribute to a rejection of the female role and a preference for the masculine one.

Assuming that there is indeed a greater frequency of masochistic trends in neurotic women than in neurotic men, how may it be accounted for? Rado and Deutsch try to show that specific factors in feminine development are responsible. I refrain from discussing these attempts because both authors introduce as the basic factor the lack of a penis, or the girl's reactions to the discovery of this fact, and I believe this to be a wrong presupposition. In fact, I do not believe it is possible at all to find specific factors in feminine development which lead to masochism, for all such attempts rest on the premise that masochism is essentially a sexual phenomenon. It is true that the sexual aspect of masochism, as it appears in masochistic fantasies and perversions, is its most conspicuous part and was the first to attract the attention of psychiatrists. I hold, however —and this contention will be elaborated later on—that masochism is not a primarily sexual phenomenon, but is rather the result of certain conflicts in interpersonal relations. When masochistic tendencies are once established they may prevail also in the sexual sphere and here may become the condition for satisfaction. From this point of view masochism cannot be a specifically feminine phenomenon, and the analytical writers who have tried to find specific factors in feminine development accounting for masochistic attitudes in women are not to be blamed for the failure to find them.

In my opinion, one has to look not for biological reasons but for cultural ones. The question then is whether there are cultural factors which are instrumental in developing masochistic trends in women. The answer to this question depends on what one holds to be essential in the dynamics of masochism. My concept, briefly, is that masochistic phenomena represent the attempt to gain safety and satisfaction in life through inconspicuousness and dependency. As will be discussed later on, this fundamental attitude toward life determines the way in which individual problems are dealt with; it leads, for instance, to gaining control over others through weakness and suffering, to expressing hostility through suffering, to seeking in illness an alibi for failure.

If these presuppositions are valid there are indeed cultural factors fostering masochistic attitudes in women. They were more relevant for the past generation than for the present one, but they still throw their shadow today. They are, briefly, the greater dependency of woman; the emphasis on woman's weakness and frailty; the ideology that it is in woman's nature to lean on someone and that her life is given content and meaning only through others: family, husband, children. These factors do not in themselves bring about masochistic attitudes. History has shown that women can be happy, contented and efficient under these conditions. But factors like these, in my judgment, are responsible for the prevalence of masochistic trends in feminine neuroses when neuroses do develop.

Freud's contention that woman's basic fear is that of losing love is in part not separate from, for it is implicitly contained in, the postulate that there are specific factors in feminine development leading to masochism. Inasmuch as masochistic trends, among other characteristics, signify an emotional dependence on others, and inasmuch as one of the predominant masochistic means of reassurance against anxiety is to obtain affection, a fear of losing love is a specific masochistic feature.

It seems to me, however, that in contrast to Freud's other two contentions concerning feminine nature—that of penis-envy and that of a specifically feminine basis for masochism—this last one has some validity also for the healthy woman in our culture. There are no biological reasons but there are significant cultural factors which lead women to overvaluate love and thus to dread losing it.

Woman lived for centuries under conditions in which she was kept away from great economic and political responsibilities and restricted to a private emotional sphere of life. This does not mean that she did not carry responsibility and did not have to work. But her work was done within the confines of the family circle and therefore was based only on emotionalism, in contradistinction to more impersonal, matter of fact relations. Another aspect of the same situation is that love and devotion came to be regarded as specifically feminine ideals and virtues. Still another aspect is that to woman—since her relations to men and children were her only gateway to happiness, security and prestige—love represented a realistic value, which in man's sphere can be compared with his activities relating to earning capacities. Thus not only were pursuits outside the emotional sphere factually discouraged, but in woman's own mind they assumed only secondary importance.

Hence there were, and to some extent still are, realistic reasons in our culture why woman is bound to over-rate love and to expect more from it than it can possibly give, and why she is more afraid of losing love than man is.

The cultural situation which has led woman to regard love as the only value that counts in life has implications which may throw light on certain characteristics of modern woman. One of them is the attitude toward aging: woman's age phobia and its implications. Since for such a long time woman's only attainable fulfillments—whether they involved love, sex, home or children—were obtained through men, it necessarily became of paramount importance to please men. The cult of beauty and charm resulting from this necessity might be registered, at least in some respects, as a good effect. But such a concentration on the importance of erotic attractiveness implies an anxiety for the time when it might eventually diminish in value. We should consider it neurotic if men became frightened or depressed when they approached the fifth decade. In a woman this is regarded as natural, and in a way it is natural so long as attractiveness represents a unique value. While age is a problem to everyone it becomes a desperate one if youthfulness is the center of attention.

This fear is not limited to the age which is regarded as ending woman's attractiveness, but throws its shadow over her entire life and is bound to create a great feeling of insecurity toward life. It accounts for the jealousy often existing between mothers and adolescent daughters, and not only helps to spoil their personal relationships but may leave a remnant of hostility toward all women. It prevents woman from evaluating qualities which are outside the erotic sphere, qualities best characterized by the terms maturity, poise, independence, autonomy in judgment, wisdom. Woman can scarcely take the task of the development of her personality as seriously as she does her love life if she constantly entertains a devaluating attitude toward her mature years, and considers them as her declining years.

The all-embracing expectations that are joined to love account to some extent for that discontentment with the female role which Freud ascribes to penis-envy. From this point of view the discontentment has two main reasons. One is that in a culture in which human relationships are so generally disturbed it is difficult to attain happiness in love life (by that I do *not* mean sexual relations). The other is that this situation is likely to create inferiority feelings. Sometimes the question is raised whether in our culture men or women suffer more from inferiority feelings. It is difficult to measure psychic quantities, but there is this difference: as a rule man's feeling of inferiority does not arise from the fact that he is a man; but woman often feels inferior merely because she is a woman. As mentioned before, I believe that feelings of inadequacy have nothing to do with femininity but use cultural implications of femininity as a disguise for other sources of inferiority feelings which, in essence, are identical in men and women. There remain, however, certain cultural reasons why woman's self-confidence is easily disturbed.

A sound and secure self-confidence draws upon a broad basis of human qualities, such as initiative, courage, independence, talents, erotic values, capacity to master situations. As long as homemaking was a really big task involving many responsibilities, and as long as the number of children was not restricted, woman had the feeling of being a constructive factor in the economic process; thus she was provided with a sound basis for self-esteem. This basis, however, has gradually vanished, and in its departure woman has lost one foundation for feeling herself valuable.

As far as the sexual basis of self-confidence is concerned, certainly the puritanical influences, however one may evaluate them, have contributed toward the debasement of women by giving sexuality the connotation of something sinful and low. In a patriarchal society this attitude was bound to make woman into the symbol of sin; many such allusions may be found in early Christian literature. This is one of the great cultural reasons why woman, even today, considers herself debased and soiled by sexuality and thus lowered in her own self-esteem.

There remains, finally, the emotional basis of self-confidence. If, however, one's self-confidence is dependent on giving or receiving love, then one builds on a foundation which is too small and too shaky—too small because it leaves out too many personality values, and too shaky because it is dependent on too many external factors, such as finding adequate partners. Beside, it very easily leads to an emotional dependence on other people's affection and appreciation, and results in a feeling of unworthiness if one is not loved or appreciated.

As far as the alleged given inferiority of woman is concerned, Freud has, to be sure, made a remark which it is quite a relief to hear from him: "You must not forget, however, that we have only described women in so far as their natures are determined by their sexual function. The influence of this factor is, of course, very far-reaching, but we must remember that *an individual woman may be a human being apart from this*" (italics mine). I am convinced that he really means it, but one would like to have this opinion of his assume a broader place in his theoretical system. Certain sentences in Freud's latest paper on feminine psychology indicate that in comparison with his earlier studies he is giving additional consideration to the influence of cultural factors on women's psychology: "But we must take care not to underestimate the influence of social conventions, which also force women into passive situations. The whole thing is still very obscure. We must not overlook one particularly constant relation between femininity and instinctual life. The repression of their aggressiveness, which is imposed upon women by their constitutions and by society, favors the development of strong masochistic impulses, which have the effect of binding erotically the destructive tendencies which have been turned inwards."

But since he has a primarily biological orientation Freud does not, and on the basis of his premises cannot, see the whole significance of these factors. He cannot see to what extent they mold wishes and attitudes, nor can he evaluate the complexity of interrelations between cultural conditions and feminine psychology.

I suppose everyone agrees with Freud that differences in sexual constitution and functions influence mental life. But it seems unconstructive to speculate on the exact nature of this influence. The American woman is different from the German woman; both are different from certain Pueblo Indian women. The New York society woman is different from the farmer's wife in Idaho. The way specific cultural conditions engender specific qualities and faculties, in women as in men—this is what we may hope to understand.

RELATED READINGS

Bardwick, Judith M. *Psychology of Women: A Study of Biocultural Conflicts*. New York: Harper and Row Publishing Company, 1971.

————— *et al. Feminine Personality and Conflict*. Monterey, California: Brooks-Cole (Wadsworth), 1970.

Blum, Harold P. (ed.). *Female Psychology*. New York International Universities Press, Inc., 1977.

Chesler, Phyllis. *Women and Madness*. New York, Avon Books, 1972.

Claremont De Castillego, Irene. *Knowing Woman*. New York: C. G. Jung Foundation Publications, 1973.

Cox, Sue. *Female Psychology: The Emerging Self*. Chicago: Science Research Associates, 1976.

Deutsch, Helene. *The Psychology of Women*. New York: Grune and Stratton, c/o Academic Press, 1944.

Foreman, Ann. *Women and the Family in Marxism and Psychoanalysis*. New York: Urizen Books, 1977.

Franks, Violet and Burtle, Vasanti (eds.). *Women in Therapy: New Psychotherapies*. New York: Brunner-Mazel, Inc., 1974.

Friday, Nancy. *My Mother My Self*. New York: Dell Publishing Company, 1977.

Harding, Esther M. *The Way of All Women*. New York: C. G. Jung Foundation Publications, 1970.

Hubbard, Ruth *et al.* (eds.). *Women Look at Biology Looking at*

Women: A Feminist Critique. Cambridge: Schenkman Publishing Company, 1979.

Johnson, Robert A. *She: Understanding Feminine Psychology.* New York: Harper and Row Publishing Company, 1977.

Luria, Gina and Tiger, Virginia. *Everywoman.* New York: Random House, Inc., 1977.

Miles, Judith. *The Feminine Principle.* Minneapolis: Bethany Fellowship Inc., 1975.

Miller, Jean. *Toward a New Psychology of Women.* Boston: Beacon Press, 1977.

———— (ed.). *Psychoanalysis and Women:* Contributions to New Theory and Therapy.

Mitchell, Juliet. *Psychoanalysis and Feminism.* New York: Pantheon Books, 1974.

Nagera, Humberto. *Female Sexuality and the Oedipus Complex.* New York: Aronson Jason, Inc., 1975.

Ruitenbeek, Hendrik M. (ed.). *Psychoanalysis and Female Sexuality.* New Haven: College and University Press, 1966.

Sherman, Julia A. *On the Psychology of Woman: A Survey of Empirical Studies.* Springfield, Illinois: Charles C. Thomas Publishing Company, 1975.

Ulanov, Ann B. *The Feminine in Jungian Psychology and in Christian Theology.* Evanston: Northwestern University Press, 1971.

Weisstein, Naomi. "Psychology Constructs the Female." In *Sex Equality,* edited by Jane English. Englewood Cliffs: Prentice-Hall, Inc., 1977, pp. 205–215.

Williams, Juanita. *Psychology of Women: Behavior in a Biosocial Context.* New York: Norton and Company, 1977.

VI
CURRENT
PHILOSOPHICAL ARTICLES

The articles in this section have been gathered from philosophers presently engaged in applying their expertise to an examination of the meaning and role of woman today. From differing perspectives, the authors scrutinize key concepts and issues, developing and defending their own views while arguing against those they consider inadequate or incorrect. Such analyses not only illustrate the essential function of philosophy, but provide a necessary propaedeutic to effective criticism and social change.

The following article—"Woman—A Philosophical Analysis" by Hilde Hein (Holy Cross College) is excerpted from *The Holy Cross Quarterly*, vol. 4, no. 4 Fall 1971, pp. 18–23.

HILDA 'Woman—
HEIN A Philosophical Analysis'

"Plus ça change, plus c'est la même chose." This traditional French phrase of urbane disillusionment expresses a jaded weariness with love as a tedious series of romances. From another point of view the same bored disenchantment is expressed by a great American hero—and darling of French society—Ben Franklin: "You can always put a bag over her head!" And so history has put bags over our heads, confined and constrained us with blindfolds for our eyes and gags for our mouths. Women have been denied consciousness; but men, incomprehensibly perverse and self-deceptive, have denied themselves consciousness. They have refused to see, to hear, to feel, and to wonder.

To a philosopher this is astounding; for, as Aristotle has noted, wonder is natural to mankind. "All men, by nature desire to know." No subject is beyond philosophical inquiry and, indeed, no mode of philosophical inquiry is itself beyond challenge and further scrutiny. When the very foundations of being are questionable, along with all those categories of reality so solidly evident to common sense—space, time, motion, the existence of the material world and myself within it; when no principle of science, or of morality, or even of logical thought can stand unsubjected to philosophical doubt, why is it that men have invariably and uniformly assumed without question and without doubt that women are inferior to themselves?

Some clever man will doubtlessly laugh and respond that female inferiority is self-evident and needs no substantiation. Would he declare that it is more obvious than the existence of the world in space and time, than his own existence, than the principle of contradiction or the regularity of nature? All of these notions have been questioned by our ancestors as well as by ourselves. Why then such unwavering acceptance of the principle of female inferiority?

Were our ancestors less enlightened than ourselves? I do not think so, but we often look back with amazement upon their ignorance and parochialism and pride ourselves upon our scientific progress and advancing consciousness. Where they failed to see the unified behavior of matter, Newton showed the way; where they failed to understand its disunity, Einstein corrected them. And what will the judgment of tomorrow be upon the failures of insight of today? Perhaps a little less pride of accomplishment is in order, and a little more humility with respect to all we do not understand: the truths we do not know, the falsities of which we are certain, the problems we fail to see, and the solutions to which we stubbornly cling. How many of the advances we claim are merely reformulations of tired old dogmas which we refuse to give up?

I maintain that the shifting history of men's philosophical attitude toward women is a case in point. The basic principle of female inferiority has never been disputed but has been retained as a presupposition underlying all rationalizations regarding human nature and the arrangements of human society. The variety of such rationalizations is remarkable; a tribute to human ingenuity. But it is also remarkable that the premise upon which that rationalization lay was itself never criticized.

I will not take time here to document this claim historically. With the recent growth of the women's liberation movement and increased interest in the facts of women's history, there is ample available evidence of oppression and of the historically prevalent prejudice against women. In all times and in all societies known, women of all ranks and levels have been subject to discriminatory law. Politically, religiously and morally, they have been denied rights and freedoms deemed to be appropriate to mankind as a whole. Psychological studies have confirmed what has long been evident through the analysis of literature, that the prevailing attitudes of the dominant western culture[1] are profoundly inimical to women and essentially misogynous. Furthermore, there is evidence of the extent to which the deprecation of women has been culturally transmitted and internalized by women themselves. They have been indoctrinated to regard themselves as lesser beings—indeed as less than human. In short, the concept of 'man' and all things pertaining to *mankind* have as the language not so misleadingly suggests, been restricted to the male of the species. I do not mean to offer additional evidence of this all-too-familiar phenomenon,[2] but to seek some explanation of how a principle so far-reaching in its implications and practical consequences, could have been left so long unexplored and unchallenged.

The notion of *explanation* itself requires clarification. I certainly do not intend it in the popular sense, equivalent to "justify." Let me make my own position clear at the outset. I find the prevailing discriminatory attitude toward women empirically baseless, intellectually unsound, economically inefficient, politically unwise, socially impractical, psychologically injurious, and morally depraved. No doubt it promotes some rewards for men. There are clear economic and political advantages following from the retention of a subject class, and some ego-gratification to be derived from the sense of one's own superiority. And the exploitation itself may be a source of physical pleasure. But I should argue that the perpetuation of the myth of male supremacy, maintained at such cost, is, in the end, as debilitating to men as it is to women.

As a philosopher, however, I am interested less in the practical consequences of the belief (which interest me very much as a woman) than in the astonishing fact that it could have been sustained at all, so universally and so long. It is worth pointing out that male supremacy is not affirmed automatically of all organic bisexual systems. There are naturally occurring species in which we find the male playing a distinctly secondary role (particularly among insects). Thus it seems to be specifically among humans that the female is held to be of lesser worth than the male.

It must also be emphasized that the pertinent distinctions are based upon differences of *gender* or sex identity, rather than upon

1. I limit my remarks to Western Culture because that is the subject of most studies with which I am familiar. From the limited evidence available, however, there is little reason to doubt that women underwent essentially the same treatment in Oriental, Middle Eastern and all other societies.

2. For the record of such evidence I refer the reader to the growing body of literature on women, the trail blazing work of Simone deBeauvoir, Kate Millett, Betty Friedan, Germaine Greer, and Mary Ellman, and recent collections from the women's movement, such as *Sisterhood is Powerful*, edited by Robin Morgan. There are also reports of professional societies and governmental agencies, such as HEW.

explicitly sexual characteristics of males and females. There is no disputing the fact that men and women are differently endowed with respect to reproductive and secondary sexual equipment. What is debatable is whether or not these biological differences have abiological consequences or even attendant differentiations that affect men and women in their non-directly reproductive activities. No sane person denies the physiological distinctions that are plain for all to see, but there is a great gap between what must be thus acknowledged and what may be therefrom inferred or may be observed as a cultural accretion. I shall maintain that "male" and "female" refer to biologically determined distinctions, but that "man" and "woman" are cultural definitions.

Let us then consider what philosophical explanations have been offered on behalf of the superiority of men over women.[3] The principle has been more assumed than defended; it is not a subject which has inspired great philosophical innovation and virtuosity. On the whole, philosophers have hewn to the dominant line: pronouncing, affirming, rationalizing, but rarely questioning the status they assign to women.

We may look to Aristotle as a terminological source.[4] In this domain, as in so many others, we are indebted to him for a vocabulary; but not for the ideas which the words enshrine. The doctrine of male supremacy clearly predates Aristotle; but as formulated by him, it presides over western thought as did his geocentric physics, his slave based economy, and his heat-activated biology. The Aristotelian categories are hard to overcome.

But it must have been long before Aristotle that the simplest explanation of female inferiority was given. The clearest distinction between male and female, apart from the obviously sexual, is a matter of sheer bulk and brute strength. Men tend, as a generality (although this is not invariably the case) to be larger and physically more powerful than their female counterparts. It does not, of course, follow with necessity that men are superior in any other sense; but it cannot be denied that under conditions in which size and strength are instrumental to survival and dominance, these features may well become prized as marks of intrinsic superiority. The argument for male supremacy is then merely a variant of the familiar (and officially disreputable) principle that *Might makes*

3. I shall omit consideration of those few unconventional philosophers who, contrary to the spirit of their own or any other time, deny male supremacy. For any doctrine, however popular, conflicting points of view can be raised and there are always a few eccentrics who do so. But my point is that even in a field so habitually critical as philosophy, the prevailing doctrines were largely upheld and any sceptical doubts were ignored.

4. Aristotle, *De Generatione Animalium*.

Right. Few men would wish to base their self-esteem on such a shaky foundation.

Male dominance receives additional support from the complex situation engendered by the roles of the sexes in childbirth. If the species is to survive, then women, particularly in their weakened condition when pregnant and lactating, must be not dominated but protected. Male dominance is defended, then, not simply as following from the right of the stronger to rule the weak, but rather as flowing from the prolonged period of dependency which women exhibit during their childbearing years. Let me point out, however, that 1) such dependency is mutual, since men are dependent upon women for the possibility of procreation, and that 2) it is only minimally inter-sexual, since women could well depend upon other, non-child-bearing women for their protection. Men are specifically required only for the act of fertilization. That they continue to provide for the welfare of their wives and young is only a variable cultural pattern. It is, however, seized upon *by men* as a justification of male supremacy.[5]

Historically, it may well be the case that men, finding women sexually gratifying, economically useful, and a means of self-perpetuation through offspring, simply assumed power and bound women to themselves as property. This is not an explanation or a justification, but simply a plausible description of how a state of affairs came into being. I will not enter into the anthropological speculation about how male dominance arose. The question is rather how have philosophers made the principle of male supremacy appear intellectually acceptable—as a state of affairs which not merely was, but *should be*. Philosophical explanations are not demonstrations, direct or indirect, of fact, but are, rather, attempts to fit such accounts of fact into a rational framework in terms of which the facts seem "correct," "necessary" "inevitable" or, better yet, "in accordance with nature." Perhaps one day, philosophers will also set their critical skills to work in this area, as they have in others, revealing the patent *evitability* and non-necessity and incorrectness of what is taken to be ineluctable fact. That is unlikely, however, as long as philosophers are mostly male or educated by men. So far, the emperor still disports himself as most fashionably attired.

Aristotle offers us a philosophical explanation of male superiority on the ground that women are in fact biologically defective males. Using the male as the standard of humanity, he regards women as deficient, and even as mutilated. In so arguing, he anticipates

5. It is not coincidental that some of the more extreme defenders of women's liberation look forward to a day when even this degree of dependency will have been rectified, when childbirth will not entail the impregnation of a woman by a man.

Freud's castration theory[6] by two-thousand years, even using much the same vocabulary to describe women as bearing a genital "wound" and being correspondingly inadequate and *envious* in all other respects. Aristotle even minimizes the female role in procreation, declaring that the woman provides only a nutrient nest in which the embryo, introduced by male semen, is stored. Aristotle is more than ready to belabor the incapacity of the women to produce offspring without the "purifying" completion of the male element, but he pays scant attention to the complementary incapacity of the male to procreate without a female counterpart.

Aristotle views women as weak-blooded; predominantly composed of elements which are cold and moist, while men are constituted by hot, fiery substances. Women are produced as a kind of embryonic deviation, caused as a genetic monstrosity through accidents of the environment. At the same time, they must be produced with some regularity and must themselves possess some of the virtues of the male. Being the mothers of men, they must have some deliberative capacity and the rationality characteristic of humans. But this possession is not sufficient, in his estimation, to render women the moral equals of men. Women, like children and slaves, are fit to be ruled. This, it should be recalled, is not due to sin or depravity, but to the intellectual inferiority which Aristotle attributes to women.

The Christian disciples of Aristotle[7] adopted Aristotelian biology *in toto* and associated the supposed absence of the higher (intellectual) faculty in women with a kind of grosser materiality and baseness of soul. Since the female principle was taken to be passive and nutritive, without form and, hence, without soul, it was evidently from the "higher" paternal principle (albeit through the material medium of semen) that offspring were "besouled." Regrettably, the greater animality of women made them an endless source of prurient fascination to men, an occasion for concupiscence and sin. According to Christian tradition[8] the moral inferiority of women was not simply a matter of intellectual defectiveness or sheer ani-

6. S. Freud, "Some Psychological Consequences of the Anatomical Distinction between the Sexes," (1925).

7. e.g. St. Thomas Aquinas, *Summa Theologica* O XCII, 1.

8. e.g. Tertullian, *De Cultu Feminarum*, "Do you not know that each one of you is an Eve? The sentence of God on this sex of yours lives in this age: the guilt must of necessity live too. You are the devil's gateway; you are the unsealer of that forbidden tree; you are the first deserter of the divine law; you are she who persuaded him whom the devil was not valiant enough to attack. You destroyed so easily God's image, man. On account of your desert, that is, death, even the Son of God had to die."

mal amorality, but rather a privative moral incompetence. Woman, the seductress, bears the guilt of man's sin.

The misogynous inclinations of the Church Fathers issued in doctrinal incongruities, however, since the denial of soul to woman also entailed the denial that she might be the cause of anything whatsoever, good or evil. Hence we might be the *occasion* of Adam's sin; but he alone must bear the responsibility of the fall of man.

Scriptural authority could be drawn upon to reinforce Aristotle's purely biological arguments for women's inferiority. Ignoring *Genesis I*, in which God is described as having produced *both* man and woman in his own image, the Doctors of the Church[9] fixed upon the later account of God's creation of Eve out of the rib of Adam. This was taken to symbolize her subordination to him and her role as helpmate. Even in this role women were reduced to baby-producers, all other activities being more effectively carried out by men. And even as baby-producers, women were burdened with guilt and shame for having evoked the concupiscence with which the act of generation was initiated. What had been a simply biological "fact" for Aristotle became, as understood by the Church, a matter of moral determination and theological necessity.

Christian doctrine was much influenced by earlier Stoic philosophy which sought to explain all phenomena in accordance with a law of Nature. Nature was taken to be normative, and was eventually personified as a prescriptive law-giver (one who was also executor of his judgments). We might note that the same argument from Natural Law which subordinates women to men has been used to defend the divine right of kings and the natural inferiority of the non-white races. According to this law natural harmony requires hierarchical authority; and so it is fitting that just as God rules over the whole of mankind, so man should rule over and as the "head" of woman. An alternative way of maintaining the same thing is to proclaim the "naturalness" of separate spheres of authority: Woman is to rule over the hearth and home, and man is to rule over everything else in the world (including woman).

The concept of natural law became once again secularized in the 17th century, but this did not significantly affect the ideological position of women. It is the case that some women achieved greater education and independence than women in former times, and so enjoyed a less oppressive pattern of life. But this was not due to a new awareness of the humanity of women. It was due, rather, to new leisure throughout society, and to new modes of social inter-action introduced by technological innovation and

9. Clement of Alexandria, *Paedagogus*, "Nothing disgraceful is proper for man who is endowed with reason; much less for woman, to whom it brings shame even to reflect of what nature she is." Similar sentiments are expressed by Tertullian, Cyprian, Commodian, and in the Apostolic Constitutions.

commerce. Women, and especially lower-class women, were as exploited as ever, but custom dictated that male gratification now required that women possess the rudiments of culture, so that they might take part appreciatively in polite society. "Naturally" their role continued to be the perpetuation of the race. And this included the provision of relaxation and recreation for men as well as the early acculturation of the very young. For this function their education was restricted to domestic skills and to those gentle expressions of appreciation which enhance social exchange. The great hero of the French Revolution, Jean-Jacques Rousseau, in his liberating educational treatise, *Emile,* explicitly prescribes that women's education be relative to their role as subordinate to men, and he violently repudiates any suggestions that women be educated for equality with men. Similar sentiments are expressed by other admirers of the "egalitarian" revolution. And such urbane philosophical sceptics as David Hume and Immanuel Kant, whose philosophical scrutiny ranged over the principle of causality, the substantive identity of the self, the foundations of morality and the truths of religion, blithely echoed the conventionalities of society with respect to women. "Bless their pretty little heads, they were not made for serious thought, the principled action or noble endeavor"[10]. Women's role was to be "merry" and amiable, not too sharp and not too witty, but ever ready with comfort, cheer and encouragement for man, that noble creature. Thus did nature reveal herself [sic] to the men of the Enlightenment.

But as David Hume himself has taught, natural law is disclosed not by *a priori* reasoning or by revelation, but by inferences drawn from the observation of nature. By nature, whatever is, is natural. To the rationalists of the Enlightenment, democratic egalitarianism was as "natural" as the sovereign rights of kings had been to their predecessors: but it was an egalitarianism that did not extend to women or children or to those property-less men of color, who, like women and children, were themselves regarded as property. Thus yesterday's Nature is tomorrow's abomination.

It is not puzzling that male supremacy, like the carnivorous nature of some organisms should be explained naturalistically if by that is meant only that the prevailing practise is indeed natural—if

10. Immanuel Kant, *Observations on the Feeling of the Beautiful and Sublime.* "Deep meditation and a long-sustained reflection are noble but difficult, and do not well befit a person in whom unconstrained charms could show nothing else than a beautiful nature. Laborious learning or painful pondering, even if a woman should greatly succeed in it, destroy the merits that are proper to her sex, and because of their rarity they can make of her an object of cold admiration; but at the same time they will weaken the charms with which she exercises her great power over the other sex. A woman—might as well have a beard; for perhaps that would express more obviously the mien of profundity for which she strives."

that is not a redundancy. But it is puzzling that what is "natural" in this sense should be further identified as right—and that solely by virtue of its naturalness. Surely there are a great many natural wrongs in the world, (disease—to name but one example) and if to be is a sufficient guarantee of naturalness, then there are a great many natural things which we are committed to wiping out. There is no necessary connection between naturalness and goodness, though there is also no necessary antagonism between them. Yet we might recall that one of the strongest arguments ever made in favor of "over-coming" the natural is to be found in the Gospel according to John. It follows that even if male supremacy were demonstrably natural, this would constitute no ground for holding it to be desirable or inevitable.

One of the first women defenders of women's rights, however, Mary Wollstonecraft,[11] did base her argument upon the doctrine of natural equality as embodied in the French Revolutionary Declaration of the Rights of Man. Noting that natural equality could be realized only in an atmosphere of equal opportunity, she insisted that women must have access to the same freedom and education which would permit the flowering of reason and virtue in all. Deprived of that, women would remain small-minded and would poison the atmosphere of sweet reason for everyone. Wollstonecraft was no political agitator. She was not calling upon women to mount the barricades. She did not demand suffrage or even the right to own property or administer an income. She was content that women occupy their traditional familial role, but only insisted that as long as they were consigned to a state of infantilism, they could not be happy or competent persons and could not even intelligently carry out the duties of housewife and mother. Least of all could they be reasonable companions to intelligent men.

In the 19th century, particularly in England and America, demands began to be made for the political and economic equality of women. And they were resisted by philosophical defense of the status quo. The Mills, Harriet Taylor and John Stuart, argued that by virtue of their humanity, women were entitled to equal rights with men with regard to labor, property and political governance.[12]

11. Mary Wollstonecraft, *A Vindication of the Rights of Woman.*

12. John Stuart Mill made these arguments in an important but little known speech to the British Parliament in 1867. (Suffrage for Women.) The points had been made however, in an earlier essay, *Enfranchisement of Women* (1851), which was most probably written by his wife, Harriet Taylor Mill. The content of the earlier essay is significantly more radical in its point of view than that of the 1867 speech. (e.g. Education is regarded in the earlier work as significant only if coupled with the real potentiality of its application in the world). There is also a stylistic discrepancy between the earlier essay and the later, as well as other, more familiar works of J. S. Mill.

Above all, they should enjoy the freedom of disposition of their own lives, unconfined by legal constraints which rendered them the helpless chattel of fathers and husbands. However benignly a man might rule, they argued, the uncontested authority invested in him by law reduced women to a state of dependency, servility and social inferiority. However, petted and adored, in fact, women were legally at the mercy of men. The claims for legal equality were greeted with horror. But while earlier rejections of women's rights had been based upon a depiction of women as weak-minded and morally depraved, the 19th century apologists of male dominance rested their arguments upon a representation of women as too refined, too sensitive, too spiritual to be sullied by the crass demands of the common world of commerce and politics. Had the nature of women changed? Had they somehow been transformed to sublimely intuitive angels from the dull-witted, carnal creatures of the medieval philosophers? That is not likely; but at all events, the net consequence of the male estimate of their nature was to deprive them of a place in human history and of the recognition of their own humanity.[13]

Philosophical arguments against equality for women were based upon moral and psychological characterizations of great empirical obscurity. One wonders where those remarkable creatures presumably encountered by romantic poets might have come from, and how Schopenhauer[14] could have been so unfortunate as to meet such an assortment of unpleasant people. And poor Neitzsche surely suffered from regrettable needs. All of us, of course, have the misfortune occasionally of being exposed to disagreeable persons of the same, or the opposite sex as ourselves, but what on earth could possess anyone to make such vast generalizations on the basis of a necessarily limited acquaintance? We must suspect a certain unscientific hubris on the part of the philosophers. ("Seen one, seen 'em all".) It is a pity that such irresponsible empiricism continues to prevail among us. It is of course the same phenomenon that gives us "shiftless, hippie-commies" and the standard string of stereotypes. In addition to the moral and psychological characterizations, philosophers grounded their discrimination against women upon what they took to be a metaphysical base. Kierkegaard, whose

13. F. Engels, *The Origin of the Family, Private Property and the State.* Engels speaks of the rise of the modern family as marking "the world historical defeat of the female sex" which degraded the position of women to servitude. Women became slaves to the lust of men, and instruments for the production of children. As for the rewards to women, "[she] only differs from the ordinary courtesan in that she does not let out her body on piece-work as a wage-worker, but sells it once and for all into slavery."

14. Arthur Schopenhauer, *On Women.*

legacy remains with us in various forms of Existentialism, declared that the essence of woman was in her absolute "alterity"—her otherness.[15] (And isn't it just like a woman to violate the laws of logic and be just plain *other*, when anything else would, in accordance with proper grammar, be *other than* something?) Kierkegaard means that women, measured against the norm of humanity (i.e. men) are of their very essence "being for another." Unlike men, who strive for self-realization in the uniqueness of their individuality, women, we are to suppose, achieve their identity only through another. And that other—a man, of course. How else are we to explain the ever-feminine tendency toward self-sacrifice, self effacement and the merging of her personality into that of her lover, husband, children? Could it be that she has been given no other choice? No. It must be some profound facet of her very being.

Having generated the myth of "otherness" and having persuaded themselves *and women* that it is true, men are cast in a dilemma of their own creation. Fearful of the alien spawned by their own metaphysics, they protect themselves and their responsibility by showing contempt for women or by raging against what they do not comprehend with brutality.

There has been no end to the endeavors of philosophical, male supremacists to rationalize their prejudice in folds of doctrine. Freudian misogyny is well known and is without any subtlety. But there are many others—including Erik Erikson's claim that women relate to "inner space" as opposed to the "outer space" of the aggressive, world-oriented male.[16] Other theorists distinguish between men's analytic mind and the knowledge by intuitive acquaintance characteristic of women. Still others refer to male bonding and female uncooperativeness. Most recently, while writing this paper, I encountered the position of Episcopalian archbishop C. Kilmer Meyers of San Francisco, who opposed women's assuming a place in the clergy on the ground that the godhead is a masculine, aggressive principle.[17]

15. S. Kierkegaard, *Either/Or*. Note, despite their differences, the seducer of Vol. I and the more staid *paterfamilias* of Vol. II are in agreement on the matter of feminine "otherness."

16. E. Erikson, "Womanhood and the Inner Space" in *Identity, Youth and Crisis*: "But how does the identity formation of women differ by dint of the fact that their somatic design harbors an "inner space" destined to bear the offspring of chosen men and, with it, a biological, psychological, and ethical commitment to take care of human infancy? Is not the disposition for this commitment (whether it be combined with a career, and even whether or not it be realized in actual motherhood) the core problem of female fidelity?

17. According to Jungian psycho-therapeutic theory, as symbolized in the dogma of the Assumption of Mary, the goal of psychotherapy is achieved in

The resistance against demythologizing is great in the matter of women's status, as in so many areas. It is easier to put woman on a pedestal than to consider her as a human equal. But even this time-honored prejudice is at last yielding to philosophical scrutiny. But the adoption of truths is ultimately determined by the satisfaction they afford to human inquiry and human need. It is gratifying to believe that one day it will be universally understood that the worth of a human being is not contingent upon sex any more than upon color, class, or property. It would be interesting to be alive in such a world.

*   *   *

The following article—"A Contemporary Approach to Sex-Identity," by Christine Allen (Concordia University)—is excerpted from *Values & the Quality of Life.*

CHRISTINE ALLEN   'A Contemporary Approach to Sex-Identity'

Theories about sex-identity and personal identity can be divided roughly as follows:

1. Women and men do not differ significantly.
    a. Women and men are persons by virtue of being human.
    b. Women and men can become persons by an effort of the will.
2. Women and men differ significantly.
    a. Men are persons and women less than persons.
    b. Women are persons and men are less than persons.
    c. Women and men are equally persons.

1. WOMEN AND MEN DO NOT DIFFER SIGNIFICANTLY

a. *Women and men are persons by virtue of being human.* The view that sex differences are not philosophically significant is per-

---

the acceptance of bi-sexuality. Feminine consciousness is redeemed. This view does represent a repudiation of misogyny, but it too rests upon a view of the feminine as fundamentally in opposition, albeit complementary to, the dominant (male) character of the psyche. cf. James Hillman, "First Adam, then Eve" Fantasies of Female Inferiority in Changing Consciousness." *Art International* XIV, 7 (1970).

haps the most commonly held position in contemporary philosophy. The philosopher is called to articulate the human condition without concern for the differences between people of different nationalities, age, or sex. It is the universal qualities of human life which concern him or her: for Heidegger it is the search for Being, for Strawson the quest for the fundamental categories of descriptive metaphysics, for Husserl the phenomenological analysis of the contents of consciousness, for Wittgenstein the uncovery of the complex character of language. We do not find any reference to significant differences between women and men. Two different conclusions can be reached from this lack of attention to sex-identity: that sex-identity is not a concern of philosophy, or that sex-identity was not a concern of these particular philosophers. Unfortunately, many professional philosophers adopt the first conclusion. In doing so they inadvertently shut off a rich area of investigation. For example, it might be very interesting to consider how Strawson's P-predicates (predicates which attribute states of consciousness to persons) break down sexually so that some cannot be applied to one sex. Imagine: "She asked the doctor for a vasectomy and he asked the doctor for a hysterectomy." To undergo the vasectomy or the hysterectomy would be described by an M-predicate (predicates which ascribe material attributes); but to ask for one is another thing altogether. Similarly to develop a Heideggarian analysis of *dasein* in its sexual dimension, to show how language mirrors the world of sex-identity in a Wittgensteinian way, or to give a phenomenological critique of the sexual contents of consciousness would enrich philosophic activity. We cannot conclude from the lack of mention of sex-identity by some important philosophers that sex-identity is not a proper concern of philosophy. One can only conclude that it did not interest these philosophers.

Another way of considering sex-identity as irrelevant to personal identity is to consider sex-identity as a legitimate philosophical concern, but to argue for the disappearance of sex-identity in social and ethical values. In this way one is asked to ignore sex-differences, particularly to fight against institutional sex-discrimination, and even to hold open the possibility that there should be human beings who are neither female nor male biologically, but to whom we might like to apply the category classification 'person.' This argument is developed by Alison Jaggar who holds that sex-identity is primarily a biological category, whereas personal identity is primarily a moral category "with attendant rights and responsibilities." Except for living beings who are defective at birth or by accident, all adult human beings are persons. No sex difference should be institutionally recognized. Jaggar agrees with philosophers who believe that women and men do not differ significantly, but she holds that sex-identity should not be ignored as a philosophical issue but faced and overcome. In this way, she proposes to live out what she considers to be one of the responsibilities of social philosophers, viz., the call to effect change in society.

b. *Women and men can become persons by an effort of the will.* The view that women and men *become* persons by an act of will is found primarily in existentialist theory. This claim is described by Sartre when he says that existence comes before essence. Human beings are thrown into the world, into a situation which they did not choose. Their primary philosophical task becomes one of self-definition; they must become a man or a woman. To be a person is an evaluative description of someone who has successfully continued the process of self-definition. To be a woman or a man similarly becomes an evaluative judgment about the success of female or male human beings taking responsibility for their own identity. The only difference between women and men is in the data they were given to work within the process of self-definition. They do not differ significantly, however, because both are called to create their identity. In this way they differ from the rest of the world, from physical objects which are defined completely by consciousness outside of themselves and from other forms of animate life which merely exist in the moment but are unable to project goals into the future, goals which could act on their own self-definition.

Sometimes the process of self-definition is described by saying that female human beings become women. Simone de Beauvoir claims that one is not born but becomes a woman. This can be understood either negatively (that one is socialized into a certain identity) or positively (that one must take responsibility for becoming an individual woman). At other times the process is described as saying that a woman becomes a person. The implication here is that women could exist without self-definition, but that persons are more fully developed. The central point is the same in both descriptions; namely, women and men both have the responsibility to exercise their will over a lifetime in order to be truly called 'persons.' In this way the view which dominated the history of philosophy, the claim that sex-identity and personal identity was fixed by something outside the person, is rejected. Instead one emerges into a personal identity. The model which is most often used to describe the process of self-creation is artistic. The person fashions the self much as an artist molds a piece of soapstone. The crucial factor is the role of the will in active self-determination. The artistic model of personal identity replaces a naturalistic model in which the person was considered to be more or less like any other natural being. Just as the acorn seed grows into the oak tree, so the person, man or woman, emerges out of the fetus. With the rejection of the view that the Forms, God, or Nature are responsible for personal identity, the primary responsibility for becoming a person rests on the shoulders of the individual.

2. WOMEN AND MEN DIFFER SIGNIFICANTLY

a. *Men are persons and women less than persons.* If we turn from the theories which claim that women and men do not differ significantly to those which claim that they do, we notice that in some cases the claim is made that men are persons but women are not. One of the most striking examples is the famous decision reached by the Canadian Supreme Court in 1926 that women were not persons in specific reference to the eligibility for being a member of the Senate. In a general way this sort of theory identifies what it is to be a man with what it is to be a person. We found several examples of this in the history of philosophy. Whether the quality of being able to reflect, of being capable of ethical judgments, or of transcendent self-creation, the particular philosopher implied that persons must be men. Stated in another way, the qualities of persons were analytically male. The prescriptive force of the identification of persons with men led to a situation where the question: 'Why are there not female persons?' was like asking "Why are there no female bass singers?"

Why should this have occurred? Some seek a reason in language, in the double use of the word 'man' to represent all humans and male humans. Others blame the predominance of patriarchy and claim that oppressors always see themselves as the ultimate example of humanity. Some suggest that the term 'person' denotes a public entity and that the split of public and private or the means of reproduction is at heart a sexist split with a subsequent devaluation of the private. In any event, there is no doubt that historically personal identity frequently meant male identity.

One of the consequences of this is that women who began to feel a call to full personal identity got caught in a conflict. To be a person demanded to forsake being a woman. De Beauvoir expresses this existentially as the conflict between being dependent and passive on the one hand and active on the other. Judith Bardwick in *Ambivalence: The Socialization of Women* describes the conflict as having sociological dimensions. If a woman chooses a career, and does not marry, she is not fulfilled as a woman; if she chooses marriage over a career, she is not fulfilled as a person; and if she chooses both she cannot do either well. Men are socialized to fear failure, women to fear success. In the following list of characteristics which describe girls and boys one can see significant differences in the sexes and that the males more properly approximate persons. Girls show dependence, passivity, fragility, non-competitiveness, non-aggression, empathy, sensitivity, subjectivity, inability to risk; boys show independence, aggression, competitiveness, leadership, innovation, self-discipline, activity, objectivity, courage, unsentimentality, and confidence. Even more interesting is the recent discovery by psychologists that characteristics associated with healthy mature women are the same as those which are considered sick if used to describe a person, whereas those which are used to describe a healthy person are the same as those for a healthy mature man. In particular a healthy mature woman is more submissive, less independent, less adventurous, more easily influenced, less aggressive, less competitive, more emotional, and less objective than a healthy man. The discoveries of sociologists about sex-role stereotyping in schools or of psychologists about sex-identity expectations in the therapeutic relationship reinforce the original insight of de Beauvoir that there is a conflict between being a woman and being a person in the situation where criteria for personal identity are made analytically similar to criteria for male identity.

b. *Women are persons and men are less than persons.* In direct contrast to the view that men only can be persons we find today in some philosophers the opposite claim. This position accepts many of the same sex-identity characteristics as the above group, but they devalue those characteristics associated with men. In particular they imply that aggression and competitiveness are more properly seen as animalistic or inferior human traits. The basic male drive for power is blamed for many of the problems in the world. Gentleness, sensitivity, and communality is considered to be better and more human. To be a person means to relinquish the desire to oppress, to control, or to dominate. Mary Daly in *Beyond God the Father* describes this as calling for the sisterhood of man. She believes that it is only through women developing their specific identity as women in separation from men that the world might be saved. Men will learn how to be persons from women. It does not appear that the identity of the person is analytically female. It is not logically impossible for a man to be a person by her criteria. Rather it takes a series of acts of the will to transform his identity from being predominantly male. The sex-identity is empirical or synthetic. It can be changed.

c. *Women and men are equally persons.* The position I should like to propose is that women and men are equally persons, and that there are significant differences between the two sexes. One of the characteristics which makes them equally persons is the fact that they are capable of making decisions. I would argue further that human beings are even persons when for some reason or other they appear to be incapable of making decisions, for reasons of illness or socialized debilitation. There is often no way that one can tell in invalids, retarded children, or those classified as pathologically insane whether decisions are being made. In particular, the decision about what kind of person one will be can be made and remade thousands of times throughout a lifetime. It is perhaps these decisions which form the ground for the most important decision of all.

Furthermore, it is precisely through recognizing the person in the human being when it appears absent that the most profound personal identity is discovered. The lack of visible response in no way proves the absence of a decision. Persons often make decisions about their own identity which for several reasons cannot be carried through at the moment.

There is an infinite variety in the character of persons. Some of this variety is able to be classified. English Canadians are different from French Canadians, Montrealers are different from rural farm dwellers, the rich are different from the poor, the healthy are different from the sick, old people are different from children, and so on. There is no doubt that nationality, class, age, the place one holds in sibling relationships, etc. all play a part in the formation of personal identity. In focusing on the factor of sex-identity in personal identity, I am intentionally selecting one element. The *significance* of the factor is determined by something other than factor itself. This means that there are some contexts in which sex-identity is not significant at all as there are contexts in which age or class is irrelevant. To say that there are significant differences between women and men is to claim that there are *some* contexts in which sex plays an important role. I am arguing against both those who maintain that it is significant in every situation and those who claim that it is not significant in any situation.

Those who argue that sex-identity is significant in every situation (male chauvinists as well as radical feminists) consider the differences between women and men to be analytic. This means that there are some necessary *a priori* characteristics which fundamentally separate women from men in everything they do. Those who argue that sex-identity is not significant in any situation (many moderates or liberals) believe that the differences between women and men are *synthetic*. This means that the characteristics which happen to belong to women or men are *a posteriori* and not necessary. I claim that there is a third alternative. There are characteristics of women and men which are not merely synthetic, that is, which have a stronger tie to sex-identity than length of hair or the kind of clothes one wears. These characteristics are looser than analytic, for it is possible to consider someone as a woman or as a man even if they do not have a characteristic frequently found in one sex or the other. The degree of frequency varies depending on the characteristic. In developing this third approach I follow a suggestion made by Michael Scriven in "The Logic of Criteria." He calls these characteristics 'normical' and attempts to work out a theory of definition which loosens up the traditional split between analytic and synthetic properties. I am not convinced that attempting to discover a definition of woman or of man is a fruitful way to approach sex-identity; and in the remainder of this chapter I intend to explore some of the significant differences between women and men without trying to tie them down to a specific definition. Any theory of definition must contain within it openness to change, for in the area of sex-identity there are a great many unknowns. The need for open-ended or flexible definitions merely restates the fundamental situation, namely that women and men can make decisions about the kind of person they want to be.

To claim that women and men can to some extent decide their sex-identity is to raise interesting philosophical problems. How does woman's context differ from man's? Can there ever be a time when her situation will be identical to man's, or will woman always be different in some significant way? The particular factors of the context of sex-identity I willl mention here are body, language, immediate past, inherited past, and future options. This list is not meant to be exhaustive, but serves to point the way to further inquiry. In this area of research, philosophers are dependent on progress in biology, psychology, linguistics, political science, religion, history, and sociology.

The body and sex-identity. Differences between a woman's body and a man's body can be classified as genetic, anatomical, and hormonal. Where the physical sex-identity is clearly male or female, these three factors balance and function throughout a lifetime in a particular way. The fetus is sexually undifferentiated anatomically for the first several weeks so that the same physical body could become male or female depending upon the messages which are transmitted to it from the brain. This is the reason why the male body has a residue of nipples which remain undeveloped, and the woman's outerlips remain open rather than closed in a scrotum. In one sex certain primary and secondary anatomical sex characteristics develop while others remain dormant. The chromosomes of the female body and male body have a different cellular structure. This is described by calling the female chromosomes xx and the male xy. There appear to be two specific periods during which messages from the brain are transmitted to the body to effect change in sex-development. The first period is during gestation when the anatomical body is formed into the primary sex characteristics, when males develop the penis, the scrotum, and the testes and females develop the uterus, ovaries, vagina, and clitoris. These sexually differentiated physical characteristics are developed from sexually undifferentiated gonads. The second period of formation is during adolescence during which both hormonal and anatomical changes are effected, again by messages sent from the brain. Through the production of different androgens secondary male characteristics such as the formation of semen, bodily and particularly facial and pubic hair, voice changes etc. are affected. In women, menstruation commences, the breasts begin to enlarge, and bodily hair forms. The androgen which particularly effects the male sex-identity is testosterone, and those which effect female sex-identity are estrogen and progesteron. All the androgens are present in both sexes, only the amount differs. In particular, it appears that male sex-identity takes an additional element. If the fetus is not given an addition of male hormones, it will remain genetically female. This had led some theorists to claim that the male is a more precarious kind of being than the female. In any event, a biological description of sex-identity reveals some complex and fascinating factors in the determination of sex-identity.

If the development is irregular then decisions have to be made about whether the person should develop as a man or woman. For example, the anatomical structure of the body may be partially formed into one sex or the other. Or the anatomical structure may be one sex in the fetus but the second state of development in adolescence the opposite sex. In each case a decision must be made about which sex-identity the person should have, and an operation or change in hormone can be used to clarify the sex-identity. In some cases where the child grew up with a female sex-identity, then began developing a male body in puberty, doctors discovered that it was easier to change physical structure of the body making the person anatomically female than to change the conscious sex-identity of being female into being male. The identity as a woman is not complete in this change because ovulation and menstruation do not occur, but the anatomic structure of the body is female. From the philosophical point of view it is interesting that the conscious sex-identification is more central to the personal identity than the bodily sex-identification.

Nonetheless, in situations where sex-identity is not as radically unsettled, but where there is a certain deviance from what a society takes as normally associated with being a woman or a man, a bodily 'defect' can cause a crisis in conscious sex-identity. For example, in women with high levels of testosterone who have facial hair, or women who are unable to become pregnant because of lack of proper ovulation or inadequately developed reproductive organs, or even in women whose breasts have not developed, there is often a residual fear of 'not being a woman.' The same is true of men whose voice remains high, who fail to develop sufficient amount of bodily hair, who develop breasts, or who are unable to develop enough sperm to fertilize in reproduction. Furthermore, sex-identity seems often to be so closely related to being able to reproduce that a female is considered a woman when she begins to menstruate and sexless after her menopause; and many men whose sex-identities are weak go through identity crises after having a vasectomy.

Therefore, the question of the relation of the body with one's sex-identity is an extremely complicated one. Many of the general philosophical problems of the nature of a person can be studied in terms of sex-identity. For instance what is the relation between the hormonal and the conscious life of a person? Do hormones cause conscious changes? Certainly doctors who give menopausal women an additional supply of estrogen on the assumption that in menopause women are passing through 'drug withdrawal symptoms' because their bodies are no longer producing a drug which it produced for 30 years believe that hormones cause a change in the conscious identity. Can the mind cause a change in the balance in the hormones? Experiments which demonstrate that people under tension produce larger amounts of hormones imply a mind causal factor. Even more interesting is the recent discovery that the mind can regulate symptoms of certain diseases through biofeedback sensitivity and even affect the progress of such serious diseases as cancer. Does this mean that there is an interaction between the mind and body? Is there some truth in the Cartesian model of the person with the pituitary gland being replaced by a more contemporary area of the brain called the hypothalmus? Or is the image of Spinoza more accurate? Do the mind and body function in a parallel way, so that mental and chemical changes occur simultaneously?

In addition to the many philosophical problems which arise in the consideration of sex-identity and personal identity, there is an area of 'lived experience' which has distinct male or female characteristics: it 'feels' different to be a woman or a man. The female body and the male body give rise to different experiences in the world. In activities as simple as walking, sitting, running, the female body moves differently from the male body. Some of this difference can be attributed to socialization, but some of it is due to the anatomical structure of the body itself. In more specific activities which are shared by both sexes such as making love, the experience of one's body as male or female is definitely determined by one's sex-identity. In a whole range of experiences which women are specifically able to have, such as pregnancy, giving birth, and nursing, to be a woman offers the possibility of a range of experiences which are different from those open to men. This difference in no way negates the similarities of lived experience which face all persons, such as the possibility of disease, the inevitability of death, the need for nourishment, and so forth. Rather it enriches the human context by its variety. In addition to specific male and female possibilities of experience by virtue of a particular kind of body, women and men are given different contexts within which they must make decisions—the effects of different sorts of birth control on the body and on personal identity, whether to work when nurturing infants, whether to have a child affect women and men differently.

Finally, the whole area of rights and discrimination on the basis of sex is a central area of philosophical concern. The practice of not allowing sufficient maternity leave with safeguards for rehiring, the question of whether men should be allowed paternity leave, the attempt to eliminate prejudice toward women on the basis that their hormonal cycles interfere with their efficiency are important. Recent investigation has shown that men pass through cycles in hormone and mood change as regularly as women. These cycles appear to be daily, monthly, and yearly and are being investigated as other 'biorhythms' present in human life.

Language and sex-identity. One of the contemporary interests of philosophers is the relation between language, thought, and the world. In many languages a sexual component is built-in because of the gender endings of nouns and adjectives. There appears to be some controversy about whether gender endings of words was caused by a sexual identification or by other considerations entirely separate from sex. For example, words may have certain endings because of the sound preference, or because of other more complex grammatical structures. Regardless of the *origin* of the gender identification, there is no doubt that once a language has developed, words with feminine or masculine endings can have a particular *effect* on the formation of female and male identity. For example, in French grammar the practice of allowing the presence of one male person in a room of 1000 females to change the ending of a word from feminine to masculine could imply to women that their presence is non-powerful in the face of the male. An indication of this is the textbook used in French elementary schools which shows a woman falling over dead at the entrance of the man.

In English the sex structure of the language is not as obvious as in French. Nonetheless there is a definite sexual basis to many words in the language. The first example is the use of 'man' to represent all persons as well as the masculine sex. It is further seen in the claim that all persons are 'brothers,' or that 'he' represents women or men. The subsequent development of the words 'chairman,' 'foreman,' or 'ombudsman,' for either women or men further indicate the disappearance of the female into the male. Some changes have been made recently to rebalance this aspect of language. The word 'human' or 'person' is replacing 'man' as the species word: 'brothers and sisters,' 'friends,' or 'comrades' are used to address mixed audiences; and 'director,' 'supervisor,' or 'arbitrator' are used instead of words with the ending 'man.' Furthermore, different writers are experimenting with the use of he/she, one, and even a new series of words 'tey,' 'tem,' and 'ter(s),' to represent he or she, him or her, and his and hers.

The second way in which words are related to sex-identity in the English language is through an identification of one sex with a particular function. The riddle in which a boy and his father are in an automobile accident, the father is killed, the boy is taken to an emergency entrance to the hospital, the surgeon on duty looks down at him and says, 'My God, it is my son,' and the person is asked how this is possible, shows the identification of surgeons with men in the common North American mind. We know that doctors are men and nurses are women, lawyers men and secretaries women, principals men and teachers women, and store 'managers' men and clerks women and so on. Each person who takes a function which is outside the expected sex identification usually has to pass through a personal sex-identity crises before being able to continue comfortably in the work. This is true for women lawyers as for male nurses. Again, the insistence that jobs not be closed to either sex, coupled with the attempt to change sex-role stereotyping in children's stories and textbooks, indicates a change in society which should be reflected in a change in language at some future time.

Still another way in which sex-identity is found in the English language is in the hidden feminine or masculine aspect of certain words. For example, someone may refer to the Church—she, God—He, my car—she, and so on. Most often it is a man who refers to something as feminine. Recently I have heard an escalator repairman at the university shout to a partner: "Turn her off," and a farmer say of a violent thunder storm, "She is really coming down." It may be an interesting linguistic study to trace how often and in what context sex-identification occurs, and the philosophers could consider the significance of the particular examples from the point of view of sex-identity.

Another way in which sex-identity is reflected in the English language is found in specific words. Take the custom of dividing women between Mrs. and Miss, while men are considered Mr. Women are defined by their marital status whereas men are not. The introduction and immediate acceptance of the word Ms. to apply to women is an attempt to reflect a basic change in society itself, namely that women are emerging with independent sex-identities. Second, the phrase "women's liberation" which emerged in the 1960's as a description of both a political movement and a general social phenomena is frequently referred to as 'women's lib.' This shortening of the phrase, unthinkable in the case of black liberation, indicates the traditional attitude towards women as 'cute' or 'inessential.'

Again, as in the relation between the body and sex-identity, we find that language presents a context in which women and men must make certain decisions. The context is different for each sex. Just as women had to decide whether to use birth control, or even whether to have children, so they have decided how to speak and even what words to use to describe themselves, as well as humanity in general. The same is true for men. What is different is the meaning that the words hold for each particular sex. Furthermore, the basic philosophical questions which focus on the relation between language and personal identity can be raised with the focus on sex-identity. Specifically, should philosophy concentrate on ordinary use of language? Should it attempt to create new language when ordinary language is found to be defective for ethical or political reasons? How does language function in the world? Should philosophers describe the world as it is, or should they try to change the world?

The immediate past and sex-identity. By 'immediate past' I mean the whole range of experiences which one has had since birth and which are particularly related to being considered a boy or girl. A great deal of contemporary research in psychology and sociology is being done on the process of socialization as it effects sex-identity. The most obvious discovery is that most girls are brought up to identify with the weaker element of a patriarchal society, whereas most boys are brought up to identify with the stronger element. Even where there appears to be equality in the power structure or in families where the woman is the stronger, outside the home the patriarchal structure is found in stores, schools, hospitals, on television, and so on. It is clear that in general the men rule and the women obey. As the child grows up, the sex-identification as oppressor or as oppressed becomes more and more internalized. To be a man means to be in a position of superiority, whereas to be a woman means to work as a helpmate to some man.

The effects of patriarchy can be analyzed economically. Women are 'the last hired and the first fired' in the public market. They provide a cheap labour pool for the most basic tasks. At home many of them work without any set pay. In this way business gets two workers for the price of one. It makes woman dependent upon the good will of men for her economic security; and it encourages the development of false charm and deviousness in the securing of money. A great deal of contemporary research in political science and sociology is being done on the *politics* of the relations between women and men. In a society where capital is as important as it is in North America, what is the relation between economic inde-

pendence and personal identity? Is any one economically independent in capitalism where a few international monopolies control
the flow of capital? Should housework be shared by all members of
the household, so that it no longer remains the responsibility of
women alone? Are women defined as houseworkers, and should
they be paid by the state for their labor? Is housework outside the
market or is it at the center? These abstract questions are concretely
translated in every life of a woman or man who is living in a household with at least one other person. Decisions must be made daily
about who will cook, shop, clean, take care of the children. Women
are often faced with the situation where they are expected to take
this responsibility, where they have been trained to do so, and
where they feel compelled to teach others to share the housework.
Men, on the other hand, have not for the most part been taught
how to do housework, feel a certain uneasiness about being men
if they do work which has traditionally been identified with
women, and frequently need reminding if they are to break out of
housework 'blindness,' that is, not even seeing what needs to be
done.

In addition to the effects of patriarchy on sex-identity in the
recent past of the formation of personal identity, there are many
sex-role or sex-behavior characteristics which have become identified with one sex or the other. Psychologist Olga Favreau in *Sex
Differences in Behavior* has given a careful analysis of some of
these characteristics such as mathematical abilities, spatial abilities,
verbal abilities, manual dexterity, bonding, and aggression in terms
of their claimed sexual component. She has shown that the expectation of the researcher frequently contaminates the results, that
it is practically impossible to separate cultural prejudice from what
are believed to be 'innate differences,' and that the reporting of
statistically significant conclusions of experiments is highly mis-
leading. Contemporary research on textbooks used in schools reveals built-in sex stereotypes both in the pictures of women and
men in the books, as well as in the particular verbal examples of
behavior in mathematics and science. Since history describes for
the most part the actions of men in wars and political struggles,
it is not surprising that girls choose literature as a field where they
can develop their identity.

Philosophically all the questions which are considered in terms
of the recent past and personal identity can be asked in terms of
sex-identity as well. How do we learn to make decisions? When
do we decide what kind of person we will be? Sartre suggests that
it occurs around 10 years of age, Freud that it occurs before 5,
and de Beauvoir that it is a decision which is made continually
throughout a lifetime. When do we accept our sex-identity? How
is this identity evaluated? Is it good or bad to be a woman or man?

How free are we to change our evaluation of our sex-identity? Did it used to be bad to be a woman, but now it is good? How free are we to change our concept of what a woman or man is? How free are we to be a different kind of woman or man? How will sex-identity and personal identity be affected by our death?

The inherited past and sex-identity. By 'inherited past' I mean all the images, archetypes, or concepts of one sex or the other which are in the world when one is born into it and which seem to re-appear generation after generation in myths and symbols. Jung called these images 'archetypes' of the unconscious which became conscious and concrete in different cultures at different times in history. He believed that just as the body contained physical characteristics from preceding generations, so the psyche contained within it certain imprints of archetypes. Philosophically, there is no way that one can prove the existence or non-existence of these contents of the psyche. Nonetheless, it is helpful when considering the factors which form the situation for decisions about sex-identity to examine some of the ways in which symbols of women or men have perpetuated themselves throughout Western history. For many people questions of identity reduce to questions of stereotypes, so that they relate both to themselves and to others in terms of projected images, instead of a more flexible and realistic openness to the unified unique combination of qualities in a mature and fulfilled personal identity.

In uncovering the inherited history of woman, it must be kept in mind that most of history was written by men, so that the archetypes are for the most part male projections which have become incorporated by women. Some of the archetypes worth investigating are: woman as an evil temptress, virgin goddess, earth mother, passive object, genius, and political activist. Different manifestations can be found in different periods in history. The evil temptress is found in Pandora, Eve, prostitutes, witches, the 'femme fatale,' and so on. The common thread is the view that women lead men to their doom. The virgin goddess, on the other hand, is the medium through which men are saved. These archetypes are found in religion and literary myths as well as in every day life. For example, in contemporary court cases of rape, it appears that only the young virginal girl is considered innocent, whereas a woman who had some sexual experience is considered to be the *cause* of the rape. Women become split in men's minds between the two poles of evil temptress and virgin goddess, and they internalize this polarization. There is not a corresponding male polarity even in Jung's description of the archetypes, for the wise man leads men to higher things and the trickster fools men as well.

The earth mother can be studied in her symbolic form as nurturer and source of life or in her more static philosophical identification

with matter. Women's identity with the earth and with motherhood can be traced historically through its transformation into the
housewife where she is cut off from the earth and married to a
house. The role of woman in the evolution of the family can be
studied in terms of the controversy about the original relation between matriarchy and patriarchy, or in terms of the evolution of
the family through the extended family, to the nuclear family, and
to the breakdown of family ties altogether. The relation between
technology and woman's identity as mother can be considered. The
role of money in the family is still another subject for investigation.
Finally, the earth mother can be seen as a correlate archetype to
the male archetype of spirit. Here instead of a polarization between
two kinds of women we find a polarity between the male and
female.

The woman as a passive object is without doubt the predominant
image of woman in the history of philosophy. She is passive in two
different ways: either she is without life altogether, much as matter
is completely devoid of life without form, or she is passive in the
way that uncontrolled emotions or passions are unregulated by the
will or the intellect. She is passive in relation to herself. This passivity can be studied in metaphysics in terms of matter vs. form,
in epistemology in terms of intuition or sensation vs. reflection, in
ethics in terms of obedience vs. power to rule, in politics in terms
of dependence as man's property, and so on.

The different forms of woman's genius can be studied as muse,
or as sophia (wisdom). She can be considered as forced into anonymity in her art forms (needlepoint, crocheting, weaving, braid-
ing, etc.). The history of her education can be examined to show
how she was denied access to the skills she might need to excel in
what has traditionally been accepted as areas of male genius.
Finally contemporary forms of female genius can be studied.

Woman as political activist can be viewed in examples of women
ruling men (Joan of Arc), or women ruling both women and men
(Judith). Why did this occur in some situations and not in others?
When did women begin to consider organizing women? What
occurred in the suffragette movement? Why did it fail to achieve
a significant change in women's identity? What are the theoretical
and practical differences in the conflicting ideologies of contemporary women's liberation organizations?

One can place the study of archetypes in a wider context of the
general history of woman. Here the central focus is not exceptional
or individual women, but the struggles and changes in the lives of
the masses of women. This 'inherited past' includes the myths,
symbols and archetypes which appear to be abstracted in some
way from every day life, as well as the situation of women in Western civilization. Two sorts of comparisons then become possible:

first, with men in Western civilization, and second with both women and men from other parts of the world. In all these areas of study the central philosophical question is: How free are we to form our particular sex-identity within the context of an inherited past which specifies certain images for women and men.

The future and sex-identity. The claim made in this section was that women and men are equally persons although there are significant differences between them. The characteristic which makes them persons was that they are capable of making decisions about their identity. The significant differences lie in the contexts of those decisions. In many central ways, the context of sex-identity for the contemporary Western woman differs from that of the contemporary Western man. The consequence is that the future offers different calls for the two. Sex-identity is changing in some fundamental ways, so that what it will mean to be a woman will be very different from what it will mean to be a man.

Women and men are born into the world with a particular body, a special relation to language, an inherited past, and soon acquire a different range of experiences. They have no choice about this context. Their responsibility lies in the particular meaning they give to it. They can choose to ignore it as far as possible and conclude that there are no significant differences between women and men; they can choose to see the differences as so significant that there is no real possibility of personal relationships of care or openness between the two sexes; or they can decide to explore the differences, deepen their consciousness of their particular sex-identity, and transcend their limitations.

Sex-identity is directly related to the conscious integration of the factors which specifically belong to each sex. This means that the more fully women uncover their own past as well as the possibilities of their contemporary situation, the more fully they will participate in the emerging identity of woman. The same holds true for men. Ignorance of one's historical and present context leads to a poverty in conscious personal identity. This same claim has been made recently by French Canadians who desire an awakening of national identity as well as by blacks who desire an awakening in racial identity. The implication is that if one has no consciousness of one's unique history and contemporary situation then one merely has inherited consciousness whereby the oppressed only see themselves through the eyes of those who have defined them. The decision, then, to learn about one's sex-identity can lead to personal fulfillment.

One of the consequences of this view is that the claim that 'after the revolution' there will be only persons or that sex will be ignored in the future is both impossible and undesirable. It is impossible because what women or men will become is decided in different contexts. It is undesirable because the unique past and present situation of woman and man can enrich the core of human experience. This enrichment can be found in science, the arts, religion, personal relationships, and politics. Personal identity emerges from a past that is different for women and men.

At the same time it is important to recognize that the individual person is faced with the task of integrating several factors of which sex is only one. One should always ask the significance of sex-identity. When one is considering class, religion, or race, the significance of sex-identity may be negligible; at other times it may be very important. The choice as to the significance of sex-identity is a very personal one. There are times when one will want to transcend sex-identity, to overlook its particularity; there will be other times when one will want to focus completely on it. For the majority of people who do not desire personal integration, the ultimate significance of sex-identity will either be ignored or left ambivalent. For those people, however, who seek to integrate their various orientations in the world, the struggle for a personal identity becomes the road to fulfillment.

❊   ❊   ❊

The following selection, "Natural Law Language and Women," by Christine Pierce, is excerpted from *Women in Sexist Society: Studies in Power and Powerlessness,* edited by Vivian Gornick and Barbara K. Moran. New York: Basic Books, Inc., Publishers, 1971, Chapter 10.

CHRISTINE PIERCE   'Natural Law Language and Women'

"Nature" or "human nature" must be among the most enigmatic concepts ever used. Often, when the "natural" is invoked, we are left in the dark as to whether it is meant as an explanation, a recommendation, a claim for determinism, or simply a desperate appeal, as if the "natural" were some sort of metaphysical glue that could hold our claims or values together.

For centuries people have appealed to the "natural" to back up their moral and social recommendations. The ordinary uses of the term which everyone hears from time to time demonstrate that such efforts are still very much with us. We are told, for example, that suicide, birth control and homosexuality are wrong because they are unnatural. Now and then the use takes a positive form; mother-hood is natural and hence the duty of women.

My major intent is to examine the language of "proper sphere," role, or function, showing its relationship to the language of natural law and pointing out problems in this kind of reasoning that are overlooked in the discussions of those who use this type of argument against women.

The following three examples characterize in a more extensive way the type of argument to be analyzed here. [1] in 1872, Myra Bradwell was refused admission to the Illinois bar by the state supreme court even though she had passed the bar entrance examination. Her suit, based upon the supposed right of every person, man or woman, to engage in any lawful employment for a livelihood, was denied. Justice Bradley, in his concurring opinion, opposed the idea that women might be attorneys on grounds that both God and nature disapprove.

> The civil law, as well as nature herself, has always recognized a wide difference in the respective spheres and destinies of man and woman. Man is, or should be, woman's protector and defender. The natural and proper timidity and delicacy which belongs to the female sex evidently unfits it for many of the occupations of civil life. The constitution of the family organization, which is founded in the divine ordinance, as well as in the nature of things, indicates the domestic sphere as that which properly belongs to the domain and functions of womanhood.[1]

[2] In a statement denouncing abortion, Pope Pius XI assumed that nature assigns duties to women. "However much we may pity the mother whose health and even life is gravely imperiled in the performance of *the duty allotted to her by nature,* nevertheless what could ever be a sufficient reason for excusing in any way the direct murder of the innocent?"[2] [3] A paragraph from Étienne Gilson's commentary on Aquinas illustrates the incredible implications of a well-known view that identifies natural sexuality with the reproductive function. On this concept of nature, rape is preferable to masturbation.

> . . . To violate nature is to set oneself against God who has ordained nature. Now the worst way of violating nature is to

1. *Bradwell v. The State,* 83 U.S. 130, 141 (1872).

2. *Encyclical Letter of Pope Pius XI on Christian Marriage,* St. Paul Editions (Boston, n.d.), p. 32. Emphasis added.

> carry corruption into its very principle. Fornication, rape, adultery, incest, respect nature's order in the performing of the sexual act. Unnatural vice, however, refuses to respect this order. The worst form of luxury is bestiality, and after it, sodomy, irregularities in the sexual act and onanism. . . .[3]

Rape, a violent action, is not recommended, but it is not as bad as consensual sodomy or interrupting heterosexual intercourse, because heterosexual rape allows for the possibility of fulfilling the purpose of sexuality, namely, procreation. At the very least, it seems somewhat peculiar to prefer sexual acts which are by definition unloving, violent abuses of persons to acts which need not be, and may be quite the contrary. Here we see the natural defined as function or purpose and applied to the sexual organs. It is assumed that procreation is the only purpose of sexual activity, and that fulfilling its function is what makes an act morally good and deviating from that function is what makes an act morally bad.

As a preface to analyzing these kinds of arguments, it is important to stress how difficult it is for anyone in any social or moral context to say what they mean by "natural" and why it recommends itself as good. Two distinct steps are involved here: defining what is meant by "natural" and arguing that what is natural is good. . . .

It is often assumed that the word "natural" has an automatic "plus" value tag which does not have to be argued for on independent grounds. In other words, it is taken for granted that if one persuades us that " 'X' is natural," he has also persuaded us that " 'X' is good." The Vatican's position on birth control reflects this: *Humanae Vitae* assumes that it is sufficient to point out that artificial means of birth control interrupt the natural order of things. The most significant question of all, "Why is 'natural order' a good thing?" is never asked. Apparently, what the "natural order" means in this case is that which will happen if untouched by human invention. This definition, however, yields absurd consequences if we try to use it as a prescription. If "natural order" is a good thing, and we must assume it is because we are told not to interrupt it, why isn't shaving a moral issue? Clearly, it is natural for hair to grow on a man's face, and shaving introduces an artificial means to disrupt the natural order of things.

One thing is evident: we cannot discuss whether the natural is good until we are able to state what we mean by the term. "Natural" can mean "untouched by human invention," but this use is not a coherent basis for normative judgments. A second meaning of "natural" sometimes applied to human beings is that human nature is everything that human beings do. As an explanation, this

3. Étienne Gilson, *The Christian Philosophy of Saint Thomas Aquinas*, trans. L. K. Shook (New York: Random House, 1956), p. 298.

use is simply vacuous; if meant as a justification, however, it would justify everything. If things are morally right because they are natural, and if everything human beings do is natural, then every-thing human beings do is morally justified. The third and fourth meanings that I want to consider are particularly interesting, not only because of their relevance to arguments for women's inequal-ity, but because both definitions are currently in use and yet clearly incompatible. Human nature is construed to be either what human beings have in common with the rest of the animal world or what distinguishes human beings from the rest of the animal world.

One of the most amusing efforts to make the third use work against women is the following comment by Mary Hemingway: "Equality, what does it mean? What's the use for it? I've said it before and I'll repeat: Women are second-class citizens and not only biologically. A female's first duty is to bear children and rear them. With the exception of a few fresh water fish, most animals follow this basic rule."[4] Unfortunately, the most obvious conse-quence of Hemingway's argument is that a few fresh water fish are immoral! What she meant to say, however, was that human duties somehow can be determined by observing animal behavior. *Prima facie,* it seems odd to claim that the meaningfulness of moral termi-nology could be derived from a realm to which moral vocabulary does not apply. We must insist that people who talk this way be able to make sense of it. What does it mean, for example, to say that nature intends for us to do certain things? We know what it means to say that "I intend to pack my suitcase," but what sense can it make to say that nature intends for us to do one thing rather than another? The above use of "natural" reduces to saying "this is what most animals do." To the extent that this is the meaning of the term, it will be hard to get a notion of value out of it. The fact that something happens a lot does not argue for or against it.

Interchanging words like "normal" and "natural" illustrates prej-udice for the statistically prevalent as opposed to the unusual, the exception. The unusual *qua* unusual, however, cannot be ruled out as bad; it can be alternatively described as "deviant" or "original," depending on whether or not we like it. Nothing prevents describ-ing the so-called sexual deviant as a sexual original except most people's inability to tolerate any unusual behavior in this area; hence, they use statistical concepts with bad connotations (unnatu-ral, abnormal) to discuss it, instead of those with good connotations (original, exceptional).

The fourth meaning of "natural," that which distinguishes human beings from the rest of the (animal) world, reaches back to Plato. For Plato, to state the nature of any given class of things was to

4. Mary Hemingway, *Look,* September 6, 1966, p. 66.

state the features of that class which distinguished it from all other classes of things. Although Plato did not claim that men and women have different natures, but rather referred to human beings as the class with the capacity to reason, his use of "natural" lends itself to the defining of classes of things according to function or role that is frequently used to restrict women. In order to understand how similar our way of talking and explaining things is to the Platonic view, it is first necessary to grasp how the latter has been historically conceived. An increased awareness of the natural law basis of the language of function should help us to be more critical of the language we take for granted, and to see what kinds of philosophical commitment we perhaps unwittingly make.

The Greek method of explanation for questions of the sort, "What is the nature of 'X'?" was teleological; explanations were given in terms of function, role, end or purpose, as opposed to mechanistic explanations. The difference between these explanations can easily be illustrated by comparing their answers to a simple question such as "What is a lawnmower?" A teleologist will explain: a lawnmower is something that is used to cut grass; a mechanist will explain about pulleys, plugs, and metal "teeth." Manufactured items lend themselves to the former type of explanation because hopefully we have in mind what the function of something is going to be before we start making any of it. Such explanation, however, is not so easily forthcoming for questions like, "What is the nature of human beings?" However, Plato was interested in this type of question; he wanted to explain the "natural" world. In this realm of nonmanufactured items, functions and roles are discovered, not created.

Although Plato thought he could answer the question concerning the nature of human beings, for the moment what concerns us is not the content of his answer, but the additional philosophical mileage we can expect from success in providing this type of answer. To be able to say what a thing is in terms of its function or purpose is simultaneously to set up standards for its evaluation. Once we can state the function of any "X," we can say what a good "X" is, or more precisely, we can say that "X" is good to the extent that it fulfills its function. We still have this use of "good" in English; we say, for example, that a good lawnmower is one that cuts grass well, that is, one that fulfills its function.

Plato's effort to apply this teleological framework to human beings consists of his functional analysis of the soul as reason, spirit, and desire. These are analogous to functioning units in the state, namely, philosopher-kings, soldiers, and artisans. Even as the function of a philosopher-king is to rule the state, implicit in the notion of reason as a function is the ability to rule, govern, or control the rest of the soul or personality. When anything does its work well, it is virtuous or excellent. In this case, when reason as well as every other functioning unit is working well and working together, the result is harmony or an order of soul to which Plato gives the name of the overarching virtue, justice. Reason, then, is the ordering principle; a good person is one who has an ordered soul, whose personality is controlled by reason.

Aristotle's agreement with both the teleological method and Plato's application of it to reason is evident when he says, "It is both natural and expedient for the body to be ruled by the mind, and for the emotional part of our natures to be ruled by that part which possesses reason, our intelligence."[5] But, for Aristotle, the soul's capacities vary for different classes of people. While the parts of the soul are present in women, slaves and children, "the slave has no deliberative faculty at all, the woman has, but it is without authority, and the child has, but it is immature."[6]

Plato may be the only philosopher to have held a doctrine of natural place which assigns social roles on the basis of individual merit rather than assigning places to whole classes of people as illustrated by the commonplace statement, "woman's place is in the home." According to Plato, the nature (distinctive function) of human beings is reason, and a whole spectrum of rational abilities are distributed among human beings. One's nature, then, can be determined only by discovering one's talents, and, as Plato put it, "many women are better than many men in many things."[7] Aristotle believed the more familiar doctrine that whole classes of people—women, slaves—have their natural places: "as between male and female the former is by nature superior and the ruler, the latter inferior and subject."[8]

When the class of human beings is divided into men and women (or, perhaps better rendered, when women are not considered full human beings), the method of determining the essence of each often remains teleological, but for women the natural is no longer the rational but the biological. This type of move usually results in defining women as childbearers and reserving rationally oriented roles for men. The biological interpretation of women's nature distorts the Platonic enterprise insofar as reproduction is not a function peculiar to human beings.

5. Aristotle, *The Politics*, 1254b5 (trans. T. A. Sinclair).

6. Aristotle, *The Politics*, 1260a13 (trans. Benjamin Jowett). Sinclair translates this passage: "the deliberative faculty in the soul is not present at all in a slave; in a female it is inoperative, in a child underdeveloped."

7. Plato, *Republic*, 455d (trans. Allan Bloom). A full discussion of Plato's argument appears in my essay, "Equality: *Republic V*," *The Monist* 57:1, January, 1973.

8. Aristotle, *The Politics*, 1254b14.

Assigning to women the same function as would be appropriate to a female of any species has serious consequences, since in citing the function or role of something, we are setting certain standards which it must measure up to in order to be called good. If we are suspicious of teleology, the quarrel is not with the fact that a use of "good" is generated by defining things in terms of function; the quarrel concerns what sort of "good" we are talking about. Are the standards referred to in maintaining that a good "X" is one that functions well moral standards or simply standards of efficiency? They are at least the latter; the worry is they are perhaps only that. When we say a good lawnmower is one that cuts grass well, we clearly mean good in the sense of efficient or effective. If, to take another example, we define poison in terms of its function, good poison is that which does an effective, that is, quick and fatal, job. The good referred to is clearly not moral good. However, this does not imply that a teleological or instrumental use of "good" could not also be a moral use.

There may be cases where the word "good" serves both functions. For example, when Lon Fuller, a Professor of Jurisprudence at Harvard Law School, defines good law as laws that are clear, public, consistent, he is claiming that such standards are necessary for moral, that is fair, laws as well as effective ones. Laws that are unclear, secret, and inconsistent are not only ineffective, but unjust. Although some jurisprudential scholars have argued against Fuller by maintaining that an instrumental use of good cannot be a moral use, there seems to be no *a priori* reason why a word cannot function simultaneously in more than one way. Granting this, the criticism of teleology is not as dramatic as some would have it. Morality based on teleology cannot be scrapped merely because we claim to have discovered that the teleological use of "good" is not a moral use but simply means that things are efficient. However, we must always be on guard to discover from context which use is intended since we can not assume that fulfilling a function or role is necessarily good in any moral sense.

For example, even if it is accepted that a good woman is one who fulfills her role, it may well be that "good" means nothing more than contributing to efficiency. Morton Hunt, in the May, 1970, issue of *Playboy*, argues against husband and wife sharing equally in all tasks (career and home) on the grounds that "when there is no specialization of function, there is inefficient performance. . . ."[9] Although specialization is supposedly one essential aspect of all successful human groups (the other being a system of leadership), it is quite conceivable that a group of two (as opposed to a large corporation) might not prize efficiency as its highest value.

9. Morton Hunt, "Up Against the Wall, Male Chauvinist Pig." *Playboy*, May, 1970, p. 209.

Much depends upon what is meant by "success." Liberty or freedom of role choice may not be very "successful" if success is measured in terms of efficiency. Freedom has never been known for its
efficiency; it is always getting in the way of the smooth operations
of orderly systems. The conflict between freedom and efficiency
can be illustrated by marriage, but is hardly confined to it. It may
be inefficient for any one person (married, single, or living in a
commune) to teach in a university, write articles, buy groceries, do
karate, and demonstrate for political rights, but if a choice must
be made between the freedom to do all these things and efficiency,
the choice should at least be portrayed as a legitimate one.

Hunt argues not only that specific roles contribute to efficiency,
but that they are (as opposed to unisex) attractive. "It feels good,
and is productive of well-being, for man and woman to look different, smell different, act somewhat different."[10] He quotes Dr. Benjamin Spock to the effect that the sexes are "more valuable and
more pleasing" to one another if they have "specialized traits and
. . . roles to play for each other's benefit—gifts of function, so to
speak, that they can give to each other." We cannot argue against
the claim that specialization of function or role yields efficiency.
We can, however, question the importance of efficiency; we can
also ask, as we shall see later, efficient for whom? We cannot deny
that many men and women find complementarity of role attractive.
Some people even find inferiority attractive. Note once again the
remarks of Mary Hemingway: "Equality! I didn't want to be
Ernest's equal. I wanted him to be the master, to be the stronger
and cleverer than I, to remember constantly how big he was and
how small I was."[11] However, arguing that specific roles are efficient and attractive does not in and of itself determine who is to
do what. Telling us in advance what woman's gift of function is
going to be makes Hunt's argument typical of anti-women's liberation arguments that are couched in the language of role.

The *essential* content of woman's role is probably best characterized by the concept of "support"—a concept that usually does
not get, but certainly deserves, much analysis. What do people
mean by the "supportive role"? Why do they think it belongs to
women? Hunt, after characterizing the roles of husband and wife
as analogous to those of President and Speaker of the House respectively, concedes that "although the man is the head, he owes
much to his wife's managerial support."[12] To prove the value of
support, he appeals to a remark once made by Senator Maurine
Neuberger that her greatest single need as a senator was for a good

10. *Ibid.*, p. 207.

11. Hemingway, p. 66.

12. Hunt, p. 209.

"wife." Neuberger's comment certainly proves that the supportive role aids efficiency; it is undeniably easier to be a senator if one has someone to shake hands, smile with you on campaign posters, repeat your ideas to groups you have not time for, and answer your dinner invitations. That playing the supporting role aids efficiency cannot be questioned; however, the question remains efficient for whom? It must be remembered that efficiency only requires that *someone* play the supportive role, belong to the maintenance class, devote [his or her life] psychologically and physically to making sure that other people get done whatever they want done. As long as women as a class play supportive roles, they contribute to the efficiency of a power structure that excludes them from freedom of role choice.

Carried to the harshest extreme, slaves played a very important supportive role for their masters; from the masters' point of view, society was the more efficient and hence more desirable for it. Aristotle attests to the efficiency, if not the morality, of his view of natural arrangements when he says that slaves would not be needed if looms would weave by themselves.[13] In its weakest version, playing the supportive role can mean as little as the truism that everyone likes to be fussed over. What Hunt has in mind is something between the two and closer to the former, since he points to the current system as admittedly unfair, but more workable and satisfying than any other alternatives. Part of what he means by "supportive" can be gleaned from the fact that for the most part he is thinking in terms of cases involving children (although not all of his illustrations bear this out—for example, Neuberger). His perspective, then, centers around the social alternatives of the married woman. They are: the state may take care of the children, hired help may take care of the children, or we can introduce some notion of equality between men and women with regard to whatever tasks confront them, but this, as we have seen, will be inefficient.

Being an essentially pragmatic society, we often buy without question the latter half of the teleological framework: that good things are those that function well; we fail to scrutinize what we mean by "good." We easily overlook that having a function, even a so-called natural one, does not entail that those having it *ought* to use it. As we have seen, to use "X" when "X" is defined as functional is to have a good "X" in some sense of the word. We can explain what poison is by citing its function, but it does not necessarily follow that it ought (in any moral sense) to function. Having children is also a natural function; whether it is good to make use of this function is a separate issue. Given our current population

13. Politics, 1253b38.

problems, we might well decide that childbearing is not good in either the moral or efficient use of that word.

One might, at this point, legitimately object that the well-being of human beings is more complicated than that of lawnmowers and poisons. If a lawnmower does not function well or is never used to cut grass, the lawnmower is not worse off for it. However, one might say, indeed Freudian conservatives have said, that the human being's biological potential is so integrated that when it is not realized, some kind of "maladjustment" or "unhappiness" results. Of course, some maintain that no such frustration ensues; obviously, to the extent that this is correct, there is no problem, and, for example, people can decide whether or not to have children on the basis of values already discussed (efficiency, morality) since their "happiness" or "adjustment" is not at stake.

However, if we accept the Freudian conservatives' view, we must apply it consistently. Freudians have also taught us that suppression of sexual and aggressive impulses was necessary for the development of civilization. Even though suppression may result in frustration, we are told that in some cases this is the price that must be paid to purchase other goals. It is certainly not a new observation that one pays in some way for everything that one gets. Certainly, in recent times, humanity has paid in increased anxiety, frustration, and, most probably, neuroses, for its advanced technological society. Freudians must allow the same perspective on the question of childbearing as on the questions of sexuality and aggressiveness. In the latter case, we realize that some sort of suppression, probably resulting in some unhappiness, is required for civilization and/or technology. Some women's deliberate suppression of their biological potential should be regarded as an enhancement of the civilized and rational aspects of experience. If there is some biological or psychological frustration involved in the suppression of biological potential, only the individual woman should decide how she wishes to balance her desire for biological "completion" and her desire to experience the world as an independent human being. To recognize the possibility of such unhappiness is not to condone social arrangements which intensify the either/or character of this choice, but to elucidate once again the importance of liberty, and to complicate values (liberty, morality, efficiency) by which we decide which units capable of functioning ought to function.

In the conclusion of his article, Hunt once more calls upon natural law, assuring us that we need not fear the eradication of all sex-role differences because "nothing as joyless and contrary to our instincts is likely to become the pattern of the majority."[14] The language of "instinct," a somewhat modern way to refer to those things

14. Hunt, p. 209.

that we want to call "natural," is usually attached to some variation of philosophical determinism. "Instincts" are not considered to be matters of value choice, but a small class of desires that are some-how given. Some uses of "natural" lose their force without this built-in determinism; for example, excusing an action on the grounds that one was jealous, and "jealous is only natural," will work only if the people listening accept the reasoning, "I couldn't help myself." If we do not buy the determinism, we do not buy the excuse.

Hunt's argument, and similar arguments from instinct, assume that that which is not the result of human effort is impervious to human control, since he moves from the claim that these instincts are "natural" (meaning by "natural," something that happens with-out our doing anything to bring it about) to the claim that they are unalterable. That is an empirical assumption which is extremely dubious; it would commit us to the position that, since gravity "nat-urally" keeps us on the ground, we could never raise ourselves off the ground. Natural instinct may be just as open to control through education and training as our response to gravity is to the tech-nology of air travel. However, if we assume that the behavior re-lated to instincts is unalterable and inevitable, we can guarantee much more in that their obliteration will not become "the pattern of the majority." As John Stuart Mill argued a hundred years ago in *The Subjection of Women*, if the "proper sphere" of women is naturally determined, there will be no need for social and legal coercion to insure that women stay in that sphere. We need not fear that women will do what they cannot do. There is no point in recommending that people desire what they inevitably will desire, so, insofar as we recommend that people adopt certain roles, we are assuming that those roles are, at least to some extent, items of choice. So, he cannot have it both ways: as soon as one uses a claim of naturalness to entail a claim of inevitability, one shows it to be inappropriate as a support for a recommendation to be natural.

In psychoanalytic literature, the notion of instinct is frequently replaced by that of unconscious desire. Freud, in this *New Intro-ductory Lectures on Psycho-Analysis*, defined the unconscious as follows: ". . . We call a psychical process unconscious whose exis-tence we are obliged to assume—for some such reason as that we infer it from its effects—but of which we know nothing."[15] In other

---

15. Sigmund Freud, *New Introductory Lectures on Psycho-Analysis* (1933), reprinted in E. Kuykendall, *Philosophy in the Age of Crisis* (New York: Harper & Row, 1970), p. 122. To philosophers the above sounds like the kind of move John Locke made when he posited the existence of material substance as an explanatory account for why collections of qualities regularly occur to-gether. To the extent that the move is similar to Locke's, it is, of course, subject to the same types of criticisms.

words, the unconscious is not a thing, not some kind of container filled with desires that "drive" us to do this or that, but rather an explanatory device, not itself empirically evident, but *needed* to explain certain behavior which is. "Needed," that is, in the sense that there are certain "effects" that defy explanation, that simply cannot be accounted for unless we posit an unconscious. For example, if people say they desire one thing, but act as if they desired the contrary, and we know they are not lying, we may be tempted to say that they are somehow unaware of what their "real" motivation is.

If Susan says she wants a career more than anything else in the world, but she does nothing all day except stay home and put on make-up, we are puzzled and desire an explanation. If she is not lying or frivolous, we still lack an explanation; anything, including childhood and gene structure, is fair game as far as possible explanations go. But if Leslie has spent eight years preparing for a career and assures a prospective employer that she is serious about it, she does not deserve as an answer: "I would like to believe you, my dear, but all women really desire to devote their lives to men and children. . . ." Such a remark is unwarranted because there are no "effects" in this case that need to be explained. (Of course, external evidence of competence, such as Ph.D.'s and M.D.'s, do help when one wants to be taken seriously. The undergraduate argument, "she only went to college to find a husband," does not seem so plausible when applied to Ph.D.'s. There simply has to be an easier way to get a husband!)

.   .   .   .

I have tried to show some of the muddles that language of the "natural" gets us into. Except in cases where the natural is defined in terms of purpose or function, it carries no automatic value tag, and in no case carries an automatic moral implication. After finding out what a person means by "natural," we then have to decide on independent grounds whether what is meant is in any sense good. For example, why is it good to do what animals do, or to avoid invented devices which interrupt what ordinarily happens? Why is what ordinarily happens considered to be a good thing? What is so good about order? Teleological uses of "natural" automatically set up an evaluative context; knowing the function of "X" makes it possible for us to evaluate "X" on grounds of functioning well. But as we have seen, teleological uses have to be morally evaluated: a good bomb is one that destroys, but is a good bomb morally good?

There is no reason to assume that the problem of evaluation would change because some things are created by persons and others are not. Many people, for example, argue that nature is good because God made it. This, of course, precipitates the old problem of evil. How can earthquakes and birth defects be good? The answer does not abandon the language of purpose, but rather tells us in Platonic fashion that all of "creation" functions for some good end; however, humans are incapable of knowing this end or purpose. Indeed, part of what it means to have faith is to believe that all natural (that is, created) purposes (in humans or otherwise) are good purposes, and work together toward some larger purpose. Since human beings cannot know this larger end, there is no way that they can evaluate it. This, however, does not eliminate the problem of evaluation. It does not eliminate the question, "In what sense are things that function well good?" It simply tells us that there is no cognitive answer, or more precisely, that only the faithful, after they have been faithful in believing the acceptability of God's answer, will receive an answer. The position comes to this: because we believe in God, we should believe that nature is good in some good sense.

Theological positions, however, in no way exempt us from either defining what we mean by "natural" or appraising it. Indeed, even if the ultimate evaluation is said to be a matter of faith, the task that Thomas Aquinas referred to as natural or rational theology (the spelling out of the ends of things that are imprinted on the natures of things) is something that human beings must be prepared to perform without divine assistance. This task brings us right back to the beginning of our inquiry, namely, what in the world do people mean when they say that "X" is natural"?

*　　*　　*

The following article—"Sex Roles: The Argument from Nature," by Joyce Trebilcot (Washington University)—is excerpted from *Ethics* 85 (1975), pp. 249–55.

JOYCE TREBILCOT　'Sex Roles: the Argument from Nature'

I am concerned here with the normative question of whether, in an ideal society, certain roles should be assigned to females and others to males. In discussions of this issue, a great deal of attention is given to the claim that there are natural psychological differences between the sexes. Those who hold that at least some roles should be sex roles generally base their view primarily on an appeal to such natural differences, while many of those advocating a society without sex roles argue either that the sexes do not differ in innate psychological traits or that there is no evidence that they do.[1] In this paper I argue that whether there are natural psychological differences between females and males has little bearing on the issue of whether society should reserve certain roles for females and others for males.

Let me begin by saying something about the claim that there are natural psychological differences between the sexes. The issue we are dealing with arises, of course, because there are biological differences among human beings which are bases for designating some as females and others as males. Now it is held by some that, in addition to biological differences between the sexes, there are also natural differences in temperament, interests, abilities, and the like. In this paper I am concerned only with arguments which appeal to these psychological differences as bases of sex roles. Thus I exclude, for example, arguments that the role of jockey should be female because women are smaller than men or that boxers should be male because men are more muscular than women. Nor do I discuss arguments which appeal directly to the reproductive functions peculiar to each sex. If the physiological process of gestation or of depositing sperm in a vagina are, apart from any psychological correlates they may have, bases for sex roles, these roles are outside the scope of the present discussion.

It should be noted, however, that virtually all those who hold that there are natural psychological differences between the sexes assume that these differences are determined primarily by differences in biology. According to one hypothesis, natural psychological differences between the sexes are due at least in part to differences between female and male nervous systems. As the male fetus develops in the womb, the testes secrete a hormone which is held to influence the growth of the central nervous system. The female fetus does not produce this hormone, nor is there an analogous female hormone which is significant at this stage. Hence it is suggested that female and male brains differ in structure, that this difference is due to the prenatal influence of testicular hormone, and that the difference in brains is the basis of some later differences in behavior.[2]

A second view about the origin of allegedy natural psycho-

1. For support of sex roles, see, for example, Aristotle, *Politics*, book 1; and Erik Erikson, "Womanhood and the Inner Space," *Identity: Youth and Crisis* (New York: W. W. Norton & Co., 1968). Arguments against sex roles may be found, for example, in J. S. Mill, "The Subjection of Women," in *Essays on Sex Equality: John Stuart Mill and Harriet Taylor Mill*, ed. Alice S. Rossi (Chicago: University of Chicago Press, 1970), and Naomi Weisstein, "Psychology Constructs the Female," in *Women in Sexist Society*, ed. Vivian Gornick and Barbara K. Moran (New York Basic Books, 1971).

2. See John Money and Anke A. Ehrhardt, *Man and Woman, Boy and Girl* (Baltimore: Johns Hopkins Press, 1973).

logical differences between the sexes, a view not incompatible with the first, is psychoanalytical. It conceives of feminine or masculine behavior as, in part, the individual's response to bodily structure. On this view, one's more or less unconscious experience of one's own body (and in some versions, of the bodies of others) is a major factor in producing sex-specific personality traits. The classic theories of this kind are, of course, Freud's; penis envy and the castration complex are supposed to arise largely from perceptions of differences between female and male bodies. Other writers make much of the analogies between genitals and genders: the uterus is passive and receptive, and so are females; penises are active and penetrating, and so are males.[3] But here we are concerned not with the etiology of allegedly natural differences between the sexes but rather with the question of whether such differences, if they exist, are grounds for holding that there should be sex roles.

That a certain psychological disposition is natural only to one sex is generally taken to mean in part that members of that sex are more likely to have the disposition, or to have it to a greater degree, than persons of the other sex. The situation is thought to be similar to that of height. In a given population, females are on the average shorter than males, but some females are taller than some males, as suggested by figure 1. The shortest members of the population are all females, and the tallest are all males, but there is an area of overlap. For psychological traits, it is usually assumed that there is some degree of overlap and that the degree of overlap is different for different characteristics. Because of the difficulty of identifying natural psychological characteristics, we have of course little or no data as to the actual distribution of such traits.

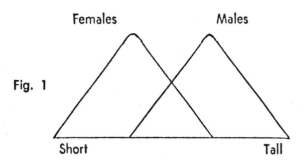

Fig. 1

Females   Males

Short   Tall

3. For Freud, see, for example, "Some Psychological Consequences of the Anatomical Distinctions between the Sexes," in *Sigmund Freud: Collected Papers*, ed. James Strachey (New York: Basic Books, 1959), 5:186–97. See also Karl Stern, *The Flight from Woman* (New York: Farrar, Straus & Giroux, 1965), chap. 2; and Erikson.

I shall not undertake here to define the concept of role, but examples include voter, librarian, wife, president. A broad concept of role might also comprise, for example, being a joker, a person who walks gracefully, a compassionate person. The genders, femininity and masculinity, may also be conceived as roles. On this view, each of the gender roles includes a number of more specific sex roles, some of which may be essential to it. For example, the concept of femininity may be construed in such a way that it is necessary to raise a child in order to be fully feminine, while other feminine roles—teacher, nurse, charity worker—are not essential to gender. In the arguments discussed below, the focus is on sex roles rather than genders, but, on the assumption that the genders are roles, much of what is said applies, *mutatis mutandis,* to them.

A sex role is a role performed only or primarily by persons of a particular sex. Now if this is all we mean by "sex role," the problem of whether there should be sex roles must be dealt with as two separate issues: "Are sex roles a good thing?" and "Should society enforce sex roles?" One might argue, for example, that sex roles have value but that, even so, the demands of individual autonomy and freedom are such that societal institutions and practices should not enforce correlations between roles and sex. But the debate over sex roles is of course mainly a discussion about the second question, whether society should enforce these correlations. The judgment that there should be sex roles is generally taken to mean not just that sex-exclusive roles are a good thing, but that society should promote such exclusivity.

In view of this, I use the term "sex role" in such a way that to ask whether there should be sex roles is to ask whether society should direct women into certain roles and away from others, and similarly for men. A role is a sex role then (or perhaps an "institutionalized sex role") only if it is performed exclusively or primarily by persons of a particular sex *and* societal factors tend to encourage this correlation. These factors may be of various kinds. Parents guide children into what are taken to be sex-appropriate roles. Schools direct students into occupations according to sex. Marriage customs prescribe different roles for females and males. Employers and unions may refuse to consider applications from persons of the "wrong" sex. The media carry tales of the happiness of those who conform and the suffering of the others. The law sometimes penalizes deviators. Individuals may ridicule and condemn role crossing and smile on conformity. Societal sanctions such as these are essential to the notion of sex role employed here.

I turn now to a discussion of the three major ways the claim that there are natural psychological differences between the sexes is held to be relevant to the issue of whether there should be sex roles.

1. *Inevitability.*—It is sometimes held that if there are innate psychological differences between females and males, sex roles are inevitable. The point of this argument is not, of course, to urge that there should be sex roles, but rather to show that the normative question is out of place, that there will be sex roles, whatever we decide. The argument assumes first that the alleged natural differences between the sexes are inevitable; but if such differences are inevitable, differences in behavior are inevitable; and if differences in behavior are inevitable, society will inevitably be structured so as to enforce role differences according to sex. Thus, sex roles are inevitable.

For the purpose of this discussion, let us accept the claim that natural psychological differences are inevitable. We assume that there are such differences and ignore the possibility of their being altered, for example, by evolutionary change or direct biological intervention. Let us also accept the second claim, that behavioral differences are inevitable. Behavioral differences could perhaps be eliminated even given the assumption of natural differences in disposition (for example, those with no natural inclination to a certain kind of behavior might nevertheless learn it; but let us waive this point). We assume then that behavioral differences, and hence also role differences, between the sexes are inevitable. Does it follow that there must be sex roles, that is, that the institutions and practices of society must enforce correlations between roles and sex?

Surely not. Indeed, such sanctions would be pointless. Why bother to direct women into some roles and men into others if the pattern occurs regardless of the nature of society? Mill makes the point elegantly in *The Subjection of Women:* "The anxiety of mankind to interfere in behalf of nature, for fear lest nature should not succeed in effecting its purpose, is an altogether unnecessary solicitude."[4]

It may be objected that if correlations between sex and roles are inevitable, societal sanctions enforcing these correlations will develop because people will expect the sexes to perform different roles and these expectations will lead to behavior which encourages their fulfillment. This can happen, of course, but it is surely not inevitable. One need not act so as to bring about what one expects. Indeed, there could be a society in which it is held that there are inevitable correlations between roles and sex but institutionalization of these correlations is deliberately avoided. What is inevitable is presumably not, for example, that every woman will perform a certain role and no man will perform it, but rather that most women will perform the role and most men will not. For any

4. Mill, p. 154.

individual, then, a particular role may not be inevitable. Now suppose it is a value in the society in question that people should be free to choose roles according to their individual needs and interests. But then there should not be sanctions enforcing correlations between roles and sex, for such sanctions tend to force some individuals into roles for which they have no natural inclination and which they might otherwise choose against.

I conclude then that, even granting the assumptions that natural psychological differences, and therefore role differences, between the sexes are inevitable, it does not follow that there must be sanctions enforcing correlations between roles and sex. Indeed, if individual freedom is valued, those who vary from the statistical norm should not be required to conform to it.

2. *Well-being.*—The argument from well-being begins with the claim that, because of natural psychological differences between the sexes, members of each sex are happier in certain roles than in others, and the roles which tend to promote happiness are different for each sex. It is also held that if all roles are equally available to everyone regardless of sex, some individuals will choose against their own well-being. Hence, the argument concludes, for the sake of maximizing well-being there should be sex roles: society should encourage individuals to make "correct" role choices.

Suppose that women, on the average, are more compassionate than men. Suppose also that there are two sets of roles, "female" and "male", and that because of the natural compassion of women, women are happier in female than in male roles. Now if females and males overlap with respect to compassion, some men have as much natural compassion as some women, so they too will be happier in female than in male roles. Thus, the first premise of the argument from well-being should read: Suppose that, because of natural psychological differences between the sexes, *most* women are happier in female roles and *most* men in male roles. The argument continues: If all roles are equally available to everyone, some of the women who would be happier in female roles will choose against their own well-being, and similarly for men.

Now if the conclusion that there should be sex roles is to be based on these premises, another assumption must be added—that the loss of potential well-being resulting from societally produced adoption of unsuitable roles by individuals in the overlapping areas of the distribution is *less* than the loss that would result from "mistaken" free choices if there were no sex roles. With sex roles, some individuals who would be happier in roles assigned to the other sex perform roles assigned to their own sex, and so there is a loss of potential happiness. Without sex roles, some individuals, we assume, choose against their own well-being. But surely we are not now in a position to compare the two systems with respect to the number of mismatches produced. Hence, the additional premise required for the argument, that overall well-being is greater with sex roles than without them, is entirely unsupported.

Even if we grant, then, that because of innate psychological differences between the sexes members of each sex achieve greater well-being in some roles than in others, the argument from well-being does not support the conclusion that there should be sex roles. In our present state of knowledge, there is no reason to suppose that a sex role system which makes no discriminations within a sex would produce fewer mismatches between individuals and roles than a system in which all roles are open equally to both sexes.

3 *Efficiency.*—If there are natural differences between the sexes in the capacity to perform socially valuable tasks, then, it is sometimes argued, efficiency is served if these tasks are assigned to the sex with the greatest innate ability for them. Suppose, for example, that females are naturally better than males at learning foreign languages. This means that, if everything else is equal and females and males are given the same training in a foreign language, females, on the average, will achieve a higher level of skill than males. Now suppose that society needs interpreters and translators and that in order to have such a job one must complete a special training program whose only purpose is to provide persons for these roles. Clearly, efficiency is served if only individuals with a good deal of natural ability are selected for training, for the time and effort required to bring them to a given level of proficiency is less than that required for the less talented. But suppose that the innate ability in question is normally distributed within each sex and that the sexes overlap (see fig. 2).

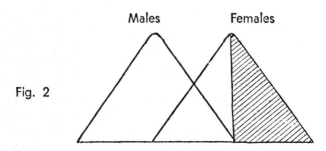

Fig. 2   Males   Females

If we assume that a sufficient number of candidates can be recruited by considering only persons in the shaded area, they are the only ones who should be eligible. There are no men in this group. Hence, although screening is necessary in order to exclude nontalented women, it would be inefficient even to consider men, for it is known that no man is as talented as the talented women.

In the interest of efficiency, then, the occupational roles of inter-
preter and translator should be sex roles; men should be denied
access to these roles but women who are interested in them, especially talented women, should be encouraged to pursue them.

This argument is sound. That is, if we grant the factual assumptions and suppose also that efficiency for the society we are concerned with has some value, the argument from efficiency provides
one reason for holding that some roles should be sex roles. This
conclusion of course is only prima facie. In order to determine
whether there should be sex roles, one would have to weigh efficiency, together with other reasons for such roles, against reasons
for holding that there should not be sex roles. The reasons against
sex roles are very strong. They are couched in terms of individual
rights—in terms of liberty, justice, equality of opportunity. Efficiency by itself does not outweigh these moral values. Nevertheless,
the appeal to nature, if true, combined with an appeal to the value
of efficiency, does provide one reason for the view that there
should be sex roles.

The arguments I have discussed here are not the only ones
which appeal to natural psychological differences between the sexes
in defense of sex roles, but these three arguments—from inevitability, well-being, and efficiency—are, I believe, the most common
and the most plausible ones. The argument from efficiency alone,
among them, provides a reason—albeit a rather weak reason—for
thinking that there should be sex roles. I suggest, therefore, that the
issue of natural psychological differences between women and men
does not deserve the central place it is given, both traditionally
and currently, in the literature on this topic.

It is frequently pointed out that the argument from nature functions as a cover, as a myth to make patriarchy palatable to both
women and men. Insofar as this is so, it is surely worthwhile ex-
ploring and exposing the myth. But of course most of those who use
the argument from nature take it seriously and literally, and this
is the spirit in which I have dealt with it. Considering the argument in this way, I conclude that whether there should be sex
roles does not depend primarily on whether there are innate psychological differences between the sexes. The question is, after
all, not what women and men naturally are, but what kind of
society is morally justifiable. In order to answer this question, we
must appeal to the notions of justice, equality, and liberty. It is
these moral concepts, not the empirical issue of sex differences,
which should have pride of place in the philosophical discussion
of sex roles.

*   *   *

The following articles—"'Because You Are a Woman'", by Joseph R. Lucas (Youngstown State University), and "Woman's Place," by Trudy R. Govier (Trent University)—are excerpted, respectively, from *Philosophy* 48, 1973, pp. 161–171, and *Philosophy* 44, 1974, pp. 303–309.

JOSEPH R. LUCAS 'Because You Are a Woman'

Plato was the first feminist. In the *Republic* he puts forward the view that women are just the same as men, only not quite so good. It is a view which has often been expressed in recent years, and generates strong passions. Some of these have deep biological origins, which a philosopher can only hope to recognize and not to assuage. But much of the heat engendered is due to unnecessary friction between views which are certainly compatible and probably correct. And here a philosopher can help. If we can divide the issues neatly, at the joints, then we need not quarrel with one another for saying something, probably true, because what is being maintained is misconstrued and taken to mean something else, probably false.

The feminist debate turns on the application of certain concepts of justice, equality and humanity. Should the fact—'the mere fact'—of a person's being a woman disqualify her from being a member of the Stock Exchange, the Bench of Bishops or the House of Lords, or from obtaining a mortgage, owning property, having a vote or going to heaven? Is it not, say the feminists, just as irrational and inequitable as disqualifying a man on the grounds of the colour of his hair? Is it not, counter the anti-feminists, just as rational as drawing a distinction between men on the one hand and children, animals, lunatics, Martians and computers on the other? Whereupon we come to enunciate the formal platitude that women are the same as men in some respects, different from them in others, just as men are the same in some respects as children, animals, lunatics, Martians and computers, and different in others. And then we have to embark on more substantial questions of the respects in which men and women are the same, and those in which they are different; and of whether any such differences could be relevant to the activity or institution in question, or could be comparable to the differences, generally acknowledged to exist, between *homo sapiens* and the rest of creation. Even if women are different from men, a feminist might argue, why should this be enough to debar them from the floor of the Stock Exchange, when, apparently, there is no objection to the presence of computers?

We are faced with two questions. We need to know first what exactly are the ways in which women differ from men, and this in turn raises issues of the methods whereby such questions may be answered. Only when these methodological issues have been discussed can we turn to the more substantial ones of morals and politics concerned with whether it can ever be right to treat a woman differently from a man on account of her sex, or whether that is a factor which must always be regarded as in itself irrelevant.

I

The facts of femininity are much in dispute. The development of genetic theory is some help, but not a decisive one. We know that men differ from women in having one Y-chromosome and only one X-chromosome whereas women have two X-chromosomes. Apart from the X- and Y- chromosomes, exactly the same sort of chromosomes turn up in men and women indifferently. The genetic make-up of each human being is constituted by his chromosomes, which occur in pairs, one of each pair coming from the father, the other from the mother. Men and Women share the same gene pool. So far as chromosomes, other than the X- and Y- ones, are concerned, men and women of the same breeding community are far more alike than members of different species, or even men of different races. This constitutes a powerful argument against the doctrine, attributed by some to the Mahometans, that women have no souls; contrary to the view of many young males, they are not just birds; or, in more modern parlance, it gives empirical support to arguments based on the principle of Universal Humanity. Women are worthy of respect, for the same reasons as men are. If it is wrong to hurt a man, to harm him, humiliate him or frustrate him, then it is wrong to hurt, harm, humiliate or frustrate a woman; for she is of the same stock as he, and they share the same inheritance and have almost all their chromosometypes in common.

Early genetic theory assumed a one-one correlation between pairs of hereditary genetic factors and their manifested effects in the individual. Whether I had brown eyes or blue eyes depended on whether I had the pair of factors BB, Bb or bB, in all of which cases I should have brown eyes, or whether I had bb, in which case I should have blue eyes. No other genetic factor was supposed to be relevant to the colour of my eyes, nor was the possession of a B or a b gene relevant to anything else about me. If this theory represented the whole truth, the feminist case would be simple. Sex is irrelevant to everything except sex. The fact of a man's being male or a woman's being female would be a 'mere fact' with no bearing on anything except sexual intercourse and the procreation of children. It would be rational to hold that only a male could be guilty of rape, and it might be permissible to have marriage laws which countenanced only heterosexual unions, and to look for proofs of paternity as well as of maternity. Perhaps we might go a very little further, and on the same grounds as we admit that negroes are not really eligible for the part of Iago, admit that males could not really expect to be employed as models for female fashions, and *vice versa*. Beyond these few and essentially unimportant exceptions, it would be as wrong for the law to discriminate between the sexes as it would be if it were to prefer blondes.

Simple genetic theory is, however, too simple. It needs to be complicated in two ways. First, although chromosomes occur in pairs, each single one being inherited more or less independently of every other one, each chromosome contains not just one, but many, many genetic factors, and these are not all independently inherited, and some, indeed, like the one responsible for haemophilia, are sex-linked. There are, so far as we know, relatively few effects—and those mostly bad—which are caused by factors contained in the Y-chromosome, and there is a slight *a priori* argument against many features being thus transmitted (because the Y-chromosome is much smaller than the others, and so, presumably, carries less genetic information): but there could well be more complicated effects due to a relatively rare recessive gene not being marked in the male as it probably would have been in the female. Mathematical talent might be like haemophilia or colour-blindness: it is consonant with what we know of genetic theory that only one in a thousand inherit the genetic factor, which if it is inherited by a boy then becomes manifest, but which if it is inherited by a girl, still in 999 cases out of a thousand is marked by a dominant unmathematicality. The second complication is more fundamental than the first. Genetic factors not only are not inherited independently of the others, but do not operate independently of the others. What is important is not simply whether I have BB, Bb, or bb, but whether I have one of these pairs in conjunction with some set of other pairs of factors. In particular, whether a person is male or female may affect whether or not some other hereditary factor manifests itself or not. Only men go bald. There are many physical features and physiological processes which are affected by whether a person is male or female. So far as our bodies are concerned, the fact of a person's being a man or a woman is 'a mere fact' but a fundamental one. Although there are many similarities between men and women, the differences are pervasive, systematic and of great biological significance. Almost the first question a hospital needs to ask is 'M or F?'.

Many feminists are dualists, and while conceding certain bodily differences between men and women, deny that there is any inheritance of intellectual ability or traits of character at all. Genetic theory, as far as it goes, is against them. There is reasonable evidence for the inheritance of skills and patterns of behavior in other animals, and in particular of those patterns of behaviour we should normally ascribe to the maternal instinct. Human beings are far too complicated to manifest many abilities or traits of character that are simple enough to be susceptible of scientific test; and although we often detect family resemblances in ways of walking and talking, as well as in temperament and emotion, it is not clear how far these are due to inherited factors and how far they have been acquired by imitation or learning. It is, however, a common experience to note resemblances between different members of the same family who have never seen each other and have had no opportunity of imitating one another. Such instances, when cited, are often dismissed as mere anecdotes, belonging to mythology rather than science, and unworthy of the attention of modern-minded thinkers in this day and age. It is difficult to stand one's ground in the face of the charge of being unscientific, for the word 'scientific' has strong evaluative overtones, and to be 'unscientific' smacks of quackery and prejudice. But it remains the case that all discussions about political and social issues must be 'unscientific' in that they are not exclusively based on the measurable results of repeatable experiments. For what we are concerned with is what people feel, decide, and ought to do about these things, and people are different, and feel differently and decide to do different things. If we refuse to admit to the argument any evidence other than the measurable results of reputable experiments, we may still be able to discuss questions of public health, but cannot even entertain those of justice or the political good. And if the feminist rejects all anecdotal evidence on principle, then she is making good her dualism by stipulation, because she is not prepared to recognize intellectual abilities or traits of character in the way in which they normally are recognized. This, of course, is not to urge that every story a boozy buffer cares to tell should be accepted as true or relevant; but only that the word 'scientific' needs to be handled with caution, and not used to rule out of court whole ranges of evidence and whole realms of experience. The canons of scientific evidence are, very properly, strictly drawn; and scientists accept the corollary that the topics amenable to scientific research are correspondingly limited. There are many discussions which cannot be evaluated within the canon of scientific argument upon the basis of scientific observations alone, among them discussions about what is right and good for individuals and societies. But they need not be any the worse for that, although they will be if the participants do not show the same fairness and reasonableness in their discussions as scientists do in their researches.

Another methodological issue is raised by those who acknowledge that there have been and are differences in the intellectual achievements and the typical behaviour of women as compared with men, but attribute all of them exclusively to the social pressures brought to bear upon women which have prevented them from exercising their talents to the full or giving rein to their natural inclinations. When the advocate of male supremacy marshals his masses of major poets against a solitary Sappho, the feminist explains that women have been so confined by domestic pressures and so inhibited by convention that those few with real poetic talent have never had the opportunity to bring it to flower. Poets might be poor, but at least they could listen to the Muse undistracted by baby's cries: whereas potential poetesses, unless their lot were cast in Lesbos, were married off and made to think of clothes and nappies to the exclusion of all higher thoughts.

It is difficult to find hard evidence either for or against this thesis. In this it is like many rival explanations or interpretations in history or literature. What moves us to adopt one rather than another is that it seems to us more explanatory or more illuminating than the alternative; and what seems to us more explanatory or illuminating depends largely on our own experience and understanding— and our own prejudices. But although we are very liable to be swayed by prejudice, it does not follow that we inevitably are, and although we are often guided by subjective considerations in deciding between various hypotheses, it does not follow that there is nothing, really, to choose between them. We can envisage evidence, even if we cannot obtain it, which would decide between the two alternatives. The feminist claim would be established if totally unisex societies sprang up and flourished; or if there were as many societies in which the roles of men and women were reversed as there were traditional ones. Indeed, the existence of any successful and stable society in which the roles of the sexes are reversed is evidence in favour of the claim. Evidence against is more difficult to come by. Few people deny that social pressures have a very considerable bearing on our behaviour and capacities. Some people argue from the analogy with other animals, whose behaviour is indubitably determined genetically and differs according to their sex; or argue, as I have done, by extrapolation from purely physical features. Both arguments are respectable, neither conclusive. Man is an animal, but very unlike other animals, particularly in respect of the extreme plasticity of human behaviour, nearly all of which is learned. Very few of our responses are purely instinctive; and it is unsafe to claim confidently that maternal feelings must be. What would constitute evidence against the feminist claim would be some intellectual ability or character trait which seemed to be both relatively independent of social circumstance and distributed unevenly between the sexes. Mathematical talent might be a case in point. It seems to be much more randomly distributed in the population than other forms of intellectual ability. If Ramanujan could triumph over his circumstances, then surely numerate sisters to Sappho should abound. But this is far from being a conclusive argument.

There are no conclusive arguments about feminine abilities and attitudes. But the discoveries of the scientists, so far as they go, lend some support to traditional views. It could well be the case that intellectual and psychological characteristics are, like physical ones, influenced by genetic factors. If this is so, the way in which a particular pair of genes in an individual genotype will be manifested in the phenotype will depend on the other genes in the genotype, and may depend greatly on whether there are two X chromosomes or one X and one Y. It could be that the masculine mind is typically more vigorous and combative, and the feminine mind typically more intuitive and responsive, with correspondingly different ranges of interests and inclinations. It would make evolutionary sense if it were, and would fit in with what else we know about the nature of man: but it is still possible to maintain the contrary view; and even if there are in fact differences between men and women, it does not follow that their treatment should be different too.

II

If it could be established that there were no innate intellectual or emotional differences between men and women, the feminists' case would be pretty well made; but it does not follow that to admit that there are differences carries with an adequate justification for every sort of discrimination, and it is useful to consider what sort of bearing various types of difference might have. Suppose, for example, that mathematical ability were distributed unevenly and according to the same pattern as haemophilia, so that only one in n males have it and only one in n^2 females. This would be a highly relevant factor in framing our educational policy. It would justify the provision of far more opportunities for boys to study higher mathematics than for girls. But it would not justify the total exclusion of girls. Most girls prefer nursing to numeracy, but those few who would rather solve differential equations ought not to be prevented from doing so on the grounds that they are female. Two principles underlie this judgment. First that the connexion between sex and mathematical ability is purely contingent; and secondly that we are in a position in which considerations of the individual's interests and deserts are paramount. Even if there are very few female mathematicians, there is no reason why any particular woman should not be a mathematician. And if any particular woman is, then her being a woman is irrelevant to her actual performance in mathematics. Her being a woman created a presumption, a purely contingent although usually reliable presumption, that she was no good at mathematics. It is like presumptive evidence in a court of law, which could be rebutted, and in this case was, and having been rebutted is of no more relevance in this individual situation, which is all we are concerned with.

Female mathematicians are rare. Few disciplines are so pure as mathematics. In most human activities—even in most academic pursuits—the whole personality is much more involved, and the irrelevance of a person's sex is far more dubious. Differences between the sexes are likely to come into play most in ordinary human relations where one person tells another what to do, or persuades, or cajoles or encourages or warns or threatens or acquiesces. In so far as most positions in society are concerned with social relations, it cannot be argued that the differences between the sexes are, of necessity, irrelevant. Although it might be the case that working men would as readily take orders from a fore-woman as a fore-man, or that customers would be as pleased to find a handsome boy receptionist as a pretty girl, there is no reason to suppose that it must be so. Moreover, life is not normally either an examination or a trial. It is one of the disadvantages of our meritocratic age that we too readily assume that all social transactions are exclusively concerned with the individual, who needs to be given every opportunity and whose rights must be zealously safeguarded. But examinations and trials are artificial and cumbersome exceptions to the general rule, in which no one individual is the centre of concern. To deny people the fruits of their examination success or to deprive them of their liberty on any grounds irrelevant to their own desert is wrong: but it is not so evidently wrong to frustrate Miss Amazon's hopes of a military career in the Grenadier Guards on the grounds not that she would make a bad soldier but that she would be a disturbing influence in the mess room. Laws and institutions are characteristically two-faced. They set norms for the behaviour of different parties, and need to take into consideration the interests and claims of more than one person. They also need to apply generally, and cannot be tailor-made to each particular situation: they define roles rather than fit actual personalities, and roles need to fit the typical rather than the special case. Even if Miss Amazon is sure not to attract sidelong glances from the licentious soldiery, her sisters may not be; and it may be easier to operate an absolute bar than leave it to the recruiting officer to decide whether a particular woman is sufficiently unattractive to be safe. This type of case turns up in many other laws and public regulations. We lay down rigid speed limits because they are easier to apply. There are many towns in which to drive at 30 mph would be dangerous, and many suburbs in which to drive at 45 mph would sometimes be safe. Some boys of ten are better informed about public affairs than other voters of thirty. But the advantage of having a fixed speed limit or a fixed voting age outweighs its admitted unfairness.

We can now see what sort of facts would bring what sort of principles to bear upon our individual decisions and the general structure of our laws and institutions. We need to know not only whether there are differences, but whether these differences are integrally or only contingently connected with a person's sex, and whether they apply in all cases or only as a rule. The more integrally and the more invariably a difference is connected with a person's sex, the more we are entitled to insist that the mere fact of being male or female can constitute a conclusive reason against being allowed to do something. The less integral a difference is, the more the arguments from Formal Equality (or Universalizability) and from Justice will come into play, requiring us to base our decisions only on the features relevant to the case in hand. The less invariable a difference is, the more the arguments from Humanity and again from Justice will come into play, requiring us to pay respect to the interests and inclinations of each individual person, and to weigh her actual interests, as against those of the community at large, on the basis of her actual situation and actual and reasonable desires.

However much I, a male, want to be a mother, a wife or a girlfriend, I am disqualified from those roles on account of my sex, and I cannot reasonably complain. Not only can I not complain if individuals refuse to regard me as suitable in those roles, but I have to acknowledge that it is reasonable for society generally to do so, and for the state to legislate accordingly. The state is justified in not countenancing homosexual 'marriages', because of our general understanding of what marriage really is, and the importance we attach to family life. For exactly the same reasons, women are debarred from being regarded in a fatherly or husbandly light; and hence also in those parts of the Christian Church that regard priests as being essentially fathers in God from being clergymen or bishops. How far roles should be regarded as being integrally dependent on sex is a matter of dispute. In very intimate and personal relationships it is evident that the whole personality is involved, and that since a man—or at least many, non-Platonic men— responds to a woman in a different way from that in which he responds to a man or a woman to a woman, it is natural that these roles should be essentially dependent on sex. But as the roles become more limited, so the dependence becomes less. I could hardly complain if I was not given the part of Desdemona or a job as an *au pair* boy on account of my sex: but if I had very feminine features and had grown my hair long and golden, or if I were particularly deft at changing nappies, I might feel a little aggrieved, and certainly I could call in question any law that forbade a man to play the part of a woman or be a nursemaid. Some substantial public good would need to be shown to justify a legal decision enforceable by penal sanctions being uniformly based not on my actual inability to fill the role required but only my supposed unsuitability on account of my sex. We demand a higher standard of cogency in arguments justifying what laws there should be than in those concerned only with individual decisions; and although this standard can be satisfied, often by admitting considerations of the public good, yet the arguments need to be adduced, because, in framing laws, we need to be sensitive to individual rights and careful about our criteria of relevance. Although it may be the case that a nurse is a better nurse for having the feminine touch, we hesitate to deem it absolutely essential; and although many more women than men have been good nurses, we do not believe that it must invariably be so. There are male nurses. We reckon it reasonable to prefer a woman in individual cases, but do not insist upon it in all cases by law. We are reluctant to impose severe legal disqualifications, but equally would hesitate to impose upon employers an obligation not to prefer women to play female parts or to be nurses or to join a family in an *au pair* capacity. For we recognize that a person's sex can reasonably be regarded as relevant to his or her suitability for particular posts, and that many institutions will operate on this basis, and are entitled to. I am justified in refusing to employ a male *au pair* girl or a female foreman, although if there are many males anxious to be looking after young children or many women anxious to supervise the work of others, it may be desirable on grounds of Humanity to establish special institutions in which they can fulfil their vocations. If we will not let Miss Amazon join the Grenadier Guards, let there be an ATS or WRAC for her to join instead.

Although we are rightly reluctant to impose legal disqualifications on individuals on grounds extraneous to their individual circumstances, it is inherent in all political thinking that we may find considerations of the general case over-riding those of the individual one; and often we frame our laws with an eye to what men and women are generally like rather than what they invariably are. A man may not adopt an infant girl unless she is more than twenty-five years younger than he; for some men might otherwise use adoption to acquire not so much a daughter as a wife. In many societies women have less freedom in disposing of their property than men; for else, things being as they are, some women would be prevailed upon to divest themselves of it to their long-term disadvantage. Ardent feminists have chafed at the shackles of marriage, and demand freedom from this degrading institution for their sisters as well as themselves. But if this freedom were established it would be the libertine males who would enjoy the benefits of liberation, being then free to leave the women to bear the burdens of parenthood all on their own. If most mothers care more for their children and their homes than most fathers do, then in the absence of institutions that recognize the fact they will in fact be disadvantaged. Some discrimination is needed to redress the balance. But discrimination, even positive discrimination, can work to the disadvantage of individuals, however much it may benefit most people on the whole.

The would-be female Stakhanovite is penalized by the law forbidding firms to employ female labour for sixty hours a week, just as the youthful entrepreneur is handicapped by his legal incapacity, as a minor, to pledge his credit except for the necessities of life, and the skilled racing motorist by the law forbidding him to drive, however safely, at more than 70 miles per hour. In each case the justification is the same: the restriction imposed on the individual, although real and burdensome, is not so severe as to outweigh the benefits that are likely to accrue in the long run to women in general, or to minors, or to motorists. It is in the nature of political society that we forgo some freedoms in order that either we ourselves or other people can secure some good. All we can in general demand is that our sacrifices should not be fruitless, and that if we give up some liberty or immunity it is at least arguable that it will be on balance for the best.

Arguments in politics are nearly always mixed, and involve appeals to different principles, according to how the question is construed. We can elucidate some canons of relevance for some of the principles which may be invoked. Where the principle is that of Universal Humanity, the reason 'Because you are a woman' is always irrelevant to its general applicability, though it may affect the way it is specified: perhaps women feel more strongly about their homes than men do, so that although we ought not, on grounds of humanity, to hurt either men or women, deprivation of her home would constitute a greater hurt to a woman than to a man. The principle of Universal Humanity is pervasive in its applications, but is conclusive only over a much more limited range. It is always wrong to torture; but often we cannot help hurting people's feelings or harming their interests if other values—justice, liberty, the public good—are to be preserved. And therefore arguments based on the principle of universal humanity may be overridden by ones based on other principles, also valuable. When the principle invoked is that of Formal Equality (or Universalizability) the reason 'Because you are a woman' cannot be dismissed out of hand as necessarily irrelevant. A person's sex is not a 'mere fact', evidently and necessarily separate from all other facts, and such that it is immediately obvious that no serious argument can be founded upon it. Particularly with those roles that involve relationships with other people, and especially where those relationships are fairly personal ones, it is likely to matter whether it is a man or a woman that is chosen. When some principle of Justice is at stake, the criteria of relevance become fairly stringent. We are concerned only with the individual's actions, attitudes and abilities, and the reason 'Because you are a woman' must either be integrally connected with the matter in issue (as in 'Why cannot I marry the girl I love?') or be reliably, although only contingently, connected with it (as in 'Why cannot I get myself employed for 60 hours a week?'); and in the latter case we feel that Justice has been compromised, although perhaps acceptably so, if there is no way whereby an individual can prove she is an exception to the rule and be treated as such. As the interests of the individual become more peripheral, or can be satisfied in alternative ways that are available, the principle of justice recedes, and we are more ready to accept rules and institutions based on general principles of social utility or tradition, and designed only to fit the general case. It is legitimate to base public feeling on such differences as seem to be relevant, but the more a law or an institution is based on merely a contingent, and not an integral, concomitance, the more ready we should be to cater for exceptions.

With sufficient care we may be able to disentangle what is true in the feminists' contention from what is false. At least we should be able to avoid the dilemma, which seems to be taken for granted by most participants in the debate, that we must say that women either are in all respects exactly the same as men or else are in all respects different from, and inferior to, them, and not members of the same universe of discourse at all. I do not share Plato's feelings about sex. I think the sexes are different, and incomparable. No doubt, women are not quite as good as men, *in some respects;* but since men are not nearly as good as women in others, this carries with it no derogatory implication of uniform inferiority. Exactly what these differences are, and, indeed, what sort of differences they are, is a matter for further research; and exactly what bearing they should have in the application of the various principles we value in making up our mind about social matters is a matter for further philosophical thought. But without any further thought we can align our emotions with the proponents of Women's Lib on the most important issue of all. What angers them most is the depersonalization of women in the Admass society: and one cannot but sympathize with their protest against women being treated as mere objects of sexual gratification by men; but cannot avoid the conclusion that their arguments and activities in fact lead towards just that result which they deplore. If we are insensitive to the essential feminity of the female sex, we shall adopt an easy egalitarianism which, while denying that there are any genetic differences, allows us to conclude in most individual cases that women, judged by male standards of excellence, are less good than their male rivals. Egalitarianism ends by depersonalizing women and men alike.

*   *   *

TRUDY R. GOVIER ' "Woman's Place" '

In 'Because You are a Woman' (*Philosophy*, April 1973) J. R. Lucas reaches the conclusion that some characteristics which are connected 'more integrally' and more invariably to a person's sex than others can provide a justification for certain types of sexual discrimination. Lucas distinguishes two questions basic to what he terms the feminist debate. What are the ways in which women differ from men? And could it ever be right to treat a woman differently from a man, simply because she is a woman? I shall argue that, despite Lucas's promise to discuss his topic as dispassionately as the subject allows, his account is biased in favour of the tradition of male domination. Furthermore he does not succeed in providing a justification for discrimination on the basis of sex in any of the areas he mentions.

The first section of Lucas's paper contains a discussion of the facts of femininity which offers a bewildering combination of layman's science, agnosticism, and traditional wisdom about the two sexes. Men and women, Lucas reminds us, differ genetically only in that men have a Y-chromosome in one pair where women have an X-chromosome. Chromosomes control many genetic factors each, and we know that some genetically carried features of human beings are sex-linked, as, for example, are colour-blindness and haemophilia. Lucas rightly points out that, in view of the genetically linked character of some human characteristics and in view of the genetic difference, albeit a small one, which does exist between men and women, it is unreasonable to reject in principle any systematic difference in intellectual capacities between the sexes. For feminists to be *a priori* dualists is both arbitrary and unscientific. So far, so good. As far as present scientific evidence goes, it is possible that some of these are inherited and even possible that some of these are inherited in a way which is sex-linked. Musical genius might appear genetically only in females, or genuine understanding of human problems only in males. These are possibilities.

But there are possibilities and possibilities. The two just mentioned are my own creations and do not appear in Lucas's article. The possibilities to which he devotes his attention are more conventional ones.

> Mathematical talent might be like haemophilia or colour-blindness: it is consonant with what we know of genetic theory that only one in a thousand inherit the genetic factor, which if it is inherited by a boy then becomes manifest but which if it is inherited by a girl, still in 999 cases out of a thousand is marked by a dominant unmathematicality. . . .
>
> It could be that the masculine mind is typically more vigorous and combative, and the feminine mind typically more intuitive and responsive, with a correspondingly different range of interest and inclinations.

In the face of the surface agnosticism expressed about what science tell us as to the 'facts of femininity', it is indeed suspicious to see that the possibilities singled out for special attention coincide so nicely with traditional beliefs about masculine and feminine traits.

Furthermore, intellectual capacities like mathematical ability or linguistic ability are not simple characteristics. They encompass complex patterns of behavior and in many of these a considerable amount of learning is necessary even if not sufficient. Perhaps for this reason, scientists have made no progress in isolating intellectual capacities and finding out which chromosomes, if any, might carry them or whether they have a substantial genetic component at all. The idea that mathematical ability might be as genetic and sex-linked as haemophilia should thus be approached with caution.

But suppose, just suppose, that genetic science had advanced to the point of being able to make perfect predictions about an individual's capacities from the chromosomal configuration of a cell in a human embryo. Such a degree of knowledge would face us with the thorny issue of genetic control. Just suppose that mathematical ability, which was still of some advantage to an individual, were genetic and sex-linked to the male. Why not alter the female's chromosomal configuration so as to give her this asset also? It is arguable that to refuse to do this would be tantamount to discrimination. At any rate, with the degree of genetic knowledge envisaged, the genetic facts about a person are not going to be brute unalterable facts any more than his shortsightedness is at present.

This brings us to a consideration of the second section of Lucas's paper, where the question of differential treatment of the sexes is explicitly raised. Lucas's overall response to this issue is indicated by his statement that 'The more integrally and the more invariably a difference is connected with a person's sex, the more we are entitled to insist that the mere fact of being male or female can constitute a conclusive reason against being allowed to do something'. Lucas does not really tell us what it is for a difference to be connected integrally with one's sex: he only contrasts *integral* connection with *purely contingent* connection. This raises a host of problems. Presumably having a vagina would be an integral feature of being female. Would having an Adam's apple be an integral feature of being male? Only men have these, but a man who had his Adam's apple surgically removed would not *ipso facto* cease to be a man. Given actual medical practice (not to mention medical possibilities) it is questionable whether any difference between the sexes is fully integral to them, if an integral difference is one which is logically essential to being of the sex in question. There are women without uteri. There are persons born with penises who develop breasts and arrange to have artificial vaginas constructed. Of course, some feature could be selected to provide the defining difference between the sexes, and then the possession of *that* feature by each sex would be integral to it. But the alliance of such a conventionally selected feature with any other would be at the mercy of medical technology. So even when we restrict our attention to purely physical characteristics, the distinction between features integral to a sex and those merely contingent to it is too wobbly to do any work at all.

Lucas's position does not rest to any great degree on this distinction, so far as I can make out. One of the confusing aspects of his paper is that it presents a variety of not very carelly distinguished reasons for discriminating between the sexes. Five of these can be distinguished: two rest on implausible empirical assumptions, two result from faulty methodology, and the fifth cannot properly operate on its own.

I. *Assumed Public Good.* If a substantial public good is at stake, Lucas maintains, individuals may rightly be denied positions in society which they would be perfectly competent to hold. This suggests that Lucas puts considerations of utility, or something like it, above those of justice—a priority which might be questioned. For the moment I shall ignore that difficulty and shall also forbear attempting to resolve any difficulties which might arise from the obscurity of the notion of the public good. Even granting these points, the claim remains problematic. Lucas seems willing to accept the empirical hypothesis that a certain amount of social disequilibrium (too much to bear, in fact) would result if women were priests or grenadiers, or if men were nursemaids. But as an empirical prediction, this is not very plausible. In the United States, Negroes are now dentists, Congressmen, professors, lawyers, and mayors of large cities. Yet forty years ago someone might have argued that their occupation of such positions would be against the public good because even though individuals might be qualified, the attitudes of many white people, and even some Negroes themselves, were such that the public good would not be served by such changes. Lucas says that some positions involve a person's whole personality and that sex is relevant to the way in which others will react to such a person. So it is. So too is race. But this fact does not license dire predictions of chaos ensuing when social changes are brought about. People's attitudes can and do change; when there are some Negro mayors, one is not prevented from respecting the mayor simply because he is a Negro. Similarly, if there were women priests it would not be long before people were able to confide in them.

So far my debate with Lucas on 'the public good' has been conducted on an empirical level. But let us suppose that Lucas is correct on the empirical question and (to take an example that he gives) that men would be seriously disturbed if women were to become priests. Would this justify excluding women from the priesthood? It is not clear that it would. The people who would be upset by the change are accustomed to having only men in this position, and some of their expectations would not be met if women began to take on the function also. Beliefs and attitudes would have to change and some frustration would doubtless be a feature of the transitional period. But if this kind of imbalance were enough to justify maintaining the *status quo,* it is difficult to see how any social change seeking to rectify injustices could ever be morally justified. In the short run, such changes are bound to cause some confusion and frustration, but past experience suggests that these need not be lastingly harmful to anyone.

2. *Protectivism.* Lucas cites some laws which are intended to protect women in particular and argues that these are justified because they benefit women generally although they might occasionally work against the interests of a particular woman. He cites property laws imposing restrictions on the way in which women may dispose of their property, differential treatment in marriage laws in case 'most mothers care more for their children and their homes than most fathers do', and labour laws limiting the number of hours women may work per week. In every one of these cases it would be possible and useful to formulate the law without reference to sex. After all, we can all use protection against con-men who masquerade as romantic partners: men, like women, might be 'prevailed upon to divest themselves of their property to their long-term disadvantage'. And working over sixty hours a week is not likely to be good for anyone's health. Lucas seems to assume that this would be too hard for women, but not too hard for men. But women out-

live men, suffer less from ulcers and heart disease, and are stronger in several non-muscular respects. A man's health is not less vulnerable than a woman's and there is no obvious reason why it should be denied equal legal protection.

The matter of marriage laws is more complicated because the whole institution of marriage has until quite recently been based upon traditional assumptions about male-female roles. If, as so often happens, a woman ceases to work outside the home when she marries, she is dependent upon her marriage for her economic subsistence in a way in which a man is not. She is more vulnerable to the dissolution of the marriage in that, having dropped out of the labour force in order to work in her home, she may later find it difficult to support herself. These factors might explain why some people, of whom Lucas appears to be one, believe that women care more about their homes and children than men do.

But the factors which have made it seem that women need special protection in marriage laws are economic vulnerability and the responsibility of children. A person whose economic self-sufficiency is limited by marriage needs and deserves some special assistance when that marriage ends. And a person who is left with the responsibility of children needs and deserves means to meet that responsibility. These factors could be incorporated into marriage law without reference to sex, and the law would then be fairer both to men and to women than it has been.

Human beings in some kinds of situations particularly need protection, but it is their situation and not their sex *per se* which makes them need it especially. It is better for the law to describe the situation in general terms than to name one sex and leave the other unprotected, even in those cases where prevailing social customs have meant that individuals of one sex are in that situation more frequently than individuals of the other.

3. *What 'We' Think.* Sometimes Lucas appeals to what 'we' think in apparent obliviousness of the fact that 'we'—whoever we are—could be floundering in moral confusion and error. The most flagrant example of this mistake is found in the following passage:

> The state is justified in not countenancing homosexual 'marriages', because of our general understanding of what marriage really is and the importance we attach to family life.

But 'our' understanding of what marriage really is is far from unanimous or perfect. Marriage typically involves companionship, child rearing, economic interdependence, sexual activity, and the sexual production of children. Only the last of these functions would be strictly impossible within a homosexual marriage, and whether this

400 CURRENT PHILOSOPHICAL ARTICLES

function is essential to marriage is certainly debatable. Many heterosexual couples avoid it through choice or necessity. As far as
the value 'we' attach to family life is concerned, there is no unan-
imity on this topic either, as the rising divorce rate and increasing
number of experimental communes indicate.

In the context of discussing the morality of sexual roles it is particularly otiose to appeal to what 'we' think. Not only is this logically irrelevant to moral questions about what these roles ought
to be, but there is just no consensus to appeal to. And yet Lucas
repeatedly speaks of what 'we' think: '*we* demand a higher standard of cogency in arguments justifying what laws there should
be than in those concerned only with individual decisions'; '*we*
reckon it reasonable to prefer a woman in individual cases (as a
nurse) but do not insist upon it in all cases by law'; '*we* recognize
that a person's sex can reasonably be regarded as relevant to him
or her suitability for particular posts, and that many institutions
will operate on this basis and are entitled to'. (All these insidious
uses of 'we' are found on a single page of the article.)

4. *Slippery Definitions.* Lucas says 'However much I, as a male,
want to be a mother, a wife, or a girlfriend, I am disqualified from
these roles on account of my sex and I cannot reasonably complain'. Now the word 'mother', 'wife', and 'girlfriend' are normally
used in such a way that to apply them to a person of the male sex
would constitute a logical error. So it might appear that a man
who complains that he cannot be someone's mother is complaining
about his inability to satisfy a logically contradictory description.
This would indeed be unreasonable. However a man might, due
to individual constitution or unfortunate personal circumstances,
urgently desire to fill the social role of a mother. If laws or extreme
social pressure prevent his having any chance of being allotted the
responsibility of (e.g.) cuddling, bathing, feeding, and playing
with his infant child, he may well complain. And there is no logical
truth about the femaleness of mothers which shows that *this* complaint is unreasonable.

The existence of sex-connoting labels serving to designate social
functions is not in itself sufficient to justify limiting those functions
to persons of the sex so singled out. For instance, consider the terms
'fireman' and 'midwife'. These strongly suggest, or perhaps even
logically require, individuals of the male and female sexes respectively. Yet for a woman to do what a fireman does would not be
impossible, either logically or physically. And if women took on
these functions, our language would probably shift so that 'fireman'
would less strongly connote a person of the male sex. Or perhaps
a new term would be developed. Already it appears that the meaning of the word 'chairman' is such that it is not logically impossible

for a chairman to be female. But if anything could lead one into sympathy with those who endorse such awkward terms as 'chairperson' and 'alterperson', it is the existence of arguments which purport to limit social functions to those of a single sex on the basis of analytic considerations about a language which was developed during periods when sexual roles were sharply stereotyped.

5. *The Necessary Generality of Laws and Institutions.* Lucas reminds us that laws and institutions cannot be tailor-made to fit every individual case. They have a necessary generality and, given this, it is inevitable that on occasion they will work against the interests of some. We are too concerned with individuals in our moral thinking, he says. Now it is true that laws and institutions must be based on principles formulated in general terms and it is true that, given this fact, we cannot avoid unfortunate consequences when these laws and institutions come to bear on highly unusual individual cases. These considerations would show that if there were other reasons for having sexually discriminatory laws, the injustices thereby done to a few exceptional women or men might be inevitable and excusable. But Lucas has not succeeded in putting forward any good reason for such laws. There is no demonstrated need to call his reasoning about general laws and the individual case into play.

The analogies Lucas offers in this connexion are poor ones, as they do not involve the injustices which sexually discriminatory laws would. (It is worth noting that Lucas himself admits that considerations of justice and equality weigh against sexually discriminatory laws.) No boy of ten can vote, although some boys of ten are better informed about political affairs than some men of forty-five, virtually all of whom can vote. This is unfair, in a way. But an individual has only to go on existing in order to be in a position where he will not suffer from the injustice any longer. Such a claim could not be made about a sexually discriminatory law. Another example Lucas offers by way of analogy is that of speed limits. There is a uniform speed limit in various locations but varying speeds would be safe at different locations. Now this case as Lucas sees it would give a good example of the generality of laws versus the variations of particular cases. But as far as justice is concerned, it is quite unproblematic. The law applies to everyone and quite probably benefits everyone. Any 'injustice' would have to be suffered by a location!

I have shown, I think, that Lucas does not offer any good reasons for his version of inegalitarianism. But before concluding, I cannot forbear commenting on the condescension manifested in the penultimate sentence of his article. 'If we are insensitive to the essential femininity of the female sex, we shall adopt an easy egalitarianism which, while denying that there are genetic differences, allows us to conclude in most individual cases that women, judged by male standards of excellence, are less good than their male 'rivals'. What are male standards of excellence? If they are not those currently embodied in educational, medical, legal, and other institutions, it is difficult to see the relevance of this remark. And if they are those current standards—as I suspect they must be—it is indeed revealing that Lucas is so sure that women will compare unfavourably to their male 'rivals'. It is also revealing that Lucas should identify the standards with *male* standards of excellence. *A priori*, there seems no special reason to think that university level examinations in biochemistry or ancient philosophy embody a standard of excellence which has any sexual orientation at all.

By now my own bias on this issue must be apparent. But, as Lucas does, I shall strive to express my conclusion as agnostically as possible: no good reason has been advanced for having laws or social institutions which discriminate between the sexes. That we do, in fact, have such laws and institutions is undeniable.

*   *   *

The following article is drawn from the *International Socialist Review*, September 1970.

EVELYN REED   'Women: Caste, Class or Oppressed Sex?'

The new stage in the struggle for women's liberation already stands on a higher ideological level than did the feminist movement of the last century. Many of the participants today respect the Marxist analysis of capitalism and subscribe to Engels's classic explanation of the origins of women's oppression. It came about through the development of class society, founded upon the family, private property, and the state.

But there still remain considerable misunderstandings and misinterpretations of Marxist positions, which have led some women who consider themselves radicals or socialists to go off course and become theoretically disoriented. Influenced by the myth that women have always been handicapped by their childbearing functions, they tend to attribute the roots of women's oppression, at least in part, to biological sexual differences. In actuality its causes are exclusively historical and social in character.

Some of these theorists maintain that women constitute a special class or caste. Such definitions are not only alien to the views of Marxism but lead to the false conclusion that it is not the capitalist system but men who are the prime enemy of women. I propose to challenge this contention.

The findings of the Marxist method, which have laid the groundwork for explaining the genesis of woman's degradation, can be summed up in the following propositions:

First, women were not always the oppressed or "second" sex. Anthropology, or the study of prehistory, tells us the contrary. Throughout primitive society, which was the epoch of tribal collectivism, women were the equals of men and recognized by man as such.

Second, the downfall of women coincided with the breakup of the matriarchal clan commune and its replacement by class-divided society with its institutions of the patriarchal family, private property and state power.

The key factors which brought about this reversal in woman's social status came out of the transition from a hunting and food-gathering economy to a far higher mode of production based upon agriculture, stock raising and urban crafts. The primitive division of labor between the sexes was replaced by a more complex social division of labor. The greater efficiency of labor gave rise to a sizable surplus product, which led first to differentiations and then to deepgoing divisions among the various segments of society.

By virtue of the directing roles played by men in large-scale agriculture, irrigation and construction projects, as well as in stock raising, this surplus wealth was gradually appropriated by a hierarchy of men as their private property. This, in turn, required the institution of marriage and the family to fix the legal ownership and inheritance of a man's property. Through monogamous marriage the wife was brought under the complete control of her husband who was thereby assured of legitimate sons to inherit his wealth.

As men took over most of the activities of social production, and with the rise of the family institution, women became relegated to the home to serve their husbands and families. The state apparatus came into existence to fortify and legalize the institutions of private property, male dominion and the father-family, which later were sanctified by religion.

This, briefly, is the Marxist approach to the origins of woman's oppression. Her subordination did not come about through any biological deficiency as a sex. It was the result of the revolutionary social changes which destroyed the equalitarian society of the matriarchal gens or clan and replaced it with a patriarchal class society which, from its birth, was stamped with discriminations and inequalities of many kinds, including the inequality of the sexes. The growth of this inherently oppressive type of socioeconomic organization was responsible for the historic downfall of women.

But the downfall of women cannot be fully understood, nor can a correct social and political solution be worked out for their liberation, without seeing what happened at the same time to men. It is too often overlooked that the patriarchal class systems which crushed the matriarchy and its communal social relations also shattered its male counterpart, the fratriarchy—or tribal brotherhood of men. Woman's overthrow went hand in hand with the subjugation of the mass of toiling men to the master class of men.

The import of these developments can be more clearly seen if we examine the basic character of the tribal structure which Morgan, Engels and others described as a system of "primitive communism." The clan commune was both a sisterhood of women and a brotherhood of men. The sisterhood of women, which was the essence of the matriarchy, denoted its collectivist character. The women worked together as a community of sisters; their social labors largely sustained the whole community. They also raised their children in common. An individual mother did not draw distinctions between her own and her clan sisters' progeny, and the children in turn regarded all the older sisters as their mutual mothers. In other words, communal production and communal possessions were accompanied by communal child-raising.

The male counterpart of this sisterhood was the brotherhood, which was molded in the same communal pattern as the sisterhood. Each clan or phratry of clans comprising the tribe was regarded as a "brotherhood' from the male standpoint just as it was viewed as a "sisterhood" or "motherhood" from the female standpoint. In this matriarchal-brotherhood the adults of both sexes not only produced the necessities of life together but also provided for and protected the children of the community. These features made the sisterhood and brotherhood a system of "primitive communism."

Thus, before the family that had the individual father standing at its head came into existence, the functions of fatherhood were a *social,* and not a *family* function of men. More than this, the earliest men who performed the services of fatherhood were not the mates or "husbands" of the clan sisters but rather their clan brothers. This was not simply because the processes of physiological paternity were unknown in ancient society. More decisively, this fact was irrelevant in a society founded upon collectivist relations of production and communal child-raising.

However odd it may seem to people today, who are so accustomed to the family form of child-raising, it was perfectly natural in the primitive commune for the clan brothers, or "mothers' brothers," to perform the paternal functions for their sisters' children that were later taken over by the individual father for his wife's children.

The first change in this sister-brother clan system came with the growing tendency for pairing couples, or "pairing families" as Morgan and Engels called them, to live together in the same community and household. However, this simple cohabitation did not substantially alter the former collectivist relations or the productive role of the women in the community. The sexual division of labor which had formerly been allotted between clan sisters and brothers became gradually transformed into a sexual division of labor between husbands and wives.

But so long as collectivist relations prevailed and women continued to participate in social production, the original equality between the sexes more or less persisted. The whole community continued to sustain the pairing units, just as each individual member of these units made his and her contribution to the labor activities.

Consequently, the pairing family, which appeared at the dawn of the family system, differed radically from the nuclear family of our times. In our ruthless competitive capitalist system every tiny family must sink or swim through its own efforts—it cannot count on assistance from outside sources. The wife is dependent upon the husband while the children must look to the parents for their subsistence, even if the wage earners who support them are stricken by unemployment, sickness or death. In the period of the pairing family, however, there was no such system of dependency upon "family economics," since the whole community took care of each individual's basic needs from the cradle to the grave.

This was the material basis for the absence, in the primitive commune, of those social oppressions and family antagonisms with which we are so familiar.

It is sometimes said or implied that male domination has always existed and that women have always been brutally treated by men. Contrariwise, it is also widely believed that the relations between the sexes in matriarchal society were merely the reverse of our own—with women dominating men. Neither of these propositions is borne out by the anthropological evidence.

It is not my intention to glorify the epoch of savagery nor advocate a romantic return to some past "golden age." An economy founded upon hunting and food-gathering is the lowliest stage in human development, and its living conditions were rude, crude and harsh. Nevertheless, we must recognize that male and female relations in that kind of society were fundamentally different from ours.

Under the clan system of the sisterhood of women and the brotherhood of men there was no more possibility for one sex to dominate the other than there was for one class to exploit another. Women occupied the most eminent position because they were the chief producers of the necessities of life as well as the procreators of new life. But this did not make them the oppressors of men. Their communal society excluded class, racial or sexual tyranny.

As Engels pointed out, with the rise of private property, monogamous marriage and the patriarchal family, new social forces came into play in both society at large and the family setup which destroyed the rights exercised by earliest womankind. From simple cohabitation of pairing couples there arose the rigidly fixed, legal system of monogamous marriage. This brought the wife and children under the complete control of the husband and father who gave the family his name and determined their conditions of life and destiny.

Women, who had once lived and worked together as a community of sisters and raised their children in common, now became dispersed as wives of individual men serving their lords and masters in individual households. The former equalitarian sexual division of labor between the men and women of the commune gave way to a family division of labor in which the woman was more and more removed from social production to serve as a household drudge for husband, home and family. Thus women, once "governesses" of society, were degraded under the class formations to become the governess of a man's children and his chief housemaid.

This abasement of women has been a permanent feature of all three stages of class society, from slavery through feudalism to capitalism. So long as women led or participated in the productive work of the whole community, they commanded respect and esteem. But once they were dismembered into separate family units and occupied a servile position in home and family, they lost their prestige along with their influence and power.

Is it any wonder that such drastic social changes should bring about intense and long-enduring antagonism between the sexes? As Engels says:

> "Monogamy then does by no means enter history as a reconciliation of man and wife, and still less as the highest form of marriage. On the contrary, it enters as the subjugation of one sex by the other, as the proclamation of an antagonism between the sexes unknown in all preceding history. . . . The first class antagonism appearing in history coincides with the development of the antagonism of man and wife in monogamy, and the first class oppression with that of the female by the male sex" (*Origin of the Family, Private Property, and the State*).

Here it is necessary to note a distinction between two degrees of women's oppression in monogamous family life under the system of private property. In the productive farm family of the pre-industrial age, women held a higher status and were accorded more respect than they receive in the consumer family of our own city life, the nuclear family.

So long as agriculture and craft industry remained dominant in the economy, the farm family, which was a large or "extended" family, remained a viable productive unit. All its members had vital functions to perform according to sex and age. The women in the family helped cultivate the ground and engaged in home industries as well as bearing children, while the children and older folks produced their share according to ability.

This changed with the rise of industrial and monopoly capitalism and the nuclear family. Once masses of men were dispossessed from the land and small businesses to become wage earners in factories, they had nothing but their labor power to sell to the capitalist bosses for their means of subsistence. The wives of these wage earners, ousted from their former productive farm and homecraft labors, became utterly dependent upon their husbands for the support of themselves and their children. As men became dependent upon their bosses, the wives became more dependent upon their husbands.

By degrees, therefore, as women were stripped of their economic self-dependence, they fell ever lower in social esteem. At the beginning of class society they had been removed from *social* production and social leadership to become farm-family producers, working through their husbands for home and family. But with the displacement of the productive farm family by the nuclear family of industrial city life, they were driven from their last foothold on solid ground.

Women were then given two dismal alternatives. They could either seek a husband as provider and be penned up thereafter as housewives in city tenements or apartments to raise the next generation of wage slaves. Or the poorest and most unfortunate could go as marginal workers into the mills and factories (along with the children) and be sweated as the most downtrodden and underpaid section of the labor force.

Over the past generations women wage workers have conducted their own labor struggles or fought along with men for improvements in their wages and working conditions. But women as dependent housewives have had no such means of social struggle. They could only resort to complaints or wrangles with husband and children over the miseries of their lives. The friction between the sexes became deeper and sharper with the abject dependency of women and their subservience to men.

Despite the hypocritical homage paid to womankind as the "sacred mother" and devoted homemaker, the *worth* of women sank to its lowest point under capitalism. Since housewives do not produce commodities for the market nor create any surplus value for the profiteers, they are not central to the operations of capitalism. Only three justifications for their existence remain under this system: as breeders, as household janitors, and as buyers of consumer goods for the family.

While wealthy women can hire servants to do the dull chores for them, poor women are riveted to an endless grind for their whole lives. Their condition of servitude is compounded when they are obliged to take an outside job to help sustain the family. Shouldering two responsibilities instead of one, they are the "doubly oppressed."

Even middle-class housewives in the Western world, despite their economic advantages, are victimized by capitalism. The isolated, monotonous, trivial circumstances of their lives lead them to "living through" their children—a relationship which fosters many of the neuroses that afflict family life today. Seeking to allay their boredom, they can be played upon and preyed upon by the profiteers in the consumer goods fields. This exploitation of women as consumers is part and parcel of a system that grew up in the first place for the exploitation of men as producers.

The capitalists have ample reason for glorifying the nuclear family. Its petty household is a goldmine for all sorts of hucksters from real estate agents to the manufacturers of detergents and cosmetics. Just as automobiles are produced for individual use instead of developing adequate mass transportation, so the big corporations can make more money by selling small homes on private lots to be equipped with individual washing machines, refrigerators, and other such items. They find this more profitable than building large-scale housing at low rentals or developing community services and child-care centers.

In the second place, the isolation of women, each enclosed in a private home and tied to the same kitchen and nursery chores, hinders them from banding together and becoming a strong social force or a serious political threat to the Establishment.

What is the most instructive lesson to be drawn from this highly condensed survey of the long imprisonment of womankind in the home and family of class society—which stands in such marked contrast to their stronger, more independent position in preclass society? It shows that the inferior status of the female sex is not the result of their biological makeup or the fact that they are the childbearers. Childbearing was no handicap in the primitive commune; it *became* a handicap, above all, in the nuclear family of our times. Poor women are torn apart by the conflicting obligations of taking care of their children at home while at the same time working outside to help sustain the family. Women, then, have been condemned to their oppressed status by the same social forces and relations which have brought about the oppression of one class by another, one race by another, and one nation by another. It is the capitalist system—the ultimate stage in the development of class society—which is the fundamental source of the degradation and oppression of women.

Some women in the liberation movement dispute these fundamental theses of Marxism. They say that the female sex represents a separate caste or class. Ti-Grace Atkinson, for example, takes the position that women are a separate *class:* Roxanne Dunbar says that they comprise a separate *caste*.[1] Let us examine these two theoretical positions and the conclusions that flow from them.

First, are women a caste? The caste hierarchy came first in history and was the prototype and predecessor of the class system. It arose after the breakup of the tribal commune with the emergence of the first marked differentiations of segments of society according to the new divisions of labor and social functions. Membership in a superior or inferior station was established by being born into that caste.

It is important to note, however, that the caste system was also inherently and at birth a class system. Furthermore, while the caste system reached its fullest development only in certain regions of the world, such as India, the class system evolved far beyond it to become a world system, which engulfed the caste system.

This can be clearly seen in India itself, where each of the four chief castes—the Brahmans or priests, the soldiers, the farmers and merchants, and the laborers, along with the "out-castes" or pariahs—had their appropriate places in an exploitative society. In India today, where the ancient caste system survives in decadent forms, capitalist relations and power prevail over all the inherited precapitalist institutions, including the caste relics.

However, those regions of the world which advanced fastest and farthest on the road to civilization bypassed or overleaped the castle system altogether. Western civilization, which started with ancient Greece and Rome, developed from slavery through feudalism to the maturest stage of class society, capitalism.

Neither in the caste system nor the class system—nor in their combinations—have women comprised a separate caste or class. Women themselves have been separated into the various castes and classes which made up these social formations.

1. Cf. Atkinson, "Radical Feminism," *supra,* and Dunbar, "Female Liberation as the Basis for Social Revolution" in *Sisterhood Is Powerful,* edited by Robin Morgan, Vintage Books 1970, pp. 477–92.

The fact that women occupy an inferior status as a *sex* does not *ipso facto* make women either an inferior caste or class. Even in ancient India women belonged to different castes, just as they belong to different classes in contemporary capitalist society. In the one case their social status was determined by birth into a caste; in the other it is determined by their own or their husband's wealth. But the two can be fused—for women as for men. Both sexes can belong to a superior caste and possess superior wealth, power and status.

What, then, does Roxanne Dunbar want to convey when she refers to all women (regardless of class) as comprising a separate caste? And what consequences for action does she draw from this characterization? The exact content of both her premise and her conclusions are not clear to me, and perhaps to many others. They therefore deserve closer examination.

Speaking in a loose and popular way, it is possible to refer to women as an inferior "caste"—as is sometimes done when they are also called "slaves" or "serfs"—when the intent is merely to indicate that they occupy the subordinate position in male-dominated society. The use of the term "caste" would then only expose the impoverishment of our language, which has no special word to indicate womankind as the oppressed sex. But more than this seems to be involved, if we judge from the paper by Roxanne Dunbar dated February 1970 which supersedes her previous positions on this question.

In that document she says that her characterization of women as an exploited caste is nothing new; that Marx and Engels likewise "analyzed the position of the female sex in just such a way." This is simply not the case. Neither Marx in *Capital,* nor Engels in *The Origin of the Family, Private Property, and the State,* nor in any writings by noted Marxists from Lenin to Luxemburg on this matter, has woman been defined by virtue of her sex as a "caste." Therefore this is not a mere verbal squabble over the misuse of a term. It is a distinct departure from Marxism, although presented in the name of Marxism.

I would like clarification from Roxanne Dunbar on the conclusions she draws from her theory. For, if all women belong to an inferior caste, and all men belong to the superior caste, it would consistently follow that the central axis of a struggle for liberation would be a "caste war" of all women against all men to bring about the liberation of women. This conclusion would seem to be confirmed by her statement that "we live under an international caste system. . . ."

This assertion is equally non-Marxist. What Marxists say is that we live under an international *class* system. And they further state that it will require not a caste war, but a *class struggle*—of all the

oppressed, male and female alike—to consummate women's liberation along with the liberation of all the oppressed masses. Does
Roxanne Dunbar agree or disagree with this viewpoint on the paramount role of the class struggle?

Her confusion points up the necessity for using precise language
in a scientific exposition. However downtrodden women are under
capitalism, they are not chattel slaves any more than they are feudal
serfs or members of an inferior caste. The social categories of slave,
serf and caste refer to stages and features of past history and do
not correctly define the position of women in our society.

If we are to be precise and scientific, women should be defined
as an "oppressed *sex*."

Turning to the other position, it is even more incorrect to characterize women as a special "class." In Marxist sociology a class
is defined in two interrelated ways: by the role it plays in the
processes of production and by the stake it has in the ownership
of property. Thus the capitalists are the major power in our society
because they own the means of production and thereby control
the state and direct the economy. The wage workers who create
the wealth own nothing but their labor power, which they have to
sell to the bosses to stay alive.

Where do women stand in relation to these polar class forces?
They belong to all strata of the social pyramid. The few at the
top are part of the plutocratic class; more among us belong to the
middle class; most of us belong to the proletarian layers of the
population. There is an enormous spread from the few wealthy
women of the Rockefeller, Morgan and Ford families to the millions of poor women who subsist on welfare dole. *In short, women,
like men, are a multiclass sex.*

This is not an attempt to divide women from one another but
simply to recognize the actual divisions that exist. The notion that
all women as a sex have more in common than do members of the
same class with one another is false. Upper-class women are not
simply bedmates of their wealthy husbands. As a rule they have
more compelling ties which bind them together. They are economic, social and political bedmates, united in defense of private
property, profiteering, militarism, racism—and the exploitation of
other women.

To be sure, there can be individual exceptions to this rule, especially among young women today. We remember that Mrs.
Frank Leslie, for example, left a $2 million bequest to further the
cause of women's suffrage, and other upper-class women have
devoted their means to secure civil rights for our sex. But it is
quite another matter to expect any large number of wealthy women
to endorse or support a revolutionary struggle which threatens
their capitalist interests and privileges. Most of them scorn the

liberation movement, saying openly or implicitly, "What do we need to be liberated from?"

Is it really necessary to stress this point? Tens of thousands of women went to the Washington antiwar demonstrations in November 1969 and again in May 1970. Did they have more in common with the militant men marching beside them on that life-and-death issue—or with Mrs. Nixon, her daughters, and the wife of the attorney general, Mrs. Mitchell, who peered uneasily out of her window and saw the specter of another Russian Revolution in those protesting masses? Will the wives of bankers, generals, corporation lawyers, and big industrialists be firmer allies of women fighting for liberation than working-class men, black and white, who are fighting for theirs? Won't there be both men and women on both sides of the class struggle? If not, is the struggle to be directed against men as a sex rather than against the capitalist system?

It is true that all forms of class society have been male-dominated and that men are trained from the cradle on to be chauvinistic. But it is not true that men as such represent the main enemy of women. This crosses out the multitudes of downtrodden, exploited men who are themselves oppressed by the main enemy of women, which is the capitalist system. These men likewise have a stake in the liberation struggle of the women; they can and will become our allies.

Although the struggle against male chauvinism is an essential part of the tasks that women must carry out through their liberation movement, it is incorrect to make that the central issue. This tends to conceal or overlook the role of the ruling powers who not only breed and benefit from all forms of discrimination and oppression but are also responsible for breeding and sustaining male chauvinism. Let us remember that male supremacy did not exist in the primitive commune, founded upon sisterhood and brotherhood. Sexism, like racism, has its roots in the private property system.

A false theoretical position easily leads to a false strategy in the struggle for women's liberation. Such is the case with a segment of the Redstockings who state in their *Manifesto* that "women are an oppressed *class*." If all women compose a class then all men must form a counterclass—the oppressor class. What conclusion flows from this premise? That there are no men in the oppressed class? Where does this leave the millions of oppressed white working men who, like the oppressed blacks, Chicanos and other minorities, are exploited by the monopolists? Don't they have a central place in the struggle for social revolution? At what point and under what banner do these oppressed peoples of all races and both sexes join together for common action against their common enemy? To oppose women as a class against men as a class can only result in a diversion of the real class struggle.

Isn't there a suggestion of this same line in Roxanne Dunbar's assertion that female liberation is the basis for social revolution? This is far from Marxist strategy since it turns the real situation on its head. Marxists say that social revolution is the basis for full female liberation—just as it is the basis for the liberation of the whole working class. In the last analysis the real allies of women's liberation are all those forces which are impelled for their own reasons to struggle against and throw off the shackles of the imperialist masters.

The underlying source of women's oppression, which is capitalism, cannot be abolished by women alone, nor by a coalition of women drawn from all classes. It will require a worldwide struggle for socialism by the working masses, female and male alike, together with every other section of the oppressed, to overthrow the power of capitalism, which is centered today in the United States.

In conclusion, we must ask, what are the connections between the struggle for women's liberation and the struggle for socialism?

First, even though the full goal of women's liberation cannot be achieved short of the socialist revolution, this does not mean that the struggle to secure reforms must be postponed until then. It is imperative for Marxist women to fight shoulder to shoulder with all our embattled sisters in organized actions for specific objectives from now on. This has been our policy ever since the new phase of the women's liberation movement surfaced a year or so ago, and even before.

The women's movement begins, like other movements for liberation, by putting forward elementary demands. These are: equal opportunities with men in education and jobs; equal pay for equal work; free abortions on demand; and child-care centers financed by the government but controlled by the community. Mobilizing women behind these issues not only gives us the possibility of securing some improvements but also exposes, curbs and modifies the worst aspects of our subordination in this society.

Second, why do women have to lead their own struggles for liberation, even though in the end the combined anticapitalist offensive of the whole working class will be required for the victory of the socialist revolution? The reason is that no segment of society which has been subjected to oppression, whether it consists of Third World people or of women, can delegate the leadership and promotion of their fight for freedom to other forces—even though other forces can act as their allies. We reject the attitude of some political tendencies that say they are Marxists but refuse to acknowledge that women have to lead and organize their own independent struggle for emancipation, just as they cannot understand why blacks must do the same.

The maxim of the Irish revolutionists—"who would be free themselves must strike the blow"—fully applies to the cause of women's liberation. Women must themselves strike the blows to gain their freedom. And this holds true after the anticapitalist revolution triumphs as well as before.

In the course of our struggle, and as part of it, we will reeducate men who have been brainwashed into believing that women are naturally the inferior sex due to some flaws in their biological makeup. Men will have to learn that, in the hierarchy of oppressions created by capitalism, their chauvinism and dominance is another weapon in the hands of the master class for maintaining its rule. The exploited worker, confronted by the even worse plight of his dependent housewife, cannot be complacent about it—he must be made to see the source of the oppressive power that has degraded them both.

Finally, to say that women form a separate caste or class must logically lead to extremely pessimistic conclusions with regard to the antagonism between the sexes in contrast with the revolutionary optimism of the Marxists. For unless the two sexes are to be totally separated, or the men liquidated, it would seem that they will have to remain forever at war with each other.

As Marxists we have a more realistic and hopeful message. We deny that women's inferiority was predestined by her biological makeup or has always existed. Far from being eternal, woman's subjugation and the bitter hostility between the sexes are no more than a few thousand years old. They were produced by the drastic social changes which brought the family, private property and the state into existence.

This view of history points up the necessity for a no less thoroughgoing revolution in socioeconomic relations to uproot the causes of inequality and achieve full emancipation for our sex. This is the purpose and promise of the socialist program, and this is what we are fighting for.

✽   ✽   ✽

PROLOGUE

This concluding selection may be viewed as an invitation to continue pondering the question asked throughout this book. "The woman question," like "the man question" or "the human question," will need to be examined so long as there are women who uniquely live its answer in a changing world. It is a question whose relevance is obvious as we move into the area of concern to which Gould's article directs us—to the social and political forum where people are practically affected by concepts such as those in this book, and where their own concepts are bound to affect the lives of others. Analysis and assessment of such concepts remains the philosophical tasks of each of us. Thus the proper study of mankind, as Pope suggests, continues to be man and woman.

The article is excerpted from *Women and Philosophy* by Carol Gould and Max Wartofsky.

CAROL C. GOULD 'The Woman Question: Philosophy of Liberation and the Liberation of Philosophy'

INTRODUCTION

Is the woman question a philosophical question? Can philosophy deal with such issues as women's social role, their oppression and liberation?[1] I shall argue against a prevailing view that it cannot

1. "The Woman Question" as it will be used in this paper denotes the range of issues which concerns women's social and economic oppression and exploitation, historically and in the present; their liberation; their roles in society, in the family; relations between the sexes; sexual equality; and the question of what constitutes women as a gender. I leave out biological characteristics as such for the reasons given in fn. 6 below. My use of the term "The Woman Question" differs from its historical usage within the Marxist tradition. In that tradition, the term has been used in both anthropological and social-political discussion. It connotes a "special" question, generally subsumed under the "more universal" issue of class-oppression and to be explained or elucidated in

and try to show how a critical philosophy can do so.

The woman question is a paradigm of the sort of question which concerns a particular and limited part of society or of humanity (like questions concerning race or social class), or a particular and limited historical or social form (like capitalism or liberal democracy). In attempting to treat such questions philosophically, one is often faced with a standard methodological objection: namely, that the woman question like these others is too "special," "limited" or "partial," and therefore it is not a properly philosophical question because it does not deal with an appropriately universal subject matter.[2] Philosophy's concern, it is argued, is with the human *qua* human, or with human nature as such, rather than with such "particular" and "applied" social questions, or with such "accidental" differences as gender. An appropriate philosophical subject matter, the objection continues, is defined by a criterion of universality which abstracts from such differences.

My argument (in Part I) will begin with a reconstruction of this objection stated in its methodologically sharpest form. I shall then attempt to refute it It will be seen that what is at issue is the criterion of universality itself—or rather, two opposed criteria of universality. The first—that of the objectors—I shall characterize as *abstract universality*. This will be the subject (a) an analytical critique, and (b) of a critique of its ideological and practical consequences. The alternative which I shall propose, taken from the Hegelian and Marxist dialectical tradition, is that of *concrete universality*. I hope to show that on this criterion, the woman question *is* a philosophical question, and further, that on this

---

terms of it. Thus, women's liberation has typically been subsumed under the more general concern for the liberation of the working class from capitalist exploitation. "The Woman Question" therefore has the "special" status accorded to other class-subordinate questions such as "The Jewish Question," "The National Question," etc. Now although I agree that the liberation of women is closely tied to general human emancipation from exploitation, I do not hold that all forms of the oppression and exploitation of women are to be accounted for by class-exploitation or what derives from it. Thus, in using the term "The Woman Question" to denote a broad range of issues, I propose to free the question from this narrow context, while retaining whatever useful connotations the term has as designating a social, historical and economic question.

2. While it is true that most philosophers do not self-consciously go about justifying what they do on some appeal to an adequate universality of scope— they rather just do what they do, either within established norms or beyond them—the objection to treating the woman question as a philosophical question is widely met in discussion (although not explicitly in print). Even among those who do not openly raise such objections, there is often tacit consent to its inappropriateness, witnessed in part by the *fact* that the question has barely been discussed.

criterion, the task of giving a philosophical critique of the present social reality becomes a viable and necessary function of philosophy. I shall then propose, programmatically (in Part II), in a critique of the concept of the family, and of women's role in contemporary society, *how* such a philosophical approach to the woman question may be carried out. Thus what I take the women question to be, both in form and content, will emerge in this second part of the paper. The criterion of concrete universality will provide the methodological guidelines for what I propose as the proper philosophical approach.

It will be seen, therefore, that I take the woman question to be not simply an abstract question (about the concept or definition of "woman" or about the "nature of woman"), but rather a question which grows out of the concrete social and historical facts of the oppression and exploitation of women and their struggle for liberation. It is thus concerned with such issues as the changing social roles of women in society, in the family and in relations between the sexes; sexual equality; the historically and socially evolved characteristics which constitute women as a gender; and present forms of domination and exploitation. Fundamentally, it is the question of how to critically understand and change the realities of woman's life in society.

Feminists have taken the woman question to be a philosophical question in two very different ways. The first approach addresses the problem of universality in the following way: since women, like men, are persons or human beings, they have all and only those rights which apply universally to humans *qua* human. The differences between men and women beyond the "real," i.e., biological, differences are interpreted as *"merely"* social, cultural and historical. On this view, being a woman is an accidental, and neither a universal nor an essential property of being human, since one may be human and not female.[3] These feminists argue further, that to recognize a sexual polarity between men and women beyond the biological differences leaves women open to continued unequal treatment and to the continued institutionalization of these sex differences. On this view, although there are of course some philosophical issues which arise from and bear on the situation of women, women as such cannot constitute a philosophical notion or category.[4] Other feminists have argued that the sexual polarity

3. Whereas contemporary usage frequently takes "male" and "female" to refer to biological sex differences, and "man" and "woman" to refer to social and cultural sex differences, in this article I am interpreting "female" as "woman," and therefore will use the terms interchangeably. Thus, glossing the usage distinction follows from my argument, since as will be seen, I am interpreting sex difference as fundamentally social and not *fundamentally* biological in nature.

establishes fundamental categories of human nature, and that therefore there is no common universal human nature, but only male nature and female nature. This view implies that "woman" is a fundamental philosophical notion, insofar as it establishes sex difference as essential or categorical.[5]

My position is distinct from both of these. Although I want to hold that the question of women *is* philosophical (as on the second view), this does not commit me to the claim that the differences between men and women are fundamental differences of natures. Instead, while arguing that the question of women is philosophical, I also want to claim (as on the first view), that the oppression of women as well as all significant differences between men and women are *thoroughly historical, social and cultural*.[6] Now I can

4. Alison Jaggar's discussion is paradigmatic. See "On Sexual Equality," in *Ethics*, July 1974.

5. This position is implied in the writings of several radical feminists, e.g., Robin Morgan, "Introduction," *Sisterhood is Powerful* (N. Y., Vintage, 1970), but it has rarely been proposed by feminist philosophers. A modified form of this position is presented by Christine Allen in "Women and Persons," in *Mother was not a Person*, ed. by Margaret Andersen (Montreal, Content Publishing and Black Rose Books, 1972). Allen suggests that the sexual polarity is fundamental, although she regards it as the product not only of physiological factors, but also the "self-determining" identity which women have achieved through the history of their struggles and oppression. Thus Allen here appears to make sex difference a function not of nature (except in the sense of anatomical difference) but of history. However, her understanding of the difference remains abstract and ahistorical, because it is seen as determined not by the interrelations of the sexes, but rather by "self-determination," where this is understood in the existentialist sense of the creation of essence by activity. However, a question of consistency arises with respect to her work: how can sex-polarity be "fundamental," if each person is uniquely self-determining? How does the self-determining, self-creating individual achieve anything but an individual nature or essence? In terms of the woman question, we might ask: why should we suppose that an anatomically "female" person should determine herself as a woman, rather than as either a man or an androgyne? Why should she accept her heritage? The connection between Allen's claim that sex difference is fundamental, and her claim that a woman, *qua* person, is basically self-determining, remains obscure.

6. In claiming that significant differences between men and women are thoroughly historical, social and cultural, I am indeed denying that the difference is fundamentally or significantly biological. That there *are* biological differences between men and women is obviously true. The point is that there are infinitely many differences among individuals, any of which is logically an equal candidate for making group distinctions among humans. So for example, left- and right-handedness, hair color, the number of hairs on one's head, the religion of one's mother and one's place of birth are all distinctions of this sort. But only some of them have been selected out for importance. Which ones have been selected is a function of the historical, social and cultural role which has been assigned to the characteristic in question. Thus, in denying that the biological difference is an essential or fundamental difference, I am asserting

maintain these seemingly incompatible positions at the same time because I would claim that social, cultural and historical differences can be relevant philosophical differences. Or to put it differently, that being human is essentially a social, historical and cultural matter, and that differences which are rooted in such contexts are therefore philosophically relevant differences.

PART I

A. *The Criterion of Abstract Universality as a Methodological Criterion for what is 'Philosophical'*

The objection raised at the outset claims that a properly universal subject matter cannot be constituted by "particular" or "accidental" social or historical differences. Rather, it insists on a criterion of universality which abstracts from differences in gender and therefore excludes the woman question as a philosophical one. I call this the criterion of *abstract universality*. I shall begin with a reconstruction of the argument (in the form of premises and conclusion) on which the objection is based. I shall call this the *Essentialist* argument[7] and attempt to show how it can be refuted on its own grounds.

Essentialist Premise 1. Unlike the special sciences, or the practical arts, philosophy is the study of first principles, i.e., of those universal principles which are common to all knowledge. The appropriate subject matter of philosophy, therefore, is that which is universal and essential, and excludes particular and accidental differences, which cannot be the subject of universal principles or laws.

Essentialist Premise 2. In the domain of the human, or of the social, philosophy therefore studies what is common to all human beings or to all societies at all times, and does not take as its subject merely local or accidental parts or aspects of the human or social.

---

that it becomes one only through its historical and cultural development, and therefore that the gender distinction between men and women is thoroughly a product of this development, and not a given fact of nature. This paper does not attempt to prove this point in a direct way, although it supports this claim indirectly. Further arguments are offered by Ruth Herschberger, *Adam's Rib* (New York, Harper & Row, 1970), and by Eva Figes, in *Patriarchal Attitudes* (New York, Fawcett Books, 1971). See also Gina Bari Kolata, "Kung Hunter-Gatherers, Feminism, Diet and Birth Control," in *Science*, Vol. 185, Sept. 1974, pp. 932 ff.

7. In this discussion, I shall be using the term "universality" (in the phrases "abstract universality" and "concrete universality" in its strong sense, to mean the same as "essentiality," and not in the weaker senses of accidental universality or as merely designating what is the same in all cases of a given sort.

It studies the human *qua* human, or human nature as such.

Essentialist Premise 3. Gender (i.e., being male or being female), is an accidental and not an essential or universal property of human beings, since one may be human and not female, or human and not male. Whereas it is true that being either male or female (i.e., having *some* gender), is a necessary property, being male or being female are not each necessary properties.

Conclusion. Since being a woman is such an accidental property, the question of women is not a philosophical question, because the domain in question is not appropriately universal or essential, in the sense required by Premises 1–3.

This conclusion may be strengthened by analogy: All human beings have language and therefore it is a proper philosophical question to discuss the nature of language, but it is not a proper philosophical question to discuss the nature of the English or Chinese languages. Similarly, although all human beings have gender, it is not a proper philosophical question to discuss the specific differences of being male or being female. Such questions are 'special' questions for applied or technical knowledge. Thus it is appropriate for linguistics to discuss the English and Chinese languages, but not for the philosophy of language (except perhaps as examples of more general principles). Similarly, it is appropriate for endocrinology or psychology of personality to discuss sex-differentiation, but not for philosophy.

Now let us examine the methodological premises of such an Essentialist view: What is universal, and therefore the proper subject matter for philosophical inquiry, consists in what is common or the same in all members of a given class. But this cannot be merely an accidental universality, i.e., it cannot be merely contingently the case that all members of a given class share some property in common. Rather, the universal properties must also be necessary, i.e., those without which the individuals would not be members of a given class, and therefore those properties which make them the kinds of things they are.[8] Furthermore, such an essential property must be unique to the members of that class, shared by members of that class only. These conditions of universality, necessity and uniqueness determine what the essential properties are.[9]

8. Cf. Plato, *Republic,* I, 352: ". . . a thing's function is the work that it alone can do or can do better than anything else." Here Plato, in distinguishing carving knives, chisels and pruning knives, makes "proper function" the basis for what kind of a thing something is. Aristotle (*Nichomachean Ethics,* I, 7) similarly defines the distinctive human function to be an activity involving reason, since reason is what distinguishes humans from all other beings and therefore makes them the kind of things they are.

9. In describing *a priori* knowledge Kant says, "Necessity and strict universality are thus sure criteria of *a priori* knowledge and are inseparable from

In order to establish such essential properties, one must abstract from all differences among members of a class, or regard these differences as *indifferent*.[10] Differences are therefore taken to be accidental, and only what is universal in the strong or nomic sense is taken to be essential.[11] As a consequence, in considering the human, all historical and social differentiation drops out and only those abstracted properties which remain invariant for all humans and in all societies count as essential. The term "abstract" here is contrasted with its opposite, "concrete," where "concrete" denotes those properties which individuate human beings or societies or which differentiate them, that is, which make them the particular individuals or societies they are.

However, this exclusion of the concrete, the different, the individual from the domain of philosophy may occasion a certain philosophical uneasiness. Suppose the objection were to be raised against Essentialism that it is too rigorously abstract in insisting on universality; that since it is not concerned with the concrete and particular relations existing among individuals in society at a given time, it will be incapable of dealing with specific social and historical problems or with present life.

To such an objection the Essentialist could reply: "But why should one burden *philosophy* with such a specific task? Why not leave it to politics, economics, history, sociology and psychology? Why conflate philosophy with the social or human sciences, as special sciences? Indeed, if the critique of the present is really a matter of *applied* critique, as it must be, why not leave the real critique to political and social practice or to action?" A socially-

---

one another." (*Critique of Pure Reason*, B4). By "strict universality" he means not that universality derived inductively from experience which he called "only assumed or comparative universality," but that in which "no exception is allowed as possible." Where Kant is using the terms "necessity" and "universality" to refer to conditions which a judgment must meet if it is to be one which represents *a priori* knowledge, I am using these terms to denote the conditions a property must have if it is to be essential.

10. Cf. Descartes' discussion of the piece of wax in the *Meditations* ("Second Meditation"). Descartes is attempting to discover the essential property of the wax. He first lists all the "accidental" properties and then removes them, in imagination, by bringing the wax close to the fire. Taste, color, odor, shape vanish; size increases; the wax becomes liquid; it grows hot. Still, we have a clear and distinct idea that it is the "same" piece of wax through all these changes. Thus, according to Descartes, "by rejecting everything that does not belong to the wax, to see what remains, we are led to the essential properties." This reduction and exclusion of "accidental" properties is classically Essentialist.

11. Cf. Ernest Nagel, *The Structure of Science* (New York, Harcourt Brace and World, Inc., 1961), pp. 56 ff.

conscious Essentialist might point out that a criterion of abstract universality itself has a critical social function, on the following grounds: "A really universal view of what is human treats all humans as (abstractly) equal in capacities, rights, obligations, etc. The abstractness is no weakness, but a strength. For example, if gender differences are not to be taken into account in defining the essence of humanity, then to the degree that the accidental difference of being a woman keeps her from full equality of rights, the society falls short of being just. In this way, abstract universality has an implicitly critical function: it presents the norm by which to measure the achievements of a given society in overcoming those differences which are accidental and which therefore should not count.[12] It is the abstract universals, and not the differences, which serve as a critical measure for existing social reality. Let us take the *philosophical* task to be the establishment, by analysis and construction, of such norms. And let it be the task of applied social practice and the social sciences to see how far such norms are fulfilled."

I have thus far presented the methodological premises and some arguments of Essentialism. I shall argue that if the Essentialist is to carry out the project of Essentialism itself—namely, the determination and investigation of essential properties, then he cannot exclude accidental differences from the domain of what is properly philosophical. If this is so, then the Essentialist argument fails, and the conclusion which excludes the woman question as properly philosophical is not warranted.

The first way in which one may show that the Essentialist argument fails is to demonstrate that the premises of the argument are incoherent or inconsistent. This may be seen as follows; Premise 2 excludes the consideration of accidental differences from philosophy. Premise 3 names and characterizes just such a difference—i.e., gender. But on a strict reading of Premise 2, Premise 3 falls outside the domain of philosophy proper, since it describes an accidental difference; therefore strictly speaking, Premise 3 is unstateable philosophically. If Premise 3 smuggles in a non-philosophical description as the basis for a philosophical argument, it violates Essentialism's own exclusion of such subject matter. But the con-

12. Cf. Plato, *Republic*, V, 472. To Glaucon's question concerning how the ideal state could ever exist, Socrates explains that the idea (or norm) was presented so that it might serve as a measure or pattern for existing states (and individuals): ". . . When we set out to discover the essential nature of justice and injustice and what a perfectly just and a perfectly unjust man would be like, supposing them to exist, our purpose was to use them as ideal patterns. . . . We did not set out to show that these ideas could exist in fact. . . . We have been constructing in discourse the pattern of an ideal state. Is our theory any the worse, if we cannot prove it possible that a state so organized should be actually founded?"

clusion of the argument depends on Premise 3, and without it the argument fails.

It may be objected that this is a sophistical argument or a dialectical ploy which may easily be countered. Thus the Essentialist might respond as follows: "the *naming of* accidental differences such as gender doesn't constitute treating them philosophically, but only serves to identify what is to be excluded from such treatment. Knowing *that* something is an accidental property is not yet investigating or establishing *what* that property is in any philosophical sense. Just as one may name things which don't exist (e.g., unicorns) without ontological commitment, so one may name accidental properties (e.g., gender) without methodological commitment to any philosophical treatment. So if one says, for example, that 'The woman question is not a philosophical question,' that doesn't amount to treating the woman question philosophically."

Against this defense, I shall argue that the Essentialist cannot exclude accidental properties from philosophical consideration if his task is the determination of which properties are essential. Consider the case of establishing the essential properties of the class of humans: such properties must be shown to be *universal*, i.e., shared by all human beings, and *necessary*, such that anything which lacks such properties is not human. Furthermore, since an essence determines what kind of thing something is, it can be shared by things of that kind only. That is, an essential human property is one which only humans have; it is *unique* to humans. Therefore, the Essentialist attempts to discover a criterion for what is essentially human which will be able to *exclude* anything which is not human, as well as to *include* everything which is. Without such exclusion (e.g., of the property "having a heart," which although universal and necessary for humans is not exclusively human), all animals, for example, would have to be included as human, and his criterion would be inadequate. Moreover, the Essentialist's criterion has to exclude those accidental properties which only some human beings have (like "speaking English"), on the grounds that such properties are neither universal or necessary, although they may be uniquely human.

In examining any human property, the Essentialist does not know *a priori* whether it meets these conditions.[13] Since such properties do not come marked as "essential" or "accidental," he cannot know in advance whether he is examining an essential or an accidental property. His investigation (whether conceptual or empirical) has

13. One Essentialist move, not considered here, is that in which the claim is made that essences are intuited *a priori*, and therefore that no "procedure" for discovering essences is viable, since it is at best inductive. I am assuming here that this argument is not made by the Essentialist in question. This argument would require a separate treatment which I am not undertaking here.

to establish this. The Essentialist therefore has to be able to demarcate essential from accidental properties and exclude the accidental properties *as accidental*, he has to be able to recognize both the (human) instances in which these properties occur and those in which they do not occur (to determine that the properties are neither necessary nor universal). In addition, he has to be able to recognize non-human cases in which they occur (to determine that the properties are not uniquely human).

For example, suppose that the Essentialist were trying to discover whether right-handedness is an essential or an accidental human property. First of all, he would have to be able to recognize right-handedness in all the human cases in which it occurs. He would also have to be able to tell that it does *not* occur in all cases, i.e., that it is absent in a given case. Moreover, he would have to be able to recognize whether such a property as right-handedness occurs in non-human cases, in order to establish whether or not it is uniquely human. Since he cannot know in advance of his investigation whether right-handedness is an essential or accidental property, he must have knowledge of this property in order to carry out his investigation. That is to say, he must know what the concept right-handedness means, i.e., he must be able to use it to refer to actual cases. As we know, right-handedness is an accidental property. Yet in order to establish that it is and thereby to exclude it from the domain of essential properties, the Essentialist needs to have knowledge of this accidental property. Therefore, he cannot exclude such knowledge of accidental properties from his philosophical task of discovering the essential properties.

But what if the property he is investigating is essential, although he does not know this at the outset? In that case, will it be necessary for the Essentialist to have knowledge of (or be able to recognize) accidental properties in order to recognize the essential one? Here he may argue that he only has to recognize that the property (e.g., speech) is shared by all and only humans; and therefore, although he has to recognize cases in which this essential property is lacking (i.e., the non-human ones, in order to establish its uniqueness and its necessity), he does not have to recognize accidental properties at all. We might agree that in such a circumstance the Essentialist would happily have hit upon a case in which knowledge of accidental properties is not required.[14] How-

14. This point—that accidental properties can be excluded from consideration when one is investigating an essential property—need not be conceded so readily. On one view (e.g., that of Leibniz or of Hegel), if something fails to have a certain property, it is not simply a case of the absence of a property, but rather a case in which that thing is a different thing because it is lacking the given property. This follows on a view which holds that things are constituted by their properties, or alternatively, are constituted by their relations to

ever, since the Essentialist cannot know in advance whether the properties under investigation are essential or accidental (for otherwise his investigation would be unnecessary), he would still have to meet the requirements of the first case (right-handedness) in order to exclude the accidental properties. But as we have seen, to fulfill these requirements he must have knowledge of the accidental properties.

In summary, in order for the Essentialist to recognize which human properties are essential, he has to be able to consider *any* human property. But unless all human properties are essential—which is absurd—the Essentialist will have to include accidental properties in his investigation. Therefore, the Essentialist will have to know such properties in order to be able to established that they are accidental. The Essentialist therefore has to be able to recognize not only what is the same in all human cases, but also what is different—what is different in some human cases of what is different between human and non-human cases. Similarly, in order to demarcate essential from accidental properties, the Essentialist has to be able to recognize not only what remains invariant, but also what changes. This is exemplified in the case of the wax in Descartes' *Meditations:* specifically, Descartes has to be able to apprehend such accidental properties as color, shape and smell, in order to eliminate them as accidental (after perceiving that they changed, or were absent), and in order to establish which property (extension, in this case) remains invariant.[15]

I have argued that the Essentialist has to include consideration of accidental properties as part of his philosophical task. If my argument is correct, then Premises 1 and 2, which state that philosophy is to be concerned only with essential properties and not with accidental ones, are false about Essentialism's own procedure, or beg the question, since we cannot know in advance of philosophical inquiry which properties are accidental and which are essential. But if Premises 1 and 2 are false as procedural premises, or beg the question, the argument fails.

The Essentialist may resort to still one more argument: he may concede that he has to know which properties are accidental and

---

all other things, where different relations determine different properties. Thus, in noting that a property is absent, one is noting a difference. In the case where the property in question is an essential property, in order to be able to tell when it is absent (to establish its necessity or uniqueness), one has to recognize the case of its absence as the *positive* case of a different property and one which is accidental relative to the essential one. The development of this point goes beyond what can be suggested here however. Cf. Leibniz, *Discourse on Metaphysics, Monadology,* and Hegel, "Doctrine of Essence" in *Science of Logic.*

15. Descartes, *Meditations,* II.

that therefore knowledge of such accidental properties is required. But he may argue that such knowledge comes from outside philosophy proper, that it is derived from common sense or from science. (Similarly, he might argue that the initial determination of essential properties, prior to a systematic conceptual analysis, is background knowledge and not itself part of philosophy, but rather what philosophy presupposes). So he may argue, "Everyone knows that gender is an accidental property, since everyone knows that not all humans are female and that one may be non-female and still human. This isn't philosophical knowledge, but common sense."

I would argue that here the Essentialist is not only appealing to extra-philosophical premises, but that he is accepting them uncritically. Now there is hardly a question that gender is in fact an accidental property (to use the Essentialist's terms). But whether it is or not, is beside the point, since what is at issue is a methodological argument concerning whether the philosopher can rely on common sense or science for the determination of accidental properties. *Uncritical* acceptance by philosophy of either common sense judgments or scientific judgments is problematic, since both common sense and science have yielded false judgments. For example, at one time it was a common sense belief that the earth was stationary; and much of pre-modern physics asserted that atoms were hard, impenetrable substances. Furthermore, if the Essentialist were only to codify what common sense or scientific beliefs take to be essential or accidental, he could hardly be said to be fulfilling the task set by Essentialism. For in that case Essentialism would be redundant.

However, do common sense and science in fact deliver such distinctions between essence and accident? In the example of gender, it is not at all clear that common sense makes this distinction. Rather, common sense often characterizes the distinction between men and women as an ultimate or essential distinction and doesn't regard it as indifferent. Thus men are viewed as dominant, women as subordinate; one as the "stronger," the other as the "weaker" sex; one is capable of leadership and rule, the other as primarily assigned to following and serving. Common sense is thus neither consistent nor articulate in the way required to make the Essentialist's distinction concerning the accidental property of gender—namely, that it is accidental because men and women are equally and essentially human and that the difference makes no difference. A similar case might be made for science, inasmuch as the history of the discussion of sex-difference (in, for example, endocrinology or psychology) includes a set of views which regard the gender difference as biologically or psychologically essential. Although I would disagree with such views, they certainly do not conform to the Essentialist's understanding of gender as an accidental difference. Thus science also does not yield a consistent understanding of this distinction[16] and the Essentialist therefore cannot uncritically rely on it either.

Therefore, the Essentialist cannot evade the task of determining philosophically which differences are accidental, either a) by his general methodological claim that differences are to be excluded and only essences considered (as we have shown), or b) by appealing to some extra- or non-philosophical account of accidental properties. His task would rather seem to be to question critically the uncritical accounts of common sense and the often uncritical accounts of science. However, this requires that he undertake a philosophical investigation of the properties as well as these accounts of them, in order to establish whether they are accidental or essential.

Here another difficulty presents itself for the Essentialist which we may call "Hair, Mud, Dirt" difficulty, after Plato's account of it in the *Parmenides*. In Parmenides' critique of the theory of Forms, the issue arises whether there are universal forms or essences for such lowly things as hair, mud and dirt. Socrates is unwilling to concede that there are, but cannot answer why there should not be.[17] A similar problem arises for the Essentialist when he attempts to demarcate essential from accidental properties. Specifically, one may ask (with respect to *any* essential property): "Why stop there?" Why, for example, should "human" be taken to be essential, and "male" or "female" accidental? May we not take "animal" as essential, and "human" as an accidental property (together with, say, "bovine" or "reptilian")? Most important for our purposes, why not take "male" and "female" as essential properties, since these have sometimes been taken to constitute an essential distinction of a cosmic sort (e.g., in Pythagorean dualism, or in Yin and Yang cosmology). I would hold that such an essential distinction of gender is wrong. Nonetheless, this argument suggests that the Essentialist has no methodogical way to exclude such alternative demarcations of essence and accident. Moreover, he cannot argue that what is taken to be an essence is relative, or that one person's essence is another person's accident, because on his view what is essential is not a matter of choice or convention, but rather of the way things are.

The exclusion of gender as an accidental property and thus as not appropriate subject matter for philosophical discourse is therefore unfounded on the grounds of the relativity of essential proper-

16. Cf. Ruth Herschberger, *op. cit.*

17. Plato, *Parmenides*, 130 c-d.

ties. Since one can argue, like Parmenides, that essential properties may be established for *any* class of things and thus not only for gender, but for more "local" properties such as red-headedness, English-speaking, or being an inhabitant of New York City, the force of the Essentialist's exclusion of gender is lost. But if this is so, then the whole Essentialist enterprise as expressed in the reconstructed Premises 1, 2 and 3 is ill-founded, and certainly one cannot sustain Premise 3, concerning gender as an accidental property. The conclusion which excludes the woman question from philosophy therefore fails.

One further thing might be said in this context: if one can establish an essence for any class of things, then the Essentialist's choice of one property as essential, with respect to which certain others are accidental, does not depend on methodological considerations alone; rather, this choice must depend on other factors, if it is not a random choice. But if, as we have suggested, the Essentialist's choice depends on the uncritical acceptance of the common sense or scientific beliefs of his time as to what is essential and what accidental, then he is open to the intrusion of the uncriticized dominant beliefs or social prejudices of his own time or of his social context. What he takes to be the essential properties as well as his characterization of them may then reflect such contingent social and historical beliefs or prejudices. It is this phenomenon which I shall investigate in the following section.

Finally, we may note yet another sort of argument against Essentialism to be taken up later. It concerns the use of abstract universal criteria as norms. The socially conscious Essentialist has argued that abstract universal norms (for example, "equal justice for all") are effective social instruments. Such norms are based on the view that what is essentially human determines the equal ontological status of all human beings in all societies at all time. Equal rights, obligations, opportunities are in turn based upon this equal ontological status. Such abstract principles, e.g., of equality, permit one to establish violations of the norm simply on the grounds that human beings are not treated equally *qua* human (leaving all inessential differences aside). My criticism is not of this function of Essentialist norms. But as I hope to show later, this very strength can also be regarded as a weakness in practical contexts; for, in practice, what is at issue is not only that an injustice has been done, but also what the source or character of the injustice has been. This distinction between abstract justice (the equal treatment of human beings *qua* human regardless of differences) and concrete cases of injustice (e.g., sex discrimination, racism, etc.) will be seen to be important in the subsequent discussion of universal norms in the section on concrete universality.

B. *A Critique of Abstract Universality in Practice; Human Nature—Universal or Male?*

There is a further practical criticism of the criterion of abstract universality: namely, that its use to determine essential human properties is not a value-free, but a value-laden one, that it reflects the interests, needs and prejudices of particular social groups. This is problematic for two reasons: (1) Such prejudices may introduce distortions into the very understanding of what is essential. But this is not decisive, for it could be argued that any philosophical approach is subject to the unintended intrusion of interests and needs, and that this is only what one might expect. However, (2) I shall argue further that Essentialism reflects such interests in a particularly harmful way, because it tends to mask them under the guise of universality and therefore is deceptive. I am not claiming that the criterion of abstract universality lends itself to such distortion or deception because it is somehow inherently vicious or because it is consciously conceived to make particular interests under the guise of universality. Rather, I hope to show that it is the very abstractness of the criterion which opens it to such distortion, and this by way of its exclusion of concrete social and historical differences as accidental and therefore philosophically irrelevant.

In particular, I shall suggest that the criterion of abstract universality, in actual philosophical practice, turns out to choose those properties as essentially and universally human which the philosophers themselves have either explicitly identified as male properties, or which were associated with roles and functions in which males predominated. As a critique of abstract universality, I hope to show how allegedly transhistorical, necessary and universal properties which are chosen to characterize human nature as such, in fact turn out upon examination to be something less than universal; in fact, they reflect the historical and social limitations and prejudices of their time, and specifically the sex-bias or male-domination of their social context. Thus instead of being necessary and universal, such properties are in fact contingent and particular. But if this is so, then the claim of universality itself masks this one-sidedness. However, since there is no doubt that the philosophers to be examined here were pursuing the essential in a systematically rigorous way, we may wonder why they were prone to such distortion. In the course of the discussion which follows, I shall present some hypotheses to explain this.

The discussion in this section can be understood to point two ways: first, it continues the critique of abstract universality, but here in terms of its practical effects, rather than in terms of its formal inadequacies as a descriptive or normative criterion; second, the discussion leads to the proposal for an alternative criterion of universality which is capable of taking actual differences into account, and is therefore capable of including the woman question as a critical philosophical one. The following discussion does not attempt to be demonstrative, but only suggestive. Consequently, I shall put forth hypotheses in rather bald form, as possible directions for future inquiry.

In the first set of cases to be examined, the connection between human nature and male nature is either explicitly made or implied, with women characterized quite differently. The case of Kant is perhaps paradigmatic here. According to Kant in the *Fundamental Principles of the Metaphysics of Morals*,

> "That is practically *good*, however, which determines the will by means of the conceptions of reason . . . on principles which are valid for every rational being as such. It is distinguished from the *pleasant* as that which influences the will only by means of sensation from merely subjective causes, valid only for the sense of this or that and not as a principle of reason which holds for every one."[18]

> "Now I say: man and generally any rational being exists as an end in himself."[19]

But if we turn to Kant's *Observations on the Feeling of the Beautiful and the Sublime* (admittedly an early work), we find that women lack these humanly essential characteristics and most clearly they lack the sort of moral agency which is characteristic of human nature (*qua* rational). Thus Kant writes,

> "Women will avoid the wicked not because it is unright, but only because it is ugly. . . . Nothing of duty, nothing of compulsion, nothing of obligation! . . . They do something only because it pleases them. . . . I hardly believe that the fair sex is capable of principles."[20]

Rather, "Her philosophy is not to reason, but to sense."[21] Furthermore,

18. Kant, *Fundamental Principles of the Metaphysic of Morals* (Indianapolis, Bobbs-Merrill, 1949), p. 30.

19. *Ibid.*, p. 45.

20. Kant, *Observations on the Feeling of the Beautiful and the Sublime*, trans. by John Goldthwait (Berkeley, Univ. of Calif., 1960), p. 81.

21. *Ibid.*, p. 79.

"All the other merits of a woman should unite solely to enhance the character of the beautiful which is the proper reference point; . . . all education and instruction must have [this]
before its eyes. . . . Deep meditation and long-sustained
reflection are noble but difficult, and do not well befit a person
in whom unconstrained charms should show nothing else than
a beautiful nature. A woman who has a head full of Greek,
like Mme. Dacier, or carries on fundamental controversies
about mechanics, might as well have a beard."[22]

A similar prejudice is revealed by Fichte who, when speaking of
"our race" in *The Vocation of Man*, writes:

"I must be free; for that which constitutes our true worth is
not the mere mechanical act, but the free determination of
free will, for the sake of duty. . . ."[23]

but who, when speaking of woman in *The Science of Rights* claims
that

"[she] is subjected through her own necessary wish—a wish
which is the condition of her morality—to be subjected. . . ."[24]

Furthermore,

"The woman who thus surrenders her personality, and yet
retains her full dignity in so doing, necessarily gives up to
her lover all that she has. For, if she retained the least of her
own self, she would thereby confess that it had a higher value
for her than her own person; and this undoubtedly would be a
lowering of that person. . . . The least consequence is, that she
should renounce to him all her property and all her rights.
Henceforth . . . her life has become a part of the life of
her lover. (This is aptly characterized by her assuming his
name.)"[25]

Or, compare Rousseau in *The Social Contract:*

22. *Ibid.,* pp. 76–78.

23. Fichte, *The Vocation of Man* (Indianapolis, Bobbs-Merrill, 1956),
p. 117.

24. Fichte, *The Science of Rights* (Philadelphia, Lippincott & Co., 1869),
First Appendix, sec. 3, Part III, p. 441; cf. also sec. 1, Part II–Part VII, pp.
396–403.

25. *Ibid.,* section 1, Part VI, pp. 401–402. Cited by E. Figes, *op. cit.,* p. 124.

"To renounce one's liberty is to renounce one's quality as a man, the rights and also the duties of humanity."[26]

with the suggestion on the education of women in the *Emile:*

"They must be trained to bear the yoke from the first, so that they may not feel it, to master their own caprices and to submit themselves to the will of others."[27]

For Schopenhauer also, in his essay "On Women," (though not in *The World as Will and Representation*), it is quite clear that women lack essential human properties. He writes that woman

"is in every respect backward, lacking in reason and reflection . . . a kind of middle step between the child and the man, who is the true human being. . . . In the last resort, women exist solely for the propagation of the race."[28]

These quotations suggest that human nature or essence, whether it be construed as freedom or reason or in some other way, is a sex-linked characteristic, since it is found only or truly in men and not women; or at the very least, that this nature is actualized only by men.[29] (Fichte's position is ambiguous because the continuous wishing to be subjected which he requires of women would seem to necessitate that they possess the human property of freedom in order to wish not to possess it.)[30] In all these cases, however, the philosopher's prejudices about women seem clearly at odds with their systematic philosophy which doesn't discrimi-

26. Rousseau, *The Social Contract,* Book I, Chap. 4.

27. Rousseau, *Emile,* Book V. Cited by E. Figes, *op. cit.,* pp. 98–99.

28. Schopenhauer, "On Women," in *Selected Essays,* ed. by E. B. Bax (London, George Bell, 1900), pp. 338–346. But when talking of the hereditary nature of qualities, Schopenhauer presents a contradictory account, arguing that the faculty of reason and intelligence, and thus the capacity for reflection and deliberation are inherited from the mother, whereas the moral nature, character and heart and will are inherited from the father. (*The World as Will and Representation,* New York, Dover, 1958, Vol. II, pp. 517–520.) See also E. Figes' discussion, *op. cit.,* pp. 121–123.

29. In treating these authors together, I do not mean to compare their systematic philosophies, nor to suggest that they are Essentialists in the rigorous sense discussed in Part IA of this paper.

30. It should be noted that Fichte himself at a few points seems to be aware of this contradiction. See *Science of Rights, op. cit.,* First Appendix, sec. 1, Part IV, p. 400 and sec. 2, Part VII, p. 418. Cf. related point in E. Figes, *op. cit.,* p. 125.

nate between the sexes. Is it the case then, that all we have here is a plain expression of the cultural prejudices of the time, in even so rational a group of philosophers? That they, like most people, are often inconsistent in their beliefs; and that they therefore simply fail to meet the very criterion of universality which they propose? Such an explanation, though common-sensical and plausible, can be shown to be too simple. Instead, let me propose another interpretation of the discrepancy.

These quotations show two things: (a) that these philosophers' views regarding universal human nature are simply contradicted by their views of concrete individuality in the case of women and that therefore their philosophical universalism is no protection against the crassest prejudices and (b) that their statements regarding women are ideological, in the sense of both reflecting and supporting the oppression of women, and that this ideological position is masked by the abstract universality which is proclaimed in their principles. (What I mean here by ideology will be discussed shortly.)

Either interpretation lends support to the critique of abstract universality: (a) The first possibility suggests that because of the abstractness of the universal principle, because it has no bridge to the concrete, the conceptions of concrete individuality of the philosophers in question remain accidental and uncriticized. Thus despite its claims to normative status, the abstract universal principle lacks critical force.

However, it would appear that this sort of discrepancy between the abstract universal principle and concrete prejudices can be overcome within Essentialism, by simply insisting on greater consistency in the interpretation of the universal principle, (supposing that the practitioners were cleansed of their male-dominating tendencies), and by requiring bridge laws to the concrete. While greater attention to consistency is desirable, in that it may force the Essentialist to reject those of his statements which contradict his principles, still he has no way of bringing to bear any critical reflections on the genesis or sources of his prejudice. His consistency becomes at best a formal matter of correcting a mistake of reasoning, but does not constitute a recognition of the substance of the error, nor of its cause. He remains open to the intrusion of further prejudices. As to bridge laws to the concrete: unless the Essentialist can take the concrete present or actual circumstances into account philosophically, i.e., systematically, such bridge laws are anchored only at one end and do not extend beyond what is systematically philosophical. But the Essentialist cannot take such concrete circumstances into account without violating his own premises (i.e., that such considerations are philosophically irrelevant because accidental). He cannot be self-critical with regard to his prejudices, because it is precisely the concrete present or the contemporary social context which generates these prejudices, and this context lies beyond him *qua* philosopher. Therefore, his philosophy is critically defenseless against the intrusion of such prejudices.

(b) The second possibility suggests that the discrepancy between universal and female nature is an ideological distortion. I will use the term ideological to denote a case in which a particular or partial aspect of social reality is taken to be the universal and essential characterization of that reality on the basis of particular interests. The form of such ideological distortion is to take (or mistake), unreflectively and therefore uncritically, the part for the whole, the particular for the universal and essential, or the present for the eternal. There are two sorts of distortion possible here on ideological grounds: first, the deliberate use of ideological distortion as an instrument for domination; second—and more significant because more pervasive—the unconscious ideological distortions which come from the uncritical acceptance of whatever partial view is expedient or current. Accordingly, in the instances examined here, we may distinguish ideological distortions in a strong and a weak sense. The strong sense takes them to be instrumentalities in the subordination of women. This interpretation is suggested, e.g., in Kant's and Rousseau's recommendations for educating women or in Fichte's fervent argument that for a woman to do less than submit and lose herself entirely (including all her property and rights) would undoubtedly be a lowering of her person.

On the other hand, it might be more appropriate to interpret the remarks as ideological in the weaker sense—in the sense of passively reflecting the subordination of women in a male-dominated society, but not actively encouraging such subordination. On this hypothesis, we might interpret Kant's view—that rationality is the dominant and essential human characteristic and male, while beauty or aesthetic sensibility is a subordinate characteristic and female—in the following way: At a given historical stage—namely that of the development of civil society and the state—the trait of rationality (and a similar argument could be made for the traits of contracting, and of freedom, and of productive labor) became the dominant one required for social life and for political rule and therefore it was raised to the level of *the* essential human characteristic. On this view, by an inversion of Plato's approach, the state is not "man writ large," but rather what is essentially human or "man" is the state writ small. As the priorities of changing forms of society themselves change, what are taken to be "essentially human characteristics" change with them. In the case at hand, we may hypothesize that since in historical fact, (1) rationality played the dominant role in social life and political rule in the transition to civil society and the political state, and (2) since males were dominant in that social and political life of that society, therefore rationality became identified not only as the essential human trait, but by association as a male trait. Thus it is not because male nature is rational that men become rulers, but it is because men rule that rationality is assigned as a male trait.

What's lacking, therefore, in this alleged essential characterization of human nature are those traits which were historically and contingently subordinate in civil society and in the political state, and which were associated with women, e.g., aesthetic sensitivity, intuition, caring, etc.,[31] which were historically characterized by Kant for example, as non-rational (if not irrational), or as part of the life of sentiment or of the affections, by contrast to the life of reason or intellect. Therefore, though the abstract universalist does not deny that these allegedly subordinate and female traits are human, he gives them a subordinate status and doesn't see them as essential. Here, we may further hypothesize that the historically contingent fact that women played a subordinate role in social and political life therefore led to the identification of such traits as aesthetic sensitivity and intuition as feminine characteristics. Thus it is not (1) because women are intuitive and aesthetically sensitive and (2) because these traits are of secondary importance to society, that women are assigned a subordinate role, but rather (1) because women are subordinate and (2) because these traits are of secondary importance, that these traits are assigned to women as "feminine" characteristics. On this hypothesis it can be seen that the assignment of "male" and "female" characteristics as respectively dominant or subordinate, or essential and accidental, is a product of contingent priorities at a given historical stage of social and political development.

Now this is not to deny that rationality is a universal and necessary human property. However, my argument suggests that the subordination of other essential properties to this one, the rank order of properties, so to speak, is not given by an *a priori* intuition, but rather by the relative roles and priorities which these properties had in a given social system.

However, what about cases where a consistent universalism does not assign the essential human traits to males, but simply characterizes them as human? Aren't such cases free of sex-bias? An examination of some instances of this sort suggests that even here sex-bias operates, insofar as the characterization of universal human

31. Indeed, sensitivity to human differences, such as I argue for in this paper, has been characteristic especially of women. By contrast, what has had priority in the state and civil society—external contracting between self-interested individuals—has been characteristic especially of men.

nature or essence is modeled after activities performed by men in male-dominated societies. One such case is the theory of the genesis of the state in a social contract; this theory universalizes an activity—contracting—which was an activity of men only, from which women were excluded. Similarly, the universality of the Greek notion that education is for citizenship is belied by the fact that women could not be citizens, and their "education," such as it was, was not for citizenship. Furthermore, these theories made the male-dominated activity of ruling or participating in government the central consideration in political activity. Since women could not rule or govern, since they were excluded from participation in governance, and since such participation was taken to be the essence or nature of the human as *zoon politikon*, women were taken to be not fully human.[32]

More generally, we find that the nature and functioning of the state tends to be characterized in terms of various activities in which males for historical reasons have tended to predominate and from which women have been excluded—specifically the activities of rule, contract, the making of laws and production. For example, in Hegel's *Philosophy of Right*, the sphere of the family and of marriage is specifically excluded from the domain of right, i.e., from the public sphere of civil society and the state.[33] Further, for much of political economy, production in the narrow sense, understood in terms of the activity of men, has been taken as the model of universal human economic activity. Indeed, political economic theories often omit entirely the broader sense of production in which domestic labor might be considered productive.

This narrow understanding of production is manifest even in Engel's *Origin of the Family, Private Property and the State*, and in this case leads to distortion in the theory. For, as we shall see, in discussing how a male activity became in fact a dominant one, Engels does not show *why* it became dominant, except for the reason that it was male. That it was both male and dominant is a matter of historical fact. But Engels' explanation of this fact begs the question. Thus Engels' attempts to explain how with the domestication of animals, property rights fell to the man; he writes,

"To produce the necessities of life had always been the busi-

32. Cf. Christine Allen's discussion of Aristotle's concept of woman in "Can a Woman be Good in the Same Way as a Man?" in *Dialogue*, Vol. X, No. 3, 1971, pp. 534–544.

33. Hegel, *Philosophy of Right*, trans. by T. M. Knox (Oxford University Press, 1969), pp. 106–122.

ness of the man; he produced and owned the means of doing
so . . . ."[34]

But we may wonder why "procuring the necessities of life" is
accomplished through food-*getting* rather than food-*processing*.
Indeed, Engels goes on to define the "getting" as socially productive labor whereas he claims that domestic labor is not. Why
aren't domestic utensils also regarded as means of production?
Moreover, Engels gives no reasoned argument as to why one should
regard as "non-productive" the curing of meat, the dressing of
hides and the transforming of raw material into food. Following
this line of reasoning, we wonder why the herding of sheep is to
be considered any more a claim to property rights in the herd than
the processing of milk, carding of wool, etc. Instead, it would appear that the "property rights" associated with the surplus produced by the domestication of animals has no more intrinsic or
social source in the male activity than in the female (domestic) activity. The claim to that property does not seem to lie in some
intrinsic distinction between "procuring the necessities of life" as
herding, etc., or "procuring the necessities of life" as domestic
processing.

In the historical cases of ideological distortion which we have
examined, we find the projection of a specific and historically contingent social form—male-domination and the subordination of
women—as a universal and unchanging one,[35] and as a result, the
projection of those characteristics which have priority in such a
social form as the essential and dominant features of human nature
itself. The criterion of abstract universality is open to such ideological distortion precisely because it assigns historical and social
difference to the realm of the accidental. As a consequence, it cannot see the historical contingency of its own time and its own society, and therefore it may uncritically adopt the dominant social
relations as eternal and unchanging ones.

In this section, I have presented a sequence of interpretations of
obviously sex-biased views by otherwise universalist philosophers.
Our discussion proceeded from a simple hypothesis about the
weakness of human nature and the coexistence of sheer prejudice
with rational thought, to a more complex hypothesis—namely, that
such prejudice is a case of ideological distortion against which the
criterion of abstract universality has no protection. This distortion

34. Engels, *The Origin of the Family, Private Property and the State* (New
York, International Publishers, 1942), p. 147.

35. Although one would hardly include Engels in this group, there are instances, as in the example in question, where even this critic of male-domination shows the limitations and influences of this ideology.

was presented in its strong (deliberate and instrumental) form and in its weak (unconscious) form. I then traced this distortion to its possible sources in the historically dominant and subordinate roles of the sexes in various forms of social organization. The identification of essential traits as those associated with dominant and male social roles was thus seen to be an ideological reflection of social and historical priorities, even within allegedly bias-free universalist theories.

C. *Universality with a Difference*

We have seen that according to the Essentialist, concrete social questions such as the woman question cannot be included as philosophical on a criterion of abstract universality. But I have shown that the exclusion of such questions is ill-founded on philosophical grounds—specifically, that unless accidental differences are taken into account philosophically, it is impossible to achieve the very aims which Essentialism sets for itself. As a consequence, the Essentialist objection to the inclusion of the woman question as a philosophical question was seen to fail.

This failure which follows from a strictly construed Essentialism puts in question the very concept of universality at work here.[36] What is at issue, then, is this concept of universality itself. We have two choices: (1) to give up the criterion of universality altogether, and either opt for a strict nominalism, which takes only particular and concrete individuals to exist, and which sees "universals" only as names or marks to represent similarities or family-resemblances among such individuals, or opt for existentialism, which in a similar way takes only unique individuals to exist, and

36. I do not mean to imply that these difficulties inherent in the criterion of abstract universality have gone unnoticed by philosophers, including Essentialists themselves. Essentialism has historically been aware of it as the problem in instantiation or of the principle of individuation. As I mentioned in the text, in the *Parmenides,* Plato has Parmenides question Socrates as to whether there are universal forms for such "concrete" and "particular" existences as hair, mud and dirt.

Leibniz introduces a critique of abstract universality in the following passage: "Never are two eggs, two leaves, or two blades of grass in a garden to be found exactly similar to each other. So perfect similarity occurs only in incomplete and abstract concepts, where matters are conceived, not in their totality but according to a certain single viewpoint, as when we consider only figures and neglect the figured matter. So geometry is right in studying similar triangles, even though two perfectly similar material triangles are never found." ("First Truth," in *Philosophical Papers and Letters,* ed. by Leroy E. Loemker, Chicago, Univ. of Chicago Press, 1956.)

Hegel proposes a radically different concept of essence and of universality as a dialectical critique of the insufficiencies of abstract universality, in the *Logic.* Finally, Marx reinterprets the problem of abstract universality as one which shows the limits of traditional philosophy, and marks its incapacity to go beyond a contemplative stance and to become critical.

which sees essences, universals or natures as creations of these existing individuals. Or alternatively, (2) we can reinterpret or radically revise the concept of universality itself so that it includes differences in a systematic way. I will propose the latter course, and argue that an alternative criterion—that of concrete universality—is both philosophically more adequate and also permits a critical and philosophical approach to such questions as the woman question.

The foregoing critique of Essentialism already suggests how we might proceed. For our alternative criterion has to be able to overcome those weaknesses which we have criticized in Essentialism. We may summarize them as follows: In failing to treat accidental properties philosophically, Essentialism cannot arrive at an adequate account of essences either. Moreover, Essentialism is not able to make a fully critical application of its universal norms and lends itself to unreflective and uncritical acceptance of particular interests and prejudices.

These difficulties first of all suggest the need for a revision in the concept of universality and of essence, since the very concept entails that actual differences play a role in the determination of what is universal. Furthermore, these weaknesses in Essentialism give rise to the idea that philosophy must address itself critically to its own present and to the concrete problems of its social reality, and overcome the one-sidedness which expresses itself in ideological distortion. In the following discussion, I shall focus on the first of these suggestions, with only brief consideration of the second.

What is the alternative notion of concrete universality? The concept of universality is retained but it is radically transformed. Whereas the criterion of abstract universality is concerned only with what is essentially the same and excludes accidental differences, the criterion of concrete universality is concerned also with human and social differences, and includes them not simply as accidents, but as aspects which constitute the universal or the essence itself. What is universal is differently conceived on each view: On the Essentialist view, the universal is what remains after all particular and non-necessary differences have been removed. On the alternative view, it is the totality of all the features—both those which are shared in common, and those which are different or individuating—which constitute the universality itself. The universal is therefore identical with this totality, where this totality is constituted by the unity of all the differences.[37] The totality (or uni-

---

37. The universal is not something apart from the differences exhibited by members of a given class; rather, it is this class with its differences included. This unity of what is the same and what is different constitutes the concrete universal. As an abstract universal, the class of humans, for example, is con-

versality) is therefore an internally differentiated unity in which differences are preserved. A feature of traditional Essentialism is that the universal is abstracted or conceived apart from the individuals who exemplify it and apart from their differences, and is therefore taken in itself. On the concrete view, the universal cannot be abstracted or conceived apart from these differences, but exists only in and through them.

The most crucial difference between the two views, however, is that in the first, the differences themselves have no systematic relationship to each other or to the universal. They are literally "accidents." But it is these so-called "accidents" which are the characteristic feature of historical change and of actual social life. Thus concrete universality reinterprets accidental differences to be systematically related to each other; further, it takes such differences to be constitutive of the universal itself. Correlatively, the Essentialist view construes the universal as a fixed and unchanging essence, since on its definition, what is essential is what remains the same or invariant against a background of accidental changes. On the alternative view the universal is seen not as a fixed essence, but rather as one which develops in time, and which is concretely located in history and in society. On this second view, then, universals or essences themselves emerge and change.

Concrete universality thus implies an alternative conception of the nature of history itself. As against the view that historical events are exemplifications of *fixed, a priori* essences, this view regards essences, as well as history itself, as constituted or created by the actions of individuals. Concrete universality conceives the present as the moment in which individuals create history through their interaction with each other and with the objective world. It sees

---

stituted by those individuals who share an essential property (or properties), where these individuals are identified only by virtue of this property. They are not further individuated (except by numerical difference); therefore, they are abstract individuals, one identical to the other in the only relevant respect. The universal is this abstractable essential property which is instantiated in each member of the class equally. All other properties which such individuals have are irrelevant. They are regarded as accidental properties and they determine the differences among such individuals. On such a criterion of abstract universality, therefore, such differences are philosophically dispensible. On the other hand as a *concrete* universal, the class of humans is identical with all the individuals in the class, including both the properties which they share in common and all those which individuate or differentiate each one from each other one. These individuals are therefore fully individuated concrete individuals. Their essence is not only the same abstract property which they share, but also the concrete property of being that particular class of individuals, with all the individual differences included. The distinction between essence and accident is reconstrued here: the essence is nothing apart from the totality of differences which constitute the individuals in the class. The unity of the class is therefore a unity of differences.

the past as the set of interactions which provides the circumstances for present action. This action transforms these circumstances in accordance with future possibilities envisioned by these agents. This transformative activity is thus the process of history itself, which is marked by genuine novelty. This activity also constitutes essences. That is, common features of social life are generated and maintained through the actions of individuals.

On this second conception, society is understood not as a change-less set of relations among individuals who are all essentially the same at all times, but rather as a changing set of relations among individuals who are very different, in part because of these relations themselves. Whereas Essentialist political theory construes society on the model of a contract among equals, concrete univer-sality conceives of society as a totality constituted by social dif-ferences, where these differences are acknowledged to be the essen-tial charactristic of that society. In a class society, for example, the relationship between exploiters and exploited (a) is a social dif-ference which constitutes the essence of that social form (b) is a difference which is not present throughout time, but which devel-oped historically, and (c) is a relationship which characterizes the individuals in terms of this difference and therefore in terms of their interactions with each other. Thus the universal form or essence of a class society involves an internal differentiation (be-tween exploiter and exploited) and a systematic interrelation be-tween the two. Likewise, the "essence" of the family is constituted not simply by the same relation that all members of a family bear to each other, but also by the internal differences in role, function, power.

Similarly, if an Essentialist were to admit sex difference at all, he would construe male and female as fixed essences or natures; each would be defined independently of the other and apart from any particular historical or social context. By contrast, on the cri-terion of concrete universality, this difference itself would be seen as one which has emerged historically and which is constituted by the concrete forms of social interaction between men and women. Thus sexual polarity would be understood to be fundamentally a function of historical, social and cultural relations between men and women—including such relations as domination and subordi-nation, the division of labor, the various historical forms of love and dependence, and social forms of relation like the family, slavery and concubinage. Furthermore, the relations between men and women would be seen as intersecting with other general relations like that of exploiter and exploited.

Thus the identity of an individual (like that of a social class or of society as a whole) cannot be established abstractly, but rather by taking into account how he or she is related to others. Being a woman, therefore, is not an abstract property of some individuals, but rather a property whose definition depends on the relations among women themselves and between women and men in concrete social life. Only in the ensemble or totality of these relations does either group have its "essential" character. These relations or interrelations are therefore not external relations between individuals who are already independently defined by some criterion. That is, it is not the case that men and women, as fully defined individuals with essential male and female properties, then enter into relations with each other in which these properties remain unchanged. Rather, the very properties themselves are constituted in the course of such relations. Men become men, and women become women, in the course of these interrelations. In this sense, the relations are "internal," or constitutive of the very properties themselves.

The criterion of concrete universality permits a different interpretation of universal norms, on the grounds of its alternative concept of universality. As we have seen, the Essentialist conception of abstract universal norms was based on the exclusion of accidental differences among human beings as irrelevant for the determination of rights. These universal rights are held to pertain to human beings *qua* human, i.e., essentially. By contrast, since the concrete universal is conceived to be embodied in society and history, the concrete differences which are excluded by the criterion of abstract universality are included here. Accordingly, a concrete universal norm is formulated not simply in terms of what is the same, but in terms of relevant differences; these differences specify the conditions for applying the norm.

Indeed, if we examine the ordinary cases in which universal norms are stated, we find that the formulation of the norm often includes an explicit specification of differences. Thus in practice, the universal norm of equal justice or equal rights almost never stands alone; rather, it is followed by an exclusionary phrase such as "regardless of race, sex, creed, or country of origin," or "regardless of previous condition of servitude." Why should such additions be made if the "all" in "equal justice for all" is sufficient to assure universal application without regard to differences?

The problem is that "all" has not always meant "all" in a strictly universal sense; rather, it has been interpreted in a less than universal way. For example, the Declaration of Independence states the universal principle that "all men are created equal." Yet the Constitution originally excluded women and slaves from the fundamental equal right of suffrage. In this case, the interpretation of "all" had to be enlarged by the Fourteenth and Nineteenth Amendments. Similarly, when the Napoleonic Code specified for the first time that Jews were to have equal rights as citizens, it made clear that the prior conception of the universal rights of man and of the citizen in practice had not included Jews. This suggests that the concept "all" in, e.g., "equal justice for all" has (in its application) been an historically changing concept, and not always universal in scope. Therefore, corrections are needed in order to make the universal norm more truly universal. However, such a critical correction cannot be made simply by a repetition of the abstract norm, but rather requires a concrete specification to the effect that what has been excluded should be included.

But let us grant that such social or historical limitations can be overcome and that the abstract norm of equal justice is fully universal in scope. Would it then be adequate? Such an abstract norm will indeed be able to reveal when an injustice has been done, simply by showing that some human being has not been treated equally. We will then know *that* a violation of universality has occurred. But we will not know *why* or on what *grounds*. I would propose that it is important to know the sources of a case of injustice. Such knowledge is required if one is concerned not only with rectifying the specific case of injustice, but with eliminating the conditions which give rise to the injustice in the first place.

Thus an abstract norm of justice may permit one to deal with the effects of injustice, but not with its causes. In a case of discriminatory treatment, for example, the abstract norm can reveal that some universal human right has been violated, but it does not permit the recognition that this discrimination is on the basis of e.g., sex or race. Since the abstract norm treats all such cases as extensionally equivalent, it cannot recognize the intensional distinctions Thus motives or interests which lead to sex-discrimination go unnoted in the application of the norm and as a consequence, they cannot become the object of specific social critique and action.[38] By contrast, a criterion of concrete universality recognizes the specific differences which play a part in actual cases of injustice and discrimination. Such a criterion therefore enables one to focus on the causes of the injustice, and permits a criticism of the social

_____

38. There is a further problem with abstract justice or abstract rights: namely, that its failure to take differences into account serves to mask concrete inequalities. For example, equal employment opportunities mean that all qualified applicants for a position will have an equal opportunity to apply and be considered for that position. But in the case of a profession or trade from which a particular group like women or Blacks have been excluded in the past, this abstract right simply serves to preserve an existing inequality; for in fact, women and Blacks will not have had the equal opportunity to qualify as applicants. In such cases, the virtue of an abstract universal norm of equality is that it disregards irrelevant differences and therefore assures in principle that they will not be taken into account. But at the same time, because it is blind to differences, it cannot recognize those existing inequalities which make its application less than equal.

reality in terms of the specific ways in which it falls short of the universal norms of justice and equality.

It is this capacity to be critical of present social reality which I have suggested is also required if philosophy is to be self-critical and self-correcting with regard to those prejudices and ideological distortions which flaw its very quest for universality. A criterion of concrete universality, by contrast to an abstract criterion, takes the social and historical differences of the philosopher's time and place as a clue to understanding and eliminating bias. It takes the task of philosophy to be the critical analysis of the present social reality. This concrete domain thus becomes the subject of philosophical activity proper—i.e., of criticism. But this criticism is no longer the criticism only of concepts, but also of the reality in which these concepts emerge.

It should be clear from the above that one of the central questions concerning present social reality is what I have characterized as the woman question. As I have shown in this section, it is just this sort of question which a criterion of concrete universality specifies as within the domain of philosophy. My argument has further shown that to construe the woman question as a philosophical question in this sense is to say that the conception of philosophy itself is changed.

PART II

A. *A Programmatic Sketch for a Philosophical Approach to the Woman Question*

However, to show *that* it is, is not yet to show *in what way* it is, that the question of women is of philosophical interest. But the criterion of concrete universality suggests some guidelines for theory and practice. First of all, it leads to an anti-separatist approach, both in the analysis and critique of women's situation in the present and in programs of action for the women's movement. A separatist approach conceives of women abstracted from their concrete interrelations; in practice, such a conception leads to separatist politics and organization, on the grounds that women alone can solve the problems of women. By contrast, the criterion suggests that women are to be conceived as social beings, not as isolated, but in definite relations to other women and to men. Furthermore, concrete universality implies that women are to be understood in relation to the totality or concrete whole of which they are a part. For most women, the primary and most immediate locus of their functioning has been the family, and *via* the family, women are related also to social class and to society as a whole. Because of this centrality, the family is the proper focus for theoretical and practical critique.

A related error of abstraction is to conceive women and their oppression ahistorically; rather, the family and the special exploitation and oppression of women have varied historically and although there are formal continuities, the differences are especially significant. Therefore, to understand women concretely in the present is to understand not only their special historically developed capacities and their oppression by men—the two most common approaches to the woman question—but also to understand the particular form which these capacities and this oppression take in the capitalist form of organization, and the ways in which these continue or are transformed in present socialist forms of organization. In the last part of this paper, I shall suggest how such a theory might begin. Moreover, this approach suggests that women's liberation must not be considered alone, but in terms of its relation to human liberation, that is, the liberation of all human beings from varied forms of oppression.

To argue that the approach should be anti-separatist is not yet sufficient. It still remains to be shown *how* the inclusion of women as a proper philosophical subject is to be critically and positively undertaken. Insofar as traditional philosophy has distorted the theoretical account of social reality by leaving women out, the critical inclusion of women as a philosophical subject matter must begin with a critique of philosophy. I have already begun this critique in the previous argument, where the traditional criterion of universality was shown to be in part ideological, serving to exclude the topic of women from philosophical discourse.

If we are now to include it critically, we may suggest certain guidelines for such an approach and various topics for philosophical consideration:

(1) As we have already indicated, women must be considered in their concrete social and historical relations to men, other women, class and social institutions; and in the first place to the family, as the historically dominant context of women's place in society, and the arena in which the crisis is now most acute.

(2) Philosophy would take the form of critique of the past and present situation of women and would attempt a critical analysis of the special oppression and exploitation of women; to this end, it should reconstruct a critical history of women's oppression, and of the conceptual justifications which supported such oppression.

(3) The use of philosophical tools to criticize and analyze social reality needs to be supplemented by a metacritique of philosophy, both of the history of philosophy and contemporary philosophy. Such a metacritique should attempt to reveal and correct the one-sidedness or partiality of philosophical theories of human na-

ture and sex-differences as well as social and political theory, insofar as these theories have been distorted because of either omitting
or misrepresenting the position of women or the family.

(4) Such philosophical analysis and critique should be guided
throughout by a practical interest in the emancipation of women.
It should be concerned not only with understanding the special
oppression of women, but also with changing the existing social
reality, in which this oppression takes its specific and contemporary
forms. This interest in women's emancipation raises a further set
of questions for philosophers to consider. These are the questions
concerned with "what is to be done?," with social, ethical and
political issues. Such questions include not only the common ones
of abortion and the so-called "right to one's body," compensatory
discrimination and maternal obligations. More fundamental still
are questions concerning whether the recognition of equal rights
is sufficient, the relation of equal opportunity and social equality,
the political changes necessary to promote social equality, the relation of exploitation and injustice, the meaning of liberation and
the basic question of the relation of woman's liberation to human
liberation. There is also the necessity for considering the implications for philosophy and philosophizing raised by the movement
for women's liberation.

B. *The Woman Question and the Family:*
   Demystification in Theory and Practice

To exemplify what I mean by a critical analysis of the concrete
situation of women, as well as the metacritique of philosophy, I
shall now consider a leading example of philosophical theorizing
on the family: Hegel's discussion in the *Philosophy of Right*.[39] My
aim is to criticize Hegel's understanding of the modern family,
which is still to a surprising extent a prevailing interpretation of it.
The critique will lead to an alternative analysis. Moreover, since
I take the role of woman in the contemporary family to provide
the central focus for a theoretical understanding and critique of
the present situation, this case study may also serve as the beginning for a theory of women's special oppression, especially as her
oppression in the family is related to her oppression in other
spheres. In focusing on Hegel's understanding of the family, I do
not mean to suggest that the actual form of the family has persisted
unchanged since his time. Rather, it is the mystifications[40] present

---

39. Hegel, *op. cit.*, pp. 106–122.

40. "Mystification," used sparsely as a term in this section, needs demysti-
fying. The term is borrowed from the Hegelian and Marxist mode of discus-

in Hegel's theory—e.g., the privacy of the family—which persist in contemporary interpretations and which obscure its present actuality as well. In the following section, I shall describe these mystifications of the family and of woman, and their contemporary counterparts. The point here is to reveal and thereby to demystify the nature of the actual functioning of the woman in the contemporary family, in its capitalist form.

In the Greek *polis*, as Aristotle described it, the household was the center of the economy. By contrast, for Hegel, in his reflections upon the modern state, the family no longer serves this function; instead, the economic realm is removed to and develops in civil society. Consequently, instead of the Greek division of institutions into family and the *polis*, there is for Hegel a three-fold distinction into family, civil society and the state.

Accordingly, for Hegel in the *Philosophy of Right*, the family is not defined in terms of its economic functions. Rather is it understood as the domain of love and immediacy, as fundamentally private, whose main function is that of the socialization of children. The family is based on the sentiment of love. The state also for Hegel is based on sentiment, in this case that of patriotism. Both of these sentimental realms are contrasted by Hegel with civil society which is based on need and labor, rather than on sentiment. Now Karl Marx—in *On the Jewish Question* and in *The Critique of Hegel's Philosophy of Right*—criticized Hegel's notion of the state by showing that Hegel's understanding of it as autonomous and as a realm of (patriotic) sentiment was only an appearance. In reality, the state could only be rightly understood as dominated by its relation to civil society, i.e., the sphere of economic needs and interests.[41] However, Marx never carried out a similar critique of Hegel's notion of the family, and I think he ought to have.[42]

---

sion. To be mystified is to be dominated by an illusion, by a particular appearance or image of a thing. A mystification functions to mask the reality from view, by taking its (usually distorted) reflection or its symbolic surrogate in place of it. Thus, Marx talks of the relationship of exchange of commodities, which is portrayed by classical political economy as an exchange of equivalent values, as such a "mystification," in that it masks what he considers to be the real relations of exploitation, i.e., of unequal exchange of values. It is in this sense that I am speaking of Hegel's theory of the family as a "mystification."

41. Thus Marx writes in *On The Jewish Question:* "The political state, in relation to civil society, is just as spiritual as is heaven in relation to earth. It stands in the same opposition to civil society, and overcomes it in the same manner as religion overcomes the narrowness of the profane world; i.e., it has always to acknowledge it again, re-establish it, and allow itself to be dominated by it." (In Robert Tucker, ed., *The Marx-Engels Reader,* New York, Norton, 1972, p. 32.) My claim in this paper is that this remark could just as well apply to the family.

42. This claim needs qualification. My point is that although Marx makes

I would argue that the family, like the state, is pervaded throughout by bourgeois or civil society, and that the characterization of the family as a domain of love, privacy, and immediacy is largely a *mystification*, masking the intricate and intimate relations in which the family stands to capital and to production. As such, the ascription of sentiment—i.e., of love—as the tie that binds serves to conceal the concrete nature of the family as a social and political institution under capitalism.

Let's begin with Hegel's account. Since the husband and wife were tied by bonds of love, Hegel did not regard marriage as a contract. The family was outside the domain of right. But this view serves to remove the first right conferred on women, which also brought them into civil society—namely, contractual marriage, with its attendant rights (for the woman, to be supported, and for the man, the right to consummate the marriage, among many others) and obligations (to love, honor and obey). Indeed, marriage is so clearly a contract that society recognizes *only* a contract, as marriage. That it is a contract, an agreement of both parties to conditions explicitly stated, is evidenced by the words "I do"; and that this contract has the status of law is evident from the extensive body of marital law of religious and civil authority. Hegel's romantic claim here—that the family is outside the domain of right—can only be understood as reflecting the patriarchal character of the German family. On this view, the so-called immediacy of the family reduces to the claim that Papa was boss. That it is not in the civil realm amounts to saying that nobody has any business telling the man not to rule his wife. The grimness of this situation is then ameliorated by saying that the family is an ethical and spiritual realm. If we understand the economic and political realms to be realms where you agree by contract to do something, then on this view the ethical realm becomes one where you have to do what someone tells you to do because it is right to do it, and the spiritual realm is one where you undertake to do what someone wants you to do without his even having to tell you.

Love and privacy, then, are the *religion* of the family, its "fantastic" or illusory reality, "its moral sanction, its solemn complement, its general basis of consolation and justification, . . . its spiritual aroma."[43] These notions continue to mystify the present

some suggestive remarks about women and the family, he offers no systematic critique of the family comparable to that which he provides for the state. Engels' discussion in *Origin of the Family* is of a different sort, focusing on an anthropological account of the origin of the family and only briefly on its modern form.

43. "Contribution to a Critique of Hegel's Philosophy of Right: Introduction" in Tucker, *op. cit.*, p. 12.

functions of the family as well. Peggy Morton[44] and Mariarosa Dalla Costa[45] among others have argued that the family serves the central economic function of producing and reproducing labor-power or workers; that the central task of the wife in the family, through which she becomes essential to capital, is to ready the worker for work each day by shopping, cleaning, cooking, etc.; insofar as she does this she contributes to the profits of the capitalist by reducing his costs. As such, part of her work is also unpaid. Because of this, the wages which the husband gets buys the labor of two, and insofar as he in his person incorporates (literally) her work, part of which is unpaid, she also is exploited by the capitalist through him.[46]

The wife also reproduces labor power by raising the children, by "socializing them." But this socialization is closely related to the needs of capital, for as we know, the children as future workers must learn the requisite qualities of possessiveness, obedience to authority, and the treatment of people as commodities and understood in terms of money. Indeed, as Firestone,[47] R. D. Laing[48] and others have pointed out, "love" in the family is made a tool in the production of these characteristics. It is used as a device to manipulate children.

Furthermore, the family as the consuming unit is a major market for capital and the woman is especially significant here for she does the shopping. Consequently, all her qualities and characteristics as well as her domestic labor are understood as commodities. By an

44. Peggy Morton, "A Woman's Work is Never Done" in Altbach, ed., *From Feminism to Liberation* (Cambridge, Schenkman, 1971), pp. 211–227.

45. Mariarosa Dalla Costa, "The Power of Women and the Subversion of the Community," Bristol, Falling Wall Press, 1972.

46. In this section, I describe the particular form which the family takes in capitalist society. Many of the functions of the capitalist family appear also in present socialist societies. But I shall not here attempt a discussion of the socialist family. We may, however, raise some questions concerning the family under socialism: first, is Engels' description of the family as "the productive unit of society" no longer applicable? If so, what are the functions of the family under socialism? Further, if these are economic functions, why have they been incompletely socialized, contrary to Engels' prediction? Moreover, although in socialist countries many women work, the larger part of the task of reproducing workers still falls to women and not to men; we may wonder why this is, and whether it can be explained adequately as being simply a residue of earlier modes of social organization.

47. Firestone, *The Dialectic of Sex: The Case for Feminist Revolution* (New York, Bantam Books, 1970), chapter 4.

48. R. D. Laing, *The Politics of Experience* (New York, Ballantine Books, 1967), chapter 3.

inversion of the "fetishism of commodities"—the case in which human relations (of exploitation) in the political economic sphere are masked or appear only in their economically abstracted form as relations among commodities—here, in the family, the commodity or production relations are masked or appear only as "sentimental" relations, i.e., in the form of love, care for children, etc. The "fetishism of love" plays an analogous role, in the bourgois ideology of the family, to that which the fetishism of commodities plays in the sphere of political economy.

But in all of these ways, the woman is no longer a person but an instrument of production.[49] The family is fundamentally economic and in this sense public.[50] Instead of being a haven of love protecting the worker from the ravages of bourgeois society, the family is thoroughly in the service of capital. It is not merely being used by capital, but in its present form it is necessary to capital, for its functions of reproducing labor power are essential economic functions. As performing these functions, the relations between family members are hardly "immediate," but are rather mediated through and through by their relation to capital. Correlatively, the family itself and the housewife at its center mediate the functioning of the economy. However, it should be clear that I do not mean to imply that human relations within the family are impossible; in fact, love and care for children may take place even within the constraints of social and economic role. But the family, as a unit of social reality, serves a different purpose.

Insofar as the woman in the family is exploited (by performing unpaid labor) and oppressed (by having to take the money from her husband, by being commodified and manipulated by advertisements and the media, by being coerced to raise the children by herself and in "appropriate" ways), the political emancipation of the woman, as well as the assurance of equal opportunity for her, reveals itself to be inadequate. Minimally we might say that concrete emancipation requires the overcoming of the dependence of the family on capital. Much more needs to be said of the nature of her

49. Cf. Marx and Engels, *Manifesto of the Communist Party*, Tucker, *op. cit.*, p. 350.

50. In the text, I follow the now common usage of having "public" refer to the political-economic realm as a whole, reserving the word "private" for the domestic sphere, i.e., the allegedly purely personal and extraeconomic functioning of individuals in the family. It is in this sense that I have argued that the family in its actual functions is not a private domain, but rather public. Furthermore, my argument suggests that, except as a conceptual or terminological distinction, a sharp distinction between the public and private realms is, at least in present actuality, a myth. There is another use of "public" and "private" however, in which the state is understood as the public sphere, as distinct from civil society as the private sphere.

specific exploitation, and I have only presented some preliminary considerations.

The exploitation and oppression of women in the family, and of all women insofar as all women are understood as potentially housewives,[51] is thus fully social and historical; all of women's relations take on a form specific to capital; women's function is the reproduction of labor power. However, this social and cultural character of woman's work is mystified and hidden from us and this mystification takes two fundamental forms.

The first mystification—present already in Hegel—is the glorification and spiritualization of love, marriage, child-raising and housekeeping. Woman here is understood as super-human; she is a heavenly or mysterious creature—love goddess, madonna or earth mother. Woman's relation to nature and her body take on a spiritual form. This spiritualization of woman, including the spiritualization of her body, here obscures the social and economic functioning of women in the family. It keeps her unaware of her exploitation and also provides a compensatory fantasy (as well as an atonement) for her repressed humanity. This spiritualization also serves to justify to woman her non-effectuality in the running of things; it hides her instrumentality in a process of production which is not of her own making and not under her control. It also fills up the isolation of existence in the family with a fantasy world of social participation manufactured in the image of true romances. Indeed, this mystification of woman's exploitation is itself exploited in turn. Woman as love goddess gives rise to the romance industry, and attractiveness becomes a matter of commodity production; thus fashions and cosmetics, dietetic foods and exercise equipment are represented by the media as necessary and indispensable if one is to be thin, young and beautiful and thus loved.

The first mystification of woman as love goddess and madonna—in which even her natural functioning is spiritualized and glorified—is complemented by a second, equally pervasive mystification. Here the social and historical exploitation of women is hidden under the guise of its being her natural biological inheritance to bear and raise children, to be a housewife. This mystification seeks to keep woman in her place by making it her lot; it seeks to make her role acceptable by making it inevitable. Woman is regarded as by nature a childbreeder. In this way, woman is kept out of the

51. The expectation that the woman should function as a housewife affects professional women also. It shows itself in the lower salary scale of women professionals and in the supportive roles which women professionals are sometimes expected to play. The understanding of woman as housewife is found also in the jobs in which women tend to be employed—as secretaries, salesgirls, school teachers and garment workers—jobs which parallel women's functions in the home

public sphere, she is restrained from relating to other women and from becoming a public force, because she is understood as a creature not of discourse but of intercourse. This mystification treats woman as closer to animal than human nature. Like the slave, she is regarded as having no will of her own. That she is a natural rather than human being, and that she is a creature without a will serves to rationalize using the woman as an instrument of production, as instrumental to the process of producing and reproducing the worker's life and that of future workers. Thus the myth of woman's naturalness, like that of her spirituality, serves to conceal the social and historical character of her real life, which although founded on a natural basis, nonetheless transcends it. And just as the myth of the spiritual love goddess and Madonna was itself exploited by being commodified, so here too the myth of the woman as natural and as animal is put to economic use in sex-ploitation and in prostitution.

Demystification, therefore, means a return from the "heaven" of spiritualized femininity, and the "hell" (or "jungle") of sheer animality, to a changed social reality, in which the very basis for these mystifications is eliminated. If we ask *why* the woman has come to be regarded either as Madonna or as whore, we then begin to raise a problem concerning the concrete social reality itself which requires these mystifications—i.e., we begin to do *critical* philosophy. The negative aspect of philosophy as critique is the elimination of illusions and specifically of those illusions which bind us all to exploitation. But philosophy as critique also has a positive dimension. As for human liberation in general, to be liberated from such illusions now makes women free to discover and to *choose* what they want to become. It is the first step in such a choice—the ground-clearing for making what was previously regarded as "natural," or what was previously imposed on women in the form of social exploitation, a matter for their own determination.

ADDITIONAL CURRENT ARTICLES

The following articles are listed because of their overall pertinence to the theme of this book. Articles mentioned in the "Related Readings" of preceding selections are not repeated.

Agonito, Rosemary. "The Concept of Inferiority: When Women Are Men." *Journal of Social Philosophy* VIII, 1 (Jan. 1977), pp. 8–13.

Baker, Robert. "Pricks and Chicks": A Plea for "Persons." In *Philosophy and Sex*, edited by Robert Baker and Frederick Elliston. Buffalo: Prometheus Books, 1975, pp. 45–64.

Barnhart, J. E. and Barnhart, Mary Ann. "The Myth of the Complete Person." In *Feminism and Philosophy*, edited by M. B. Vetterling, F. Elliston, and J. English. Totowa, New Jersey: Littlefield, Adams and Company, 1977.

Bartky, Sandra Lee. "Towards a Phenomenology of Feminist Consciousness." *Social Theory and Practice* 3 (Fall 1975), pp. 425–439.

Beardsley, Elizabeth. "Referential Genderization." In *Women and Philosophy*, edited by C. Gould and M. Wartofsky. New York: G. P. Putnam and Sons, 1976, pp. 285–293.

_____. "Traits and Genderization." In *Feminism and Philosophy*, edited by M. Vetterling, F. Elliston, and J. English. Totowa, New Jersey: Littlefield, Adams and Company, 1977.

Bhattacharya, Debee Rajlukshmee. "Because He Is a Man." *Philosophy* 49 (1974), p. 96 (reply to Lucas).

Blackstone, William. "Freedom and Women." *Ethics* 85 (1975), pp. 243–48.

Clark, Lorenne. "The Rights of Women: The Theory and Practice of the Ideology of Male Supremacy." In *Contemporary Issues in Political Philosophy*. New York: Neal Watson Academic Publications, 1976.

Cooper, William E. "What Is Sexual Equality and Why Does Tey Want It?" (a reply to Jaggar). *Ethics* 85 (1975), pp. 256–257.

Dickason, Anne. "The Feminine as a Universal." In *Feminism and Philosophy*, edited by M. Vetterling, F. Elliston, and J. English. Totowa, New Jersey: Littlefield, Adams and Company, 1977.

Eames, Elizabeth R. "Sexism and Woman as Sex Object" (a reply to Ryskamp). *Journal of Thought* 11 (April 1976), pp. 140–143.

Haack, Susan. "On the Moral Relevance of Sex" (a reply to Lucas). *Philosophy* 49 (1974), pp. 90–95.

Held, Virginia. "Men, Women, and Equal Liberty." In *Promise and Problems of Human Equality*, edited by Walter Feinberg. Urbana: University of Illinois Press, 1976.

Jaggar, Alison. "On Sexual Equality" (a reply to Lucas, Blackstone, and Cooper). *Ethics* 84 (1974), pp. 275–292.

Ketchum, Sara Ann and Pierce, Christine. "Implicit Racism." *Analysis* 36 (Jan. 1976), pp. 91–95.

Lucas, J. R. "Vive La Difference." *Philosophy* 53 (July 1978), pp. 363–73.

Lyons, Dan. "Action, Excellence, and Achievement." *Inquiry* 19 (Fall 1976), pp. 277–297.

MacGuigan, Maryellen. "Is Woman a Question?" *International Philosophical Quarterly* 13 (1973), pp. 485–505.

Mahowald, Mary B. "Feminism, Socialism and Christianity." *Cross Currents* XXV, 1 (Spring 1975), pp. 33–50.

Markovíc, Mihailo. "Women's Liberation and Human Emancipation". In *Women and Philosophy,* edited by C. Gould and M. Wartofsky. New York: G. P. Putnam and Sons, 1976, pp. 145-167.

Mastandrea, Jamie and Duggan, Mary K. "Language and the Oppression of Women." *Dialogue* 19 (Oct. 1976), pp. 7–14.

Moulton, Janice. "The Myth of the Neutral 'Man.'" In *Feminism and Philosophy,* edited by M. Vetterling, F. Elliston, and J. English. Totowa, New Jersey: Littlefield, Adams and Company, 1977.

————. "Sex and Reference." In *Philosophy and Sex,* edited by R. Baker and F. Elliston. Buffalo: Prometheus Books, Inc., 1976, pp. 34–44.

Ryskamp, John. "The Women's Movement and the Dialectic of Sex: The Failure of Positive Schism." *Journal of Thought* 10 (1975), pp. 46–57.

Solomon, Robert. "Sexual Paradigms." *Journal of Philosophy* 71 (1974), pp. 336–345.

Trebilcot, Joyce. "Two Forms of Androgynism." *Journal of Social Philosophy* VIII, 1 (Jan. 1977), pp. 4–8.

Whitbeck, Caroline. "The Maternal Instinct." *Philosophical Forum* 6 (Winter-Spring, 1974-75), pp. 265–272.

White, Stephen W. "Beautiful Losers: An Analysis of Radical Feminist Egalitarianism." *Journal of Value Inquiry* (Winter 1977), pp. 264–283.